The Zohar

by

Rav Shimon bar Yochai

From The Book of Avraham

with

The Sulam Commentary

by

Rav Yehuda Ashlag

The First Ever Unabridged
English Translation with Commentary

Published by
The Kabbalah Centre International Inc.
Dean Rav S. P. Berg Shlita

Edited and Compiled by
Rabbi Michael Berg

Published by
The Kabbalah Centre International Inc.

155 E. 48th St., New York, NY 10017
1062 S. Robertson Blvd., Los Angeles, CA 90035

Director Rav Berg

First Printing 2001
Revised Edition 2008

Printed in USA

ISBN: 1-57189-183-8

May the Light of the Zohar
bring redemption to humanity,
Immortality,
And no more chaos.

Rivka

APPLYING THE POWER OF THE ZOHAR

The Zohar is a book of great mystical power and wisdom. It is Universally recognized as the definitive work on the Kabbalah – and it is also so Much more.

The Zohar is a wellspring of spiritual energy, a fountainhead of metaphysical power that not only reveals and explains, but literally brings blessing, protection, and well-being into the lives of all those who read or peruse its sacred texts. All that is required is worthy desire, the certainty of a trusting heart, and an open and receptive mind. Unlike other books, including the great spiritual texts of other traditions, The Zohar is written in a kind of code, through which metaphors, parables, and cryptic language at first conceal but ultimately reveal the forces of creation.

As electrical current is concealed in wire and cable before disclosing itself as an illuminated light bulb, the spiritual Light of the Creator is wrapped in allegory and symbolism throughout the Aramaic text of the Zohar. And while many books contain information and knowledge, the Zohar both expresses and embodies spiritual Light. The very letters on its pages have the power to bring spiritual wisdom and positive energy into every area of our lives.

As we visually scan the Aramaic texts and study the accompanying insights that appear in English, spiritual power is summoned from above – and worlds tremble as Light is sent forth in response.

It's primary purpose is not only to help us acquire wisdom, but to draw Light from the Upper Worlds and to bring sanctification into our lives. Indeed, the book itself is the most powerful of all tools for cleansing the soul and connecting to the Light of the Creator. As you open these pages, therefore, do not make understanding in the conventional sense your primary goal.

Although you may not have a knowledge of Aramaic, look first at the Aramaic text before reading the English. Do not be discouraged by difficulties with comprehension. Instead, open your heart to the spiritual transformation the Zohar is offering you.

Ultimately, the Zohar is an instrument for refining the individual soul – for removing darkness from the earth – and for bringing well being and blessing to our fellow man.

Its purpose is not only to make us intellectually wise, but to make us spiritually pure.

Glossary of Hebrew words

Torah

Also known as the Five Books of Moses, the Torah is considered to be the physical body of learning, whereas the Zohar is the internal soul. The literal stories of the Torah conceal countless hidden secrets.` The Zohar is the Light that illuminates all of the Torah's sublime mysteries.

Beresheet	Genesis
Shemot	Exodus
Vayikra	Leviticus
Bemidbar	Numbers
Devarim	Deuteronomy

Prophets

Amos	Amos
Chagai	Haggai
Chavakuk	Habakkuk
Hoshea	Hosea
Malachi	Malachi
Melachim	Kings
Michah	Micah
Nachum	Nahum
Ovadyah	Obadiah
Shmuel	Samuel
Shoftim	Judges
Tzefanyah	Zephaniah
Yechezkel	Ezekiel
Yehoshua	Joshua
Yeshayah	Isaiah
Yirmeyah	Jeremiah
Yoel	Joel
Yonah	Jonah
Zecharyah	Zechariah

Writings

Daniel	Daniel
Divrei Hayamim	Chronicles
Eicha	Lamentations
Ester	Esther
Ezra	Ezra
Nechemiah	Nehemiah
Iyov	Job
Kohelet	Ecclesiastes
Mishlei	Proverbs
Rut	Ruth
Sir Hashirim	Songs of Songs
Tehilim	Psalms

The Ten Sfirot – Emanations

To conceal the blinding *Light* of the Upper World, and thus create a tiny point into which our universe would be born, ten *curtains* were fabricated. These ten *curtains* are called Ten Sfirot. Each successive Sfirah further reduces the emanation of *Light*, gradually dimming its brilliance to a level almost devoid of *Light* – our physical world known as *Malchut*. The only remnant of Light remaining in this darkened universe is a *pilot light* which sustains our existence. This Light is the life force of a human being and the force that gives birth to stars, sustains suns and sets everything from swirling galaxies to busy ant hills in motion. Moreover, the Ten Sfirot act like a prism, refracting the Light into many *colors* giving rise to the diversity of life and matter in our world.

The Ten Sfirot are as follows:

Keter	Crown
Chochmah	Wisdom
Binah	Understanding
Da'at	Knowledge
Zeir Anpin	Small Face,
	(includes the next six Sfirot):
Chesed	Mercy (Chassadim - plural)
Gvurah	Judgment (Gvurot - Plural)
Tiferet	Splendor
Netzach	Victory (Eternity)
Hod	Glory
Yesod	Foundation
Malchut	Kingdom

The Partzufim - Spiritual forms

One complete structure of the Ten Sfirot creates a *Partzuf* or Spiritual Form. Together, these forces are the building blocks of all reality. As water and sand combine to create cement, the Ten Sfirot combine to produce a Spiritual Form *[Partzuf]*. Each of the Spiritual Forms below are therefore composed of one set of Ten Sfirot.

These Spiritual Forms are called:

Atik	Ancient
Atik Yomin	Ancient of Days
Atika Kadisha	Holy Ancient
Atik of Atikin	Anceint of Ancients
Aba	Father
Arich Anpin	Long Face
Ima	Mother
Nukva	Female
Tevunah	Intelligence
Yisrael Saba	Israel Grandfather
Zachar	Male

These names are not meant to be understood literally. Each represents a unique spiritual force and building block, producing a substructure and foundation for all the worlds make up reality.

The Five Worlds

All of the above Spiritual Forms *[Partzufim]* create one spiritual world. There are Five Worlds in total that compose all reality, therefore, five sets of the above Spiritual Forms are required.

Our physical world corresponds to the world of: Asiyah – Action

Adam Kadmon	Primordial Man
Atzilut	Emanation
Briyah	Creation
Yetzirah	Formation
Asiyah	Action

The Five Levels of the soul

Nefesh	First, Lowest level of Soul
Ruach	Second level of Soul
Neshamah	Third level of Soul
Chayah	Fourth level of Soul
Yechidah	Highest, fifth level of Soul

Names of God

As a single ray of white sunlight contains the seven colors of the spectrum, the one Light of the Creator embodies many diverse spiritual forces. These different forces are called *Names of God.* Each Name denotes a specific attribute and spiritual power. The Hebrew letters that compose these Names are the interface by which these varied Forces act upon our physical world. The most common Name of God is the Tetragrammaton (the four letters, *Yud Hei Vav Hei* יהוה.) Because of the enormous power that the Tetragrammaton transmits, we do not utter it aloud. When speaking of the Tetragrammaton, we use the term *Hashem* which means, *The Name.*

Adonai, El, Elohim, Hashem, Shadai, Eheyeh, Tzevaot, Yud Hei Vav Hei

People

Er	The son of Noach
Rabbi Elazar	The son of Rabbi Shimon bar Yochai
Rabbi Shimon bar Yochai	Author of the Zohar
Shem, Cham, Yefet	Noach's children
Shet	Seth
Ya'akov	Jacob
Yishai	Jesse (King David's father)
Yitzchak	Isaac
Yosef	Joseph
Yitro	Jethro
Yehuda	Judah

Angels

Angels are distinct energy components, part of a vast communication network running through the upper worlds. Each unique Angel is responsible for transmitting various forces of influence into our physical universe.

Adriel, Ahinael, Dumah (name of Angel in charge of the dead), Gabriel, Kadshiel, Kedumiel, Metatron, Michael, Rachmiel,

Raphael, Tahariel, Uriel

Nations

Nations actually represent the inner attributes and character traits of our individual self. The nation of Amalek refers to the doubt and uncertainty that dwells within us when we face hardship and obstacles. Moab represents the dual nature of man. Nefilim refers to the sparks of Light that we have defiled through our impure actions, and to the negative forces that lurk within the human soul as a result of our own wrongful deeds.

Amalek, Moab, Nefilim

General

Aba	Father Refers to the male principle and positive force in our universe. Correlates to the proton in an atom.
Arvit	The Evening prayer
Chayot	Animals
Chupah	Canopy (wedding ceremony)
Et	The
Avadon	Hell
Gehenom	Hell
Sheol	Hell The place a soul goes for purification upon leaving this world.
Ima	Mother The female principle and minus force in our universe. Correlates to the electron in an atom.
Kiddush	Blessing over the wine
Klipah	Shell (negativity)
Klipot	Shells (Plural)
Kriat Sh'ma	The Reading of the Sh'ma
Mashiach	Messiah
Minchah	The Afternoon prayer
Mishnah	Study
Mochin	Brain, Spiritual levels of Light
Moed	A designated time or holiday
Negev	The south of Israel
Nukva	Female
Partzuf	Face
Shacharit	The Morning prayer
Shamayim	Heavens (sky)
Shechinah	The Divine presence, The female aspect of the Creator
Tefilin	Phylacteries
The Dinur river	The river of fire
Tzadik	Righteous person
Zion	Another name for Jerusalem
Yisrael	The land of Israel The nation of Israel or an individual Israelite
Zohar	Splendor

The Hebrew vowels

Chirik אִ, Cholam אוֹ אֹ, Kamatz אָ, Patach אַ, Segol אֶ, Sh'va אְ, Shuruk אוּ אֻ, Tzere אֵ.

The Twelve Tribes

Asher, Dan, Ephraim, Gad, Issachar, Judah, Levi, Menasheh, Naphtali, Reuben, Shimon, Zebulun

Jewish Holidays

Rosh Hashanah	The Jewish New Year
Yom Kippur	Day of Atonement
Sukkot	Holiday of the Booths
Shmini Atzeret	The day of Convocation
Simchat Torah	Holiday on which we dance with the Torah
Pesach	Passover
Shavout	Holiday of the Weeks

כרך יט

פרשת בלק

Vol. XIX

Balak

A Prayer from The Ari

To be recited before the study of the Zohar

Ruler of the universe, and Master of all masters, The Father of mercy and forgiveness, we thank You, our God and the God of our fathers, by bowing down and kneeling, that You brought us closer to Your Torah and Your holy work, and You enable us to take part in the secrets of Your holy Torah. How worthy are we that You grant us with such big favor, that is the reason we plead before You, that You will forgive and acquit all our sins, and that they should not bring separation between You and us.

And may it be your will before You, our God and the God of our fathers, that You will awaken and prepare our hearts to love and revere You, and may You listen to our utterances, and open our closed heart to the hidden studies of Your Torah, and may our study be pleasant before Your Place of Honor, as the aroma of sweet incense, and may You emanate to us Light from the source of our soul to all of our being. And, may the sparks of your holy servants, through which you revealed Your wisdom to the world, shine.

May their merit and the merit of their fathers, and the merit of their Torah, and holiness, support us so we shall not stumble through our study. And by their merit enlighten our eyes in our learning as it stated by King David, The Sweet Singer of Israel: “Open my eyes, so that I will see wonders from Your Torah” (Tehilim 119:18). Because from His mouth God gives wisdom and understanding.

“May the utterances of my mouth and the thoughts of my heart find favor before You, God, my Strength and my Redeemer” (Tehilim 19:15).

Balak

Names of the articles

1. The bird

A Synopsis

Rabbi Shimon says that Balak saw a real vision with the eyes of Wisdom, and that he saw it through one of the windows to Chochmah. We learn that Balak was a son of Tzipor, meaning bird, and that all his witchcraft was done through birds. Rabbi Shimon describes the origin and nature of the bird that he used for his sorcery, and says that that name of the bird was Yadua, meaning 'known'. Balak knew everything through the bird, which spoke great things on her own.

1. וַיַּרְא בָּלָק בֶּן צִפּוֹר וְגוֹ'. ר' שִׁמְעוֹן אָמַר, וַיַּרְא, מַאי רְאִיָּה חָמָא. רְאִיָּה וַדַּאי מַמָּשׁ חָמָא בְּמַשְׁקוּפָא דְחָכְמְתָא, וְחָמָא בְּעֵינוֹי. חָמָא בְּמַשְׁקוּפָא דְחָכְמְתָא, כְּמָה דִכְתִּיב וַיַּשְׁקֵף אֲבִימֶלֶךְ מֶלֶךְ פְּלִשְׁתִּים בְּעַד הַחַלּוֹן. מַאי בְּעַד הַחַלּוֹן. כד"א בְּעַד הַחַלּוֹן נִשְׁקְפָה וַתְּיַבֵּב אֵם סִיסְרָא אֶלָּא וַדַּאי חַלּוֹן דְחָכְמְתָא דִזְנָבֵי שׁוּלֵיהוֹן דְכֹכְבַיָּא, וְאִינּוּן חַלּוֹנֵי דְחָכְמְתָא. וְחַד חַלּוֹן אִית דְּכָל חָכְמְתָא בֵּיהּ שַׁרְיָא, וּבָהּ חָמֵי מַאן דְחָמֵי בְּעִקָּרָא דְחָכְמְתָא. אוּף הָכָא וַיַּרְא בָּלָק, בְּחָכְמְתָא דִילֵיהּ.

1. "And Balak the son of Tzipor saw" (Bemidbar 22:2). Rabbi Shimon said, he "saw." What did he see? HE RESPONDS: It is definitely a real vision. He perceived through the gaze of Chochmah and he saw with his eyes, MEANING THE EYES OF CHOCHMAH. He noticed through the perception of wisdom, as it says that "Abimelech, king of the Philistines looked out at a window" (Beresheet 26:8). What is the meaning of: "out at a window"? It is as is written: "The mother of Sisera looked out at the window" (Shoftim 5:28). It is assuredly the window of Chochmah at the rim of the edges of the stars. THAT IS THE WINDOW THAT IS MENTIONED WITH REFERENCE TO SISERA'S MOTHER AND ABIMELECH, and these are the windows TO Chochmah, MEANING THAT THERE EXIST MANY WINDOWS and there is one window where all wisdom are. Whoever looks at the essence of wisdom can look through it. Here too: "And Balak...saw" through his wisdom, MEANING HIS OWN PRIVATE WINDOW.

2. בֶּן צִפּוֹר, כְּמָה דְאָמְרוּ. אֲבָל בֶּן צִפּוֹר מַמָּשׁ, דְּהָא חֲרָשׁוֹי הֲווֹ בְּכַמָּה זִינִין דְּהַהוּא צִפּוֹר, נָטִיל צִפּוֹר, מְכַשְׁכֵּשׁ בְּעִשְׂבָּא, מְפָרַח בַּאֲוִירָא.

עָבֵיד עוֹבָדִין וְלָחִישׁ לְחִישֵׁי, וְהַהוּא צִפּוֹר הֲוָה אָתֵי, וְהַהוּא עִשְׂבָּא בְּפוּמֵיהּ, מְצַפְצְפָא קַמֵּיהּ. וְאָעִיל לֵיהּ בִּכְלוּב חַד. מְקַטֵר קְטַרְתִּין קַמֵּיהּ, וְאִיהוּ אוֹדַע לֵיהּ כַּמָּה מִלִּין. עָבֵיד חֲרָשׁוֹי, וּמְצַפְצְפָא עוֹפָא, וּפָרַח וְטָס לְגַבֵּי גִּלּוּי עֵינַיִם, וְאוֹדַע לֵיהּ. וְאִיהוּ אָתֵי. וְכָל מִלּוֹי בְּהַהוּא צִפּוֹר הֲווֹ.

2. "The son of Tzipor" is as they said, THAT HE WAS A DESCENDANT OF JETHRO WHO WAS ALSO CALLED 'TZIPOR'. However, he was literally "the son of Tzipor (lit. 'bird')," MEANING THAT ALL HIS DEALINGS WERE WITH BIRDS, since his witchcraft dealt with different kinds of that bird. He took a bird, struck about with grass, and let it fly in the air. He performed acts and whispered incantations, and the bird would return with the grass in its mouth, chirping at him. He would then put her into a cage and burn incense before her, and she would inform him certain things. He would then perform witchcraft and that fowl, MEANING THE BIRD, chirped and flew swiftly to the one whose eyes were open, who gave her his message, and she would return. All his words came through that bird.

3. יוֹמָא חַד עֲבַד עוֹבָדוֹי, וְנָטִיל הַהוּא צִפּוֹר, וּפָרַח וְאָזִיל וְאִתְעַכָּב, וְלָא אָתָא. הֲוָה מִצְטַעֵר בְּנַפְשֵׁיהּ. עַד דְּאָתָא, חָמָא חַד שַׁלְהוֹבָא דְּאֶשָּׁא דְּטָס אֲבַתְרֵיהּ, וְאוֹקִיד גַּדְפּוֹי. כְּדֵין חָמָא מַה דְּחָמָא, וְדָחִיל מִקַּמַּיְיהוּ דְּיִשְׂרָאֵל. מַה שְׁמֵיהּ דְּהַהוּא צִפּוֹר. יָדוּ"עַ. וְכָל אִינּוּן דִּמְשַׁמְשֵׁי וְיַדְעֵי לְשַׁמְשָׁא בְּהַהוּא צִפּוֹר, לָא יַדְעִין חֲרָשׁוֹי, כְּמָה דַּהֲוָה יָדַע בָּלָק.

3. One day, he performed his acts and took the bird. She flew away and left, tarried and did not return TO HIM. Balak was saddened and, before her return, saw a flame of fire that flew AFTER THE BIRD and scorched her wings. He then saw what he saw and was afraid of Yisrael. What is the name of that bird? It is known (Heb. *yadua*). None of those who make use of and know how to make use of that bird know its witchcraft as well as Balak knew it.

4. וְכָל חָכְמְתָא דַּהֲוָה יָדַע, בְּהַהוּא צִפּוֹר הֲוָה יָדַע. וְהָכִי הֲוָה עָבֵיד.

גָּחִין קַמֵּיהּ, וְקָטִיר קְטַרְתָּא חָפֵי רֵישֵׁיהּ, וְגָחִין וְאָמַר. אִיהוּ אָמַר הָעָם, וְצִפָּרָא אָתִיב יִשְׂרָאֵל, אִיהוּ אָמַר מְאֹד, וְצִפָּרָא אָתִיב רַב. עַל שׁוּם רַב עִלָּאָה דְּאָזִיל בְּהוּ. שַׁבְעִין זִמְנִין צִפְצְפוּ דָּא וְדָא. אִיהוּ אָמַר דַּל, וְצִפָּרָא אָמַר רַב. כְּדֵין דָּחִיל, דִּכְתִיב וַיָּגָר מוֹאָב מִפְּנֵי הָעָם מְאֹד כִּי רַב הוּא, רַב הוּא וַדַּאי.

4. All of the wisdom that he acquired came from that bird. This is what he used to do: he bowed down before THE BIRD, burned incense, covered his head, bent over and spoke. He would say, 'The nation', and the bird would reply to him, 'Yisrael'. He would say, 'Much', and the bird would respond, 'Many (Heb. *rav*)' in commemoration of the great one (Heb. *rav*) that traveled among them. They whispered to each other seventy times, BALAK AND THE BIRD. He would say, 'poor', and the bird would say, 'Great (Heb. *rav*)'. He then was afraid, as is written: "And Moab was sore afraid of the people, because they were many (Heb. *rav*)" (Bemidbar 22:3), assuredly *rav*.

5. וּבְזִינֵי חַרְשִׁין דְּקַסְדִּיאֵ"ל קַדְמָאָה, אַשְׁכְּחָן, דְּצִפְּרָא דָּא הֲווֹ עַבְדִּין לֵיהּ בִּזְמְנִין יְדִיעָן, מִכֶּסֶף מְעֳרָב בְּדַהֲבָא, רֵישָׁא דְּדַהֲבָא. פּוּמָא דְּכֶסֶף. גַּדְפּוֹי מִנְּחֹשֶׁת קָלָל מְעֳרָב בְּכַסְפָּא. גּוּפָא דְּדַהֲבָא, נְקוּדִין דְּנוֹצֵי בְּכֶסֶף. רַגְלִין דְּדַהֲבָא. וְשַׁוְיָין בְּפוּמָא לִישָׁן דְּהַהוּא צִפּוֹר יָדוּ"עַ.

5. In the variety of witchcraft of ancient Kasdiel, we first found that this bird was produced at specific times from silver mixed with gold. SILVER IS THE SECRET OF THE RIGHT COLUMN, CHASSADIM, AND GOLD IS THE LEFT COLUMN, CHOCHMAH, AND THEY USED IT TO PRODUCE AND PUT TOGETHER THAT BIRD TO BE LIKENED TO HOLINESS, AS A MONKEY TO PEOPLE. JUST LIKE IN HOLINESS CHOCHMAH OF THE LEFT IS BLENDED WITH CHASSADIM OF THE RIGHT, THEY WANTED TO DRAW IT THAT WAY. HOWEVER, SINCE THEY DID NOT HAVE THE POWER OF UNIFICATION OF THE CENTRAL COLUMN, EVERYTHING RESULTS IN THE ASPECT OF REFUSE. The head, THE FIRST THREE SFIROT OF THE BIRD, is made of gold, MEANING THE REFUSE OF GOLD. Her mouth is made of silver, MEANING FROM SILVER REFUSE, and her wings, CHESED AND GVURAH, from light copper, THAT IS LEFT, blended with silver, THAT IS RIGHT,

SINCE EACH ONE IS COMPRISED OF RIGHT AND LEFT. The body is of gold with round points of silver in her feathers. Her legs, NETZACH, HOD AND YESOD, are from gold and they place in her mouth the tongue of that bird Yadua, SINCE THE TONGUE IS DA'AT. AND SINCE THE KLIPOT HAVE NO DA'AT, THEY HAVE INSTEAD KNOWN (HEB. *YADUA*).

6. וְשַׁוְיָן לְהַהוּא צִפָּרָא בְּחַלּוֹן חַד. וּפַתְחִין כַּוִּין לְקַבֵּל שִׁמְשָׁא. וּבְלֵילְיָא פַּתְחִין כַּוִּין לְסִיהֲרָא. מְקַטְּרִין קְטַרְתִּין, וְעַבְדִין חַרְשִׁין, וְאוּמָאן לְשִׁמְשָׁא. וּבְלֵילְיָא אוּמָאן לְסִיהֲרָא, וְדָא עַבְדִין שִׁבְעָה יוֹמִין. מִכָּאן וּלְהָלְאָה, הַהוּא לִישָׁנָא מְכַשְׁכְּשָׁא בְּפוּמָא דְּהַהוּא צִפָּרָא, נַקְדִין לְהַהוּא לִישָׁנָא בְּמַחֲטָא דְּדַהֲבָא, וְהִיא מְמַלְּלָא רַבְרְבָן מִגַּרְמָהּ, וְכֹלָּא הֲוָה יָדַע בָּלָק בְּצִפּוֹר דָּא. עַ"ד בֶּן צִפּוֹר, וּבְגִין כַּךְ חָמָא, מַה דְּבַ"נ אַחֲרָא לָא יָכִיל לְמִנְדַּע, וְלָא יָכִיל לְמֶחֱמֵי.

6. They place that bird in that one window, OF THE ONES MENTIONED ABOVE, AND DURING THE DAY they open the window in the direction of the sun THAT RULES BY DAY. At night, they open the window in the direction of the moon, WHICH RULES BY NIGHT, and they burn incense and perform witchcraft. DURING THE DAY, they conjure the sun TO BESTOW ITS ABUNDANCE and at night they conjure the moon. And so they perform for seven days. From then on, that tongue is already rattling in the mouth of the bird, BUT IS STILL UNABLE TO SPEAK. THEN they puncture her tongue with a golden needle and she speaks great things on her own. Everything that Balak knew came from that bird. Therefore, HE WAS CALLED 'the son of bird' and he saw what other people were unable to know and could not see.

2. Sihon and Og

A Synopsis

Rabbi Shimon says that God can do anything immediately, but because people don't fully believe, they think that it will take years to fulfill a wish, and so it does. Although the lives of people are fleeting, they are sanctified with repentance and prayer and good deeds and tears, since God commits Himself to do as they wish. We hear about Og the King of Bashan and Sihon the King of the Amorites, with whom Moses waged war. Sihon was destroyed by a flame from the King of Heaven and it could not therefore be rebuilt. Rabbi Shimon says that the children of Yisrael overthrew the rulers below in this world and also in the world above. He tells us why Esau did not receive his birthright even though he was the eldest.

7. כְּתִיב אָמַר יְיָ׳ מִבָּשָׁן אָשִׁיב אָשִׁיב מִמְּצוּלוֹת יָם. אִית לָן לְשַׁוָּאָה לִבָּא לִמְהֵימְנוּתָא דְקוּדְשָׁא בְּרִיךְ הוּא, דְּכָל מִלּוֹי מִלֵּי קְשׁוֹט, וּמְהֵימְנוּתָא סַגִּיא. דְּכֵיוָן דְּמִלָּה אָמַר, כֹּלָּא אִתְעָבֵיד, וְדָא בַּר נָשׁ דָּחִיק לִבָּא, וְאָמַר לְכַמָּה שְׁנִין, וּלְכַמָּה זִמְנִין יִשְׁתְּלִם דָּא, דְּאִיהוּ כַּךְ. כְּפוּם רַבְרְבָנוּ דִּילֵיהּ, דְּכָל עָלְמִין מַלְיָא יְקָרֵיהּ, הָכִי הוּא. מִלּוֹי בַּר נָשׁ זְעֵיר, וְכָל מִלּוֹי אִינּוּן לְפוּם שַׁעֲתָא, הָכִי הוּא לְפוּם שַׁעֲתָא. אֲבָל בְּתִיּוּבְתָּא, וּבָעוּתָא, וּבְעוֹבָדִין טָבִין, וּבְדִמְעִין סַגִּיאִין, אִיהוּ קַדִּישָׁא רַב וְעִלָּאָה עַל כָּל עָלְמָא, אַזְהִיר נְהוֹרֵיהּ, וְקָמִיט קְדוּשָׁתֵיהּ, לְגַבֵּיהּ דב״נ, לְמֶעְבַּד רְעוּתֵיהּ.

7. It is written: "Hashem said, 'I will bring back from Bashan, I will bring them back from the depths of the sea'" (Tehilim 68:23). We must pay attention to the Faith in the Holy One, blessed be He, since all His words are spoken with truth and great Faith. As soon as He utters something, it is immediately completely accomplished. If a person who is narrow of heart says that it will take several years, and a certain time to fulfill his wish, that is what happens, with THE HOLY ONE, BLESSED BE HE, in accord with His dominion that all the universe is filled with His glory, it is surely so. A person's words are of small consequence and all his words are of a temporary nature. Similarly, he himself is of a temporary nature, LIKE A PASSING SHADOW. However, he is sanctified with repentance and prayer and good deeds and many tears, SINCE the Supernal One who is higher than all the world lights His lamp and contracts His Holiness to that person to do his wish.

8. אָמַר יְיָ', לִזְמְנָא דְּאָתֵי, זַמִּין קוּדְשָׁא בְּרִיךְ הוּא לְאַתְעֲרָא וּלְאַתָבָא מִבָּשָׁן, כָּל אִינּוּן דְּקַטְלוּ לוֹן חֵיוַת בָּרָא וְאַכְלוּ לוֹן. בְּגִין דְּאִית בְּעָלְמָא אֲתָר מוֹתְבָא, דְּכָל חֵיוָן רַבְרְבָן, וְטוּרִין רָמָאִין וְסַגִּיאִין, וּטְמִירִין אִלֵּין בְּאִלֵּין. וְעָרוֹד מַדְבְּרָא תַּקִּיפָא תַּמָּן, אִיהוּ עוֹג בֵּין עֲרוֹדֵי דְּמַדְבְּרָא הֲוָה, וּשְׁכִיחַ תַּמָּן תּוּקְפָּא דִּילֵיהּ, בְּגִין דַּהֲוָה מֶלֶךְ הַבָּשָׁן, דְּכָל מַלְכֵי עָלְמָא, לָא יַכְלִין לְאַגָּחָא קְרָבָא בֵּיהּ, בְּגִין תּוּקְפָּא דְּבָשָׁן. וְאָתָא מֹשֶׁה, וְאָגַח בֵּיהּ קְרָבָא.

8. NOW HE EXPLAINS THE VERSE: "Hashem said" is in the future to come. The Holy One, blessed be He, will arise and bring back from Bashan all those whom the wild beasts killed and devoured, SINCE "*MI* (ENG. 'FROM') BASHAN" IS SPELLED WITH THE SAME LETTERS OF *MIBEIN SHINEI* (LIT. 'FROM BETWEEN THE TEETH OF') THE BEASTS. There exists in the world a dwelling place where all the great beasts and the great high mountains are, and these are hidden in those, THE BEASTS HIDE IN THE MOUNTAINS. THAT PLACE IS CALLED 'BASHAN'. There is the strong wild desert donkey. This is Og, who dwelt among the wild desert asses. There lies his strength, because he was the King of Bashan, MEANING THE KING OF THAT AREA, and none of the world's kings could fight with him due to the powerful might of Bashan. Moses came and waged war with him.

9. סִיחוֹן: סַיְיחָא דְּמַדְבְּרָא הֲוָה סִיחוֹן. וְרָחְצָנוּ דְּמוֹאָב עֲלֵיהּ הֲוָה. כִּי אַרְנוֹן גְּבוּל מוֹאָב בֵּין מוֹאָב וּבֵין הָאֱמוֹרִי. ת"ח, בְּשַׁעֲתָא דְּחָרִיבוּ יִשְׂרָאֵל קַרְתָּא דְּסִיחוֹן, כָּרוֹזָא אִתְעֲבַר בְּמַלְכוּ דִּשְׁמַיָּא, אִתְכְּנָשׁוּ גֻּבְרִין שַׁלְטָנִין עַל שְׁאַר עַמִּין, וְתֶחֱמוּן מַלְכוּ דֶּאֱמוֹרָאָה הֵיךְ אִתְחָרַב בְּמַלְכוּ.

9. Sihon was the desert colt and Moab's security depended on him. "For Arnon is the border of Moab, between Moab and the Amorites" (Bemidbar 21:13), MEANING THAT HE WAS HIS NEIGHBOR AND GUARDED HIS BORDER. Come and see: When Yisrael destroyed the city of Sihon, the proclamation went forth in the Heavenly Kingdom, MEANING AMONG THE SEVENTY CHIEFTAINS OF THE SEVENTY NATIONS: Gather together, you mighty who rule over other nations, and see how the Emorite kingdom is destroyed.

10. בְּהַהִיא שַׁעֲתָא, כָּל אִינּוּן שָׁלְטָנִין דַּהֲווֹ מְמָנִין עַל שֶׁבַע עֲמָמִין אִתְכְּנָשׁוּ, וּבָעוּ לְאַהַדְּרָא מָלְכוּ לְיוֹשְׁנָהּ. כֵּיוָן דְּחָמוּ תֻּקְפָּא דְּמֹשֶׁה, אָהַדְרוּ לַאֲחוֹרָא. הה״ד, עַל כֵּן יֹאמְרוּ הַמּוֹשְׁלִים בֹּאוּ חֶשְׁבּוֹן, אִינּוּן שִׁלְטוֹנִין מְמָנָן עֲלַיְיהוּ דְּאִתְכְּנָשׁוּ, וַהֲווֹ אַמְרֵי בֹּאוּ חֶשְׁבּוֹן, מַאן הוּא דֵּין דְּחָרִיב לָהּ. תִּבָּנֶה וְתִכּוֹנֵן כִּדְבְקַדְמֵיתָא, וְתֶהְדַּר מַלְכוּ לְיוֹשְׁנָהּ.

10. At that moment, all the rulers who were appointed over the seventy nations gathered and wanted to restore the kingdom of Sihon to its prior state. As soon as they saw Moses' might, they retreated. That is the meaning of the words: "Wherefore they who speak in similes say, 'Come to Heshbon'" (Ibid. 27). These are the appointed ministers over the nations, who gathered and said, "Come to Heshbon." Who is he who destroyed it? Let it "be built and established" (Ibid.) as originally, and let the kingdom be reinstated as before.

11. כַּד חָמוּ גְּבוּרְתָּא דְּמֹשֶׁה, וְשַׁלְהוֹבָא דְּמַלְכוּ, אָמְרוּ כִּי אֵשׁ יָצְאָה מֵחֶשְׁבּוֹן לֶהָבָה מִקִּרְיַת סִיחוֹן. כֵּיוָן דִּכְתִּיב מֵחֶשְׁבּוֹן, אֲמַאי מִקִּרְיַת סִיחוֹן. דְּהָא קִרְיַת סִיחוֹן חֶשְׁבּוֹן הֲוָה, דִּכְתִּיב כִּי חֶשְׁבּוֹן עִיר סִיחוֹן מֶלֶךְ הָאֱמוֹרִי.

11. When they saw Moses' might and the flame of his kingdom, they said, "For there is a fire gone out of Heshbon, a flame from the city of Sihon" (Ibid. 28). HE ASKS: If it already says "from Heshbon," why the additional "from the city of Sihon"? Isn't the city of Sihon Heshbon, as it says, "For Heshbon was a city of Sihon the king of the Amorites" (Ibid. 26).

12. אֶלָּא, שַׁלְהוֹבָא דְּמַלְכָּא שְׁמַיָּא נָפַק, וְחָרִיב כֹּלָּא. בְּשַׁעֲתָא דְּאִינּוּן אַמְרִין תִּבָּנֶה וְתִכּוֹנֵן עִיר סִיחוֹן סְתָם, וְלָא אָמְרוּ חֶשְׁבּוֹן, דְּחָשִׁיבוּ דִּבְגִין כַּךְ יִתְבְּנֵי לְמוֹתָבָא דֶּאֱמוֹרָאָה, כְּדֵין אָתִיבוּ וְאָמְרוּ, לָא יָכִילְנָא.

מ״ט. בְּגִין דְּכָל אָרְחִין וּשְׁבִילִין אִסְתְּתָמוּ בְּתֻקְפָּא דְּרַב עִלָּאָה דִּלְהוֹן. אִי נֶהְדַּר וְנֵימָא וְנִדְכַּר חֶשְׁבּוֹן דְּתִבָּנֶה, הָא אֵשׁ יָצְאָה מֵחֶשְׁבּוֹן. אִי נֶהְדַּר וְנֵימָא קִרְיַת סִיחוֹן, הָא לֶהָבָה יָצְאָה מִקִּרְיַת סִיחוֹן וַדַּאי. כֵּיוָן דְּהַהִיא שַׁלְהוֹבָא דְּאֶשָּׁא שַׁרְיָא תַּמָּן עָלָהּ, לֵית מַאן דְּיָכִיל לָהּ לְאַהְדְּרָא לָהּ לְיוֹשְׁנָהּ, דְּהָא מִכָּל סִטְרִין לֵית לָן רְשׁוּ.

12. HE REPLIES: It is only that a flame from the King of Heaven went and destroyed everything. When they said, "Let the city of Sihon be built and established" simply, and did not specify Heshbon, it is because they figured that it would be rebuilt for the Amorites' dwelling place. Then they replied and said, 'We cannot'. What is the reason? It is because all the roads and paths were sealed by the might of their higher authority. If we say and mention again that Heshbon should be built, did not "a fire gone out of Heshbon"? And if we say again 'the city of Sihon', surely a flame started out from the city of Sihon. Since that flame of fire still prevails there, there is nobody who can return it to its prior state, because we have no permission from any side.

13. מִכָּאן וּלְהָלְאָה אוֹי לְךָ מוֹאָב, דְּהָא הַהוּא דַּהֲוָה מָגֵן עֲלָךְ, אַתְּבָּר. ובג״כ מוֹאָב כֵּיוָן דְּחָמוּ דְּמָגֵן דִּלְהוֹן אִתְּבַּר, כְּדֵין וַיָּגָר מוֹאָב מִפְּנֵי הָעָם מְאֹד. מַאי מְאֹד, יַתִּיר מִמּוֹתָא.

13. From here on, woe to you Moab, since your protector has been broken. Therefore, as soon as Moab saw that their defense was breached, then "Moab was sore (Heb. *meod*) afraid of the people" (Bemidbar 22:3). What is "*meod*"? It means very, that is, more than death, SINCE *MEOD* ALLUDES TO THE ANGEL OF DEATH.

14. כִּי רַב הוּא. דְּהָא כְּדֵין אִיהוּ הֲוָה רַב, וְרַב הֲוָה זְעִיר, דִּכְתִּיב הִנֵּה קָטֹן נְתַתִּיךָ בַּגּוֹיִם. וְיִשְׂרָאֵל הֲוָה רַב בַּאֲתַר עֵשָׂו, דִּכְתִּיב בֵּיהּ וְרַב. מ״ט. בְּגִין דְּחָמוּ דְּשַׁלְטוּ יִשְׂרָאֵל, עֵילָּא וְתַתָּא. דִּכְתִּיב אֵת כָּל אֲשֶׁר עָשָׂה יִשְׂרָאֵל לָאֱמוֹרִי. אֲשֶׁר עָשָׂה יִשְׂרָאֵל מִבָּעֵי לֵיהּ, מַאי אֵת כָּל. לְאַסְגָּאָה עֵילָּא וְתַתָּא, עֵילָּא, דַּאֲפִילוּ מִשַּׁלְטָנֵיהוֹן רַבְרְבָנִין וְשָׁלְטָנִין

דִּלְעֵילָּא. וַאֲפִילּוּ מִשָּׁלְטָנֵיהוֹן רַבְרְבָנִין וְשָׁלְטָנִין דִּלְתַּתָּא. וע״ד אֵת כָּל אֲשֶׁר עָשָׂה. וע״ד כִּי רַב הוּא, בַּאֲתַר דְּרַב בּוּכְרָא קַדִּישָׁא, דִּכְתִּיב בְּנִי בְכוֹרִי יִשְׂרָאֵל.

14. "Because they were many (Heb. *rav*)" (Ibid.). At earlier times, ESAU was great (Heb. *rav*) and great is small, as it is written: "Behold, I will make you small among the nations" (Ovadyah 1:2). Yisrael became great instead of Esau, as is written about him: "And the elder (Heb. *rav*)," MEANING: "AND THE ELDER SHALL SERVE THE YOUNGER" (BERESHEET 25:23). What is the reason THEY CONSIDERED YISRAEL AS GREAT? It is because they saw that Yisrael were dominant above and below, as is written: "All that Yisrael had done to the Amorites" (Bemidbar 22:2). It should have said, 'That which Yisrael had done'. What is "all that (Heb. *et*)"? It is to also include above and below, that they toppled THEIR chiefs and rulers above from their domination and also knocked down the chiefs and rulers below, IN THIS WORLD. Therefore, IT IS WRITTEN: "All that (Heb. *et*) Yisrael had done." That is why THEY SAID, "Because they were many (Heb. *rav*)" instead of 'the rav', which would have meant the holy firstborn IN PLACE OF ESAU'S BIRTHRIGHT, as is written: "Yisrael is My son, My firstborn" (Shemot 4:22).

15. וְאִי תֵּימָא דְקוּדְשָׁא בְּרִיךְ הוּא בָּעָא הָכִי, וְלָאו מִן דִּינָא. ת״ח, עֵשָׂו קְלִיפָּה הֲוָה, וְסִטְרָא אַחֲרָא הֲוָה. כֵּיוָן דְּנָפַק קְלִיפָּה וְאִתְעֲבַר, הָא מוֹחָא שְׁכִיחָא, עָרְלָה קַדְמָאָה קָאֵי לְבַר. בְּרִית אִיהוּ יַקִּירָא מִכֹּלָּא, וְאִיהוּ אִתְגְּלֵי לְבָתַר.

15. You might say that the Holy One, blessed be He, desired it that way, TO GIVE THE BIRTHRIGHT TO YISRAEL, yet it was not according to justice. Come and see that Esau was a Klipah of the Other Side AND IT IS KNOWN THAT THE SKULL (HEB. *KLIPAH*) PRECEDED THE BRAIN. THEREFORE, HE EMERGED FIRST. As soon as the skull came out and removed, the brain was found. The foreskin come first, THAT IS ESAU, found externally; THEREFORE, HE EXITED FIRST. The of circumcised member that is most precious, MEANING JACOB, is revealed later. THEREFORE, ESAU'S PRIOR APPEARANCE IS NOT CONSIDERED AS THE BIRTHRIGHT SINCE THE

KLIPAH AND THE FORESKIN HAVE NO VALUE IN COMPARISON TO THE BRAIN AND THE CIRCUMCISED MEMBER. NOT ONLY THAT, HE WAS FIRST TO EXIT FOR THAT SAME REASON, SINCE THE SHELL COMES BEFORE THE FRUIT.

3. “And he showed me Joshua the High Priest”

A Synopsis

Rabbi Chiya tells us that a person is tried many times during his lifetime and after death, and he says that God is always filled with compassion and does not want to judge people according to their deeds. Rabbi Shimon talks about three levels of compassion, and he tells us about the members of the Yeshivah above that gather to consider a person’s sentence.

16. וַיֹּאמֶר מוֹאָב אֶל זִקְנֵי מִדְיָן עַתָּה יְלַחֲכוּ וְגוֹ׳. ר׳ חִיָּיא פָּתַח, וַיַּרְאֵנִי אֶת יְהוֹשֻׁעַ הַכֹּהֵן הַגָּדוֹל עוֹמֵד לִפְנֵי מַלְאַךְ יְיָ׳ וְגוֹ׳. כַּמָּה אִית לֵיהּ לב״נ, לְאִסְתַּמְּרָא אוֹרְחוֹי בְּהַאי עָלְמָא, וּלְמֵהַךְ בְּאֹרַח קְשׁוֹט. בְּגִין דְּכָל עוֹבָדוֹי דב״נ כְּתִיבִין קַמֵּי מַלְכָּא, וּרְשִׁימִין קַמֵּיהּ, וְכֻלְּהוּ בְּמִנְיָינָא. נְטוּרֵי תַּרְעֵי קַיְימִין וְסָהֲדִין, קַיְימֵי וְתָבְעֵי דִּינָא תְּרִיצִין. וְדַיָּינָא קַיְּימָא לְקַבְּלָא סַהֲדוּתָא, וְאִינּוּן דְּטַעֲנוּ טַעֲנְתָּא מְרַחְשָׁן, וְלָא יְדִיעַ אִי יְהָכוּן מִימִינָא, וְאִם יִשְׂמָאֲלוּן מִשְּׂמָאלָא.

16. “And Moab said to the elders of Midian, ‘Now shall this company lick up...’” (Bemidbar 22:4). Rabbi Chiya opened the discussion with the verse: “And he showed me Joshua the High Priest standing before the angel of Hashem” (Zecharyah 3:1). How much should a man watch his ways in this world and walk in a true path, since all the actions of a person are recorded before the King and are inscribed before Him, and all are counted. The guards at the gates stand and give evidence and request true justice, and the judge is ready to receive the evidence. Those who have claims FOR THEIR JUSTIFICATION murmur and do not know if they should go from the right or turn to the left side.

17. דְּהָא כַּד רוּחֵי בְּנֵי נָשָׁא נָפְקֵי מֵהַאי עָלְמָא, כַּמָּה אִינּוּן מְקַטְרְגִין דְּקַיְימִין קַמַּיְיהוּ, וְכָרוֹזִין נָפְקִין הֵן לְטָב הֵן לְבִישׁ, כְּפוּם מַה דְּנָפִיק מִן דִּינָא. דְּתַנְיָא, בְּכַמָּה דִּינִין אִתְּדָן ב״נ בְּהַאי עָלְמָא, בֵּין בְּחַיּוֹי, בֵּין לְבָתַר. דְּהָא כָּל מִלּוֹי בְּדִינָא אִינּוּן. וְקוּדְשָׁא בְּרִיךְ הוּא תָּדִיר בְּרַחֲמָנוּ, וְרַחֲמוֹי עַל כֹּלָּא, וְלָא בָּעֵי לְדַיְּינָא בְּנֵי נָשָׁא כְּפוּם עוֹבָדֵיהוֹן, דְּהָכִי

אָמַר דָּוִד, אִם עֲוֺנוֹת תִּשְׁמָר יָהּ יְיָ' מִי יַעֲמוֹד. הָכָא אִית לְאִסְתַּכְּלָא, כֵּיוָן דְּאָמַר אִם עֲוֺנוֹת תִּשְׁמָר יָ"הּ, אֲמַאי אֲדֹנָי.

17. When the human spirits exit from this world, many accusers stand up about them and proclamations go out, both for their benefit and for their detriment, in accordance with the outcome of their trial; we are taught that a person is tried many times in this world, both during his lifetime and also afterwards, since all his words are through judgment. The Holy One, blessed be He, is always filled with compassion, and His mercy is over all, and He does not wish to judge people according to their deeds. This is what David said, "If You, Yah, should mark iniquities, Adonai, who could stand" (Tehilim 130:3). Here we must observe, since he said Yud-Hei. Why DID HE SAY IN ADDITION Adonai? IT WOULD HAVE BEEN SUFFICIENT TO SAY, 'IF YOU, YAH, SHOULD MARK INIQUITIES, WHO COULD STAND'.

18. אֶלָּא, תְּלָת דַּרְגִּין דְּרַחֲמֵי אַדְכַּר דָּוִד הָכָא. אִם עֲוֺנוֹת תִּשְׁמָר יָהּ, אִם חוֹבִין סַגִּיאוּ, עַד דְּסַלְּקִין לְעֵילָּא לְגַבֵּי אַבָּא וְאִמָּא, הָא אֲדֹנָי דְּאִיהוּ רַחֲמֵי. וְאִי שְׁמָא דָּא, אע"ג דְּאִיהוּ רַחֲמֵי, יִתְּעַר בְּדִינָא וְכָל דַּרְגִּין אַסְתִּימוּ בְּדִינָא, דַּרְגָּא חֲדָא אִית דְּנֶהְדַּר לְגַבֵּיהּ, דְּכָל אַסְוָותִין מִינֵּהּ נָפְקִין, אִיהוּ יָחוּס עֲלָן, וּמַאן אִיהוּ, מִי. מִ"י יַעֲמוֹד וַדַּאי. מִ"י יִרְפָּא לָךְ. וע"ד יָהּ אֲדֹנָי אִי אִלֵּין שְׁמָהָן יִסְתְּמוּן מִנָּן, מִ"י יַעֲמוֹד, דְּכָל אׇרְחִין דִּתְיוּבְתָּא פְּתִיחָן מִנֵּיהּ.

18. HE RESPONDS: It is because there are three levels of compassion that David mentions here, WHICH ARE YUD-HEI, ADONAI AND 'WHO.' "If You, Yah, should mark iniquities": THAT IS ABA AND IMA REFERRED TO BY YUD-HEI AS EXPLAINED. If the iniquities are so many that they have ascended above to Aba and Ima, then it is "Adonai," which is Mercy. Although this name ADONAI is merciful, it will be aroused in judgment, and all the levels will be blocked through Judgment. Yet there is still one level that we can turn to, as all the remedies emanate from it, that one should have mercy on us. That one is 'WHO' THAT IS BINAH, "who could stand" FOR US assuredly, as it says, "Who can heal you" (Eichah 2:13). Therefore, if these TWO names, Yud-Hei Adonai, were sealed and hidden from him, "who could stand," because all the roads to repentance are open from it.

19. ת"ח, יְהוֹשֻׁעַ בֶּן יְהוֹצָדָק צַדִּיק גָּמוּר הֲוָה, גַּבְרָא דַּהֲוָה עָאל לִפְנַי לִפְנִים, דְּעַיְילוּהוּ לִמְתִיבְתָּא דִּרְקִיעָא. אִתְכְּנָשׁוּ כָּל בְּנֵי מְתִיבְתָּא תַּמָּן, לְעַיְּינָא בְּדִינֵיהּ. וְכַךְ אָרְחוֹי דְּהַהוּא מְתִיבְתָּא דִּרְקִיעָא, כַּד עַיְילֵי לֵיהּ לְדִינָא, כָּרוֹזָא נָפִיק וְאַכְרִיז, כָּל בְּנֵי מְתִיבְתָּא עוּלוּ. לְאִדָּרָא טְמִירָא. וּבֵי דִּינָא מִתְכַּנְּשֵׁי.

19. Come and see Joshua, son of Yehotzedek, was entirely righteous, a man that used to enter to the innermost sanctum. They raised him up to the Yeshivah up in the heavens, and all the members of that Yeshivah were gathered to consider his sentence. Such are the ways of that Yeshivah of the firmament, when they bring in A PERSON'S SPIRIT to be judged. A proclamation is sounded, all the members of the Yeshivah enter into a concealed chamber and the court is gathered into session.

4. All the members of the Yeshivah gathered to study the trial

A Synopsis

This section tells us about the trial after death, and we learn that the angel Metatron, who is the head of the Yeshivah of Heaven, pronounces the sentence over everything.

20. וְהַהוּא רוּחָא דְּבַר נָשׁ סַלְּקָא ע״י דִּתְרֵי מְמָנָן, כֵּיוָן דְּעָאל, קָרִיב לְגַבֵּי חַד עַמּוּדָא דְּשַׁלְהוֹבָא מְלָהֲטָא דְּקַיְּימָא תַּמָּן, וְאַגְלִים בְּרוּחָא דַּאֲוִירָא דְּנָשִׁיב בְּהַהוּא עַמּוּדָא, וְכַמָּה אִינּוּן דְּסַלְּקִין לוֹן תַּמָּן. בְּגִין דְּכָל אִינּוּן דְּמִשְׁתַּדְּלֵי בְּאוֹרַיְיתָא, וּמְחַדְּשֵׁי בָּהּ חִדּוּשִׁין, מִיַּד אַכְתּוּב לְגַבֵּי בְּנֵי מְתִיבְתָּא אִינּוּן מִלִּין, כְּדֵין כָּל אִינּוּן בְּנֵי מְתִיבְתָּא אָתָאן לְמֶחֱמֵי לֵיהּ. אִינּוּן תְּרֵין מְמָנָן נָפְקִין, וְסַלְּקִין לֵיהּ לְהַהוּא מְתִיבְתָּא דִּרְקִיעָא, מִיַּד קָרִיב לְגַבֵּי הַהוּא עַמּוּדָא, דְּאַגְלִים תַּמָּן.

20. The spirit of the person is raised up by two appointees. As it enters, it approaches a pillar of glowing flame that stands there, covered in the air of the wind that blows in that pillar. And now many that are raised up there... (MISSING HERE)... Since all those who study Torah and have new insights about her, the maters are immediately written and recorded for those members of that Yeshivah. Then all the members of the Yeshivah come to see him and those two appointed MENTIONED ABOVE exit and raise him up above to the Yeshivah of the firmament. He immediately approaches that pillar, MENTIONED ABOVE, where he is dressed IN THAT GARMENT MENTIONED ABOVE.

21. עָאל לִמְתִיבְתָּא, וְחָמָאן לֵיהּ, אִי מִלָּה כַּדְקָא יָאוּת זַכָּאָה אִיהוּ, כַּמָּה עִטְרִין מְנַצְּצָן, מְעַטְּרִין לֵיהּ כָּל בְּנֵי מְתִיבְתָּא. וְאִי מִלָּה אַחֲרָא הֲוָה, וַוי לֵיהּ לְהַהוּא כִּסּוּפָא, דַּחְיָין לֵיהּ לְבַר, וְקָאֵים גּוֹ עַמּוּדָא, עַד דְּעַיְילֵי לֵיהּ לְדִינָא, רַחֲמָנָא לִשֵׁיזְבָן.

21. AFTER DRESSING IN THOSE GARMENTS, he enters into the Yeshivah and THE MEMBERS OF THE YESHIVAH observe him. If the matters OF NEW INSIGHT are appropriate, happy is he, since all the members of the session will adorn him with many laurels. If it is something else, MEANING TO SAY

THAT IT DOES NOT FOLLOW THE PATHS OF HOLINESS, woe to him, to that embarrassment and shame. He is pushed outside and goes to stand next to the pillar MENTIONED ABOVE, until they bring him in for trial and judgment. May the Merciful One save us.

22. **וְאִית אַחֲרָנִין דְּסַלְקִין לוֹן תַּמָּן, כַּד קוּדְשָׁא בְּרִיךְ הוּא בִּפְלוּגְתָּא בִּבְנֵי מְתִיבְתָּא, וְאַמְרֵי מַאן מוֹכַח, הָא פְּלוֹנִי דְּאוֹכַח מִלָּה. כְּדֵין סַלְקִין לֵיהּ תַּמָּן, וְאוֹכַח הַהוּא מִלָּה בֵּין קוּדְשָׁא בְּרִיךְ הוּא וּבֵין בְּנֵי מְתִיבְתָּא. וְאִית אַחֲרָנִין דְּסַלְקִין לוֹן תַּמָּן לְדִינָא, וְדַיְינִין לֵיהּ תַּמָּן, לְבָרְרָא לוֹן, וּלְלַבְּנָא לוֹן.**

22. There are others that are raised up there when the Holy One, blessed be He, is in a disputation with the members of the Yeshivah, WHETHER THE ITEM IS PERMISSIBLE OR PROHIBITED. They say, Who shall decide THE LAW? Here is so-and-so, THE WISE MAN FROM THIS WORLD, let him come and determine this matter, HOW TO CARRY OUT THE LAW. Then they raise THAT WISE MAN up, there, and he decides by evidence that legal dispute between the Holy One, blessed be He, and the members of the Yeshivah. There are others that are raised up there for trial and are judged there, to be refined and purified.

23. **אָ"ל ר' יוֹסֵי, א"ה בְּלָא דִּינָא אִתְפְּטַר בַּר נָשׁ וְאִסְתַּלָּק מֵהַאי עָלְמָא. וְאִי בְּדִינָא אִסְתַּלָּק, אֲמַאי אִתְדָּן זִמְנָא אַחֲרִינָא. אָ"ל, הָכִי אוֹלִיפְנָא, וְהָכִי שְׁמַעְנָא, דְּהָא וַדַּאי בְּדִינָא אִסְתַּלָּק ב"נ מֵהַאי עָלְמָא, אֲבָל עַד לָא יֵיעוּל לִמְחִיצָתְהוֹן דְּצַדִּיקַיָּא, סַלְקֵי לֵיהּ לְדִינָא, וְתַמָּן אִתְדָּן בְּהַהוּא מְתִיבְתָּא דִּרְקִיעָא.**

23. Rabbi Yosi said to him, If so, IT WOULD SEEM that a person leaves and departs this world without trial. If he does depart by trial, THAT IS, HE ALREADY WAS JUDGED ABOVE, why then is he on trial a second time IN THE YESHIVAH OF THE FIRMAMENT? He replied to him, That is the way I was taught and so I heard. Surely a person who departs from this world is judged. However, prior to entering the presence of the righteous, he is raised for A SECOND trial for a decision in that Yeshivah of the firmament.

24. וְתַמָּן קַיְּימָא הַהוּא מְמָנָא דְּגֵיהִנָּם לְאַסְטָאָה. זַכָּאָה אִיהוּ מַאן דְּזָכֵי מִן דִּינָא, וְאִי לָאו הַהוּא מְמָנָא דְּגֵיהִנָּם נָטִיל לֵיהּ, בְּשַׁעֲתָא דְּמַסְרִין לֵיהּ בִּידוֹי, וּמִקְלַע לֵיהּ מִתַּמָּן לְתַתָּא, כְּמַאן דְּמִקְלַע אַבְנָא בְּקוּסְפִתָא דִּכְתִּיב וְאֵת נֶפֶשׁ אוֹיְבֶיךָ יְקַלְּעֶנָּה בְּתוֹךְ כַּף הַקָּלַע וְגוֹ׳. וְשַׁדֵּי לֵיהּ לְגֵיהִנָּם, וְקַבִּיל עוֹנְשֵׁיהּ כְּפוּם מַה דְּאִתְדָּן.

24. AT THE YESHIVAH OF THE FIRMAMENT stands the appointee of Gehenom to prosecute. Happy is the one who was found guiltless in that trial. If not, that appointee of Gehenom takes him when they hand him over to him and slings him downward, like someone who hurtles a stone with a sling, as is written: “And the souls of your enemies, them shall he sling out, as out of the hollow of a sling...” (I Shmuel 25:29). The appointee throws him into Gehenom and he receives his punishment corresponding to his sentence.

25. ת״ח, וַיַּרְאֵנִי אֶת יְהוֹשֻׁעַ הַכֹּהֵן הַגָּדוֹל עוֹמֵד לִפְנֵי מַלְאַךְ וְגוֹ׳, דְּסָלִיקוּ לֵיהּ לְדִינָא, גּוֹ הַהוּא מְתִיבְתָּא דִּרְקִיעָא, בְּשַׁעֲתָא דְּאִתְפְּטָר מֵהַאי עָלְמָא. עוֹמֵד לִפְנֵי מַלְאַךְ יְיָ׳, דָּא הוּא הַהוּא נַעַר, רֵישׁ מְתִיבְתָּא, דְּאִיהוּ חָתִיךְ דִּינָא עַל כֹּלָּא.

25. Come and see: “And he showed me Joshua the High Priest standing before the angel of Hashem” (Zecharyah 3:1) means that they have raised him up above for trial in the Yeshivah of the firmament, after he was gone from the world. “Standing before the angel of Hashem”: That is the same youth, MEANING THE ANGEL METATRON, THAT IS CALLED ‘YOUTH’, who is the head of the Yeshivah IN THE YESHIVAH OF THE FIRMAMENT. And he pronounces the sentence over everything.

5. "Hashem rebuke you, O adversary"

A Synopsis

Rabbi Shimon talks about the adversary who is appointed over the souls in Gehenom. The Satan transforms into the form of an ox; since Balak knew about this he was a wise man, and that very knowledge enabled him to perform his witchcraft.

26. וְהַשָּׂטָן, מַאן וְהַשָּׂטָן. הַהוּא דִּמְמָנָא, עַל נַפְשָׁתָא בְּגֵיהִנָּם, דְּתִיאוּבְתֵּיה לְמֵיסַב לֵיהּ, וְתָדִיר קַיְימָא וְאָמַר הַב הַב, הָבוּ חַיָּיבִין לְגֵיהִנָּם. לְשִׂטְנוֹ, לְאַדְכְּרָא חוֹבוֹי. כְּדֵין וַיֹּאמֶר יְיָ׳ אֶל הַשָּׂטָן יִגְעַר בְּךָ הַשָּׂטָן וְיִגְעַר ה׳ בְּךָ, תְּרֵין גְּעָרוֹת אַמַּאי. אֶלָּא חַד לְדוּמָה. וְחַד, לְהַהוּא דְּנָפְקָא מִגֵּיהִנָּם, דְּקַיְימָא תָּדִיר לְאַסְטָאָה.

26. HE INQUIRES ABOUT WHAT IT SAYS: "And the adversary (Heb. *Satan*) STANDING AT HIS RIGHT HAND TO THWART HIM" (ZECHARYAH 3:1). What is "the adversary"? HE REPLIES: That one who is appointed over the souls in Gehenom, whose desire is to take him TO GEHENOM, who is always present and says, Give, give the wicked to Gehenom. "To thwart him" means to mention his iniquities. Then, "Hashem said to the adversary, 'Hashem rebuke you, O adversary; even Hashem...rebuke you'" (Ibid.). HE ASKS: Why two rebukes? HE REPLIES: One FOR THE ANGEL Dumah, THAT IS THE CHIEF APPOINTEE OF GEHENOM, and one for that one that leaves Gehenom, who is constantly ready to thwart, MEANING THE ADVERSARY.

27. ת״ח, הַהוּא שָׂטָן עִלָּאָה נָחִית כְּמָה דְּאוּקְמוּהָ, דְּאַגְלִים בְּדִיוּקְנָא דְּשׁוֹר, וְכָל אִינּוּן רוּחִין בִּישִׁין, דְּאִתְדָּנוּ לְאַעֲלָא בַּגֵּיהִנָּם, לָחִיךְ לוֹן בְּרִגְעָא חֲדָא, וְחָטַף לוֹן, וְנָחִית וְיָהַב לוֹן לְדוּמָה, לְבָתַר דְּבָלַע לוֹן. וְדָא הוּא דִּכְתִּיב, וַיֹּאמֶר מוֹאָב אֶל זִקְנֵי מִדְיָן עַתָּה יְלַחֲכוּ הַקָּהָל אֶת כָּל סְבִיבוֹתֵינוּ כִּלְחוֹךְ הַשּׁוֹר, דְּאִשְׁתְּמוֹדַע, הַשּׁוֹר דְּקַיְימָא לְבִישׁ עַל כָּל בְּנֵי עָלְמָא. אֵת יֶרֶק הַשָּׂדֶה, אִינּוּן רוּחִין דִּבְנֵי נָשָׁא, דְּאִינּוּן יֶרֶק הַשָּׂדֶה. הַשָּׂדֶה, הַהוּא שָׂדֶה דְּאִשְׁתְּמוֹדַע.

27. Come and see, the celestial adversary descends, as we have already explained, being transformed into the image of an ox. All these evil spirits that were sentenced to be entered into Gehenom, he licks them up in an instant and grabs them, and descends and gives them over to Dumah, after he swallows them up. This is what is said: "And Moab said to the elders of Midian, 'Now shall this company lick up all that are round about us, as the ox licks up...'" (Bemidbar 22:4). That is that known ox, WHICH IS THE ADVERSARY, that stands constantly ready to cause evil for all the world's inhabitants. "The grass of the field" (Ibid.), are the spirits of people, who are the grass of the field. "The field" is that certain field, MEANING MALCHUT.

28. א״ר יוֹסֵי, א״ה, חַכִּים הֲוָה בָּלָק. אָ״ל וַדַּאי, וְהָכִי אִצְטְרִיךְ לֵיהּ לְמִנְדַּע כָּל אָרְחוֹי דְּהַהוּא שׁוֹר, וְאִי לָא יַדְעֵי לְהוּ, לָא יָכִיל לְמֶעְבַּד חֲרָשׁוֹי וְקִסְמוֹי. א״ר יוֹסֵי וַדַּאי הָכִי הוּא, וְיָאוּת אֲמָרְת. וְתוּקְפֵּיהּ דְּהַהוּא שׁוֹר, מִכִּי מַכְרִיזוּ עַל הַתְּבוּאָה. כָּל אִינּוּן יוֹמִין דְּמַכְרִיזִין וְכָל יוֹמִין דְּמַכְרִיזֵי עַל רוּחֵיהוֹן דִּבְנֵי נָשָׁא. וְאִינּוּן יוֹמֵי נִיסָן, וְיוֹמֵי תִּשְׁרֵי, וְהָא אִתְּמַר.

28. Rabbi Yosi says, If so, Balak was a wise man, SINCE HE WAS AWARE THAT THE SATAN TRANSFORMS INTO THE FORM OF AN OX. He said to him most certainly HE WAS WISE. Similarly, he needed to know all the habits of that ox and if he had not been familiar with them, he would not have been able to perform his witchcraft and magic. Rabbi Yosi said, That is certainly so, and you spoke well. The might of that ox is, when they proclaim about the grain crops... (SOMETHING MISSING) ...all these days that are being proclaimed, and all the days that they proclaim about spirits of people. They are the days of Nissan and the days of Tishrei, as we have already learned.

6. The child (Yenuka)

A Synopsis

Rabbi Yitzchak and Rabbi Yehuda encounter the small son of Rav Hamnuna Saba, and find that he is preternaturally wise. The child rebukes them for not having read the Kriat Sh'ma and for having started to say grace while their hands were still dirty. He talks about the five fingers on the hand, the five bars of acacia wood, and the five hundred years, and he concludes from this that all the blessings of the priest are dependent on the fingers. The boy discusses the grace before the meal and the grace after the meal. When his mother begs the rabbis to look at her son with a benevolent eye, the child says he is not afraid of an evil eye because he is the son of a great and worthy fish, and a fish has no harm from the evil eye as the water acts as a protection for it. He talks about the fact that Malchut is called 'angel' when she is an emissary from Aba and Ima, but when she is at rest over the two Cherubim she is called Adonai. We read that Malchut appeared to Moses as an angel but to Abraham as Adonai, and that Jacob called to Malchut in the name of angel when he died. Moses joined with Malchut during his lifetime while still in his body but Jacob joined with her only in spirit after he died. We read about Metatron and Sandalphon who are from the great ocean, Malchut, and that they are fruitful and multiply in the land. When the wise boy says the blessing over the cup of blessing he speaks of Rabbi Yitzchak's nearness to death and says that he should find a guarantor down below, meaning Rabbi Shimon. The rabbis leave the boy's house, and Rabbi Shimon, when encountered, says that the boy will not live long. Next the rabbis wonder why Moses' merit did not protect the Midianites from destruction even though Ruth and Naamah protected Moab from destruction. Rabbi Shimon explained that Moab had not yet produced Ruth and her offspring so it had to be protected. Three of the rabbis return to see the boy, who welcomes them and who knows without being told that they have been talking about Amon and Moab. He discusses the secret of the wave offering and why barley is offered. They talk about wheat, saying that it is the Tree of Knowledge of Good and Evil. We hear that the Other Side has a part – the chaff – in all the five kinds of grain, and the chaff is exempt from tithe because it has no share in holiness. The boy says that even if the snake had not tempted Eve, Adam would still have produced offspring immediately, due to God's commandment to be fruitful and multiply. The boy talks about the grapevine known as sanctity and the grapevine of the Other Side; he tells why water must be added to wine for the blessing after the meal, to add compassion to mercy. We hear about the bad advice that the elders of Midian gave to Moab, and how they were punished. The boy informs the rabbis that Moab was punished later by David after Ruth had come out of that country. Generations later the Midianites were still longing to attack Yisrael. We learn that King David summoned the hosts of heaven and included his soul with them to bless God, and that later Yisrael took over the task of the serving angels. The boy and Rabbi Elazar talk about sanctification and blessings and about the mighty ones who perform God's bidding. Finally we hear about the great importance of teaching the Torah to one's son.

29. רִבִּי יִצְחָק וְרִבִּי יְהוּדָה הֲווֹ אָזְלֵי בְּאוֹרְחָא, מָטוּ לְהַהוּא אֲתָר דִּכְפַר סִכְנִין, דַּהֲוָה תַּמָּן רַב הַמְנוּנָא סָבָא, אִתְאֲרָחוּ בְּאִתְּתָא דִּילֵיהּ, דַּהֲוָה לָהּ בְּרָא חֲדָא זְעֵירָא, וְכָל יוֹמָא הֲוָה בְּבֵי סִפְרָא, הַהוּא יוֹמָא סָלִיק מִבֵּי סִפְרָא, וְאָתָא לְבֵיתָא, חָמָא לוֹן לְאִלֵּין חַכִּימִין. אָ״ל אִמֵּיהּ, קָרִיב לְגַבֵּי אִלֵּין גּוּבְרִין עִלָּאִין וְתִרְווּח מִנַּיְיהוּ בִּרְכָאָן. קָרִיב לְגַבַּיְיהוּ, עַד לָא קָרִיב, אַהֲדָר לַאֲחוֹרָא. אָ״ל לְאִמֵּיהּ, לָא בָּעֵינָא לְקָרְבָא לְגַבַּיְיהוּ. דְּהָא יוֹמָא דָּא לָא קָרוּ ק״ש, וְהָכִי אוֹלְפֵי לִי, כָּל מַאן דְּלָא קָרֵי ק״ש בְּעוֹנָתֵיהּ, בְּנִדּוּי הוּא כָּל הַהוּא יוֹמָא.

29. Rabbi Yitzchak and Rabbi Yehuda were walking along the road. They reached the place of the village Sachnin, where Rav Hamnuna Saba (the elder) lived, and they were guests of his wife who had a small boy. Every day he went to school, and when he came home from school that day, he saw these sages. His mother told him to approach these lofty people and receive blessings from them. He approached them. As he was approaching, he retreated and said to his mother, I do not wish to approach them, since they did not read Kriat Sh'ma this day and they taught me that whoever does not recite the Sh'ma at its appropriate time is banned all that day.

30. שָׁמְעוּ אִינּוּן, וְתַוְוהוּ, אָרִימוּ יְדַיְיהוּ וּבָרִיכוּ לֵיהּ. אָמְרוּ וַדַּאי הָכִי הוּא. וְיוֹמָא דָּא אִשְׁתַּדַּלְנָא בַּהֲדֵי חָתָן וְכַלָּה, דְּלָא הֲוָה לוֹן צָרְכַיְיהוּ, וַהֲווֹ מִתְאַחֲרָן לְאִזְדַּוְּוגָא, וְלָא הֲוָה ב״נ לְאִשְׁתַּדְּלָא עָלַיְיהוּ, וַאֲנָן אִשְׁתַּדַּלְנָא בְּהוּ, וְלָא קָרֵינָן ק״ש בְּעוֹנָתֵיהּ, וּמַאן דְּאִתְעַסַּק בְּמִצְוָה,

פָּטוּר מִן הַמִּצְוָה. אָמְרוּ לֵיהּ, בְּרִי, בְּמָה יַדְעַת. אָ"ל, בְּרֵיחָא דִּלְבוּשַׁיְיכוּ יְדַעְנָא, כַּד קָרִיבְנָא לְגַבַּיְיכוּ. תַּוְוהוּ. יָתְבוּ, נַטְלוּ יְדַיְיהוּ וְכָרִיכוּ רִפְתָּא.

30. They heard and marveled. They raised their hands and blessed him. They said, It is certainly true THAT WE DIDN'T READ THE KRIAT SH'MA, because today we were busy with a groom and a bride that did not have their minimum needs, and were thus being delayed in their marriage. There was no one to take up their cause and we did our best for them. THEREFORE, we could not read the Kriat Sh'ma at its appropriate time. And whoever performs a precept is exempt from a precept. They said to him, son how did you know? He said to them, By the fragrance of your garments I knew, when I approached you. They marvelled, sat down, washed their hands and ate bread.

31. ר' יְהוּדָה הֲווֹ יְדוֹי מְלוּכְלְכָן, וְנָטִיל יְדוֹי, וּבָרִיךְ עַד לָא נָטִיל. אָ"ל, אִי תַּלְמִידֵי דְּרַב שְׁמַעְיָה חֲסִידָא אַתּוּן, לָא הֲוָה לְכוּ לְבָרְכָא בְּיָדַיִם מְזוּהֲמוֹת, וּמַאן דְּבָרִיךְ בְּיָדַיִם מְזוּהֲמוֹת, חַיָּיב מִיתָה.

31. Rabbi Yehuda's hands were dirty. He washed his hands but said the grace before he washed his hands. THE CHILD told them, If you are the disciples of Rav Shmaya the pious, you would not have blessed when your hands were still filthy. Whoever says the benediction with unclean hands deserves death.

32. פָּתַח הַהוּא יַנּוּקָא וְאָמַר, בְּבֹאָם אֶל אֹהֶל מוֹעֵד יִרְחֲצוּ מַיִם וְלֹא יָמוּתוּ וְגוֹ'. יַלְפֵינָן מֵהַאי קְרָא, דְּמַאן דְּלָא חָיִישׁ לְהַאי, וְיִתְחֲזֵי קַמֵּי מַלְכָּא בִּידִין מְזוּהֲמָן, חַיָּיב מִיתָא. מ"ט. בְּגִין דִּידוֹי דב"נ יַתְבִין בְּרוּמוֹ שֶׁל עוֹלָם. אֶצְבְּעָא חֲדָא אִית בִּידָא דב"נ, וְאִיהוּ אֶצְבְּעָא דְּאָרָמָא מֹשֶׁה.

32. The child opened the discussion with the verse: "When they go into the Tent of Meeting, they shall wash with water, that they die not" (Shemot 30:20). We learn from this verse that whoever is not careful of this, and appears before the King with soiled hands, deserves to die. What is the reason? It is because a person's hands dwell at the top of the world. There is one finger on the hand of a person and that is the finger that Moses raised, MEANING THE MIDDLE FINGER THAT CORRESPONDS TO MOSES, WHO IS THE CENTRAL COLUMN, AS WILL BE EXPLAINED.

33. כְּתִיב וְעָשִׂיתָ בְרִיחִים עֲצֵי שִׁטִּים חֲמִשָּׁה לְקַרְשֵׁי צֶלַע הַמִּשְׁכָּן הָאֶחָד וַחֲמִשָּׁה בְרִיחִים לְקַרְשֵׁי צֶלַע הַמִּשְׁכָּן הַשֵּׁנִית. וּכְתִיב וְהַבְּרִיחַ הַתִּיכוֹן בְּתוֹךְ הַקְּרָשִׁים מַבְרִיחַ מִן הַקָּצֶה אֶל הַקָּצֶה. וְאִי תֵּימָא, דְּהַהוּא בָּרִיחַ הַתִּיכוֹן אַחֲרָא הוּא, דְּלָא הֲוָה בִּכְלָלָא דְּאִינּוּן חֲמִשָּׁה. לָאו הָכִי. אֶלָּא הַהוּא בְּרִיחַ הַתִּיכוֹן, מֵאִינּוּן חֲמִשָּׁה הֲוָה. תְּרֵין מִכָּאן, וּתְרֵין מִכָּאן, וְחַד בְּאֶמְצָעִיתָא. הָא הֲוָה בְּרִיחַ הַתִּיכוֹן, עַמּוּדָא דְּיַעֲקֹב, רָזָא דְּמֹשֶׁה, לָקֳבֵל דָּא, חָמֵשׁ אֶצְבְּעָאן בִּידָא דְּבַר נָשׁ. וְהַבְּרִיחַ הַתִּיכוֹן בְּאֶמְצָעִיתָא, רַב וְעִלָּאָה מִכֹּלָּא, בֵּיהּ קַיְימִין שְׁאַר אַחֲרָנִין.

33. It is written: "And you shall make bars of acacia wood; five for the boards of the one side of the tabernacle, and five bars for the boards of the other side of the tabernacle... And the middle bar in the midst of the boards shall reach from end to end" (Shemot 26:26-28). If you say that middle bar is another one and is not included in the five BARS, it is not so. Rather, that middle bar is one of the five BARS. Two BARS are from this side, two are from that side and one is in the middle. That was the middle bar, the pillar of Jacob, the secret of Moses, MEANING TIFERET, BECAUSE THE TWO BARS IN FRONT OF IT ARE CHESED AND GVURAH AND THE TWO BARS BEHIND IT ARE NETZACH AND HOD. Corresponding to this, there are five fingers on a person's hand and the middle bar, MEANING THE MIDDLE FINGER, is in the middle, larger and longer than the rest. All other FINGERS are supported by it, SINCE TIFERET IS INCLUSIVE OF ALL THE SIX ENDS.

34. וְאִינּוּן חָמֵשׁ בְּרִיחִין, דְּאִקְרוּן חָמֵשׁ מְאָה שְׁנִין, דְּאִילָנָא דְּחַיֵּי אָזִיל בְּהוּ. וּבְרִית קַדִּישָׁא אִתְעַר, בְּחָמֵשׁ אֶצְבְּעָן דִּיְדָא. וּמִלָּה סְתִימָא הוּא עַל מַה דְּאַמְרַת. וע״ד כָּל בִּרְכָאן דְּכַהֲנָא, בְּאֶצְבְּעָן תַּלְיָין. פְּרִישׂוּ דִּיְדָא דְּמֹשֶׁה עַ״ד הֲוָה.

34. These five bars are referred to as five hundred years – MEANING CHESED, GVURAH, TIFERET, NETZACH AND HOD OF ZEIR ANPIN,

WHICH IS THE SECRET OF FIVE HUNDRED YEARS, since the Tree of Life THAT IS ZEIR ANPIN goes in them [meaning included in them]. The holy covenant is aroused by the five fingers of the hand, SINCE YESOD COMPRISES WITHIN IT CHESED, GVURAH, TIFERET, NETZACH AND HOD, and that is a concealed matter about which I spoke. Therefore, all the blessings of the priest are dependent on the fingers. And the spreading of hands of Moses, MEANING WHERE IT SAYS: "AND SPREAD OUT HIS HANDS TO HASHEM..." (SHEMOT 9:33) was because of this.

35. אִי כָּל דָּא אִית בְּהוּ, לֵית דִּינָא לְמֶהֱוֵי בְּנַקְיוּ, כַּד מְבָרְכִין בְּהוּ לְקוּדְשָׁא בְּרִיךְ הוּא. בְּגִין דִּבְהוּ, וּבְדוּגְמָא דִּלְהוֹן, מִתְבְּרַךְ שְׁמָא קַדִּישָׁא. וע"ד אַתּוּן דְּחַכְמִיתּוּ טוּבָא, הֵיךְ לָא אַשְׁגַּחְתּוּן לְהַאי. וְלָא שַׁמַּשְׁתּוּן לְר' שְׁמַעְיָה חֲסִידָא, וְאִיהוּ אָמַר, כָּל טִנּוּפָא, וְכָל לִכְלוּכָא, סָלִיקוּ לֵיהּ לְסִטְרָא אַחֲרָא, דְּהָא סִטְרָא אַחֲרָא מֵהַאי טִנּוּפָא וְלִכְלוּכָא אִתְזָן. וְעַל דָּא מַיִם אַחֲרוֹנִים חוֹבָה, וְחוֹבָה אִינּוּן.

35. If all this is inherent IN THE FINGERS, it is redundant to say that they must be clean when blessing the Holy One, blessed be He. Through them and their counterparts, MEANING THE UPPER CHESED, GVURAH, TIFERET, NETZACH AND HOD, THAT ARE INDICATED THROUGH THEM, the Holy Name is blessed. Therefore, you who are so wise, why did you not pay attention to this? And you did not pay service to Rabbi Shmaya the pious, who declared any filth or stain rises to the Other Side, since the Other Side is sustained from that filth and dirt. Consequently, final water washings are obligatory and required.

36. תַּוְוהוּ וְלָא יָכִילוּ לְמַלְּלָא. א"ר יְהוּדָה, בְּרִי, שְׁמָא דְּאָבוּךְ מַאן הוּא. שָׁתִיק יַנּוּקָא רִגְעָא חֲדָא, קָם לְגַבֵּיהּ אִמֵּיהּ וְנָשַׁק לָהּ, אָ"ל אִמִּי, עַל אַבָּא שָׁאִילוּ לִי אִלֵּין חַכִּימִין, אֵימָא לוֹן. אָ"ל אִימֵּיהּ, בְּרִי, בַּדְקַת לְהוּ. אָמַר הָא בָּדָקִית, וְלָא אַשְׁכָּחִית כַּדְקָא יָאוּת. לְחִישָׁא לֵיהּ אִמֵּיהּ, וְאַהְדָּר לְגַבַּיְיהוּ, אָ"ל אַתּוּן שְׁאֶלְתּוּן עַל אַבָּא, וְהָא אִסְתַּלַּק מֵעָלְמָא, וּבְכָל יוֹמָא דְּחַסִידֵי קַדִּישִׁין אָזְלִין בְּאָרְחָא, אִיהוּ טַיָּיעָא אֲבַתְרַיְיהוּ. וְאִי אַתּוּן קַדִּישֵׁי עֶלְיוֹנִין, הֵיךְ לָא אַשְׁכַּחְתּוּן לֵיהּ, אָזִיל טַיָּיעָא אֲבַתְרַיְיכוּ.

36. They marveled, and could not speak. Rabbi Yehuda said, My son, what is your father's name? The boy was quiet for a moment. He rose AND WENT to his mother and kissed her. He said to her, Mother, these sages asked me about my father. Should I tell them? His mother said to him, My son, have you examined them, IF THEY ARE WORTHY? He said, Here, I checked them and did not find them to be proper. His mother whispered into his ears and he returned to them. He said to them, You have asked me about my father but he has already departed from the world. Every day that devout holy pious men walk the roads, he travels after them on a she-mule. If you are holy and elevated, why did you not notice him walking along and traveling after you on a she-mule?

37. אֲבָל בְּקַדְמֵיתָא חֲמֵינָא בְּכוּ, וְהַשְׁתָּא חֲמֵינָא בְּכוּ, דְּאַבָּא לָא חָמָא חֲמָרָא דְּלָא טָעִין אֲבַתְרֵיהּ חֲמָרָא, לְמִסְבַּל עוּלָּא דְּאוֹרַיְיתָא. כֵּיוָן דְּלָא זְכִיתּוּן דְּאַבָּא יַטְעוּן אֲבַתְרַיְיכוּ, לָא אֵימָא מַאן הוּא אַבָּא. אָמַר רִבִּי יְהוּדָה לְר׳ יִצְחָק, כִּדְדָמֵי לָן, הַאי יַנּוּקָא לָאו בַּר נָשׁ הוּא. אַכְלוּ. וְהַהוּא יְנוֹקָא הֲוָה אָמַר מִלֵּי דְּאוֹרַיְיתָא, וְחִדּוּשֵׁי אוֹרַיְיתָא. אָמְרוּ, הַב וְנִבְרִיךְ. אָמַר לְהוּ, יָאוּת אֲמַרְתּוּן. בְּגִין דִּשְׁמָא קַדִּישָׁא לָא מִתְבָּרַךְ בִּבְרָכָה דָּא, אֶלָּא בְּהַזְמָנָה.

37. At first, I saw THAT YOU DID NOT READ THE SH'MA and now I see THAT YOU ARE NOT HOLY AND ELEVATED; since my father did not see A HOLY MAN RIDING ON an donkey, without bringing after him an donkey, to carry the burden of Torah. Since you were not meritorious enough that my father should follow after you on an donkey, I will not tell you who my father is. Rabbi Yehuda said to Rabbi Yitzchak, It seems to us that this boy is not human. They ate. The boy was speaking words of Torah and giving new insights in the Torah. They said, Let us bless. He said to them, You spoke well, since the Holy Name is not get blessed through this blessing only by summons.

38. פָּתַח וְאָמַר, אֲבָרְכָה אֶת יְיָ׳ בְּכָל עֵת וְגוֹ׳. וְכִי מַה חָמָא דָּוִד לוֹמַר אֲבָרְכָה אֶת יְיָ׳. אֶלָּא, חָמָא דָּוִד דְּבָעֵי הַזְמָנָה, וְאָמַר אֲבָרְכָה. בְּגִין דִּבְשַׁעֲתָא דְּבַר נָשׁ יָתִיב עַל פָּתוֹרָא, שְׁכִינְתָּא קַיְּימָא תַּמָּן, וְסִטְרָא אַחֲרָא קַיְּימָא תַּמָּן. כַּד אַזְמִין בַּר נָשׁ לְבָרְכָא לְקוּדְשָׁא בְּרִיךְ הוּא,

שְׁכִינְתָּא אִתְתְּקָנַת לְגַבֵּי עֵילָּא, לְקַבְּלָא בִּרְכָאן, וְסִטְרָא אַחֲרָא אִתְכַּפְיָיא. וְאִי לָא אַזְמִין ב״נ לְבָרְכָא לְקוּדְשָׁא בְּרִיךְ הוּא, סִטְרָא אַחֲרָא שָׁמַע וּמְכַשְׁכְּשָׁא לְמֶהֱוֵי לֵיהּ חוּלָקָא בְּהַהִיא בְּרָכָה.

38. He opened the discussion with the verse: "I will bless Hashem at all times..." (Tehilim 34:2). HE INQUIRES: Why did David see fit to say, "I will bless Hashem"? HE REPLIES: It is because David realized that a summoning is required and he therefore said, "I will bless," since when a person sits at his table, the Shechinah dwells there and the Other Side stands there. When a person summons to bless the Holy One, blessed be He, the Shechinah is restored to the supernal levels, TO ZEIR ANPIN, to receive blessings, and the Other Side is subdued. If a person does not summon others to bless the Holy One, blessed be He, the Other Side listens and is happy, because it will have a part in that blessing.

39. וְאִי תֵּימָא, בִּשְׁאַר בִּרְכָאן אֲמַאי לָא אִית הַזְמָנָה. אֶלָּא הַהוּא מִלָּה דִּבְרָכָה, דְּקָא מְבָרְכִין עָלָהּ, אִיהוּ הַזְמָנָה. ות״ח דְּהָכִי הוּא, דְּהַאי דִּמְבָרֵךְ עַל פְּרִי, הַהוּא פְּרִי אִיהוּ הַזְמָנָה, וּמְבָרְכִין עָלֵיהּ. וְלֵית לֵיהּ חוּלָקָא לְסִטְרָא אַחֲרָא. וְקוֹדֶם דָּא, דְּהֲוָה הַהוּא פְּרִי בִּרְשׁוּת דְּסִטְרָא אַחֲרָא, לָא מְבָרְכִין עָלֵיהּ. וּכְתִיב לֹא יֵאָכֵל, בְּגִין דְּלָא יְבָרְכוּן עַל הַהוּא פְּרִי, וְלָא יִתְבָּרַךְ סִטְרָא אַחֲרָא. כֵּיוָן דְּנָפַק מֵרְשׁוּתֵיהּ, יֵאָכֵל, וּמְבָרְכִין עָלֵיהּ. וְאִיהוּ הַזְמָנָא לְבִרְכָתָא. וְכֵן כָּל מִילִּין דְּעָלְמָא דְּקָא מְבָרְכִין עֲלַיְיהוּ. כֻּלְּהוּ הַזְמָנָה לְבִרְכָתָא. וְלֵית בְּהוּ חוּלָקָא לְסִטְרָא אַחֲרָא.

39. You might ask why there is no requirement for summoning others in the rest of the blessings. HE REPLIES: It is because these words of blessings, about which the grace is to be given, are in themselves the summons. Come and see that it is so, because when one says a blessing over a fruit, that fruit is the summons for grace. The Other Side has no part in it. However, prior to that, when that fruit is in the domain of the Other Side, no grace is to be recited over it, as is written: "IT BE AS UNCIRCUMCISED UNTO YOU. They shall not be eaten" (Vayikra 19:23), BECAUSE IT IS IN THE DOMAIN OF THE OTHER SIDE. On that fruit, no grace is given, so that the Other Side should not get blessed. As soon as it is out of its domain, of THE OTHER SIDE AFTER THE REQUIRED FORBIDDEN YEARS OF ORLA, he may eat and give grace for it. The fruit becomes the summons for grace, and similarly, all things in the world over which a blessing is said are an invitation for blessings. They have no part for the Other Side.

40. וְאִי תֵּימָא, אוּף הָכִי לְבִרְכַּת זִמּוּן כַּסָּא דְּבִרְכָתָא הֲוָה הַזְמָנָה, אֲמַאי הַב וְנִבְרִיךְ. אֶלָּא, הוֹאִיל וּבְקַדְמֵיתָא כַּד הֲוָה שָׁתֵי, אָמַר בּוֹרֵא פְּרִי הַגֶּפֶן. הָא הַזְמָנָה הֲוֵי. וְהַשְׁתָּא לְבִרְכַּת מְזוֹנָא, בָּעֵינָן שִׁנּוּי, לְהַזְמָנָה אַחֲרָא, דְּהָא כַּסָּא דָּא לְקוּדְשָׁא בְּרִיךְ הוּא הֲוֵי, וְלָאו לִמְזוֹנָא, ובג״כ בָּעֵי הַזְמָנָה דְּפוּמָא.

40. You might say that the blessing after the meal is also similar to it, since the cup of blessing is considered the summons. Why do they say, Let us bless, FOR THE PURPOSE OF INVITATION? HE RESPONDS: It is only because at the beginning, when he drank, he said, 'Who creates the fruit of the vine' so, THE WINE ALREADY SERVED ITS PURPOSE FOR an invitation and now at the blessing after the meal we require something else for a different summons, since the cup is for the Holy One, blessed be He, and not for the meal. Therefore, the summoning must be by mouth.

41. וְאִי תֵּימָא, נְבָרֵךְ שֶׁאָכַלְנוּ מִשֶּׁלּוֹ, דָּא הוּא הַזְמָנָה, בָּרוּךְ שֶׁאָכַלְנוּ דָּא הוּא בְּרָכָה. הָכִי הוּא וַדַּאי. אֲבָל נְבָרֵךְ, הַזְמָנָה אַחֲרָא אִיהוּ, הַזְמָנָה דְּבוֹרֵא פְּרִי הַגֶּפֶן. דְּקַדְמֵיתָא אִיהִי הַזְמָנָה לְכוֹס דִּבְרָכָה סְתָם. וְהִיא כּוֹס, כֵּיוָן דְּאַנְטִיל אִיהוּ הַזְמָנָה אַחֲרָא בְּמִלָּה דִּנְבָרֵךְ לְגַבֵּי עָלְמָא עִלָּאָה דְּכָל מְזוֹנִין וּבִרְכָאן מִתַּמָּן נָפְקִין, ובג״כ אִיהוּ בְּאֹרַח סָתִים, דְּעָלְמָא עִלָּאָה סָתִים אִיהוּ, וְלֵית לְגַבֵּיהּ הַזְמָנָה. אֶלָּא בְּדַרְגָּא דָּא כּוֹס דִּבְרָכָה. א״ר יְהוּדָה, זַכָּאָה חוּלָקָנָא, דְּמִן יוֹמָא דְּעָלְמָא עַד הַשְׁתָּא, לָא שְׁמַעְנָא מִלִּין אִלֵּין, וַדַּאי הָא אֲמֵינָא דְּדָא לָאו ב״נ אִיהוּ.

41. You might say that 'Let us bless Him of whose bounty we have eaten' is the invitation, and 'blessed is He of whose bounty we have eaten' is the blessing. AND IF SO, WHY IS IT NECESSARY TO SAY BEFORE THESE: LET

US BLESS? HE RESPONDS: That is certainly so; however, let us bless HIM OF WHOSE BOUNTY WE HAVE EATEN, is another invitation. It is an invitation for He who creates the fruit of the vine. At first, WHEN HE SAID, LET US BLESS, it is a general invitation for the cup of blessing, WHICH IS THE SECRET OF MALCHUT. As soon as this cup is received, there is another additional invitation in the phrase: Let us bless. That is for the supernal world, WHICH IS ZEIR ANPIN, whence all the sustenance and blessings emanate. Thus, it is done in a concealed manner, AS THE NAME IS NOT MENTIONED IN IT, BUT RATHER SIMPLY, LET US BLESS HIM OF WHOSE BOUNTY WE HAVE EATEN. The higher realm is concealed and no OPEN invitation is to be given EXCEPT through this level ONLY, but with the cup of blessing THERE IS AN OPEN INVITATION. Rabbi Yehuda said, Praised is our lot, for from this day that I am in this world until now, I have not heard these things. Certainly it is like I said, that this one is not human.

42. אָ"ל, בְּרָא, מַלְאָכָא דַּיְיָ', רְחִימָא דִּילֵיהּ, הַאי דְּאַמְרַת וְעָשִׂיתָ בְרִיחִים עֲצֵי שִׁטִּים חֲמִשָּׁה לְקַרְשֵׁי צֶלַע הַמִּשְׁכָּן וְגוֹ', וַחֲמִשָּׁה בְרִיחִים וְגוֹ', וַחֲמִשָּׁה בְּרִיחִים לַיַּרְכָתַיִם יָמָּה. הָא בְּרִיחִים טוּבָא אִיכָּא הָכָא, וְיָדַיִם אִינּוּן תְּרֵין. אָמַר לֵיהּ, דָּא הוּא דְּאַמְרִין, מִפּוּמֵיהּ דְּבַר נָשׁ אִשְׁתְּמַע מַאן אִיהוּ. אֲבָל הוֹאִיל וְלָא אַשְׁגַּחְתּוּן אֲנָא אֵימָא.

42. He said to him, Son, angel of Hashem, His beloved, that which you said, "And you shall make bars of acacia wood, five, for the boards of the one side of the tabernacle...and five bars...and five bars...for the side westward" (Shemot 26:26-28). We find here a great number of bars but there are only two hands, THAT CONTAIN ONLY TWO TIMES FIVE FINGERS. THE BOY said to him, That is what they say, From a person's mouth it is known who he is. However, since you have not observed TO BE ABLE TO UNDERSTAND, I will speak.

43. פָּתַח וְאָמַר, הֶחָכָם עֵינָיו בְּרֹאשׁוֹ וְגוֹ'. וְכִי בְּאָן אֲתָר עֵינוֹי דב"נ, אֶלָּא בְּרֹאשׁוֹ, דִּילְמָא בְּגוּפוֹ אוֹ בִּדְרוֹעֵיהּ, דְּאַפִּיק לֶחָכָם יַתִּיר מִכָּל בְּנֵי עָלְמָא. אֶלָּא קְרָא הָכִי הוּא וַדַּאי, דִּתְנָן, לָא יְהַךְ בַּר נָשׁ בְּגִלּוּי דְּרֵישָׁא ד' אַמּוֹת. מ"ט. דִּשְׁכִינְתָּא שַׁרְיָא עַל רֵישֵׁיהּ, וְכָל חַכִּים, עֵינוֹי וּמִלּוֹי בְּרֹאשׁוֹ אִינּוּן, בְּהַהוּא דְּשַׁרְיָא וְקַיְּימָא עַל רֵישֵׁיהּ.

43. He opened the discussion with the verse: "The wise man's eyes are in his head" (Kohelet 2:14). HE INQUIRES: IT SAYS, "in his head:" are the eyes of a man in any other place, are they in his body, or in his arm, that the wisest of men is letting us know!? But the meaning in the scripture is surely this, that we were taught a person should not walk more than four cubits with an uncovered head. Why is this? It is because the Shechinah dwells upon his head, and any wise man's eyes and thoughts are in his head, that is, upon that which dwells and remains over his head, WHICH IS THE SHECHINAH.

44. וְכַד עֵינוֹי תַּמָּן, לִינְדַּע דְּהַהוּא נְהוֹרָא דְּאַדְלִיק עַל רֵישֵׁיהּ, אִצְטְרִיךְ לְמִשְׁחָא, בְּגִין דְּגוּפָא דב"נ אִיהוּ פְּתִילָה, וּנְהוֹרָא אַדְלִיק לְעֵילָּא, וּשְׁלֹמֹה מַלְכָּא צָוַוח וְאָמַר, וְשֶׁמֶן עַל רֹאשְׁךָ אַל יֶחְסָר, דְּהָא נְהוֹרָא דִּבְרֹאשׁוֹ, אִצְטְרִיךְ לְמִשְׁחָא וְאִינּוּן עוֹבָדִין טָבָאן. וע"ד הֶחָכָם עֵינָיו בְּרֹאשׁוֹ, וְלָא בַּאֲתָר אַחֲרָא.

44. When his eyes are there on the head, WHICH IS THE SHECHINAH, he should be aware that the light that is lit over his head needs oil, since the person's body is the wick and the light is lit on the top, IN THE WICK. King Solomon cried out and said, "Let your head lack no oil" (Kohelet 9:8), since the light in his head requires oil, and that is good deeds. About this, HE SAYS, "The wise man's eyes are in the head" and in no other place.

45. אַתּוּן חַכִּימִין, וַדַּאי שְׁכִינְתָּא שַׁרְיָיא עַל רֵישַׁיְיכוּ, הֵיךְ לָא אַשְׁגַּחְתּוּן לְהַאי, דִּכְתִּיב וְעָשִׂיתָ בְרִיחִם וְגוֹ', לְקַרְשֵׁי צֶלַע הַמִּשְׁכָּן הָאֶחָד. וַחֲמִשָּׁה בְּרִיחִם לְקַרְשֵׁי צֶלַע הַמִּשְׁכָּן הַשֵּׁנִית. הָאֶחָד וְהַשֵּׁנִית אָמַר קְרָא, שְׁלִישִׁית וּרְבִיעִית לָא אָמַר קְרָא. דְּהָא אֶחָד וְשֵׁנִית, דָּא חָשִׁיבוּ דִּתְרֵין סִטְרִין, ובג"כ עָבֵיד חוּשְׁבָנָא בִּתְרֵין אִלֵּין.

45. You are certainly wise men and the Shechinah dwells upon your heads. How is it that you have not noticed what is written: "And you shall make bars of acacia wood; five for the boards of the one side of the Tabernacle, and five bars for the boards of the other side of the Tabernacle"? The first and second side of the Tabernacle are mentioned in the scripture, but the third and fourth sides are not mentioned in the scripture. For the first and second of the two sides are the reckoning of the two sides, RIGHT AND LEFT, WHICH ARE CHESED AND GVURAH THAT ARE CALLED 'TWO HANDS'. AND THE THIRD, WHICH IS ON THE WEST, HE DOES NOT COUNT, SINCE IT ONLY RECEIVES FROM THESE TWO SIDES. Therefore, he accounted ONLY FOR these two THAT ARE THE SECRET OF THE TWO HANDS.

46. אָתוּ אִינּוּן וּנְשָׁקוּהוּ, בָּכָה רִבִּי יְהוּדָה, וְאָמַר, ר' שִׁמְעוֹן זַכָּאָה חוּלָקָךְ, זַכָּאָה דָּרָא, דְּהָא בִּזְכוּתָךְ אֲפִילּוּ יַנּוּקֵי דְּבֵי רַב, אִינּוּן טִנָּרִין רָמָאִין תַּקִּיפִין. אָתָאת אִמֵּיהּ, אָמְרָה לוֹן רַבּוֹתַי, בְּמָטוּ מִנַּיְיכוּ, לָא תִּשְׁגְּחוּן עַל בְּרִי, אֶלָּא בְּעֵינָא טָבָא. אָמְרוּ לָהּ, זַכָּאָה חוּלָקָךְ אִתְּתָא כְּשֵׁרָה, אִתְּתָא בְּרִירָא מִכָּל שְׁאַר נָשִׁין, דְּהָא קוּדְשָׁא בְּרִיךְ הוּא בָּרִיר חוּלָקָךְ, וְאָרִים דִּגְלָךְ עַל כָּל שְׁאַר נָשִׁין דְּעָלְמָא.

46. They approached and kissed him. Rabbi Yehuda cried and said, Rabbi Shimon, praised is your lot and praised is YOUR generation, since because of your merit, even school children are high and mighty mountains. His mother approached and said to them, My teacher, I beg of you, Look at my son only with a benevolent eye. They said to her, Praised is your lot, worthy woman. You are a distinguished woman above all other women, since the Holy One, blessed be He, chose your lot and raised your banner over all other women of the world.

47. אָמַר יַנּוּקָא, אֲנָא לָא מִסְתַּפֵינָא מֵעֵינָא בִּישָׁא, דְּבַר נוּנָא רַבָּא וְיַקִּירָא אֲנָא, וְנוּנָא לָא דָּחִיל מֵעֵינָא בִּישָׁא, דִּכְתִּיב וְיִדְגּוּ לָרוֹב בְּקֶרֶב הָאָרֶץ, מַאי לָרוֹב, לְאַסְגָּאָה עַל עֵינָא. וְתָנֵינָן, מַה דָּגִים דְּיַמָּא מַיָּא חָפֵי עֲלֵיהוֹן, וְלֵית עֵינָא בִּישָׁא וְכוּ'. לָרוֹב וַדַּאי, בְּקֶרֶב הָאָרֶץ, בְּגוֹ בְּנֵי אֱנָשָׁא עַל אַרְעָא. אָמְרוּ, בְּרָא, מַלְאָכָא דַּיְיָ', לֵית בָּנָא עֵינָא בִּישָׁא, וְלָא מִסִּטְרָא דְּעֵינָא בִּישָׁא אֲתֵינָן. וְקוּדְשָׁא בְּרִיךְ הוּא חָפֵי עֲלָךְ בְּגַדְפּוֹי.

47. The child said, I am not afraid of the evil eye, since I am a son of a great and worthy fish, and a fish has no fear from the evil eye, as is written: "And let them grow into a multitude (lit. 'as fish') in the midst of the earth"

(Beresheet 48:16). What is "multitude"? That includes also the eye, MEANING TO SAY THAT NO HARM SHALL BEFALL THEM DUE TO THE EVIL EYE. We were taught, just like fish in the sea, that the water acts as a cover for them, and no evil eye HAS AN EFFECT ON THEM, SO THE EVIL EYE WILL HAVE NO POWER OVER THEM. THEREFORE, it is "multitude" assuredly. "In the midst of the earth" means within the people that are dwelling on the land, MEANING THAT THE EVIL EYE WILL NOT HARM THEM, EVEN THOUGH THEY ARE NOT COVERED AS ARE FISH. They said TO HIM, Son, angel of Hashem, we do not have an evil eye and neither do we come from the side of the evil eye. The Holy One, blessed be He, covers you with His wings.

48. פָּתַח וְאָמַר הַמַּלְאָךְ הַגּוֹאֵל אוֹתִי מִכָּל רָע יְבָרֵךְ וְגוֹ'. הַאי קְרָא אָמַר יַעֲקֹב בְּרוּחַ קוּדְשָׁא, אִי בְּרוּחַ קוּדְשָׁא אָ"ל, רָזָא דְּחָכְמְתָא אִית בֵּיהּ. הַמַּלְאָךְ, קָרֵי לֵיהּ מַלְאָךְ. וְקָרֵי לֵיהּ שְׁמָהָן אַחֲרָנִין. הָכָא, אֲמַאי אִקְרֵי מַלְאָךְ. אֶלָּא כַּד אִיהוּ שְׁלִיחָא מִלְּעֵילָּא, וְקַבִּילַת זְהֲרָא מִגּוֹ אַסְפַּקְלַרְיָא דִּלְעֵילָּא, דִּכְדֵין מְבָרְכִין אַבָּא וְאִמָּא לְהַאי, אַמְרֵי לָהּ בְּרַתִּי, זִילִי נְטוּרִי בֵּיתֵיךְ, פְּקִידִי לְבֵיתֵיךְ. הָכִי עֲבִידִי לְבֵיתֵיךְ. זִילִי וְזוּנִי לוֹן. זִילִי, דְּהַהוּא עָלְמָא דִּלְתַתָּא מְחַכֶּא לָךְ, בְּנֵי בֵּיתָךְ מְחַכָּאן מְזוֹנָא מִנָּךְ, הָא לָךְ כָּל מַה דְּתִצְטָרְכִי לְמֵיהַב לוֹן, כְּדֵין אִיהִי מַלְאָךְ.

48. He opened the discussion with the verse: "The angel who redeemed me from all evil, bless..." (Ibid.). Jacob said this verse in the Holy Spirit and if he said it to him in the Holy Spirit, it must contain the secret of wisdom. "The angel": HE ASKS: He calls MALCHUT an angel, and calls it also other names. Why has he here called her, MALCHUT, an angel? HE REPLIES: It is only WHEN MALCHUT is a messenger from above and receives splendor from the mirror above that Aba and Ima bless her, and say to her, My daughter, go and watch your home, MEANING THE WORLD. Visit your household. That is what you should do to your household. Go and sustain them. Go, since the world below waits for you and the members of your household are waiting for food from you. You have all you need to give to them. Then MALCHUT IS CALLED 'an angel' (also: 'messenger').

49. וְאִי תֵּימָא, וְהָא בְּכַמָּה דוּכְתֵּי אִקְרֵי מַלְאָךְ, וְלָא אָתֵי לְמֵיזָן

עָלְמִין. וְעוֹד, דְּבִשְׁמָא דָּא לָא זָן עָלְמִין, אֶלָּא בִּשְׁמָא דַּיְיָ׳. הָכִי הוּא וַדַּאי, כַּד שָׁלִיחַ מִגּוֹ אַבָּא וְאִמָּא, אִקְרֵי מַלְאָךְ, וְכֵיוָן דְּשָׁארִי עַל דּוּכְתִּין, עַל תְּרֵין כְּרוּבִין אֲדֹנָי שְׁמֵיהּ.

49. You may wonder that we find that MALCHUT is called ‘angel’ in several places, and yet is not sent to sustain the worlds. Furthermore, with this name, ANGEL, she does not sustain the worlds, but rather by the name of Yud Hei Vav Hei. HE RESPONDS: It definitely is so. When she is an emissary from Aba and Ima, she is called ‘angel’ and when she is at rest in her own place over the two Cherubs, Adonai is her name.

50. לְמֹשֶׁה כַּד אִתְחֲזֵי לֵיהּ בְּקַדְמֵיתָא, אִקְרֵי מַלְאָךְ לְיַעֲקֹב לָא אִתְחֲזֵי הָכִי, אֶלָּא בְּדוּגְמָא, דִּכְתִּיב וְרָחֵל בָּאָה, דָּא דְּיוּקְנָא דְּרָחֵל אַחֲרָא, דִּכְתִּיב כֹּה אָמַר יְיָ׳ קוֹל בְּרָמָה נִשְׁמָע וְגוֹ׳. רָחֵל מְבַכָּה עַל בָּנֶיהָ. וְרָחֵל בָּאָה סְתָם, עִם הַצֹּאן דַּרְגִּין דִּילָהּ. אֲשֶׁר לְאָבִיהָ וַדַּאי. וְכֻלְּהוּ אִתְמְנוּן וְאִתְפַּקְּדוּן בִּידָהָא. כִּי רוֹעָה הִיא, אִיהִי מְנַהֲגָא לוֹן, וְאִתְפַּקְדָא עָלַיְיהוּ.

50. When THE SHECHINAH first appeared to Moses, She is called ‘an angel’, AS IT SAYS, “AND THE ANGEL OF HASHEM APPEARED TO HIM IN THE FLAME OF FIRE” (SHEMOT 3:2). To Jacob, She did not appear like that, except in a likeness, MEANING IN RACHEL BELOW, WHO IS THE LIKENESS OF RACHEL ABOVE, WHICH IS MALCHUT. It is written: “Rachel came” (Beresheet 29:9), which is the form of another Rachel ABOVE, WHICH IS MALCHUT, as is written: “Thus says Hashem; A voice is heard in Ramah... Rachel weeping for her children” (Yirmeyah 31:14). THIS RACHEL IS THE SECRET OF MALCHUT. HERE TOO, “Rachel came” unspecified INDICATES MALCHUT. “With sheep” (Beresheet 29:9): These are the levels OF MALCHUT. “Her father’s” (Ibid.), surely, SINCE ABA, THAT IS CHOCHMAH, ESTABLISHED THE DAUGHTER, WHICH IS MALCHUT. And all, THAT IS, ALL THE WORLDS, were appointed and assigned to her hands, “for she kept them.” She also leads them and has been assigned over them.

51. וְהָכִי בְּמֹשֶׁה כְּתִיב, וַיֵּרָא מַלְאַךְ יְיָ׳ אֵלָיו בְּלַבַּת אֵשׁ. וְאִי תֵּימָא יַתִּיר הוּא שְׁבָחָא דְּאַבְרָהָם, דְּלָא כְּתִיב בֵּיהּ מַלְאָךְ, אֶלָּא וַיֵּרָא אֵלָיו יְיָ׳

בְּאֵלוֹנֵי מַמְרֵא וְגוֹ׳. הָתָם בְּאַבְרָהָם, אִתְחֲזֵי לֵיהּ אֲדֹנָי, בְּאָלֶף דָּלֶת, בְּגִין דִּבְהַהוּא זִמְנָא קַבִּיל בְּרִית, וּמַה דַּהֲוָה אִתְכַּסֵּי עַד כְּעָן מִנֵּיהּ, אִתְחֲזֵי לֵיהּ רִבּוֹן וְשָׁלִיט, וְהָכִי אִתְחֲזֵי, דְּהָא כְּדֵין בְּהַהוּא דַּרְגָּא אִתְקָשַׁר, וְלָא יַתִּיר. וּבג״כ, בִּשְׁמָא דַּאֲדוֹן רִבּוֹן עָלֵיהּ.

51. So it was written about Moses: "And the angel of Hashem appeared to him in a flame of fire." SINCE THE FIRST TIME, MALCHUT APPEARED TO HIM IN THE ASPECT OF AN ANGEL, AS MENTIONED ABOVE, AND THAT IS MORE IMPORTANT THAN THE VISION OF JACOB, THAT WAS ONLY A LIKENESS. You might say that Abraham's praise is greater than his, since no angel is mentioned in relation to him, but rather: "And Hashem appeared to him by the oak of Mamre..." (Beresheet 18:1). HE RESPONDS: The name of Adonai appeared to Abraham, which is with Aleph-Dalet-Nun-Yud, AS IS WRITTEN: "MY MASTER, (HEB. *ADONAI*), PASS NOT AWAY, I PRAY YOU, FROM YOUR SERVANT" (IBID. 3). It is because during this period he received the covenant, and what was concealed from him up to then was PRESENTLY visible to him, the Master and ruler, WHICH IS ADONAI. He was worthy of that, since he was then connected to that level, MALCHUT, but not further. Therefore, HASHEM WAS REVEALED TO HIM by the name of Master and ruler, THAT IS, BY THE NAME OF ADONAI.

52. אֲבָל מֹשֶׁה דְּלָא הֲוָה בֵּיהּ פֵּרוּדָא, דִּכְתִיב מֹשֶׁה מֹשֶׁה דְּלָא פָּסְקָא טַעֲמָא. כְּמָה דִּכְתִיב אַבְרָהָם אַבְרָהָם, דְּפַסְקָא טַעֲמָא. בְּגִין דְּהַשְׁתָּא שְׁלִים, מַה דְּלָא הֲוָה מִקַּדְמַת דְּנָא. פְּרִישׁוּ אִית בֵּין אַבְרָהָם דְּהַשְׁתָּא, לְאַבְרָהָם דְּקַדְמֵיתָא. אֲבָל מֹשֶׁה, מִיַּד דְּאִתְיְילִיד, אַסְפַּקְלַרְיָאָה דְּנַהֲרָא הֲוָת עִמֵּיהּ, דִּכְתִיב וַתֵּרֶא אוֹתוֹ כִּי טוֹב הוּא. וּכְתִיב וַיַּרְא אֱלֹהִים אֶת הָאוֹר כִּי טוֹב. מֹשֶׁה מִיָּד אִתְקְשַׁר בְּדַרְגָּא דִּילֵיהּ וּבג״כ מֹשֶׁה מֹשֶׁה, וְלָא אַפְסִיק טַעֲמָא.

52. However, there was no division in Moses, as is written: "Moses" (Shemot 3:4), without any dividing mark, as it is written regarding Abraham: "Abraham, Abraham" (Beresheet 22:11), with a separating punctuation mark to make a division. THE DIVISION MARK ALLUDES TO THE SECOND 'ABRAHAM', who is now perfected, which was not the case with the earlier Abraham. There is a difference between Abraham at present to Abram of the past. However, at the instant Moses was born, the shining mirror was already with him, WHICH IS THE LIGHT OF ZEIR ANPIN, as is written: "And when she saw that he was goodly" (Shemot 2:2). It is also written: "And Elohim saw the light, that it was good" (Beresheet 1:4), WHICH ALLUDES TO ZEIR ANPIN. HERE TOO, "GOODLY" ALLUDES TO ZEIR ANPIN, because Moses was immediately connected to his own level THAT IS ZEIR ANPIN. Therefore it says, "Moses Moses," without a separating punctuation mark BETWEEN MOSES AND MOSES.

53. וע״ד לְגַבֵּי דְּמֹשֶׁה, אַזְעִיר גַּרְמֵיהּ, דִּכְתִּיב מַלְאַךְ יְיָ׳. יַעֲקֹב קָרָא לֵיהּ, בְּשַׁעֲתָא דַּהֲוָה סָלִיק מֵעָלְמָא, מַלְאָךְ. מ״ט. בְּגִין דִּבְהַהִיא שַׁעֲתָא הֲוָה יָרִית לָהּ, לְשַׁלְטָאָה. מֹשֶׁה בְּחַיָּיו. יַעֲקֹב, לְבָתַר דְּסָלִיק מֵעָלְמָא. מֹשֶׁה בְּגוּפָא. יַעֲקֹב בְּרוּחָא. זַכָּאָה חוּלָקָא דְּמֹשֶׁה.

53. Therefore, MALCHUT reduced herself towards Moses, WHO WAS ALWAYS ON THE LEVEL OF ZEIR ANPIN, as is written: "The angel of Hashem" AND NOT HER OWN NAME, SINCE MALCHUT RECEIVES FROM ZEIR ANPIN. Jacob called MALCHUT at the time he departed from the world, by the name of angel, LIKE MOSES. What is the reason? At that time, he was inheriting her to rule, AS MOSES DID, SINCE Moses JOINED WITH MALCHUT during his lifetime, but Jacob WAS JOINED WITH HER ONLY after departing from the world. Moses WAS WITH MALCHUT WHILE STILL in his body, Jacob ONLY in spirit AFTER IT LEFT THE BODY. Praised is the lot of Moses.

54. הַגּוֹאֵל אוֹתִי מִכָּל רָע, דְּלָא אִתְקְרִיב לְעָלְמִין לְגַבֵּי סִטְרָא דְּרַע, וְלָא יָכִיל רַע לְשַׁלְטָאָה בֵּיהּ. יְבָרֵךְ אֶת הַנְּעָרִים, כְּדֵין יַעֲקֹב הֲוָה מְתַקֵּן לְבֵיתֵיהּ, כב״נ דְּאָזִיל לְבֵיתָא חַדְתָּא, וּמְתַקֵּן לָהּ בְּתִקּוּנוֹי, וּמְקַשֵּׁט לָהּ בְּקִשּׁוּטוֹי. יְבָרֵךְ אֶת הַנְּעָרִים, אִינּוּן דְּאִשְׁתְּמוֹדְעָן, אִינּוּן דְּאִתְפָּקְדָן עַל עָלְמָא, לְאִתְמַשְּׁכָא מִנַּיְיהוּ בִּרְכָאן, תְּרֵין כְּרוּבִין אִינּוּן. וְיִקָּרֵא בָהֶם שְׁמִי, הַשְׁתָּא אַתְקִין בֵּיתֵיהּ, וְאִיהוּ אִסְתַּלָּק בְּדַרְגֵּיהּ, בְּגִין דְּחִבּוּרָא בְּיַעֲקֹב הֲוֵי. גּוּפָא, אִתְדַּבַּק בַּאֲתָר דְּאִצְטְרִיךְ, וּתְרֵין דְּרוֹעִין בַּהֲדֵיהּ.

54. "Who redeemed me from all evil" (Beresheet 48:16), MEANING that he never came close to the side of evil and evil had no domination over him. "Bless the lads" (Ibid.): PRIOR TO HIS DEPARTURE, Jacob established his household, MEANING MALCHUT, like a person who moves to a new house, who makes his own arrangements and decorates it. "Bless the lads": That means the known LADS, who were appointed over the world so as to draw blessings from them. These are the two Cherubs, METATRON AND SANDALPHON. "And let my name be named on them" (Ibid.), MEANING TIFERET, THE QUALITY OF JACOB. Now that he constructed his abode, WHICH IS MALCHUT, and he rose to his own level, WHICH IS TIFERET, since MALCHUT is connected with Jacob, WHO IS TIFERET. The body, WHICH IS TIFERET, is joined where it should, MEANING IN MALCHUT, with the two arms with it. THAT IS "THE NAMES OF MY FATHERS" (IBID.) WHICH ARE CHESED AND GVURAH.

55. לְבָתַר דְּאִינּוּן נְעָרִים מִתְבָּרְכָן כַּדְּקָא יָאוּת, כְּדֵין וְיִדְגּוּ לָרוֹב בְּקֶרֶב הָאָרֶץ. אָרְחָא דְּנוּנִין לְאַסְגָּאָה גּוֹ מַיִין, וְאִי נַפְקָן מִגּוֹ מַיָּא לְיַבֶּשְׁתָּא, מִיָּד מֵתִין. אִלֵּין לָאו הָכִי, אֶלָּא אִינּוּן מִן יַמָּא רַבָּא, וּסְגִיאוּ דִּלְהוֹן לְאַפָּשָׁא וּלְאַסְגֵּי בְּקֶרֶב הָאָרֶץ אִיהוּ. מַה דְּלֵית הָכִי לְכָל נוּנִין דְּעָלְמָא.

55. After these lads, METATRON AND SANDALPHON, are blessed as required, then, "let grow into a multitude (lit. 'like fish') in the midst of the earth," since it is the manner of fish to multiply AND BE FRUITFUL inside water. If they leave the water for dry land, they soon die. These are not like that. They are, however, from that great ocean, MEANING FROM MALCHUT. Their increase is by being fruitful and multiplying in the land, MEANING IN THE LOWER WORLDS THAT ARE DRAWN DOWN FROM MALCHUT, which is not the case for all the fish in the world.

56. מַה כְּתִיב לְעֵילָּא, וַיְבָרֶךְ אֶת יוֹסֵף וַיֹּאמַר, וְלָא אַשְׁכְּחָן לֵיהּ הָכָא בִּרְכָאן, דְּהָא לְבָתַר בָּרִיךְ לֵיהּ, דִּכְתִּיב בֵּן פּוֹרָת יוֹסֵף. אֶלָּא, כֵּיוָן דְּבָרִיךְ לְאִלֵּין נְעָרִים, לְיוֹסֵף בְּרִיךְ. דְּהָא לָא יַכְלִי לְאִתְבָּרְכָא, אֶלָּא מִגּוֹ יוֹסֵף, וּמִגּוֹ דְּאִיהוּ בִּטְמִירוּ, וְלָא אִתְחֲזֵי לְאִתְגַּלָּאָה, כְּתִיב בִּטְמִירוּ, וְיִקָּרֵא בָהֶם שְׁמִי וְשֵׁם אֲבוֹתַי, מִן הָאָבוֹת מִתְבָּרְכָן, וְלָא מֵאֲתָר אַחֲרָא. בְּקֶרֶב הָאָרֶץ, דָּא הוּא כִּסּוּיָא לְחָפָאָה מַה דְּאִצְטְרִיךְ.

56. It is written before: "And he blessed Joseph, and said" (Ibid. 15), yet we don't find any blessings here. It is only later that he blessed him, as it says, "Joseph is a fruitful bough" (Beresheet 49:22). HE RESPONDS: It is because by blessing these lads, he also was giving a blessing to Joseph. They could only be blessed through Joseph, SINCE MALCHUT HAS NOTHING OF HER OWN EXCEPT WHAT JOSEPH, WHO IS YESOD OF ZEIR ANPIN, GIVES HER. THEREFORE, HE GAVE HIS BLESSING TO JOSEPH, WHO BESTOWED IT ON MALCHUT, AND MALCHUT TO THE LADS, WHICH ARE METATRON AND SANDALPHON. Because YESOD is hidden, and it is improper to uncover it, FOR FEAR THAT THE FORESKIN SHOULD COME NEAR AND SUCKLE FROM IT, it is written in a hidden form, because "and let my name be named on them, and the name of my fathers." They are blessed from the fathers, WHO ARE CHESED, GVURAH AND TIFERET, and from no other place. "In the midst of the earth": That is the cover, to cover that which needs covering, WHICH IS YESOD THAT MALCHUT, THAT IS CALLED 'EARTH', COVERS. THEREFORE, JOSEPH IS ALSO ALLUDED TO IN THE SCRIPTURE, HOWEVER, IN A HIDDEN WAY. THAT IS A DIFFERENT EXPLANATION THAN THE ONE MENTIONED NEARBY.

57. אָתוּ וּנְשָׁקוּהּ כְּמִלְקַדְּמִין, אָמְרוּ, הָבוּ וּנְבָרִיךְ. אָמַר אִיהוּ, אֲנִי אֲבָרֵךְ, דְּכָל מַה דִּשְׁמַעְתּוּן עַד הָכָא מִנַּאי הֲוָה, וַאֲקַיֵּים בִּי טוֹב עַיִן הוּא יְבוֹרָךְ, קְרֵי בֵּיהּ יְבָרֵךְ. מ״ט. בְּגִין דְּנָתַן מִלַּחְמוֹ לַדָּל. מִלַּחְמָא וּמֵיכְלָא דְּאוֹרַיְיתָא דִּילִי אֲכַלְתּוּן. א״ר יְהוּדָה. בְּרָא רְחִימָא דְקוּדְשָׁא בְּרִיךְ הוּא, הָא תָּנֵינָן בַּעַל הַבַּיִת בּוֹצֵעַ וְאוֹרֵחַ מְבָרֵךְ. אָ״ל, לָאו אֲנָא בַּעַל הַבַּיִת, וְלָאו אַתּוּן אוֹרְחִין. אֲבָל קְרָא אַשְׁכַּחְנָא, וַאֲקַיֵּים לֵיהּ. דְּהָא אֲנָא טוֹב עַיִן וַדַּאי, בְּלָא שָׁאִילוּ דִּלְכוֹן אֲמֵינָא עַד הַשְׁתָּא, וְלַחְמָא וּמֵיכְלָא דִּילִי אֲכַלְתּוּן.

57. They approached and kissed him again. They said, Let us bless. THE CHILD said, I will say the blessing, since everything that you heard up until now, YOU HEARD from me, and I shall fulfill in me: "He that has a generous eye shall be blessed" (Mishlei 22:9). Pronounce it "shall bless." What is the reason? "For he gives of his bread to the poor" (Ibid.) and you ate and received my bread and victuals of the Torah. Rabbi Yehuda said, Beloved son of the Holy One, blessed be He, were we not taught that the master of the household cuts the bread and the guest says the blessing after the meal?

He replied to them, I am not the master of the household and you are not guests. However, I shall fulfill the verse that I have found, since I certainly have a generous eye. Without your request, I spoke OF NEW INSIGHTS IN THE TORAH until now, and you ate my bread and food.

58. נָטַל כַּסָּא דְּבִרְכָתָא וּבָרִיךְ, וִידוֹי לָא יַכְלֵי לְמִסְבַּל כַּסָּא, וַהֲווֹ מְרַתְּתֵי. כַּד מָטָא לְעַל הָאָרֶץ וְעַל הַמָּזוֹן, אָמַר, כּוֹס יְשׁוּעוֹת אֶשָּׂא וּבְשֵׁם יְיָ' אֶקְרָא. קַיְּימָא כַּסָּא עַל תִּקּוּנֵיהּ, וְאִתְיְשַׁב בִּימִינֵיהּ, וּבָרִיךְ. לְסוֹף אָמַר, יְהֵא רַעֲוָא דִּלְחַד מֵאִלֵּין, יִתְמַשְׁכוּן לֵיהּ חַיִּין, מִגּוֹ אִילָנָא דְּחַיֵּי, דְּכָל חַיִּין בֵּיהּ תַּלְיָין. וְקוּדְשָׁא בְּרִיךְ הוּא יֶעֱרַב לֵיהּ, וְיִשְׁכַּח עָרֵב לְתַתָּא, דְּיִסְתַּכַּם בְּעַרְבוּתֵיהּ, בַּהֲדֵי מַלְכָּא קַדִּישָׁא.

58. He took the cup of blessing and said the blessing. His hands could not carry the cup and were shaking. When he reached: 'for the land and for the nourishment', he said, "I will raise the cup of salvation, and call upon the name of Hashem" (Tehilim 116:13). He placed the cup in its place and settled to the right and continued the blessings. At the end, he said, May it please You that to one of these, MEANING RABBI YITZCHAK, life would be drawn from the Tree of Life, upon which all life is dependent, and the Holy One, blessed be He would be his surety, so he would find a guarantor down below, MEANING RABBI SHIMON, who would agree to be a guarantor together with the Holy King, AS IT IS WRITTEN THAT RABBI YITZCHAK WAS CLOSE TO DEATH. YET RABBI SHIMON HELD ON TO HIM AND WAS HIS SURETY, AND HE REMAINED ALIVE.

59. כֵּיוָן דְּבָרִיךְ, אַסְתִּים עֵינוֹי רִגְעָא חֲדָא, לְבָתַר פָּתַח לוֹן, אָמַר חַבְרַיָּיא, שְׁלוֹם לְכוֹן מֵרִבּוֹן טַב, דְּכָל עָלְמָא דִּילֵיהּ הוּא. תַּוְּוהוּ, וּבָכוּ, וּבָרִיכוּ לֵיהּ. בָּתוּ הַהוּא לֵילְיָא. בְּצַפְרָא אַקְדִּימוּ וְאַזְלוּ. כַּד מָטוּ לְגַבֵּי ר"ש, סָחוּ לֵיהּ עוֹבָדָא. תָּוָּה ר' שִׁמְעוֹן, אָמַר בַּר טְנָרָא תַּקִּיפָא אִיהוּ, וְיָאוּת הוּא לְכַךְ, וְיַתִּיר מִמַּה דְּלָא חָשִׁיב ב"נ, בְּרֵיהּ דְּרַב הַמְנוּנָא סָבָא הוּא, אִזְדַּעְזָע ר' אֶלְעָזָר, אָמַר, עָלַי לְמֵיהַךְ לְמֶחֱזֵי לְהַהוּא בּוֹצִינָא דְּדָלִיק. אָמַר ר' שִׁמְעוֹן, דָּא לָא סָלִיק בִּשְׁמָא בְּעָלְמָא, דְּהָא מִלָּה עִלָּאָה אִית בֵּיהּ. וְרָזָא אִיהוּ, דְּהָא נְהִירוּ מְשִׁיחוּ דַּאֲבוֹי מְנַהֲרָא עָלֵיהּ,

וְרָזָא דָּא לָא מִתְפַּשְּׁטָא בֵּין חַבְרַיָּיא.

59. When he completed saying the blessing, he closed his eyes for a moment and opened them afterward. He said, Friends, you have a message of peace from the good Master, to whom the entire universe belongs. They marveled and wept, and blessed him. They slept over that night. In the morning, they rose early and left. When they reached Rabbi Shimon, they related the episode to him. Rabbi Shimon wondered and said, He is a son of a strong rock and he is deserving of it, even more than one could imagine. He is the son of Rav Hamnuna Saba. Rabbi Elazar was shaken. He said, It is incumbent upon me to go and see this lit candle. Rabbi Shimon said, This one will not rise in renown in this world, MEANING TO SAY, HE WILL NOT LIVE LONG, since he has in him something supernal. The illumination of his father's oil shines on him and this secret should not be spread among the friends.

60. יוֹמָא חֲדָא, הֲווֹ חַבְרַיָּיא יַתְבִין וּמִתְנַגְּחִין אִלֵּין בְּאִלֵּין, וַהֲווֹ תַּמָּן ר׳ אֶלְעָזָר, וְר׳ אַבָּא, וְר׳ חִיָּיא, וְר׳ יוֹסֵי, וּשְׁאַר חַבְרַיָּיא. אָמְרוּ הָא כְּתִיב אַל תָּצַר אֶת מוֹאָב וְאַל תִּתְגָּר בָּם מִלְחָמָה וְגוֹ׳. בְּגִין רוּת וְנַעֲמָה, דַּהֲווֹ זְמִינִין לְנָפְקָא מִנַּיְיהוּ. צִפּוֹרָה אִתַּת מֹשֶׁה דַּהֲוַת מִמִּדְיָן, וְיִתְרוֹ וּבְנוֹי דְּנַפְקוּ מִמִּדְיָן, דַּהֲווֹ כֻּלְּהוּ זַכָּאֵי קְשׁוֹט עאכ״ו. וְתוּ מֹשֶׁה דְּרַבִּיאוּ לֵיהּ בְּמִדְיָן, וְאָמַר לֵיהּ קוּדְשָׁא בְּרִיךְ הוּא, נְקוֹם נִקְמַת בְּנֵי יִשְׂרָאֵל מֵאֵת הַמִּדְיָנִים אִי הָכִי מַשּׂוֹא פָּנִים אִית בְּמִלָּה, דְּיַתִּיר אִתְחָזוּ בְּנֵי מִדְיָן לְשֵׁזָבָא מִן מוֹאָב.

60. One day, the friends were sitting and contending with each other, MEANING THEY WERE HAVING A DISCUSSION AMONG THEMSELVES. Rabbi Elazar, Rabbi Aba, Rabbi Chiya, Rabbi Yosi and the rest of the friends were present. They said that it is written: "Do not harass Moab, nor contend with them in battle..." (Devarim 2:9). That was for the sake of Ruth and Naamah, who were destined to come from their midst. AND IF SO, Tziporah, the wife of Moses who came from Midian, and Jethro and his offspring, who came out of Midian, who were all truly just, most certainly SHOULD HAVE PROTECTED MIDIAN. Furthermore, Moses grew up in Midian and still, the Holy One, blessed be He, told him, "Execute the vengeance of the children of Yisrael on the Midianites" (Bemidbar 31:2), YET MOSES' MERIT DID NOT PROTECT THEM. Therefore, there is an inappropriate bias in this matter, since Midian appeared worthier to be saved than Moab.

61. אָמַר ר׳ שִׁמְעוֹן, לָא דָּמֵי מַאן דְּזַמִּין לְמִלְקַט תְּאֵנֵי, לְמַאן דִּכְבַר לָקִיט לוֹן. אָ״ל רִבִּי אֶלְעָזָר, אע״ג דִּכְבַר לָקִיט לוֹן, שְׁבָחָא אִיהוּ. אָ״ל, מַאן דְּלָא לֶקֶט תְּאֵנֵי, נָטִיר תְּאֵנָה תָּדִיר, דְּלָא יְהֵא בָּהּ פְּגָם, בְּגִין תְּאֵנֵי דִּזְמִינַת לְאַיְיתָאָה. כֵּיוָן דְּלָקִיט תְּאֵנֵי, שָׁבִיק לָהּ לַתְּאֵנָה, וְתוּ לָא נָטִיר לָהּ.

61. Rabbi Shimon said, There is no comparison between he who is going to gather the figs and he who already gathered them, SINCE RUTH AND NAAMAH HAD NOT YET COME OUT FROM AMON AND MOAB, WHICH IS NOT THE CASE WITH TZIPORAH, WHO HAD ALREADY EMERGED FROM MIDIAN. Rabbi Elazar said to him, Although they already gathered THE FIGS, it is still a merit AND THEY SHOULD HAVE BEEN SAVED DUE TO THEIR MERIT. He said to him, Whoever has not collected the figs yet constantly guards that fig tree, so that it should not get any harm for the sake of the figs that are still to grow. He abandons the tree and does not watch it after collecting the figs.

62. כַּךְ מוֹאָב, דִּזְמִינָא לְאַיְיתָאָה אִינּוּן תְּאֵנֵי, נָטַר לֵיהּ קוּדְשָׁא בְּרִיךְ הוּא, דִּכְתִיב אַל תָּצַר אֶת מוֹאָב. מִדְיָן דְּקָא יְהִיבַת תְּאֵנֵי, וְאַלְקִיטוּ לוֹן, כְּתִיב צָרוֹר אֶת הַמִּדְיָנִים. דְּהָא מִכָּאן וּלְהָלְאָה, תְּאֵנָה דָּא לָא זְמִינַת לְאַיְיתָאָה פֵּירִין, ובג״כ אִתְחַזְיַית לִיקִידַת אֶשָּׁא. פָּתַח וְאָמַר, וַיֹּאמֶר מוֹאָב אֶל זִקְנֵי מִדְיָן וְגוֹ׳, מוֹאָב אִינּוּן שָׁארִי, וּבְגִין אִינּוּן תְּאֵנֵי, דְּזַמִּין מוֹאָב לְאַפָּקָא לְעָלְמָא, אִשְׁתֵּזִיבוּ מֵעוֹנְשָׁא.

62. So with Moab, that was to produce in the future these figs, RUTH, AND HER OFFSPRING, the Holy One, blessed be He, guarded them, as it says, "Do not harass Moab." Midian had already produced the figs and they were collected, as it is written: "Vex the Midianites" (Bemidbar 25:17), since from here on, this fig tree will no longer produce fruit. Therefore, it deserves to be burned by fire. He opened the discussion saying, "And Moab said to the elders of Midian..." (Bemidbar 22:4). Moabites are the ones who started TO DISTRESS YISRAEL. For the sake of the figs, RUTH AND HER OFFSPRING, that Moab will produce in the future, they were saved from punishment.

63. רִבִּי אֶלְעָזָר בָּעָא לְמֶיחֱמֵי לְר׳ יוֹסֵי בַּר׳ שִׁמְעוֹן בֶּן לָקוּנְיָא חָמוּי. וַהֲווֹ אָזְלֵי ר׳ אַבָּא וְר׳ יוֹסֵי בַּהֲדֵיהּ, אָזְלוּ בְּאָרְחָא, וַהֲווֹ אַמְרֵי מִלֵּי דְּאוֹרַיְיתָא כָּל הַהוּא אָרְחָא.

63. Rabbi Elazar wished to see Rabbi Yosi, son of Rabbi Shimon ben Lakunya, his father-in-law. Rabbi Aba and Rabbi Yosi accompanied him. They went along the road and were speaking of Torah matters all along the journey.

64. א״ר אַבָּא, מַאי דִּכְתִּיב, וַיֹּאמֶר יְיָ׳ אֵלַי אַל תָּצַר אֶת מוֹאָב וְאַל תִּתְגָּר בָּם מִלְחָמָה וְגוֹ׳, וּכְתִיב וְקָרַבְתָּ מוּל בְּנֵי עַמּוֹן וְגוֹ׳, מִלָּה דָּא כְּמִלָּה דָּא, מַה הֶפְרֵשׁ בֵּין דָּא לְדָא, אֶלָּא אִתְחֲזֵי דִּשְׁקוּלֵי הֲווֹ. וְתָנֵינָן, כַּד הֲווֹ מְקָרְבֵי לְגַבֵּי בְּנֵי מוֹאָב, הֲווֹ יִשְׂרָאֵל אִתְחַזְיָין לְגַבַּיְיהוּ בְּכָל מָאנֵי קְרָבָא, כִּדְבָּעוּ אִתְגַּרְיָין בְּהוּ. וּלְגַבֵּי בְּנֵי עַמּוֹן, הֲווֹ יִשְׂרָאֵל מִתְעַטְּפֵי בְּעִטּוּפַיְיהוּ, וְלָא אִתְחֲזֵי מָאנֵי קְרָבָא כְּלָל. וּקְרָאן מוֹכָחָן בִּשְׁקוּלָא דָּא כְּדָא.

64. Rabbi Aba said that it is written: "And Hashem said to me, 'Do not harass Moab, nor contend with them in battle...'" It is also written: "And when you come near, opposite the children of Amon, harass them not, nor contend with them" (Devarim 2:19). The injunction ABOUT AMON'S CHILDREN was similar to this one, WITH MOAB. What difference was there between the one and the other? They seem of equal weight. We were taught that when YISRAEL approached the children of Moab, Yisrael displayed themselves to them in all their battle gear, as if they wished to provoke them. As for the Amonites, Yisrael were covered in their clothing and the battle gear was not visible at all. Yet, the scriptures seem to indicate that they were equal.

65. אָמַר ר׳ אֶלְעָזָר, וַדַּאי הָכִי הוּא. וְתָנֵינָן, דְּדָא דַּהֲוַת חֲצִיפָא,

וְאַמְרַת מוֹאָב, דִּכְתִּיב וַתִּקְרָא אֶת שְׁמוֹ מוֹאָב. אִתְחָזוּן יִשְׂרָאֵל חֲצִיפוּ לְגַבַּיְיהוּ, כְּמָה דְּאִיהִי הֲוַת חֲצִיפָא, דְּאַמְרַת מוֹאָב, מֵאָב הֲוָה בְּרָא דָּא. אֲבָל זְעֶרְתָּא, דְּאַמְרַת בֶּן עַמִּי, וְכַסִּיאַת אָרְחָהָא, יִשְׂרָאֵל הֲווֹ מְכַסְּיָין אָרְחַיְיהוּ לְגַבַּיְיהוּ, מְעַטְּפֵי עִטּוּפָא בְּטַלִּית, וְאִתְחָזוּן קַמַּיְיהוּ כְּאַחִין מַמָּשׁ. וְהָא אוּקְמוּהָ.

65. Rabbi Elazar said, Certainly it is so. We were also taught that the one was impudent, as is written: "And called his name Moab" (Beresheet 19:37). Yisrael appeared impudently before them as she was impudent and said, 'Moab,' meaning I have this son from my father (Heb. *me'av*). However, the younger one, who said "Ben Ami" (Ibid. 38), 'son of my nation,' was discreet in her manners; Yisrael, too, were discreet in their manners to her, that they were enveloped in the cover of a Talit and appeared to them as real brothers. We have already explained this.

66. עַד דַּהֲווֹ אָזְלֵי, אִדְכַּר ר׳ אֶלְעָזָר מֵהַאי יַנּוּקָא, סָטוּ מֵאָרְחָא ג׳ פַּרְסֵי, וּמָטוּ לְהָתָם. אִתְאֲרָחוּ בְּהַהוּא בֵּיתָא, עָאלוּ וְאַשְׁכָּחוּ לְהַהוּא יַנּוּקָא, דַּהֲוָה יָתִיב, וּמְתַקְּנִין פָּתוֹרָא קַמֵּיהּ. כֵּיוָן דְּחָמָא לוֹן, קָרִיב גַּבַּיְיהוּ, אָ״ל, עוּלוּ חֲסִידֵי קַדִּישִׁין, עוּלוּ שְׁתִילִין דְּעָלְמָא, אִינּוּן דְּעֵילָּא וְתַתָּא מְשַׁבְּחִין לוֹן. אִינּוּן דַּאֲפִילּוּ נוּנֵי יַמָּא רַבָּא, נָפְקִין בְּיַבֶּשְׁתָּא לְגַבַּיְיהוּ. אָתָא ר׳ אֶלְעָזָר וּנְשָׁקֵיהּ בְּרֵישֵׁיהּ. הָדַר כְּמִלְּקַדְּמִין, וּנְשָׁקֵיהּ בְּפוּמֵיהּ. א״ר אֶלְעָזָר נְשִׁיקָה קַדְמָאָה עַל נוּנִין דְּשָׁבְקִין מַיָּא, וְאַזְלִין בְּיַבֶּשְׁתָּא. וּנְשָׁקֵיהּ תִּנְיָינָא עַל בִּיעִין דְּנוּנָא, דְּעָבְדוּ אִיבָּא טָבָא בְּעָלְמָא.

66. While walking, Rabbi Elazar remembered about the child. They went out of their way, three leagues, and reached there. They visited that house, entered and found the child, who was sitting at the table being prepared for him. As soon as he saw them, he approached them and said to them, Enter, holy pious men; enter, plants of the world. Those above and below exalt you, those for whom even the fish of the great ocean leave for dry land. HE NOW SAW IN THEM THAT HIS FATHER RAV HAMNUNA APPEARED TO THEM. Rabbi Elazar approached and kissed him on the head. He then again kissed him on the lips. Rabbi Elazar said, The first kiss was for the fish that left the water and went to dry land, MEANING FOR RAV HAMNUNA WHO APPEARED TO THEM. And the second kiss was for the eggs of the fish that produced good offspring in the world, MEANING FOR THE SAKE OF THE CHILD HIMSELF, WHO WAS THE SON OF RAV HAMNUNA.

67. אָמַר הַהוּא יַנּוּקָא, בְּרֵיחָא דִּלְבוּשַׁיְיכוּ חֲמֵינָא, דְּעַמּוֹן וּמוֹאָב מִתְגָּרָן בְּכוּ, הֵיךְ אִשְׁתְּזֵבְתּוּן מִנַּיְיהוּ. מָאנֵי קְרָבָא לָא הֲווֹ בִּידַיְיכוּ. וְאִי לָאו, לְרָחְצָנוּ תֵּהֲכוּן, בְּלָא דְּחִילוּ. תַּוְּוהוּ ר׳ אֶלְעָזָר וְר׳ אַבָּא וְחַבְרַיָּיא. אָמַר רִבִּי אַבָּא, זַכָּאָה אָרְחָא דָּא, וְזַכָּאָה חוּלָקָנָא דְּזָכֵינָא לְמֶיחֱמֵי דָּא, אַתְקִינוּ פָּתוֹרָא כְּמִלְקַדְמִין.

67. The child said, By the fragrance of your clothes, I see that Amon and Moab were provoking you. How did you save yourselves from them? You had no battle gear in your hands. Without it, HOW did you travel securely without fear? Rabbi Elazar and Rabbi Aba and the friends marveled. Rabbi Aba said, Praised is this road and praised is our lot that we were worthy of seeing this. They prepared the table again.

68. אָמַר, חַכִּימִין קַדִּישִׁין. תִּבְעוּ נָהֲמָא דְּתַפְנוּקֵי בְּלָא קְרָבָא, וּפָתוֹרָא דְּמָאנֵי קְרָבָא. אוֹ נָהֲמָא דִּקְרָבָא. אוֹ תִּבְעוּן לְבָרְכָא לְמַלְכָּא בְּכָל מָאנֵי קְרָבָא דְּהָא פָּתוֹרָא לָא אִסְתָּלִיק בְּלָא קְרָבָא. אָמַר ר׳ אֶלְעָזָר, בְּרָא רְחִימָא חֲבִיבָא קַדִּישָׁא, הָכִי בָּעֵינָן, בְּכָל הָנֵי זִינֵי קְרָבָא אִשְׁתָּדַּלְנָא בְּהוּ, וְיַדְעֵינָן לְאַגָּחָא בְּחַרְבָּא, וּבְקַשְׁתָּא, וּבְרוֹמְחָא, וּבְאַבְנִין דְּקִירְטָא. וְאַנְתְּ רַבְיָא, עַד לָא חָמֵית, הֵיךְ מַגִּיחִין קְרָבָא, גּוּבְרִין תַּקִּיפִין דְּעָלְמָא.

68. THE CHILD said, Holy sages, do you wish for dainty dishes without battle or a table of war utensils and dishes of war, or do you wish to praise the King in complete battle gear, since the table does not rise without battle. Rabbi Elazar said, Beloved and precious holy son, this is the way we wish; we strive with all these battle gear. We know how to do battle by sword, by bow, by lance, by sling stones. But you are a child. You have not seen yet how mighty men wage battle.

69. חַדֵּי הַהוּא יַנּוּקָא, אָמַר וַדַּאי לָא חֲמֵינָא, אֲבָל כְּתִיב אַל יִתְהַלֵּל

חוֹגֵר כִּמְפַתֵּחַ. אַתְקִינוּ פָּתוֹרָא בְּנַהֲמָא, וּבְכָל מַה דְּאִצְטְרִיךְ. א״ר אֶלְעָזָר, כַּמָּה חֵדוּ אִית בְּלִבָּאִי בְּרַבְיָא דָּא, וְכַמָּה חִדּוּשִׁין יִתְחַדְּשׁוּן עַל פָּתוֹרָא דָּא, וע״ד אֲמָרִית, דְּיָדַעְנָא דְּזָגֵי פַּעֲמוֹנֵי רוּחָא קַדִּישָׁא, הֲווֹ אָזְלִין בֵּיהּ.

69. That child was glad and said, Certainly I have not observed HOW MIGHTY MEN WAGE BATTLE. However, it is written: "Let not him that girds on his harness boast himself as he that takes it off" (I Melachim 20:11). FIRST, HEAR SOMETHING AND THEN YOU CAN CONGRATULATE YOURSELVES. They prepared the table with bread and all that is necessary. Rabbi Elazar said, How much gladness there is in my heart with this child and how many new insights will be remarked at this table. Therefore, I know that bells of the Holy Spirit are pealing WITHIN THAT CHILD.

70. אָמַר הַהוּא יַנּוּקָא, מַאן דְּבָעֵי לְנַהֲמָא, עַל פּוּם חַרְבָּא יֵיכוּל. חַדֵּי ר׳ אֶלְעָזָר, אַהְדָּר וְקָרִיב יַנּוּקָא לְגַבֵּיהּ, אָ״ל, בְּגִין דְּשַׁבְחַת גַּרְמָךְ, אִית לָךְ לְמֵיגַּח קְרָבָא בְּקַדְמֵיתָא, וַאֲנָא אֲמָרִית בְּקַדְמֵיתָא, דִּקְרָבָא לֶיהֱוֵי בָּתַר אֲכִילָה. אֲבָל הַשְׁתָּא, מַאן דְּבָעֵי סוֹלְתָּא, יֵיתֵי מָאנֵי קְרָבָא בִּידוֹי. אָמַר ר׳ אֶלְעָזָר, לָךְ יֵאוֹת לְאַחֲזָאָה מֵאִינּוּן מָאנֵי קְרָבָא דִּילָךְ.

70. The child said, Whoever wishes to eat bread, let him eat it by the sword. Rabbi Elazar was glad and again brought the child close to him. He said to him, Since you praised yourself, you have to begin the battle. At first, I said that the battle will begin after the meal. However, whoever wishes for fine flour, SIFTED OUT OF HUSKS THAT ARE THE KLIPOT, shall bring the gear of battle in his hands. Rabbi Elazar said, It is appropriate for you to show us what battle gear you possess.

71. פָּתַח הַהוּא יַנּוּקָא וְאָמַר, וְהָיָה בַּאֲכָלְכֶם מִלֶּחֶם הָאָרֶץ תָּרִימוּ תְרוּמָה לַיְיָ׳. קְרָא דָּא עַל עוֹמֶר הַתְּנוּפָה אִתְּמַר, מַאי תְּנוּפָה, אִי בְּגִין דְּאָנִיף לֵיהּ כַּהֲנָא לְעֵילָּא אִיהִי תְּנוּפָה. מַאי אִכְפַּת לָן, אִי אָנִיף אִי מָאִיךְ.

71. The child opened the discussion with the verse: "Then it shall be, that, when you eat of the bread of the land, you shall offer up a gift to Hashem"

(Bemidbar 15:19). This verse, ALTHOUGH IT PERTAINS TO DOUGH, was said of the Omer of the wave offering. What is the wave offering? Because the priest waved it up high, it is called 'wave offering'. What does it concern us if that offering of the Omer was waved or lowered?

72. אֶלָּא וַדַּאי אִצְטְרִיךְ לְאַרְמָא לָהּ לְעֵילָּא, וְהַיְינוּ תְּרוּמָה. ואע״ג דְּדַרְשִׁינָן תְּרֵי מִמְּאָה, וְהָכִי הוּא, אֲבָל תְּנוּפָה מַאי דָּא הוּא אֲרָמוּתָא. וְרָזָא דְּחָכְמְתָא הָכָא. אִי חֲסִידֵי קַדִּישִׁין, מָארֵי דְּרוֹמְחִין, לָא שְׁמַשְׁתּוּן לְר׳ שְׁמַעְיָה חֲסִידָא, דְּאִי לָאו תִּנְדְּעוּן תְּנוּפָה מַאי הִיא. חִטָּה מַאי הִיא. שְׂעוֹרָה מַאי הִיא.

72. HE RESPONDS: Assuredly one has to raise it up high. Hence, it is a heave offering, FOR THIS IT SHOULD HAVE BEEN CALLED *TRUMAH* (ENG. 'HEAVE OFFERING) DERIVED FROM *HARAMAH* (ENG. 'RAISING UP') AND NOT *TNUFAH* (ENG. 'WAVING'), although we explained THAT TRUMAH IS SPELLED WITH THE LETTERS OF tri mime'ah (Aramaic two out of a hundred) and that is so indeed. NONETHELESS, THE PRIMARY MEANING OF *TRUMAH* COMES FROM *HARAMAH* – RAISING UP. Wherefore IS IT CALLED 'wave' then, if it means here raising up? IT SHOULD HAVE BEEN CALLED *TRUMAH* THEN. HE RESPONDS: Here lies the secret of wisdom. Woe, pious holy men, masters of lance, for not having served Rabbi Shmaya the pious. Had it not been for that, you would have known what a wave offering is, what is wheat and what is barley.

73. תְּנוּפָה דְּקָאָמְרֵינָן, הַיְינוּ תְּנ״ו פֶּ״ה. וְרָזָא דִּילֵיהּ תְּנוּ כָּבוֹד לַיְיָ׳ אֱלֹהֵיכֶם. דְּהָא פֶּה הַיְינוּ כָּבוֹד, דְּבָעֵינָן לְמֵיהַב לֵיהּ לְקוּדְשָׁא בְּרִיךְ הוּא. וע״ד אִבְעֵי לָן לְאַרְמָא לְעֵילָּא, לְאַחֲזָאָה דִּילֵיהּ אֲנָן יָהֲבִין לְהַאי פֶּה. דְּלֵית שְׁבָחָא לְמַלְכָּא עִלָּאָה, אֶלָּא כַּד יִשְׂרָאֵל מְתַקְּנֵי לֵיהּ לְהַאי כָּבוֹד, וְיָהֲבֵי לֵיהּ לְמַלְכָּא כָּבוֹד. וְדָא הוּא תְּנוּ פֶּה, תְּנוּ כָּבוֹד, וְאַרְמָא אִיהוּ וַדַּאי.

73. Tnufah (Eng. 'wave offering') that we mentioned MEANS, *tnu peh* (Eng. 'give mouth'), WHICH ARE SPELLED WITH THE LETTERS OF TNUFAH. The secret meaning of it is: "Give glory to Hashem, your Elohim" (Yirmeyah

13:16), since mouth is glory, WHICH IS MALCHUT CALLED 'GLORY', that should be given to the Holy One, blessed be He, MEANING TO RAISE AND UNITE MALCHUT WITH ZEIR ANPIN. That is why we are required to raise it up above, TOWARDS ZEIR ANPIN, to indicate that we are giving to him, TO ZEIR ANPIN, this mouth, WHICH IS MALCHUT, since the Supernal King, ZEIR ANPIN, has no praise except when Yisrael prepare this glory, WHICH IS MALCHUT, and give it to the King of glory, ZEIR ANPIN. That is 'give mouth', "give glory," and that is definitely raising, MEANING TO RAISE UP MALCHUT TO ZEIR ANPIN.

74. קְרָא דְּשָׁרֵינָן בֵּיהּ, וְהָיָה בַּאֲכָלְכֶם מִלֶּחֶם הָאָרֶץ. וְכִי לָכֶם הָאָרֶץ שְׂעוֹרָה אִיהוּ, לָאו הָכִי. וַאֲנָן שְׂעוֹרָה מְקָרְבֵינָן, בְּגִין דִּשְׂעוֹרָה קַדְמָאָה לִשְׁאַר נָהֲמָא דְּעָלְמָא. שְׂעוֹרָה אִיהוּ שִׁיעוּר הֵ״א, דְּהָא אֲתָר יְדִיעַ הוּא, בְּשִׁיעוּרָא דְּהֵ״א. חִטָּה נְקוּדָה בְּאֶמְצָעִיתָא, דְּלֵית חוּלָקָא לְסִטְרָא אַחֲרָא דְּחוֹבָא תַּמָּן. חִטָּה בְּרָתָא דְּמִתְחַטְּאָה לְקַמֵּי אֲבוּהָ, וְעָבֵד לָהּ רְעוּתָא, וּמַה חִטָּה. כְּלָלָא דכ״ב אַתְוָון.

74. LET US RETURN TO the verse we began with: "Then it shall be, that, when you eat of the bread of the land." HE ASKS: Was the bread of the land just barley AND NOTHING ELSE? THIS VERSE, EVEN THOUGH IT IS MENTIONED TO BE THE PRECEPT OF DOUGH CONTRIBUTION, ALLUDES TO THE OMER OF THE WAVE OFFERING, AND THAT OMER OF THE WAVE OFFERING WAS OFFERED AS BARLEY. HE RESPONDS: It is not so, SINCE THERE ARE FIVE KINDS OF GRAINS and we offer barley because it is the first of the other kinds of bread in the world. *Seorah* (Eng. 'barley') is the letters of *shiur Hei* (Eng. 'measure of Hei'), which occupies a known measure in the Hei, WHICH IS MALCHUT. *Chitah* (Eng. 'wheat') is the central point, where the Other Side of the scale of guilt has no place. *Chitah* is a daughter that asks petulantly (Heb. *mitchat'ah*) before her father and he does her will. What is *chitah*? It has the numerical value of the 22 letters.

75. א״ר אֶלְעָזָר, אע״ג דַּהֲוָה לָן לְמִשְׁמַע. הָכָא אִית לָן לְמֵימַר, וּלְדַרְכָּא קַשְׁתָּא. אָמַר הַהוּא יַנּוּקָא, הָא מָגִנָּא לָקֳבֵל גִּירָא. אָמַר רִבִּי אֶלְעָזָר, וַדַּאי חִטָּה הָכִי קָרֵינָן לָהּ. אֲבָל חֲמֵינָן בִּשְׁבָטִים כֻּלְּהוּ דְּלֵית בְּהוּ חֵ״ט, וּבָהּ אִית חֵ״ט, וְקָרֵינָן חִטָּה. אָמַר הַהוּא יַנּוּקָא, וַדַּאי הָכִי

הוּא, דְּהָא חֵ״ט שַׁרְיָא סָמִיךְ לָהּ. בְּהוּ בְּשִׁבְטִין, לָא הֲווֹ אַתְוָון אִלֵּין, דְּקָא אָתוּ מִסִּטְרָא דִּקְדוּשָּׁה דִּלְעֵילָּא, אֲבָל לְגַבָּהּ שַׁרְיָא.

75. Rabbi Elazar said, Although we should listen TO YOUR WORDS, we have something to say here and draw our bow (Heb. *keshet*), WHICH IS DERIVED FROM DIFFICULTY (HEB. *KUSHIYA*). The child said, Behold a shield against that arrow, MEANING TO SAY THAT HE WOULD BE READY TO EXPLAIN AWAY THAT DIFFICULTY. Rabbi Elazar said, Certainly we call it *chitah*. However, we notice that among all the tribes, there are no LETTERS Chet and Tet IN THEIR NAMES, BECAUSE THEY ARE INDICATIVE OF SIN (HEB. *CHET*, CHET TET ALEPH) AND A HOLD FOR THE EXTERNAL FORCES. Yet, IN *CHITAH*, there are Chet and Tet, because we call her chitah. IF SO, THERE IS SOMETHING THAT GIVES A HOLD FOR THE OUTER FORCES, AND NOT LIKE THE CHILD SAID THAT THE OTHER SIDE OF GUILT HAS NO PART THERE. That child replied, It is definitely so. The Chet and Tet THAT INDICATE THE HOLD OF THE OTHER SIDE prevail close by, THAT IS, NEAR TO MALCHUT. Within them, among the tribes, those letters did not dwell, because they emanated from the side of holiness that is above, SINCE THE TWELVE TRIBES ARE DRAWN FROM THE TWELVE ASPECTS THAT ARE IN MALCHUT THAT RESULT FROM THE TWELVE PERMUTATIONS OF YUD HEI VAV HEI, ALL OF WHICH ARE HOLINESS. However, near her, NEAR MALCHUT THAT IS CALLED '*CHITAH*' THE LETTERS CHET AND TET do dwell, WHICH INDICATE THE HOLD OF THE OUTER FORCES.

76. וְאִי בָּעִית לְאַפָּקָא חַרְבָּא, וְתֵימָא אֲמַאי נָקְטַת אַתְוָון אִלֵּין הַהִיא בְּרַתָּא, אֶלָּא אִי תִּנְדַּע חוֹבָא דְּאָדָם הָרִאשׁוֹן, דְּאָמְרוּ חִטָּ״ה הֲוָה, תִּנְדַּע הָא. וְאִילָנָא דָּא כַּד נָצַח, כֹּלָּא סִטְרָא דְּטוֹב, נָקִיט לְכָל סִטְרָא אַחֲרָא, וְכַפְיָיא לֵיהּ.

76. You might wish to draw the sword and wonder why that daughter holds on to these letters, CHET AND TET, IF THERE IS A HOLD FOR THE OUTER FORCES. However, if you know the sin of Adam, which they said THAT THE TREE OF KNOWLEDGE OF GOOD AND EVIL was wheat, you will understand this. When this tree, MALCHUT, is victorious, everything is on the good side, as it takes everything from the Other Side and suppresses it. THEREFORE, HE SAID THAT THE OTHER SIDE HAS NO HOLD ON THE

WHEAT GRAIN.

77. חַבְרַיָּיא קַדְמָאֵי פְּרִישׁוּ מִלָּה דָּא, וְשָׁרוּ לָהּ מֵרָחִיק, חִטָּה סְתָם. אָתוּ בַּתְרָאֵי וְאָמְרוּ, חִטָּה מַמָּשׁ. אָתָא יְשַׁעְיָה וּפָרִישׁ לָהּ, דִּכְתִּיב וּמִמְּחִתָּה כִּי לֹא תִקְרַב אֵלָיִךְ, וע״כ נְקוּדָה בְּאֶמְצָעִיתָא, דְּלָא יְהֵא חַטָּאָה, דְּאִלּוּ נְקוּדָה לָא הֲוֵי, חַטָּאָה לֶהֱוֵי. וְחִלּוּפָא בֵּין ט׳ לְת׳, תָּבִירוּ לְסִטְרָא אַחֲרָא, בְּרִירוּ דִּילָהּ.

77. The friends of old have explained this matter, IN SAYING THAT THE TREE OF KNOWLEDGE OF GOOD AND EVIL WAS WHEAT. They began from a distance, MEANING TO SAY, WITH A VAGUE EXPLANATION, saying simply wheat, MEANING THAT *CHITAH* CONTAINS THE LETTERS OF SIN (HEB. *CHET*) AND INDICATES SIN. THERE IS NO INTENTION OF ACTUAL WHEAT, BUT MERELY AN ALLUSION TO IT. Then, the latter came and said actual wheat. THAT IS, IT ALLUDES TO YESOD OF MALCHUT, AS MENTIONED, THAT SHE IS CALLED 'THE TREE OF KNOWLEDGE OF GOOD AND EVIL', AS MENTIONED. Isaiah came and explained it: "And from terror (Heb. *mechitah*, spelled with Chet and Tav); then it shall not come near you" (Yeshayah 54:14). Therefore, WHEAT is the central point in order that there should be no sin, since without this point, there would have been sin. And the substituting of Tet and Tav is a guarding against the Other Side and the cleansing thereof.

78. אַתּוּן חַבְרַיָּיא, דְּלָא שִׁמַּשְׁתּוּן לְר׳ שְׁמַעְיָה חֲסִידָא, אַמְרִין דִּבְחֲמֵשֶׁת זִינֵי דָּגָן, לָא אִית חוּלָקָא לְסִטַר אַחֲרָא. וְלָאו הָכִי, דְּהָא כָּל מַה דְּאִתְבְּלֵי בְּאַרְעָא, לְסִטַר אַחֲרָא אִית בֵּיהּ חוּלָקָא. וּמַאן חוּלָקָא אִית לֵיהּ. מוֹץ דְּתִדְּפֶנּוּ רוּחַ, דִּכְתִּיב לֹא כֵן הָרְשָׁעִים כִּי אִם כַּמּוֹץ אֲשֶׁר תִּדְּפֶנּוּ רוּחַ. וְדָא הוּא רוּחָא דִּקְדוּשָׁא, וּכְתִיב כִּי רוּחַ עָבְרָה בּוֹ וְאֵינֶנּוּ וְגוֹ׳. בְּגִין דְּרוּחַ קֻדְשָׁא מְפַזֵּר לֵיהּ בְּכָל סִטְרִין דְּעָלְמָא, דְּלָא יִשְׁתְּכַח. דָּא בְּנוּקְבָּא. דְּכוּרָא מַאי הוּא. תֶּבֶן.

78. You friends, who have not served Rabbi Shmaya the pious, you mentioned that the five kinds of grains, WHICH ARE WHEAT, BARLEY, RYE,

RICE AND MILLET, have no portion for the Other Side. However, it is not so, since the Other Side has a part in anything that rots on earth. What is its part? "The chaff which the wind drives away," as is written: "Not so the wicked: but they are like the chaff which the wind (Heb. *ruach*) drives away" (Tehilim 1:4). That is the Holy Spirit (Heb. *Ruach*), WHICH IS MALCHUT, as is written: "For the wind passes over it, and it is gone" (Tehilim 103:16). The Holy Spirit THAT IS MALCHUT scatters it in every direction, so it should no longer exist. Chaff is the female OF THE KLIPAH. What is the male OF THE KLIPAH? It is straw.

79. וּמוֹץ וְתֶבֶן כַּחֲדָא אַזְלִין, וְעַל דָּא פָּטוּר מִמַּעֲשֵׂר. דְּלֵית בְּהוּ חוּלָקָא בִּקְדוּשָּׁה. ה׳, דָּגָן בִּנְקִיוּ בְּלָא תֶּבֶן וּמוֹץ. חֵ״ט דְּכַר וְנוּקְבָא, מוֹץ וְתֶבֶן, ה: בִּנְקִיוּ דְּדָגָן. וע״ד שְׁלִימוּ דְּאִילָנָא חִטָּה אִיהוּ וְאִילָנָא דְּחָטָא בֵּיהּ אָדָם הָרִאשׁוֹן חִטָּה הֲוָה. דְּכֹלָּא אִיהוּ בְּרָזָא, וּבְמִלָּה דְּחִטָּה. תָּוָּה ר״א, וְתַוְּוהוּ חַבְרַיָּיא, א״ר אֶלְעָזָר, וַדַּאי הָכִי הוּא.

79. Chaff and straw, WHICH ARE THE MALE AND FEMALE OF THE KLIPAH, go together. Therefore, they are exempt from tithe, because they do not contain any part in holiness. Hei OF CHITAH is the cleaned grain without the straw and chaff. Chet and Tet OF CHITAH are male and female, chaff and straw. IF Hei too IS INCLUDED WITH CHET AND TET, it indicates refined grain, and hence the perfection of the tree, THAT IS MALCHUT, is the wheat grain, WHICH IS INDICATIVE OF REFINED GRAIN WITHOUT KLIPOT. The tree by which Adam sinned was wheat, since everything is contained in the secret and in the word chitah. Rabbi Elazar wondered and the friends marveled. Rabbi Elazar said, It definitely is so.

80. אָמַר הַהוּא יַנּוּקָא, הָכִי הוּא וַדַּאי, קְרָא דְּשָׁרֵינָן בֵּיהּ, דְּהָא שְׂעוֹרָה אַקְדִּים לְמֵיתֵי לְעָלְמָא. וְאִיהוּ מְתַתְקָן לְמֵיכְלָא דִּבְעִירָא סְתָם, אִיהוּ רָזָא דַּאֲלַף הָרִים, דְּמְגַדְּלִין בְּכָל יוֹמָא, וְהִיא אָכְלָה לוֹן. וְאִקְרֵי לֶחֶם תְּרוּמָה, מֵיכְלָא דְּהַהוּא תְּרוּמָה, וְאִתְקְרִיב בְּלֵילְיָא, דְּהָא כְּתִיב וּבָא הַשֶּׁמֶשׁ וְטָהֵר וְאַחַר יֹאכַל מִן הַקֳּדָשִׁים כִּי לַחְמוֹ הוּא. מִן הַקֳּדָשִׁים דָּא תְּרוּמָה. מִן הַקֳּדָשִׁים, וְלָא קֳדָשִׁים, דְּהָא קֹדֶשׁ סְתָם לָא אִקְרֵי תְּרוּמָה, דְּחוֹמֶר בַּקֹּדֶשׁ מִבַּתְּרוּמָה תְּנָן.

80. That child said, This is definitely the meaning of the verse with which we began, because barley appeared first in the world. It is only good for animal food, MEANING MALCHUT THAT IS CALLED 'BEAST' (HEB. *BEHEMAH*) THAT EQUALS IN NUMERICAL VALUE 52, YUD HEI VAV HEI FULLY SPELLED WITH HEI'S. AND BARLEY is the secret of thousand mountains, WHICH IS THE SECRET OF CHOCHMAH THAT IS CALLED 'THOUSAND' that is grown every day, and she, MALCHUT, eats them. She is called 'loaves offering', which is the food of that offering, WHICH IS MALCHUT, that is offered at night, SINCE CHOCHMAH WITHOUT CHASSADIM IS THE SECRET OF DARKNESS, BECAUSE CHOCHMAH CANNOT SHINE WITHOUT CHASSADIM. THEREFORE, THE TIME WHEN IT IS REVEALED IS AT NIGHT, WHICH IS THE SECRET OF DARKNESS, WITHOUT CHASSADIM THAT ARE THE LIGHT OF DAY. It is written: "And when the sun is down, he shall be clean, and shall afterwards eat of the holy things; because it is his food" (Vayikra 22:7). "Of the holy things" indicates offering. "Of the holy things" and not just 'the holy things', since just any holy thing is not considered an offering (Heb. *trumah*). We have studied the ritual restrictions of holiness over *trumah*.

81. אַרְעָא קַדִּישָׁא בִּרְשׁוּ דְקוּדְשָׁא בְּרִיךְ הוּא הֲוַת, וּרְשׁוּ אַחֲרָא לָא עָאל תַּמָּן. הֵיךְ אִתְבְּדִיקַת אַרְעָא, אִי קַיְימַת בִּמְהֵימְנוּתָא, וְלָא אִתְחַבְּרַת בִּרְשׁוּ אַחֲרָא, בְּקְרִיבוּ דִּתְרוּמָה דָּא דִּשְׂעוֹרִים, כְּגַוְונָא דְּרָזָא דְּסוֹטָה. א״ר אַבָּא, וַדַּאי שִׁנָּנָא דְּחַרְבָּא לְגַבָּךְ, אָמַר הַהוּא יַנּוּקָא, וַדַּאי אִתָּקְפְנָא בְּמָגֵן וְצִינָּא לְאַגָּנָא מִנֵּיהּ. א״ר אַבָּא, אַרְעָא קַדִּישָׁא לֵית בָּהּ רְשׁוּ אַחֲרָא, וְלָא עָאל תַּמָּן. מוֹץ וְתֶבֶן מִמַּאן הֲווֹ.

81. The Holy Land THAT IS MALCHUT is under the authority of the Holy One, blessed be He, and no other authority enters there. How is the land tested if it keeps its Faith? MEANING TO SAY, IF SHE IS FAITHFUL TO HER HUSBAND, WHO IS THE CENTRAL COLUMN, WHO FIXES IT SO THAT CHOCHMAH SHOULD NOT ILLUMINATE ON THE LEFT EXCEPT FROM BELOW UPWARDS? She was not joined to another authority, THAT IS THE OTHER SIDE, WHOSE MANNER IS TO DRAW CHOCHMAH DOWNWARDS, IN REVERSE TO THE MANNER SET UP BY THE CENTRAL COLUMN, THAT IS ZEIR ANPIN. THE TEST IS by this offering of barley, similar to the secret meaning of the test of the sotah (lit. 'wife suspected of idolatry'). Rabbi Aba spoke, Definitely the edge of the sword is before you. That child replied, I certainly was strengthened with a shield and breastplate to be protected from it. Rabbi Aba said, Isn't the Holy Land clear of any other dominion, WHICH IS THE OTHER SIDE that does not enter therein? AND IF SO, Where did chaff and straw, WHICH ARE KLIPOT, come from?

82. פָּתַח הַהוּא יַנּוּקָא וְאָמַר, וַיִּבְרָא אֱלֹהִים אֶת הָאָדָם בְּצַלְמוֹ וְגוֹ'. וּכְתִיב וַיֹּאמֶר לָהֶם אֱלֹהִים פְּרוּ וּרְבוּ. וְכִי אִי לָאו דְּאָתָא נָחָשׁ עַל חַוָּה לָא יַעֲבִיד תּוֹלְדִין לְעָלְמָא, אוֹ אִי לָא חָאבוּ יִשְׂרָאֵל בְּעוֹבָדָא דְּעֶגְלָא, לָא יַעַבְדוּן תּוֹלְדִין. אֶלָּא וַדַּאי, אִי לָא יֵיתֵי נָחָשׁ עַל חַוָּה, תּוֹלְדִין יַעֲבִיד אָדָם מִיָּד וַדַּאי, דְּהָא גְּזֵרָה אִתְגְּזַר מִיָּד דְּאִתְבְּרֵי, דִּכְתִּיב פְּרוּ וּרְבוּ וּמִלְאוּ אֶת הָאָרֶץ. וְאִינּוּן תּוֹלְדִין יְהוֹן כֻּלְּהוֹן בְּנְקִיוּ בְּלָא זוּהֲמָא כְּלָל. אוֹף הָכִי אַרְעָא קַדִּישָׁא, דְּהָא לָא עָאל בָּהּ רְשׁוּ אַחֲרָא, אִית בָּהּ מוֹץ וְתֶבֶן, דְּלָאו מֵהַהוּא סְטָר. וּלְבַר מֵאַרְעָא, הַהוּא מוֹץ וְתֶבֶן דִּסְטָר אַחֲרָא הֲוֵי, דְּאַזְלָא בָּתַר קְדוּשָּׁה, כְּקוֹף בָּתַר בְּנֵי נָשָׁא.

82. The child opened the discussion with the verse: "So Elohim created man in His own image...and Elohim said to them, 'Be fruitful and multiply'" (Beresheet 1:27-28). HE ASKS: If the serpent had not tempted Eve, there would have been no procreation in the world or if Yisrael had not sinned by the golden calf, they would not have produced any offspring. YET THE VERSE SAYS: "AND ELOHIM SAID TO THEM, 'BE FRUITFUL AND MULTIPLY.'" It is therefore certain that even if the serpent had not come upon Eve, Adam would have produced offspring immediately, since that was the pronounced decree as soon as he was created, as is written: "Be fruitful and multiply, replenish the earth." HOWEVER, these offspring would all have been entirely clean without any filth. There is an analogy with the Holy Land, where no other dominion enters, but it contains chaff and straw that do not result from the OTHER Side. And outside the country, that chaff and straw is of the Other Side that follows the holiness like a monkey after men.

83. אָתוּ ר"א וְחַבְרַיָּיא וּנְשָׁקוּהוּ, א"ל, דְּאָמֵי לִי, דְּרַווּחְנָא בְּמָאנֵי קְרָבָא, נָהֲמָא דְּפָתוּרָא. א"ר אֶלְעָזָר וַדַּאי הָכִי הוּא, דְּהָא כָּל זֵינֵי קְרָבָא בִּידָךְ אִינּוּן, וּמַצְלְחָן בִּידָךְ, אָתוּ וּנְשָׁקוּהוּ כְּמִלְּקַדְמִין.

83. Rabbi Elazar and the friends came and kissed him. THE CHILD said to them, It seems to me that I have earned with my battle gear the bread on the table. Rabbi Elazar said, Certainly so, since all the weapons are in your hand, and are successful in your hands. They again came and kissed him.

84. פָּתַח אִיהוּ וְאָמַר, וּבַגֶּפֶן שְׁלשָׁה שָׂרִיגִים וְגוֹ׳. עַד הָכָא חֶזְוֹנָא דְּמִלָּה, דְּהָא מִכָּאן וּלְהָלְאָה חֶזְוֹנָא דִּילֵיהּ הֲוָה, דִּכְתִּיב וְכוֹס פַּרְעֹה בְּיָדִי. אֲבָל חֶזְוֹנָא דְּמִלָּה, בְּגִינֵיהּ דְּיוֹסֵף הֲוָה וּלְבַשְּׂרָא לֵיהּ, דְּיִשְׁמַע יוֹסֵף וְיִנְדַּע.

84. THE CHILD opened the discussion with the verse: "And on the vine were three tendrils..." (Beresheet 40:10). Up until here is the subject of the vision OF HIS DREAM, WHICH IS THE GRAPEVINE, THREE TENDRILS AND THE GRAPES. From here on, it is his own vision, as is written: "And Pharaoh's cup was in my hand" (Ibid. 11), MEANING WHAT HE HIMSELF DID. However, the vision's subject THAT WAS IN HIS DREAM was for Joseph, to inform him so that Joseph would hear it and know.

85. תָּנֵינָן, שִׁבְעָה רְקִיעִין אִינּוּן, וְאִינּוּן שִׁבְעָה הֵיכָלִין. וְשִׁית אִינּוּן, וַחֲמֵשׁ אִינּוּן, וְכֻלְּהוּ נַפְקֵי מִגּוֹ עַתִּיקָא עִלָּאָה. הַהוּא יַיִן מָשִׁיךְ לֵיהּ יַעֲקֹב מֵרָחִיק, וְסָחִיט לֵיהּ מֵעֲנָבִים דְּהַהוּא גֶּפֶן. כְּדֵין, יַעֲקֹב אַמְשִׁיךְ לֵיהּ הַהוּא יַיִן דְּקָא אִתְחֲזֵי לֵיהּ, וְחַדֵּי וְשָׁתָה. הה״ד, וַיָּבֵא לוֹ יַיִן וַיֵּשְׁתְּ. הָכָא אִתְכְּלִיל עֵילָּא וְתַתָּא. וע״ד אַרְחִיק מִלָּה, וּמָשִׁיךְ לָהּ בְּמְשִׁיכוּ דִּתְרֵי תְּנוּעֵי, וְהַיְינוּ לוֹ. לֵיהּ לְתַתָּא, לֵיהּ לְעֵילָּא.

85. We were taught that there are seven firmaments, and there are seven chambers, and they are six, and they are five, and all emanate from the supernal Ancient One. Jacob draws that wine from a distance and squeezes them from the grapes of that grapevine. Then Jacob draws that wine that is suitable FOR ISAAC, and he joyously drinks it. This is what it says, "And he brought him wine, and he drank" (Beresheet 27:25). Here, the upper and the lower were included together. Therefore, one stretches the word and draws it out by a lengthy TUNE, over two vowels, THAT ARE THE DOUBLE *MERCHA* CANTILLATION MARK, and that is THE WORD "him," OF "AND HE BROUGHT HIM WINE," THAT IT HAS A DOUBLE SOUND MARK UNDER IT, "him" below and "him" above.

86. חֲנוֹךְ מְטַטְרוֹן אָמַר, וַיָּבֵא לוֹ יַיִן, דְּאַרְמֵי מַיָּא בְּהַהוּא יַיִן, וְאִי לָאו דְּאַרְמֵי בֵּיהּ מַיִם, לָא יָכִיל לְמִסְבַּל, וְשַׁפִּיר אָמַר חֲנוֹךְ מְטַטְרוֹן. ובג״כ אַמְשִׁיךְ לוֹ בִּתְרֵי טַעֲמֵי, דְּהָא בִּתְרֵין סִטְרִין אָחִיד, וְהַהוּא יַיִן אָזִיל מִדַּרְגָּא לְדַרְגָּא, וְכֻלְּהוּ טַעֲמִין בֵּיהּ, עַד דְּיוֹסֵף צַדִּיקָא טָעִים לֵיהּ, דְּאִיהוּ דָּוִד נֶאֱמָן, הה״ד כְּיֵין הַטּוֹב הוֹלֵךְ לְדוֹדִי לְמֵישָׁרִים. מַהוּ כְּיֵין הַטּוֹב. דְּאָתָא יַעֲקֹב וְאַרְמֵי בֵּיהּ מַיָּא, דָּא הוּא יֵין הַטּוֹב וְהָכִי הוּא, כְּמָה דְּאָמַר חֲנוֹךְ מְטַטְרוֹן. תָּוָה ר׳ אֶלְעָזָר, וְתַוָּוה ר׳ אַבָּא, אָמְרוּ הָא חַמְרָא דִּילָךְ, הוּא נַצְחַת מַלְאָכָא קַדִּישָׁא, אַפּוּמָא דְּרוּחַ קוּדְשָׁא.

86. Enoch, who is Metatron, THE ONE THAT IS THE HEAD OF THE YESHIVAH OF THE FIRMAMENT, said that "and he brought him wine" means that he blended that wine with water, and if he would not have put water into it, he would not have been able to stand it. Enoch Metatron spoke well. That is the reason that THE WORD "him" gets drawn out longer with a double cantilation mark when pronouncing it, MEANING THE DOUBLE *MERCHA*, AS MENTIONED ABOVE since he is connected to both directions, TO THE RIGHT AND TO THE LEFT. That wine flows from level to level, all having a taste of it until Joseph the just, WHO IS YESOD OF ZEIR ANPIN, tastes of it, who is the faithful David. This is what is written: "Like the best wine, that goes down sweetly for my beloved" (Shir Hashirim 7:10). What is the "best wine"? It means that Jacob blended water into it and that is the good wine. And this is so, as Enoch Metatron has said. Rabbi Elazar and Rabbi Aba marveled. They said to him, With your good wine, you triumphed over a holy angel by the Holy Spirit, MEANING THAT YOU REVEALED THE CONCEALED WORDS OF THE ANGEL METATRON.

87. אָ״ל, עַד כְּעַן הַהוּא גֶּפֶן מְחַכָּא לְמֶעְבַּד פֵּירִין. וּבַגֶּפֶן: דָּא אִיהוּ גֶּפֶן דְּאִשְׁתְּמוֹדְעָא בְּקוּדְשָׁא. בְּגִין דְּאִית גֶּפֶן אַחֲרָא, דְּאִיהוּ אִקְרֵי גֶּפֶן נָכְרִיָּה. וַעֲנָבִים דִּילָהּ לָא אִינּוּן עֲנָבִים, אֶלָּא קַשְׁיָן, אֲחִידִין לִבָּא, נַשְׁכִין כְּכַלְבָּא. אִינּוּן עֲנָבִים אִקְרוּן, סוּרֵי הַגֶּפֶן נָכְרִיָּה. אֲבָל גֶּפֶן דָּא, עָלָהּ כְּתִיב וּבַגֶּפֶן, הַהִיא דְּאִשְׁתְּמוֹדְעָא. הַהִיא דְּכָל קַדִּישִׁין טָעֲמוּ חַמְרָא עַתִּיקָא, חַמְרָא טָבָא, חַמְרָא דְּיַעֲקֹב יָהִיב בֵּיהּ מַיָּא, עַד דְּכָל

אִינּוּן דְּיַדְעִין לְטַעְמָא חַמְרָא, טָעֲמוּ לֵיהּ, וַהֲוָה טַב לְחִכָּא.

87. THE CHILD told him, Up until now, that grapevine is waiting to produce fruits, MEANING THAT THE ILLUMINATION OF CHOCHMAH, ITS FRUITS, SHOULD BE REVEALED IN IT, AS MENTIONED. "And on the vine" refers to the grapevine known for its sanctity, WHICH IS MALCHUT. There exists another grapevine, which is a foreign grapevine, whose grapes are not proper grapes, but are only hard and sour to the heart and bite THE PALATE like a dog. These grapes are considered "the degenerate plant of a strange vine" (Yirmeyah 2:21), WHICH IS THE OTHER SIDE. However, it is written about this grapevine, MALCHUT: "And on the vine," meaning that known one, the one from which all the saints get to taste the ancient wine, the good wine, the wine into which Jacob added water, AS MENTIONED ABOVE, until all those who know how to taste wine get to taste it, and it is pleasant to the palate.

88. וְהַהִיא גֶּפֶן, כַּד מָטָא לְגַבָּהּ, אוֹשִׁיטַת תְּלָתָא שָׂרִיגִין, וְאִינּוּן תְּלַת דְּיוּקְנָא דַּאֲבָהָן, דְּאִתְקַדְּשַׁת בְּהוּ. וְלֵית קְדוּשָּׁה אֶלָּא בְּיַיִן, וְלֵית בִּרְכָתָא אֶלָּא בְּיַיִן. בַּאֲתָר דְּחֶדְוָה שָׁארֵי. וְהִיא כְּפוֹרַחַת, כְּכַלָּה דְּאִתְקַשְּׁטַת וְעָאלַת בִּרְחִימוּ, בְּחֶדְוָה דְּהַהוּא יַיִן דְּאִתְעֲרָב בְּמַיָּא. כְּדֵין עָלְתָה נִצָּהּ, סְלִיקַת רְחִימוּ דִּילָהּ לְגַבֵּי דּוֹדָהּ, וְשָׁרִיאַת לְנַגְּנָא וּלְאַעֲלָא בִּרְחִימוּ. וּכְדֵין, אִתְמַלְיָין וְאִתְבַּשְּׁלָן אִינּוּן עֲנָבִין, רְכִיכָן, וּמַלְיָין מֵהַהוּא חַמְרָא טָבָא עַתִּיקָא חַמְרָא דְּיַעֲקֹב אַרְמֵי בֵּיהּ מַיָּא.

88. When that grapevine, WHICH IS MALCHUT, is reached, it sends out three tendrils, which are the forms of the three patriarchs, WHICH ARE THE THREE COLUMNS, by which it is sanctified, since there is no sanctification except through wine, and there is no blessing except by wine, where there is joy, MEANING WINE THAT MAKES MERRY, AS EXPLAINED ABOVE. "And it was as though it budded" (Beresheet 40:10), MEANING like an adorned bride that approaches with love and gladness of wine, THAT IS THE ILLUMINATION OF CHOCHMAH that is blended with water, WHICH ARE CHASSADIM. "And its blossoms shot forth" (Ibid.), meaning that her love reaches to her beloved, ZEIR ANPIN, and she begins to play music and enter with love. Then "IT BROUGHT FORTH RIPE GRAPES" (IBID.), AS these young grapes have become full and ripened and are full of that fine old wine, the wine which Jacob has blended with water.

89. וְעַל דָּא מַאן דִּמְבָרֵךְ עַל הַיַּיִן, וּמָטֵי עַל הָאָרֶץ, אִצְטְרִיךְ לְמִרְמֵי בֵּיהּ מַיָּא, בְּגִין דְּלֵית לֵיהּ לְבָרְכָא רַחֵם ה׳ עַל יִשְׂרָאֵל עַמָּךְ, בַּר בְּמַיָּא גּוֹ חַמְרָא. וְאִי לָאו, מַאן יָכִיל לְמִסְבַּל. דָּא הֲוָה לְבַשְּׂרָא לְיוֹסֵף, בְּגִין דְּבֵיהּ הֲוָה תַּלְיָא מִלְּתָא.

89. Therefore, whoever says the blessing AFTER THE MEAL over wine and reaches 'for the land' needs to add water to it, since he should not say the blessing of: 'Have mercy, Hashem, our Elohim, upon Yisrael, Your people' unless there is water added to that wine. MEANING TO SAY, AS LONG AS THE ILLUMINATION OF CHOCHMAH IN THE LEFT, WHICH IS THE SECRET OF WINE, IS NOT BLENDED WITH CHASSADIM THAT ARE ON THE RIGHT, WHICH IS THE SECRET OF WATER, THERE IS NO MERCY IN MALCHUT. AND IT IS EXCLUSIVELY JUDGMENT WITHOUT MERCY. If he does not POUR WATER INTO IT who could stand THE JUDGMENTS OF MALCHUT! That was what he, THE CHIEF WINE STEWARD, had to inform Joseph, WHO IS YESOD OF ZEIR ANPIN, since it was dependent on him, MEANING TO SAY THAT HE WAS THE ONE BESTOWING EVERYTHING ON MALCHUT.

90. חֲנוֹ״ךְ מְטַטְרוֹ״ן אָמַר, שְׁלֹשָׁה שָׂרִיגִים וַדַּאי. לָקֳבֵל תְּלַת אֲבָהָן, וְהָא אַרְבַּע אִינּוּן דִּילָהּ. אֶלָּא דָּא הוּא דִּכְתִּיב, וְהִיא כְפוֹרַחַת. בְּזִמְנָא דְּאִיהִי סְלִיקַת וּפַרְחַת בְּכַנְפָּהָא לְסַלְּקָא, כְּדֵין עָלְתָה נִצָּהּ, דָּא הוּא הַהוּא רְבִיעָאָה דְּאִשְׁתְּאַר, דְּסָלִיק בַּהֲדָהּ, וְלָא אִתְפְּרַשׁ מִנָּהּ. הה״ד, וַיִּרְכַּב עַל כְּרוּב וַיָּעֹף. כַּד יָעוּף. כְפוֹרַחַת, בְּזִמְנָא דְּפוֹרַחַת. וְשַׁפִּיר אָמַר חֲנוֹךְ מְטַטְרוֹן, וְהָכָא הוּא.

90. Enoch Metatron said, Three tendrils definitely correspond to the three patriarchs THAT ARE THREE COLUMNS – WHICH ARE MICHAEL, URIEL, RAPHAEL. HE ASKS, Does she not have four ANGELS, MICHAEL, GABRIEL, URIEL AND RAPHAEL, AND WHY DOES IT SAY THREE? HE REPLIES: It must be in accordance with what is written, "And it was as though it budded," because during the time when she rises and soars with her wings so as to rise up, MEANING WHEN SHE SHINES UPWARDS, then "its blossoms shot forth." That is the fourth one that remained, MEANING GABRIEL, who rises with her and does not abandon her, SINCE GABRIEL IS FROM THE LEFT COLUMN, AND SO IS MALCHUT FROM THE LEFT COLUMN. THEREFORE, HE DOESN'T SEPARATE FROM HER, MEANING THAT GABRIEL TOO COULD NOT RULE, EXCEPT WHEN MALCHUT FLIES AND SHINES UPWARD. This is what is written: "And He rode upon a Cherub and did fly" (II Shmuel 22:11). THAT MEANS, WHEN MALCHUT is flying, SHE THEN RIDES ON A CHERUB, THAT IS GABRIEL, THAT IS "its blossoms shot forth," MEANING THIS HAPPENS WHEN SHE SHINES UPWARDS, SINCE THE LEFT IS NOT CAPABLE OF SHINING EXCEPT UPWARDS. Enoch Metatron spoke well and so it is.

91. תָּוַוה רִבִּי אֶלְעָזָר, וְתַוָּוה רִבִּי אַבָּא, אָמְרוּ, מַלְאָכָא קַדִּישָׁא, שְׁלִיחָא מִלְּעֵילָּא, הָא חַמְרָא דִּילָךְ, הוּא, נָצַחְתְּ בְּרָזָא דְּרוּחַ קֻדְשָׁא. אָתוּ כֻּלְּהוּ חַבְרַיָּיא וּנְשָׁקוּהוּ. א״ר אֶלְעָזָר, בְּרִיךְ רַחֲמָנָא דְּשַׁדְּרַנִי הָכָא.

91. Rabbi Elazar wondered and Rabbi Aba marveled. They said to him, Holy angel, emissary from above, here is your wine. It is that which was victorious in the secret of the Holy Spirit. All the friends approached and kissed him. Rabbi Elazar said, Blessed is the Holy One, blessed be He, that sent me here.

92. אָמַר הַהוּא יַנּוּקָא, חַבְרַיָּיא. נַהֲמָא וְחַמְרָא עִיקָּרָא דִּפְתוֹרָא אִינּוּן, כָּל שְׁאַר מֵיכְלָא אֲבַתְרַיְיהוּ אִתְמְשַׁךְ. וְהָא אוֹרַיְיתָא רַוְוחַת לוֹן, וְדִילָהּ אִינּוּן. אוֹרַיְיתָא בָּעָאת מִנַּיְיכוּ, בְּבָעוּ, בִּרְחִימוּ, וְאָמְרָה לְכוּ לַחֲמוּ בְלַחְמִי וּשְׁתוּ בְּיַיִן מָסָכְתִּי. וְהוֹאִיל וְאוֹרַיְיתָא זְמִינַת לְכוּ, וְהִיא בָּעָאת מִנַּיְיכוּ מִלָּה דָּא, אִית לְכוּ לְמֶעְבַּד רְעוּתָא דִּילָהּ. בְּמָטוּ מִנַּיְיכוּ, הוֹאִיל וְאִיהִי זְמִינָא לְכוּ, דְּתַעַבְדוּן רְעוּתָהּ. אָמְרוּ הָכִי הוּא וַדַּאי. יָתְבוּ וְאַכְלוּ וְחַדוּ בַּהֲדֵיהּ. כֵּיוָן דְּאָכְלוּ אִתְעַכְּבוּ עַל פָּתוֹרָא.

92. The child spoke, saying, Friends, bread and wine are the main part of the meal. All the rest of the foods are accessories to them. The Torah has earned them, BREAD AND WINE, and they belong to her. The Torah requests of you graciously with love, and says, "Come, eat of my bread, and drink of the wine which I have mixed" (Mishlei 9:5). Since the Torah has invited you and requests of you this matter, you are obliged to do her wish. I beg of you, since she invited you, to do her bidding. They replied, Definitely. They sat and ate and rejoiced with him. After they completed the meal, they remained at the table. He began the discussion.

93. פָּתַח אִיהוּ וְאָמַר. וַיֹּאמֶר מוֹאָב אֶל זִקְנֵי מִדְיָן וְגוֹ'. וַיֹּאמְרוּ זִקְנֵי מוֹאָב וְאֶל זִקְנֵי מִדְיָן לָא כְּתִיב, אֶלָּא וַיֹּאמֶר מוֹאָב. עוּלֵמִין נַטְלוּ עֵיטָא מִסַבְיָא, וְסַבְיָא אִתְמְשָׁכוּ אֲבַתְרַיְיהוּ, וְאִינּוּן יַהֲבוּ לוֹן עֵיטָא. מַאי עֵיטָא יָהֲבוּ לוֹן. עֵיטָא בִּישָׁא נַטְלוּ לְגַרְמַיְיהוּ. אָמְרוּ לוֹן לְמוֹאָב, גְּדוּלָא בִּישָׁא גַּדַּלְנָא בֵּינָנָא. וּמַנוּ. מֹשֶׁה רַבֵּיהוֹן. עַל חַד כּוּמָרָא דַּהֲוָה בֵּינָנָא, דְּרַבֵּי לֵיהּ וְגַדִּיל לֵיהּ בְּבֵיתֵיהּ, וְיָהַב לֵיהּ בְּרָתֵיהּ לְאִנְתּוּ. וְלֹא עוֹד, אֶלָּא יָהַב לֵיהּ מָמוֹנָא, וְשָׁדַר לֵיהּ לְמִצְרַיִם, לְשֵׁיצָאָה כָּל אַרְעָא. וְאִיהוּ, וְכָל בֵּיתֵיהּ, אִתְמְשָׁכוּ אֲבַתְרֵיהּ. אִי לְהַהוּא רַבֵּיהוֹן, נֵיכוּל לְאַעְקְרָא מִן עָלְמָא, כָּל עַמָּא דִּילֵיהּ יִתְעַקְרוּן מִיָּד מֵעָלְמָא. וְכָל עֵיטָא בִּישָׁא מֵהַהוּא מִלָּה דִּפְעוֹר, מִמִּדְיָן הֲוָה.

93. He opened by saying, "And Moab said to the elders of Midian" (Bemidbar 22:4). HE ASKS: It does not say, 'The elders of Moab said to the elders of Midian', but "Moab said." That means that the young OF MOAB took counsel of the elders OF MIDIAN, and the older ones followed after THE WISHES OF THE YOUNGER ONES and gave them advice. What was the advice with which they counseled them? They took for themselves bad advice. The ELDERS OF MIDIAN said to Moab, We have grown a bad crop among us. And who is it? It is their master, Moses. There was among us a priest who took care of him and supported him in his house and gave him his daughter for a wife. Furthermore, he gave him money and sent him to Egypt to destroy the whole country. And he, THE PRIEST, and his entire household got carried away after him. If we could root out from the world that master of theirs, all his people would be uprooted from the world. The entire disastrous advice in the matters of Pe'or stemmed from Midian.

94. ות"ח, דְּכֹלָּא הֲוָה מִמִּדְיָן. וְכָל עֵיטָא דִּלְהוֹן עַל מֹשֶׁה הֲוָה. וּבְעֵיטָא דִּלְהוֹן, שָׂכְרוּ לְבִלְעָם. כֵּיוָן דְּחָמוּ דְּבִלְעָם לָא יָכִיל, נַטְלוּ עֵיטָא אַחֲרָא בִּישָׁא לְגַרְמַיְיהוּ, וְאַפְקִירוּ נָשַׁיְיהוּ וּבְנָתַיְיהוּ יַתִּיר מִמּוֹאָב, דְּהָא עַל

נְשֵׁי מִדְיָן כְּתִיב, הֵן הֵנָּה הָיוּ לִבְנֵי יִשְׂרָאֵל וְגוֹ'. וְכֹלָּא מִמִּדְיָן הֲוָה. נַטְלוּ עֵיטָא בַּהֲדֵי נְשִׂיאָה דִּלְהוֹן, דְּיַפְקִיר בְּרָתֵּיהּ. דַּחֲשִׁיבוּ לְנַטְלָא לְמֹשֶׁה בְּרִשְׁתֵּיהוֹן, בְּכַמָּה זִינֵי חַרְשִׁין אַעֲטְרוּ לָהּ, דְּיִתָּפֵס רֵישָׁא דִּלְהוֹן. וְקוּדְשָׁא בְּרִיךְ הוּא מֵשִׁיב חֲכָמִים אָחוֹר.

94. Come and see that everything stemmed from Midian; the thrust of their counsel was about Moses, and with the advice of Midian they hired Bilaam. When they realized that Bilaam was incapable, they followed another bad idea, and they freely loosened their women and daughters even more than Moab. About the women of Midian, it is written: "Behold, these caused the children of Yisrael..." (Bemidbar 31:16). Everything stemmed from Midian. They took counsel with their chief that he should loosen his daughter, since they were plotting to ensnare Moses in their net. They adorned her with many spells, so she should successfully catch the head OF YISRAEL. And the Holy One, blessed be He, "turns wise men back" (Yeshayah 44:25).

95. אִינּוּן חָמָן דְּרֵישָׁא יִתָּפֵס בְּרִשְׁתָּא דִּלְהוֹן, וְלָא יָדְעוּ, חָמוּ וְלָא חָמוּ. חָמוּ רֵישָׁא דְּעַמָּא דְּנָפִיל בַּהֲדָהּ, וְכַמָּה אַלְפִּין אוֹחֲרָנִין, וַחֲשִׁיבוּ דְּמֹשֶׁה הֲוָה, אַפְקִירוּ לָהּ, וּפָקִידוּ לָהּ עַל מֹשֶׁה, דְּלָא תִּזְדַּוְּוגֵי לְאַחֲרָא, אֶלָּא בֵּיהּ. אָמְרָה לוֹן, בְּמָה אֶנְדַּע. אָמְרוּ הַהוּא דְּתֶחֱמֵי דְּכֹלָּא קַיְימֵי קַמֵּיהּ, בֵּיהּ תִּזְדַּוְּוגֵי, וְלָא בְּאַחֲרָא. כֵּיוָן דְּאָתָא זִמְרִי בֶּן סָלוּא, קָמוּ קָמֵיהּ אַרְבְּעָה וְעֶשְׂרִים אֲלַף, מִשִּׁבְטָא דְּשִׁמְעוֹן, בְּגִין דַּהֲוָה נְשִׂיאָה דִּלְהוֹן, וְהִיא חֲשִׁיבַת דְּהוּא מֹשֶׁה, וְאִזְדַּוְּוגַת בֵּיהּ. כֵּיוָן דְּחָמוּ כָּל אִינּוּן שְׁאָר לְדָא, עָבְדוּ מַה דְּעָבְדוּ, וַהֲוָה מַה דַּהֲוָה.

95. They envisioned that the head would be caught in their net, yet they did not know WHO IT WAS. They saw, yet saw not. They had a vision that the chief of the people would fall with her, WITH KOZBI, and several thousand others. They thought it would be Moses, so they let her loose, and gave her orders about Moses, so that she should not couple with another but only with him. She asked them, How will I be able to tell him apart? They said to her, The one that you'll notice, that everyone stands up before, you will engage yourself with him and with nobody else. Once Zimri son of Salu came, 24,000 people from the tribe of Shimon stood up in his honor, since he was their chief. She assumed that he was Moses and she mated with him. When all those 24,000 saw this, they carried on with whatever they saw fit, and that was the cause of everything that happened after that.

96. וְכֹלָּא הֲוָה מִמִּדְיָן, בְּכַמָּה זִינִין, ובג״כ אִתְעֲנָשׁוּ מִדְיָן. וְקוּדְשָׁא בְּרִיךְ הוּא אָמַר לְמֹשֶׁה, נְקוֹם נִקְמַת בְּנֵי יִשְׂרָאֵל מֵאֵת הַמִּדְיָנִים. לָךְ אִתְחֲזֵי, וְלָךְ יֵאוֹת. לְמוֹאָב אֲנָא שָׁבִיק לוֹן לְבָתַר דְּיִפְּקוּן תְּרֵין מַרְגְּלָאן מִנַּיְיהוּ, הָא דָּוִד בְּרֵיהּ דְּיִשַׁי, דְּאִיהוּ יִנְקוֹם נוּקְמִין דְּמוֹאָב, וְיִסְחֵי קְדֵירָה דְּמַלְיָא טִנּוּפָא דִּפְעוֹר, הה״ד מוֹאָב סִיר רַחְצִי וַדַּאי, וְעַד דְּאִינּוּן תְּרֵין מַרְגְּלָאן לָא נַפְקוּ, לָא אִתְעֲנָשׁוּ, כֵּיוָן דְּנַפְקוּ, אָתָא דָּוִד וְאַסְחֵי קְדֵירָה מִטִּנּוּפָא דִּלְהוֹן. וְכֻלְּהוּ אִתְעֲנָשׁוּ. מִדְיָן בְּיוֹמֵי מֹשֶׁה. מוֹאָב בְּיוֹמֵי דָּוִד.

96. Everything originated in Midian in several ways. Therefore, Midian was punished and the Holy One, blessed be He, said to Moses, "Execute the vengeance of the children of Yisrael on the Midianites" (Bemidbar 31:2). For you, it is appropriate and becoming. As for Moab, I leave them alone until the two jewels will come out from among them. Here's David son of Yishai who will take revenge on Moab, and will rinse the loaded pot of filth from Pe'or. This is what it says, "Moab is My washpot" (Tehilim 60:10) assuredly. As long as these two jewels did not come out of there, they were not punished. As soon as they came out, David came and washed clean the pot from their filth, and all received their punishment, Midian during the time of Moses and Moab during the time of David.

97. ת״ח, חַיָּיבַיָּא דְּמִדְיָן, עַכ״ד לָא שְׁבִיכוּ מִכָּל בִּישִׁין דִּלְהוֹן. לְבָתַר דָּרִין דְּחָמוּ דְּמִית יְהוֹשֻׁעַ, וְכָל אִינּוּן זְקֵנִים דְּאִתְחָזוּ לְמֶעְבַּד נֵס עַל יְדַיְיהוּ, אָמְרוּ, הַשְׁתָּא שַׁעֲתָא קַיְימָא לָן. מָה עַבְדוּ אָתוּ לְגַבֵּי עֲמָלֵק, אָמְרוּ אִית לְכוֹן לְאַדְכְּרָא, מָה עַבְדוּ לְכוֹן בְּנֵי יִשְׂרָאֵל, וּמֹשֶׁה רַבֵּיהוֹן, וִיהוֹשֻׁעַ תַּלְמִידָא דִּילֵיהּ, דְּשֵׁיצֵי לְכוֹן מֵעָלְמָא, הַשְׁתָּא הוּא עִדָּנָא דְּלֵית בְּהוּ מַאן דְּאָגִין עָלַיְיהוּ, וַאֲנָן בַּהֲדַיְיכוּ, דִּכְתִיב מִדְיָן וַעֲמָלֵק וּבְנֵי קֶדֶם וְגוֹ׳, מִפְּנֵי מִדְיָן עָשׂוּ לָהֶם בְּנֵי יִשְׂרָאֵל אֶת הַמִּנְהָרוֹת וְגוֹ׳. לָא הֲוָה בְּעָלְמָא, מַאן דְּיַעֲבִיד בִּישָׁא בְּכֹלָּא, כְּמִדְיָן. וְאִי תֵּימָא עֲמָלֵק.

בְּגִין קִנְאַת בְּרִית דְּקָרִיבוּ לְגַבֵּי בְּרִית. וע״ד קַנֵּי קוּדְשָׁא בְּרִיךְ הוּא קִנְאָה עָלְמִין, דְּלָא יִתְנְשֵׁי. אָמְרוּ וַדַּאי הָכִי הוּא, וְלֵית הָכָא סְפֵקָא בְּעָלְמָא.

97. Come and see that, in spite of all this, the wicked of Midian did not rest from all their evil. Generations later, when they saw that Joshua had died, together with all the elders who were worthy to have miracles performed through them, they figured that the time was now opportune. What did they do? They approached Amalek and told them, It is worth it for you to remember what the children of Yisrael and their master Moses and his disciple Joshua have brought upon you that will destroy you. Now is the opportune time, for they have no one to shield them. We will go and accompany you, as is written: "Midian and Amalek and the children of the east..." (Shoftim 6:33). "And because of Midian Yisrael made for themselves the tunnels..." (Ibid. 2). There was no one in the world who wished to harm the children of YISRAEL like Midian. You might say Amalek; because of jealousy of the covenant, they approached the covenant TO HARM IT. Therefore, the Holy One, blessed be He, took everlasting vengeance, which was not to be forgotten. They agreed that it was certainly so and there was no doubt at all.

98. פָּתַח וְאָמַר, וַיֹּאמֶר יְיָ׳ אֵלַי אַל תָּצַר אֶת מוֹאָב וְגוֹ׳. וַיֹּאמֶר יְיָ׳ אֵלַי, וְכִי עַד הַשְׁתָּא לָא יְדַעְנָא דְּעִם מֹשֶׁה הֲוָה מְמַלֵּל קוּדְשָׁא בְּרִיךְ הוּא, וְלָא עִם אַחֲרָא, דִּכְתִיב וַיֹּאמֶר יְיָ׳ אֵלַי. אֵלַי לָמָּה. אֶלָּא לְמֹשֶׁה פָּקִיד קוּדְשָׁא בְּרִיךְ הוּא, דְּלָא לְאַבְאָשָׁא לְמוֹאָב. אֲבָל לְאַחֲרָא לָא, לְדָוִד לָא פָּקִיד דָּא, ובג״כ אֵלַי אַל תָּצַר אֶת מוֹאָב, אֲפִילוּ לְתְחוּם זְעֵירָא דִּלְהוֹן. דְּהָא מִנַּיְיכוּ יִפּוֹק מַאן דְּיִתֵּן נוּקְמִין לְיִשְׂרָאֵל, וְיִנְקוֹם נוּקְמַיְיהוּ, וְאִיהוּ דָּוִד דְּאָתָא מֵרוּת הַמּוֹאָבִיָּה.

98. He opened the discussion with the verse: "And Hashem said to me, 'Do not harass Moab'" (Devarim 2:9). HE INQUIRES: Until now, didn't we know that the Holy One, blessed be He, talked to Moses and not with anyone else, that the verse needed to inform us that? "Hashem said to me"? Why "to me"? HE RESPONDS: It is only to Moses that the Holy One, blessed be He, gave the command not to lay siege to Moab; to anyone else,

He did not GIVE SUCH A COMMAND. He did not give this command to David. Therefore, IT IS WRITTEN: "And Hashem said to me, 'Do not harass Moab'", not even a small part of their boundary, because from them will come out the one who will provide vindication for Yisrael and provide them with revenge ON MOAB. That is David, who is a descendant of Ruth the Moabite.

99. וְאַל תִּתְגָּר בָּם מִלְחָמָה, כָּל דָּא אִתְפְּקַד לְמֹשֶׁה, הָא לְאַחֲרָא שָׁרֵי. וְאִי תֵּימָא, לִיהוֹשֻׁעַ וּלְאִינּוּן זְקֵנִים דַּהֲווֹ דְּאָרִיכוּ יוֹמִין בַּתְרֵיהּ שָׁרֵי. לָאו הָכִי. בְּגִין דְּכֻלְּהוּ מִבֵּי דִּינָא דְּמֹשֶׁה הֲווֹ, וּמַה דְּאִתְסָר לְמֹשֶׁה, אִתְסָר לְהוּ וְעוֹד דְּלָא נַפְקוּ עֲדַיִין אִינּוּן מַרְגְּלָאן טָבָאן, דְּהָא בְּיוֹמֵיהוֹן דְּשׁוֹפְטִים נָפְקָא רוּת. וּבְרָתֵיהּ דְּעֶגְלוֹן מַלְכָּא דְּמוֹאָב הֲוַת. מִית עֶגְלוֹן, דְּקָטִיל לֵיהּ אֵהוּד. וּמָנוּ מֶלֶךְ אַחֲרָא, וְדָא בְּרָתֵיהּ אִשְׁתְּאָרַת, וַהֲוַת בְּבֵי אוּמָנָא, וּבִשְׂדֵי מוֹאָב. כֵּיוָן דְּאָתָא תַּמָּן אֱלִימֶלֶךְ, נַסְבָּהּ לִבְרֵיהּ.

99. "Nor contend with them in battle" (Ibid.): All this was a command to Moses; however, someone else was permitted. If you would venture to say that Joshua and the elders, who lived long after him, were also permitted, it is not so. All were from the original courthouse of Moses and whatever was forbidden to Moses was also forbidden to them. Furthermore, the goodly jewels have not yet come out from among them, since Ruth came in the days of the Judges and she was the daughter of Eglon, king of Moab. Eglon died because Ehud killed him and another king was appointed. This daughter of Eglon remained and was in the hands of a nurse, in the fields of Moab. As soon as Elimelech arrived there, he took her for his son.

100. וְאִי תֵּימָא דְּגַיְירָהּ אֱלִימֶלֶךְ תַּמָּן. לָא. אֶלָּא כָּל אוֹרְחֵי בֵּיתָא, וּמֵיכְלָא וּמִשְׁתְּיָא אוֹלִיפַת. אֵימָתַי אִתְגַּיְירַת. לְבָתַר כַּד אַזְלַת בְּנָעֳמִי, כְּדֵין אַמְרַת, עַמֵּךְ עַמִּי וֵאלֹהַיִךְ אֱלֹהָי. נַעֲמָה בִּבְנֵי עַמּוֹן בְּיוֹמֵי דְּדָוִד נָפְקָא.

100. If you say that Elimelech converted her there, it is not so. However, she was taught all the household customs, including permissible food and drink. When did she get converted? Later on, when Naomi left. Then she said, "Your people shall be my people, and your Elohim my Elohim" (Rut 1:16). Naomi,

WHO CAME OUT from the offspring of Amon, came out at the time of David.

101. כְּדֵין שָׁרָאת רוּחַ קוּדְשָׁא עַל דָּוִד. אָ"ל, דָּוִד, כַּד כָּל עָלְמָא מָדִידְנָא, וְאַפִּילְנָא עַדְבִין, יִשְׂרָאֵל חֶבֶל נַחֲלָתוֹ הֲווֹ, דָּכִירְנָא מַה דְּעָבְדוּ מוֹאָב בְּחֶבֶל נַחֲלָתוֹ. מַה כְּתִיב, וַיְמַדְּדֵם בַּחֶבֶל. בְּהַהוּא חֶבֶל נַחֲלַת יְיָ'. כָּל אִינּוּן דַּהֲווֹ מֵהַהוּא זַרְעָא, הַהוּא חֶבֶל אָחִיד בְּהוּ.

101. At that time, the Holy Spirit rested on David. THE HOLY SPIRIT, THAT IS MALCHUT, said to him,: David, when I measured the entire universe and threw lots, and Yisrael was "the lot (Heb. *chevel*) of His inheritance" (Devarim 32:9), I remember what Moab did to "the lot of His inheritance." It is written: "And measured them with a line (Heb. *chevel*)" (II Shmuel 8:2), meaning with the very measuring line of Hashem's inheritance THAT IS YISRAEL. That line was hanging on to all those who issued from that seed OF MOAB THAT DID HARM YISRAEL IN THE DAYS OF MOSES.

102. כְּתִיב מְלֹא הַחֶבֶל. מַהוּ מְלֹא הַחֶבֶל. אֶלָּא הַהוּא דִּכְתִּיב, מְלֹא כָל הָאָרֶץ כְּבוֹדוֹ. וַהֲוָה אָמַר, דָּא הוּא לְאַחֲיָיא, וְדָא הוּא לְקַטְלָא. וְהַהוּא חֶבֶל אָחִיד בְּאִינּוּן דְּאִתְחָזוּן לְקַטְלָא. בג"כ אָחִיד בְּחֶבֶל, וּפָשִׁיט חֶבֶל, עַל מַה דְּעַבְדוּ בְּהַהוּא חֶבֶל נַחֲלַת יְיָ'.

102. It is written: "One full line" (Ibid.): What is the meaning of "one full line"? This is what is written: "The whole earth is full of His glory" (Yeshayah 6:3). THAT IS MALCHUT, which decreed one to life and another to death. That line was attached to those who deserved to be killed. Therefore, he held that rope and extended the line, due to what he caused to that line of Hashem's inheritance.

103. וּמִדְיָן, גִּדְעוֹן שָׁצֵי כָּל הַהוּא זַרְעָא, דְּלָא אַשְׁאִיר מִנַּיְיהוּ, מִכָּל אִינּוּן דְּאַבְאִישׁוּ לְיִשְׂרָאֵל בְּעֵיטָא, אוֹ בְּמִלָּה אַחֲרָא. וּלְכֻלְּהוּ דְּאַבְאִישׁוּ לְיִשְׂרָאֵל, קוּדְשָׁא בְּרִיךְ הוּא נָטִיר לוֹן דְּבָבוּ, וְנָטַל מִנַּיְיהוּ נוּקְמִין. אֲבָל אִי זַמְנִין לְמֵיתֵי מִנַּיְיהוּ טַב לְעָלְמָא, אָרִיךְ רוּגְזֵיהּ וְאַפֵּיהּ עִמְּהוֹן, עַד דְּיָפִּיק הַהוּא טַב לְעָלְמָא, וּבָתַר כֵּן נָטִיל נוּקְמָא וְדִינָא מִנַּיְיהוּ. א"ר אֶלְעָזָר, הָכִי הוּא וַדַּאי, וְדָא הוּא בְּרִירוּ דְּמִלָּה. אָמַר הַהוּא יַנּוּקָא,

מִכָּאן וּלְהָלְאָה, חַבְרַיָּיא, אַתְקִינוּ מָאנֵי קְרָבָא בִּידַיְיכוּ, וְאַגָּחוּ קְרָבָא.

103. Gideon was destroying all that seed of Midian, so that he left none of those who planned to harm Yisrael by counsel or in any other way. To all those that caused harm to Yisrael, the Holy One, blessed be He, will reserve hate for them and be vindictive to them. However, if good is destined to emerge from them, He will be long-suffering and extend the period of His anger to them, until that good will come into the world. Then he will carry out their sentence of vengeance. Rabbi Elazar said, That is definitely the meaning and that is the clarification of it. That child said, From here on friends, prepare your weapon to do battle.

104. פָּתַח ר׳ אֶלְעָזָר וְאָמַר, בָּרְכוּ יְיָ׳ מַלְאָכָיו גִּבּוֹרֵי כֹחַ וְגוֹ׳. דָּוִד מַלְכָּא זַמִּין לְבָרְכָא לְקוּדְשָׁא בְּרִיךְ הוּא, זַמִּין לְחֵילֵי שְׁמַיָּא, דְּאִינּוּן כֹּכָבַיָּא וּמַזָּלֵי, וּשְׁאַר חַיָּילִין, וְשָׁתַף לְנִשְׁמְתָא דִּילֵיהּ בַּהֲדַיְיהוּ, לְבָרְכָא לְקוּדְשָׁא בְּרִיךְ הוּא. הה״ד, בָּרְכוּ יְיָ׳ כָּל מַעֲשָׂיו בְּכָל מְקוֹמוֹת מֶמְשַׁלְתּוֹ בָּרְכִי נַפְשִׁי אֶת יְיָ׳ חָתִים בְּנַפְשֵׁיהּ כָּל בִּרְכָאן.

104. Rabbi Elazar opened the discussion with the verse: "Bless Hashem, you angels of His, you mighty ones..." (Tehilim 103:20). King David summoned to bless the Holy One, blessed be He. He summoned the hosts of heaven, which are the stars and constellations, and other armies, and included his soul with them to bless the Holy One, blessed be He. This is what is written: "Bless Hashem, all His works in all places of His dominion. Bless Hashem, O my soul" (Ibid. 22). He concluded all the blessings with his soul.

105. זַמִּין לְמַלְאֲכֵי מְרוֹמָא לְבָרְכָא לֵיהּ, דִּכְתִּיב בָּרְכוּ יְיָ׳ מַלְאָכָיו וְגוֹ׳, וְעַד לָא אָתוּ יִשְׂרָאֵל, מַלְאֲכֵי מְרוֹמָא הֲווֹ עַבְדֵּי וְשַׁלְמֵי עֲשִׂיָּה. כֵּיוָן דְּאָתוּ יִשְׂרָאֵל, וְקַיְימוּ עַל טוּרָא דְּסִינַי, וְאָמְרוּ נַעֲשֶׂה וְנִשְׁמָע, נַטְלֵי עֲשִׂיָּיה מִמַּלְאֲכֵי הַשָּׁרֵת, אִתְכְּלִילוּ בִּדְבָרוֹ. וּמִכְּדֵין, עֲשִׂיָּה הֲוַת בְּאַרְעָא דְּיִשְׂרָאֵל בִּלְחוֹדַיְיהוּ, וּמַלְאָכִין קַדִּישִׁין בִּלְחוֹדַיְיהוּ. יִשְׂרָאֵל גַּמְרִין וּשְׁלֵמִין עֲשִׂיָּיה. וע״ד גִּבּוֹרֵי כֹחַ עוֹשֵׂי דְבָרוֹ בְּקַדְמֵיתָא, וּלְבָתַר לִשְׁמוֹעַ. זַכָּאִין אִינּוּן יִשְׂרָאֵל, דְּנָטְלוּ עֲשִׂיָּיה מִנַּיְיהוּ, וְאִתְקַיָּים בְּהוּ.

105. He invited the lofty angels to bless Him, as it is written: "Bless Hashem, you angels of His...." Before Yisrael arrived on the scene, the lofty angels in heaven used to prepare and complete this work. As soon as Yisrael arrived and stood at Mount Sinai and said, "Will we do and obey (lit. 'listen')" (Shemot 24:7), they took over this task from the ministering angels and became part of His world. Since then, that task on earth was exclusively Yisrael's, the holy angels were on their own and Yisrael would complete and perfect this work. Therefore, at first, PRIOR TO THE ARRIVAL OF YISRAEL, WERE "mighty ones who perform His bidding" (Tehilim 103:20), and after that, THE ANGELS WERE ONLY "hearkening TO THE VOICE OF HIS WORD" (IBID.), BUT THOSE "WHO PERFORM HIS BIDDING" WERE YISRAEL. Praised are Yisrael, who took over this service from them. It was kept up through them.

106. אָמַר הַהוּא יַנּוּקָא, נְטַר גַּרְמָךְ וְאַצְלַח בְּמָאנָךְ. וְכִי שְׁבָחָא דָּא בִּלְחוֹדוֹי נָטְלוּ יִשְׂרָאֵל, וְלָא אַחֲרָא. אָמַר שְׁבָחָא דָּא אֶשְׁכַּחְנָא, וְלָא אַחֲרָא. אָמַר הַהוּא יְנוּקָא, כֵּיוָן דְּחַרְבָּא דִּילָךְ לָא אַצְלַח. אוֹ אַנְתְּ לָא מְנַעְנְעָא לֵיהּ כַּדְקָא חֲזֵי, שְׁבַק חַרְבָּא לְמַאן דְּאַגָּח קְרָבָא.

106. That boy said, Watch yourself now, and be successful with your battle-gear. Is this the only praise that Yisrael gained and no other praise? He said, This praise I discovered, and no other. That child said, Since your sword is not accomplishing anything or you are not brandishing it effectively, leave the sword to someone who is capable of waging war with it.

107. שְׁבָחָא עִלָּאָה דְּלָא אִתְמְסַר לְמַלְאֲכֵי עִלָּאֵי בִּלְחוֹדַיְיהוּ, אֶלָּא בַּהֲדֵי יִשְׂרָאֵל, מַאן אִיהוּ. קָדוֹשׁ. בְּרָכָה אִתְמְסַר לוֹן בִּלְחוֹדַיְיהוּ, כְּמָה דְּאִתְמְסַר לְיִשְׂרָאֵל. אֲבָל קָדוֹשׁ, לָא אִתְמְסַר לוֹן בִּלְחוֹדַיְיהוּ, אֶלָּא בַּהֲדֵי יִשְׂרָאֵל. דְּלָא מְקַדְּשֵׁי קְדוּשָּׁה, אֶלָּא בַּהֲדֵי יִשְׂרָאֵל. וְאִי תֵּימָא, וְהָא כְּתִיב וְקָרָא זֶה אֶל זֶה וְאָמַר, אֵימָתַי בְּזִמְנָא דְּיִשְׂרָאֵל מְקַדְּשֵׁי לְתַתָּא. וְעַד דְּיִשְׂרָאֵל לָא מְקַדְּשֵׁי לְתַתָּא, אִינּוּן לָא אַמְרֵי קְדוּשָּׁה.

107. What is the highest praise that is not passed on to the angels exclusively, except in conjunction with Yisrael? It is 'holy'. Blessings were given to them alone, as they were given to Yisrael. However, 'holy' was not handed to them alone, but only accomplished together with Yisrael, since they do not sanctify the holiness, except together with Yisrael. You might ask why it is written: "And one cried to another, and said..." (Yeshayah 6:3). HE REPLIES: When did this happen? That is at the same time that Yisrael do the sanctification below. Until Yisrael do not sanctify below, they cannot say sanctification either.

108. בְּגִין דִּקְדוּשָּׁה מִתְּלַת עָלְמִין סַלְּקָא, וְלָא מִתְּרֵין, וְהַיְינוּ, וְקָרָא זֶה, הָא חַד. אֶל זֶה, הָא תְּרֵין. וְאָמַר, הָא תְּלָתָא. תְּלַת עָלְמִין, אִינּוּן לְקָבְלַיְיהוּ תְּלַת קְדוּשּׁוֹת. ובג"כ שְׁבָחָא דְּיִשְׂרָאֵל דְּנַטְלִין קְדוּשָּׁא לְתַתָּא בִּלְחוֹדָיְיהוּ.

108. The sanctification arises from the three realms, WHICH ARE THE SECRET OF THE THREE COLUMNS, and not from two realms, AND NOT FROM TWO COLUMNS. That is the meaning of: "And one cried." Here we have one, WHICH IS THE RIGHT COLUMN; in "to another" we have two, WHICH IS THE LEFT COLUMN. "And said": Here we have a third, WHICH IS THE CENTRAL COLUMN. The three realms correspond to the three sanctities and this is due to the praise of Yisrael, because they exclusively take that sanctity that is below, WHICH IS THE CENTRAL COLUMN, AS IS MENTIONED NEARBY.

109. א"ר אֶלְעָזָר, הָכִי הוּא וַדַּאי, וּמִלִּין אִלֵּין אוֹקִימְנָא לוֹן. וְתוּ אוֹקִימְנָא, דְּהָא תְּלַת קְדוּשּׁוֹת אִתְמְסָרוּ לְיִשְׂרָאֵל לְתַתָּא. מִן הַאי קְרָא, וְהִתְקַדִּשְׁתֶּם וִהְיִיתֶם קְדוֹשִׁים, כִּי קָדוֹשׁ אֲנִי יְיָ'. וְהִתְקַדִּשְׁתֶּם חַד. וִהְיִיתֶם קְדוֹשִׁים תְּרֵין. כִּי קָדוֹשׁ אֲנִי יְיָ', הָא תְּלָתָא. הָכָא אִתְמְסַר לוֹן קְדוּשָּׁה. אָ"ל יָאוּת. וְהָא לָא אִדְכַּרַת מֵרוּמְחָא, עַד דְּנַטְלַת לֵיהּ אֲנָא מִבָּתַר כִּתְפָךְ, וְשַׁוֵּי לָךְ בִּידָךְ. מִכָּאן וּלְהָלְאָה תִּדְכַּר לְרוּמְחָא, דְּאִיהוּ בִּידָךְ. תּוּב לְאַתָר דְּשַׁבְקַת.

109. Rabbi Elazar said, It is definitely so and these matters I have already explained. I further explained that the three sanctities were given to Yisrael below, as is apparent from these verses: "You shall therefore sanctify yourselves, and you shall be holy; for I am holy" (Vayikra 20:7). "You shall therefore sanctify yourselves" is one, "and you shall be holy" is two and "for I am holy" is the third. Here the sanctification was granted to us. THE CHILD said to him, That is lovely, but you did not remind yourself of the lance until I took it off your back and handed it to you. From here on, remember that the lance is in your hand. Return to where you left off, MEANING TO THE INTERPRETATION, WHICH HE BEGAN.

110. א"ר אֶלְעָזָר, מִלִּין דַּאֲנָן בְּהוּ, בִּבְרָכָה אִינּוּן. בָּרְכוּ, מַאי בָּרְכוּ. מְשִׁיכוּ בִּרְכָאן, מֵאֲתָר דְּכָל בִּרְכָאן נָפְקִין, עַד דְּיִתְעַבְדוּן בְּרֵכָה. בִּסְגִיאוּ מְשִׁיכוּ דְּאִתְמְשִׁיךְ, וּמִגּוֹ סְגִיאוּ דְּמַיִין בְּהַהִיא בְּרֵכָה, מִיַּד יִפְּשׁוּן מַיִין נוּנֵי סַגִּיאִין, לְכַמָּה זִינִין. וְהַהוּא מְשִׁיכוּ מַאי הוּא. ה' מְשִׁיכוּ דִּנְהוֹרָא דְּנָהִיר, מִגּוֹ הַהוּא אַסְפַּקְלַרְיָאה דְּנַהֲרָא, דְּאִתְמְשָׁךְ מֵעֵילָּא לְתַתָּא.

110. Rabbi Elazar said, The discussion we are in deals with blessings (Heb. *brachah*). What is the meaning of "bless," THAT IS drawing down blessings from where all blessings emanate, MEANING FROM BINAH until they form a pool from that abundant drawing, and the massing of water in that pool (Heb. *brechah*), MEANING, THAT FROM THAT GREAT ABUNDANCE, that water increased a great number of fish, THAT IS, MANY LEVELS, of several varieties. And what is that drawing? It is the Hei, WHICH IS MALCHUT, that draws forth the light that shines from that mirror that illuminates, THAT IS ZEIR ANPIN, that is flowing from above, FROM BINAH, downward TO MALCHUT.

111. הַאי לְמַלְאֲכֵי עִלָּאֵי, דְּאִינּוּן בְּבֵי מְרוֹמָא דְּאִדָּרָא עִלָּאָה, אִתְּמַר בָּרְכוּ יְיָ'. אֲנָן דְּיַתְבֵי לְתַתָּא, אֲמַאי בָּרְכוּ אֶת יְיָ'. בְּגִין דַּאֲנָן צְרִיכִין לְאַמְשָׁכָא עֲלָן, לְהַאי אֶת, וּבָהּ נֵיעוּל לְגַבֵּי מַלְכָּא, לְאַחֲזָאָה אַנְפּוֹי. וע"ד אָמַר דָּוִד, אֲנִי בְּצֶדֶק אֶחֱזֶה פָּנֶיךָ, אֲנִי בְּצֶדֶק וַדַּאי. ובג"כ, שֵׁירוּתָא דִּצְלוֹתָא, בָּרְכוּ אֶת יְיָ', לְאַמְשָׁכָא עַל רֵישָׁן הַאי אֶת. וְכֵיוָן דַּאֲנָן מַשְׁכָן לְהַאי אֶת עֲלָנָא, אִית לָן לְמֵימַר צְלוֹתָא, וּלְשַׁבְּחָא.

111. That flowing tide is to the lofty angels, up higher, that are at the top of the upper chamber. To them, it is said, "Bless Hashem." We who dwell below, why do we say, "Bless (*et*) Hashem"? It is because we need to draw and bring forth upon us the particle "Et," WHICH IS MALCHUT, and with her we can approach the King, ZEIR ANPIN, to see His face. Therefore, David said, "I will behold Your face in righteousness" (Tehilim 17:15), WHICH IS MALCHUT THAT IS CALLED 'RIGHTEOUSNESS' assuredly, MEANING TO SAY, THROUGH RIGHTEOUSNESS THAT IS MALCHUT: "I WILL BEHOLD YOUR FACE." Therefore, the beginning of the prayer is: "Bless (*et*) Hashem" in order to bring upon our heads this Et THAT IS MALCHUT. After drawing that Et upon us, we may say that prayer and praise.

112. ובג״כ אָסוּר לְבָרְכָא לב״נ, עַד לָא יִצְלֵּי ב״נ צְלוֹתֵיהּ, וְיַמְשִׁיךְ עַל רֵישֵׁיהּ לְהַאי אֶת. וְאִי יַקְדִּים וִיבָרֵךְ לב״נ בְּקַדְמֵיתָא, הָא אַמְשִׁיךְ לְהַהוּא ב״נ בָּמָה עַל רֵישֵׁיהּ, בַּאֲתָר דְּהַאי אֶת.

112. Therefore, it is forbidden to greet a person before a person says his prayers and draws upon his head this Et, WHICH IS MALCHUT. If he hurries and greets him before that, it is as if he draws that person upon his head like an altar instead of this Et THAT IS REQUIRED TO BE OVER HIM. THEREFORE, IT SEEMS AS IF HE HAS CONSTRUCTED AN ALTAR FOR HIMSELF.

113. וּבְגִין כַּךְ, לְמַלְאֲכֵי עִלָּאֵי כְּתִיב בָּרְכוּ יְיָ׳. וַאֲנָן אֶת יְיָ׳ לְתוֹסֶפֶת אָמַר הַהוּא יַנּוּקָא, וַדַּאי הָא יְדַעְנָא דְּמָאנֵי קְרָבָא דִּילָךְ טָבִין אִינּוּן, אִתְדְּכַר מִנְּהוֹן וְלָא תִּנְשֵׁי לוֹן, וַדָּאי גְּבוּרָה דְּבַר נָשׁ דְּאַגָּח קְרָבָא בְּרוּמְחָא וְחַרְבָּא אִיהוּ. אֲבָל מַהוּ גִּבּוֹרֵי כֹחַ עוֹשֵׂי דְבָרוֹ לִשְׁמוֹעַ בְּקוֹל דְּבָרוֹ. א״ר אֶלְעָזָר הָא אֲמָרִית. אָמַר הַהוּא יַנּוּקָא, הָא יְדַעְנָא דְּחֵילָא דִּדְרוֹעָא דִּילָךְ אִתְחֲלָשׁ. הַשְׁתָּא אִיהוּ עִדָּנָא, דְּלָא לְאַמְתְּנָא, אֶלָּא לְאַלְקָאָה בְּקִירְטָא, אַבְנָא בָּתַר אַבְנָא. כד״א בַּקֶּלַע וְאֶבֶן. בִּבְהִילוּ דָּא בָּתַר דָּא. חַדֵּי ר״א. וְחַדּוּ ר׳ אַבָּא וְחַבְרַיָּא.

113. Therefore, it is written for the high angels: "Bless Hashem" and for us: "*Et* Hashem" in addition, BECAUSE WE HAVE TO DRAW UPON US MALCHUT FIRST. The child said, I definitely knew that your weapons were fine. Remember them and do not forget them. Certainly, the strength of a man of war is by the lance and sword. But what is the meaning of "mighty ones who perform His bidding, hearkening to the voice of His word"? Rabbi Elazar replied, I have already spoken OF THE EXPLANATION. The child said,

I already realize that the strength of your arm is weakened (SINCE HE SAID, THIS I FOUND AND NO OTHER; ALSO, HE FORGOT THE THREE SANCTIFICATIONS.) Now is no time to delay, but strike with the sling, stone after stone, as it says, "With a sling and with a stone" (I Shmuel 17:50) rapidly, without interruption, one after the other. Rabbi Elazar rejoiced and Rabbi Aba and the friends also rejoiced.

114. פָּתַח הַהוּא יַנּוּקָא וְאָמַר, שְׁחוֹרָה אֲנִי וְנָאוָה בְּנוֹת יְרוּשָׁלַםִ וְגוֹ'. אַל תִּרְאוּנִי שֶׁאֲנִי שְׁחַרְחֹרֶת וְגוֹ'. מִלִּין אִלֵּין הָא אוּקְמוּהָ. אֲבָל בְּשַׁעֲתָא דְּאִיהִי גּוֹ רְחִימוּ סַגִּי לְגַבֵּי רְחִימָהָא, מִגּוֹ דְּחִיקוּ רְחִימוּ, דְּלָא יַכְלָה לְמִסְבַּל, אַזְעִירַת גַּרְמָהּ בִּזְעִירוּ סַגִּי, עַד דְּלָא אִתְחֲזִיאַת מִנָּהּ, אֶלָּא זְעִירוּ דִּנְקוּדָה חֲדָא, וּמַאי אִיהִי י'. כְּדֵין אִתְכַּסְיָא מִכָּל חֵילִין וּמַשִׁרְיָין דִּילָהּ. וְאִיהִי אַמְרַת שְׁחוֹרָה אֲנִי, דְּלֵית בְּאָת דָּא חִוָּורָא בְּגַוֵּויהּ, כִּשְׁאַר אַתְוָון. וְדָא שְׁחוֹרָה אֲנִי, וְלֵית לִי אֲתָר לְאַעֲלָא לְכוֹן תְּחוֹת גַּדְפָּאי. כְּאָהֳלֵי קֵדָר, תָּנֵינָן, דָּא י', דְּלֵית בָּהּ חִוָּורוּ לְגוֹ. כִּירִיעוֹת שְׁלֹמֹה, דָּא ו'.

114. The child opened the discussion with the verse: "I am black, but comely, O daughters of Jerusalem... Do not gaze upon me, because I am black..." (Shir Hashirim 1:5-6). These things were already explained. However, during the period when MALCHUT is full of great love for her beloved, ZEIR ANPIN, through the pressure of her love because she is unable to stand BEING APART, she diminishes herself significantly until she is reduced to the smallness of one point. What is that? That is the letter Yud. At that point, she is concealed from all her legions and camps, and says, "I am black," for there is no internal whiteness in this letter YUD as there is in the rest of the letters. That is what she means WHEN SHE SAYS, "I am black" and I have no room to bring them under my wings. "the tents of Kedar" (Ibid.), we are taught, are Yud, which has no whiteness in it, while "the curtains of Solomon" (Ibid.) are Vav.

115. ובג"כ אַל תִּרְאוּנִי. לָא תֶּחֱמוּן בִּי כְּלָל, דַּאֲנָא נְקוּדָה זְעֵירָא. מֶה עָבְדִין גֻּבְרִין תַּקִּיפִין, חַיָּילִין דִּילָהּ. שָׁאֲגִין כְּאַרְיָין תַּקִּיפִין, כד"א, הַכְּפִירִים שׁוֹאֲגִים לַטָּרֶף. וּמִגּוֹ קָלִין וְשָׁאֲגִין תַּקִּיפִין, דְּקָא מְשָׁאֲגִין כְּאַרְיָין גּוּבְרִין תַּקִּיפִין דְּחֵילָא, שָׁמַע רְחִימָא לְעֵילָּא, וְיָדַע דִּרְחִימָתֵיהּ

הִיא בִּרְחִימוּ כְּוָותֵיהּ, מִגּוֹ רְחִימוּ עַד דְּלָא אִתְחֲזִיאַת מִדְּיוּקְנָא וּשְׁפִירוּ דִּילָהּ כְּלָל.

115. Due to that, "do not gaze upon me." You cannot see me at all, since I am but a tiny point. What do her strong and mighty legions do? They roar like powerful lions, as it says, "The young lions roar after their prey" (Tehilim 104:21). From the sounds and roars that they emit like powerful and mighty lions, her beloved listens above and knows that His beloved is in love with Him like He is. SHE LOWERED HERSELF due to His love, until none of her form and beauty was apparent.

116. וּכְדֵין, מִגּוֹ קָלִין וְשַׁאֲגִין דְּאִינּוּן גִּבָּרֵי חֵילָא דִּילָהּ, נָפִיק דּוֹדָהּ רְחִימְאָה מִגּוֹ הֵיכָלֵיהּ, בְּכַמָּה מַתְנָן, בְּכַמָּה נְבִזְבְּזָן, בְּרֵיחִין וּבוּסְמִין וְאָתֵי לְגַבָּהּ, וְאַשְׁכַּח לָהּ שְׁחוֹרָה זְעֵירָא, בְּלָא דְּיוּקְנָא וּשְׁפִירוּ כְּלָל, קָרִיב לְגַבָּהּ, מְחַבֵּק לָהּ, וּמְנַשֵּׁיק לָהּ, עַד דְּאַתְעָרַת זְעֵיר זְעֵיר מִגּוֹ רֵיחִין וּבוּסְמִין. וּבְחֶדְוָה דִּרְחִימָהָא דְּעִמָּהּ, וְאִתְבְּנִיאַת, וְאִתְעֲבֵידַת בְּתִקּוּנָהָא, בְּדִיוּקְנָהָא, בִּשְׁפִירוּ דִּילָהּ, ה' כְּמִלְּקַדְמִין.

116. Then, from the sounds and roars that stream out from these mighty ones of hers, her beloved lover, ZEIR ANPIN, goes out of His chamber with many gifts and presents and with spices and fragrances. He comes to her and finds her black and small without form and beauty at all. He approaches her, hugs and kisses her, until she slowly and continuously gets aroused from these fragrances and spices and from the happiness of her lover, ZEIR ANPIN, THAT IS with her. She is transformed and regains her shape and beautiful form, AND BECOMES Hei OF YUD HEI VAV HEI as before.

117. וְדָא גִּבּוֹרֵי כֹחַ, עָשׂוּ לָהּ, וְאַהְדָּרוּ לָהּ לְדִיוּקְנָהָא וּשְׁפִירוּ דִּילָהּ, דְּתוּקְפָּא וּגְבוּרְתָּא דִּלְהוֹן גְּרִימוּ דָּא. וְעַ"ד כְּתִיב, גִּבּוֹרֵי כֹחַ עוֹשֵׂי דְבָרוֹ. עוֹשֵׂי דְבָרוֹ וַדַּאי, דִּמְתַקְּנִין לֵיהּ לְהַאי דָּבָר, וּמְהַדְּרִין לֵיהּ לְדִיוּקְנָא קַדְמָאָה. כֵּיוָן דְּאִתַּקְנַת וְאִתְעֲבֵידַת בְּדִיוּקְנָהָא שַׁפִּירָא כְּמִלְּקַדְמִין, כְּדֵין אִינּוּן, וְכָל שְׁאַר חֵילִין, קַיְימִין לִשְׁמוֹעַ, מַה דְּאִיהִי אַמְרַת, וְאִיהִי קַיְימָא כְּמַלְכָּא גּוֹ חֵילֵיהּ, וְדָא הוּא עוֹשֵׂי דְבָרוֹ וַדַּאי.

117. This was done for her by the mighty ones, who have returned her to her stature and beauty. Their strength and might caused this. Therefore, it is written: "You mighty ones who perform His bidding" (Tehilim 103:20). Assuredly, they "perform His bidding," because they restore this bid (word), WHICH IS MALCHUT CALLED 'WORD'. They bring her back to her original form and, as soon as she is restored to her original beautiful form, they and all the rest of the hosts stand ready to hearken to whatever she says, MEANING "HEARKENING TO THE VOICE OF HIS WORD." And she stands like a king amidst his legions, which is specifically the meaning of "who perform His bidding," BECAUSE THEY PERFORM AND MAKE MALCHUT.

118. כְּגַוְונָא דָּא לְתַתָּא, בִּזְמְנָא דְּחַיָּיבִין בְּדָרָא, אִיהִי אִתְכַּסְיָא וְאַזְעִירַת גַּרְמָהּ, עַד דְּלָא אִתְחֲזִיאַת מִכָּל דִּיוּקְנָהָא, בַּר נְקוּדָא חֲדָא. וְכַד אָתָאן גִּבּוֹרֵי כֹּחַ, וְזַכָּאֵי קְשׁוֹט, כִּבְיָכוֹל, עוֹשִׂים לְהַאי דָּבָר. וְאַנְהִירַת זְעֵיר זְעֵיר, וְאִתְעֲבֵידַת בְּדִיוּקְנָהָא בְּשְׁפִּירוּ דִּילָהּ ה׳ כְּמִלְּקַדְּמִין.

118. Similarly, here below, at a time when there are evil people in a generation, that one, MALCHUT, gets covered and reduces herself until nothing is visible from her entire form, except a point. When the mighty powerful and truly just, so-to-speak, arrive, they perform this word, WHICH IS MALCHUT CALLED 'WORD', and she starts shining slowly. Then she returns to her former stature and beauty and becomes Hei OF YUD HEI VAV HEI, as before.

119. אָתוּ חַבְרַיָּיא וּנְשָׁקוּהּ, א״ר אֶלְעָזָר, אִלְמָלֵא יְחֶזְקֵאל נְבִיאָה אָמַר דָּא, תַּוְּוהָא הֲוֵי בְּעָלְמָא, נַטְלֵיהּ ר״א, וּנְשָׁקֵיהּ כְּמִלְּקַדְּמִין, אָמַר הַהוּא יַנּוּקָא אֲנָא אֲבָרֵךְ. אָמְרוּ, אַתְּ בְּרִיךְ, וְלָךְ יָאוּת לְבָרְכָא. אָמַר כַּמָּה אַתּוּן קַדִּישִׁין, כַּמָּה בְּרָכוֹת זְמִינִין לְכוּ, מֵאִימָא קַדִּישָׁא, בְּגִין דְּלָא מְנַעְתּוּן לִי לְבָרְכָא.

119. The friends approached and kissed him. Rabbi Elazar said, If Ezekiel, the prophet, would have said this, it would have been a great marvel in the world. Rabbi Elazar took him and kissed him again. The child said, I will say the blessing. They said, You say the blessing and it behooves you to bless. He said, How holy you are and how MANY blessings are destined for you from holy Ima, THAT IS BINAH, because you have not restrained me from blessing.

120. פָּתַח וְאָמַר, מוֹנֵעַ בָּר יִקְּבוּהוּ לְאֹם וּבְרָכוֹת לְרֹאשׁ מַשְׁבִּיר. הַאי קְרָא כְּמַשְׁמָעוֹ. אֲבָל תָּנֵינָן, כָּל בַּר נָשׁ חַיָּיב בְּבִרְכַּת הַמָּזוֹן. וְאִי לָא יָדַע, אִתְּתֵיהּ, אוֹ בְּנוֹי, מְבָרְכִין לֵיהּ וְתָבֹא מְאֵרָה לְהַהוּא גַּבְרָא, דְּלָא יָדַע לְבָרְכָא, עַד דְּיִצְטְרִיךְ לְאִתְּתֵיהּ וְלִבְנוֹי דִּיבָרְכוּן לֵיהּ.

120. He opened the discussion with the verse: "He who holds back corn, the people shall curse him: but blessing shall be upon the head of him who sells freely" (Mishlei 11:26). This verse means simply what it says, but we were taught that every person is obligated to say the blessing after the meal. If he is not versed in it, his wife and children bless in his stead. May a curse come upon that person who needs his wife and children to bless in his stead, because he does not know how to make that blessing.

121. וְאִי הוּא יָדַע, אִצְטְרִיךְ לְחַנְכָא לִבְרֵיהּ, וּלְמֵהַב לֵיהּ כַּסָּא לְבָרְכָא. וּמַאן דְּמָנַע לֵיהּ, דְּלָא יִתְחַנֵּךְ, יִקְּבוּהוּ לְאוֹם. מוֹנֵעַ בָּר דְּלָא לְבָרְכָא לְקוּדְשָׁא בְּרִיךְ הוּא, וְלָא יִתְחַנֵּךְ בְּמִצְוֹת. יִקְּבוּהוּ לְאֹם, יִקְּבֵהוּ מִבָּעֵי לֵיהּ, אוֹ יִקְּבוּהוּ לְאוּמִּים, דְּהָא לְאֹם חַד הוּא, כד״א וּלְאֹם מִלְאֹם יֶאֱמָץ, מַאי יִקְּבוּהוּ לְאֹם. אֶלָּא לְאֵם כְּתִיב, לְאִימָא קַדִּישָׁא. יִקְּבוּהוּ לְהַאי בָּר נָשׁ, דְּמָנַע לְהַהוּא בַּר מִלְּבָרְכָא לְקוּדְשָׁא בְּרִיךְ הוּא.

121. If he does know, he is required to teach his son and give him the cup to make the blessing. Whoever prevents his son from getting an education, "the people shall curse him." "He who holds back corn (Heb. *bar*)," MEANING THAT HE PREVENTS HIS SON (ARAM. *BAR*) from blessing the Holy One, blessed be He, and being trained in the precepts, "the people shall curse him." HE ASKS: either "shall curse (plur.)" should have been in the singular form, or it should have said "the peoples shall curse (plur.) him," since "people" is one NATION, as it says, "And the one people shall be stronger than the other people" (Beresheet 25:23). Why is it "the people (sing.) shall curse (plur.) him"? HE REPLIES: It is written: "le'om," BECAUSE IT REFERS TO holy mother (Heb. *la'em*), THAT IS MALCHUT, who will curse that person that prevented that son from giving blessings to the Holy One, blessed be He, MEANING HE WAS CURSED TO MALCHUT, SO THAT SHE WILL NOT PROVIDE HIM BLESSINGS.

122. אֲנָא בְּרָא יְחִידָא הֲוֵינָא לְאִמִּי, הָבוּ לִי כַּסָּא וַאֲבָרֵךְ לְמַלְכָּא קַדִּישָׁא, דְּיָהַב בְּבֵיתָא דְּאִמִּי, גּוּבְרִין דְּחֵילָא, דְּמַלִּילְנָא קַמַּיְיהוּ מִלִּין תַּקִּיפִין, וְזָכֵינָא לוֹן. ובג״כ אֲנָא אֲבָרֵךְ. וְקוֹדֶם דָּא אִתְיָשֵׁב קְרָא עַל תִּקּוּנֵיהּ, הָא דְּשָׁרֵינָן בֵּיהּ.

122. I am an only son to my mother. Hand me a cup so that I can give blessings to the Holy King, who presented the mighty ones at my mother's residence. I have spoken in their presence of difficult matters and was successful over them. Because of that, I will say the blessing and prior to that, I will interpret in its proper setting that scripture with which we began.

123. מוֹנֵעַ בָּר יִקְּבוּהוּ לְאֹם, מַאן דְּאַמְנַע בַּר כְּמָה דְּאִתְּמַר, יִקְּבוּהוּ לְאֹם. כד״א, וַיִּקּוֹב בֶּן הָאִשָּׁה הַיִּשְׂרְאֵלִית אֶת הַשֵּׁם. אוּף הָכָא יִקְּבוּהוּ, וַיְפָרְשׁוּן לֵיהּ לְאֵם, יְפָרְשׁוּ חֶטְאוֹי לְאִמָּא קַדִּישָׁא. וּבְרָכָה לְרֹאשׁ מַשְׁבִּיר, לְהַהוּא ב״נ דִּיחָנֵךְ בְּרֵיהּ לְבָרְכָא לְקוּדְשָׁא בְּרִיךְ הוּא, וּלְחַנְכָא לֵיהּ בְּפִקּוּדֵי אוֹרַיְיתָא.

123. "He who holds back corn, the people shall curse him (Heb. *yik'vuhu*)": That is, whoever prevents his son FROM BLESSING, as we were taught "the people shall curse him." This is as is written: "And that son of the Yisraelite woman, blasphemed (Heb. *vayikov*) the name" (Vayikra 24:11). "*VAYIKOV*" MEANS, HE PRONOUNCES. Here too, they will specify him to the mother, meaning they will tell his sins in detail to holy Ima, WHICH IS MALCHUT. "But blessing shall be upon the head of him who sells freely": This applies to that person that will educate his son to give blessings to the Holy One, blessed be He, and teach him the precepts of the Torah.

124. וְרָזָא דְּמִלָּה, כְּתִיב בְּרָזָא דִּלְעֵילָּא, מַה שְּׁמוֹ וּמַה שֶּׁם בְּנוֹ כִּי תֵדָע. הַהוּא שֵׁם יְדִיעָא, יְיָ׳ צְבָאוֹת שְׁמוֹ. שֶׁם בְּנוֹ. יִשְׂרָאֵל שְׁמוֹ. דִּכְתִיב בְּנִי בְכֹרִי יִשְׂרָאֵל. וְהָא יִשְׂרָאֵל, כָּל מַפְתְּחָן דִּמְהֵימְנוּתָא בֵּיהּ תַּלְיָין. וְאִיהוּ מִשְׁתְּבַּח וְאָמַר, יְיָ׳ אָמַר אֵלַי בְּנִי אַתָּה. וְהָכִי הוּא וַדַּאי,

דְּהָא אַבָּא וְאִמָּא עֲטְרוּ לֵיהּ, וּבָרִיכוּ לֵיהּ בְּכַמָּה בִּרְכָאן, וְאָמְרוּ וּפָקִידוּ לְכֹלָּא, נַשְּׁקוּ בַר, נַשְּׁקוּ יְדָא לְהַאי בַּר. כִּבְיָכוֹל, שָׁלְטָנוּ יָהַב לֵיהּ עַל כֹּלָּא, דְּכֹלָּא יִפְלְחוּן לֵיהּ. פֶּן יֶאֱנַף, בְּגִין דְּאַעְטָרוּ לֵיהּ בְּדִינָא וְרַחֲמֵי. מַאן דְּזָכֵי לְדִינָא לְדִינָא, מַאן דְּזָכֵי לְרַחֲמֵי לְרַחֲמֵי.

124. The secret of this matter is written in the secret above: "What is His name and what is the name of His son, if you can tell" (Mishlei 30:4). That name is known: Hashem Tzva'ot is His name, WHICH IS BINAH, AS ALL THE LEGIONS (HEB. *TZVA'OT*) ARE HERS, the name of His son: that is, Yisrael is his name, WHICH IS ZEIR ANPIN, CALLED 'YISRAEL', as is written: "Yisrael is My son, My firstborn" (Shemot 4:22). Here we have Yisrael with all the keys of the Faith, MEANING ALL THE LEVELS OF MALCHUT CONSIDERED FAITH, hanging from him – ZEIR ANPIN CALLED 'YISRAEL'. He praises himself and says, "Hashem has said to me, 'You are My son'" (Tehilim 2:7). THAT IS, YUD HEI VAV HEI THAT IS BINAH SAID TO ZEIR ANPIN, YOU ARE MY SON. And it is definitely so, since Aba and Ima, WHICH IS RIGHT AND LEFT OF BINAH THAT ARE CALLED 'YISRAEL–SABA AND TEVUNAH', AND ALSO 'ABA' AND 'IMA', have adorned ZEIR ANPIN and blessed Him with many blessings, SINCE ALL MOCHIN OF ZEIR ANPIN ARE FROM YISRAEL–SABA AND TEVUNAH. They commanded everyone to "worship (also: 'kiss') in purity (Heb. *bar*)" (Ibid. 12), meaning kiss the hand of this son (Aram. *bar*), THAT IS, ZEIR ANPIN, MEANING it is as if He gave him dominion over everything, so that all shall serve him. "Lest He be angry" (Ibid.), because ABA AND IMA have adorned him, ZEIR ANPIN, with Judgment and Mercy. Whoever deserves Judgment is for Judgment and whoever deserves Mercy is for Mercy.

125. כָּל בִּרְכָאן דִּלְעֵילָּא, וְתַתָּא לְהַאי בַּר סַלְּקִין וּמִתְעַטְּרָן. וּמַאן דְּמָנַע בִּרְכָאן מֵהַאי בַּר, יְפָרְשׁוּן חֶטְאוֹי קַמֵּי מַלְכָּא קַדִּישָׁא, לְאֵם מַמָּשׁ. וּבְרָכָה לְרֹאשׁ מַשְׁבִּיר, מַאן דִּמְבָרֵךְ וְאַזְמִין בְּכַסָּא דִּבְרָכָה לְמַאן דְּאִצְטְרִיךְ לֵיהּ, בְּהַאי אִתְבַּר סִטְרָא אַחֲרָא וְאִתְכַּפְיָא בִּתְבִירוּ. וְאִסְתְּלַק סְטָר קְדוּשָׁה. וְדָא הוּא דִּכְתִיב, וּבְרָכָה לְרֹאשׁ מַשְׁבִּיר. כְּמָה דְּאִיהוּ מְסַלֵּק וּמְבָרֵךְ לְקוּדְשָׁא בְּרִיךְ הוּא, וְעָבֵיד לִסְטַר אַחֲרָא דְּיִתְבַּר, הָכִי קוּדְשָׁא בְּרִיךְ הוּא מָשִׁיךְ עָלֵיהּ בִּרְכָאן מִלְעֵילָּא, וְהַהוּא דְּאִקְרֵי בְּרָכָה, שַׁרְיָא עַל רֵישֵׁיהּ.

125. All the blessings of the above and below are ascending to this son, ZEIR ANPIN, and get adorned. Whoever prevents blessings from this son will spread out his sins in the presence of the holy King, meaning to the mother actually, WHICH IS BINAH. HENCE, IT SAYS, "HE WHO HOLDS BACK CORN, THE PEOPLE SHALL CURSE HIM." "But blessing shall be upon the head of him who sells freely": That is the one who gives the grace and invites with the cup of blessing whoever he should, MEANING THE HOLY ONE, BLESSED BE HE. Through this, the Other Side is broken. By its breaking, it is subdued and the side of holiness is raised. This is what is written: "But blessing shall be upon the head of him who sells freely (Heb. *mashbir*)." As he uplifts and blesses the Holy One, blessed be He, and causes the Other Side to break down (Heb. *shever*), in accordance, the Holy One, blessed be He, draws blessings upon him from above and the one who is called 'blessing, WHICH IS MALCHUT, prevails upon his head.

126. מִכָּאן וּלְהָלְאָה חַבְרַיָּיא, הָבוּ וְנִבְרִיךְ. יָהֲבוּ לֵיהּ כַּסָּא דִּבְרָכָה, וּבָרִיךְ. וְחַבְרַיָּיא כֻּלְּהוּ הֲוֵי בְּחֶדְוָה, דְּהָא מִיּוֹמָא דְּהִלּוּלָא דְּר׳ אֶלְעָזָר, לָא חֲדוּ חַבְרַיָּיא, כְּהַהוּא יוֹמָא דְּיָתְבוּ תַּמָּן. אַקְדִּימוּ וּבָרִיכוּ לֵיהּ בְּחֶדְוָה בִּרְעוּ דְּלִבָּא. אָמַר הַהוּא יַנּוּקָא, לֵית לְכוּ לְאִתְפָּרְשָׁא, אֶלָּא מִגּוֹ מִלֵּי אוֹרַיְיתָא, וְהָכִי תָּנֵינָן.

126. From here on, friends, let us bless. They handed him the cup of blessing and he made the blessings. All the friends were rejoicing that they had not been so happy since the wedding celebration of Rabbi Elazar. They were first to greet him with happiness and willingly. That child told them, You should not part from me except by words of Torah, for that is the way we were taught.

127. פָּתַח וְאָמַר וַיְיָ׳ הוֹלֵךְ לִפְנֵיהֶם יוֹמָם בְּעַמּוּד עָנָן וְגוֹ׳. וַיְיָ׳, זָקִיף טַעֲמָא לְעֵילָּא, אֲמַאי. אֶלָּא, בְּהַהוּא שַׁעֲתָא כַּמָּה יָאוּת וּשְׁפִּירוּ הֲוַת לְהַאי כַּלָּה, דְּאִתְכַּפִּיאַת עַד הַשְׁתָּא בְּגָלוּתָא, וְהַשְׁתָּא אַזְלַת בִּזְקִיפוּ דְּרֵישָׁא בְּאֲכְלוּסָהָא בְּחֶדְוָה.

127. He opened the discussion with the verse: "And Hashem went before them by day, in a pillar of a cloud..." (Shemot 13:21). That "and Hashem," THAT ALLUDES TO MALCHUT, has above it a tuning sound, MEANING,

THAT CANTILATION MARK OF PAZER IS WRITTEN ABOVE IT, WHICH IS ERECT. Why? HE RESPONDS: It is only because at that period, how lovely and beautiful it was for this bride, WHICH IS MALCHUT, who was subdued until now in exile. Now she walks joyfully with an upright raised head within her multitudes.

128. בְּוַיְיָ' זָקִיף טַעֲמָא לְעֵילָּא, הוֹלֵךְ לִפְנֵיהֶם יוֹמָם. עַד הָכָא לָא יָדַע, אִי הַאי כַּלָּה אַזְלַה לְקַמַּיְיהוּ, אִי לָא, דְּהָא טַעֲמָא אַפְסִיק בְּוַיְהוָ"ה, אֶלָּא אִיהִי הֲוַת תַּמָּן, אֲבָל מַאן דְּאָזִיל קַמַּיְיהוּ, סָבָא עִלָּאָה, מָארֵיהּ דְּבֵיתָא, הַהוּא דְּאוֹמֵי לֵיהּ קוּדְשָׁא בְּרִיךְ הוּא. וּמַנוֹ. אַבְרָהָם. דִּכְתִיב, יוֹמָם יְצַוֶּה יְיָ' חַסְדּוֹ. וּכְתִיב אִם לֹא בְרִיתִי יוֹמָם וָלָיְלָה. יוֹמָא דְּכָל יוֹמִין כְּלִילָן בֵּיהּ. יוֹמָא דִּשְׁאַר יוֹמִין, אִיהוּ שְׁאַר כָּל יוֹמִין וַדַּאי. וְעַל דָּא אִקְרֵי יוֹמָם, וְלָא יוֹם. ובג"כ הוֹלֵךְ לִפְנֵיהֶם יוֹמָם, הוּא אָזִיל בִּימָמָא, וְכַלָּה אַזְלַת בְּלֵילְיָא, דִּכְתִיב וְלַיְלָה בְּעַמּוּד אֵשׁ לְהָאִיר לָהֶם, דָּא כַּלָּה, כָּל חַד כִּדְקָחֲזֵי לֵיהּ. וְאַתּוּן חַבְרַיָּיא, יוֹמָם וָלַיְלָה יְהֵא קַמַּיְיכוּ, בְּכָל שַׁעֲתָא. נָשְׁקוּהוּ, וּבֵרְכוּהוּ כְּמִלְּקַדְּמִין, וְאַזְלוּ.

128. By "And Hshem," the sound mark is erect above it, AND AFTER THIS IS WRITTEN: "Went before them by day." Up to this point, it is not known if the bride, WHICH IS MALCHUT, THAT IS ALLUDED TO IN THE NAME OF "AND HASHEM," goes before them or not, since there is a separating musical mark in "and Hashem," WHEN SINGING THIS PAZER CANTILATION MARK THAT SEPARATES "AND HASHEM" – WHICH IS MALCHUT, FROM "WENT BEFORE THEM BY DAY." HE RESPONDS: It is only that she, MALCHUT, INDICATED BY THE NAME "AND HASHEM," was there, but he who goes "before them," is the elder of the household, the owner, to whom the Holy One, blessed be He swore. And who is that? That is Abraham, MEANING CHESED OF ZEIR ANPIN, as it says, "Yet Hashem will command His steadfast love (Heb. *Chesed*) in the daytime (Heb. *yoman*)" (Tehilim 42:9). SIMILARLY, "If My covenant be not day and night" (Yirmeyah 33:25), OF WHICH CHESED IS CONSIDERED DAY because it is a day in which all the days, MEANING ALL THE SFIROT OF ZEIR ANPIN, are included, IN CHESED, a day of the other days, which is definitely all the other days. Therefore, it is called 'Yomam' (alluding plural form) and not the accustomed Yom. Because of this, it is written: "Went before them by day (Heb. *yomam*)." He, CHESED OF ZEIR ANPIN, walks by day and the bride, INDICATED BY "AND HASHEM," walks by night, as is written: "And by night in a pillar of fire, to give them light" (Shemot 13:21). That is the bride, WHICH IS MALCHUT; everyone in his place, SINCE ZEIR ANPIN IS THE DOMINION OF THE DAY AND MALCHUT IS THE DOMINION OF THE NIGHT. Friends, day and night may they be ever before you. They kissed him, blessed him again and left.

129. אָתוּ לְגַבֵּי רִבִּי שִׁמְעוֹן, וְסָחוּ לֵיהּ עוֹבְדָא. תָּוָּה, אָמַר כַּמָּה יָאוּת הוּא. אֲבָל לָא סָלִיק בִּשְׁמָא. אָעָא דָּקִיק, כַּד סָלִיק נְהוֹרֵיהּ, סָלִיק לְפוּם שַׁעֲתָא, וּמִיַּד כָּבָה וְאִשְׁתְּקַע. וְתוּ הָא אֲמֵינָא נְהוֹרָא דָּא מִמָּה הֲוֵי.

129. They came before Rabbi Shimon and related the episode to him. He marveled and said, How proper that is, but he will not rise in fame. When a delicate tree grows, its light rises temporarily and soon it dims and sinks. In addition, I already said where that light came from, THAT HE WAS THE SON OF RAV HAMNUNA.

130. פָּתַח וְאָמַר, גִּבּוֹר בָּאָרֶץ יִהְיֶה זַרְעוֹ דּוֹר יְשָׁרִים יְבוֹרָךְ. כַּד בַּר נָשׁ אִיהוּ גִּבּוֹר בָּאָרֶץ, גִּבּוֹר בְּאוֹרַיְיתָא, גִּבּוֹר בְּיִצְרֵיהּ, גִּבּוֹר בָּאָרֶץ וַדַּאי. סָלִיק נְהוֹרֵיהּ, וְאִתְמְשַׁךְ בֵּיהּ מְשִׁיכוּ סַגִּי, כְּדֵין דּוֹר יְשָׁרִים יְבֹרָךְ, יְבָרֵךְ כְּתִיב.

130. He opened with the verse: "His seed shall be mighty upon earth: the generation of the upright shall be blessed" (Tehilim 112:2). When a man is "mighty upon earth" and strong in Torah, mighty over his Evil Inclination, he is then certainly mighty upon earth, since his light rises continuously and abundantly. Then, "the generation of the upright shall be blessed," spelled "will bless." HE SAID THAT ABOUT RAV HAMNUNA, THAT BECAUSE HE WAS MIGHTY UPON EARTH, THEREFORE THE GENERATION OF THE UPRIGHT SHALL BLESS, IN THAT HE MERITED TO HAVE SUCH A SON.

131. אָמַר רִבִּי אַבָּא, וְהָא חֲמֵינָן יַנּוּקֵי דְּאַמְרִין מִלִּין עִלָּאִין, וְקַיְימִין לְבָתַר רֵישִׁין דְּעָלְמָא. א"ל, יַנּוּקָא דְּאָמַר מִלָּה חֲדָא, אוֹ תְּרֵין, לְפוּם שַׁעֲתָא, בְּלָא כַּוָּונָה דִּלְהוֹן, מוּבְטָח בַּר נָשׁ בְּדָא, דְּיִזְכֵּי לְמֵילַף

אוֹרַיְיתָא בְּיִשְׂרָאֵל. אֲבָל דָּא, דִּנְהוֹרָא דִּילֵיהּ קַיְּימָא עַל קִיּוּמֵיהּ בְּדַעְתָּא שְׁלִים, לָאו הָכִי. וְתוּ, דְּהָא קוּדְשָׁא בְּרִיךְ הוּא וְתִיאוּבְתֵּיהּ דִּילֵיהּ, לְאַרְחָא בְּתַפּוּחָא דָּא, זַכָּאָה חוּלָקֵיהּ.

131. Rabbi Aba said, But we see children speaking eloquently of lofty matters, and then they become world leaders. He said to them, Children that speak of one or two things for a while, without specific intention, a person can be secure by that Torah will be taught in Yisrael. But this CHILD, whose light has reached a mature stature with perfect logic is not so. Furthermore, the Holy One, blessed be He, desires to smell this apple. THEREFORE, IT IS IMPERATIVE THAT HE WILL DEPART. Praised is his lot.

132. זַכָּאִין אַתּוּן צַדִּיקַיָּיא, דִּכְתִיב בְּכוּ, וְיָסְפָה פְּלֵיטַת בֵּית יְהוּדָה הַנִּשְׁאֶרֶת שֹׁרֶשׁ לְמַטָּה וְעָשָׂה פְּרִי לְמָעְלָה. שֹׁרֶשׁ לְמַטָּה, כְּגוֹן אֲבוֹי, דְּאִסְתַּלָּק מֵעָלְמָא, וְאִיהוּ שֹׁרֶשׁ לְמַטָּה, בִּמְתִיבְתָּא דִּרְקִיעָא. וְעָשָׂה פְּרִי לְמָעְלָה, בִּמְתִיבְתָּא עִלָּאָה. כַּמָּה טָבָא שָׁרְשָׁא וְאִיבָּא. וְאִי לָאו דְּלָא אֱהֵא מְקַטְרְגָא לְקוּדְשָׁא בְּרִיךְ הוּא, הוֹאִיל וְתִיאוּבְתֵּיהּ לְאַרְחָא בֵּיהּ, לָא הֲוָה מַאן דְּיֵיכוּל לְשַׁלְטָאָה בֵּיהּ. אֲבָל יְהֵא רַעֲוָא, דְּאִמֵּיהּ לָא תֶּחֱמֵי צַעֲרָא עָלֵיהּ, וְכֵן הֲוָה.

132. Praised are you, the righteous, that it is written about you: "And the remnant that is escaped of the house of Judah, shall yet again take root downward, and bear fruit upward" (II Melachim 19:30). "Root downward": He is like his father, RABBI HAMNUNA, who departed from the world and he is a "root downward" in the Yeshivah of the firmament, WHICH IS THE YESHIVAH OF METATRON. "And bear fruit upward" in the higher Yeshivah, WHICH IS THE YESHIVAH OF THE HOLY ONE, BLESSED BE HE. How fine this root and fruit are. If I would not have felt that the Holy One, blessed be He, has a desire to smell him I WOULD HAVE ARRANGED IT that no one would have any power over him, MEANING THAT HE WOULD LIVE LONG. However, let it be His wish that his mother shall not see any pain, because of him. And so it was THAT HE DIED.

7. "So he sent messengers to Bilaam"

A Synopsis

Rabbi Shimon tells how Balak sent a message to Bilaam to ask him to curse the children of Yisrael, since Balak knew about Bilaam's high level of sorcery. We hear about the table that was prepared by the sorcerer for the defiled spirits to draw them near, and then about the table of acacia wood in the tabernacle that was made to draw the Holy Spirit from above.

133. וַיִּשְׁלַח מַלְאָכִים אֶל בִּלְעָם בֶּן בְּעוֹר וְגוֹ'. הָכָא אִית עֶשְׂרִין וּתְמַנְיָא תֵּיבִין, לָקֳבֵל כ"ח דַּרְגִּין דְּחַרְשֵׁי קוֹסְמִין דְּצִפּוֹר. וְאִית לְאִסְתַּכְּלָא, מַאן דְּבָעָא לְמַלְּלָא בֵּיהּ בְּבִלְעָם, וּלְאִתְחַבְּרָא בַּהֲדֵיהּ, אַמַּאי שָׁדַר לֵיהּ מִיַּד, עַד לָא יֵיתֵי לְגַבֵּיהּ, מִלִּין בְּפֵירוּשָׁא, דְּקָאָמַר הִנֵּה עַם יָצָא מִמִּצְרַיִם וְעַתָּה לְכָה אָרָה לִי, הֲוָה לֵיהּ לְאִתְחַבְּרָא בַּהֲדֵיהּ בְּקַדְמֵיתָא, וּלְפַיְּיסָא וּלְשׁוֹחֲדָא לֵיהּ, וּלְבָתַר לְאוֹדָעָא לֵיהּ מִלּוֹי.

133. "So he sent messengers to Bilaam the son of Beor" (Bemidbar 5-6). There are 28 words here, corresponding to the 28 levels of witches and magic sorcerers using a bird. We need to wonder why whoever wished to speak to Bilaam and join with him sent clear instructions immediately before approaching him, by saying, "Behold, there is a people come out from Egypt... Come now therefore, I pray you, curse me" (Ibid. 6). He should first have joined with him, ingratiated himself, bribed him and then informed him of what he wished to do.

134. אֶלָּא אָמַר רִבִּי יוֹסֵי, מֵהָכָא אִשְׁתְּמוֹדַע דְּהָא יָדַע בָּלָק רְעוּתֵיהּ דְּהַהוּא רָשָׁע, דְּבָעָא לְאִתְיַקְּרָא תָּדִיר בְּמִלִּין רַבְרְבִין, וְלֵית לֵיהּ תִּיאוּבְתָּא, אֶלָּא כַּד עָבֵיד בִּישִׁין.

134. HE RESPONDS: Yet Rabbi Yosi said that from here, it is recognizable that Balak was already aware of the desires of that evildoer, and that he wished to be apportioned great projects; his only ambition is to do evil deeds. THEREFORE, HE WAS EXALTING HIM AS IF THE REINS ARE IN HIS HANDS, AND TO WHOM HE WISHES HE CAN SEND BLESSINGS OR CURSES AND IT WILL BE ACCOMPLISHED. ALSO, HE INFORMED HIM OF HIS OWN

DESIRE TO CURSE YISRAEL, SINCE HE KNEW THAT HIS ENTIRE WISH WAS ONLY TO DO EVIL AND HARM.

135. בָּלָק קָסַם קְסָמִין וְעָבֵיד חַרְשִׁין וְאַתְקִין צִפֳּרָא. וְיָדַע דְּדַרְגִּין דְּמֹשֶׁה עִלָּאִין וְיַקִּירִין, וְחָרַשׁ בְּחַרְשׁוֹי וְקָסַם בִּקְסָמוֹי, וְיָדַע דְּדַרְגִּין דְּבִלְעָם הֲווֹ לָקֳבְלַיְיהוּ, מִיַּד וַיִּשְׁלַח מַלְאָכִים אֶל בִּלְעָם בֶּן בְּעוֹר.

135. Balak performed sorcery and witchcraft and constructed a bird. He was aware that Moses' levels were lofty and precious; he crafted with his witchery, and performed magical sorcery, and was aware that Bilaam's levels were corresponding TO THE LEVELS OF MOSES. Immediately, "he sent messengers to Bilaam the son of Beor."

136. פְּתוֹרָה: שְׁמָא דְּאַתְרָא הֲוָה. כד"א, מִפְּתוֹר אֲרַם נַהֲרַיִם לְקַלְלֶךָּ. אֲמַאי אִקְרֵי הָכִי. בְּגִין דִּכְתִּיב, הָעוֹרְכִים לַגַּד שֻׁלְחָן. וּפְתוֹרָא הֲוָה מְסַדֵּר תַּמָּן כָּל יוֹמָא. דְּהָכִי הוּא תִּקּוּנָא דְּסִטְרִין בִּישִׁין, מְסַדְּרִין קַמַּיְיהוּ פְּתוֹרָא בְּמֵיכְלָא וּבְמִשְׁתְּיָיא, וַעֲבְדִּין חַרְשִׁין, וּמְקַטְרִין לְקַמֵּי פְּתוֹרָא, וּמִתְכַּנְּשִׁין תַּמָּן כָּל רוּחִין מִסְאֲבִין, וְאוֹדְעִין לוֹן מַה דְּאִינּוּן בָּעָאן. וְכָל חַרְשִׁין וְקוֹסְמִין דְּעָלְמָא עַל הַהוּא פְּתוֹרָא הֲווֹ, ובג"כ אִקְרֵי שְׁמָא דְּאַתְרָא הַהוּא פְּתוֹרָא. דְּהָכִי קוֹרִין בַּאֲרַם נַהֲרַיִם לַשֻּׁלְחָן פְּתוֹרָא.

136. Petor is a name of a place, as is written: "From Petor of Aram Naharaim (Eng. 'two rivers') to curse you" (Devarim 23:5). Why was it called that way? Because it is written: "That set out a table for Fortune" (Yeshayah 65:11). He set a table there every day, since that is the custom of the evil sides. They set up for them a table with food and drink, performed sorcery, and smoked incense before that table. Then all the defiled spirits gathered there and informed them of whatever they wished. And all the magic and sorcery in the world were on that table, which is why the name of the place was called 'Petorah', since a table is called 'Petora' in Aram Naharaim (Eng. 'two rivers').

137. פָּתַח וְאָמַר וְעָשִׂיתָ שֻׁלְחָן עֲצֵי שִׁטִּים וְגוֹ'. וּכְתִיב וְנָתַתָּ עַל הַשֻּׁלְחָן לֶחֶם פָּנִים וְגוֹ'. כָּל אִינּוּן מָאנֵי קוּדְשָׁא, בָּעָא קוּדְשָׁא בְּרִיךְ

הוּא לְמֶעְבַּד קַמֵּיהּ, לְאַמְשָׁכָא רוּחָא קַדִּישָׁא מֵעֵילָּא לְתַתָּא. הַהוּא רָשָׁע דְּבִלְעָם, הֲוָה מְסַדֵּר הָכִי לְסִטְרָא אַחֲרָא. וַהֲוָה מְסַדֵּר שֻׁלְחָן, וְנַהֲמָא דְּאִקְרֵי לֶחֶם מְגוֹאָל, כְּמָה דְּאִתְּמַר. דְּהָכִי אָזִיל סְטַר אַחֲרָא בָּתַר קְדוּשָּׁה, כְּקוֹף בָּתַר בְּנֵי נָשָׁא. וּשְׁלֹמֹה מַלְכָּא צָווח וְאָמַר, כִּי מֶה הָאָדָם שֶׁיָּבֹא אַחֲרֵי הַמֶּלֶךְ אֵת אֲשֶׁר כְּבָר עָשׂוּהוּ. וְהָא אִתְּמַר קְרָא דָּא.

137. He opened the discussion with the verse: “You shall also make a table of acacia wood” (Shemot 25:23) and: “And you shall set upon the table shewbread...” (Ibid. 30). The Holy One, blessed be He, wished to have all these holy utensils made for Him, in order to draw the Holy Spirit from above downward. The wicked Bilaam prepared similarly for the Other Side, and he prepared a table and bread that is called “disgusting bread” (Malachi 1:7). As we were taught, the Other Side follows the holiness like a monkey after people. And King Solomon cried and said, “For what can the man do who comes after the king? Even that which has already been done” (Kohelet 2:12), WISHING TO IMITATE HIM, AND BE LIKE HIM, and we were already taught this verse.

8. “And rose up from Seir to them”

A Synopsis

We are told that God first offered the Torah to the children of Esau and then to the children of Ishmael, all of whom refused it, before He offered it to the children of Yisrael. Rabbi Shimon clarifies a point by saying that the refusal of the inhabitants of Seir and Paran enabled God to add their light and love to the children of Yisrael. We hear a dialogue between God and Samael wherein God offers the Torah to Samael who of course refuses it because of its stricture against killing. Samael suggests that God give the Torah to the children of Yisrael because he thinks that would ensure that Yisrael would never be capable of surviving or ruling – in effect, that the Torah would make them weak. Samael removes his own light and gives it to God to add to the light of Yisrael. The same thing happens with Rachav, the higher minister of Ishmael, who refuses the Torah because of its prohibition against adultery, and who also gives his light to God for Yisrael. Eventually we learn that from the other nations of the world God also took gifts on behalf of the children of Yisrael. Thus Yisrael inherited the Torah with no disagreement from anyone above or below. When Yisrael sinned and went into exile, all their gifts were removed from them, but in the future these gifts will be returned to them.

138. ת״ח, כְּתִיב יְיָ׳ בְּצֵאתְךָ מִשֵּׂעִיר בְּצַעְדְּךָ מִשְּׂדֵה אֱדוֹם אֶרֶץ רָעָשָׁה וְגוֹ׳. בְּשַׁעֲתָא דְּבָעָא קוּדְשָׁא בְּרִיךְ הוּא לְמֵיהַב אוֹרַיְיתָא לְיִשְׂרָאֵל, אָזַל וְזַמִּין לְהוּ לִבְנֵי עֵשָׂו, וְלָא קִבְּלוּהָ. כד״א יְיָ׳ מִסִּינַי בָּא וְזָרַח מִשֵּׂעִיר לָמוֹ, וְלָא בָּעוּ לְקַבְּלָהּ. אָזַל לִבְנֵי יִשְׁמָעֵאל, וְלָא בָּעוּ לְקַבְּלָהּ, דִּכְתִיב הוֹפִיעַ מֵהַר פָּארָן. כֵּיוָן דְּלָא בָּעוּ, אַהְדָּר לוֹן לְיִשְׂרָאֵל, הָכִי תָּנֵינָן.

138. Come and see that it is written: “Hashem, when You did go out of Seir, when You did march out of the field of Edom, the earth trembled...” (Shoftim 5:4). When the Holy One, blessed be He, wished to give the Torah to Yisrael, He went and invited the children of Esau, but they did not accept it, as it says, “Hashem came from Sinai, and rose up from Seir to them” (Ibid.). They refused to accept her. He went to the children of Ishmael and they refused to accept her, as it says, “He shone forth from Mount Paran” (Devarim 33:2). Since they refused, He returned to the children of Yisrael as we were taught.

139. הַשְׁתָּא אִית לְשָׁאֲלָא, וְהָא תָּנֵינָן דְּלֵית חַטָּאָה כַּד בַּר נָשׁ מְדַקְדֵּק דִּיּוּקִין דְּאוֹרַיְיתָא, וַיִּשְׁאַל שְׁאֶלְתּוֹי לְאַנְהֳרָא מִלּוֹי. הַאי קְרָא לָא אִתְיַישְׁבָא, וְאִית לְשָׁאֲלָא. קוּדְשָׁא בְּרִיךְ הוּא כַּד אָזַל לְשֵׂעִיר, לְמַאן נְבִיאָה דִּלְהוֹן אִתְגְּלֵי. וְכַד אָזַל לְפָארָן, לְמַאן נְבִיאָה דִּלְהוֹן אִתְגְּלֵי. אִי תֵּימָא דְּאִתְגְּלֵי לְכֻלְּהוּ, לָא אַשְׁכְּחָן דָּא לְעָלְמִין. בַּר לְיִשְׂרָאֵל בִּלְחוֹדַיְיהוּ, וע״י דְּמֹשֶׁה. וְהָא אִתְּמַר דְּהָכִי מִבָּעֵי קְרָא לְמֵימַר, יְיָ׳ לְסִינַי בָּא, וְזָרַח לְשֵׂעִיר לָמוֹ, הוֹפִיעַ לְהַר פָּארָן, מַהוּ מִשֵּׂעִיר לָמוֹ, וּמַהוּ מֵהַר פָּארָן. כֹּלָּא אִית לְמִנְדַּע וּלְאִסְתַּכְּלָא, וְהָא שָׁאִילְנָא, וְלָא שְׁמַעְנָא, וְלָא יְדַעְנָא.

139. Since we learned that it is not considered a sin, if a person is very meticulous about the details of the Torah and is asking his questions to clarify, this scripture is difficult to understand and the question needs to be asked. When the Holy One, blessed be He, went to Seir, to which prophet of theirs did He appear? And when He approached Paran, to which prophet of theirs did He reveal Himself? If you say that He revealed Himself to the whole nation, we find that it happened only to Yisrael alone and through Moses. FURTHERMORE, we were taught that this is what the scripture should have said, 'Hashem came to Sinai, and rose up to Seir to them; He shone forth to Mount Paran'. What is meant by: "From Seir to them...from Mount Paran"? All this must be known and be observed. Though I asked, I have not yet heard.

140. כַּד אָתָא רִבִּי שִׁמְעוֹן, אָתָא וְשָׁאִיל מִלָּה כְּמִלְּקַדְּמִין, אָ״ל הָא שְׁאֶלְתָּא דָּא אִתְאַמְרַת. יְיָ׳ מִסִּינַי בָּא: כד״א הִנֵּה אָנֹכִי בָּא אֵלֶיךָ בְּעַב הֶעָנָן, וּמִסִּינַי בָּא וְאִתְגְּלֵי עֲלַיְיהוּ. וְזָרַח מִשֵּׂעִיר לָמוֹ, מִמַּה דְּאָמְרוּ בְּנֵי שֵׂעִיר, דְּלָא בָּעָאן לְקַבְּלָא, מֵהַאי, אַנְהַר לוֹן לְיִשְׂרָאֵל, וְאוֹסִיף עֲלַיְיהוּ נְהוֹרָא וְחָבִיבוּ סַגִּיא. אוּף הָכִי, הוֹפִיעַ וְאַנְהַר לְיִשְׂרָאֵל מֵהַר פָּארָן, מִמַּה דְּאָמְרוּ בְּנֵי פָּארָן, דְּלָא בָּעוּ לְקַבְּלָא, מֵהַאי. אוֹסִיפוּ יִשְׂרָאֵל חֲבִיבוּ וּנְהִירוּ יַתִּיר כַּדְּקָא יָאוּת.

140. When Rabbi Shimon came, he approached and asked this again. RABBI SHIMON said to him, This inquiry has been settled, as "Hashem came from

Sinai" is as it says, "Lo, I come to you in a thick cloud" (Shemot 19:9) and "came from Sinai" and appeared over them, "and rose up from Seir to them," WHICH MEANS THAT because the inhabitants of Seir said that they do not wish to accept the Torah, He shone upon Yisrael, and added light, and great love, to them. Similarly, He "shone forth" and brightened the light from the mountain of Paran; additional love and bright light was available from the inhabitants of Paran's refusal to accept the Torah, and that was given to Yisrael as well, as is proper.

141. וּמַה דְּשָׁאַלְתְּ עַל יְדָא דְּמַאן אִתְגְּלֵי עֲלַיְיהוּ. רָזָא עִלָּאָה אִיהוּ, וְאִתְגְּלֵי מִלָּה עַל יְדָךְ. אוֹרַיְיתָא נַפְקַת מֵרָזָא עִלָּאָה, דְּרֵישָׁא דְּמַלְכָּא סְתִימָא, כַּד מָטָא לְגַבֵּי דְּרוֹעָא שְׂמָאלָא, חָמָא קוּדְשָׁא בְּרִיךְ הוּא בְּהַהוּא דְּרוֹעָא, דָּמָא בִּישָׁא דַּהֲוו מִתְרַבֵּי מִתַּמָּן. אָמַר, אִצְטְרִיךְ לִי לְבָרְרָא וּלְלַבְּנָא דְּרוֹעָא דָּא. וְאִי לָא יַמְאִיךְ הַהוּא דָּמָא בִּישָׁא, יַפְגִּים כֹּלָּא. אֲבָל אִצְטְרִיךְ לְבָרְרָא מֵהָכָא כָּל פְּגִימוּ.

141. You asked through whom He was revealed to them. That is a high secret and it will be uncovered through you; THAT IS, THROUGH YOUR INQUIRY. The Torah came out from the highest mystery, from the concealed head of the King, WHICH IS BINAH. When it reached the left arm, WHICH IS ISAAC, MEANING GVURAH, the Holy One, blessed be He, saw in that arm bad blood, that was increasing from there, WHICH IS ESAU, MEANING SAMAEL AND THE OTHER SIDE. He said, 'I need to refine and clarify this arm and if I do not take off that defective blood, it will injure everything. Indeed, it is necessary to refine every defect from here.'

142. מָה עֲבַד. קָרָא לְסָמָאֵל, וְאָתָא קַמֵּיהּ, וְאָמַר לֵיהּ תִּבְעֵי אוֹרַיְיתָא דִּילִי. אָמַר, מַה כְּתִיב בָּהּ. אָמַר לֵיהּ, לֹא תִרְצַח. דָּלִיג קוּדְשָׁא בְּרִיךְ הוּא לַאֲתָר דְּאִצְטְרִיךְ. אָמַר ח"ו, אוֹרַיְיתָא דָּא דִּילָךְ הִיא, וְדִילָךְ יְהֵא, לָא בָּעֵינָא אוֹרַיְיתָא דָּא. אָתִיב וְאִתְחַנַּן קַמֵּיהּ, אָמַר מָארֵיהּ דְּעָלְמָא, אִי אַתְּ יָהֲבָהּ לִי, כָּל שָׁלְטָנוּ דִּילִי אִתְעֲבַר, דְּהָא שָׁלְטָנוּ דִּילִי עַל קְטוּלָא אִיהוּ, וּקְרָבִין לָא יֶהֱוֹן וְשֻׁלְטָנוּ דִּילִי עַל כֹּכָבָא דְּמַאֲדִים, א"ה כֹּלָּא אִתְבְּטַל מֵעָלְמָא.

142. What did He do? He called Samael, ESAU'S MINISTER ABOVE, who came before Him. He said to him, 'Do you want My Torah?' And he said, What is written in her? He said, "You shall not murder" (Shemot 20:13), since the Holy One, blessed be He, skipped to show him the necessary place – HE SKIPPED TO THE COMMANDMENT THAT HE KNEW HE WOULD NOT BE ABLE TO KEEP. SAMAEL said, Heaven forbid, this Torah is Yours and Yours it shall remain. I do not desire such a Torah. He again beseeched of Him saying, Master of the world, if You give me THIS TORAH, my entire government will cease, since my entire domination is based on killing. AND IF I ACCEPT THE TORAH, there will no longer be wars. My rule is over the planet *Maadim* (Mars) THAT INDICATES SPILLING OF BLOOD. If so, all becomes void from the world.

143. מָארֵיהּ דְּעָלְמָא, טוֹל אוֹרַיְיתָךְ, וְלָא יְהֵא חוּלָקָא וְאַחֲסָנָא לִי בָּהּ. אֲבָל אִי נִיחָא קַמָּךְ, הָא עַמָּא בְּנוֹי דְּיַעֲקֹב, לוֹן אִתְחֲזֵי. וְאִיהוּ חָשִׁיב דְּהָא דַּלְטוֹרָא אָמַר עֲלַיְיהוּ. וְדָא הוּא וְזָרַח מִשֵּׂעִיר לָמוֹ, מִשֵּׂעִיר מַמָּשׁ נָפַק נְהוֹרָא לוֹן לְיִשְׂרָאֵל. אָמַר סָמָאֵ״ל וַדַּאי, אִי בְּנוֹי דְּיַעֲקֹב יְקַבְּלוּן דָּא, יִתְעָבְרוּן מֵעָלְמָא, וְלָא יִשְׁלְטוּן לְעָלְמִין. אָתִיב לֵיהּ כַּמָּה זִמְנִין, וְאָמַר דָּא, וְאָמַר לֵיהּ אַנְתְּ בּוּכְרָא, וְלָךְ אִתְחֲזֵי. אָמַר לֵיהּ, הָא לֵיהּ בְּכִירוּתָא דִּילִי, וְהָא אִזְדְּבַן לֵיהּ, וַאֲנָא אוֹדֵיתִי. אָמַר לֵיהּ הוֹאִיל וְלָא בָּעִית לְמֶהֱוֵי לָךְ בָּהּ חוּלָקָא, אִתְעֲבַר מִנָּהּ בְּכֹלָּא. אָמַר יָאוּת.

143. Master of the universe, take for Yourself that Torah of Yours. I do not want any part or portion in her. However, if it suits You, here are the people, the children of Jacob, for whom THIS TORAH is suitable. He thought that he said about them some derogatory accusation, which is the meaning of: "And rose up from Seir to them." Actually "from Seir" light went out for Yisrael, MEANING FROM SAMAEL, THE CHIEF MINISTER OF SEIR. Samael said TO HIMSELF, Certainly, if Jacob's children will accept THE TORAH, they will cease to exist in the world and will never be capable of ruling. THE HOLY ONE, BLESSED BE HE, responded several times and said the following, 'You are the firstborn, BECAUSE ESAU WAS THE FIRSTBORN and THE TORAH befits you.' He said to him, My birthright belongs to him, since it was sold to him and I gave my consent. THE HOLY ONE, BLESSED BE HE, then said, 'Since you don't wish to have any part IN THE TORAH, remove yourself from her altogether.' He said, Fine.

144. אֲמַר לֵיהּ, הוֹאִיל וְכָךְ, הַב לִי עֵיטָא, אֵיךְ אַעְבִּיד דִּיקַבְּלוּן לָהּ בְּנוֹי דְּיַעֲקֹב דְּאַתְּ אָמֵר. אֲמַר לֵיהּ מָארֵיהּ דְּעָלְמָא, אִצְטְרִיךְ לְשַׁחֲדָא לוֹן, טוֹל נְהוֹרָא מִנְּהִירוּ דְּחֵילֵי שְׁמַיָּא, וְהַב עֲלַיְיהוּ, וּבְדָא יְקַבְּלוּן לָהּ, וְהָא דִּילִי יְהֵא בְּקַדְמֵיתָא. אַפְשִׁיט מִנֵּיהּ נְהִירוּ דְּחַפְיָא עָלֵיהּ, וְיָהַב לֵיהּ, לְמֵיהַב לוֹן לְיִשְׂרָאֵל, הה"ד וְזָרַח מִשֵּׂעִיר לָמוֹ. מִשֵּׂעִיר מַמָּשׁ דָּא סָמָאֵ"ל. דִּכְתִּיב וְנָשָׂא הַשָּׂעִיר עָלָיו. לָמוֹ לְיִשְׂרָאֵל.

144. THE HOLY ONE, BLESSED BE HE, said to him, 'Since it is so, give Me advice on what I should do, so that the children of Jacob would accept her, as you say.' SAMAEL said to him, Master of the universe, there is a need to bribe them. Take light from the light of the legions in heaven and impart it to them. By this, they will accept her and here is some OF MY LIGHT, which I will give first. He removed from himself the light that enveloped him and gave it TO THE HOLY ONE, BLESSED BE HE, TO present it to Yisrael. This is what is meant by: "And rose up from Seir to them"; "from Seir" actually is Samael. It is written about him: "And the goat (Heb. *sair*) shall bear upon it" (Vayikra 16:22). "To them" MEANS to Yisrael.

145. כֵּיוָן דְּבִיעֵר דָּא, וְאַעְבַּר דָּמָא בִּישָׁא מִדְּרוֹעָא שְׂמָאלָא, אַהְדָּר לִדְרוֹעָא יְמִינָא חָמָא בֵּיהּ אוּף הָכִי, אָמַר הָכִי נָמֵי אִצְטְרִיךְ לְנַקְיָיא, מִדָּמָא בִּישָׁא, דְּרוֹעָא דָּא. קָרָא לְרַהַ"ב אָמַר לֵיהּ, תִּבְעֵי אַתְּ אוֹרַיְיתָא דִּילִי. אָמַר לֵיהּ, מַה כְּתִיב בָּהּ. דָּלִיג לֵיהּ, וְאָמַר לֹא תִּנְאָף. אָמַר וַוי אִי יְרוּתָא דָּא יַחֲסִין לִי קוּדְשָׁא בְּרִיךְ הוּא, יְרוּתָא בִּישָׁא, דְּיִתְעֲבַר בָּהּ כָּל שָׁלְטָנִי, דְּהָא בִּרְכָתָא דְּמַיָּא נְטִילְנָא, בִּרְכָתָא דְּנוּנֵי יַמָּא, דִּכְתִּיב פְּרוּ וּרְבוּ וְגוֹ'. וּכְתִיב וְהִפְרֵיתִי אוֹתוֹ וְהִרְבֵּיתִי אוֹתוֹ וְגוֹ' וּכְתִיב וְהוּא יִהְיֶה פֶּרֶא אָדָם.

145. As soon as He removed that one, SAMAEL, and cleaned out the bad blood from the left arm, THAT IS ISAAC, WHICH IS GVURAH, He turned to the right arm, WHICH IS ABRAHAM, AND HE IS CHESED. He noticed in it also DEFECTIVE BLOOD THAT IS ISHMAEL. He said, 'This arm too needs to have the bad blood cleaned out of it.' The Holy One, blessed be He, called to Rahav, THE MINISTER OF ISHMAEL. He said to him, 'Do you want My Torah?' RAHAV said to Him, What is written in it? He skipped EVERYTHING ELSE and said TO HIM, "You shall not commit adultery" (Shemot 20:13). He said to Him, Woe FOR ME. If that is the legacy the Holy One, blessed be He, wishes me to inherit, that would be an evil legacy for me, since it would remove my entire dominion WHICH IS BASED ON ADULTERY. Since I took the blessings of the water, the blessing reserved for the fish of the sea, as is written: "Be fruitful (Heb. *pru*) and multiply" (Beresheet 1:22) and: "and will make him fruitful, and will multiply him..." (Beresheet 17:20). It is further written: "And he will be a wild (Heb. *pere*) man" (Beresheet 16:12).

146. שָׁארִי לְאִתְחַנְּנָא קַמֵּי מָארֵיהּ, אָמַר לֵיהּ, מָארֵי דְעָלְמָא, תְּרֵין בְּנִין נָפְקָנָא מֵאַבְרָהָם, הָא בְּנוֹי דְיִצְחָק, הַב לוֹן, וְלוֹן אִתְחֲזֵי. אָמַר לֵיהּ, לָא יָכִילְנָא, דְאַנְתְּ בּוּכְרָא, וְלָךְ אִתְחֲזֵי, שָׁארִי לְאִתְחַנְּנָא קַמֵּיהּ, וְאָמַר מָארֵיהּ דְעָלְמָא, בְּכֵירוּתָא דִילִי יְהֵא דִילֵיהּ, וְהַאי נְהוֹרָא דַאֲנָא יָרִיתְנָא עַל דָא, טוֹל וְהַב לוֹן, וְכַךְ עָבֵד, הֲדָא הוּא דִכְתִיב, הוֹפִיעַ מֵהַר פָּארָן.

146. He began to beseech his Master and said to him, Master of the universe, two children came out of Abraham. Here are the children of Isaac, give it to them, for she is suitable for them. THE HOLY ONE, BLESSED BE HE, said to him, 'I can't, since you are the firstborn and THE TORAH is suitable for you.' He began to plead before Him and said, Master of the universe, let the rights of the firstborn be his. That light which I inherited as a legacy thereby due to that RIGHTS OF THE FIRSTBORN, take and give to them. And so, THE HOLY ONE, BLESSED BE HE, did. This is what is written: "He shone forth from Mount Paran" (Devarim 33:2).

147. מַאי שְׁנָא בְּסָמָאֵ"ל כְּתִיב וְזָרַח, וּבְרַהַ"ב כְּתִיב הוֹפִיעַ. אֶלָּא נָטַל בְּהַהוּא נְהִירוּ דְאַפְשִׁיט מִנֵּיהּ סָמָאֵ"ל, חֶרֶב וְקָטוֹלָא, לְקָטְלָא בְּדִינָא, וּלְקַטְלָא כַּדְקָא יָאוּת. הֲדָא הוּא דִכְתִיב, וַאֲשֶׁר חֶרֶב גַּאֲוָתֶךָ. אע"ג דְלָא הֲוָה דִילָךְ. וְנָטַל בְּהַהוּא בִרְכָתָא דְאַפְשִׁיט מִנֵּיהּ רַהַ"ב, זְעֵיר, כְּמָאן דְהוֹפִיעַ זְעֵיר מִבִּרְכָתָא דִלְהוֹן, לְמֶעְבַּד פְּרִיָה וּרְבִיָּה. בְּגִין כַּךְ הוֹפִיעַ מֵהַר פָּארָן, וְלָא כְּתִיב וְזָרַח.

147. What changed, in that by Samael, it says, "Rose up" and by Rahav, it is written: "Shone forth"? HE RESPONDS: It is only that He took with that light, which He removed from Samael, the sword and the killing, to kill with sentencing by judgment and to do the killing properly, as is written: "And One that is the sword of your excellency" (Devarim 33:29), though it is not belonging to you. From that blessing which He removed from Rahav, He took only a little, like someone that only shone a little of their blessing, meaning just enough to be able to produce and multiply. Therefore, IT IS WRITTEN: "He shone forth from Mount Paran" and it is not written: "Rose up," WHICH MEANS INCREASE LIKE BY SAMAEL.

148. כֵּיוָן דְּנָטַל מַתְּנָן אִלֵּין לְיִשְׂרָאֵל, מֵאִינּוּן רַבְרְבָנִין שָׁלְטָנִין, אָתָא וְקָרָא לְהוּ לְכָל רִבְבוֹת קֹדֶשׁ, דִּמְמָנָן עַל שְׁאַר עַמִּין, וְאָתִיבוּ לֵיהּ אוּף הָכִי. וּמִכֻּלְּהוּ קַבִּיל וְנָטִיל מַתְּנָן, לְמֵיהַב לוֹן לְיִשְׂרָאֵל. לְאַסְיָא, דַּהֲוָה לֵיהּ חַד מָאנָא מַלְיָא מִסַּמָּא דְּחַיֵּי, וְנָטִיר לֵיהּ לִבְרֵיהּ. בָּעָא לְמֵיהַב לֵיהּ לִבְרֵיהּ, הַהוּא פְּלַיְיטוֹן דְּסָמָא דְּחַיֵּי. אַסְיָא הֲוָה חַכִּים, אָמַר עַבְדִּין בִּישִׁין אִית בְּבֵיתִי, אִי יִנְדְּעוּן דַּאֲנָא יָהִיב לִבְרִי נְבַזְבְּזָא דָּא, יַבְאִישׁ בְּעֵינַיְיהוּ, וְיִבְעוּן לְקַטְלָא לֵיהּ.

148. As soon as THE HOLY ONE, BLESSED BE HE, took these gifts to Yisrael from these chief ministers that rule OVER ESAU AND ISHMAEL, He approached and called all the "holy multitudes" (Ibid. 2) that are appointed over the rest of the nations. They also replied to Him similarly AS SAMAEL AND RAHAV. From all of them, He took and accepted gifts on behalf of Yisrael. THIS IS LIKE a doctor who had one vial full of medicine of life and kept it for his son. He wished to give his son those medicine of life, but the doctor was wise and thought about the evil servants in his household. If they notice that I give this gift to my son, they will be jealous and will want to kill him.

149. מָה עֲבַד. נָטַל זְעֵיר מִסַּמָּא דְּמוֹתָא, וְשַׁוֵּי אַפִּתְחָא דְּמָאנָא, קָרָא לְעַבְדוֹי, אָמַר לוֹן, אַתּוּן מְהֵימְנָן קֳדָמַי, תִּבְעוּן לְהַהוּא סַמָּא. אָמְרוּ נֶחֱמֵי מַאי הִוא. נַטְלוּ לְמִטְעַם, עַד לָא אַרְחוּ, בָּעוּ לְמֵימַת, אָמְרוּ בְּלִבַּיְיהוּ, אִי הַאי סַמָּא יָהִיב לִבְרֵיהּ, וַדַּאי יָמוּת וַאֲנָן נִירַת לְרִבּוֹנָנָא.

אָמְרוּ קַמֵּיהּ, מָרָנָא, סַמָּא דָּא לָא אִתְחָזֵי אֶלָּא לִבְרָךְ, וְהָא אַגְרָא דִּפוּלְחָנָנָא שְׁבַקְנָא גַּבָּךְ, זִיל וְהַב לֵיהּ לְשׁוֹחֲדָא, דִּיקָבֵּל סַמָּא דָּא.

149. What did he do? He took a little bit of deadly poison spices and put it at the opening of that vessel, then called his servants and said to them, You faithful of mine, would you like to have some of this potion? They said, Let's see what it consists of. They took a bit of it to taste and, even before that, when they only smelled it, they felt like they were going to die. They figured to themselves, If he gives that potion to his son, he would certainly die, and we will inherit our lord's goods. They said to him, Our lord, this potion is only proper and suitable for your son. Here are some of our wages. Give it as a bribe to your son so that he will accept this potion.

150. כַּךְ קוּדְשָׁא בְּרִיךְ הוּא, הוּא אַסְיָא חַכִּים, יָדַע דְּאִי יָהִיב אוֹרַיְיתָא לְיִשְׂרָאֵל, עַד לָא אוֹדַע לוֹן, בְּכָל יוֹמָא הֲווֹ רַדְפִין לוֹן לְיִשְׂרָאֵל עָלָהּ, וְקַטְלִין לוֹן. אֲבָל עֲבַד דָּא, וְאִינּוּן יָהֲבוּ לֵיהּ מַתְנָן וּנְבִזְבְּזָן, בְּגִין דִּיקַבְּלוּן לָהּ. וְכֻלְּהוּ קַבִּיל לוֹן מֹשֶׁה, לְמֵיהַב לְהוּ לְיִשְׂרָאֵל, הה״ד עָלִיתָ לַמָּרוֹם שָׁבִיתָ שֶּׁבִי וְגוֹ׳. וּבְגִין כַּךְ יַרְתּוּ יִשְׂרָאֵל אוֹרַיְיתָא, בְּלָא עִרְעוּרָא, וּבְלָא קִטְרוּגָא כְּלָל. בְּרִיךְ הוּא, בְּרִיךְ שְׁמֵיהּ, לְעָלַם וּלְעָלְמֵי עָלְמַיָּא.

150. So too, the Holy One, blessed be He, is a wise healer and knew if He gave the Torah to Yisrael before He informed THE CHIEF MINISTERS, they would pursue Yisrael for her sake every day, and kill them. But instead, HE INVITED THEM AND THEY REFUSED and they gave Him offerings and gifts so that YISRAEL should accept her. Moses accepted all of them to give to Yisrael. This is what is written: "You have ascended on high, you have led captivity captive: you have received gifts..." (Tehilim 68:19). Therefore, Yisrael inherited the Torah without any disagreement and without any accusation at all. Praised is He and praised is His name forever and ever.

151. ת״ח, עֶדְיָם דִּבְנֵי יִשְׂרָאֵל, אִלֵּין מַתְנָן וּנְבִזְבְּזָן דְּקַבִּילוּ. וּבג״כ, לָא הֲוָה שַׁלִּיט עֲלַיְיהוּ מוֹתָא, וְלָא סִטְרָא אַחֲרָא, וְלָא דַּי לוֹן דַּי נַטְלוּ אוֹרַיְיתָא בְּלָא עִרְעוּרָא כְּלָל, אֶלָּא דְּקַבִּילוּ נְבִזְבְּזָן וּמַתְּנָן מִכֻּלְּהוּ. כֵּיוָן

דְּחָטוּ מַה כְּתִיב, וַיִּתְנַצְּלוּ בְנֵי יִשְׂרָאֵל אֶת עֶדְיָם. אִינּוּן מַתָּנוֹת בָּאָדָם. מַה אִשְׁתְּאַר מִנְּהוֹן. הַהוּא שְׁבִי, דִּכְתִיב עָלִיתָ לַמָּרוֹם שָׁבִיתָ שֶּׁבִי וְגוֹ'.

151. Come and see the offerings and gifts that Yisrael received from the CHIEFS OF THESE NATIONS, because of which neither death nor the Other Side could dominate them, and not only that, they received the Torah without any protest. They also received gifts and presents from all. When they sinned, it is written: "And the children of Yisrael stripped themselves of their ornaments" (Shemot 33:6), which are "gifts from men," WHICH THEY RECEIVED. What was left of them? Just that captivity, which is written: "You have ascended on high, you have led captivity captive, YOU HAVE RECEIVED GIFTS FROM (ALSO: 'WITH') MEN."

152. אוֹסִפוּ וְחָטוּ, מַה כְּתִיב וַיִּשְׁמַע הַכְּנַעֲנִי מֶלֶךְ עֲרָד. וּכְתִיב, וַיִּלָּחֶם בְּיִשְׂרָאֵל וַיִּשְׁבְּ מִמֶּנּוּ שֶׁבִי וְכָל זִמְנָא דְּיִשְׂרָאֵל תָּבִין לַאֲבוּהוֹן דְּבִשְׁמַיָּא, אִינּוּן נִבְזְבְּזָן יִתְהַדַּר לְגַבַּיְיהוּ, וְאִתְחַפְּיָין בֵּיהּ. וּלְזִמְנָא דְּאָתֵי, כֹּלָּא יִתְהַדַּר דִּכְתִיב וְשָׁב ה' אֱלֹהֶיךָ אֶת שְׁבוּתְךָ וְגוֹ'. מִכָּאן וּלְהָלְאָה אֵימָא מִילָּךְ.

152. When they sinned again, it is written: "And when the Canaanite, the king of Arad...heard...then he fought against Yisrael, and took some of them prisoners" (Bemidbar 21:1), MEANING THAT HE TOOK FROM THEM THEIR REMAINING CAPTIVITY. As long as Yisrael will repent before their Father in heaven, these gifts will be returned to them and they will shelter them. In the future to come, everything will be returned, as is written: "And then Hashem your Elohim will return your captivity..." (Devarim 30:3). From here on, speak your words.

9. "The earth feared, and was still"

A Synopsis

Rabbi Yosi opens by saying that God told the earth that if Yisrael accepted the Torah all would be well, but if not He would return the earth to its formless condition. Because of this the earth trembled in fear that Yisrael would not accept, but when Yisrael said they would obey the Torah, the earth became still. After Yisrael accepted, they were no longer afraid of witchcraft or sorcery, because God removed its power over them when He led them out of Egypt. Balak knew this immediately when he arrived, so he needed advice from Bilaam. Next Rabbi Elazar is persuaded by the other rabbis to reveal the secret of the joy that God experiences in the Garden of Eden with the righteous.

153. א״ר יוֹסֵי, יְיָ׳ בְּצֵאתְךָ מִשֵּׂעִיר בְּצַעְדְּךָ מִשְּׂדֵה אֱדוֹם אֶרֶץ רָעָשָׁה. בְּשַׁעֲתָא דְקוּדְשָׁא בְּרִיךְ הוּא תָּב מִשֵּׂעִיר, דְּלָא קַבִּילוּ אוֹרַיְיתָא, אֶרֶץ רָעָשָׁה וְגוֹ׳. מ״ט רָעָשָׁה. בְּגִין דְּבָעָאת לְאַהַדְרָא לְתוֹהוּ וָבוֹהוּ, דְּהָכִי אַתְנֵי קוּדְשָׁא בְּרִיךְ הוּא בְּעָלְמָא, אִי יְקַבְּלוּן בְּנֵי יִשְׂרָאֵל אוֹרַיְיתָא, מוּטָב. וְאִם לָאו, אַהְדָּר עָלְמָא לְתוֹהוּ וָבוֹהוּ. כֵּיוָן דְּחָמָאת אַרְעָא, דְּהָא אַזְמִין קוּדְשָׁא בְּרִיךְ הוּא לְכָל עַמְמַיָא דִּיְקַבְּלוּ אוֹרַיְיתָא, וְלָא קַבִּילוּ. וּמִכָּל עַמְמַיָא לָא אִשְׁתָּאֲרוּ אֶלָּא יִשְׂרָאֵל בִּלְחוֹדַיְיהוּ, חֲשִׁיבַת אַרְעָא, דְּיִשְׂרָאֵל לָא יְקַבְּלוּ כְּוָותַיְיהוּ, ובג״כ אֶרֶץ רָעָשָׁה. כֵּיוָן דְּאָמְרוּ נַעֲשֶׂה וְנִשְׁמָע, מִיָּד שָׁקָטָה, הה״ד אֶרֶץ יָרְאָה וְשָׁקָטָה. יָרְאָה בְּקַדְמֵיתָא, וּלְבַסּוֹף וְשָׁקָטָה.

153. Rabbi Yosi said, "Hashem, when you did go out of Seir, when you did march out of the field of Edom, the earth trembled..." (Shoftim 5:4). That was during the time when the Holy One, blessed be He, returned from Seir, because they didn't accept the Torah. "The earth trembled": What is the reason that it trembled? It is because it wanted to return to formlessness and void. The Holy One, blessed be He, made a condition with the world that if the children of Yisrael accept the Torah, it is good but if not, I will return you to formlessness and void. When the earth noticed that the Holy One, blessed be He, invited all the nations to accept the Torah, but they didn't accept, and from all the nations, only Yisrael were left, the earth thought that Yisrael, too, would refuse to accept the Torah as the others did. Due to this, "the earth trembled"; as soon as YISRAEL said, "Will we do, and obey" (Shemot 24:7) immediately, it quieted down. This is what is written: "The earth feared, and was still." First it "feared," then "was still" (Tehilim 76:9).

154. ות"ח, בְּגִין דְּיִשְׂרָאֵל אָמְרוּ נַעֲשֶׂה, לָא דַּחֲלִין מִן כָּל עֲשִׂיָּיה, דְּיֵכְלוּן כָּל חֲרָשֵׁי דְּעָלְמָא לְמֶעְבַּד, וְלָא מִכָּל קִסְמִין וְחַרְשִׁין דְּעָלְמָא. מ"ט. חַד, בּגּ"ד. וְחַד, בְּגִין דְּכַד אַפִּיק לוֹן קוּדְשָׁא בְּרִיךְ הוּא מִמִּצְרַיִם, תָּבַר קַמַּיְיהוּ כָּל זִינֵי חַרְשֵׁי וּקְסָמִין, דְּלָא יַכְלִין לְשַׁלְטָאָה עֲלַיְיהוּ, וְהַהִיא שַׁעֲתָא דְּאָתָא בָּלָק, הֲוָה יָדַע דָּא. מִיָּד וַיִּשְׁלַח מַלְאָכִים אֶל בִּלְעָם בֶּן בְּעוֹר פְּתוֹרָה אֲשֶׁר עַל הַנָּהָר וְגוֹ'. מַאי פְּתוֹרָה. אֶלָּא דְּיַתְקִין פְּתוֹרָא, וְיִבְעֵי מִתַּמָּן עֵיטָא, מַה יַעְבִיד. אֲשֶׁר עַל הַנָּהָר, עַל הַנְּהָרִים מִבָּעֵי לֵיהּ, מַאי עַל הַנָּהָר. וַדַּאי הָכִי הוּא, דְּעַל חַד נַהֲרָא קַיְימָא תָּדִיר.

154. Come and see: Because Yisrael said, "will we do," they were neither afraid of any deeds that the practitioners of witchcraft of the world were capable of doing nor of any sorcerers in the world. What is the reason? One is THAT THEY SAID, "WILL WE DO" and one is because the Holy One, blessed be He, broke all the witchcraft and sorcery before the children of Yisrael, when He took them out of Egypt, so that they should have no effect on them. When Balak came, he was aware of it. Immediately, "he sent messengers to Bilaam the son of Beor to Petor, which is by the river" (Bemidbar 22:5). What is Petor? It is that he prepared a table (Aram. *Ptora*) from which to ask for counsel as to what to do. "by the river": HE ASKS: It should have said 'two rivers (Heb. *naharaim*)', SINCE HE WAS FROM ARAM NAHARAIM (ENG. 'TWO RIVERS'). HE REPLIES: He certainly dwells at all times on one river, MEANING TO SAY THE TABLE OF THE KLIPAH, WHICH IS MALCHUT OF KLIPAH, STANDS ABOVE ONE RIVER OF THAT KLIPAH, WHICH IS YESOD OF THE KLIPAH.

155. רִבִּי אֶלְעָזָר וְרִבִּי אַבָּא, הֲווֹ אָזְלֵי לְמֶיחֱמֵי לְרִבִּי יוֹסֵי בְּר' שִׁמְעוֹן בֶּן לָקוּנְיָא, חַמוֹי דְּרִבִּי אֶלְעָזָר, קָמוּ בְּפַלְגוּת לֵילְיָא לְמִלְעֵי בְּאוֹרַיְיתָא, יָתְבוּ. א"ר אֶלְעָזָר, הַשְׁתָּא הוּא עִדָּנָא, דְּקוּדְשָׁא בְּרִיךְ הוּא עָאל

בְּגִנְתָּא דְעֵדֶן, לְאִשְׁתַּעְשְׁעָא בְּצַדִּיקַיָּיא דְתַמָּן. א"ר אַבָּא, שַׁעֲשׁוּעָא דָא מַאי הוּא, וְהֵיךְ יִשְׁתַּעְשַׁע בְּהוּ. א"ר אֶלְעָזָר, מִלָּה דָא רָזָא סְתִימָא אִיהוּ, טְמִירָא לְגַבֵּי, דְּלָא יְדִיעַ. א"ל, וְכִי בְּרֵיקַנַיָּא הֲווֹ סַמְכִין רַבְרְבִין דְּמִקַּדְמַת דְּנָא בְּהַאי עָלְמָא, דְּלָא יָדְעוּ, וְלָא רָדְפוּ אֲבַתְרָהּ לְמִנְדַּע עַל מַה קַיְימִין בְּהַאי עָלְמָא, וּמַה הֲווֹ מְחַכָּאן בְּהַהוּא עָלְמָא.

155. Rabbi Elazar and Rabbi Aba went to see Rabbi Yosi, son of Rabbi Shimon ben Lakunya, father-in-law of Rabbi Elazar. They rose at midnight to study the Torah. They sat. Rabbi Elazar said, Now is the time that the Holy One, blessed be He, enters the Garden of Eden to be merry with the righteous that are there. Rabbi Aba said, What is this joy and how does He rejoice in them? Rabbi Elazar said, This matter is a secret sealed with me that is not known TO ALL, AND HE DID NOT WANT TO DIVULGE IT. RABBI ABA said to him, Were then the great pillars in the world before us empty, THAT YOU SAY that they did not know OF THIS SECRET AND IT IS IMPROPER TO REVEAL IT? HAD THEY not pursue the knowledge of the reason of their existence in this world, and what they can expect in the World to Come. THEN MOST DEFINITELY, THEY TOO WERE AWARE OF THIS SECRET; THEREFORE, YOU ARE REQUIRED TO DIVULGE IT.

10. "Hashem, You are my Elohim; I will exalt You"

A Synopsis

Rabbi Elazar explains the secret of the high point that is concealed and unknown, and the level where inquiry may first be made. He talks about the word of Melchizedek the High Priest, that corresponds to Chesed of Zeir Anpin standing over Malchut. We hear the three meanings of "You" in the title verse, and Rabbi Elazar goes on to give two explanations of "For You have done wonderful things." He says that the actual form of the aleph is the beginning of the higher secret of primordial man, and he tells us why it has a numerical value of one. We learn that the prophets receive from Netzach and Hod that are called 'counsels'. Rabbi Elazar says that the title verse is a concise vehicle for the entire concealed secret meaning of the faith, in that Hashem is Chochmah, "my Elohim" is Binah, "You" is Chesed, "wonder" is the three Columns Chesed Gvurah and Tiferet, "counsel from afar" is Netzach and Hod, "faithfulness" is Malchut, and "truth" is Yesod.

156. פָּתַח רִבִּי אֶלְעָזָר וְאָמַר, יְיָ׳ אֱלֹהַי אַתָּה אֲרוֹמִמְךָ אוֹדֶה שִׁמְךָ כִּי עָשִׂיתָ וְגו׳. הַאי קְרָא רָזָא דִּמְהֵימְנוּתָא אִיהוּ. יְיָ׳, רָזָא עִלָּאָה, שֵׁירוּתָא דִּנְקוּדָה עִלָּאָה סְתִימָא דְּלָא יְדִיעַ. אֱלֹהַי, רָזָא קוֹל דְּמָמָה דַּקָּה, וְאִיהוּ שֵׁירוּתָא דְּקַיְימָא לְשָׁאֲלָא, וְאַסְתִּים וְלָא יְדִיעַ, וְלֵית מַאן דְּאָתִיב עָלֵיהּ, בְּגִין דְּאִיהוּ סָתִים וְטָמִיר וְגָנִיז.

156. Rabbi Elazar opened the discussion with the verse: "Hashem, You are my Elohim; I will exalt You, I will praise Your name; for You have done..." (Yeshayah 25:1). This verse in the scripture is the secret of the Faith. Yud Hei Vav Hei is the top secret and is the beginning of the higher point that is concealed and not known, THAT IS, ABA AND IMA UP HIGH, WHO ARE THE SECRET OF CHOCHMAH. AND THEY ARE CONCEALED FROM CHOCHMAH, ENTIRELY UNKNOWN. "My Elohim" is the secret meaning of "a still small voice" (I Melachim 19:12) THAT IS YISRAEL-SABA AND TEVUNAH, WHICH IS THE SECRET MEANING OF BINAH. That is the beginning of that which may be inquired into. HOWEVER, it becomes concealed and unknown, and there is no one that responds to it; ALTHOUGH IT IS AVAILABLE FOR INQUIRY, AVAILABLE TO BE REVEALED BUT RATHER IN THE PLACE OF ZEIR ANPIN AND MALCHUT, because it is concealed, covered and hidden.

157. אַתָּה, דָּא יְמִינָא, שֵׁירוּתָא דְּקַיְּימָא לְשָׁאֳלָא, וּלְאַתְבָא בֵּיהּ, וְהוּא כֹּהֵן עִלָּאָה. כד"א אַתָּה כֹהֵן לְעוֹלָם עַל דִּבְרָתִי מַלְכִּי צֶדֶק. מַאן עַל דִּבְרָתִי מַלְכִּי צֶדֶק. אֶלָּא כֹּהֵן עִלָּאָה דָּא, אִיהוּ דְּקַיְּימָא עַל דָּבָר, בְּגִין דְּהַהוּא דָּבָר לָא קַיְּימָא, אֶלָּא בִּימִינָא. וְהַהוּא דָּבָר מַאן אִיהוּ. מַלְכִּי צֶדֶק, כַּךְ שְׁמֵיהּ. וּמַאי דְּאָמַר דִּבְרָתִי, בְּגִין דְּאִתְקְשַׁר בֵּיהּ בְּדָוִד. וְכָל מִלֵּי שְׁבָחָא דִילֵיהּ, בְּהַהוּא דָּבָר אַתְיָין. וְעַל דָּא דִּבְרָתִי. ובג"כ, אַתָּה דָּא כֹּהֵן. וְהָא אוֹקִימְנָא, דִּתְלַת דוּכְתֵּי אִינּוּן, דְּאִקְרֵי כָּל חַד אַתָּה.

157. AFTER EXPLAINING THAT YUD HEI VAV HEI IS THE SECRET OF ABA AND IMA THAT STAND ABOVE ANY QUESTIONING, AND "MY ELOHIM," THAT SECRET OF YISRAEL-SABA AND TEVUNAH THAT ARE AVAILABLE FOR INQUIRY, BUT THERE IS NO ONE TO RESPOND TO IT, HE EXPLAINS NOW: "You" that is right, MEANING CHESED OF ZEIR ANPIN, is the start of what is available for inquiry and for a response to it. HOWEVER, THAT IS MERELY THE BEGINNING OF THIS REVELATION, BUT IS NOT YET REVEALED IN IT, ONLY WHEN IT IS IN MALCHUT. That is CALLED 'the High Priest', as it says, "You shall be a priest forever, after the manner of Melchizedek" (Tehilim 110:4). HE INQUIRES: What is the meaning of: "After the manner (lit. 'word') of Melchizedek"? HE RESPONDS: This is the supernal priest, CHESED OF ZEIR ANPIN, that is standing over the word, WHICH IS MALCHUT, because this word does not endure except through the right, WHICH IS CHESED. What is that word? That is Melchizedek, the name OF MALCHUT. The reason it says "*divrati* (lit. 'word of' also: 'my word')" INSTEAD OF '*DAVAR*' IS because it was connected with David, SINCE DAVID WAS THE CHARIOT TO MALCHUT. All the words of DAVID'S praise came through that word and, therefore, it says, "My word," MEANING MY MALCHUT. As a result of this, "you" is a priest, WHICH IS CHESED. We have already explained that there are three areas and each one is called "you," BECAUSE CHOCHMAH IS CALLED "YOU" AND CHESED IS CALLED "YOU," AS IS WRITTEN HERE. AND MALCHUT IS CALLED "YOU."

158. אֲרוֹמִמְךָ כְּלָּא כַּחֲדָא. אוֹדֶה שִׁמְךָ כַּדְקָא יָאוּת, וְהַאי שֵׁם יְדִיעַ. כִּי עָשִׂיתָ פֶּלֶא, כִּסּוּיָא וּלְבוּשָׁא, לְאִתְלַבְּשָׁא נְהוֹרָא סְתִימָא עַתִּיקָא, רֵאשִׁיתָא דַּרְגָּא עִלָּאָה, אָדָם קַדְמָאָה, טְמִירָא בְּכִסּוּיָא דִּנְהוֹרָא אַחֲרָא.

158. NOW HE EXPLAINS THE WORDS: "I WILL EXALT YOU" THAT IS IN THE VERSE MENTIONED ABOVE. HE SAYS, "I will exalt You," meaning in all THREE NAMES, YUD HEI VAV HEI, "MY ELOHIM," AND "YOU," and together "I will praise Your name" as proper. That name is known TO BE MALCHUT CALLED 'NAME'. "For You have done wonderful things" (Yeshayah 25:1): "WONDERFUL" IS A LANGUAGE OF CONCEALMENT THAT MEANS THAT YOU HAVE MADE a cover and attire to the concealed light of Atika, WHICH IS BINAH. The beginning of the top level, WHICH IS THE CHOCHMAH CONTAINED WITHIN, IS REFERRED TO AS concealed primordial man, so that he will be attired with a cover of another light THAT IS CHASSADIM.

159. ד"א כִּי עָשִׂיתָ פֶּלֶא, כִּי עָשִׂיתָ אָלֶ"ף. וּמַהוּ אָלֶף. הָא תָּנֵינָן, אָלֶ"ף בֵּי"ת, אָלֵף בִּינָה. אֲבָל דִּיוּקְנָא דְּא', אִיהוּ תְּלַת סִטְרִין. רֵאשִׁית דְּרָזָא עִלָּאָה דְּאָדָם קַדְמָאָה. בְּגִין, דִּבְדִיוּקְנָא דְּא', אִית תְּרֵין דְּרוֹעִין, חַד מִכָּאן, וְחַד מִכָּאן, וְגוּפָא בְּאֶמְצָעִיתָא, וְכֹלָּא רָזָא חֲדָא. וְאִיהוּ רָזָא דְּיִחוּדָא, א'. ובג"כ אָלֶף לְחוּשְׁבְּנָא אֶחָד, וְהַיְינוּ כִּי עָשִׂיתָ פֶּלֶא. וְרַב הַמְנוּנָא סָבָא אָמַר הָכִי, כִּי עָשִׂיתָ פֶּלֶא, פֶּלֶא דָּא הוּא חַד דַּרְגָּא מֵאִינוּן פְּלָאוֹת חָכְמָה. וּמַאן אִיהוּ. דָּא נָתִיב לֹא יְדָעוֹ עָיִט. וְאִיהוּ פֶּלֶא.

159. Another explanation of: "For You have done wonderful things (Heb. *pele*)": NAMELY, You have made Aleph, SINCE *PELE* IS SPELLED WITH THE SAME LETTERS OF ALEPH. What is the meaning of Aleph? We learned that Aleph Bet MEANS Aleph Binah, (lit. 'teach to understand'). Yet the form of the Aleph is three side, RIGHT, LEFT AND CENTER, that is the start of the higher secret of the primordial man. THAT IS THE THREE COLUMNS IN BINAH, THE SOURCE OF THE IMAGE OF MAN, WHO IS MOCHIN OF ZEIR ANPIN. For in the form of the Aleph there are two arms, one from each side, THAT ARE THE TWO COLUMNS OF CHESED AND GVURAH THAT ARE THE UPPER YUD AND HER LOWER YUD, and the body in the centre; THAT IS THE VAV BETWEEN THE TWO YUD'S. All has one secret meaning, THAT IT IS IN ONE MEANING WITH THE EXPLANATION THAT *PELE* IS CHOCHMAH BEING CLOTHED IN CHASSADIM, SINCE THIS CLOTHING DOES NOT HAPPEN EXCEPT THROUGH THE THREE COLUMNS. That is the secret of unification of this Aleph and that is also why Aleph HAS A NUMERICAL VALUE OF one. That is the meaning of: "For You have done wonderful things (Heb. *pele*)," WHICH IS THE SECRET OF ALEPH. And Rav Hamnuna Saba (the elder) said this, "For You have done wonderful things." This wonder is one level from these hidden wonders of Chochmah. Which one is it? "There is a path which no bird of prey knows" (Iyov 28:7), WHICH IS THE FIFTIETH GATE. And that is a wonderful thing.

160. עֵצוֹת מֵרָחוֹק קָרָא לְהַאי בְּקַדְמֵיתָא פֶּלֶא, וְהָכָא אָמַר פֶּלֶא עֵצוֹת מֵרָחוֹק. אֶלָּא הָתָם אִצְטְרִיךְ לְמִמְנֵי שִׁית סִטְרִין לְדַרְגִּין עִלָּאִין, פֶּלֶא יוֹעֵץ אֵל גִּבּוֹר אֲבִי עַד שַׂר שָׁלוֹם. וְהָכָא, לָא אָתָא לְמִמְנֵי חוּשְׁבְּנָא. אֲבָל עֵצוֹת מֵרָחוֹק מַאי נִינְהוּ. תְּרֵי בַּדֵּי עֲרָבוֹת. דְּכָל עֵיטָא דִּנְבִיאֵי מִתַּמָּן אַתְיָא. אִינּוּן אִקְרוּן עֵצוֹת מֵרָחוֹק. אֱמוּנָה אוֹמֶן, תְּרֵין דְּאִינּוּן חַד, נָהָר וְגַן. דָּא נָפִיק מֵעֵדֶן, וְדָא אִשְׁתְּקֵי מִינֵּיהּ. הָא הָכָא, כָּל רָזָא סְתִימָא דִּמְהֵימְנוּתָא.

160. "Counsels from afar" (Yeshayah 25:1): HE ASKS: First he calls it "wonderful" AND DOES NOT SAY THERE 'COUNSELS OF OLD', yet here he says: "wonderful things – counsels of old (also: 'from afar')." WHAT IS THE DIFFERENCE? HE RESPONDS: It is because there he had to count the six ends of the higher levels. THEREFORE, HE SAYS, "Wonderful (Heb. *pele*), counselor, a mighty El, the everlasting father, prince of peace" (Yeshayah 9:5). EL IS CHESED, MIGHTY IS GVURAH, THE FATHER IS TIFERET, EVERLASTING IS NETZACH, PRINCE IS HOD, AND PEACE IS YESOD. And here, he does not come to count THE LEVELS. HE ASKS: However, what are "counsels from afar"? HE REPLIES: They are the two willow branches, WHICH ARE NETZACH AND HOD AND ARE CALLED 'COUNSELS', since all the counsels of the prophets stem from there and are called 'counsels from afar' SINCE THE PROPHETS RECEIVE FROM NETZACH AND HOD. "In faithfulness and truth" (Yeshayah 25:1): These are two that are one, SINCE THEY ARE the river and the Garden THAT ARE YESOD AND MALCHUT. This RIVER, YESOD, comes out from Eden and this GARDEN, WHICH IS MALCHUT, gets watered from it. We find here IN THIS SCRIPTURAL VERSE: "HASHEM YOU ARE MY ELOHIM," the entire concealed secret meaning of the Faith, AS DEFINED SINCE HASHEM IS CHOCHMAH; "MY ELOHIM" IS BINAH; 'YOU' IS CHESED; 'WONDERFUL' IS THE THREE COLUMNS, CHESED, GVURAH AND TIFERET; 'COUNSEL FROM AFAR' ARE NETZACH AND HOD; 'FAITHFULNESS' IS MALCHUT; AND 'TRUTH' IS YESOD.

11. "Bilaam also, of the son of Beor did...slay with the sword"

A Synopsis

Rabbi Elazar asks how Bilaam was killed, and he receives a superficial explanation from Rabbi Yitzchak that says he was killed by Pinchas and his people. Rabbi Elazar is not satisfied with this, and Rabbi Shimon says that Bilaam was as powerful and wise in the aspect of the left as Moses was in the higher levels; the question is, then, how were they able to kill him? As Bilaam had praised himself so much, Rabbi Shimon speaks about the verse in Mishlei to do with praising oneself, saying that a person should speak about the Torah so that people will know who he is from his words.

161. א״ר אֶלְעָזָר, בִּלְעָם חַיָּיבָא מַאן קָטִיל לֵיהּ, וְהֵיךְ אַקְטִיל. א״ר יִצְחָק, פִּנְחָס וְסִיעָתֵיהּ קַטְלוּהוּ. דִּכְתִּיב הָרְגוּ עַל חַלְלֵיהֶם. וְתָנֵינָן, בְּקַרְתָּא דְּמִדְיָן הֲוָה עָבֵיד בְּחָכְמְתָא דְּחַרְשׁוּי, דְּטָאסִין בַּאֲוִירָא הוּא וּמַלְכֵי מִדְיָן. וְאִלְמָלֵא צִיץ דִּקְדוּשָׁא, וּצְלוֹתָא דְּפִינְחָס, דַּאֲפִילוּ לְהוֹן עַל קְטִילַיָּיא, הה״ד עַל חַלְלֵיהֶם. וּכְתִיב וְאֶת בִּלְעָם בֶּן בְּעוֹר הַקּוֹסֵם הָרְגוּ בֶּחָרֶב. אָ״ל ר׳ אֶלְעָזָר, כָּל דָּא יְדַעְנָא.

161. Rabbi Elazar asked about Bilaam the wicked, who killed him and how he got killed. Rabbi Yitzchak said, Pinchas and his people killed him, as it says, "And they slew...beside the rest of them" (Bemidbar 31:8). We were taught that in the city of Midian, Bilaam was performing with his witchcraft and that he was flying in the air together with the kings of Midian. If not for the holy gold plate and the prayer of Pinchas that made them drop TO THE GROUND over their slain, THEY WOULD NOT HAVE BEEN VICTORIOUS OVER THEM. That is what is written: "AND THEY SLEW THE KINGS OF MIDIAN, beside the rest of them" and: "Bilaam also, of the son of Beor, the soothsayer, did the children of Yisrael slay with the sword" (Yehoshua 13:22). Rabbi Elazar said to him, I know all this.

162. אר״ש, אֶלְעָזָר, כָּל מִלּוֹי דְּבִלְעָם חַיָּיבָא, תַּקִּיפִין אִינּוּן, וְהָא אוּקְמוּהָ חַבְרַיָּיא, דִּכְתִיב וְלֹא קָם נָבִיא עוֹד בְּיִשְׂרָאֵל כְּמֹשֶׁה, וְאָמְרוּ, בְּיִשְׂרָאֵל לֹא קָם אֲבָל באו״ה קָם, וּמַנוּ. בִּלְעָם, וְהָא אוּקִימְנָא מִלָּה,

מֹשֶׁה לֵית דִּכְוָותֵיהּ, בְּכִתְרִין עִלָּאִין. בִּלְעָם לֵית דִּכְוָותֵיהּ, בְּכִתְרִין תַּתָּאִין. דָּא בְּסִטְרָא דִּקְדוּשָּׁה, וְדָא בְּסִטְרָא דִּשְׂמָאלָא. וְאִי כָּל דָּא הֲוָה בִּידֵיהּ, וכ״כ תַּקִּיף בְּחָכְמְתָא, גְּבַר דְּיִשַׁבַּח גַּרְמֵיהּ בְּחֵילָא תַּקִּיף, דִּכְתִּיב וְאָנֹכִי אִקָּרֶה כֹּה, אַעְקַר לְכֹה מֵהַאי. הֵיאַךְ יָכִילוּ לְקַטְלָא לֵיהּ.

162. Rabbi Shimon said, Elazar, all the sayings of Bilaam the wicked are harsh. The friends already explained them, as it is written: "And there arose not a prophet since in Yisrael like Moses" (Devarim 34:10). They said that one such did arise but not in Yisrael, rather among the nations of the world. Who was he? That was Bilaam. We have already explained this matter that just as there is no one like Moses in the higher crowns, there is no one like Bilaam in the lower crowns, this one in the aspect of holiness and that one in the aspect of the left since he had all this in his power and he was so strong in wisdom, a person who boasted with great power, as is written: "While I go to the meeting yonder (Heb. *coh*)" (Bemidbar 23:15). THE MEANING IS THAT HE MEANT TO SAY, I will uproot coh, WHICH IS MALCHUT, from here. How were they able, then, to kill him?

163. אֶלָּא בְּסִפְרָא דְּחָכְמְתָא דִּשְׁלֹמֹה מַלְכָּא הָכִי אָמַר, תְּלַת סִימָנִין אִינּוּן. סִימַן לַעֲבֵרָה, יְרָקוֹן. סִימַן לַשְּׁטוּת, מִלִּין. סִימַן דְּלָא יָדַע כְּלוּם, שַׁבּוּחֵי. וְדָא אַכְרַע לִשְׁאַר, שׁוֹטֶה בְּכָל עֲבֵירוֹת, כֹּלָּא אִית בֵּיהּ.

163. HE RESPONDS: However, in the book of wisdom of King Solomon, it says as follows that there are three indications, an indication of transgression is jaundice, an indication of nonsense is TOO MUCH talk and an indication that he knows nothing is one who keeps boasting. This one WHO BOASTS has outdone the rest, since he is a fool. He is SUSPECTED in all sinful transgressions and has everything in him.

164. וְהָא כְּתִיב יְהַלֶּלְךָ זָר וְלֹא פִּיךָ, וְאִם לָא זָר. פִּיךָ. לָאו הָכִי. אֶלָּא אִי לָא הֲוֵי מַאן דְּאִשְׁתְּמוֹדַע לָךְ, אַפְתַּח פּוּמָךְ לְמַלְּלָא בְּאוֹרַיְיתָא, וּלְאוֹדָעָא מִלֵּי קְשׁוֹט בְּאוֹרַיְיתָא. וּכְדֵין פְּתִיחוּ דְּפוּמָךְ בְּאוֹרַיְיתָא, יְשַׁבְּחוּן מִילָךְ, וְיִנְדְּעוּן מַאן אַנְתְּ, דְּלֵית מִלָּה בְּעָלְמָא דְּיִשְׁתְּמוֹדְעוּן לֵיהּ לב״נ, אֶלָּא בְּזִמְנָא דְּאַפְתַּח פּוּמֵיהּ. פּוּמֵיהּ הוֹדַע לִבְנֵי נָשָׁא מַאן הוּא.

11. "Bilaam also, of the son of Beor did...slay with the sword"

164. HE ASKS: Yet it is written: "Let another man praise you, and not your own mouth" (Mishlei 27:2), WHICH MEANS that if there is no stranger to praise you, then let your own mouth. HE RESPONDS: It is not so. However, THE EXPLANATION IS if there is no one who recognizes you, open your mouth to speak in matters of Torah. Inform the true things that are in the Torah and then, by opening your mouth in Torah matters, they will praise your words and they will know who you are. There is nothing in the world that tells as much about a person as when he opens his mouth, and his mouth informs people who he is.

12. "Who hears the words of El"

A Synopsis

Rabbi Shimon explains the great power that Bilaam had to influence people by his speech, in which he included a good deal of truth. People thought he was the greatest prophet in the world, and in fact he was able to speak with the highest El, but it was a strange El from the Other Side, not "the" El. We hear about the higher ones who rule over the levels of defilement, to whom Bilaam was connected. When Bilaam was giving speeches about levels of defilement people thought he was speaking about the highest sanctity. Rabbi Shimon shows how the parts of the names Balak and Bilaam were included in each other and in the name Amalek.

165. הַהוּא רָשָׁע דְּבִלְעָם, שַׁבּוּחֵי מְשַׁבַּח גַּרְמֵיהּ בְּכֹלָּא. ועכ"ד, גְּנִיבוּ דְּדַעְתָּא קָא גָּנִיב, וְאִסְתַּלָּק בְּמִלּוֹי. בְּמִלִּין זְעִירִין, הֲוָה עָבֵיד רַבְרְבִין. מַה דְּאָמַר עַל אִינּוּן דַּרְגִּין מִלִּין מְסָאֲבִין הֲוָה אָמַר, וּקְשׁוֹט אָמַר. אֲבָל הַהוּא רָשָׁע הֲוָה אָמַר וּמְשַׁבַּח גַּרְמֵיהּ בְּאֹרַח סָתִים, וְאִסְתַּלָּק בְּמִלּוֹי, דְּכָל מַאן דַּהֲוָה שָׁמַע, חָשִׁיב דְּאִסְתַּלָּק עַל כָּל נְבִיאֵי עָלְמָא, דִּכְתִיב שׁוֹמֵעַ אִמְרֵי אֵל וְיוֹדֵעַ דַּעַת עֶלְיוֹן. מַאן גֶּבֶר בְּעָלְמָא, דַּהֲוָה שָׁמַע מִפּוּמֵיהּ מִלִּין אִלֵּין, דְּלָא חָשִׁיב דְּלֵית בְּעָלְמָא נְבִיאָה מְהֵימָנָא כְּגִינֵיהּ.

165. The evil Bilaam used to praise himself in everything. With all these, he used to deceive people's minds and reached a high level with his RHETORICAL speeches. He used to make mountains out of molehills. Whatever he said was about these levels of filthy speech, and he spoke the truth. However, that wicked one used to speak and heap praise upon himself disguised manner and arrogantly speak highly UNTIL whoever listened to him would think that he had exceeded above all the prophets of the world, as it says, "The saying of him, who hears the words of El, and knows the knowledge of the most High" (Bemidbar 24:16). Who in the world could hear such talk, and imagine any other prophet in the world as trustworthy.

166. וּקְשׁוֹט הֲוָה, וְהָכִי הֲוָה. נְאֻם שׁוֹמֵעַ אִמְרֵי אֵל, הָכִי הֲוָה. וְיוֹדֵעַ דַּעַת עֶלְיוֹן הָכִי הֲוָה. וְהַהוּא רָשָׁע הֲוָה אָמַר עַל דַּרְגִּין דְּאִתְדְּבַק בְּהוּ,

שׁוֹמֵעַ אִמְרֵי אֵל, מִלָּה דְּאִיהוּ בִּסְלִיקוּ עִלָּאָה.

166. It was indeed true and so it was. "The saying of him who hears the words of El," so it was "And knows the knowledge of the most high," so it was. This evil man was speaking of the levels to which he was attached. "Who hears the words of El." He heard matters that are of the highest level, AND THERE IS NOTHING ELSE LIKE THEM.

167. וְהָכִי אָמַר, שׁוֹמֵעַ אִמְרֵי אֵל, הָאֵל לָא כְּתִיב, דְּהָא הָאֵל תָּמִים דַּרְכּוֹ. אֲבָל סְתָם אֵל, אֵל אַחֵר אִיהוּ. כִּי לֹא תִשְׁתַּחֲוֶה לְאֵל אַחֵר שׁוֹמֵעַ אִמְרֵי אֵל, מִלָּה זְעֵירָא אִיהִי. וְדָמֵי לְמַאן דְּלָא יָדַע, דְּאִיהוּ רַב וְעִלָּאָה. שׁוֹמֵעַ אִמְרֵי אֵל, הַהוּא דְּאִקְרֵי אֵל אַחֵר, דִּכְתִיב כִּי לֹא תִשְׁתַּחֲוֶה לְאֵל אַחֵר.

167. So he said, "Who hears the words of El." It is not written: 'the El' since "as for the El, His way is perfect" (Tehilim 18:31). However, simply, "El," which is another El, AS IS WRITTEN: "for you shall worship no other El" (Shemot 34:14). THEREFORE, "who hears the words of El" is merely a minor thing, yet to whoever is unaware and does not recognize it, it seems that it is a great and high achievement. "Who hears the words of El" means that which is called a strange El, is as written: "For you shall worship no other El."

168. וְיוֹדֵעַ דַּעַת עֶלְיוֹן, עַל כָּל דַּרְגִּין דִּמְסָאֲבוּ, אִינּוּן דִּמְנַהֲגֵי אַרְבָּא דְּיַמָּא וּסְעָרָא. אַרְבְּעִין חָסֵר חַד אִינּוּן. וְהַהוּא רַב הַחוֹבֵל, דְּכֻלְּהוּ מִתְנַהֲגֵי עַל יְדוֹי, אִיהוּ עֶלְיוֹן עַל כֻּלְּהוּ. בְּדָא הֲוָה מִתְדַּבַּק הַהוּא רָשָׁע, וְאָמַר דְּהֲוָה יָדַע דַּעַת עֶלְיוֹן, דַּרְגָּא דְּאִיהוּ עֶלְיוֹן עַל כֻּלְּהוּ מְנַהֲגֵי אַרְבָּא. מַאן שָׁמַע הָכִי דְּלָא אִתְבְּהִיל בְּדַעְתֵּיהּ, וְיֵימָא דְּלָא הֲוָה כְּגִינֵיהּ בְּעָלְמָא. אֶלָּא הַהוּא רָשָׁע מְשַׁבַּח גַּרְמֵיהּ בְּאֹרַח סָתִים וְאָמַר מִלֵּי קְשׁוֹט, וְגָנִיב דַּעְתָּא דִּבְנֵי עָלְמָא.

168. "And knows the knowledge of the most High." THE EXPLANATION IS that THE HIGHEST over all the levels of defilement are the ones that steer and lead the ship of the sea and the storm WINDS. They are forty minus one.

The captain of the ship, who leads them all, is the highest over all. In that HIGHEST one, this wicked one was connected, and about him he said that he knows "the knowledge of the most High," meaning the highest level of all those who steer the ships OF DEFILEMENT. Who could hear his talk and would not become afraid in his mind and say that there was no one like him! However, that wicked one used to acclaim himself in a vague manner and speak truthful words, except that he used to deceive the minds of the people BECAUSE HE USED TO SPEAK ABOUT LEVELS OF DEFILEMENT. AND THE ONES WHO LISTENED THOUGHT THAT HE WAS SPEAKING ABOUT THE HIGHEST SANCTITY.

169. אֲשֶׁר מַחֲזֵה שַׁדַּי יֶחֱזֶה, מַאן דְּשָׁמַע דָּא, חָשִׁיב דְּהֲוָה חָמֵי מַה דְּלָא חָמֵי אַחֲרָא בְּעָלְמָא. מַחֲזֵה שַׁדַּי, דָּא עַנְפָּא חֲדָא, מֵאִינּוּן עַנְפִּין דַּהֲווֹ נָפְקִין מִשַּׁדַּי. וְלָמָּה. דִּבְחָכְמְתָא דָּא, אַחְזֵי תְּלַת, לָקֳבֵל ש׳ דְּשַׁדַּי, לָקֳבֵל תְּלַת עַנְפִּין דְּבֵיהּ, וְאַחְזֵי תְּרֵין נְבִיאִין, בַּדֵּי עֲרָבוֹת, דְּתַמְכִין בֵּיהּ. לָקֳבֵל ע׳ תְּרֵין עַנְפִּין דְּעֵינָא בִּישָׁא, לְסַתְמָא לוֹן. כַּד אָתָא בָּלָק, אָמַר אֲנָא אֵיכוּל לוֹן. עֲמָלֵק בַּהֲדֵי חָכְמְתָא דָּא אָתָא לְגַבַּיְיהוּ, וְיָכִיל לוֹן.

169. "Who sees the vision of Shadai": Whoever hears this thinks that he actually used to see what no other visionary saw. HOWEVER, "the vision of Shadai" is one branch of the branches that emerge from the name Shadai. Why IS IT SO? Because among this wisdom OF THEIRS there are seen three BRANCHES, corresponding to the Shin of Shadai that correspond to the three branches OF THE SHIN OF SHADAI, WHICH ARE CHESED, GVURAH AND TIFERET. There are seen CORRESPONDING to the two prophets TWO twigs of the willows, WHICH ARE NETZACH AND HOD that support TIFERET AND corresponding to the 72 branches of the evil eye, WHICH CORRESPONDS TO THE NAME OF 72 OF SANCTITY, THAT IS THE SECRET OF THE BENEVOLENT EYE, to block them, AND ALL THIS EXISTS IN CHOCHMAH OF THE KLIPOT. When Balak came, he said to himself, I will be successful against them, since Amalek attacked them with this wisdom and was successful against them.

170. וְשָׁדַר לְבִלְעָם, וְאָ״ל, אֲנָא תְּרֵי אַתְוָון דַּעֲמָלֵק אִית בִּי, דְּאִינּוּן

ל״ק, דְּאִינּוּן סִיּוּמָא דַּעֲמָלֵק. אֲנָא לִי ל״ק, ועמלק ל״ק, לִי סִיּוּמָא, וּבָךְ שֵׁירוּתָא ב״ל. א״ל ר״ש, הָכִי אֵימָא שֵׁירוּתָא דְּבָלָק ב״ל, וְשֵׁירוּתָא דְּבִלְעָם ב״ל, שֵׁירוּתָא דְּבָלָק הֲוָה בֵּיהּ בְּבִלְעָם. וְסִיּוּמָא דַּעֲמָלֵק, הֲוָה בֵּיהּ בְּבָלָק, וְסִיּוּמָא דְּבִלְעָם, הֲוָה שֵׁירוּתָא דַּעֲמָלֵק.

170. He sent to Bilaam and said to him, I have within my name the two letters of Amalek, which are Lamed Kof, the ending of the name Amalek. I have Lamed Kof, and Amalek's ending is Lamed Kof. I have the ending. And you have the beginning, Bet Lamed. Rabbi Shimon said to him, Here is how I say it. The beginning of THE NAME Balak is Bet Lamed and the beginning of the name of Bilaam is Bet Lamed; hence, the beginning of Balak was with Bilaam. The ending OF THE NAME of Amalek, MEANING LAMED KOF, was in Balak and the ending of Bilaam, WHICH IS AM is in the beginning of Amalek. SO WE FIND THAT THE NAME ENDING OF BILAAM WHICH IS AM AND THE NAME ENDING OF BALAK, THAT IS LAMED KOF, SPELL AMALEK.

171. וְאִי תֵּימָא דְּלָא נֵיכוּל לְהוֹן, בְּגִין דְּחַרְשַׁיָּא דְּרַבֵּהוֹן מֹשֶׁה, דַּהֲוָה פָּשִׁיט יְדֵיהּ, הַאי יְדָא אִית בְּאִלֵּין רַבְרְבִין, דְּיַכְלֵי בְּחַרְשִׁין לְאִתְתַּקְּפָא יַתִּיר. וְהַיְינוּ דִּכְתִּיב וּקְסָמִים בְּיָדָם, בִּידֵיהֶם לָא כְּתִיב, אֶלָּא בְּיָדָם, יְדָא לָקֳבֵל יְדָא, הָכִי שָׁדַר לֵיהּ בָּלָק לְבִלְעָם.

171. You might say that we cannot succeed against them because of the witchcraft of their master Moses, when he extends his hand, MEANING "MOSES STRETCHED OUT HIS HAND OVER THE SEA" (SHEMOT 14:27) AND OTHER INSTANCES. Here, this hand exists among these chiefs, who are more powerful with witchcraft. This is what is written: "Divination in their hand" (Bemidbar 22:7). It is not written: 'in their hands', but rather: "in their hand," meaning hand against the hand OF MOSES, which is how Balak sent to Bilaam.

172. וּלְהָכִי מַחֲזֵה שַׁדַּי כִּדְאַמָרָן, וּלְהָכִי אִתְעֲנָשׁוּ, וְאִתְעֲנָשׁוּ לְעֵילָּא, וְאִקְרוּן מַחֲזֵה, כד״א וּמוּל מֶחֱזָה אֶל מֶחֱזָה. עַנְפָּא דְּנָפַק מִתַּמָּן. וּמַאן הַהוּא מַחֲזֶה עֲזָא וַעֲזָאֵל, דְּאִינּוּן נוֹפֵל וּגְלוּי עֵינָיִם, וְאִיהוּ מַחֲזֵה שַׁדַּי,

דְּהֲוָה חָמָא נוֹפֵל וּגְלוּי עֵינָיִם.

172. (SOME MISSING HERE). Therefore, "who sees the vision (Heb. *machazeh*) of Shadai" is as we explained. Therefore, they were punished and they were punished above, and they were called 'visionaries', as is written: "And light (Heb. *mechezeh*) was against light" (I Melachim 7:5), which is the branch that emerges from there. Who is that visionary? That is Uza and Azael, who are the "falling down, but having his eyes open" (Bemidbar 24:4) and that is the "the vision of Shadai," which he saw when falling down and with open eyes...(SOME MISSING HERE).

13. Tzelyah who threw down Bilaam

A Synopsis

Rabbi Shimon informs his son that Bilaam and his sons flew into the air when they saw Pinchas. A member of the tribe of Dan named Tzelyah flew into the air after him, and having found the correct secret path due to some shouted advice from Pinchas, was able to bring Bilaam to earth. The advice from Pinchas had to do with the serpent, and in the end Tzelyah was only able to kill Bilaam with a sword that had a snake engraved on either side; thus Bilaam died by means of the same force by which he had lived. Rabbi Shimon says that Bilaam's bones rotted and turned into harmful snakes, and even the worms that ate his flesh turned into snakes. The book of Asmodeus says that people can still perform powerful witchcraft with those snakes that are found near the rock where Bilaam died. Rabbi Shimon says that the only thing that has the power to catch one of those snakes is hot semen; this is a secret that Solomon told to the Queen of Sheba.

173. אָן הֲוָה בִּלְעָם בְּהַהִיא שַׁעֲתָא. אִי תֵּימָא בְּמִדְיָן, הָא כְּתִיב וְעַתָּה הִנְנִי הוֹלֵךְ לְעַמִּי. אִי אָזַל לֵיהּ, מַאן יָהֲבֵיהּ בְּמִדְיָן. אֶלָּא הַהוּא רָשָׁע, כֵּיוָן דְּחָמָא דְּנָפְלוּ מִיִּשְׂרָאֵל כ״ד אֲלַף עַל עֵיטוֹי, אִתְעַכָּב תַּמָּן וַהֲוָה בָּעֵי מִנַּיְיהוּ אַגְרוֹי. וּבְעוֹד דְּאִתְעַכָּב תַּמָּן, אָתָא פִּנְחָס וְרַבְרְבָנֵי חֵילָא לְתַמָּן.

173. HE INQUIRES: Where was Bilaam at that time? If you say in Midian, why is it written: "And now, behold, I go to my people" (Bemidbar 24:14). If he already left, who placed him in Midian? HE RESPONDS: As soon as that wicked man saw that 24,000 fell from Yisrael due to his advice, TO OFFER THE WOMEN TO PROSTITUTE WITH YISRAEL, he wished to collect from them his recompense. While he was still there, Pinchas and the chiefs of the army arrived there.

174. כֵּיוָן דְּחָמָא לְפִנְחָס, פָּרַח בַּאֲוִירָא, וּתְרֵין בְּנוֹהִי עִמֵּיהּ, יוֹנוּס וְיוֹמְבְּרוֹס. וְאִי תֵּימָא, הָא מִיתוּ בְּעוֹבָדָא דְּעֵגֶל, דְּהָא אִינּוּן עַבְדוּ. אֶלָּא הָכִי הֲוָה וַדָּאי, וְדָא הוּא דִּכְתִיב, וַיִּפּוֹל מִן הָעָם בַּיּוֹם הַהוּא כִּשְׁלֹשֶׁת אַלְפֵי אִישׁ. וְכִי לָא הֲווֹ יַדְעֵי חוּשְׁבְּנָא זְעֵירָא דָּא, וַהֲרֵי כַּמָּה חוּשְׁבָּנִין

אַחֲרָנִין, רָמָאִין עִלָּאִין וְרַבְרְבָנִין, יָדַע קְרָא לְמִמְנֵי, וְהָכָא כִּשְׁלֹשֶׁת אַלְפֵי אִישׁ. אֶלָּא אִינּוּן בְּנוֹי דְּבִלְעָם, יוּנוּ״ס וְיוֹמְבְּרוֹ״ס, דַּהֲווֹ שַׁקְלֵי כִּשְׁלֹשֶׁת אַלְפֵי אִישׁ.

174. As soon as BILAAM noticed Pinchas, he flew into the air and his two sons with him, Yunus and Yumbrus. You might say that they died during the episode of the calf, since they are the ones who created and formed THAT CALF. It was surely so, and it is written: "And there fell of the people that day about 3,000 men" (Shemot 32:28). Didn't they know how to figure and account for such a small number? Haven't we found then accounting for other higher and much greater censuses? The scripture there knew how to count and here it is written: "About 3,000 men," MEANING THAT THEY DID NOT KNOW PRECISELY. It is only because these were the sons of Bilaam, Yunus and Yumbrus, who were equal to 3,000 men.

175. אֶלָּא הַהוּא רָשָׁע, כָּל חַרְשִׁין דְּעָלְמָא הֲוָה יָדַע, וְנָטַל אוּף הָכִי חַרְשִׁין דִּבְנוֹי, דַּהֲווֹ רְגִילִין בְּהוּ, וּבְהוּ טָאס וְאִסְתְּלַק. פִּנְחָס חָמָא לֵיהּ, דַּהֲוָה ב״נ חַד טָס בַּאֲוִירָא, וַהֲוָה מִסְתְּלַק בַּאֲוִירָא מֵעֵינָא, רָמָא קָלָא לִבְנֵי חֵילָא, אָמַר אִית מַאן דְּיָדַע לְמִפְרַח אֲבַתְרֵיהּ דְּהַהוּא רָשָׁע, דְּהָא בִּלְעָם אִיהוּ, חָמוּ לֵיהּ דַּהֲוָה טָאס.

175. HE RESPONDS: It is only because that wicked man knew all the magic in the world and he even received the sorcery of his sons, in which they were accustomed. With those, he flew in the air and ascended. Pinchas saw him, a person flying in the air and vanishing in the air. He raised his voice to the members of his army and said, Is there anyone who is capable of flying and chasing after that wicked man, who is no other than Bilaam himself? They saw him flying.

176. צַלְיָה בְּרֵיהּ דְּשִׁבְטָא דְּדָן, קָם וְנָטַל שָׁלְטָנוּ דְּשַׁלִּיט עַל חַרְשִׁין, וּפָרַח בַּתְרֵיהּ. כֵּיוָן דְּחָמָא לֵיהּ הַהוּא רָשָׁע, עָבַד אָרְחָא אוּחֲרָא בַּאֲוִירָא, וּבָקַע חָמֵשׁ אֲוִירִין בְּהַהוּא אֹרַח, וְאִסְתַּלַּק וְאִתְכַּסֵּי מֵעֵינָא, כְּדֵין אִסְתַּכַּן צַלְיָה בְּהַהִיא שַׁעְתָּא, וַהֲוָה בְּצַעֲרָא דְּלָא הֲוָה יָדַע מַה יַעֲבֵיד.

13. Tzelyah who threw down Bilaam

176. Tzelyah, a member from Dan's tribe, rose and took charge of the powers that are dominant over witchcraft, and flew after him. When the wicked one noticed him, he took another course in the air and penetrated five other layers of air in that course. He rose higher and disappeared from eyesight. At that point, Tzelyah came into danger and was distressed, since he did not know what to do.

177. רָמָא לֵיהּ קָלָא פִּנְחָס וְאָמַר, טוּלָא דְּתַנִּינַיָּיא דְּרַבְעִין עַל כָּל חִוְיָין, הֲפוֹךְ בְּמִזְיָיךְ. מִיַּד יָדַע וְגַלֵּי הַהוּא אַחֲרָא, וְעָאל לְגַבֵּיהּ. מִיַּד אִתְגַּלֵּי, וְנַחְתּוּ תַּרְוַויְיהוּ קַמֵּיהּ דְּפִנְחָס.

177. Pinchas raised his voice and shouted to him, The shadow of the crocodiles that crouch over all the snakes, turn over in your hair. TZELYAH instantly knew and discovered that other path, and entered into it. BILAAM immediately appeared and they both descended in front of Pinchas.

178. תָּא חֲזֵי, הַהוּא רָשָׁע כְּתִיב בֵּיהּ וַיֵּלֶךְ שֶׁפִי, דָּא הוּא עֶלְיוֹן דְּדַרְגִּין דִּילֵיהּ, חִוְיָא דְּכוּרָא. צַלְיָה נָטַל תְּרֵין, דְּכַר וְנוּקְבָא. וּבְהַהוּא שַׁלִּיט עָלֵיהּ, בְּגִין דְּשֻׁלְטָנוּ דְּשַׁלִּיט עֲלַיְיהוּ נָטַל, וְאִתְכַּפְיָין קַמֵּיהּ. וְדָא הֲוָה שְׁפִיפוֹן עֲלֵי אֹרַח. עַל הַהוּא אֹרַח, דְּעָבֵד הַהוּא רָשָׁע, דִּכְתִּיב יְהִי דָן נָחָשׁ עֲלֵי דֶרֶךְ, דָּא שִׁמְשׁוֹן. שְׁפִיפוֹן עֲלֵי אֹרַח, דָּא צַלְיָה.

178. Come and see that wicked man, about whom it is written: "And he went to a steep place (Heb. *shefi*)" (Bemidbar 23:3). This is one of his higher levels, which is the male snake. Tzelyah took both male and female and, through this, he was able to overpower him, because he took over the charge that was dominating them and they were subjugated to him. This was "an adder (Heb. *shefifon*) in the path" (Beresheet 49:17), which is on the same path that this wicked one took, as is written: "Dan shall be a serpent by the way" (Ibid.), which refers to Samson. "An adder in the path" refers to Tzelyah.

179. הַנּוֹשֵׁךְ עִקְּבֵי סוּס, דָּא עִירָה, דַּהֲוָה בַּהֲדֵיהּ דְּדָוִד, דַּהֲוָה אָתֵי מִדָּן, וּבְגִינֵיהּ, תַּלְיָא גְּבוּרְתֵּיהּ בְּדָוִד, דִּכְתִּיב וַיְעַקֵּר דָּוִד אֶת כָּל הָרֶכֶב.

וַיִּפּוֹל רוֹכְבוֹ אָחוֹר, דָּא שְׂרָיָה, דְּזַמִּין לְמֵיתֵי בַּהֲדֵי מְשִׁיחָא דְּאֶפְרַיִם, וְאִיהוּ הֲוֵי מִשִּׁבְטָא דְּדָן, וְזַמִּין אִיהוּ לְמֶעְבַּד נוּקְמִין וּקְרָבִין בִּשְׁאַר עַמִּין. וְכַד דָּא יְקוּם, כְּדֵין מְחַכֶּא לְפוּרְקָנָא דְּיִשְׂרָאֵל, דִּכְתִיב לִישׁוּעָתְךָ קִוִּיתִי יְיָ'. ואע"ג דְּאוֹקְמוּהָ לְהַאי קְרָא, אֲבָל בְּרִירוּ דְּמִלָּה כְּמָה דְּאִתְּמַר, וּכְמָה דְּאוֹקְמוּהָ. וְעַל דָּא אָתָא קְרָא וְאוֹכַח.

179. "That bites the horse's heels" (Ibid.): This refers to Ira, who was with David, whose descent was from the tribe of Dan. Through his merit, David's might balanced in his favor, as is written: "And David lamed all the chariot horses" (II Shmuel 8:4). "So that his rider shall fall backwards" (Beresheet 49:17) refers to Srayah, who will come with Messiah, son of Ephraim. He will be a descendant of Dan's tribe and he will take revenge and do wars with the rest of the nations. When this one rises, you will wait for the redemption of Yisrael, as is written: "I wait for Your salvation, Hashem" (Ibid.). Although this verse has already been explained, the definition of it is as we mentioned and as was explained. The verse in the scripture is proof of this.

180. כֵּיוָן דְּנָחַת הַהוּא רָשָׁע לְקַמֵּי פִּנְחָס, אָמַר לֵיהּ, רָשָׁע, כַּמָּה גִּלְגּוּלִין בִּישִׁין עֲבַדְתְּ, עַל עַמָּא קַדִּישָׁא. אָמַר לֵיהּ לִצְלִיָּה, תָּא וְקַטְלֵיהּ, וְלָא בִּשְׁמָא, דְּלָא אִתְחֲזֵי הַאי, לְאַדְכְּרָא עָלֵיהּ קְדוּשָּׁה עִלָּאָה, בְּגִין דְּלָא תֵּיפּוּק נִשְׁמָתֵיהּ, וְתִתְכְּלִיל בְּמִלִּין דְּדַרְגִּין קַדִּישִׁין, וְתִתְקַיֵּים בֵּיהּ מַה דְּאָמַר תָּמוֹת נַפְשִׁי מוֹת יְשָׁרִים.

180. When the wicked man landed in front of Pinchas, he said to him, You evil man, how many evils have you inflicted on this holy nation? He told Tzelyah, Get up and kill him, but not by the Name, since he is not worthy to have high holiness mentioned upon him, in order that his soul should not depart included in words of holy levels, because the words he said will be fulfilled, "Let me die the death of the righteous" (Bemidbar 23:10).

181. בְּהַהוּא שַׁעֲתָא עָבֵד בֵּיהּ כַּמָּה זִינֵי מוֹתָא, וְלָא מִית, עַד דְּנָטַל חַרְבָּא דַּהֲוָה חָקִיק עֲלוֹי חִוְיָא מֵהַאי סִטְרָא, וְחִוְיָא מֵהַאי סִטְרָא. א"ל פִּנְחָס, בְּדִילֵיהּ קְטוֹל לֵיהּ, וּבְדִילֵיהּ יְמוּת. כְּדֵין קָטַל לֵיהּ, וְיָכִיל לֵיהּ.

דְּכַךְ אָרְחוֹי דְּהַהוּא סִטְרָא, מַאן דְּאָזַל אֲבַתְרָאָה, בָּהּ יָמוּת, וּבָהּ תִּפּוּק נִשְׁמָתֵיהּ, וּבָהּ תִּתְכְּלִיל. וְהָכִי מִית בִּלְעָם, וְדַיְינֵי לֵיהּ בְּדִינִין בְּהַהוּא עָלְמָא, וְלָא אִתְקְבִיר לְעָלְמִין. וְגַרְמוֹי כֻּלְּהוּ אִתְרְקָבוּ, וְאִתְעֲבֵידוּ כַּמָּה חִוְיָין מְזוּהֲמִין, מְנַזְקֵי שְׁאַר בִּרְיָין, וַאֲפִילוּ תּוֹלַעְתִּין דַּהֲווֹ אַכְלֵי בִּשְׂרֵיהּ, אִתְהֲדָרוּ חִוְיָין.

181. At that moment, he tried to kill him in a variety of ways, but he didn't die until he took the sword that had a snake engraved on either side. Pinchas told him, Kill him with his own and by his own he will die. He then killed him and prevailed over him, since that is the manner of that side. Whoever follows it dies through it. Through it, his soul will leave and with in it, HIS SOUL will be included. That is how Bilaam died. He is punished with punishments of that world and he was never buried. And all his bones were rotten and turned into many filthy snakes that are harmful to other creatures. Even the worms that ate his flesh turned into snakes.

182. אַשְׁכַּחְנָא בְּסִפְרָא דְּאַשְׁמוֹדָאי, דְּיָהַב לֵיהּ לִשְׁלֹמֹה מַלְכָּא, דְּכָל מַאן דַּהֲוָה בָּעֵי לְמֶעְבַּד חַרְשִׁין תַּקִּיפִין סְתִימִין דְּעֵינָא. אִי יְדַע טִנָּרָא דְּנָפַל תַּמָּן בִּלְעָם, יִשְׁכַּח מֵאִינּוּן חִוְיָין דַּהֲווֹ מִגַּרְמוֹי דְּהַהוּא רָשָׁע, אִי יַקְטִיל חַד מִנַּיְיהוּ, רֵישָׁא דִּילֵיהּ בֵּיהּ יַעְבֵּיד חַרְשִׁין עִלָּאִין, בְּגוּפָא דִּילֵיהּ חַרְשִׁין אַחֲרָנִין, בִּזְנָבָא דִּילֵיהּ חַרְשִׁין אַחֲרָנִין. תְּלַת זִינֵי חַרְשִׁין, אִית בְּכָל חַד וְחָד.

182. I found in the book of Asmodeus, which he gave to King Solomon, that whoever wants to perform powerful magic that is unobservable by the eye, if he knows the rock where Bilaam had his downfall, he will locate there some of these snakes that were made from the bones of that evil one. If he kills one of those SNAKES, he could perform high-level sorcery with its head, other magic with its body and different witchcraft with its tail. Each one contains three types of witchcraft.

183. מַלְכַּת שְׁבָא כַּד אָתַת לְגַבֵּי שְׁלֹמֹה, מֵאִינּוּן מִלִּין דְּשָׁאִילַת לִשְׁלֹמֹה, אַמְרַת, גַּרְמָא דְּחִוְיָא דִּתְלַת חַרְשִׁין בְּמַה נִתְפַּס. מִיָּד לֹא הָיָה

דָּבָר נֶעְלָם מִן הַמֶּלֶךְ אֲשֶׁר לֹא הִגִּיד לָהּ, אִיהִי שְׁאִילַת עַל דָּא, וַהֲוַת אִצְטְרִיכַת לְאִינּוּן חִוְיָין. וְלָא יָכִילַת לְנַטְלָא חַד מִנַּיְיהוּ. מָה אָתִיב לָהּ מִלִּין דַּהֲווֹ בְּלִבָּהּ. כַּךְ אוֹדַע לָהּ, דִּכְתִּיב וַיַּגֶּד לָהּ שְׁלֹמֹה אֶת כָּל דְּבָרֶיהָ. אִינּוּן חִוְיָין, לָא יַכְלִין לוֹן כָּל בְּנֵי עָלְמָא, בַּר מִמִּלָּה דְּרָזָא חֲדָא, וּמַאי אִיהוּ. שִׁכְבַת זֶרַע רוֹתַחַת.

183. When the queen of Sheba came to Solomon, ONE of the things that she asked Solomon WAS, How do you catch a bone of a snake that contains three sorceries? Instantly, "there was not anything hid from the king, which he told her not" (I Melachim 10:3). She asked about this and she required these snakes, but she could not capture one of them. What did he respond to her about these things she harbored in at her heart, AS IT SAYS, "SHE SPOKE TO HIM OF ALL THAT WAS IN HER HEART" (Ibid. 2)? This is what he informed her, as it says, "And Solomon answered her all her questions" (Ibid. 3). HE SAID, None of the world's inhabitants have power against those snakes, except for one secret thing. What is it? It is boiling hot semen.

184. וְאִי תֵּימָא מַאן יָכִיל. אֶלָּא, בְּשַׁעֲתָא דְּהַהוּא שִׁכְבַת זֶרַע אַפִּיק ב"נ, כַּד אִיהוּ בְּתִיאוּבְתָּא, אַפִּיק לָהּ לִשְׁמָא דְּהַהוּא חִוְיָא, בִּרְעוּתָא דְּתִיאוּבְתָּא. כַּד נָפִיק בִּרְתִּיחוּ, נַטְלֵי לֵיהּ מִיָּד בִּלְבוּשָׁא חֲדָא, וְהַהוּא לְבוּשָׁא זַרְקִין לְגַבֵּי חִוְיָא, מִיָּד כָּפִיף רֵישֵׁיהּ, וְתַפְסָן לֵיהּ, כְּמָה דְּתָפִיס תַּרְנְגוֹלָא דְּבֵיתָא. וְאִי בְּכָל מָאנֵי קְרָבִין דְּעָלְמָא, יִגְחוּן בְּחַד מִנַּיְיהוּ, לָא יַכְלִין לֵיהּ. וּבְהַאי, לָא אִצְטְרִיךְ ב"נ בְּעָלְמָא מָאנֵי קְרָבָא, וְלָא מִלָּה אַחֲרָא וְלָא אִצְטְרִיךְ לְאִסְתַּמְרָא מִנַּיְיהוּ דְּהָא כֻּלְּהוּ אִתְכַּפְיָין לְגַבֵּיהּ. כְּדֵין אִתְדָּבְקוּ אִינּוּן מִלִּין בִּלְבָבָהּ, וְתָאִיבַת לְהַאי.

184. If you wonder who has the power, it is only when a man is full of desire and he issues that semen that is expelled with the lustful desire for the purpose of defeating that snake. When it spurts out in boiling heat, it is captured immediately in a garment, and that garment is thrown onto the snake. Instantly, it bows down its head and is caught, like a domesticated rooster is caught. EVEN if all battle gear are prepared against one of them, it would not be successful. But when you do this, there is no need for any person in the world to use weapons, or any other thing, and he does not need to be constantly on watch against them, because they all become subservient to him. Then these words touched the heart OF THE QUEEN OF SHEBA, and she desired it.

185. מִכָּאן וּלְהָלְאָה אֶלְעָזָר בְּרִי, קוּדְשָׁא בְּרִיךְ הוּא עָבֵד מַה דְּעָבֵד בְּהַהוּא חַיָּיבָא, וְרָזִין סְתִימִין אִלֵּין, לָא אִצְטְרִיכוּ לְגַלָּאָה, אֲבָל בְּגִין דְּחַבְרַיָּיא דְּהָכָא יִנְדְּעוּן אָרְחִין סְתִימִין דְּעָלְמָא, גָּלֵינָא לְכוּ. דְּהָא כַּמָּה נִמּוּסִין סְתִימִין אִינּוּן בְּעָלְמָא, וּבְנֵי נָשָׁא לָא יַדְעִין, וְאִינּוּן פְּלִיאָן סְתִימִין, רַבְרְבָן וְעִלָּאִין. עָלֵיהּ, וְעַל דְּדָמֵי לֵיהּ, קְרָאן וְשֵׁם רְשָׁעִים יִרְקָב. זַכָּאִין אִינּוּן זַכָּאֵי קְשׁוֹט, עֲלַיְיהוּ כְּתִיב, אַךְ צַדִּיקִים יוֹדוּ לִשְׁמֶךָ וְגוֹ'.

185. From here on, my son Elazar, the Holy One, blessed be He, did what He did with that wicked one, BILAAM. There is no need to reveal these hidden secrets; however, in order that the friends here should know things that are concealed, I revealed them to you since there are so many concealed laws of which people are unaware, and they are highly concealed great wonders. About BILAAM and about those comparable to him, we say, "But the name of the wicked shall rot" (Mishlei 10:7). Praised are the truly just, for the scripture says about them: "Surely the righteous shall give thanks to Your name..." (Tehilim 140:14).

14. A prayer to Moses, a prayer to David, a prayer to the poor

A Synopsis

Rabbi Aba talks about the prayer of Moses, the prayer of David and the prayer of the poor that is the most important of the three. The prayer of the poor is heard above all others because God is always close to the broken-hearted, and destitute people are always broken-hearted. God delays all other prayers until he has heard their supplications, and, because he knew this, David referred to himself as poor when he was praying. Rabbi Elazar says that all people should do this in order to be heard.

186. וְעַתָּה לְכָה נָא אָרָה לִּי אֶת הָעָם הַזֶּה וְגוֹ׳. ר׳ אַבָּא פָּתַח, תְּפִלָּה לְעָנִי כִּי יַעֲטוֹף וְגוֹ׳, תְּלַת אִינּוּן דִּכְתִּיב בְּהוּ תְּפִלָּה. וְאוֹקְמוּהָ מִלָּה דָּא, חַד הֲוָה מֹשֶׁה, וְחַד הֲוָה דָּוִד, וְחַד עָנִי, דְּאִתְכְּלִיל בְּהוּ, וְאִתְחַבָּר בְּהוּ. וְאִי תֵּימָא, הָא כְּתִיב תְּפִלָּה לַחֲבַקּוּק הַנָּבִיא הָא אַרְבָּע אִינּוּן. אֶלָּא חֲבַקּוּק לָאו בְּגִין תְּפִלָּה הֲוָה, ואע״ג דִּכְתִּיב בֵּיהּ תְּפִלָּה, תּוּשְׁבַּחְתָּא וְהוֹדָאָה אִיהוּ לְקוּדְשָׁא בְּרִיךְ הוּא, עַל דְּאַחֲיָא לֵיהּ, וַעֲבַד עִמֵּיהּ נִסִּין וּגְבוּרָן, דְּהָא בְּרֵיהּ דְּשׁוּנַמִּית הֲוָה.

186. “Come now therefore, I pray you, curse me this people...” (Bemidbar 22:6). Rabbi Aba opened the discussion with the verse: “A prayer of the afflicted (poor), when he faints...” (Tehilim 102:1). There are three for whom the expression “prayer” is written and this subject was already explained. One is Moses, one is David and one is the poor man that was included with them and was together with them. You may say that we also find it written: “A prayer of the prophet Habakkuk” (Chavakuk 3:1), for a total of four. HE RESPONDS: that of Habakkuk is not SAID for the reason of prayer, even though the word prayer is written about it, it is rather praise and thanks for the Holy One, blessed be He, for having revived him and performed with him miracles and mighty deeds since he was the son of the Shunamite, WHOM ELISHA BROUGHT BACK TO LIFE.

187. אֲבָל ג׳ אִינּוּן דְּאִקְרוּן תְּפִלָּה. תְּפִלָּה לְמֹשֶׁה אִישׁ הָאֱלֹהִים, תְּפִלָּה דָּא דְּלֵית כְּגַוְונֵיהּ בְּבַר נָשׁ אַחֲרָא. תְּפִלָּה לְדָוִד, תְּפִלָּה דָּא אִיהִי תְּפִלָּה, דְּלֵית כְּגַוְונֵיהּ בְּמַלְכָּא אַחֲרָא. תְּפִלָּה לְעָנִי, תְּפִלָּה אִיהִי מֵאִינּוּן

ג׳. מַאן חֲשִׁיבָא מִכֻּלְּהוּ. הֲוֵי אֵימָא תְּפִלָּה דְּעָנִי. תְּפִלָּה דָּא, קָדִים לַתְּפִלָּה דְּמֹשֶׁה. וְקָדִים לַתְּפִלָּה דְּדָוִד, וְקָדִים לְכָל שְׁאַר צְלוֹתִין דְּעָלְמָא.

187. However, there are three that are considered a prayer: "A prayer of Moses the man of Elohim" (Tehilim 90:1). This prayer has no equal by any other person. "A prayer of David" (Tehilim 86:1): This prayer has no equal by any other king. "A prayer of the poor" (Tehilim 102:1) is one prayer of the three mentioned. Which is the most important? One says, "A prayer of the poor": this prayer takes priority over Moses' prayer, is before David's prayer and preempts all other prayers of the world.

188. מ״ט. בְּגִין דְּעָנִי אִיהוּ תְּבִיר לִבָּא. וּכְתִיב, קָרוֹב יְיָ׳ לְנִשְׁבְּרֵי לֵב וְגוֹ׳. וּמִסְכְּנָא עָבֵיד תָּדִיר קְטָטָה בְּקוּדְשָׁא בְּרִיךְ הוּא. וְקוּדְשָׁא בְּרִיךְ הוּא אָצִית וְשָׁמַע מִלּוֹי. כֵּיוָן דְּצַלֵּי צְלוֹתֵיהּ, פָּתַח כָּל כַּוֵּי רְקִיעִין, וְכָל שְׁאַר צְלוֹתִין דְּקָא סַלְקִין לְעֵילָּא, דָּחֵי לוֹן הַהוּא מִסְכְּנָא תְּבִיר לִבָּא, דִּכְתִיב תְּפִלָּה לְעָנִי כִּי יַעֲטוֹף. כִּי יִתְעַטֵּף מִבָּעֵי לֵיהּ, מַאי כִּי יַעֲטוֹף אֶלָּא אִיהוּ עָבֵיד עִטּוּפָא לְכָל צְלוֹתִין דְּעָלְמָא, וְלָא עָאלִין עַד דִּצְלוֹתָא דִּילֵיהּ עָאלַת.

188. HE INQUIRES: What is the reason? HE REPLIES: Because the poor man is broken-hearted and it is written: "Hashem is near to them who are of a broken heart" (Tehilim 34:19). The destitute always quarrels with the Holy One, blessed be He, and the Holy One, blessed be He, listens and pays attention to his words. As soon as the poor man says his prayer, He opens all the windows of the firmament, and all the rest of the prayers rising above are pushed away by that destitute, broken-hearted man, as is written: "A prayer of the afflicted, when he faints (Heb. *ya'atof*, also: 'delays')..." It should have said, 'When he is faint (Heb. *yit'ataf*)'. Why "when he delays"? THE MEANING IS THAT he causes the delay, because all other prayers do not enter in until his prayer enters.

189. וְקוּדְשָׁא בְּרִיךְ הוּא אָמַר, יִתְעַטְּפוּן כָּל צְלוֹתִין, וּצְלוֹתָא דָּא תֵּיעוּל לְגַבָּאי. לָא בָּעֵינָא הָכָא בֵּי דִּינָא דִּידוּנוּן בֵּינָנָא, קַמָּאי לֶיהֱווּ

תַּרְעוּמִין דִּילֵיהּ, וַאֲנָא וְהוּא בִּלְחוֹדָנָא. וְקוּדְשָׁא בְּרִיךְ הוּא אִתְיָיחָד בִּלְחוֹדוֹי, בְּאִינּוּן תּוּרְעָמִין, בְּהַהוּא צְלוֹתָא, דִּכְתִּיב וְלִפְנֵי יְיָ׳ יִשְׁפּוֹךְ שִׂיחוֹ. לִפְנֵי יְיָ׳ וַדַּאי.

189. The Holy One, blessed be He, said, 'Let all the prayers get delayed and this prayer should rise to Me. I do not require a court session to intervene between us. Let all his complaints come directly to Me, and I and he shall settle it on our own.' And the Holy One, blessed be He, is left alone with these complaints in that prayer, as is written: "And pours out his complaint before Hashem" (Tehilim 102:1), assuredly "before Hashem."

190. כָּל חֵילֵי שְׁמַיָּא שָׁאֲלִין אִלֵּין לְאִלֵּין, קוּדְשָׁא בְּרִיךְ הוּא בְּמַאי אִתְעֲסַק, בְּמַאי אִשְׁתְּדַל. אַמְרִין, אִתְיַיחֲדָא בְּתִיאוּבְתָּא בְּמָאנִין דִּילֵיהּ, כֻּלְּהוּ לָא יָדְעוּ מָה אִתְעָבֵיד מֵהַהוּא צְלוֹתָא דְּמִסְכְּנָא, וּמִכָּל אִינּוּן תּוּרְעָמִין דִּילֵיהּ. דְּלֵית תִּיאוּבְתָּא לְמִסְכְּנָא, אֶלָּא כַּד שָׁפִיךְ דִּמְעוֹי בְּתוּרְעָמוּ, קַמֵּי מַלְכָּא קַדִּישָׁא. וְלֵית תִּיאוּבְתָּא לְקוּדְשָׁא בְּרִיךְ הוּא, אֶלָּא כַּד מְקַבֵּל לוֹן, וְאוּשְׁדוּ קַמֵּיהּ וְדָא אִיהִי צְלוֹתָא, דְּעָבֵיד עִטּוּפָא לְכָל צְלוֹתִין דְּעָלְמָא.

190. All the hosts of heaven inquire one of the other; what is the Holy One, blessed be He, dealing with, what is He striving with? They reply TO THEM, He is concentrating on His vessels, MEANING THE BROKEN-HEARTED, desiring to be alone with them. No one knows what is made of the destitute's prayer and all his complaints, since the poor has no other desire except when he spills his tears in displeasure in front of the Holy King. The Holy One, blessed be He, has no other desire except when He accepts them and they are poured before Him. That is a prayer that causes delay to all the prayers of the world.

191. מֹשֶׁה צַלֵּי צְלוֹתֵיהּ, וְאִתְעַכָּב כַּמָּה יוֹמִין בְּהַאי תְּפִלָּה. דָּוִד חָמָא, דְּכָל כַּוִּין, וְכָל תַּרְעֵי שְׁמַיָּא, כֻּלְּהוּ זְמִינִין לְאַפְתְּחָא לְמִסְכְּנָא, וְלֵית בְּכָל צְלוֹתִין דְּעָלְמָא, דְּקוּדְשָׁא בְּרִיךְ הוּא אָצִית מִיָּד, כִּצְלוֹתָא דְּמִסְכְּנָא, כֵּיוָן דְּחָמֵי הַאי עָבֵד גַּרְמֵיהּ עַנְיָא וּמִסְכְּנָא פָּשַׁט לְבוּשָׁא

דְּמַלְכוּתָא, וְיָתִיב בְּאַרְעָא כְּמִסְכְּנָא. אָמַר תְּפִלָּה. דִּכְתִּיב, תְּפִלָּה לְדָוִד הַטֵּה יְיָ' אָזְנְךָ עֲנֵנִי. וְאִי תֵּימָא אֲמַאי. בְּגִין כִּי עָנִי וְאֶבְיוֹן אָנִי. אָ"ל קוּדְשָׁא בְּרִיךְ הוּא, דָּוִד, וְלָאו מַלְכָּא אַנְתְּ, וְשַׁלִּיטָא עַל מַלְכִין תַּקִּיפִין, וְאַתְּ עָבֵיד גַּרְמָךְ עָנִי וְאֶבְיוֹן. מִיַּד אַהְדָּר צְלוֹתֵיהּ בְּגַוְונָא אַחֲרָא, וְשָׁבַק מִלָּה דְּאֶבְיוֹן וְעָנִי, וְאָמַר שָׁמְרָה נַפְשִׁי כִּי חָסִיד אָנִי. ועכ"ד כֹּלָּא הֲוָה בֵּיהּ בְּדָוִד.

191. Moses poured forth his prayer and was held up for several days due to this prayer, BECAUSE OF THE BESEECHING OF THE POOR MAN. David saw that all the windows and gates of heaven were ready to open to the prayer of the poor. There exists no other prayer in the world to which the Holy One, blessed be He, will give His immediate attention as to the poor man's prayer. As soon as he noticed this, he made himself poor and destitute, removed his royal attire, sat on the ground like the destitute, and said the prayer as it is written: "A prayer of David. Incline Your ear, Hashem, hear me" (Tehilim 86:1). If you ask why, it is "for I am poor and needy" (Ibid.). The Holy One, blessed be He, replied to him, 'David, aren't you king and ruler over mighty kings? yet you make yourself out to be poor and needy.' Immediately, he prayed again in another manner and left out the words poor and needy, and said, "Preserve my soul; for I am pious" (Ibid. 2) despite all this everything was in David, BOTH POOR AND DEVOUT.

192. אָמַר לֵיהּ רִבִּי אֶלְעָזָר, שַׁפִּיר קָאֲמַרְתְּ. וְעַ"ד אִצְטְרִיךְ לֵיהּ לְבַר נָשׁ דְּצַלֵּי צְלוֹתֵיהּ, לְמֶעְבַּד גַּרְמֵיהּ עָנִי, בְּגִין דְּתֵיעוּל צְלוֹתֵיהּ בִּכְלָלָא דְּכָל עֲנִיִּים. דְּהָא כָּל נְטוּרֵי תַּרְעִין, לָא שַׁבְקִין הָכִי לְמֵיעָאל, כְּמָה דְּשָׁבְקִין לְמִסְכְּנִין, דְּהָא בְּלָא רְשׁוּתָא עָאלִין. וְאִי עָבֵיד בַּר נָשׁ גַּרְמֵיהּ, וְשַׁוֵּי רְעוּתֵיהּ תָּדִיר כְּמִסְכְּנָא, צְלוֹתֵיהּ סַלְּקָא, וְאִעֲרָעַת בְּאִינּוּן צְלוֹתִין דְּמִסְכְּנִין, וְאִתְחַבְּרַת בְּהוּ, וְסַלְּקַת בַּהֲדַיְיהוּ, וּבִכְלָלָא דִּלְהוֹן עָאלַת, וְאִתְקַבְּלַת בִּרְעוּתָא קַמֵּי מַלְכָּא קַדִּישָׁא.

192. Rabbi Elazar said to him, You spoke well. Therefore, the person who puts forth his prayers must make himself poor, so that his prayers will be worthy to enter among the prayers of all the poor. Non of the guardians of the gates allows them, THAT IS ALL THE OTHER PRAYERS IN THE WORLD, to just simply enter as they allow the poor man's prayer, since they enter without permission. If a person makes himself poor and desires constantly to be poor, his prayer ascends and meets up with the poor's prayers. It joins up with them and rises together with them, and enters combined with theirs. And it is willingly received before the Holy King.

15. Four ways: The poor, the devout, servants, those who sanctify Hashem

A Synopsis

Rabbi Elazar goes on to say that King David placed himself among the poor, the pious, the servants, and those who are willing to sacrifice their lives for the sanctification of God's name. We learn that when people are confessing and repenting they do not have to worry about the sins they don't remember, just the ones they do. Rabbi Elazar says that all people need to do as King David did, and that acting as a servant to God includes being pious, poor and willing to offer one's soul for the glorification of God. When someone has done all these things with a willing heart he is acceptable to God, and God calls him His servant and listens to his prayers. The rabbis talks further about the meaning of 'servant' and what the effect of prayer is. They describe the times each day when the Other Side wanders around the world and during which people should pray. The Other Side brings darkness but the windows of the upper lights are opened above those who are praying, and these lights are dispersed over their heads. Anyone who has not come to the synagogue at this time of prayer "walks in darkness" since he is under the dominion of the Other Side.

193. דָּוִד מַלְכָּא, שַׁוֵּי גַּרְמֵיהּ בְּאַרְבָּעָה אָרְחִין, שַׁוֵּי גַּרְמֵיהּ בַּהֲדֵי מִסְכְּנֵי. שַׁוֵּי גַּרְמֵיהּ בַּהֲדֵי חֲסִידִים. שַׁוֵּי גַּרְמֵיהּ בַּהֲדֵי עֲבָדִים. שַׁוֵּי גַּרְמֵיהּ בַּהֲדֵי אִינּוּן דְּמַסְרֵי גַּרְמַיְיהוּ וְנַפְשַׁיְיהוּ עַל קְדוּשַּׁת שְׁמֵיהּ. שַׁוֵּי גַּרְמֵיהּ בַּהֲדֵי מִסְכְּנָא. דִּכְתִּיב כִּי עָנִי וְאֶבְיוֹן אָנִי. שַׁוֵּי גַּרְמֵיהּ בַּהֲדֵי חֲסִידִים, דִּכְתִּיב שָׁמְרָה נַפְשִׁי כִּי חָסִיד אָנִי. בְּגִין דְּאִצְטְרִיךְ לֵיהּ לְבַר נָשׁ, דְּלָא לְשַׁוָּאָה גַּרְמֵיהּ רָשָׁע. וְאִי תֵּימָא אִי הָכִי לָא יְפָרֵט חֶטְאוֹי לְעָלְמִין. לָאו הָכִי. אֶלָּא כַּד יְפָרֵט חֶטְאוֹי, כְּדֵין אִיהוּ חָסִיד, דְּאָתֵי לְקַבְּלָא תְּשׁוּבָה, אַפִּיק גַּרְמֵיהּ מִסִּטְרָא בִּישָׁא, דַּהֲוָה בְּטִנּוּפָא דִּילֵיהּ עַד הַשְׁתָּא, וְהַשְׁתָּא אִתְדְּבַק בִּימִינָא עִלָּאָה, דְּאִיהִי פְּשׁוּטָה לְקַבְּלָא לֵיהּ.

193. King David has placed himself in four ways. He placed himself with the poor, he placed himself with the devout, he placed himself with the servants and he placed himself with those who are willing to sacrifice themselves and their souls for the sanctification of the name of Hashem. He placed himself with the poor, as is written: "For I am poor and needy" (Tehilim 86:1). He placed himself with the devout, as is written: "Preserve my soul; for I am pious" (Ibid. 2), since a person must not place himself as a wicked one. If you contemplate that in that case he will never confess and repent his sins, SINCE BY DOING SO, HE WILL SET HIMSELF UP AS AN EVIL ONE. It is not so. Rather if he confesses about his sins, then he is devout, since he approaches to do repentance and removes himself from the Evil Side, where he was in its filth until now. Now, he adhered to the uppermost right, WHICH IS CHESED, that is extended to receive him. AND BECAUSE HE ADHERED TO CHESED, HE IS CONSIDERED DEVOUT (HEB. *CHASID*).

194. וְלָא תֵּימָא, דְּלָא מְקַבֵּל לֵיהּ קוּדְשָׁא בְּרִיךְ הוּא, עַד דִּיפָרֵט חֶטְאוֹי מִיּוֹמָא דַּהֲוָה בְּעָלְמָא. אוֹ אִינּוּן דְּאִתְכְּסוּן מִנֵּיהּ, דְּלָא יָכִיל לְאַדְבְּקָא. אֶלָּא לָא אִצְטְרִיךְ לְפָרְשָׁא, בַּר אִינּוּן דְּיִדְכַּר מִנַּיְיהוּ. וְאִי שַׁוֵּי רְעוּתֵיהּ בְּהוּ, כָּל אַחֲרָנִין אִתְמַשְׁכָן אֲבַתְרַיְיהוּ. דְּהָא תָּנֵינָן, אֵין בּוֹדְקִין חוֹרֵי בֵּיתָא עִלָּאִין לְעֵילָּא, וְלָא אִינּוּן תַּתָּאִין לְתַתָּא בְּבִיעוּר חָמֵץ. אֶלָּא כֵּיוָן דְּבָדִיק כְּפוּם חֵיזוּ דְּעֵינוֹי מַה דְּיָכִיל לְאַדְבְּקָא, כֹּלָּא אִתְמְשַׁךְ בָּתַר דָּא, וְאִתְבְּטִיל בַּהֲדֵיהּ.

194. Do not say that the Holy One, blessed be He, will not accept him until he specifies all his sins since the day he came to this world, or even those that have been hidden from him and that he can't even remember. IT IS NOT SO. Rather, he is only required to enumerate those SINS that he remembers and if he directs his desire TO BE REGRETFUL ABOUT THEM, DURING HIS CONFESSION, all the other SINS followed them. IT IS IN THE SAME WAY that we were taught that it is not necessary to check out, WHEN GETTING RID OF LEAVENED BREAD, either the household crevices above nor the house crevices down below. As soon as he checked out in accordance with his eyesight as much as he could see, all the rest follows and is voided with it.

195. וְהָכִי גַּרְסֵינָן בִּנְגָעִים, כ"ד רָאשֵׁי אֵבָרִים אִינּוּן דְּלָא מְטַמְּאִין מִשּׁוּם מִחְיָה. וְכַהֲנָא לָא הֲוָה אַטְרַח אֲבַתְרַיְיהוּ, וְהַיְינוּ דִּכְתִּיב, לְכָל מַרְאֵה עֵינֵי הַכֹּהֵן אֲתַר דְּיָכִיל כַּהֲנָא לְמֶחֱזֵי מַכְתְּשָׁא בְּאִסְתַּכְּלוּתָא חֲדָא, וְלָא אִצְטְרִיךְ לְמַאֲכָא גַּרְמֵיהּ, וּלְאַרְמָא עֵינוֹי הָכָא וְהָכָא. אוּף

הָכִי. לָא אִצְטְרִיךְ לְפַרְטָא חֶטְאוֹי מִן יוֹמָא דַּהֲוָה, דְּאִינּוּן חוֹרֵי בֵּיתָא תַּתָּאִין, וְלָא אִינּוּן דְּאִתְכְּסוּ, דְּלָא יָכִיל לְאַדְבְּקָא, דְּאִינּוּן חוֹרֵי בֵּיתָא עִלָּאִין לְעֵילָּא. אֶלָּא לְכָל מַרְאֵה עֵינֵי הַכֹּהֵן, וְכֻלְּהוּ אִתְמַשְׁכָן אֲבַתְרַיְיהוּ. וְעַ"ד שַׁוֵּי דָּוִד גַּרְמֵיהּ גּוֹ חֲסִידִים.

195. We were similarly taught concerning plagues that there are 24 principal organs that do not cause uncleanness due to light cicatrization, where the priest does not bother himself TO OBSERVE THEM. This is what is meant by: "As far as the priest can see" (Vayikra 13:12). That is the area where the priest can see the plague AT ONCE in one glance, and does not need to bend himself and raise his eyes up or down or either way. Here too, he has no need to enumerate his sins from the day he was born, because it is LIKE the lower crevices of the house THAT REQUIRE NO EXAMINATION. Neither does he need to enumerate those sins that he has already forgotten, and can't remember, that are LIKE the upper house crevices above, only "as far as the priest can see," WHAT HE COULD OBSERVE WITH ONE GLANCE. All the rest followed them. In this way, David placed himself among the pious. HE CONFESSED HIS SINS AND ADHERED TO THE RIGHT, AS DEFINED.

196. שַׁוֵּי גַּרְמֵיהּ בַּהֲדֵי עֲבָדִים, דִּכְתִּיב הִנֵּה כְעֵינֵי עֲבָדִים אֶל יַד אֲדוֹנֵיהֶם. וּכְתִיב, הוֹשַׁע עַבְדְּךָ אַתָּה אֱלֹהַי. שַׁוֵּי גַּרְמֵיהּ בַּהֲדֵי אִינּוּן דְּמַסְרֵי נַפְשַׁיְיהוּ עַל קְדוּשַּׁת שְׁמֵיהּ. דִּכְתִּיב, שַׂמֵּחַ נֶפֶשׁ עַבְדֶּךָ כִּי אֵלֶיךָ יְיָ' נַפְשִׁי אֶשָּׂא. בְּכָל הָנֵי אַרְבַּע, עָבֵד גַּרְמֵיהּ דָּוִד מַלְכָּא קַמֵּי מָארֵיהּ.

196. FROM WHERE DO WE TAKE IT THAT he placed himself with the servants? It is written: "Behold, as the eyes of the servants look to the hand of their masters" (Tehilim 123:2) and: "O You, my Elohim, save Your servant" (Ibid. 86:2). FROM WHERE DO WE TAKE IT THAT he placed himself with those who deliver themselves to death for the sanctification of Hashem's name? That refers to what is written: "Rejoice the soul of Your servant: for to You, Hashem, do I lift up my soul" (Ibid. 4). King David made himself before his Master into all these four, WHICH ARE THE DESTITUTE, THE PIOUS, THE SERVANTS AND THOSE WHO ARE WILLING TO DIE FOR THE SANCTIFICATION OF HIS NAME.

197. אָמַר רִבִּי אֶלְעָזָר, אֲרִימִית יְדַי בִּצְלוּ לְקַמֵּי מַלְכָּא קַדִּישָׁא. דְּהָא תָּנֵינָן, אָסוּר לֵיהּ לְבַר נָשׁ לְאַרְמָא יְדוֹי לְעֵילָּא, בַּר בִּצְלוּ, וּבְבִרְכָּאן וְתַחֲנוּנִים לְמָרֵיהּ. דִּכְתִּיב, הֲרִימוֹתִי יָדִי אֶל יְיָ׳ אֵל עֶלְיוֹן, וּמְתַרְגְּמִינָן, אֲרִימִית יְדִי בִּצְלוּ, דְּהָא אֶצְבְּעָאן דְּיָדִין מִלִּין עִלָּאִין אִית בְּהוּ. וְהַשְׁתָּא אֲנָא הָכִי עֲבִידְנָא. וַאֲמֵינָא דְּכָל מַאן דְּאִלֵּין אַרְבַּע יְסַדֵּר קַמֵּי מָארֵיהּ, וְעָבֵיד גַּרְמֵיהּ בִּרְעוּתָא, בְּתִקּוּנָא דָּא כַּדְקָא יָאוּת, בְּתִקּוּנָא דָּא לָא תֵּהָדַר צְלוֹתֵיהּ בְּרֵיקָנַיָּא.

197. Rabbi Elazar said, I have raised my hands in prayer before the Holy King, since we were taught that a person is not permitted to raise his hands upward, except at prayer, at blessings and at supplications to his master. It is written: "I have raised my hand to Hashem, the most high El" (Beresheet 14:23), which was translated into Aramaic as "I have raised my hands in prayer," since the fingers of the hand contain higher things. Now I practice that, RAISING MY HANDS AT PRAYER, and I say that whoever conforms to these four MENTIONED ABOVE, THE DESTITUTE, THE PIOUS, THE SERVANTS AND THOSE WHO SUFFER FOR HIS NAME'S SANCTIFICATION, before his Master and accomplishes himself with a willing heart in this appropriate preparation here with this manner, his prayers will not return unanswered.

198. בְּקַדְמֵיתָא עֶבֶד, לְסַדְּרָא שְׁבָחָא קַמֵּי מָארֵיהּ, וּלְזַמְּרָא קַמֵּיהּ. וְדָא בְּתוּשְׁבְּחָן דְּקַמֵּי צְלוֹתָא. וּלְבָתַר עֶבֶד, לְבָתַר דְּצַלֵּי צְלוֹתָא דַּעֲמִידָה, אִיהוּ עַבְדָּא דְּסִדֵּר צְלוֹתָא דְּמָארֵיהּ. וּלְבָתַר עֶבֶד, לְבָתַר דְּצַלֵּי כָּל צְלוֹתֵיהּ, וְאָזִיל לֵיהּ, וְעַ״ד דָּוִד תְּלַת זִמְנִין עֲבַד גַּרְמֵיהּ בִּצְלוֹתָא דָּא עֶבֶד. דִּכְתִּיב הוֹשַׁע עַבְדְּךָ אַתָּה אֱלֹהַי. שַׂמֵּחַ נֶפֶשׁ עַבְדֶּךָ. וּכְתִיב תְּנָה עֻזְּךָ לְעַבְדֶּךָ. הָא תְּלַת זִמְנִין, אִצְטְרִיךְ לְשַׁוָּאָה גַּרְמֵיהּ עֶבֶד.

198. At first, HE SHOULD PLACE HIMSELF as a servant that is to offer praises to his Master and sing for Him. That refers to the praises before the prayer service. Following this, HE SHOULD CONSIDER HIMSELF a servant after he finished saying his standing prayer. He is the servant who offers prayer to his Master. Following this, HE SHOULD CONSIDER HIMSELF a servant after he completed his entire prayer, and went his way. That is why

15. Four ways: The poor, the devout, servants, those who sanctify Hashem

David considered himself a servant three times in this prayer, as is written: "O You, my Elohim, save Your servant" and "Rejoice the soul of Your servant." It is also written: "Give Your strength to Your servant" (Tehilim 86:16). We have here three occasions where one should consider oneself a servant. THAT IS BEFORE THE PRAYER, AFTER THE AMIDAH PRAYER AND AFTER THE WHOLE PRAYER SERVICE AS MENTIONED.

199. לְבָתַר לְשַׁוָּאָה גַּרְמֵיהּ גּוֹ אִינּוּן דִּמְסְרֵי נַפְשַׁיְיהוּ עַל קְדוּשַּׁת שְׁמֵיהּ, וְהַיְינוּ בְּיִחוּדָא דִּשְׁמַע יִשְׂרָאֵל, דְּכָל מַאן דְּשַׁוֵּי הָכִי רְעוּתֵיהּ בְּהַאי קְרָא, אִתְחֲשִׁיב לֵיהּ כְּאִלּוּ מָסַר נַפְשֵׁיהּ עַל קְדוּשַּׁת שְׁמֵיהּ.

199. Then, HE NEEDS to place oneself among those who have risked their lives for the sake of sanctifying the Holy Name. That is accomplished at the unification of the Sh'ma Yisrael, for whoever concentrated on it at this verse, it is considered as if he risked his life for the sanctification of Hashem's name.

200. לְבָתַר לְשַׁוָּאָה גַּרְמֵיהּ עָנִי, בְּזִמְנָא דְּעָאל וְדַפִּיק דָּשִׁין דְּרוֹמֵי מְרוֹמִים, כַּד אָמַר אֱמֶת וְיַצִּיב, וְסָמִיךְ גְּאוּלָּה לִתְפִלָּה. לְמֶהֱוֵי בִּצְלוֹתָא דַּעֲמִידָה, תָּבִיר לִבָּא, עַנְיָא וּמִסְכְּנָא. וּלְשַׁוָּאָה רְעוּתֵיהּ, לְאִתְכַּלְּלָא גּוֹ מִסְכְּנֵי, בִּתְבִירוּ דְּלִבָּא, בְּמְאִיכוּ דְּנַפְשָׁא.

200. Then he must place himself in the place of the poor, since during the time when he enters and knocks at the doors of the most high up, when he finished saying 'true and certain', and he has joined 'who has redeemed' to the Amidah prayer, he shall reach the Amidah prayer broken at heart, poor and destitute. And he shall place his will to be included among the poverty-stricken with a broken heart and humility of soul.

201. לְבָתַר לְשַׁוָּאָה גַּרְמֵיהּ גּוֹ חֲסִידִים, בְּשׁוֹמֵעַ תְּפִלָּה, לְפָרְשָׁא חֶטְאוֹי. דְּהָכִי אִצְטְרִיךְ יָחִיד בְּשׁוֹמֵעַ תְּפִלָּה, בְּגִין לְאִתְדַּבְּקָא בִּימִינָא, דִּפְשׁוּטָה לְקַבְּלָא לְאִינּוּן דְּתָבִין, וּכְדֵין אִקְרֵי חָסִיד, הָא אַרְבַּע אִלֵּין כַּדְקָא יֵאוֹת.

201. Following this, HE NEEDS to place himself among the devout before 'who hears prayer' to elucidate his sins, because this is what an individual should do when reciting 'who hears prayer' in order to adhere to the right, THAT IS CHESED, which is extended to receive the penitent. And then he is considered pious (Heb. *chasid*). Here we have the four, as is appropriate.

202. מַאן כָּלִיל לְכָל הָנֵי, הַהוּא דְּקָא אִצְטְרִיךְ לְכַלְלָא לוֹן, וְהַאי אִיהוּ עֶבֶד, דְּאַכְלִיל לְכָל שְׁאָר. תְּלַת עַבְדִּין אִינּוּן בִּתְלַת דּוּכְתִּין, וְכֻלְּהוּ חַד. וְעָלַיְיהוּ כְּתִיב, הִנֵּה כְעֵינֵי עֲבָדִים אֶל יַד אֲדוֹנֵיהֶם וְגוֹ'. בֵּין עֶבֶד לְעֶבֶד אִינּוּן אַחֲרָנִין. בֵּין עֶבֶד קַדְמָאָה, לְעֶבֶד תִּנְיָינָא, אִית לֵיהּ לְמִמְסַר נַפְשֵׁיהּ עַל יִחוּדָא דִּקְדוּשַּׁת שְׁמֵיהּ, וּלְשַׁוָּאָה גַּרְמֵיהּ עָנִי וּמִסְכְּנָא בִּצְלוֹתָא דַּעֲמִידָה, וּלְשַׁוָּאָה גַּרְמֵיהּ גּוֹ חֲסִידִים בְּשׁוֹמֵעַ תְּפִלָּה. עֶבֶד תְּלִיתָאָה בָּתַר דְּסִיֵּים וְסִדֵּר כֹּלָּא.

202. HE INQUIRES: Whoever combines all those MENTIONED ABOVE? HE RESPONDS: The one who should include them is the servant that combines all the rest, THOSE SANCTIFYING THE HOLY NAME, THE POOR, AND THE DEVOUT. "Servant" is found three times at three places and all are one. About them, it is written: 'Behold, as the eyes of the servants look to the hand of their masters'. Between each 'servant' ARE all the others, from the first servant, THAT IS BEFORE THE PRAYER SERVICE, to the last servant, AFTER THE AMIDAH PRAYER; he needs to deliver his soul for the sake of sanctifying Hashem's name. He also needs to feel himself as the poor and destitute at the Amidah prayer and place himself among the pious at 'who hears prayer'. The third servant follows after he completed and offered the entire prayer, MEANING AFTER THE COMPLETION OF THE WHOLE PRAYER.

203. תְּנָן, בְּהַהִיא שַׁעֲתָא דְּסִדֵּר בַּר נָשׁ כָּל הָנֵי סִדּוּרִין אַרְבַּע, בִּרְעוּ דְּלִבָּא, קוּדְשָׁא בְּרִיךְ הוּא נִיחָא קַמֵּיהּ, וּפָרִישׂ יְמִינֵיהּ עָלֵיהּ, בְּהַהוּא עֶבֶד תְּלִיתָאָה, וְקָרָא עָלֵיהּ וְאָ"ל, עַבְדִּי אַתָּה, דִּכְתִּיב וַיֹּאמֶר לִי עַבְדִּי אָתָּה יִשְׂרָאֵל אֲשֶׁר בְּךָ אֶתְפָּאָר. וַדַּאי צְלוֹתָא דְּהַאי בַּר נָשׁ, לָא תֶּהְדַּר בְּרֵיקָנַיָּא לְעָלְמִין. אָתָא ר' אַבָּא וּנְשָׁקֵיהּ.

203. We were taught at that moment when a man has pronounced in successive order all these four arrangements with a willing heart, it pleases the Holy One, blessed be He. And He spreads His right hand over him at that third 'servant', WHICH IS AFTER THE ENTIRE PRAYER SERVICE, and calls upon him, and says to him, "You are My servant," as it is written: "And said to me, 'You are My servant Yisrael, in whom I will be glorified'" (Yeshayah 49:3). It is certain that the prayer of this man will never be returned empty. Rabbi Aba approached and kissed him.

204. אָמַר ר׳ אֶלְעָזָר, ת״ח, תְּרֵי עֶבֶד מֵאִינּוּן תְּלָתָא, אִינּוּן דְּכָלְלֵי כָּל הָנֵי, דְּהָא תְּלִיתָאָה קַיְּימָא לְחַתְמָא בֵּיהּ חוֹתָמָא לְעֵילָּא, לְשַׁוָּאָה בֵּיהּ יְדָא מִימִינָא דְּמַלְכָּא, וּלְאִשְׁתַּבְּחָא בֵּיהּ. אֲבָל הָנֵי תְּרֵין, קַדְמָאָה וְתִנְיָינָא, אִינּוּן כְּלָלָא דְּכֹלָּא. וְדָוִד שַׁבַּח גַּרְמֵיהּ בְּהוּ, דִּכְתִּיב אָנָּא יְיָ׳ כִּי אֲנִי עַבְדֶּךָ אֲנִי עַבְדְּךָ וְגוֹ׳, דְּאִלֵּין כְּלָלֵי דְּכָל שְׁאַר. תְּלִיתָאָה כַּךְ קַיְּימָא לְמִפְרַק לִי, דִּכְתִּיב הוֹשַׁע עַבְדְּךָ אַתָּה אֱלֹהַי. מַאן דִּמְסַדֵּר דָּא, יְדִיעַ לֶיהֱוֵי לֵיהּ דְּקוּדְשָׁא בְּרִיךְ הוּא מִשְׁתַּבַּח בֵּיהּ, וְקָרָא עָלֵיהּ עַבְדִּי אָתָּה יִשְׂרָאֵל אֲשֶׁר בְּךָ אֶתְפָּאָר. אָתָא ר׳ אַבָּא וּנְשָׁקֵיהּ.

204. Rabbi Elazar said, Come and see: The two 'servant' out of those three combine within them all THE OTHER, THOSE SANCTIFYING THE NAME, THE POOR ABD THE PIOUS, because the third 'SERVANT' is there to stamp him with the celestial seal, to place on him the right hand of the King because he is acclaimed by Him. However, these two 'SERVANT', the first THAT IS PRIOR TO THE PRAYERS SERVICE and the second THAT IS AFTER THE AMIDAH PRAYER, are inclusive of all. King David glorified himself with them, as is written: "Hashem, truly I am Your servant; I am the servant..." (Tehilim 116:16), since these are inclusive of all the rest. The third 'SERVANT' FOLLOWING THE ENTIRE PRAYER SERVICE is there to redeem me, as is written: "Help Your servant, You are my Elohim" (Tehilim 86:2). Whoever offers, let him know that the Holy One, blessed be He, is glorified through him and declares about him: "You are My servant, Yisrael, in whom I will be glorified." Rabbi Aba approached and kissed him.

205. א״ר אַבָּא, עַ״ד קָרֵינָן, הַנֶּחֱמָדִים מִזָּהָב וּמִפָּז רָב וְגוֹ׳, כַּמָּה מְתִיקִין מִלִּין עַתִּיקִין דְּסִדְּרוּ קַדְמָאֵי, וַאֲנָן כַּד טַעֲמִין לוֹן, לָא יַכְלִין לְמֵיכַל. וַדַּאי הָכִי הוּא, וְהָא קְרָא אוֹכַח עַל תְּלָתָא עַבְדִּין, וְאִינּוּן חַד,

וּבַאֲתָר חַד. וּתְרֵין כִּדְקָאָמַרְתְּ, וְחַד דְּאִיהוּ לְאִתְעַטְּרָא בֵּיהּ קוּדְשָׁא בְּרִיךְ הוּא, דִּכְתִּיב כִּי לִי בְנֵי יִשְׂרָאֵל עֲבָדִים עֲבָדַי הֵם וְגוֹ׳. לֹא יִמָּכְרוּ מִמְכֶּרֶת עָבֶד. בְּגִין דְּקוּדְשָׁא בְּרִיךְ הוּא אִצְטְרִיךְ לְאִתְעַטְּרָא בְּהַאי תְּלִיתָאָה. וְעַל דָּא לֹא יִמָּכְרוּ לִשְׁמָא דְּעָבֶד, דְּהָא דְּקוּדְשָׁא בְּרִיךְ הוּא הֲוֵי.

205. Rabbi Aba said, About this, it is written: "More to be desired are they than gold, even much fine gold..." (Tehilim 19:11). How sweet are the ancient teachings that the earlier generations have arranged. When we taste them, we are unable to eat them, MEANING WE DON'T UNDERSTAND THEM. It is definitely so. The scripture indicates three servants here. They are one in one place, the second is as you mentioned and the third is for the Holy One, blessed be He, to be adorned with, as is written: "For to Me the children of Yisrael are servants; they are My servants" (Vayikra 25:55). THERE ARE TWO SERVANTS BEFORE THE PRAYER, AND AFTER THE AMIDAH PRAYER, IT IS WRITTEN: "They shall not be sold as bondsmen" (Ibid. 42), WHICH IS THE THIRD. The Holy One, blessed be He, needs to be adorned with this third SERVANT; therefore, they must not be sold for slavery, since he belongs to the Holy One, blessed be He.

206. פָּתַח ר׳ אֶלְעָזָר וְאָמַר, מִי בָכֶם יְרֵא יְיָ׳ וְגוֹ׳. מַאי שׁוֹמֵעַ בְּקוֹל עַבְדּוֹ. הַאי קְרָא אוֹקְמוּהָ חַבְרַיָּיא בִּצְלוֹתָא, וְהָכִי הוּא. מַאן דְּרָגִיל לְמֵיתֵי לְבֵי כְּנִשְׁתָּא לְצַלָּאָה, וְיוֹמָא חֲדָא לָא אָתֵי, קוּדְשָׁא בְּרִיךְ הוּא שָׁאִיל עָלֵיהּ וְאָמַר, מִי בָכֶם יְרֵא יְיָ׳ שׁוֹמֵעַ בְּקוֹל עַבְדּוֹ אֲשֶׁר הָלַךְ חֲשֵׁכִים וְאֵין נֹגַהּ לוֹ. מַאי שׁוֹמֵעַ בְּקוֹל עַבְדּוֹ. בְּמַאן. אִי תֵּימָא בִּנְבִיאָה, אוֹ גְּבַר אַחֲרָא, מַאן יָהַב נְבִיאָה, אוֹ גְּבַר אַחֲרָא לִצְלוֹתָא. דִּבְגִין דְּצַלֵּי צְלוֹתֵיהּ שׁוֹמֵעַ בְּקוֹל נְבִיאָה, אוֹ דִּגְבַר בְּעָלְמָא.

206. Rabbi Elazar opened the discussion saying, "Who is there among you that fears Hashem, THAT OBEYS THE VOICE OF HIS SERVANT, THAT WALKS IN DARKNESS AND HAS NO LIGHT? LET HIM TRUST IN THE NAME OF HASHEM AND RELY UPON HIS ELOHIM" (Yeshayah 50:10). HE ASKS: What is the meaning of: "that obeys the voice of His servant"? This verse has been explained by the friends as applicable to prayer. It is as follows, MEANING whoever is accustomed to come to the synagogue to pray, if one day he doesn't come, the Holy One, blessed be He, inquires about him and says, "Who is there among you that fears Hashem, that obeys the voice of His servant, that walks in darkness, and has no light?" HOWEVER, what is the meaning of: "that obeys the voice of His servant" – the voice of whom? If you say that of "His servant" REFERS TO a prophet or some other person, what is then the relation between the prophet or any other person and the prayer? Is it because, since he performed his prayer, He obeys the voice of a prophet or another person in the world?

207. אֶלָּא הַהוּא דְּצַלֵּי צְלוֹתִין בְּכָל יוֹמָא, אִיהוּ שׁוֹמֵעַ בְּהַהוּא קוֹל, דְּקָרֵי לֵיהּ קוּדְשָׁא בְּרִיךְ הוּא, וּמִשְׁתַּבַּח בֵּיהּ, וְאָמַר דְּאִיהוּ עַבְדּוֹ וַדַּאי. שׁוֹמֵעַ בְּקוֹל, בְּמַאי קוֹל. בְּהַהוּא דְּאִקְרֵי עַבְדּוֹ. שְׁבָחָא עִלָּאָה אִיהוּ דְּנָפִיק עָלֵיהּ קוֹל דְּאִיהוּ עַבְדּוֹ. וְתוּ, דְּקָלָא אִשְׁתְּמַע בְּכָל אִינּוּן רְקִיעִין, דְּאִיהוּ עַבְדָּא דְּמַלְכָּא קַדִּישָׁא, וְדָא הוּא שׁוֹמֵעַ בְּקוֹל עַבְדּוֹ.

207. HE RESPONDS: It is only that he who says his prayer regularly obeys that voice with which the Holy One, blessed be He, calls to him. And he takes praise in it, saying that he definitely is His servant. That is the meaning of: "That obeys (also: 'listens to') the voice." Which voice? That voice that is considered "His servant." That is the highest praise that a voice was proclaiming about him, which is His servant. Furthermore, a voice is heard in all these heavens, which is the servant in the service (of) the Holy King. This is the meaning of: "That obeys the voice of His servant."

208. אֲשֶׁר הָלַךְ חֲשֵׁכִים וְאֵין נֹגַהּ לוֹ, וְכִי בְּגִין דְּלָא אָתָא לְצַלוּיֵי הָלַךְ חֲשֵׁכִים. אֶלָּא אוּקְמוּהָ. אֲבָל עַד לָא יִתְכַּנְּשׁוּן יִשְׂרָאֵל לְבָתֵּי כְּנֵסִיּוֹת לְצַלָּאָה, סִטְרָא אַחֲרָא קַיְּימָא וְסָגִיר כָּל נְהוֹרִין עִלָּאִין, דְּלָא יִתְפַּשְּׁטוּן וְיִפְּקוּן עַל עָלְמִין. וּתְלַת זִמְנִין בְּיוֹמָא אַזְלֵי סְטַר אַחֲרָא, דְּכַר וְנוּקְבָא, וּמְשַׁטְטִין בְּעָלְמָא, וְהַהוּא עִידָּן אַתְקַן לִצְלוֹתָא, בְּגִין דְּלָא הֲוֵי תַּמָּן קִטְרוּגָא כְּלָל.

208. "That walks in darkness, and has no light." HE ASKS: Because he did not come to pray, he "walks in darkness." HE RESPONDS: It was however explained only that before Yisrael gather into the synagogues to pray, the

Other Side stands around and closes all the upper lights, so that they should not expand and be distributed over the world. Three times a day, this Other Side, which is male and female, goes and wanders around the world. That time was appropriated for prayers, because then no accusations prevail.

209. וּכְדֵין אִיהוּ עִידָּן לִצְלוֹתָא, בְּגִין דְּאִינּוּן אָזְלֵי לְמִשַׁטְטָא, בְּטוּרֵי חָשׁוּךְ, וְהַר נִשְׁפֶּה, כְּדֵין פְּתִיחִין כַּוֵּי נְהוֹרִין עִלָּאִין, וְנַפְקֵי וְשָׁרִיאָן עַל בָּתֵּי כְּנֵסִיּוֹת, בְּרֵישַׁיְהוֹן דְּאִינּוּן דְּצַלָּאן צְלוֹתִין, וּמִתְפַּלְּגָן נְהוֹרִין עַל רֵישַׁיְיהוּ. וְקוּדְשָׁא בְּרִיךְ הוּא שָׁאִיל, עַל הַהוּא דְּלָא אִשְׁתְּכַח תַּמָּן, וְאָמַר חֲבָל עַל פְּלַנְיָא, דַּהֲוָה רָגִיל הָכָא, וְהַשְׁתָּא דְּהָלַךְ חֲשֵׁכִים וְאִתְעֲבָר מִקַּמֵּי נְהוֹרִין, וְהָלַךְ לְשַׁטְטָא בְּטוּרַיָּא בְּעָלְמָא, וְנָפַק מֵהַהוּא נֹגַהּ נְהוֹרָא דְּנָהִיר, וְלֵית לֵיהּ בֵּיהּ חוּלָקָא, אֵין נֹגַהּ לוֹן, כְּמָה דְּאִתְפְּלִיג וְשַׁרְיָא עַל אַחֲרָנִין דְּתַמָּן, כַּמָּה טָבִין אִתְאֲבִידוּ מִנֵּיהּ. וְאִלּוּ הֲוָה תַּמָּן, יִבְטַח בְּשֵׁם יְיָ', בִּכְלָלָא דְּעֶבֶד קַדְמָאָה. וְיִשָּׁעֵן בֵּאלֹהָיו בְּרָזָא דְּעֶבֶד תִּנְיָינָא.

209. Then is the opportune period for prayer, because they, THE OTHER SIDE, go to loiter in the dark mountains and Mount Nishpe. At that moment, the windows of the upper lights are opened and leave to dwell upon the houses of worship on the heads of those who say prayers. And the lights are dispersed over their heads. The Holy One, blessed be He, inquires about the one who isn't there and declares, It is a pity about so-and-so who used to come here. Now, he "walks in darkness," is removed from the lights and has gone to wander in the mountains in the world, BECAUSE HE FINDS HIMSELF UNDER THE DOMINION OF THE OTHER SIDE THAT IS IN THE DARK MOUNTAINS. He left that brightness, which is the lamp that gives light IN THE HOUSE OF WORSHIP, and he has no part in it. This is what is written: "And has no light," as it was spread and laid upon the others that are there, IN THE SYNAGOGUE. How much benefit was lost to him. If he were there, "let him trust in the name of Hashem," meaning he would be included in the first servant THAT IS BEFORE THE PRAYER SERVICE "and rely upon his Elohim" in the secret meaning of the second servant, THAT IS, AFTER THE PRAYERS IN THE AMIDAH PRAYER.

210. אר"ש, אֶלְעָזָר בְּרִי, וַדַּאי רוּחַ נְבוּאָה שַׁרְיָא עֲלָךְ. א"ר אַבָּא, אַרְיָא בַּר אַרְיָא, מַאן יְקוּם קַמַּיְיהוּ, כַּד שָׁאֲגֵי לְמִטְרַף טַרְפָּא. כָּל אַרְיָין

דְּעָלְמָא תַּקִּיפִין, וְאִלֵּין יַתִּיר מִכֻּלְּהוּ. כָּל אַרְיָין דְּעָלְמָא, קַשְׁיָין לְאַפָּקָא טַרְפָּא מִפּוּמַיְיהוּ, וְאִלֵּין נוֹחִין לְאַפָּקָא מִפּוּמַיְיהוּ טַרְפָּא. אִינּוּן טַרְפֵּי טַרְפָּא, וְיָהֲבֵי לְכֹלָּא.

210. Rabbi Shimon said, My son Elazar, it is certain that the spirit of prophecy rests on you. Rabbi Aba said TO RABBI ELAZAR, A lion, the son of a lion, who would rise before them when they roar to kill for their prey? All lions are powerful, and RABBI SHIMON AND HIS SON more than all of them. It is difficult to take the prey out of the mouths of all the lions in the world, but it is easy to take out the prey, MEANING, THE TORAH INSIGHTS, from the lips of these lions; they send the prey and provide for everyone.

211. אֲשֶׁר הָלַךְ חֲשֵׁכִים, אֲשֶׁר הָלְכוּ מִבָּעֵי לֵיהּ. אָמַר רִבִּי אֶלְעָזָר, בְּגִין דְּאִינּוּן שַׁרְיָין בְּחִבּוּרָא, וּמִיָּד מִתְפָּרְשָׁן. הָלַךְ חִבּוּרָא, חֲשֵׁכִים אִתְפָּרְשָׁן. שָׁרָאן בְּחִבּוּרָא, וְאִתְפָּרְשָׁן מִיָּד. כְּגַוְונָא דָּא, רוּחַ סְעָרָה בָּאָה, כְּלַל דְּכַר וְנוּקְבָא. בָּאָה וְהִיא שַׁבְקַת לֵיהּ, מִיָּד מִתְפָּרְשָׁן.

211. "That walks in darkness (lit. 'darknesses')" HE ASKS: It should have said, 'That walk (plural)'. Rabbi Elazar said, That is because they, THE OTHER SIDE, dwell together, MALE AND FEMALE, and immediately separate. THAT IS WHAT IS WRITTEN: "walks," meaning together AND THEY ARE ONE. "DARKNESSES" refers to when they are separated already. They begin together and immediately separate, similar to this verse: "A storm wind came out" (Yechezkel 1:4). That is a combined action of male and female, OF THE OTHER SIDE THAT ARE CALLED 'STORM' AND 'WIND'. FOLLOWING THAT, IT SAYS "CAME OUT" IN SINGULAR FEMININE FORM, because THE FEMALE leaves THE MALE, since they immediately go apart.

16. "Even the sparrow has found a home"

A Synopsis

Rabbi Shimon says that the souls of the just are God's beloved, and He makes dwellings below and above for them. We hear a description of the three outer walls of the Garden of Eden, and Rabbi Shimon tells his son that some spirits are allowed to see a hidden chamber in the palace where the crowns are stored for Messiah in the time to come. The importance of having holy sons who study the Oral and Written Torahs is emphasized. Finally we hear that Balak saw a vision and knew that he would fall into the hands of Yisrael after they had first fallen into his hands.

212. וַיַּרְא בָּלָק וְגוֹ'. רִבִּי אֶלְעָזָר אָמַר, וַדַּאי מַה דְּאָמַר רִבִּי חִיָּיא, מִלָּה סְתִימָא הֲוָה. אֲבָל כְּתִיב, גַּם צִפּוֹר מָצְאָה בַיִת וּדְרוֹר קֵן לָהּ וְגוֹ'. וְכִי דָּוִד מַלְכָּא, עַל צִפָּרָא בְּעָלְמָא, הֲוָה אָמַר מִלָּה דָּא.

212. "And Balak...saw" (Bemidbar 22:1): Rabbi Elazar said, Certainly what Rabbi Chiya said ABOUT THIS VERSE: "BALAK THE SON OF TZIPOR (LIT. 'BIRD')" is a concealed matter. However, it is written: "Even the sparrow has found a home, and the swallow a nest for herself" (Tehilim 84:4). HE ASKS: Did King David then say this about a mere PHYSICAL bird?

213. אֶלָּא, כְּמָה דְּתָנֵינָן, כַּמָּה חֲבִיבִין נִשְׁמָתִין קַמֵּי קוּדְשָׁא בְּרִיךְ הוּא. אִי תֵּימָא כָּל נִשְׁמָתִין דְּעָלְמָא. לָאו הָכִי. אֶלָּא אִינּוּן נִשְׁמָתֵהוֹן דְּצַדִּיקַיָּיא, דְּתַמָּן מְדוֹרֵיהוֹן בַּהֲדֵיהּ, מָדוֹרֵיהוֹן לְעֵילָּא, וּמָדוֹרֵיהוֹן לְתַתָּא. וְהָכִי אִתְּמַר. גַּם צִפּוֹר מָצְאָה בַיִת, אִלֵּין רוּחֵיהוֹן דְּצַדִּיקַיָּיא.

213. HE RESPONDS: It is only as we were taught, how beloved are the souls to the Holy One, blessed be He. If you say all the souls, it is not so. It is only the souls of the righteous whose dwellings are with Him. Their dwellings are above and their dwellings are below, as we were taught. "Even the sparrow has found a home" refers to the spirits of the righteous.

214. תָּנֵינָן, תְּלַת שׁוּרִין אִינּוּן לג"ע, וּבֵין כָּל חַד וְחַד, כַּמָּה רוּחִין וְנִשְׁמָתִין מְטַיְּילִין תַּמָּן, וְאִתְהֲנָן מֵרֵיחָא דְּעִנּוּגִין דְּצַדִּיקַיָּיא דִּלְגוֹ,

אע"ג דְּלָא זָכוּ לְמֵיעָאל. אֲבָל עִנּוּגָא דְּרוּחֵיהוֹן דְּצַדִּיקַיָּיא דִּלְגוֹ, עַיִן לֹא רָאָתָה אֱלֹהִים וְגוֹ'.

214. We were taught that there are three outer walls to the Garden of Eden. Between each one of them, many spirits and souls walk about there and derive pleasure from the fragrance enjoyed by the righteous that are inside the Garden of Eden, although they themselves did not earn the merits to enter WITHIN. However, it is written of the enjoyable pleasure of the just that are inside: "Neither has the eye seen, that Elohim, beside You" (Yeshayah 64:3).

215. וְיוֹמִין רְשִׁימִין אִית בְּשַׁתָּא, וְאִינּוּן יוֹמֵי נִיסָן, לְיוֹמֵי תִּשְׁרֵי, דְּאִינּוּן רוּחִין מְשַׁטְטָן וּפַקְדָן לַאֲתָר דְּאִצְטְרִיךְ. וְאע"ג דִּזְמְנִין סַגִּיאִין מְשַׁטְטָן, אֲבָל יוֹמִין אִלֵּין רְשִׁימִין אִינּוּן, וְאִתְחָזוּן עַל גַּבֵּי שׁוּרִין דְּגִנְתָּא, כָּל חַד וְחַד כְּחֵיזוּ דְּצִפָּרִין מְצַפְצְפָן, בְּכָל צַפְרָא וְצַפְרָא.

215. There are designated days during the year, which are the days of Nissan and Tishrei, when these spirits wander and visit the place they should. Even though there are lots of occasions when they wander, these days are marked and are visible on the outer walls of the Garden, each one individually in a depiction of chirping birds, regularly each morning.

216. וְהַהוּא צִפְצוּפָא שְׁבָחָא דְּקוּדְשָׁא בְּרִיךְ הוּא, וּצְלוֹתָא עַל חַיֵּי בְּנֵי נָשָׁא דְּהַאי עָלְמָא. בְּגִין דְּאִלֵּין יוֹמִין, יִשְׂרָאֵל כֻּלְּהוּ מִתְעַסְּקִין בְּמִצְוֹת, וּבְפִקּוּדִין דְּמָארֵי עָלְמָא. וּכְדֵין בְּחֶדְוּ אִתְחֲזָן צִפָּרִין מְצַפְצְפָן, וע"ג שׁוּרִין דְּע"ג מְצַפְצְפָן מְשַׁבְּחָן וְאוֹדָן וּמְצַלָּן עַל חַיֵּי דְּהַאי עָלְמָא.

216. That chirping is praise to the Holy One, blessed be He, and a prayer about the lives of the human beings in this world, because in these days, Yisrael are involved in the precepts and commandments of the Master of the universe. Then, these birds appear chirping happily and they chirp and whisper praises and gratitudes and pray for the living of this world on the walls at the Garden of Eden.

217. אר"ש, אֶלְעָזָר וַדַּאי שַׁפִּיר קָאֲמַרְתְּ, דְּוַדַּאי אִינּוּן רוּחִין תַּמָּן.

אֲבָל מַה תֵּימָא וּדְרוֹר קֵן לָהּ. אָמַר, הָכִי אוֹלִיפְנָא, דָּא הִיא נִשְׁמְתָא קַדִּישָׁא, דְּסַלְקָא לְעֵילָּא, וְסַלְקָא לַאֲתַר טָמִיר וְגָנִיז, דְּעַיִן לֹא רָאָתָה אֱלֹהִים זוּלָתְךָ וְגוֹ׳.

217. Rabbi Shimon said, Elazar, you certainly spoke well, since these spirits are definitely there. But what would you say IN THE EXPLANATION OF THE VERSE: "And the swallow (Heb. *dror*) a nest for herself"? He said, This is what I was taught: that refers to the holy soul, WHICH IS CALLED '*DROR*', IT BEING THE LIGHT OF BINAH, WHICH IS FREEDOM (HEB. *DROR*) that rises above and ascends to a hidden and concealed area, where "neither has the eye seen, that Elohim, beside You..."

218. א״ר שִׁמְעוֹן, אֶלְעָזָר וַדַּאי שַׁפִּיר קָאֲמָרְתְּ, וְשַׁפִּיר אִיהוּ. אֲבָל כָּל דָּא בְּגַ״ע דִּלְתַּתָּא הִיא, וּכְמָה דְּאַמְרַת הוּא, וְהָכִי הוּא וַדַּאי, גַּם צִפּוֹר מָצְאָה בַיִת, אִלֵּין רוּחִין קַדִּישִׁין, דְּזָכוּ לְמֵיעָאל וּלְמֵיפַּק לְבָתַר, בְּגִין דִּמְשַׁטְטָן וְאִתְחָזוּן כְּחֵיזוּ דְּצִפּוֹרִין, וְאִלֵּין רוּחִין מָצְאָה בַיִת. וַדַּאי כָּל חֲדָא וַחֲדָא אִית לוֹן מָדוֹרִין יְדִיעָאן לְגוֹ.

218. Rabbi Shimon said, Elazar, you certainly spoke well and that is lovely. However, all this is in the lower Garden of Eden, and it is as you said, and most definitely so: "Even the sparrow has found a home" refers to the holy spirits that deserved afterwards to enter and leave, following their wanderings WITHOUT ANY PLACE TO SETTLE. They are depicted as birds and these spirits have now found a dwelling place. Each individual surely has a specified residence within.

219. ועב״ד, כֻּלְּהוּ נִכְוִין מֵחוּפָּה דְּחַבְרַיְיהוּ. אִינּוּן דְּאִית לוֹן דְּרוֹר, וְחֵירוּ מִכֹּלָּא. וְקוּדְשָׁא בְּרִיךְ הוּא אַחְזֵי לוֹן הֵיכָלָא טְמִירוּ חֲדָא גָּנִיז, דְּעַיִן לֹא רָאָתָה אֱלֹהִים זוּלָתְךָ, וְהַהוּא הֵיכָלָא אִקְרֵי קֵן צִפּוֹר. וּמִתַּמָּן מִתְעַטְּרִין עִטְרִין לְמָשִׁיחַ בְּזִמְנָא דְּאָתֵי, וּבְיוֹמִין רְשִׁימִין, תְּלַת זִמְנִין בְּשַׁתָּא, קוּדְשָׁא בְּרִיךְ הוּא בָּעֵי לְאִשְׁתַּעְשְׁעָא בְּאִינּוּן צַדִּיקַיָּיא, וְאַחְזֵי לוֹן הַהוּא הֵיכָלָא טְמִירָא גָּנִיז, דְּלָא יַדְעִין וְלָא אִשְׁתְּמוֹדְעָן בֵּיהּ, כָּל צַדִּיקַיָּיא דְּתַמָּן.

16. “Even the sparrow has found a home”

219. In spite of all this, ALL THESE SPIRITS get burned from the canopies of their neighbors, from these that have freedom and liberty of all. And the Holy One, blessed be He, shows them one hidden chamber that is stored away, which “neither has the eye seen, that Elohim, beside You.” That chamber is called ‘bird’s nest’ and from there come crowns that are adorned for Messiah in the future to come, because on designated days, three times a year, the Holy One, blessed be He, wishes to delight in these righteous and show them that chamber that is hidden and stored away. It is not recognized by all the righteous that are there.

220. אֲשֶׁר שָׁתָה אֶפְרוֹחֶיהָ אֶת מִזְבְּחוֹתֶיךָ, אִלֵּין אִינּוּן צַדִּיקַיָּיא, דְּאִשְׁתָּכְלָלוּ בִּבְנִין קַדִּישִׁין, דְּזָכוּ לַתּוֹרָה שֶׁבִּכְתָב, וְלַתּוֹרָה שֶׁבְּעַל פֶּה בְּהַאי עָלְמָא. וְאִלֵּין אִקְרוּן תְּרֵין מַדְבְּחָן. מִתְעַטְּרָן לְקַמֵּי מַלְכָּא קַדִּישָׁא, דְּהָא זְכוּתָא דִּבְנַיְיהוּ בְּהַאי עָלְמָא, אַגִּין עֲלַיְיהוּ, וּמְעַטְּרִין לְהוּ תַּמָּן. מַאן רוּחָא זַכָּאָה לְכָל הַאי. הַאי דְּשָׁתָה אֶפְרוֹחֶיהָ, לְאוֹלְפָא לְמִזְבְּחוֹתֶיךָ וְגוֹ׳. מִכָּאן וּלְהָלְאָה אֵימָא מִילָּךְ, דְּהָא בְּלָא כִּסּוּפָא אִתְחֲזֵינָא תַּמָּן.

220. “Where she may lay her young. Your altars” (Tehilim 84:4). These are the righteous, who laid their foundations with holy sons that merited the Written Torah and Oral Torah in this world. THE WRITTEN TORAH AND ORAL TORAH are considered two altars, AND THESE RIGHTEOUS get adorned before the Holy King, because the merits of their sons in this world protect them, and they get decorated there. Which spirit deserves all this? The one that lays her young to teach “Your altars,” WHICH ARE THE TWO TORAHS, AS MENTIONED. From here on, speak your words, so I will appear there without shame BECAUSE OF THE MERIT OF A SON LIKE YOU WHO STUDIES BOTH TORAHS.

221. פָּתַח כְּמִלְּקַדְּמִין, רִבִּי אֶלְעָזָר וְאָמַר, גַּם צִפּוֹר מָצְאָה בַיִת, דָּא יִתְרוֹ. וּדְרוֹר קֵן לָהּ, דָּא בְּנוֹי, דַּהֲווֹ בְּלִשְׁכַּת הַגָּזִית, אוּלְפֵי אוֹרַיְיתָא, וְחַתְכִין מִלִּין דְּאוֹרַיְיתָא בְּפוּמַיְיהוּ. מָצְאָה בַיִת מַהוּ. אֶלָּא בְּקַדְמֵיתָא נַטְלוּ וְשָׁארוּ בְּמַדְבְּרָא, נַטְלוּ מֵעִנּוּגָא דְּמִדְיָן, וּמִמְּתִיקוּ דְּתַמָּן, וְשָׁרוּ בְּמַדְבְּרָא. כֵּיוָן דְּחָמָא קוּדְשָׁא בְּרִיךְ הוּא, דְּעַל אוֹרַיְיתָא הֲוָה כִּסּוּפָא

דִּלְהוֹן, מַשִׁיךְ לוֹן מִתַּמָּן, וְאָעִיל לוֹן לְלִשְׁכַּת הַגָּזִית. וּדְרוֹר קֵן לָהּ, כֹּלָּא חַד. צִפּוֹר דְּרוֹר כֹּלָּא אִיהוּ חַד. חֶבֶר הַקֵּינִי. וַיֹּאמֶר שָׁאוּל אֶל הַקֵּינִי וְגוֹ׳.

221. Rabbi Elazar spoke again saying, "Even the sparrow has found a home" refers to Jethro. "And the swallow (Heb. *dror*) a nest for herself": That is his sons, who were in Cell of Gazith studying Torah, and decree Torah laws with their lips. "Find a home": What is the meaning of that? HE RESPONDS: It is because they journeyed and camped in the desert at first, then traveled from the pleasures of Midian and from their sweet life there and camped in the desert. When the Holy One, blessed be He, noticed their desire for Torah, He drew them from there and gave them a place in the Cell of Gazith. "And the swallow a nest for herself" is all one and the same, because a sparrow and swallow are both one and the same bird. AND NEST (HEB. *KEN*) IS LIKE: "Heber the Kenite" (Shoftim 4:17), and: "And Saul said to the Kenites" (I Shmuel 15:6).

222. ת״ח, מַה כְּתִיב, וַיַּרְא בָּלָק בֶּן צִפּוֹר. וְכִי מַאי שְׁנָא דְּאַדְכִּיר שְׁמָא דַּאֲבוֹי מִשְּׁאַר מַלְכִּין. אֶלָּא יִתְרוֹ אִתְמְשַׁךְ וְאִתְעֲבַר מע״ז, וְאָתָא לְאִתְדַּבְּקָא בְּיִשְׂרָאֵל, הוּא וּבְנוֹי, וְכָל עָלְמָא נַדּוּהוּ וְרַדְפוּ אֲבַתְרֵיהּ.

222. Come and see what is written: "And Balak the son of Tzipor saw." Why the difference that his father's name is mentioned rather than the rest of the other kings OF MIDIAN WHO DID NOT HAVE THEIR FATHER'S NAMES MENTIONED? HE RESPONDS: It is only because Jethro drew himself away and was removed from idol worship, and he together with his children approached Yisrael to join with them. The whole world excommunicated him and persecuted him.

223. בָּלָק מִבְּנֵי בְּנוֹי הֲוָה, וְאִתְעֲבַר מֵאָרְחָא דַּאֲבוֹי, כֵּיוָן דְּחָמוּ סָבֵי מוֹאָב וְסָבֵי מִדְיָן, דַּהֲווֹ בַּהֲדֵי הֲדָדֵי בְּאַחֲוָה דִּלְהוֹן בע״ז, בְּחוּלָקָא דִּלְהוֹן, דְּיִתְרוֹ וּבְנוֹי אִתְדַּבְּקוּ בִּשְׁכִינְתָּא, וְדָא אִתְמְשַׁךְ מִנַּהוֹן. אָתוּ וְאַמְלְכוּהוּ עֲלַיְיהוּ בְּהַאי שַׁעֲתָא, דִּכְתִּיב וּבָלָק בֶּן צִפּוֹר מֶלֶךְ לְמוֹאָב בָּעֵת הַהִיא. בָּעֵת הַהִיא הֲוָה מֶלֶךְ, מַה דְּלָא הֲוָה מִקַּדְמַת דְּנָא. וְעַל

דָּא כְּתִיב בֶּן צִפּוֹר, מַה דְּלָא אִתְחֲזֵי לְמֶעְבַּד הָכִי. וַיַּרְא בָּלָק, וַיִּשְׁמַע מִבָּעֵי לֵיהּ, מַהוּ וַיַּרְא. רְאִיָּיה חָמָא, וְיָדַע דְּזַמִּין הוּא לְמִנְפַּל בִּידָא דְּיִשְׂרָאֵל, וְיִשְׂרָאֵל לְמִנְפַּל בִּידוֹי בְּקַדְמֵיתָא, וּלְבָתַר אִיהוּ בִּידָא דְּיִשְׂרָאֵל, וַיַּרְא בָּלָק בֶּן צִפּוֹר.

223. Balak was from the descendants OF JETHRO and deviated from the ways of his father. When the elders of Moab and the elders of Midian, who were friends in their idol worship, saw that Jethro and his descendants adhered to the Shechinah, this one distanced himself from them. They came and crowned him king over them at that time, as is written: “And Balak the son of Tzipor was king of Moab at that time.” At that time, he was the king, something that he was not before then. Therefore, it is written: “the son of Tzipor” THAT ALLUDES TO JETHRO WHO WAS CALLED ‘TZIPOR’ TO INDICATE that it was not proper to do so, BECAUSE HE WAS FROM THE DESCENDANTS OF JETHRO CALLED ‘TZIPOR’. HE INQUIRES: It says, “And Balak...saw,” but it should have said ‘heard’. What is the meaning here of: “saw”? HE RESPONDS: He saw a vision and he knew that he will fall into the hands of Yisrael. Yisrael will first fall into his hands and only afterward would he fall into Yisrael’s hands. That is the reason it says: “And Balak the son of Tzipor saw.”

17. "If you know not, O you fairest among women"

A Synopsis

Rabbi Aba wonders about the meaning of Congregation, and Rabbi Shimon explains that sometimes the female, Malchut, is called Congregation; this means that she receives many blessings from above but slows down the flow to the lower grades because she finds so little faith there. Wherever she finds a little faith she drips a little dew. If the faith were as great as it is in her, the blessings would have flowed in every direction. Those people who have no faith delay the gifts from being provided below. Rabbi Shimon tells what happens when Yisrael sins, and he talks about the destruction of the two temples and the two exiles to Babylon and Edom. We hear that the Shechinah wonders how she will be able to feed her children in exile from the dew and water of Chassadim at a time when Judgment prevails. Rabbi Shimon says that Zeir Anpin tells her to gain strength for herself by listening to the children who study the Torah. Another explanation of the verse under discussion is that the Shechinah behaves kindly to her children in great secrecy. The rabbis talk about Yisrael (the son) acting rebelliously toward the Father in heaven. Finally we hear that Balak and the Amorites wanted to destroy Yisrael because Yisrael took their land and made it into pasture for their herds.

224. רִבִּי אַבָּא פָּתַח, אִם לֹא תֵדְעִי לָךְ הַיָּפָה בַּנָּשִׁים צְאִי לָךְ בְּעִקְבֵי הַצֹּאן. כְּנִישְׁתָּא דְיִשְׂרָאֵל אַמְרַת לְגַבֵּי מַלְכָּא עִלָּאָה. כְּנִישְׁתָּא דְיִשְׂרָאֵל, מַהוּ כְּנִישְׁתָּא. דָא אִיהוּ עֲצֶרֶת, כְּנִישׁוּ. כד״א, מְאַסֵּף לְכָל הַמַּחֲנוֹת. מַאן דְּכָנִישׁ לְכָל מַשְׁרְיָין עִלָּאִין לְגַבֵּיהּ.

224. Rabbi Aba opened the discussion with the verse: "If you know not, O you fairest among women, go your way forth by the footsteps of the flock" (Shir Hashirim 1:8). The Congregation of Yisrael spoke in this manner in the presence of the King up high. The Congregation of Yisrael? What is the meaning of this congregation? HE RESPONDS: That is the assembly, meaning the gathering, as it says, "Which was the rearward (gatherer) of all the camps" (Bemidbar 10:25), since it assembles to her all the higher camps, MEANING MALCHUT WHICH RECEIVES FROM ALL THE FIRST NINE SFIROT.

225. וּמִגּוֹ דִּלְזִמְנִין נוּקְבָּא אִקְרֵי כְּנִישְׁתָּא, וְאִתְּמַר עֲצֶרֶת, כד״א כִּי

עָצוֹר עָצַר יְיָ׳, דְּנָקִיט וְלָא יָהִיב. הָכִי הוּא וַדַּאי, דְּהָא מִגּוֹ מְהֵימְנוּ סַגְּיָא דִּילָהּ, דְּלָא אַשְׁכְּחָן בָּהּ מוּמָא, יָהֲבוּ לָהּ בְּלָא עִכּוּבָא כְּלָל. וְאִיהִי כַּד מָטָא לְגַבָּהּ, כָּל מַאן דִּכְנִישַׁת, עָצַר וּמְעָצֵר וּמְעַכֶּבֶת, דְּלָא נָחִית וְנָהִיר, אֶלָּא כְּפוּם טַלָּא, טִפִּין טִפִּין, זְעֵיר זְעֵיר. מ״ט. בְּגִין דְּלָא אִשְׁתְּכַח לְתַתָּא מְהֵימְנוּתָא, אֶלָּא כד״א, זְעֵיר שָׁם זְעֵיר שָׁם, זְעֵיר זְכוּתָא, וּזְעֵיר אַנְהֲרוּתָא דְּטַלָּא, מִדָּה לָקֳבֵל מִדָּה.

225. Sometimes the female, WHICH IS MALCHUT, is called by the name 'congregation', and it says ABOUT HER "assembly." THAT IS DERIVED FROM WITHHOLDING, as it says, "For Hashem has fast closed" (Beresheet 20:18), WHICH MEANS she receives and does not provide. So it is certain that, due to her great faith, there is no fault in her. She, MALCHUT, is granted without any delay and when THE ABUNDANCE reaches her, she holds in all that she gathered in, and slows down and delays it so it should not fall and shine, but rather, only as dew, drop by drop, bit by bit. What is the reason? Because she finds no faith below, except as it says: "Here a little, and there a little" (Yeshayah 28:13), MEANING a little merit and a little illumination, JUST LIKE dew, measure for measure.

226. דְּאִלְמָלֵא תִּשְׁכַּח מְהֵימְנוּתָא, כְּמָה דְּאִשְׁתְּכָחוּ בָּהּ, אֲרִיקַת בְּכָל סִטְרָא וְסִטְרָא, בְּלָא עִכּוּבָא כְּלַל, וְאִיהִי חַדָּאת. וּכְדֵין יָהֲבִין לָהּ מַתְּנָן וּנְבִזְבְּזָן סַגִּיאִין דָּא עַל דָּא, וְלָא יְהוֹן מְעַכְּבִין לָהּ כְּלַל. אֲבָל תַּתָּאִין אִינּוּן מְעַכְּבִין לוֹן, וּמְעַכְּבִין לָהּ, וּכְדֵין אִיהִי עֲצֶרֶת. עָצוֹר עָצַר יְיָ׳ וַדַּאי, כִּבְיָכוֹל, יָהִיב תַּמְצִית, וְלָא יַתִּיר.

226. If there would have been faith IN THE WORLD as it prevails in her, IN MALCHUT, it would have flowed in every direction, BOTH CHOCHMAH ON THE LEFT SIDE AND CHESED ON THE RIGHT SIDE, without any delay at all. She would have been glad and then she would have received many presents and gifts one on top of another, MEANING ONE GIFT AFTER ANOTHER, and nothing would be held back from her. However, the lower beings, IF THEY LACK FAITH, delay these GIFTS, WHICH SHOULD BE SUPPLIED IN ABUNDANCE TO MALCHUT. As a result, they hold back MALCHUT FROM PROVIDING FOR THE LOWER BEINGS. At that point, she is referred to as "*atzeret* (lit. 'assembly')." "For Hashem has fast closed (Heb. *atzar*)," He so to speak is giving the residue and nothing more.

227. ועכ"ד כְּאִימָּא יָהֲבַת לִבְנִין בִּטְמִירוּ, דְּלָא יַדְעִין בָּהּ, הָכִי עֲבִידַת לוֹן לִבְנָהָא יִשְׂרָאֵל. וְאוֹלִיפְנָא מִגּוֹ בּוּצִינָא קַדִּישָׁא, דִּבְשַׁעֲתָא דְּאִיהִי סְלִיקַת לְמִנְקַט עִנּוּגִין וְכִסּוּפִין, וּמוּמָא אִשְׁתְּכַח בְּהוּ בְּיִשְׂרָאֵל לְתַתָּא, כְּדֵין מָטֵי לְגַבָּהּ טִפָּה דְּחַרְדָּל וּמִיַּד אַעְדִּיאַת, וְיָתִיבַת עָלָהּ יוֹמִין בְּמִנְיָן. וּכְדֵין יַדְעִין לְעֵילָּא, דְּמוּמָא בְּהוּ בְּיִשְׂרָאֵל.

227. Notwithstanding all this, as a mother who provides for her children in secret so no one should notice her, so MALCHUT acts to her children, to Yisrael. I learned from the holy luminary that, when MALCHUT ascends to receive the pleasures and delights, but fault exists in Yisrael below, a tiny drop of BLOOD, AS a mustard seed, reaches her and immediately HER DOMINATION is removed. She dwells over it for several days; then they are aware above that there is fault with Yisrael.

228. וְאִתְּעַר שְׂמָאלָא מִיַּד, וּמָשִׁיךְ חוּטָא לְתַתָּא. וַתִּכְהֶיןָ עֵינָיו מֵרְאוֹת, מַה דַּהֲוָה מִסְתַּכַּל בְּעֵין שְׁפִירוּ, בִּכְלָלָא דְּאַבְרָהָם, בְּלָא דִּינָא כְּלַל, כְּדֵין וַתִּכְהֶיןָ עֵינָיו מֵרְאוֹת, מֵרְאוֹת וַדַּאי, מִלְּאִסְתַּכְּלָא בִּכְלָלָא דְּרַחֲמָנוּ. כְּדֵין אַתְּעֲרוּ דְּסָמָאֵ"ל בְּקָל תַּקִּיף, לְאִתְּעָרָא עַל עָלְמָא. כד"א וַיִּקְרָא אֶת עֵשָׂו בְּנוֹ הַגָּדוֹל וְגוֹ'. גָּדוֹל אִיהוּ לְגַבֵּי מַשִׁרְיָין דְּסִטְרָא אַחֲרָא, אִיהוּ גָּדוֹל, וְנָהִיג לְכָל אַרְבִּין דְּיַמָּא, דְּעַרְעִירָן בְּרוּחָא בִּישָׁא, לְאַטְבְּעָא לוֹן בְּעוּמְקָא דְּיַמָּא, בְּאִינּוּן מְצוּלוֹת יָם דִּילֵיהּ.

228. The left is awakened instantly, pulls a string below, "and his eyes were dim, so that he could not see" (Beresheet 27:1). Whereas he observed PREVIOUSLY with a favorable eye, in the sense of Abraham, THAT IS CHESED, without any Judgment at all, now "his eyes were dim, so that he could not see." "See": From seeing definitely, which means from looking at it with a sense of Mercy. Then there is an awakening of Samael in a strong voice to stir accusations on the world, as is said: "He called Esau, his eldest (bigger) son" (Ibid.). He is bigger, towards the camps of the Other Side he is great, and steers all the ships in the ocean that meet the evil wind, to sink them into the depth of his ocean.

229. וְכַד קוּדְשָׁא בְּרִיךְ הוּא הוּא בְּרַחֲמָנוּ, כְּדֵין כָּל חֲטָאִין וְכָל חוֹבִין דְּיִשְׂרָאֵל, יָהִיב לֵיהּ, וְאִיהוּ אַטִּיל לוֹן לִמְצוּלוֹת יָם. כָּל מַשִׁרְיָין דִּילֵיהּ מְצוּלוֹת יָם אִקְרוּן, וְאִינּוּן נַטְלֵי לוֹן, וּמְשַׁטְטֵי בְּהוֹן לְכָל שְׁאַר עַמִּין. וְכִי חֲטָאִין דְּיִשְׂרָאֵל, וְחוֹבִין דִּלְהוֹן, זַרְקִין וּמִתְפַּלְגִין לְעַמָּא דִּלְהוֹן. אֶלָּא, אִינּוּן מְחַכָּאן וּמְצַפָּאן לְמַתְּנָן דִּלְעֵילָּא, כְּכַלְבֵּי לְקַמֵּי פָּתוֹרָא. וְכַד קוּדְשָׁא בְּרִיךְ הוּא נָטִיל כָּל חוֹבַיְיהוּ דְּיִשְׂרָאֵל, וְזָרִיק עֲלַיְיהוּ, כֻּלְּהוּ חַשְׁבֵי דְּמַתְּנָן וּנְבִזְבְּזָן דְּאִיהוּ בָּעָא לְמֵיהַב לְיִשְׂרָאֵל, דְּאַעְבַּר מִנַּיְיהוּ, וְיָהִב לוֹן. וּמִיַּד כֻּלְּהוּ כַּחֲדָא זַרְקִין לוֹן עַל שְׁאַר עַמִּין.

229. When the Holy One, blessed be He, is in a state of Mercy, He hands him over all the sins and iniquities of Yisrael. He throws them into the depths of the sea, MEANING TO HIS CAMPS, since all his camps are called the depths of the sea. They take them and wander with them to all the rest of the nations. HE INQUIRES: Do the sins of Yisrael and their iniquities get thrown and divided to their nations? AND WHY SHOULD THEY DO THIS? HE RESPONDS: It is only because they wait and look for the gifts from above like dogs at the table. When the Holy One, blessed be He, takes all the sins of Yisrael and throws them to them, they all immediately think that the gifts and presents that were meant to be given to Yisrael were removed from Yisrael and were granted to them. Immediately, they all together throw them to all other nations.

230. ת"ח, כְּנִישְׁתָּא דְּיִשְׂרָאֵל, אִיהִי אַמְרַת בְּקַדְמֵיתָא, שְׁחוֹרָה אֲנִי וְנָאוָה, אַזְעִירַת גַּרְמָהּ לְקַמֵּי מַלְכָּא עִלָּאָה. וּכְדֵין שְׁאִילַת מִנֵּיהּ וְאַמְרַת, הַגִּידָה לִי שֶׁאָהֲבָה נַפְשִׁי אֵיכָה תִרְעֶה אֵיכָה תַּרְבִּיץ בַּצָּהֳרָיִם. תְּרֵין זִמְנִין אֵיכָה אֵיכָה אֲמַאי. אֶלָּא אִיהִי רְמִיזָא עַל תְּרֵין חָרְבְּנִין, דִּתְרֵין מִקְדָּשִׁין. דְּקָרָאן כֹּלָּא אֵיכָה אֵיכָה. אֵיכָה תִרְעֶה, בְּחָרְבַּן בַּיִת רִאשׁוֹן. אֵיכָה תַּרְבִּיץ, בְּחָרְבַּן בַּיִת שֵׁנִי. וְעַ"ד תְּרֵין זִמְנִין אֵיכָה אֵיכָה.

230. Come and see the Congregation of Yisrael. She said at first, "I am black, but comely" (Shir Hashirim 1:5). She diminished herself before the Supernal King up high and asked of Him, saying, "Tell me, O you whom my soul loves, where (Heb. *Eichah*) you feed, where you make your flock rest at noon" (Ibid. 7). HE INQUIRES: Why twice "*Eichah* (lit. 'how')"? HE RESPONDS: It is only that they are alluding to the two destructions of the two Temples. When everybody reads the scriptural verses of *Eichah*, *Eichah* – "where you feed" at the destruction of the first Temple and "where you make your flock rest" at the destruction of the second Temple. Therefore, it is written twice – *Eichah*, *Eichah*.

231. תִרְעֶה תַּרְבִּיץ, לָאו דָּא כְּדָא. גָּלוּתָא דְּבָבֶל, דְּאִיהִי זְמַן זְעֵיר, קָארֵי בֵּיהּ תִרְעֶה. וְעַל גָּלוּתָא דֶּאֱדוֹם, דְּאִיהוּ זְמַן סַגִּי, קָארֵי בֵּיהּ תַּרְבִּיץ. וְעַ"ד תְּרֵין זִמְנִין אֵיכָה אֵיכָה. וְתוּ תִרְעֶה תַּרְבִּיץ, יִרְעֶה מִבָּעֵי לֵיהּ, יַרְבִּיץ מִבָּעֵי לֵיהּ אוּף הָכִי, דְּהָא עַל יִשְׂרָאֵל אַמְרַת. אֶלָּא אִיהִי אַמְרַת עַל נַפְשָׁהּ אֵיכָה תִרְעֶה כַּלָּתְךָ לִבְנָהָא בְּגָלוּתָא, דִּיהוֹן בֵּין שְׁאַר עַמִּין. אֵיכָה תַּרְבִּיץ בַּצָּהֳרָיִם, הֵיךְ תַּטִּיף אִיהִי עֲלַיְיהוּ טַלִּין וּמַיִין, גּוֹ חֲמִימוּ דְּצָהֳרַיִם.

231. HE INQUIRES: "You feed" and "you make rest." One is not like the other. WHAT IS THE DIFFERENCE BETWEEN THEM? HE REPLIES: The Babylonian exile was for a short period, and it calls it: "you feed." About the Edomite exile, which is for a prolonged period, it calls it: "you make rest." Therefore, two times *Eichah, Eichah*. Another reason: "You (also: 'she will') feed" and "you make rest" should have read: 'he feeds' and 'he makes rest', since it refers to Yisrael. HE RESPONDS: Only that She, THE SHECHINAH, said it about Herself, *Eichah*, how will Your bride THAT IS THE SHECHINAH feed Her children in exile, when they will be among the other nations? How will She make rest, drip upon them dew and water, MEANING CHASSADIM, in the heat of high noon, MEANING AT A TIME WHEN JUDGMENTS ARE DOMINANT?

232. שַׁלָּמָה אֶהְיֶה כְּעוֹטְיָה, בְּשַׁעֲתָא דְּיִשְׂרָאֵל קָרָאן מִגּוֹ עָאקוּ, דְּחִיקוּ דִּלְהוֹן, וּשְׁאַר עַמִּין מְחָרְפִין וּמְגַדְּפִין לוֹן, אֵימָתַי תִּפְקוּן מִן גָּלוּתָא. אֱלָהֲכוֹן הֵיךְ לָא עָבֵיד לְכוֹן נִסִּין. וַאֲנָא יָתִיב כְּעוֹטְיָה, וְלָא יָכִילַת לְמֶעְבַּד לוֹן נִסִּין, וּלְמֵיהַב לוֹן נוּקְמִין. אִיהוּ אָתִיב לְגַבָּהּ, אִם לֹא תֵדְעִי לָךְ הַיָּפָה בַּנָּשִׁים. הַאי קְרָא הָכִי מִבָּעֵי לֵיהּ, אִם לֹא תֵדְעִי הַיָּפָה בַּנָּשִׁים. לָךְ אַמַּאי. אֶלָּא אִם לֹא תֵדְעִי לָךְ: לְאַתְקְפָא גַּרְמָךְ בְּגָלוּתָא,

וּלְאִתְּקְפָא חֵילָא, לְאַגָּנָא עַל בְּנָךְ. צְאִי לָךְ, צְאִי לָךְ לְאִתְּקְפָא בְּעִקְבֵי הַצֹּאן. אִינּוּן תִּינוֹקוֹת דְּבֵי רַבָּן, דְּאוֹלְפֵי תּוֹרָה.

232. "Why should I be like one who cloaks himself" (Ibid.), meaning when Yisrael call UPON THE HOLY ONE, BLESSED BE HE, from their distress and sorrow? The rest of the nations curse and insult them: When will you leave this exile? Why does your Elohim not perform any miracles for you? But I sit like one cloaked who cannot perform miracles for them and take revenge ON THEIR ENEMIES. He, ZEIR ANPIN, replies to her, "If you know not (lit. 'for yourself'), O you fairest among women" (Ibid. 8). He asks, What is the meaning of: "for yourself"? And he answers, "If you know not for yourself" MEANS IF YOU KNOW NOT how to gain the strength for yourself in this exile and be strengthened with power to guard over your children. Get out and be strengthened "by the footsteps of the flock" (Ibid.): This refers to the children in their master's schools, who learn and study Torah. FROM THEM, YOU WILL TAKE THE STRENGTH TO PROTECT YOUR CHILDREN.

233. וּרְעִי אֶת גְּדִיּוֹתַיִךְ, אִלֵּין עַתִּיקֵי מִשָּׁדַיִם, דְּקָא מִסְתַּלְּקֵי מֵעָלְמָא וְאִתְמַשְׁכָן לְבֵי מְתִיבְתָּא עִלָּאָה, דְּאִיהִי עַל מִשְׁכְּנוֹת הָרוֹעִים, עַל דַּיְיקָא, בְּמִשְׁכְּנוֹת הָרוֹעִים לָא כְּתִיב, אֶלָּא עַל מִשְׁכְּנוֹת הָרוֹעִים, דָּא מְתִיבְתָּא דְּמְטַטְרוֹ"ן, דְּתַמָּן כָּל תַּקִּיפִין וִינוּקִין דְּעָלְמָא, וּמַנְהִיגֵי אוֹרַיְיתָא בְּהַאי עָלְמָא בְּאִיסוּר וְהֶיתֵּר, בְּכָל מַה דְּאִצְטְרִיכוּ בְּנֵי עָלְמָא, דְּהָא עִקְבֵי הַצֹּאן אִינּוּן תִּינוֹקוֹת כִּדְאַמָרָן.

233. "And feed your kids" (Ibid.): These are the ones who were "removed from the breasts" (Yeshayah 28:9), who died and were drawn to the upper Yeshivah, which is, "besides (lit. 'above) the shepherds' tents" (Shir Hashirim 1:8). "Above" is precise. It does not say, 'By the shepherds' tents', but "above the shepherds' tents" that refers to the Yeshivah of Metatron THAT IS ABOVE THE SHEPHERDS' TENTS IN THIS WORLD, SINCE THE SHEPHERDS, WHO ARE THE LEADERS IN THIS WORLD, GO UP THERE AFTER THEIR DEMISE. There are all the powerful and children of the world, and the leaders in the Torah, who guide in matters of the forbidden and permitted of this world, and all the matters necessary for people. THEREFORE, THEY ARE REFERRED TO AS SHEPHERDS, since "the footsteps of the flock" refers to the children, as we explained. THE "SHEPHERDS" REFER TO THE LEADERS OF THE WORLD.

234. אָמַר ר׳ אֶלְעָזָר, עִקְבֵי הַצֹּאן, אִינּוּן תַּלְמִידֵי דְּבֵי רַב, דְּקָא אַתְיָין לְבָתַר בְּעָלְמָא, וְאַשְׁכְּחָן אוֹרַיְיתָא בְּאֹרַח מֵישָׁר, וְאוֹרְחָא פְּתִיחָא, וְעַל דָּא אִינּוּן מְחַדְּשָׁן מִלִּין עַתִּיקִין בְּכָל יוֹמָא, וּשְׁכִינְתָּא שַׁרְיָיא עֲלַיְיהוּ, וְצַיְיתָא לְמִלַּיְיהוֹן, כד״א וַיַּקְשֵׁב יְיָ׳ וַיִּשְׁמָע. אָמַר ר׳ אַבָּא, הָכִי הוּא וַדַּאי, וְכֹלָּא חַד מִלָּה.

234. Rabbi Elazar said, "The footsteps of the flock" are the students in the Torah academy who come afterward to the world and find the Torah in a straight open coax. Therefore, they renew ancient insights every day, and the Shechinah rests on them and listens to their words. It is written: "And Hashem hearkened, and heard it" (Malachi 3:16). Rabbi Aba said, That definitely is the case, and it all amounts to the same thing.

235. ד״א אִם לֹא תֵדְעִי לָךְ. לָךְ לָמָּה. אֶלָּא בְּכָל אֲתַר דְּיִשְׂרָאֵל בְּגָלוּתָא, אִיהִי עִמְּהוֹן בְּגָלוּתָא. וְעַ״ד כְּתִיב לָךְ, וּכְתִיב בְּכָל צָרָתָם לוֹ צָר. וְדָא הוּא לָךְ. הַיָּפָה בַּנָּשִׁים, הַיָּפָה, אִיהִי אַמְרַת דְּאִיהִי אוּכְּמְתָּא, כד״א שְׁחוֹרָה אֲנִי. וְאִיהוּ אָמַר לְגַבָּהּ, יָפָה אַתְּ, שַׁפִּירְתָּא, הַיָּפָה בַּנָּשִׁים, שַׁפִּירְתָּא אִיהִי עַל כָּל דַּרְגִּין, וּכְתִיב יָפָה אַתְּ רַעְיָתִי.

235. Another explanation of: "If you know not for yourself." Why "for yourself"? It is that wherever Yisrael are in exile, THE SHECHINAH is with them in exile. It is therefore written, "for yourself." It is also written: "In all their afflictions He is afflicted (lit. 'there is affliction for Him')" (Yeshayah 63:9). Hence, it says "for yourself," MEANING FOR YOUR SAKE, SINCE SHE TOO IS IN EXILE. "You fairest among women," "fairest": she said she was black, as it says: "I am black," and he says to her: you are comely, "you fairest among women," meaning she is prettier than all the levels, and: "You are fair, my love" (Shir Hashirim 1:15).

236. ד״א הַיָּפָה בַּנָּשִׁים, טַבְתָּא בְּטִיבוּ. דַּעֲבִידַת טִיבוּ לִבְנָהָא, בְּטְמִירוּ בִּגְנִיזוּ. וְקוּדְשָׁא בְּרִיךְ הוּא סַגִּי טָב עֲלֵיהּ, כָּל מַה דַּעֲבִידַת לִבְנָהָא

בְּטְמִירוּ בִּגְנִיזוּ, אע״ג דְּלָא מְכַשְׁרָן עוֹבָדִין. מִכָּאן דְּאִתְחֲזֵי לְאַבָּא כַּד אִמָּא רַחֲמָא עַל בְּנִין וְתָאִיב עָלֵיהּ כָּל מַה דְּעַבְדַּת לִבְנָהָא רַחֲמִין בְּטְמִירוּ אע״ג דְּלָא מְכַשְׁרָן עוֹבָדוֹי.

236. Another explanation for: "You fairest among women" means that She is good with kindness and that She is kind to Her children in a secret and hidden manner. The Holy One, blessed be He, is very good to Her for all She does for Her children in a secretly and hidden way, although deeds are improper.

237. אָמַר ר׳ אַבָּא, תַּוַּוהְנָא עַל הַהוּא דִּכְתִּיב כִּי יִהְיֶה לְאִישׁ בֵּן סוֹרֵר וּמוֹרֶה וְגוֹ׳, וְתָפְשׂוּ בוֹ אָבִיו וְאִמּוֹ וְגוֹ׳, וְתָנֵינָן, דִּבְהַהִיא שַׁעֲתָא אָמַר קוּדְשָׁא בְּרִיךְ הוּא לְמֹשֶׁה כְּתוֹב. אָמַר לֵיהּ מֹשֶׁה, מָארֵיהּ דְּעָלְמָא, שְׁבִיק דָּא, אִית אַבָּא דְּעָבֵיד כְּדֵין לִבְרֵיהּ. וּמֹשֶׁה מֵרַחִיק הֲוָה חָמֵי בְּחָכְמְתָא, כָּל מַה דְּזַמִּין קוּדְשָׁא בְּרִיךְ הוּא לִבְנֵי יִשְׂרָאֵל. אָמַר, מָארֵיהּ דְּעָלְמָא, שְׁבוֹק מִלָּה דָּא. א״ל קוּדְשָׁא בְּרִיךְ הוּא לְמֹשֶׁה, חֲמֵינָא מַה דְּאַתְּ אָמֵר, כְּתוֹב וְקַבֵּל אַגְרָא. אַתְּ יַדְעַת וַאֲנָא יְדַע יַתִּיר. מַה דְּאַתְּ חָמֵי, עָלַי הַהוּא עוֹבָדָא. דְּרוֹשׁ קְרָא וְתִשְׁכַּח.

237. Rabbi Aba said, I wonder about the verse, "If a man have a stubborn and rebellious son, who will not obey the voice of his father, or the voice of his mother, and that, when they have chastened him, will not hearken to them: then shall his father and his mother lay hold of him" (Devarim 21:18). We were taught that when the Holy One, blessed be He, said this to Moses, that he write, MEANING, RECORD THE EPISODE OF THE STUBBORN AND THE REBELLIOUS SON, Moses said to him, Master of the universe Leave this alone. Is there then a father who could do this to his son? Moses saw in advance with his wisdom everything that the Holy One, blessed be He, will do to Yisrael, MEANING TO SAY THAT HE OBSERVED THIS FROM A DISTANCE. HE NOTICED THAT THIS EPISODE OF THE STUBBORN AND REBELLIOUS SON ALLUDES TO THE MANNER THAT THE HOLY ONE, BLESSED BE HE, WILL DEAL WITH YISRAEL. THEREFORE, he said, Master of the universe, leave this thing. And the Holy One, blessed be He, replied to Moses, 'I see what you are saying, but write it down and receive your wages. You know but I know more. Whatever you see, it is for Me to act. Explain that passage through homiletical discourse, but forget ITS SECRET.'

238. בְּהַהוּא שַׁעֲתָא רָמַז לֵיהּ לְיוֹפִיאֵ"ל, רַבָּנָא דְאוֹרַיְיתָא, אָמַר לְמֹשֶׁה, אֲנָא דָרִישְׁנָא לְהַאי קְרָא כְּתִיב כִּי יִהְיֶה לְאִישׁ, דָּא קוּדְשָׁא בְּרִיךְ הוּא, דִּכְתִּיב יְיָ' אִישׁ מִלְחָמָה. בֵּן, דָּא יִשְׂרָאֵל. סוֹרֵר וּמוֹרֶה, דִּכְתִּיב כִּי כְּפָרָה סוֹרֵרָה סָרַר יִשְׂרָאֵל. אֵינֶנּוּ שׁוֹמֵעַ בְּקוֹל אָבִיו וּבְקוֹל אִמּוֹ, דָּא קוּדְשָׁא בְּרִיךְ הוּא וּכְנֶסֶת יִשְׂרָאֵל. וְיִסְּרוּ אוֹתוֹ, דִּכְתִּיב, וַיָּעַד יְיָ' בְּיִשְׂרָאֵל וּבִיהוּדָה בְּיַד כָּל נְבִיאֵי כָּל חוֹזֶה וְגוֹ'. וְלֹא שָׁמַע אֲלֵיהֶם, דִּכְתִּיב וְלֹא יִשְׁמְעוּ אֶל יְיָ' וְגוֹ'. וְתָפְשׂוּ בוֹ אָבִיו וְאִמּוֹ, בְּדַעְתָּא חֲדָא. בְּהַסְכָּמָה חֲדָא.

238. At that moment, He gestured to THE ANGEL Yofiel, the chief minister of the Torah. YOFIEL said to Moses, I explained this verse. The words: "If a man have" refer to the Holy One, blessed be He, as it says: "Hashem is a man of war" (Shemot 15:3). The son, which is Yisrael; "stubborn and rebellious," as is written: "For Yisrael is headstrong like a headstrong heifer" (Hoshea 4:16). "Who will not obey the voice of his father, or the voice of his mother": That is the Holy One, blessed be He, and the Congregation of Yisrael, WHICH IS MALCHUT. "When they have chastened him" is as is written: "Then Hashem testified against Yisrael, and against Judah, by all the prophets, and by all the seers..." (II Melachim 17:13). "Will not hearken to them," as is written: "Yet they would not hear..."; "then shall his father and his mother lay hold of him," meaning with the same mind and agreement.

239. וְהוֹצִיאוּ אוֹתוֹ אֶל זִקְנֵי עִירוֹ וְאֶל שַׁעַר מְקוֹמוֹ. אֶל זִקְנֵי עִירוֹ, אֶל זִקְנֵי עִירָם, וְאֶל שַׁעַר מְקוֹמָם, מִבָּעֵי לֵיהּ, מַאי אֶל זִקְנֵי עִירוֹ, וְאֶל שַׁעַר מְקוֹמוֹ. אֶלָּא, אֶל זִקְנֵי עִירוֹ, דָּא קוּדְשָׁא בְּרִיךְ הוּא, וְאֶל שַׁעַר מְקוֹמוֹ, דָּא כְּנֶסֶת יִשְׂרָאֵל. זִקְנֵי עִירוֹ, אִלֵּין יוֹמִין קַדְמָאִין, יוֹמִין עַתִּיקִין דְּכֹלָּא. שַׁעַר מְקוֹמוֹ, דָּא מוּסַף שַׁבָּת.

239. "And bring him out to the elders of his city, and to the gate of his place" (Devarim 21:19): HE ASKS: It should have said, 'To the elders of their city'. Why "to the elders of his city"? "And to the gate of his place," why is "his" IN SINGULAR FORM? HE RESPONDS: "To the elders of his city" refers to the Holy One, blessed be He, and "to the gate of his place" refers to the Congregation of Yisrael, MALCHUT. HE EXPLAINS, "The elders of his city" refers to the ancient times, the most ancient days of all, WHICH IS THE SECRET OF THE FIRST THREE SFIROT OF ZEIR ANPIN, BEFORE WHICH JUDGMENT IS PUT. "The gates of his place": That is the Musaf (additional prayer) of Shabbat, THE FIRST THREE SFIROT OF MALCHUT THAT ARE ADDED TO HER IN THE SHABBAT.

240. ועכ״ד, אע״ג דְּכֹּלָּא יַדְעִין, דִּינָא לְעֵילָּא אִיהוּ, בְּגִין דְּבֵי דִּינָא דְּאִמָּא קְרִיבִין אִינּוּן לְיִשְׂרָאֵל, וְאַחֲדִין בְּהוּ, וְכָל קָרִיב לָא דָּאִין דִּינָא לִקְרוֹבִים, וּפָסוּל אִיהוּ לְדִינָא. בְּקַדְמֵיתָא מַה כְּתִיב, אֶל זִקְנֵי עִירוֹ וְאֶל שַׁעַר מְקוֹמוֹ, כֵּיוָן דְּחָמָא קוּדְשָׁא בְּרִיךְ הוּא דְּאִינּוּן קְרִיבִין, מִיָּד סָלִיק דִּינָא מִשַּׁעַר מְקוֹמוֹ, מַה כְּתִיב בַּתְרֵיהּ, וְאָמְרוּ אֶל זִקְנֵי עִירוֹ לְחוֹד. וְאֶל שַׁעַר מְקוֹמוֹ לָא כְּתִיב, אֶלָּא אֶל זִקְנֵי עִירוֹ.

240. Notwithstanding all this, although everyone knows that judgment is above, NEVERTHELESS HE REMOVED THE JUDGMENT FROM THE GATE OF HIS PLACE, BECAUSE the mother's court, THAT IS MALCHUT, are related to Yisrael and are attached to them. Any close relative cannot sit in trial for relatives and is disqualified to pass sentence. THEREFORE, it is first written: "to the elders of his city" and then "to the gate of his place." As soon as the Holy One, blessed be He, saw that they were related, He immediately removed the trial from "the gate of his place," THE FIRST THREE SFIROT OF MALCHUT, WHICH ARE RELATIVES. The following verse says: "And they shall say to the elders of his city." It is not written: 'to the gate of his place', but rather "to the elders of his city" alone.

241. בְּנֵינוּ זֶה וַדַּאי, וְלָאו דִּשְׁאַר עַמִּין. סוֹרֵר וּמוֹרֶה אֵינֶנּוּ שׁוֹמֵעַ בְּקוֹלֵנוּ. מַאי שְׁנָא, דְּהָא בְּקַדְמֵיתָא לָא כְּתִיב זוֹלֵל וְסוֹבֵא, וּלְבָתַר כְּתִיב זוֹלֵל וְסוֹבֵא. אֶלָּא מַאן גָּרִים לְהוּ לְיִשְׂרָאֵל, לְמֶהֱוֵי סוֹרֵר וּמוֹרֶה לְגַבֵּי אֲבוּהוֹן דְּבִשְׁמַיָּא, בְּגִין דְּאִיהוּ זוֹלֵל וְסוֹבֵא, בִּשְׁאַר עַמִּין דִּכְתִּיב וַיִּתְעָרְבוּ בַגּוֹיִם וַיִּלְמְדוּ מַעֲשֵׂיהֶם וּכְתִיב וַיֹּאכַל הָעָם וַיִּשְׁתַּחֲווּ, דְּעִקָּרָא

וִיסוֹדָא אֲכִילָה וּשְׁתִיָּה, כַּד עַבְדִּין בִּשְׁאָר עַמִּין. דָּא גָּרִים לוֹן, לְמֶהֱוֵי בֵּן סוֹרֵר וּמוֹרֶה, לְגַבֵּי אֲבוּהוֹן דִּבִשְׁמַיָּא.

241. THEY SAY ABOUT YISRAEL: "This our son" (Devarim 21:20) and no other nation "is stubborn and rebellious, he will not obey our voice" (Ibid.). HE INQUIRES: What is the change, that at first it is not written "a glutton and drunkard," and later it is written: "he is a glutton and a drunkard" (Ibid.). HE RESPONDS: What is the cause for Yisrael to be wayward and rebellious toward their Father in heaven? It is because he is a glutton and a drunkard among the rest of the nations, as it says, "But mingled among the nations, and learned their works" (Tehilim 106:35). It is also written: "And the people ate, and bowed down" (Bemidbar 25:2), since the basis and foundation is the eating and drinking, as they did WHEN THEY WERE among the rest of the nations. That caused them to be stubborn and rebellious toward their Father in heaven.

242. וְעַ"ד וּרְגָמוּהוּ כָּל אַנְשֵׁי עִירוֹ בָּאֲבָנִים. אִלֵּין כָּל שְׁאָר עַמִּין, דַּהֲווֹ מְקַלְּעִין לְהוּ בָּאֲבָנִים, וְסַתְרִין שׁוּרִין, וּמְנַתְּצִין מִגְדָּלִין, וְלָא מֵהָנֵי לוֹן כְּלוּם. כֵּיוָן דְּשָׁמַע מֹשֶׁה כְּדֵין, כָּתַב פַּרְשְׁתָּא דָּא.

242. That is why IT IS WRITTEN: "And all the men of his city shall stone him with stones" (Devarim 21:21). This refers to the rest of the nations who were aiming and hurling stones at them. They knocked down the walls and smashed the towers. ALL THIS does not benefit them at all, BECAUSE THEY COULD NOT PREVAIL AGAINST YISRAEL. When Moses heard this, he wrote this passage.

243. וְעִם כָּל דָּא הַיָּפָה בַּנָּשִׁים, טָבָא וְיַקִּירָא בְּנָשִׁים דְּעָלְמָא. צְאִי לָךְ בְּעִקְבֵי הַצֹּאן, הָא אוּקִימְנָא, אִלֵּין בָּתֵּי כְּנֵסִיּוֹת וּבָתֵּי מִדְרָשׁוֹת. וּרְעִי אֶת גְּדִיּוֹתַיִךְ, אִלֵּין יַנּוּקֵי דְּבֵי רַב, דְּלָא טָעֲמוּ טַעַם חוֹבָא בְּעָלְמָא. עַל מִשְׁכְּנוֹת הָרוֹעִים, אִלֵּין מְלַמְּדֵי תִּינוֹקוֹת וְרֵישֵׁי יְשִׁיבוֹת.

243. Notwithstanding all this, "you fairest among women," WHICH IS MALCHUT, the best and dearest among all the women in the world, "go your way forth by the footsteps of the flock." We already explained that these are the synagogues and houses of study. "And feed your kids": these are the school children who have never tasted any taste of sin. "Besides the shepherds' tents": these are the teachers of the children and the heads of the Yeshivahs.

244. ד"א עַל מִשְׁכְּנוֹת הָרוֹעִים, חָסֵר ו'. אִינּוּן בִּישִׁין, אִלֵּין מַלְכֵי הָאֱמוֹרִי, דְּנָטְלוּ יִשְׂרָאֵל אַרְעָא דִּלְהוֹן, לְרַעְיָא מִקְנֵיהוֹן, וּלְבֵי מַרְעֶה יָהַב יִשְׂרָאֵל אַרְעָא דָּא. כְּדֵין שָׁמַע בָּלָק, דְּאַרְעָא דַּהֲוַת חֲשִׁיבָא כ"כ, עָבְדוּ יִשְׂרָאֵל קְרָבָא דָּא, וְסַתְרוּ לָהּ, עַד דְּשָׁווּ לָהּ בֵּי מַרְעֶה. כְּדֵין אִשְׁתְּדַל בְּכָל מַה דְּאִשְׁתְּדַל, וְשָׁתַף בַּהֲדֵיהּ לְבִלְעָם.

244. Another explanation of: "Besides the shepherds' (Heb. *roim*) tents": the Vav is missing IN THE WORD *ROIM* AND IT IS AS IF IT SAYS *RAIM* (LIT. 'EVIL ONES'). THIS INDICATES THAT they are evil, meaning the Amorite kings, from whom Yisrael have taken the land to give pasture to their herds. And Yisrael have turned that land to pasture land. Then Balak heard that the land that was so important, Yisrael made battle over it, and so demolished it as to make it into pasture. He then strove in whatever means was at his disposal and joined Bilaam with him.

18. "Thus says Hashem"

A Synopsis

We hear about the three gates or orders of justice: Baba Kama, Baba Metzia and Baba Batra. Rabbi Shimon says that God treats the sins of the children of Yisrael as though they were errors, not intentional acts. He talks about Balak's request to Bilaam to curse Yisrael; Balak knew that many of the people of Yisrael would fall dead because of his own armies, so he felt the time was opportune for the curse. Lastly Rabbi Shimon says that neither Balak nor Bilaam were aware that they themselves would be destroyed afterward.

245. וַיַּרְא בָּלָק, רִבִּי חִזְקִיָּה פָּתַח, כֹּה אָמַר יְיָ׳ שִׁמְרוּ מִשְׁפָּט וַעֲשׂוּ צְדָקָה כִּי קְרוֹבָה יְשׁוּעָתִי וְגוֹ׳. כַּמָּה חֲבִיבִין יִשְׂרָאֵל קַמֵּי קוּדְשָׁא בְּרִיךְ הוּא, דְּאע״ג דְּאִינּוּן חָאבוּ קַמֵּיהּ, וְחָבִין קַמֵּיהּ בְּכָל זִמְנָא וְזִמְנָא, אִיהוּ עָבֵיד לוֹן לְיִשְׂרָאֵל, זְדוֹנוֹת כִּשְׁגָגוֹת.

245. "And Balak...saw": Rabbi Chizkiyah opened the discussion saying, "Thus says Hashem, 'Keep judgment, and do justice: for My salvation is near...'" (Yeshayah 56:1). How beloved are Yisrael before the Holy One, blessed be He. Although they have sinned and are sinning constantly, He accounts their premeditated sins as errors.

246. וְהָכִי אָמַר רַב הַמְנוּנָא סָבָא, תְּלַת בָּבֵי דִּינָא, תַּקִּינוּ בְּסִדְרֵי מַתְנִיתָא, חֲדָא, קַדְמֵיתָא, בְּאַרְבַּע אָבוֹת נְזִיקִין הַשּׁוֹר וְכוּ׳. תִּנְיָינָא, טַלִּית דְּאִשְׁתְּכַח. תְּלִיתָאָה, שׁוּתָּפִין וְרָזָא דַּאֲבֵידָה. מ״ט. אֶלָּא, קוּדְשָׁא בְּרִיךְ הוּא בְּכָל זִמְנָא, עָבֵיד לוֹן לְיִשְׂרָאֵל זְדוֹנוֹת כִּשְׁגָגוֹת. וְאִינּוּן דְּסִדְּרוּ מַתְנִיתִין דִּתְלָתָא בָּבֵי, הָכִי סִדְּרוּ, אֹרַח דִּקְרָא נַקְטוּ, דִּכְתִּיב עַל כָּל דְּבַר פֶּשַׁע, וְהַאי פֶּשַׁע אִיהוּ דְּלָאו בְּזָדוֹן, וּמַאן אִיהוּ. עַל שׁוֹר, עַל חֲמוֹר, עַל שֶׂה, דָּא בָּבָא קַמָּא, דְּהָכָא הוּא בְּאִינּוּן מִלִּין. עַל שַׂלְמָה, דָּא בָּבָא מְצִיעָא, עַל כָּל אֲבֵדָה, דָּא בָּבָא תְּלִיתָאָה.

246. This is how Rav Hamnuna Saba said: Three gates of justice were composedin the orders of the Mishnah. The first one is: "The four primary causes of injury are the ox etc.," WHICH IS BABA KAMA (FIRST GATE). The second gate is A garment that was found, WHICH IS BABA METZIA (THE MIDDLE GATE). The third gate is partnerships and the meaning of a lost object, WHICH IS BABA BATRA (THE LAST GATE). What is the reason? HE RESPONDS: It is only that the Holy One, blessed be He, always accounts Yisrael's premeditated sins as errors. Those who set up the orders of the Mishnah, set it up this way in three gates OF BABA KAMA, BABA METZIA, BABA BATRA, followed the manner of the scriptures: "Manner of trespass" (Shemot 22:8). That refers to an offense that is not intentional, SINCE THE HOLY ONE, BLESSED BE HE, ACCOUNTS THE INTENTIONAL CRIME AS ERRORS. What is it, "whether it be for ox, for donkey, for sheep" (Ibid.), that is the Baba Kama, where it DISCUSSES these matters. "For a garment" is Baba Metzia THAT DISCUSSES A GARMENT THAT WAS FOUND; "or for any manner of lost thing" refers to the third gate, NAMELY IS BABA BATRA.

247. דְּאֹרַח קְרָא נַקְטוּ. דְּכַד מָטָא לְבָבָא מְצִיעָא, הֲוָה אָמַר, שֵׁירוּתָא דְּקָא נַקְטוּ בְּטַלִּית דָּא, אֲמַאי. כֵּיוָן דְּאִשְׁתְּכַח קְרָא, אָמַר, וַדַּאי דָּא הֲלָכָה לְמֹשֶׁה מִסִּינַי, וּבִיאֲרוּ כָּל מִלֵּי דְּרַבָּנָן.

247. Since they picked the order of the scriptures, when RAV HAMNUNA SABA reached Baba Metzia, the middle gate, he used to say, Why did they start with the garment, BECAUSE BABA METZIA BEGINS WITH THE SITUATION WHERE TWO ARE HOLDING ON TO THE GARMENT THAT WAS FOUND. The verse: "FOR A GARMENT," he said, most definitely is articulation dating from Moses as delivered on Mount Sinai, which all the sages' discussions were explaining.

248. כֹּה אָמַר יְיָ', מ"ש בְּכָל דוּכְתָּא דִּנְבִיאֵי, דִּכְתִּיב כֹּה אָמַר יְיָ', וּבְמֹשֶׁה לָא כְּתִיב הָכִי. אֶלָּא, מֹשֶׁה דַּהֲוַת נְבִיאוּתֵיהּ מִגּוֹ אַסְפַּקְלַרְיָאה דְּנַהֲרָא דִּלְעֵילָּא, לָא כְּתִיב בֵּיהּ כֹּה. אֲבָל שְׁאַר נְבִיאִים, דַּהֲווֹ מְנַבְּאִין מִגּוֹ אַסְפַּקְלַרְיָאה דְּלָא נַהֲרָא, נְבִיאוּ מִגּוֹ כֹּה.

248. "Thus says Hashem." HE INQUIRES: What is the difference that it is always written about the prophets: "Thus (Heb. *coh*) says Hashem," yet of Moses, this language is not used, BUT RATHER "THIS (HEB. *ZEH*) IS THE WORD." HE RESPONDS: It is only because Moses' prophecy was from a shining mirror that is light from above, THAT IS ZEIR ANPIN, so it is not written of him, Coh, WHICH IS MALCHUT THAT IS REFERRED TO BY "*COH*." However, the rest of the prophets, who used to prophecy from the dim mirror, WHICH IS MALCHUT REFERRED TO BY COH, prophesied from Coh.

249. וְעַתָּה לְכָה נָּא אָרָה לִּי אֶת הָעָם הַזֶּה וְגוֹ'. וְעַתָּה, רִבִּי אֶלְעָזָר אָמַר, אָמַר הַהוּא רָשָׁע, וַדַּאי שַׁעֲתָא קַיְּימָא לִי לְמֶעְבַּד מַה דַּאֲנָא בָּעֵי. חָמָא, וְלָא חָמָא יָאוּת. חָמָא כַּמָּה אַלְפִין נַפְלִין מִיִּשְׂרָאֵל עַל יְדוֹי לִזְמַן זְעֵיר, אָמַר וַדַּאי הַשְׁתָּא שַׁעְתָּא קַיְּימֵי לִי. ובג"כ וְעַתָּה, וְלָא בִּזְמְנָא אַחֲרָא.

249. "Come now therefore, I pray you, curse me this people" (Bemidbar 22:6). HE SAYS: Rabbi Elazar says that wicked man said, Most definitely, the time is right for me to do anything I wish. He saw, but did not see completely. He saw that several thousand of Yisrael would fall dead through him in a short time. He figured, Most definitely I have the opportune moment. Therefore, HE SAID "now" and not at any other time.

250. לְכָה, לֵךְ מִבָּעֵי לֵיהּ, מַאי לְכָה. אָמַר, נִזְדָּרֵז גַּרְמַן לְהַהוּא דְּרָחִיף בְּגַדְפּוֹי עָלַיְיהוּ, לְהַהוּא דִּשְׁמֵיהּ כֹּ"ה. וְעַתָּה לְכָה, נִגַּח קְרָבָא בְּהַהוּא כֹּ"ה.

250. HE INQUIRES: "Come now (Heb. *lechah*), but he should have said *lech*. What is "*lechah* (Lamed Kaf Hei)"? HE RESPONDS: He thought, Let us hurry up AND DO BATTLE with the one who flutters his wings over them, the one that is referred to by the name "*coh* (Kaf Hei)," MEANING MALCHUT, and now is the opportune time to do battle with that Coh.

251. אָמַר, עַד הַשְׁתָּא לָא הֲוָה בְּעָלְמָא מַאן דְּיֵיכוּל לְהוּ, בְּגִין הַהוּא פַּטְרוֹנָא דְּקַיְּימָא עָלַיְיהוּ, הַשְׁתָּא דְּשַׁעְתָּא קַיְּימָא לָן, לְכֹה נַעְבֵּיד קְרָבָא. וְכָל עֵיטָא דְּהַהוּא רָשָׁע לְכֹ"ה הֲוָה, דִּכְתִּיב וְאָנֹכִי אִקָּרֶה כֹּה אַעְקַר לְהַהוּא כֹּה מֵאַתְרֵיהּ. וְתַרְוַויְיהוּ בְּעֵיטָא בִּישָׁא לְהַאי כֹּה הֲווֹ,

כד״א עַל יְיָ׳ וְעַל מְשִׁיחוֹ, לָא יָדְעוּ דְּהָא לְבָתַר, הַאי כֹּ״ה אַעְקַר לוֹן מֵעָלְמָא.

251. He thought there was nobody in the world who would succeed against them until now, because of the protector who stands over them. Now that the moment is opportune for us, let us (Heb. *lechah*) do battle with Coh. The entire counsel of that wicked one was against Coh, as is written: “While I go to the meeting yonder (*Coh*)” (Bemidbar 23:15), meaning I will uproot that Coh from its place. Both of them participated in that wicked counsel against Coh, as it is said, “Against Hashem, and against His anointed” (Tehilim 2:2). They were not aware that afterwards this Coh would uproot them from the world following that.

19. "Come now therefore, I pray you, curse me this people"

A Synopsis

The question is asked how Balak knew that Yisrael were too mighty for him to conquer since they had never encountered each other in battle before. Rabbi Shimon says that he had seen into the future and discovered that King David, a descendant of Ruth the Moabite, would be victorious over Moab. Balak hoped that by joining with Bilaam they could destroy Yisrael before King David even came into the world. Rabbi Shimon talks about the cauldron of sorcery that Balak buried and that David exposed and cleansed with water. He explains the difference between righteousness and faithfulness, the former being judgment for the other nations, and the latter being compassion for the children of Yisrael. These also correspond to war and peace. We learn that Balak knew that Bilaam had power to bestow blessings on a very high level, and thought he would be able to uproot Yisrael from her union with Malchut.

252. כִּי עָצוּם הוּא מִמֶּנִּי. וְכִי עַד הַהוּא שַׁעֲתָא אָן אַגָּחוּ בֵּיהּ קְרָבָא וְנָצְחוּ לֵיהּ. בְּאָן אֲתָר אַעְרָעוּ בְּחַרְבָּא דִּלְהוֹן, וַהֲווֹ גַּבְרִין כְּגִבָּרִין לְאַחֲזָאָה גְּבוּרְתָּא דִּלְהוֹן. מַאי כִּי עָצוּם הוּא מִמֶּנִּי. אֶלָּא הַהוּא רָשָׁע חַכִּים הֲוָה, וְחָמֵי לְמֵרָחִיק, חָמָא לְדָוִד מַלְכָּא, דְּאָתֵי מֵרוּת הַמּוֹאֲבִיָּה, גִּיבָּר תַּקִּיף כְּאַרְיֵה, וְעָבֵיד קְרָבִין תַּקִּיפִין, וְנָצַח לְמוֹאָב, וְשַׁוֵּי לוֹן תְּחוֹת רַגְלוֹי. אָמַר עָצוּם הוּא. הַהוּא דְּיָרְתָא הַהוּא גְּבוּרְתָּא, חַד מַלְכָּא דִּלְהוֹן, מִינָן יִפּוּק לְשֵׁיצָאָה לְמוֹאָב.

252. "For they are too mighty for me" (Bemidbar 22:6). HE INQUIRES: Until that time, where had YISRAEL done battle with them, and beaten them? At which location had they met up with the sword OF YISRAEL and showed their strength like mighty men to display their power, SO THAT HE ALREADY KNEW THAT YISRAEL WAS TOO MIGHTY FOR HIM? What is the meaning of, "For they are too mighty for me"? HE RESPONDS: It is only that this wicked one was wise and foresaw in the distant future that King David, who stemmed from Ruth the Moabite, had the valor and strength of a lion. He will conduct and wage difficult wars and be victorious over Moab, and place him under his feet. THEREFORE, he said "(lit.) he is mighty" IN A SINGULAR FORM, meaning he who inherited that power, one of their kings who will stem from us, FROM RUTH THE MOABITE, to destroy Moab.

253. אוּלַי אוּכַל נַכֶּה בּוֹ. הַאי קְרָא הָכִי הֲוָה לֵיהּ לְמֵימַר, אוּלַי אוּכַל אַכֶּה בּוֹ. אוֹ אוּלַי נוּכַל נַכֶּה בּוֹ. אֶלָּא הַהוּא רָשָׁע הֲוָה חַכִּים, אָמַר, חֲמֵינָא יְדָא חֲדָא, דְּחַד אַרְיָא תַּקִּיפָא, פָּרִישׁ יְדָא, אִי אִיכוּל עִמָּךְ, דְּנִתְחַבָּר תַּרְוָונָא וְנִגְרַע מֵהַהוּא אַרְיֵה יְדָא דָּא, עַד לָא יֵיתֵי הַהוּא מַלְכָּא לְעָלְמָא, וְלָא יִתְרָךְ יַת מוֹאָב מֵאַתְרֵיהּ.

253. "Perhaps I shall prevail, that we mignt smite them" (Ibid.): HE ASKS: This verse should have read: 'Perhaps I shall prevail, that I may smite them' or 'perhaps we shall prevail, that we may smite them'. WHY DOES IT SAY: "I SHALL PREVAIL, THAT WE MAY SMITE"? HE RESPONDS: It is only that this wicked man was wise. He said, I see here one hand, MEANING ONE POWER, a powerful lion extending its paw. Maybe I can prevail with you, meaning that if we join together and cut off that lion's paw, THAT IS, THROUGH A CURSE, before that king comes into the world, he will not drive out Moab from its location. THEREFORE IT SAYS, "I SHALL PREVAIL" IN SINGULAR FORM AND "WE MAY SMITE" IN PLURAL FORM, BECAUSE THE MEANING IS, PERHAPS I COULD JOIN WITH YOU AND WE WILL BOTH SMITE IT.

254. אָרָה לִּי, מַאי אָרָה לִּי. א״ר אַבָּא, הַהוּא רָשָׁע בִּתְרֵי לִישָּׁנֵי קָאָמַר לְבִלְעָם. חַד אָמַר אָרָה לִּי, וְחַד אָמַר קָבָה לִּי. מַה בֵּין הַאי לְהַאי. אֶלָּא אָ״ל, אָרָה לִּי עַשְׂבִּין וְחַרְשִׁין דְּרֵישֵׁי דְּחִוְיָין, וְשַׁוֵּי לוֹן בַּקְּדֵרָה דְּחַרְשַׁיָּא, כֵּיוָן דְּחָמָא דְּחֵילֵיהּ יַתִּיר בְּפוּמָא, תָּב וְאָמַר, וּלְכָה נָא קָבָה לִּי.

254. HE INQUIRES: What is "curse me"? Rabbi Aba said, That wicked man said to Bilaam using two expressions, "Curse (Heb. *ara*) me" (Bemidbar 22:6) and he also said, "Curse (Heb. *kava*) me" (Ibid. 17). What is the difference between these? HE RESPONDS: It is only that he first said to him, "Curse (Heb. *ara*) me," MEANING GATHER UP FOR ME weeds and sorcery of heads of snakes to place in the cauldron of witchcraft. When he observed that his strength was greater by the power of his speech, he said again, "Come therefore, I pray you, curse (Heb. *kavah*) me."

255. וַאֲפִילּוּ הָכִי, הַהוּא רָשָׁע דְּבָלָק, לָא שָׁבַק חֲרָשׁוֹי, אֶלָּא לָקִיט כָּל זִינֵי עִשְׂבִּין, חַרְשֵׁי דְּרֵישֵׁי דְּחִוְיָין, וְנָטִיל קְדֵרָה דְּחָרְשִׁין, וְנָעִיץ לָהּ

תְּחוֹת אַרְעָא אֶלֶף וַחֲמֵשׁ מְאָה אַמִּין, וְגָנִיז לָהּ לְסוֹף יוֹמִין. כֵּיוָן דְּאָתָא דָּוִד, כָּרָא בִּתְהוֹמָא, אֶלֶף וַחֲמֵשׁ מְאָה אַמִּין, וְאַפִּיק מַיָּא מִן תְּהוֹמָא, וְנָסִיךְ עַל מַדְבְּחָא. בְּהַהוּא שַׁעֲתָא, אָמַר, אֲנָא אַסְחֵי הַהִיא קְדֵרָה, מוֹאָב סִיר רַחְצִי. סִיר רַחְצִי וַדַּאי.

255. In spite of all this, the wicked Balak did not abandon his design of sorcery, but rather he gathered up and picked all types of weeds and sorcery of snake heads, and took a cauldron of witchcraft. Balak stuck it 1,500 cubits underground and stored it for the end of days. When David came, he dug to the depth of 1,500 cubits, exposed the water from the depths and poured libations over the altar. At that moment, WHEN THE WATER LIBATIONS WERE POURED, he said, I will cleanse WITH THESE WATERS that cauldron OF SORCERY OF BALAK, as is written: "Moab is My washpot" (Tehilim 60:10), assuredly My washpot.

256. עַל אֱדוֹם אַשְׁלִיךְ נַעֲלִי, מַאי אַשְׁלִיךְ נַעֲלִי. אֶלָּא דָּא אוּף הָכִי לְמֵרָחִיק הֲוָה, דִּכְתִּיב וַיֹּאמֶר עֵשָׂו אֶל יַעֲקֹב הַלְעִיטֵנִי נָא מִן הָאָדֹם הָאָדֹם הַזֶּה כִּי עָיֵף אָנֹכִי. הַלְעִיטֵנִי: הַלְעָטָה מַמָּשׁ, פְּתִיחוּ דְּפוּמָא וּגְרוֹנָא לְמִבְלַע. אָמַר דָּוִד לְהַהוּא בַּלְעָן, מְלָעֵט הַלְעָטִין, אֲנָא אַרְמֵי עָלֵיהּ נַעֲלִי, לְמִסְתַּם גְּרוֹנֵיהּ.

256. "Over Edom will I cast My shoe" (Ibid.). HE INQUIRES: What is the meaning of: "Will I cast My shoe"? HE RESPONDS: It also refers to the one who had distant VISION, as it is written: "And Esau said to Jacob, 'Give me to swallow, I pray you, of that red pottage; for I am faint'" (Beresheet 25:30). "Give me to swallow" MEANS actually stuffing down the throat, opening wide the mouth and throat to swallow. David said to that swallower who stuffs himself, I will dump on him, THAT IS ON HIS MOUTH, "my shoe" to shut his throat. THEREFORE, "OVER EDOM WILL I CAST MY SHOE."

257. עֲלֵי פְּלֶשֶׁת אֶתְרוֹעָע, אוּף הָכִי דָּא לְמֵרָחִיק אִסְתָּכֵּי דָּוִד, אָמַר, כְּנַעַן סִטְרָא בִּישָׁא דְּסִטְרָא אַחֲרָא אִיהוּ, וּפְלִשְׁתִּים מִתַּמָּן אִינּוּן, לְסִטְרָא אַחֲרָא מַה אִצְטְרִיךְ. תְּרוּעָה. דִּכְתִּיב, וְכִי תָבֹאוּ מִלְחָמָה

בְּאַרְצְכֶם וַהֲרֵעוֹתֶם וְגוֹ׳, לְתַבְרָא חֵילֵיהּ וְתוּקְפֵּיהּ, וּבג״כ עֲלֵי פְּלֶשֶׁת אֶתְרוֹעָע, וְהָכִי אִתְחֲזֵי לוֹן.

257. "Over Philistia I will cry in triumph" (Tehilim 108:10). This too, David saw with distant vision. He said, Canaan is the bad side of the Other Side and the Philistines stem from there, FROM CANAAN (YEHOSHUA 13). What is there TO BE DONE against the Other Side? It is the blowing of the horn (Heb. truah), as it says, "if you go to war in your land...then you shall blow an alarm..." (Bemidbar 10:9). TRUAH MEANS BREAKING in order to break down his power and strength. Therefore, "over Philistia I will cry (blow) in triumph," MEANING HE WILL BREAK THEM, because that is what they deserve.

258. וְעַתָּה לְכָה נָּא אָרָה לִּי אֶת הָעָם הַזֶּה כִּי עָצוּם הוּא מִמֶּנִּי. ר׳ חִזְקִיָּה פָּתַח, וְהָיָה צֶדֶק אֵזוֹר מָתְנָיו וְהָאֱמוּנָה אֵזוֹר חֲלָצָיו. הַאי קְרָא כֹּלָּא אִיהוּ חַד. מַאי חִדּוּשָׁא אָתָא לְאַשְׁמוֹעִינָן, דְּהָא צֶדֶק הַיְינוּ אֱמוּנָה, וֶאֱמוּנָה הַיְינוּ צֶדֶק. אֵזוֹר מָתְנָיו, הַיְינוּ אֵזוֹר חֲלָצָיו, לָא אַשְׁכְּחָן קְרָא כְּהַאי גַּוְונָא.

258. "Come now therefore, curse me this people; for they are too mighty for me." Rabbi Chizkiyah opened the discussion with the verse: "And righteousness shall be the girdle of his loins, and faithfulness, the girdle of his loins" (Yeshayah 11:5). This verse is all the same. What new insight does it come to teach us, seeing that righteousness is faithfulness and faithfulness is righteousness? THEY ARE MERELY TWO NAMES OF MALCHUT. The girdle of his hips is also the girdle of his loins, and we do not find a verse like that.

259. אֶלָּא לָאו צֶדֶק כֶּאֱמוּנָה, וְאע״ג דְּכֹלָּא חַד, וְחַד דַּרְגָּא אִיהוּ. אֲבָל בְּזִמְנָא דְּקַיְּימָא בְּדִינָא קַשְׁיָא, וּמְקַבְּלָא מִסְּטַר שְׂמָאלָא, כְּדֵין אִקְרֵי צֶדֶק, דִּינָא מַמָּשׁ. וְהַיְינוּ כִּי כַּאֲשֶׁר מִשְׁפָּטֶיךָ לָאָרֶץ צֶדֶק לָמְדוּ יוֹשְׁבֵי תֵבֵל. דְּהַאי דַּרְגָּא דְּמִשְׁפָּט, רַחֲמֵי אִיהוּ. וְכַד אִתְקְרִיב מִשְׁפָּט בְּצֶדֶק, כְּדֵין אִתְבְּסַם, וְיַכְלִין בְּנֵי עָלְמָא, לְמִסְבַּל דִּינָא דְּצֶדֶק.

259. HE RESPONDS: It is that righteousness is not the same as faithfulness. Even though they are all one and the same, and are of one level, MEANING

MALCHUT, she is considered righteousness, which is the actual Judgment, during a period WHEN MALCHUT PRETAINS TO harsh Judgment and receives from the left side. That is: "For when Your judgments (lit. 'justices') are on the earth, the inhabitants of the world learn righteousness" (Ibid. 26:9). This level THAT IS CALLED 'justice' pertains to Mercy, WHICH IS ZEIR ANPIN. When that justice is approaching righteousness, WHICH IS JUDGMENT, then THAT RIGHTEOUSNESS, WHICH IS MALCHUT, is established and the world's inhabitants can withstand the Judgment of righteousness.

260. אֱמוּנָה, בְּשַׁעֲתָא דְּאִתְחַבָּר בָּהּ אֱמֶת, לְחֶדְוָה. וְכָל אַנְפִּין נְהִירִין, כְּדֵין אִקְרֵי אֱמוּנָה. וְאִית וַוּתְרָנוּתָא לְכֹלָּא, וְכָל נִשְׁמָתִין סַלְּקִין, מִתְחַיְּיבֵי בְּכַמָּה חִיּוּבִין דְּחַיָּיבִין בִּישִׁין, וְכֵיוָן דִּבְפִקָּדוֹן סַלְּקִן, אַהְדָּר לוֹן בְּרַחֲמֵי, וְחָס עֲלַיְיהוּ. וּכְדֵין אִקְרֵי אֱמוּנָה, וְלֵית אֱמוּנָה בְּלָא אֱמֶת.

260. MALCHUT IS CALLED 'Faith' at the time that she is joined with truth, WHICH IS ZEIR ANPIN, for happiness. All the faces are bright. Then MALCHUT is called 'Faith' and there is absolution for all, MEANING FORGIVENESS FOR INIQUITIES. She returns to all the souls of the wicked, WHICH ARE encumbered with many debts, with compassion and has mercy on them when they ascend and rise through committing, MEANING WHEN THEY SAY BEFORE THEIR SLEEP "INTO YOUR HAND I COMMIT MY SPIRIT" (TEHILIM 31:6). Then she is considered Faith and there is no Faith without truth, MEANING TO SAY THAT MALCHUT IS NOT CONSIDERED FAITH EXCEPT WHEN JOINED WITH ZEIR ANPIN THAT IS CALLED 'TRUTH'.

261. הַשְׁתָּא אֵזוֹר מָתְנָיו, וְאֵזוֹר חֲלָצָיו. מַהוּ תְּרֵין אֵזוֹרִין הָכָא. וּמָתְנַיִם וַחֲלָצַיִן אע״ג דְּחַד אִינּוּן, תְּרֵין דַּרְגִּין אִינּוּן, חַד לְעֵילָּא, וְחַד לְתַתָּא. לְעֵילָּא בְּשֵׁירוּתָא, אִקְרֵי מָתְנַיִם. לְתַתָּא בְּסוֹפָא, אִקְרֵי חֲלָצַיִן, כד״א וַחֲגוֹרָה עַל חֲלָצָיִם, בְּסוֹפָא, עַל רֵישׁ יְרֵכַיִם. כַּד אִתְּתָא בְּצַעֲרָא, מְתַקְּנָן אִינּוּן חֲלָצַיִם, מֵרֵישׁ יְרֵכַיִן, וְשַׁוִּיאַת יְדָהָא בְּכִאִיבָא עֲלַיְיהוּ.

261. Now, what two girdles are here when it says the girdle of his loins and the girdle of his hips? HE RESPONDS: Even though hips and loins are similar, they are two levels. One is above and one is below. Above at the top OF THE HIPS, it is called 'hips'. At the lower end OF THE HIPS, they are called 'loins', as it says, "And gird sackcloth upon your loins" (Yeshayah 32:11), WHICH MEANS TO COVER THE GENITALS. THEREFORE, HE CALLS THEM LOINS BECAUSE THEY ARE at the end OF THE HIPS and at the top of the thighs. When a woman is in the pain OF LABOR, these loins are disconnected from the tops of her thighs and she places her hands on them BECAUSE OF that pain.

262. ובג״כ לִגְבוּרָה וּלְקְרָבָא, צֶדֶק אֵזוֹר מָתְנָיו. וְהָכִי אִצְטְרִיךְ. לְרַחֲמָנוּ וּלְטָב, אֱמוּנָה אֵזוֹר חֲלָצָיו, בְּחַד דַּרְגָּא יְדִין עָלְמָא, וְשַׁלְטָא לִתְרֵין סִטְרִין, חַד רַחֲמֵי לְיִשְׂרָאֵל. וְחַד דִּינָא לִשְׁאַר עַמִּין.

262. Because of that, for strength and war, IT IS SAID, "And righteousness shall be the girdle of his hips." That is how it should be, BECAUSE THAT IS WHERE THE VIRILITY OF A MAN IS. For compassion and goodness, it is said, "And faithfulness, the girdle of his loins." In one level, MESSIAH will judge the world, MEANING WITH MALCHUT, and it dominates both sides. One, WHICH IS FAITH, THE GIRDLE OF HIS LOINS, is compassion for Yisrael and one, WHICH IS RIGHTEOUSNESS, THE GIRDLE OF HIS HIPS, is judgment for the rest of the nations.

263. וְאִי תֵּימָא, צֶדֶק דִּינָא תַּקִּיף אִיהוּ, וְהָא כְּתִיב בְּצֶדֶק תִּשְׁפּוֹט עֲמִיתֶךָ. צֶדֶק צֶדֶק תִּרְדּוֹף. וְכַמָּה אִינוּן. וַדַּאי הָכִי הוּא. דְּהָא צֶדֶק לֵית בֵּיהּ וַתְּרָנוּתָא כְּלַל. אוּף הָכִי מַאן דְּדָאִין לְחַבְרֵיהּ, לָא אִצְטְרִיךְ לְמֶעְבַּד לֵיהּ וַתְּרָנוּתָא מִן דִּינָא כְּלָל, אֶלָּא בְּצֶדֶק, דְּלָא יִשְׁגַּח לִרְחִימוּ. מֹאזְנֵי צֶדֶק, בְּלָא וַתְּרָנוּ לְהַאי סִטְרָא וּלְהַאי סִטְרָא, לְמַאן דְּיָהִיב וּלְמַאן דִּמְקַבֵּל. ובג״כ חַד דַּרְגָּא אִיהוּ, וְאִתְפְּלֵג לִתְרֵין סִטְרִין. וְהָנֵי תְּרֵין סִטְרִין, ב׳ אֱזוֹרִין, קַיְימָן, חַד לִשְׁאָר עַמִּין, וְחַד לְיִשְׂרָאֵל. וּבְשַׁעֲתָא דְּנַפְקוּ יִשְׂרָאֵל מִמִּצְרַיִם, אִתְאַזְּרוּ בְּאֵזוֹרִין אִלֵּין, חַד דִּקְרָבָא. וְחַד הֲוָה דִּשְׁלָמָא.

263. You may wonder WHY righteousness is harsh judgment, since we find written: "But in righteousness shall you judge your neighbor" (Vayikra 19:15) and "Justice (lit. 'righteousness'), only justice shall you pursue" (Devarim 16:20). There are many such VERSES. HE RESPONDS: It is definite that there is no compromise in righteousness, ONLY ACCORDANCE WITH THE LAW. Anyone who judges his neighbor must not compromise any laws for him, but judge according to righteousness, that love should not be a consideration. The scales of justice MEANS without compromise to one side or the other, neither to the one who will have to pay nor to the one who will receive. Because of this, it is one level that is divided into two directions. And these two directions THAT WE MENTIONED WHICH ARE two girdles are one for the rest of the nations and one for Yisrael. When Yisrael went out from Egypt, they were supported by these two girdles: one of war, WHICH IS RIGHTEOUSNESS, THE GIRDLE OF HIS HIPS, and one of peace, WHICH IS FAITH, THE GIRDLE OF HIS LOINS.

264. כַּד אִתְיָעַט בָּלָק, אָמַר וַאֲגָרְשֶׁנּוּ מִן הָאָרֶץ. אָמַר הַהוּא דַּרְגָּא דְּקָא אִתְאַחֲדָן בֵּיהּ, מִן הָאָרֶץ וַדַּאי. וְדָא הוּא כִּי עָצוּם הוּא מִמֶּנִּי וַדַּאי, מַאן יֵיכוּל לְאַגָּחָא וּלְקַיְּימָא בְּהוּ בְּיִשְׂרָאֵל דַּרְגָּא דִּלְהוֹן תַּקִּיף הוּא מִדִּילִי. ובג"כ, וַאֲגָרְשֶׁנּוּ מִן הָאָרֶץ. וְאִי מֵהַאי אֶרֶץ אֲגָרְשֶׁנּוּ, וְאַתְּרֵךְ יָתֵיהּ מִינֵּיהּ, אֵיכוּל לְמֶעְבַּד כָּל רְעוּתִי, חֵילָא דִּלְהוֹן בְּמָאי אִיהוּ. בְּפוּמָא, וּבְעוֹבָדָא. הָא פּוּמָא דִּילָךְ, וְעוֹבָדָא דִּילִי.

264. When Balak took counsel, he said, "That I may drive them out of the land" (Bemidbar 22:6). He figured that the level into which YISRAEL were connected was definitely of the land, WHICH IS MALCHUT REFERRED TO AS EARTH. That is the meaning of: "For they are too mighty for me." The level of whoever could wage battle and stand up to Yisrael is stronger than mine. Therefore: "that I may drive them out of the land," WHICH IS FROM THEIR LEVEL, MALCHUT. If I drive them from that land and drive them from her, MEANING I WILL MANAGE TO HAVE THEM COMMIT SINS, I will be capable of doing WITH THEM as I please. Their power is through what? Through word and deed. Here is your mouth and my deed, AND WE WILL OVERCOME HIM.

265. כִּי יָדַעְתִּי אֵת אֲשֶׁר תְּבָרֵךְ מְבוֹרָךְ וְגוֹ'. וְכִי מַאן הֲוָה יָדַע. הָא אוּקְמוּהָ, דְּהָא בְּקַדְמֵיתָא כְּתִיב, וְהוּא נִלְחַם בְּמֶלֶךְ מוֹאָב הָרִאשׁוֹן וַיִּקַּח אֶת כָּל אַרְצוֹ מִיָּדוֹ, דְּאָגַר לֵיהּ לְבִלְעָם וְכוּ'. אֲבָל כִּי יָדַעְתִּי, יְדִיעָה וַדַּאי יָדַע, בְּחָכְמְתָא דִּילֵיהּ. אֵת אֲשֶׁר תְּבָרֵךְ מְבוֹרָךְ, מַאי

אִצְטְרִיךְ הָכָא בְּרָכָה, דְּהָא בְּגִין קְלָלָה הֲוָה אָזִיל. וְאִי הַהוּא מִלָּה דַּהֲוָה יָדַע מִן בִּלְעָם בְּקַדְמֵיתָא, קְלָלָה הֲוָה, מַאי אֵת אֲשֶׁר תְּבָרֵךְ מְבוֹרָךְ.

265. "For I know that he whom you bless is blessed" (Ibid.). HE ASKS: From where did he know that? HE RESPONDS: It was already explained and it is written: "Who had fought against the former king of Moab, and taken all his land, out of his hand" (Bemidbar 21:26), since he hired Bilaam TO CURSE HIM. However, "for I know" MEANS that he had this knowledge through his wisdom. FURTHERMORE, BECAUSE IT IS WRITTEN: "He whom you bless is blessed," what was the need TO MENTION blessing here, since his aim was to curse? If his prior knowledge of Bilaam was in relation to the curse, what is the intention of: "He whom you bless is blessed"?

266. אֶלָּא מִלָּה הָכָא, וְלָא יְדַעְנָא בָּהּ, וְלָא זָכֵינָא בָּהּ, עַד דְּאָתָא רִבִּי אֶלְעָזָר וְדָרַשׁ, אֲבָרְכָה אֶת יְיָ' בְּכָל עֵת תָּמִיד תְּהִלָּתוֹ בְּפִי. וּכְתִיב אֲבָרֵךְ אֶת יְיָ' אֲשֶׁר יְעָצָנִי. מָאן דְּאִצְטְרִיךְ בִּרְכָתָא מִן תַּתָּאֵי. אֶת, דְּהָא אִתְאַחָד בְּהוּ כְּשַׁלְהוֹבָא בִּפְתִילָה. וְדָוִד דַּהֲוָה יָדַע דָּא, אָמַר אֲבָרְכָה אֶת. אָמַר הַהוּא רָשָׁע, הַהוּא דַּרְגָּא דִּלְהוֹן, אָחִיד בְּהוּ, בְּגִין בִּרְכָאן דִּלְהוֹן, דְּקָא מְבָרְכִין לֵיהּ בְּכָל יוֹמָא. חֵילָא אִית לָךְ לְבָרְכָא לְהַהוּא דַּרְגָּא, וּתְעַקַּר לָהּ מִנַּיְיהוּ וְדָא הוּא כִּי יָדַעְתִּי אֵת אֲשֶׁר תְּבָרֵךְ מְבוֹרָךְ וְגוֹ'. וּבְדָא נֵיכוּל בְּהוּ. תְּבָרֵךְ לְהַהוּא דַּרְגָּא וְתִילוּט לִפְתִילָה. וְעַל דָּא אָמַר, וְאָנֹכִי אִקָּרֶה כֹּה, אַעְקָר לָהּ מִנַּיְיהוּ, דְּלָא יִתְאֲחָד בְּהוּ.

266. HE RESPONDS: However, there is something implied here. I did not know it and I did not merit it until Rabbi Elazar arrived and interpreted the verse: "I will bless (*et*) Hashem at all times: His praise shall continually be in my mouth" (Tehilim 34:2), and: "I bless (*et*) Hashem who gives me counsel" (Tehilim 16:7). Who is it that needs blessings from the lower beings? That is the particle *Et*, WHICH IS MALCHUT, that is jointly connected to them, TO YISRAEL, as a flame to the wick. David, who knew it, said, "I will bless *Et*." The wicked man said TO BILAAM, that level of theirs, WHICH IS MALCHUT, is connected to them, because of their blessings that they bestow on her daily. IF SO, you have the power to bestow blessings on that level and you will uproot her from them. That is why it says, "For I know that (*Et*) he whom you bless is blessed." THAT IS,

HE TOO COULD BESTOW BLESSINGS ON MALCHUT REFERRED TO BY *ET*. That way, we will succeed against them. Bless that level and curse the wick THAT IS YISRAEL, TO WHICH MALCHUT IS ATTACHED LIKE A FLAME TO THE WICK. About this, he said, "While I go to the meeting yonder (Heb. *coh*)" (Bemidbar 23:15); that is, I will uproot MALCHUT THAT IS REFERRED TO BY *COH* from them, so that she should not unite with them.

267. וְתוּ אִקָּרֶה כֹּה, אַנְגִּיד וְאַמְשִׁיךְ לְהַהוּא דַּרְגָּא, בְּחוֹבִין וּמִסְאֲבִי וּבְקֶרִי וּבְטוּמְאָה דְּעָבְדוּ בְּנוֹי, וְהִיא תַּעֲבִיד עִמְּהוֹן גְּמִירָא. מִיַּד וַיֵּלְכוּ זִקְנֵי מוֹאָב וְזִקְנֵי מִדְיָן וּקְסָמִים בְּיָדָם, דְּלָא יֵימָא הַהוּא רָשָׁע דְּלָאו עִמֵּיהּ אִינּוּן זִינִין חַרְשִׁין דְּאִצְטְרִיךְ וְיִתְעַכָּב עָלַיְיהוּ.

267. Furthermore, "go to the meeting (Heb. *ikareh*) yonder (Heb. *coh*)" MEANS I will lead and pull that level down with transgressions, defilement, nightly uncleanness (Heb. *keri*) and the defilement that will be caused by His children. And she will destroy them. HE DEFINES *IKAREH* AS DERIVED FROM *KERI*. Immediately, "And the elders of Moab and the elders of Midian departed with the rewards of divinations in their hand" (Bemidbar 22:7) in order to avoid the excuses of the wicked one who says that he does not possess the particular magic which he may need, and who will thereby be able to restrain himself from joining them.

20. "Therefore fear you not, O My servant Jacob"

A Synopsis

Rabbi Shimon explains the meaning of 'you' in the title verse. We hear from Rav Hamnuna that the hardships that Yisrael underwent gave them a great many benefits over the other nations who did not undergo them. Yisrael will inherit the tabernacle of peace, the Shechinah, while the other nations will be destroyed. Rabbi Shimon says that this is because Yisrael is being punished for their sins now, little by little, and at the end their sins will be erased because they have already been cleansed in this way. At that same time Samael and all of his side and all of his nations will vanish completely from the world.

268. פָּתַח וְאָמַר, וְאַתָּה אַל תִּירָא עַבְדִּי יַעֲקֹב וְאַל תֵּחַת יִשְׂרָאֵל כִּי אִתְּךָ אֲנִי וְגוֹ'. הַאי קְרָא אִתְּמַר וְאִתְּעֲרוּ בֵּיהּ, אֲבָל עַד כְּעַן אִית לְאַתְּעָרָא יַתִּיר. אַתָּה, מַאי אִיהוּ. רָזָא אֲרוֹן הַבְּרִית. דְּדָא אִיהוּ דַּרְגָּא דְּאַזְלָא בְּגָלוּתָא בַּהֲדֵי בְּנָהָא עַמָּא קַדִּישָׁא. מֹשֶׁה בְּשַׁעֲתָא דְּבָעָא רַחֲמִין עָלַיְיהוּ דְּיִשְׂרָאֵל, מַה כְּתִיב וְאִם כָּכָה אַתְּ עוֹשֶׂה לִּי הָרְגֵנִי נָא הָרוֹג, וְאוּקְמוּהָ.

268. He opened the discussion with the verse: "'Therefore fear you not, O My servant Jacob,' says Hashem; 'neither be dismayed, O Yisrael... For I am with you'" (Yirmeyah 30:10-11). We have learned this verse and it has been discussed. However, we could now discuss it more thoroughly. What is "you"? It is the secret of the Ark of the Covenant, WHICH IS MALCHUT, that is the level that goes into exile with her children, the holy nation. At the time Moses asked mercy for Yisrael, it is written there: "And if You deal thus with me, kill me, I pray You, out of hand" (Bemidbar 11:15), as it was already explained.

269. אֲבָל הָכִי אָמַר מֹשֶׁה, דַּרְגָּא חַד דִּיְּהַבִית לִי אִקְרֵי אַתָּה, בְּגִין דְּלֵית לֵיהּ פְּרִישׁוּ מִמָּךְ. ה' דִּילָהּ אִתְאֲחָד בְּהוּ בְּיִשְׂרָאֵל. אִי אַתְּ תְּשֵׁיצֵי לוֹן מֵעָלְמָא, הָא ה' דִּשְׁמָא דָּא דְּאִתְאֲחָד בְּהוּ אִתְעֲבָר מִנֵּיהּ, אִי הָכִי אַתְּ עוֹשֶׂה לִּי, דְּה' עִקָּרָא דִּשְׁמָא דָּא אִתְעֲקָר.

269. However, this is what Moses said, One level that You granted me was called 'You', THAT IS MALCHUT, since she is not separated from You. Her Hei, MEANING THE HEI of *atah* (Eng. 'you'), was attached to Yisrael. If You destroy them, then the Hei of this name *ATAH*, which is connected to YISRAEL, will be removed FROM THE NAME *ATAH* AND *AT* WILL BE LEFT. THAT IS THE MEANING OF WHAT IS WRITTEN: "If You (Heb. *at*) deal thus with me," MEANING IF YOU DESTROY YISRAEL, the Hei that is the baasis of this name, *ATAH,* is uprooted AND ONLY *AT* IS LEFT FROM *ATAH*. THE RESULT IS THAT YOU WILL MAKE ME AN *AT* FROM *ATAH*, AND THAT IS WHAT HE SAID, "YOU (*AT*) DEAL THUS."

270. וְעַ"ד אָמַר יְהוֹשֻׁעַ לְבָתַר, וּמַה תַּעֲשֶׂה לְשִׁמְךָ הַגָּדוֹל, דְּהָא וַדַּאי שְׁמָא דָּא עִקָּרָא וִיסוֹדָא דְּכֹלָּא, אַתָּה הוּא יְיָ'. וּמֹשֶׁה אע"ג דְּקוּדְשָׁא בְּרִיךְ הוּא לָא אָ"ל, הָכִי יָדַע, דְּהָא בְּהָא תַּלְיָיא, וְחוֹבָה גָּרִים. וְאַתָּה אַל תִּירָא עַבְדִּי יַעֲקֹב וְגוֹ', כֹּלָּא חַד. כִּי אִתְּךָ אֲנִי, הָא אוֹקִימְנָא כִּי אִתִּי אַתָּה לָא כְּתִיב, אֶלָּא כִּי אִתְּךָ אֲנִי. כִּי אֶעֱשֶׂה כָלָה בְּכָל הַגּוֹיִם וְגוֹ', בְּכָל הַגּוֹיִם אֶעֱשֶׂה כָלָה.

270. Therefore, Joshua later said, "And what will You do for Your great name" (Yehoshua 7:9), MEANING TO THE NAME *ATAH*, since this name is most definitely the basis and foundation of everything, AS IT IS WRITTEN: "You are Hashem." Even though the Holy One, blessed be He, did not tell Moses THAT THE HEI WILL BE REDUCED FROM THE NAME *ATAH*, he understood that one depends on the other, THAT THE HEI OF *ATAH* DEPENDS ON YISRAEL, and the sin causes THE HEI TO GET UPROOTED FROM *ATAH*. HE RETURNS TO THE VERSE THAT HE STARTED WITH: "Therefore fear you not, O My servant Jacob" (Yeshayah 46:28). JACOB AND YISRAEL are all one. "For I am with you" (Ibid.) was already defined. It does not say, 'For you are with Me', but rather "For I am with you," INDICATING THAT THE NAME *ATAH* IS CONNECTED TO YISRAEL, AS MENTIONED ABOVE. THEREFORE, "for I will make a full end of all the nations" (Ibid.). Among all the nations I will create destruction, "YET WILL I NOT MAKE A FULL END OF YOU" (IBID.). THAT IS BECAUSE OF THE HEI OF *ATAH*, WHICH IS TIED TO YISRAEL AS MENTIONED.

271. רַב הַמְנוּנָא קַדְמָאָה אָמַר, דְּחִיקוּ וְעָאקוּ דְּיִשְׂרָאֵל, כַּמָּה טָב וְכַמָּה

תּוּעַלְתָּא גָּרִים לוֹן. רִפְיוֹן דִּשְׁאַר עַמִּין, כַּמָּה בִּישִׁין גָּרִים לוֹן. דְּחִיקוּ וְעָאקוּ דְּיִשְׂרָאֵל, גָּרִים לוֹן דְּטָב לֶיהֱוֵי וְתוּעַלְתָּא. וּמַאי נִיהוּ. כָּלָה. כֹּלָּא דָּחִיק. רִפְיוֹן דִּשְׁאַר עַמִּין, גָּרִים לוֹן רִפְיוֹן וּבִישׁ, וְהַאי אִיהוּ כָלָה. וְהָכִי אִתְחֲזֵי לוֹן, דְּהָא כָּל רִפְיוֹן בְּלָא דְּחִיקוּ דַּהֲוָה לוֹן בְּהַאי עָלְמָא, גָּרִים לוֹן רִפְיוֹן לְבָתַר בְּלָא דְּחִיקוּ, כָלָה. כִּי כָלָה וְנֶחֱרָצָה שָׁמַעְתִּי. כִּי אֶעֱשֶׂה כָלָה. כָלָה בְּרִפְיוֹן. לְיִשְׂרָאֵל דַּהֲוָה לוֹן דְּחִיקוּ וְעָאקוּ, כַּלָּה, וְכַכַּלָּה תַּעְדֶּה כֵלֶיהָ.

271. The First Rav Hamnuna said, The pressure and distress to Yisrael caused them a great many benefits and advantages. The laxity of the other nations, MEANING THAT THEY HAVE NO PRESSURE AND PAIN IN THIS WORLD, caused them many evils. HE EXPLAINS: The pressure and distress that was upon Yisrael caused them advantages and benefits. What do they consist of: *kalah* (lit. 'destruction'), as everything is strained, MEANING TO SAY THAT ALL THE LETTERS THAT ARE SOUNDED IN IT ARE STRESSED WITH A *DAGESH*, INDICATING THAT THROUGH STRESS THEY SUCCEED IN GAINING THE HIGHER *KALAH* (ENG. 'BRIDE'), WHICH IS THE SHECHINAH. The laxness of the nations, WHO HAVE NO DISTRESS OR DIFFICULTIES, yielded them slackness and evil. That is *kalah* (lit. 'destruction') WITHOUT DAGESH STRESS, and that is proper for them, because all the easiness without any difficulties that they had in this world caused them slackness without any pressure afterwards. That is *kalah* (lit. 'destruction') WITH UNSTRESSED KAF AND LAMED, AS IS WRITTEN: "For I have heard from Adonai Elohim Tzva'ot that destruction (Heb. *kalah*) is decreed" (Yeshayah 28:22). "For I will make a full end (Heb. *kalah*)" without a stress, KAF AND LAMED BEING UNSTRESSED. However, for Yisrael, who passed through strain and pressure, they will get the benefit of the bride, WITH KAF AND LAMED STRESSED WITH DAGESH, as it says, "And as a bride (Heb. *kalah*) adorns herself with her jewels" (Ibid. 61:10), KALAH BEING THE SHECHINAH.

272. מַאן כֵּלֶיהָ. אִלֵּין יִשְׂרָאֵל, דְּאִינּוּן כֵּלִים דְּהַאי כַּלָּה, יִשְׂרָאֵל דַּהֲוָה לוֹן דְּחִיקוּ וְעָאקוּ, אָקִים אֶת סֻכַּת דָּוִד הַנּוֹפֶלֶת, סֻכַּת שָׁלוֹם. לִשְׁאַר עַמִּין דַּהֲוָה לוֹן רִפְיוֹן צָרָה וְצוּקָה, כָלָה בְּרִפְיוֹן, כְּמָה דַּהֲוָה לוֹן בְּקַדְמֵיתָא. וְעַ"ד כִּי אֶעֱשֶׂה כָלָה בְּכָל הַגּוֹיִם וְגו', וְאוֹתְךָ לֹא אֶעֱשֶׂה

כָּלָה, דְּהָא לָא אִתְחֲזֵי לָךְ. דְּהָא דָּחִיק הֲוֵית בְּקַדְמֵיתָא זִמְנִין סַגִּיאִין, בִּדְחִיקוּ, דְּגָלוּתָא תָּדִיר, וְדָחִיק תִּהְיֶה כַּלָּה.

272. HE INQUIRES: Who are her jewels, AS IT SAYS, "AND AS A BRIDE (HEB. *KALAH*) ADORNS HERSELF WITH HER JEWELS"? HE RESPONDS: These refer to Yisrael, who are the adornments of this bride, THE SHECHINAH. Yisrael, who went through this distress and pressure, MERIT THE VERSE: "I will raise up the tabernacle of David that is fallen" (Amos 9:11). That is the tabernacle of peace, MEANING THE SHECHINAH. And the rest of the nations, who had respite from trouble and anguish, later deserve destruction through laxity, WITH KAF AND LAMED NOT STRESSED WITH DAGESH, as they previously enjoyed RESPITE FROM TROUBLE. The result is: "For I will make a full end of all the nations...yet will I not make a full end of you," since you do not deserve it. You already were many times earlier in distress and under the constant pressure of the exile. Therefore, you will have a bride; THAT IS, THE SHECHINAH.

273. וְיִסַּרְתִּיךָ לַמִּשְׁפָּט, הַאי קְרָא הָכִי מִבָּעֵי לֵיהּ וְיִסַּרְתִּיךָ בַּמִּשְׁפָּט, דְּהָא אֵימָתַי יִיסוּרֵי בְּשַׁעֲתָא דְּדִינָא. מַאי וְיִסַּרְתִּיךָ לַמִּשְׁפָּט. אֶלָּא כְּתִיב יְיָ׳ בְּמִשְׁפָּט יָבֹא עִם זִקְנֵי עַמּוֹ. וְהַהוּא יוֹמָא, אַקְדִּים קוּדְשָׁא בְּרִיךְ הוּא אַסְוָותָא לְיִשְׂרָאֵל, עַד לָא יֵיעֲלוּן לְדִינָא, בְּגִין דְּיֵיכְלוּן לְקַיְּימָא בֵּיהּ. וּמַאי אַסְוָותָא, הִיא דִּבְכָל שַׁעֲתָא וְשַׁעֲתָא קוּדְשָׁא בְּרִיךְ הוּא יָהִיב יִסּוּרִין לְיִשְׂרָאֵל זְעֵיר, זְעֵיר בְּכָל זִמְנָא וְזִמְנָא, וּבְכָל דָּרָא וְדָרָא בְּגִין דְּכַד יֵיעֲלוּן לְיוֹמָא דְּדִינָא רַבָּא, דְּיֵיחוּן מֵתַיָּיא, לָא יִשְׁלוֹט עֲלַיְיהוּ דִּינָא.

273. He asks, "But I will correct you in due measure (lit. 'for justice)" (Yirmeyah 30:11). This verse should read: "But I will correct you in justice," since when does one have torment? When he is sentenced on trial. So, what is the meaning of: "But I will correct you for justice"? HE ANSWERS, It is only because it is written: "Hashem will come with trial with the elders of His nation" (Yeshayah 3:14). On that day, the Holy One, blessed be He, introduce a remedy for Yisrael before they are put on trial, in order that they would be able to withstand it. What is that remedy? At every moment, the Holy One, blessed be He, provides them with a slight amount of suffering at each and every time and in each generation, in order that when they rise to the day of the great trial, AT THE TIME when the dead will be resurrected, judgment will not affect them.

274. וְנַקֵּה לֹא אֲנַקֶּךָּ, מַהוּ. אֶלָּא, כַּד יִשְׂרָאֵל בִּלְחוֹדַיְיהוּ, וְלָא עָאלִין בְּדִינָא עִם שְׁאַר עַמִּין, קוּדְשָׁא בְּרִיךְ הוּא עָבֵיד לוֹן לְגוֹ מִשּׁוּרַת הַדִּין, וְהוּא מְכַפֵּר עָלַיְיהוּ. וּבִזְמְנָא דְּעָאלִין בְּדִינָא בִּשְׁאַר עַמִּין, מֶה עָבֵיד. יָדַע קוּדְשָׁא בְּרִיךְ הוּא דְּהָא סָמָאֵ״ל אַפּוֹטְרוֹפְּסָא דְּעֵשָׂו, יֵיתֵי לְאַדְכְּרָא חוֹבֵיהוֹן דְּיִשְׂרָאֵל, וְכָנִישׁ כֻּלְּהוּ לְגַבֵּיהּ לְיוֹמָא דְּדִינָא, וְהָא קוּדְשָׁא בְּרִיךְ הוּא אַקְדִּים לְהוּ אַסְוָותָא, וְעַל כָּל חוֹבָא וְחוֹבָא לָקֵי וְנַקֵּה לְהוּ בְּיִסּוּרִין זְעֵיר זְעֵיר. וְדָא הוּא וְנַקֵּה, בְּיִסּוּרִין. וּבְגִין כַּךְ בְּדִינָא דִּקְשׁוֹט, לָא אֲנַקֶּךָּ מֵעָלְמָא בְּדִינָא בָּתַר דְּסַבָּלְתְּ יִסּוּרִין זְעֵיר זְעֵיר.

274. "And will not leave you altogether unpunished (lit. 'cleansing I will not cleanse you')" (Yirmeyah 30:11). HE ASKS: What is it? HE RESPONDS: It is that when Yisrael are by themselves and do not go to trail with the other nations, MEANING BEFORE THE END OF CORRECTION. The Holy One, blessed be He, does not apply the strict law to them and forgives them. When they do go to trail together with the other nations, AT THE END OF CORRECTION, AS MENTIONED ABOVE, what does He do? The Holy One, blessed be He, knows that Samael, who is the patron of Esau, will come to remind Him of the sins of Yisrael, and will have accumulated all THEIR INIQUITIES to himself for the day of judgment. And the Holy One, blessed be He, will give them a remedy beforehand, so that for each and every iniquity, He smote and cleansed them with sufferings, little by little. That is the meaning of "cleansing" BEFOREHAND, through sufferings. Thus, at the true trial IN THE FUTURE, "I will not cleanse you" from the world through judgment, since you have already suffered affliction AT EACH GIVEN TIME, little by little.

275. וְתוּ לָא אֲנַקֶּךָּ, אע״ג דְּאַתּוּן בָּנַי, לָא אֶשְׁבּוֹק חוֹבֵיכוֹן, אֶלָּא אִתְפְּרַע מִנְּכוֹן זְעֵיר זְעֵיר, בְּגִין דִּתְהֱווֹן זַכָּאִין לְיוֹמָא דְּדִינָא רַבָּא. כַּךְ אָתָאן לְדִינָא, אָתָא סָמָאֵ״ל, בְּכַמָּה פִּתְקִין עָלַיְיהוּ. וְקוּדְשָׁא בְּרִיךְ הוּא אַפִּיק פִּתְקִין דְּיִסּוּרִין, דְּסַבְלוּ יִשְׂרָאֵל עַל כָּל חוֹבָא וְחוֹבָא, וְנִמּוֹחוּ כָּל

חוֹבִין, וְלָא עָבֵיד לוֹן וַותְּרָנוּתָא כְּלָל. כְּדֵין תָּשַׁשׁ כֹּחֵיהּ וְחֵילֵיהּ דְּסָמָאֵל, וְלָא יָכִיל לוֹן. וְיִתְעֲבָר מֵעָלְמָא, הוּא, וְכָל סִטְרוֹי, וְכָל עַמִּין. הה"ד, וְאַתָּה אַל תִּירָא עַבְדִּי יַעֲקֹב וְגוֹ', בְּג"כ וְיִסַּרְתִּיךָ לַמִּשְׁפָּט וְנַקֵּה לֹא אֲנַקֶּךָּ.

275. "I will not cleanse you" MEANS that even though you are My children, I will not discard your wrongdoings, but rather I will make you pay Me little by little, so that you will be free of guilt at the day of the great judgment. When they come for trial, Samael will come with many writs of accusation about them. And TO COUNTER THEM the Holy One, blessed be He, will provide many writs of sufferings that Yisrael endured for each and every iniquity. All the sins were erased, and He is not being charitable at all, BECAUSE THEY HAVE ALREADY RECEIVED THEIR PUNISHMENT. Then the power and strength of Samael is weakened, and he is powerless against them. AND THEN he will vanish from the world, he and all of his aspects and all his nations. That is what it says: "Therefore fear you not, O My servant Jacob." Hence, "but I will correct you for judgment, and will not leave you altogether unpunished."

21. Balak – Ba Lak, Bilaam – Bal Am

A Synopsis

We learn about the evil partnership of Balak and Bilaam with Samael and his friends. Rabbi Elazar dissects the names Amalek, Balak and Bilaam to show their deeper meanings of destruction and confusion and hurt. Rabbi Shimon says that Samael did the action when Bilaam did the speech, so that whoever Bilaam blessed was blessed and whoever he cursed was damned. But Balak and Bilaam did not know that God would take away their power of speech and also their understanding. Finally we hear that Bilaam was impaired in his hearing and in his sight and in his leg.

276. וְדָוִד מַלְכָּא אָמַר, כִּי הִנֵּה הָרְשָׁעִים יִדְרְכוּן קֶשֶׁת כּוֹנְנוּ וְגוֹ׳. וְאַף עַל גַּב דְּהַאי קְרָא הָא אוֹקְמוּהָ, עַל שֶׁבְנָא וְיוֹאָח מִמָּנָן דְּחִזְקִיָּה אִתְּמַר, אֲבָל הַאי קְרָא עַל סָמָאֵ״ל וְסִיעָתֵיהּ אוּף הָכִי אִתְּמַר, דְּכָל עוֹבָדוֹי וְעֵיטוֹי עַל יִשְׂרָאֵל נִינְהוּ. בָּלָק וּבִלְעָם הַהוּא אֹרַח מַמָּשׁ נַקְטוּ, וְהָא אִתְּמַר דַּחֲבוּרָא בִּישָׁא עַבְדוּ. אַמְרוּ, עֲמָלֵ״ק: עָ״ם לָ״ק, עַמָּא דְּלַקָא לוֹן, כְּחִוְיָא דְּמָחֵי בִּזְנָבָא דִּילֵיהּ, הָא אֲנָן יַתִּיר. בָּלָ״ק: בָּ״א לָ״ק. אָתָא מַאן דְּלָקֵי לוֹן כִּרְעוּתֵיהּ. בִּלְעָ״ם: בַּ״ל עָ״ם, לֵית עַמָּא, וְלֵית רַעְיָא. שְׁמָא דִּילָן גָּרִים לְשֵׁיצָאָה לוֹן וּלְאַעְקְרָא לְהוּ מֵעָלְמָא.

276. King David said, "For, lo, the wicked bend the bow, they make ready their arrow..." (Tehilim 11:2). Although we already explained that this verse is about Shevna and Yoach, the chief ministers of Hezekiah, it is also said, referring to Samael and his retinue, that all his counsels and advice were against Yisrael. Balak and Bilaam tread exactly the same path, THAT OF SAMAEL AND HIS RETINUE and we learned that they formed an evil partnership. They said, Amalek IS SPELLED *am lak*, meaning a nation (Heb. *am*) that smote (Heb. *lakah*) them, like a snake that strikes with his tail. They figured that we are more THAN THEY ARE, because Balak IS SPELLED *ba lak,* meaning came (Heb. *ba*), he who smote (Heb. *lakah*) them as he wishes. Bilaam CONSISTS OF THE LETTERS *bal am,* meaning there are no (Heb. *bal*) people (Heb. *am*) and no shepherd. Our name will cause their destruction and uprooting from the world.

277. וְקוּדְשָׁא בְּרִיךְ הוּא חָשִׁיב בְּגַוְונָא אַחֲרָא שְׁמֵיהוֹן, בְּבָלָק בַּ״ל,

בְּבִלְעָם בַּ״ל, הָא בִּלְבֵּ״ל. מַה אַתְוָון אִשְׁתָּאֲרוּ עַמֶ״ק, בִּלְבֵּל עָמְקָא דְּמַחֲשָׁבָה דִּלְהוֹן, דְּלָא יִשְׁלְטוּן בְּעָלְמָא, וְלָא יִשְׁתַּאֲרוּן בְּעָלְמָא.

277. The Holy One, blessed be He, has figured their names in a different manner, since there is *bal* in Balak and in Bilaam. AND WHEN THEYARE JOINED, they form *bilbel* or confusion. What are the letters that are left WHEN YOU DEDUCT FROM THEM THE LETTERS *BILBEL*? THEY ARE Aleph Mem Kof; THAT IS, THE AYIN AND MEM FROM BILAAM AND KOF FROM BALAK. THIS COMBINATION WILL CAUSE their deep (Heb. *omek*) thinking and ideas to become confused, so that they should have no domination in the world and so that they should not remain in the world.

278. אר״ש, אֶלְעָזָר, יָאוּת אֲמַרְתְּ, אֲבָל בָּלָק, תִּפַּח רוּחֵיהּ בְּגֵיהִנָּם. וּבִלְעָם יִשְׁתַּחֲקוּן תַּמָּן גַּרְמוֹי וְרוּחֵיהּ. וְהָכִי הוּא עֵיטָא בִּישָׁא נַטְלוּ עַל פַּטְרוֹנָא. עַל הַאי כֹּה, דְּחָשִׁיבוּ לְאַעְקְרָא לְהַאי כֹּה, וְחָשִׁיבוּ לְסִטְרָא בִּישָׁא לְסַלְּקָא לֵיהּ בְּפוּמָא וּבְעוֹבָדָא.

278. Rabbi Shimon said, Elazar, you spoke well. However, let the spirit of Balak burn in Gehenom and let the bones and spirit of Bilaam be ground there, because they made a bad decision to go against the shield OF YISRAEL, meaning that *coh*, WHICH IS THE SHECHINAH REFERRED TO AS *COH*, and because they thought about uprooting that *coh* and bringing evil through speech and action.

279. אָמַר הַהוּא רָשָׁע, קַדְמָאֵי אִשְׁתַּדָּלוּ וְלָא יָכִילוּ. דּוֹר הַפְּלָגָה אִשְׁתַּדָּלוּ, וְלָא יָכִילוּ. עָבְדוּ עוֹבָדָא, וּפוּמָא חָסֵר מִנַּיְיהוּ, דְּלִישָׁנְהוֹן אִתְבַּלְבַּל, וְלָא יָכִיל. אֲבָל אַנְתְּ, הָא פּוּמָךְ שַׁנָּן, וְלִישָׁנָךְ מִתְתְּקַן בִּתְרֵין סִטְרִין אִלֵּין, אֵת אֲשֶׁר תְּבָרֵךְ מְבוֹרָךְ, וַאֲשֶׁר תָּאוֹר יוּאָר, הַהוּא סִטְרָא דְּאַתְּ בָּעֵי לְסַלְּקָא לְעֵילָא בְּפוּמָךְ וְלִישָׁנָךְ, אִסְתְּלִיק. וְהַהוּא סִטְרָא דְּאַתְּ בָּעֵי לְמֵילַט, בְּחֵילָא דְּפוּמָךְ תֵּילוֹט וְכֹלָּא בָּךְ תַּלְיָיא דְּהָא עוֹבָדָא אִתְתְּקַן. אֲבָל בְּמִלָּה תַּלְיָיא כֹּלָּא, וְעַ״ד בְּעוֹבָדָא דְּנָחָשׁ אֲנָא אַתְקִין. וְאַנְתְּ תַּשְׁלִים כֹּלָּא בְּפוּמָךְ, הַהוּא סִטְרָא דִּתְבָרֵךְ מְבוֹרָךְ, וְהַהוּא סִטְרָא דְּתָאוֹר יוּאָר.

279. The wicked man said, Ancient people tried but were unable to do that. The Generation of Separation strove but did not succeed, because they performed the deed but lacked the speech, because their languages became confused and they could not. However, BILAAM, your mouth is sharp and your tongue is equipped with these two aspects: "He whom you bless is blessed" FROM ONE ASPECT and "he whom you curse is cursed" FROM THE SECOND ASPECT (Bemidbar 22:6). The aspect that you wish to raise is uplifted through your mouth and tongue, and that aspect that you wish to curse you can curse with the strength of your mouth. Everything depends on you because the action was already done THROUGH ME. However, all the rest depends on talk. Therefore, I prepare the act of enchantment and you will complete it all with your speech. That aspect that you bless will be blessed and that aspect that you curse will be cursed.

280. וְהוּא לָא יָדַע דְּקוּדְשָׁא בְּרִיךְ הוּא מֵסִיר שָׂפָה לְנֶאֱמָנִים וְטַעַם זְקֵנִים יִקָּח, וְכֹלָּא בִּרְשׁוּתֵיהּ קַיְימָא. מֵסִיר שָׂפָה לְנֶאֱמָנִים, אִלֵּין דּוֹר הַפְלָגָה, דְּבִלְבֵּל לִישָׁנֵיהוֹן, דְּלָא יִשְׁלְטוּן בְּמִלָּה כְּלַל. דִּכְתִּיב, אֲשֶׁר לֹא יִשְׁמְעוּ אִישׁ שְׂפַת רֵעֵהוּ. וְטַעַם זְקֵנִים יִקָּח, אִלֵּין בִּלְעָם וּבָלָק דְּתַרְוַויְיהוּ הֲווֹ בְּעֵיטָא חֲדָא, דִּכְתִּיב וַיַּעַל בָּלָק וּבִלְעָם פַּר וְאַיִל בַּמִּזְבֵּחַ.

280. He did not know that the Holy One, blessed be He, "removes the speech of the trusty, and takes away the understanding of the aged" (Iyov 12:20). And everything is at His command. "He removes the speech of the trusty" refers to the Generation of Separation, whose language He confused and who could not have any control of their speech, as is written: "That they may not understand one another's speech" (Beresheet 11:7). "And takes away the understanding of the aged" refers to Bilaam and Balak, who were of one counsel, as is written: "And Balak and Bilaam offered (sing.) on every altar a bullock and a ram" (Bemidbar 23:2).

281. ת"ח, הַהוּא רָשָׁע דְּבִלְעָם, כָּל עוֹבָדוֹי לְבִישׁ, בְּרוּם לִבָּא. תַּרְוַויְיהוּ הֲווֹ סַלְקִין קָרְבְּנָא, דִּכְתִּיב וַיַּעַל בָּלָק וּבִלְעָם. וְכָל מַדְבְּחִין בָּלָק הֲוָה מְסַדֵּר, וְאִיהוּ רָשָׁע, הֲוָה מְשַׁבַּח גַּרְמֵיהּ וְאָמַר, אֶת שֶׁבַע הַמִּזְבְּחוֹת עָרַכְתִּי וָאַעַל פַּר וְאַיִל בַּמִּזְבֵּחַ. וְאִלּוּ לְבָלָק לָא שָׁתַּף בַּהֲדֵיהּ. אָמַר קוּדְשָׁא בְּרִיךְ הוּא, רָשָׁע, כֹּלָּא יְדַעְנָא, אֶלָּא שׁוּב אֶל בָּלָק, וְאַתְּ

לָא צָרִיךְ לְמַלְּלָא אֶלָּא וְכֹה תְּדַבֵּר. הה״ד, וְטַעַם זְקֵנִים יִקָּח.

281. Come and see that wicked man, Bilaam. All his activities were designed for evil, with haughtiness of heart. Both sacrificed the offerings, as it says, "And Balak and Bilaam offered." All the altars were prepared by Balak, but the wicked one, BILAAM, took praise and credit for himself, saying, "I have prepared the seven altars, and have offered upon every altar the bullock and the ram" (Ibid. 4). And he didn't include Balak with him. The Holy One, blessed be He, said, 'Wicked one, I know everything, however, return to Balak, and you won't have to speak; rather "and say thus (Heb. *coh*)" (Bemidbar 23:16), MEANING THE SHECHINAH THAT IS REFERRED TO AS *COH* WILL SPEAK INSTEAD. That is what is meant by: "And takes away the understanding of the aged."

282. ד״א וְטַעַם זְקֵנִים יִקָּח, דִּכְתִּיב וַיֵּלְכוּ זִקְנֵי מוֹאָב וְזִקְנֵי מִדְיָן וּקְסָמִים בְּיָדָם. טַעֲמָא דְּאִינּוּן זְקֵנִים נָטַל מִנַּיְיהוּ, וְלָא יָכִילוּ לְמִשְׁלַט בְּחַרְשַׁיְיהוּ כְּלַל. וַיְדַבְּרוּ אֵלָיו דִּבְרֵי בָלָק. מִלִּין בְּאִתְגַּלְיָא, וְלָא בִּלְחִישׁוּ. פָּגִים אוּדְנָא הֲוָה, וּפָגִים עֵינָא, וּפָגִים רַגְלָא. מִתְּלַת דּוּכְתִּין הֲוָה פָּגִים. מְתוּקָּן הֲוָה לְסִטְרָא אַחֲרָא, וְהָכִי אִצְטְרִיךְ לְהַהוּא סִטְרָא אַחֲרָא, אֲתָר דְּשַׁרְיָא פָּגִים, זִינָא לְזִינֵיהּ.

282. Another explanation of: "And takes away the understanding of the aged" is as is written: "And the elders of Moab and the elders of Midian departed with the rewards of divination in their hand" (Bemidbar 22:7). He took away their reasoning powers so they could not control their witchcraft at all "and spoke to him the words of Balak" (Ibid.) loudly and openly, and not quietly BECAUSE HIS HEARING WAS IMPAIRED. He had a blemish in his ear, a blemish in his eye and a blemish in his leg. In these three areas, he had a blemish AND DISABILITY, because he was equipped for the Other Side. That was necessary for the Other Side, WHICH IS a place where there is a blemish. Each kind follows its own kind.

22. "Lodge here this night"

A Synopsis

Rabbi Shimon continues with the story of Bilaam, and tells us that the Midianites would have acted appropriately if they had separated from Moab and not taken Bilaam's advice to send their women to confuse Yisrael. The Moabites who remained to hear what God had to say were not killed, and yet the Midianites who left were later killed because they didn't care. We are told that in the night Bilaam whispered and performed witchcraft, and brought on himself a higher spirit from the other side, the Elohim that was his own level.

283. וַיֹּאמֶר אֲלֵיהֶם לִינוּ פֹה הַלַּיְלָה וַהֲשִׁיבוֹתִי, אִינּוּן כְּתִיב, וַיְדַבְּרוּ אֵלָיו. וְאִיהוּ כְּתִיב, וַיֹּאמֶר אֲלֵיהֶם. לִינוּ פֹה הַלַּיְלָה, בְּגִין דְּלֵילְיָא אִיהוּ שַׁעֲתָא דְּסִטְרָא אַחֲרָא הֲוֵי, לְחַרְשַׁיָּא, בְּשַׁעֲתָא דְּמִשְׁתַּכְּחֵי וְשַׁלְטֵי סִטְרֵי בִּישִׁין וּמִתְפַּשְׁטָן בְּעָלְמָא. כַּאֲשֶׁר יְדַבֵּר יְיָ' אֵלָי. שַׁבּוּחֵי קָא מְשַׁבַּח גַּרְמֵיהּ בִּשְׁמָא דַּיְיָ'.

283. "And he said to them, 'Lodge here this night, and I will bring you back'" (Bemidbar 22:8). About them, it says, "And spoke to him" (Ibid. 7), MEANING SPEECH OF LOUD WORDS, BECAUSE HE WAS IMPAIRED IN HIS EAR. About him it says, "And he said to them," WHICH IS SAYING WITH SOFT WORDS, THE USUAL SORT OF LANGUAGE. "Lodge here this night": that is because the night is the opportune period of the Other Side and of sorcerers, because it is the time during which evil aspects are prevalent and are in control, spreading about in the world. "As Hashem shall speak to me" (Ibid. 8): he was priding himself with the name of Hashem.

284. וַיֵּשְׁבוּ שָׂרֵי מוֹאָב, וְשָׂרֵי מִדְיָן אִתְפְּרָשׁוּ מִנַּיְיהוּ, וְלָא בָּעוּ לְמֵיתַב תַּמָּן. וְסָבֵי מוֹאָב אִשְׁתָּאֲרוּ, דִּכְתִּיב וַיֵּשְׁבוּ שָׂרֵי מוֹאָב, בִּלְחוֹדַיְיהוּ. יָאוּת עַבְדֵי מִדְיָן, דְּאִתְפְּרָשׁוּ מִכָּל וְכָל מִנַּיְיהוּ. וְאִלְמָלֵא לָא הֲווֹ מָחָאן בְּסוֹפָא דַּהֲווֹ בְּעֵיטָא דְּבִלְעָם, לְשָׁלְחָא נְשֵׁיהוֹן לְיִשְׂרָאֵל בַּשִּׁטִּים לְמִטְעֵי לוֹן. וְקָרָא אוֹכַח חוֹבָא דִּלְהוֹן, דִּכְתִּיב כִּי צוֹרְרִים הֵם לָכֶם בְּנִכְלֵיהֶם אֲשֶׁר נִכְּלוּ לָכֶם עַל דְּבַר פְּעוֹר וְעַל דְּבַר כָּזְבִּי בַּת נְשִׂיא מִדְיָן אֲחוֹתָם

וְגוֹ'. בְּתְרֵין אִלֵּין חָאבוּ. וַהֲוָה חוֹבָא דִּלְהוֹן סַגִּי. מָחוּ בִּזְנָבָא לְבָתַר. ובג"כ אִלֵּין אִשְׁתְּאָרוּ בַּהֲדֵיהּ, וְאִלֵּין אָזְלוּ בִּלְחוֹדַיְיהוּ.

284. "And the princes of Moab abode" (Ibid.). However, the princes of Midian left them and did not want to remain there, although the ministers of Moab did stay, as is written: "And the princes of Moab abode" on their own. Midian would have acted appropriately IF THEY WOULD HAVE separated from them altogether, if in the end they would have caused no harm, and not eventually been in the counsel of Bilaam that sent their wives and women to Yisrael at Shitim to lead them astray. The scripture points out their sin, as is written: "For they vex you with their wiles, with which they have beguiled you in the matter of Pe'or, and in the matter of Kozbi, the daughter of a prince of Midian, their sister..." (Bemidbar 25:18). With these two things they sinned, WITH PE'OR AND KOZBI and their iniquity was great. And with their tail, THAT IS, EVENTUALLY, they struck later. Therefore, they remained with him and the Midianites left on their own.

285. ד"א וַיֵּשְׁבוּ שָׂרֵי מוֹאָב עִם בִּלְעָם, כַּמָּה יָאוֹת הֲוָה לוֹן לִבְנֵי מִדְיָן דְּאַזְלֵי, אִי רְעוּתָא דִּלְהוֹן הָכִי. אֲבָל יְשִׁיבָה דְּיָתִיבוּ אִינּוּן דְּמוֹאָב, גַּרְמָא לוֹן טַב, בְּגִין דְּאִשְׁתְּאָרוּ תַּמָּן. וּמַאן דְּאָזְלוּ אִינּוּן דְּמִדְיָן, גַּרְמֵי לוֹן בִּישׁ. מ"ט. אִלֵּין חַשְׁשׁוּ לִיקָרָא דְּמִלָּה דְּקוּדְשָׁא בְּרִיךְ הוּא, וְיָתִיבוּ. וְאִלֵּין לָא חַשְׁשׁוּ לָהּ כְּלוּם. וְאָזְלוּ לְאָרְחַיְיהוּ.

285. Another explanation of: "And the princes of Moab abode with Bilaam": It was fine for Midian to leave if that was their wish. However, the staying over of those from Moab who remained caused them to have a good reward due to their remaining there, while the Midianites' leaving caused them harm. Why is this? It is because those who stayed cared for the glory ot the words of the Holy One, blessed be He, while those who left did not care at all.

286. בְּשַׁעְתָּא דְּאָמַר הַהוּא רָשָׁע, וַהֲשִׁיבוֹתִי אֶתְכֶם דָּבָר כַּאֲשֶׁר יְדַבֵּר יְיָ'. מִיַּד אִזְדַּעֲזָעוּ אִינּוּן דְּמוֹאָב לְמִלָּה דָּא, וְיָתִיבוּ תַּמָּן. וְאִינּוּן דְּמִדְיָן לָא חַשְׁשׁוּ לְדָא כְּלוּם, וְאָזְלוּ לוֹן, וְאִתְעֲנָשׁוּ לְבָתַר. וְעַל דָּא וַיֵּשְׁבוּ שָׂרֵי מוֹאָב עִם בִּלְעָם. בְּהַהוּא לֵילְיָא, הַהוּא רָשָׁע לָחִישׁ לְחִישִׁין, וַעֲבִיד

בְּלָטִין, וְאַמְשִׁיךְ עָלֵיהּ רוּחָא מִלְעֵילָּא, מִיַּד וַיָּבֹא אֱלֹהִים אֶל בִּלְעָם, אֱלֹהִים סְתָם, דַּרְגָּא דִּילֵיהּ מִסִּטְרָא אַחֲרָא דִּשְׂמָאלָא.

286. HE EXPLAINS HIMSELF: At the time, that wicked one said: "And I will bring you back word, as Hashem shall speak to me" (Bemidbar 22:8), instantly, those of Moab were shook up to hear this and stayed there, and those of Midian did not care at all and left. THEREFORE, they were punished afterward, which is why the ministers of Moab remained with Bilaam. That night, this wicked one was whispering whispers and performed witchcraft, and brought upon himself a spirit from above. Instantly, "Elohim came to Bilaam," simply Elohim, meaning his own level, of the Other Side, that is in the left.

23. "What men are these with you"

A Synopsis

Here the Zohar tells us that God tested three men – Hezekiah, Ezekiel and Bilaam – by asking them "Can these bones live?" and only Ezekiel passed the test. Someone said to Rabbi Elazar that Bilaam was greater than Moses because God called Moses to come to him, but it seemed that God went to Bilaam. Rabbi Elazar explains that God went out to warn Bilaam rather than have him come into His holy place and defile it. We hear how arrogant Bilaam was, and how unworthy Balak was to be King of Moab.

287. וַיֹּאמֶר מִי הָאֲנָשִׁים הָאֵלֶּה עִמָּךְ. דַּרְגָּא דִּילֵיהּ, מִסִּטְרָא אַחֲרָא דִּשְׂמָאלָא הֲוָה, דְּקָא אִצְטְרִיךְ לְמִשְׁאַל. ואע"ג דְּחַבְרַיָּיא אִתְּעֲרוּ בְּדָא, בְּגַוְונָא אַחֲרָא, וְאִינּוּן אַמְרֵי דְּקוּדְשָׁא בְּרִיךְ הוּא נִסְיוֹנָא עֲבַד לֵיהּ בְּמִלּוֹי. תְּלָתָא הֲווֹ, חַד חִזְקִיָּה. וְחַד יְחֶזְקֵאל. וְחַד בִּלְעָם. תְּרֵין לָא קַיְימוּ כַּדְקָא יֵאוֹת, וְחַד קָאֵים. וּמַנּוּ. יְחֶזְקֵאל. דִּכְתִּיב, הֲתִחְיֶינָה הָעֲצָמוֹת הָאֵלֶּה, וְאִיהוּ תָּב וְאָמַר, וַיֹּאמֶר יְיָ' אֱלֹהִים אַתָּה יָדָעְתָּ. חִזְקִיָּהוּ אָמַר, מֵאֶרֶץ רְחוֹקָה בָּאוּ אֵלַי מִבָּבֶל. בִּלְעָם אָמַר בָּלָק בֶּן צִפּוֹר מֶלֶךְ מוֹאָב שָׁלַח אֵלַי, חָשִׁיב אֲנָא בְּעֵינֵי מַלְכִין וְשַׁלִּיטִין. וְקוּדְשָׁא בְּרִיךְ הוּא שָׁאִיל לֵיהּ לְמִטְעֵי לֵיהּ, דִּכְתִּיב מַשְׂגִּיא לַגּוֹיִם וַיְאַבְּדֵם וְאוֹקְמוּהָ.

287. "And said, 'What men are these with you'" (Bemidbar 22:9): That was his own level of the left side that needed to ask, BECAUSE IT DIDN'T KNOW. Although the friends remarked on this differently, they indicated that the Holy One, blessed be He, was testing him with His words, because there were three WHO ELOHIM PUT TO A TEST. One was Hezekiah, one was Ezekiel and one was Bilaam. Two of them did not stand up to the test properly and one did. Who was it? That was Ezekiel, as is written THAT THE HOLY ONE, BLESSED BE HE, ASKED HIM, "Can these bones live?" (Yechezkel 37:3). And he answered, "And I answered, Hashem, Elohim You know" (Ibid.) Hezekiah said: "They are come from a far country, from Babylon" (II Melachim 20:14). Bilaam said, "Balak the son of Tzipor, king of Moab, has sent to me" (Bemidbar 22:10) TO SHOW THAT he is important in the eyes of rulers and kings. HOWEVER, the Holy One, blessed be He, simply asked him in order to mislead him and allow him to err, as is written: "He makes nations great and destroys them" (Iyov 12:23). And this has been explained.

288. חַד כּוּתִי שָׁאִיל לְר' אֶלְעָזָר, אָ"ל, חֵילָא תַּקִּיפָא חֲמֵינָא בֵּיהּ בְּבִלְעָם, יַתִּיר מִמֹּשֶׁה. דְּאִילוּ בְּמֹשֶׁה כְּתִיב וַיִּקְרָא אֶל מֹשֶׁה. וּבְבִלְעָם כְּתִיב, וַיִּקָּר אֱלֹהִים אֶל בִּלְעָם, וּכְתִיב וַיָּבֹא אֱלֹהִים אֶל בִּלְעָם.

288. A man from Cuth asked Rabbi Elazar, saying to him, I see a greater power in Bilaam than in Moses. About Moses, it is written: "And Hashem called to Moses" (Vayikra 1:1), MEANING HE CALLED HIM TO COME OVER TO HIM. About Bilaam it says, "And Elohim met Bilaam" (Bemidbar 23:16) and: "And Elohim came to Bilaam" (Bemidbar 22:9), INDICATING THAT ELOHIM CAME TO HIM.

289. אָמַר לֵיהּ, לְמַלְכָּא דְּיָתִיב בְּהֵיכָלֵיהּ עַל כֻּרְסְיָיא, חַד סְגִיר קָרָא לְתַרְעָא. אָמַר, מַאן הוּא דְּבָטַשׁ לְתַרְעָא. אָמְרוּ, סְגִיר פְּלָן. אָמַר לָא יֵיעוּל הָכָא, וְלָא יְטַנֵּף הֵיכָלָא, יָדַעְנָא דְּאִי בִּשְׁלִיחָא אֵימָא לֵיהּ, לָא חָיִישׁ. וְיֵיזִיל בְּרִי וְיִסְתְּאַב וְיִקְרַב בַּהֲדֵיהּ. אֲבָל אֲנָא אֵיזִיל, וְאַגְזִים בֵּיהּ, דְּיִרְחַק אָרְחֵיהּ מִמּוֹתְבָא דִּבְרִי, וְלָא יְסָאֵב לֵיהּ. אַקְדִּים מַלְכָּא, וְאָתָא לְגַבֵּיהּ, וְאַגְזִים. וְאָמַר לֵיהּ, סְגִיר סְגִיר, מְנַע רַגְלָךְ מֵאָרְחָא דִּבְרִי שָׁארֵי תַּמָּן, וְאִי לָאו, אוֹמֵינָא, דְּחֲתִיכִין יַעַבְדוּן גּוּפָךְ בְּנֵי שִׁפְחוֹתַי.

289. He replied to him, THAT IS COMPARABLE to a king that was sitting in his palace on the throne. Some leper called at the door. The king responded, Who is it that knocks on my door? They replied, Some unknown leper. He said, Let him not enter this area and let him not soil the palace with filth. I understand that if I inform him through a messenger, he will have no fear of me and if my son will approach him, he will be contaminated. Rather, I will go myself and threaten him to distance him from my son so that he won't be contaminated. The king came first and approached him and warned him, Leper, leper, keep your foot away from the road where my son lives. If not, I promise you that my handmaids' sons will cut you into pieces.

290. רְחִימָא דְּמַלְכָּא קָרֵי לְדָשָׁא. אָמַר מַלְכָּא, מַאן הוּא. אָמְרוּ,

רְחִימָךְ פְּלַנְיָא. אָמַר, רְחִימָא חֲבִיבָא דְּנַפְשָׁאי, לָא יִקְרֵי לֵיהּ קָלָא אַחֲרָא, אֶלָּא אֲנָא. צָוַח מַלְכָּא וְאָמַר, פְּלַנְיָא פְּלַנְיָא עוּל, חֲבִיבָא דְּנַפְשָׁאי, רְחִימָא דִּילִי, אַתְקִינוּ הֵיכָלִין לְמַלְּלָא עִמֵּיהּ.

290. When the friend of the king calls at the gate, the king inquires, Who is it? They say to him, That is so-and-so, your friend. He replies, My most beloved soul friend, no other voice should call him but myself. The king shouts, Enter so-and-so, my friend and my soul's beloved. Prepare and make ready the chambers so that I can talk with him.

291. כַּךְ בִּלְעָם אִיהוּ סְגִיר, רְחִיקָא מִבְּנֵי נָשָׁא, קָרָא לְתַרְעָא דְּמַלְכָּא, שְׁמַע מַלְכָּא, אָמַר סְגִיר מִסְאֲבָא לָא יֵיעוּל, וְלָא יְטַנֵּף הֵיכָלָא דִּילִי. אֲנָא אִצְטְרִיךְ לְמֵיזָל לְאַגְזְמָא לֵיהּ, דְּלָא יִקְרַב לְגַבֵּי תַּרְעָא דִּבְרִי, וְלָא יְסָאַב לֵיהּ, וְעַ"ד וַיָּבֹא אֱלֹהִים אֶל בִּלְעָם וְגוֹ'. אָמַר לֵיהּ, סְגִיר סְגִיר לֹא תֵלֵךְ עִמָּהֶם, לֹא תָאוֹר אֶת הָעָם כִּי בָרוּךְ הוּא. לָא תִּקְרַב לְגַבֵּי דִּבְרִי, הֵין לְטָב הֵין לְבִישׁ, מְסָאַב אַנְתְּ בְּכֹלָּא. אֲבָל בְּמֹשֶׁה כְּתִיב, וַיִּקְרָא אֶל מֹשֶׁה, קָלָא דְּמַלְכָּא, וְלָא ע"י שְׁלִיחָא אַחֲרָא. מֵאֹהֶל מוֹעֵד מֵהֵיכָלָא קַדִּישָׁא, מֵהֵיכָלָא מְתֻקְּנָא, מֵהֵיכָלָא יַקִּירָא דְּעִלָּאִין וְתַתָּאִין תְּאִיבִין לְגַבֵּיהּ, וְלָא יַכְלִין לְמִקְרַב לְגַבֵּיהּ.

291. So too, Bilaam that leper, who is the outcast from people, calls at the king's gate. The king heard and said, This contaminated leper should not enter in here and he shall not soil my palace. I need to go and warn him that he should not approach the gate of my son, and he should not taint him. Therefore, "And Elohim came to Bilaam" saying, Leper, leper, "You shall not go with them; you shall not curse the people: for they are blessed" (Bemidbar 22:12). Do not get near my son, either for good or for bad. You are outright polluted. However, about Moses, it is written: "And...called to Moses" (Vayikra 1:1), meaning the voice of the King, and not through an emissary. "Out of the Tent of Meeting" (Shemot 30:20), MEANS from the holy palace the good chanber, the precious palace, which the upper and lower grades crave, but are unable to approach.

292. וַיֹּאמֶר בִּלְעָם אֶל הָאֱלֹהִים בָּלָק בֶּן צִפּוֹר. וְהוּא אָמַר מֶלֶךְ מוֹאָב,

מַלְכָּא חֲשִׁיבָא שָׁלַח אֵלַי. מֶלֶךְ מוֹאָב. חָמוּ גָּאוּתָא דְּהַהוּא רָשָׁע, דִּכְתִּיב מֶלֶךְ מוֹאָב, וְלָא אָמַר לְמוֹאָב, מִכְּלַל גַּבְרָא דְּלָא אִתְחֲזֵי לְמַלְכָּא, וְהָא אִתְעֲבֵיד מַלְכָּא לְמוֹאָב. קַדְמָאָה מַה כְּתִיב בֵּיהּ. וְהוּא נִלְחַם בְּמֶלֶךְ מוֹאָב הָרִאשׁוֹן, מַלְכָּא בַּר מַלְכָּא. חֲשִׁיבָא בַּר חֲשִׁיבָא. אֲבָל דָּא מֶלֶךְ לְמוֹאָב כְּתִיב. קְרָא אַסְהִיד מֶלֶךְ לְמוֹאָב. וְהָא אִתְּעַרְנָא, דְּאִתְכַּוֵּון הוּא לְגָאוּתָא לִבָּא רַב. כָּל מַלְכִין דְּעָלְמָא, שַׁלְחִין לְגַבָּאי שְׁלוּחֵיהוֹן.

292. "And Bilaam said to the Elohim, 'Balak the son of Tzipor, king of Moab...'" (Bemidbar 22:10). He mentioned the king of Moab TO SHOW THAT an important king sent for him. "King of Moab," indeed! Look at the arrogance of that wicked man, because it is written THAT HE SAID king of Moab instead of A KING over Moab, WHICH SHOULD HAVE indicated a person who is not worthy to be a king, but became a king over Moab FOR SOME REASON. Of the first KING, it is written: "Who had fought against the former king of Moab" (Bemidbar 21:26). IT DOES NOT REFER TO THE FIRST KING AS A KING OVER MOAB, AS IT IS WRITTEN: "AND BALAK THE SON OF TZIPOR WAS KING OVER MOAB" (BEMIDBAR 22:4), DUE TO THE FACT THAT THE EARLIER KING WAS a king, the son of a king, royalty descended from royalty. However, about this one, IT IS WRITTEN: "BALAK THE SON OF TZIPOR was king over Moab." The scripture testifies, "king over Moab" – THAT HE WAS NOT DISTINGUISHED, BUT BILAAM SAID TO ELOHIM, "BALAK THE SON OF TZIPOR, KING OF MOAB." Here, I remarked that he intended to give pride to his arrogant heart, SAYING LOOK HOW all the royalty of the world send me messengers.

24. "To Him who alone does great wonders"

A Synopsis

We learn first of a miracle that God had performed in the past by saving some Jews, including Rabbi Pinchas, from robbers. Rabbi Pinchas marvels that such a wonder was done for him, when he did not even know about it. He says we have no way of knowing how often God performs miracles for people because no one knows about them except God Himself. Next the Arabs, who told Rabbi Pinchas about the miracle, tell him about another, how they have just now seen a flock of birds circling around to make shade for five people sitting together. The rabbis know that Rabbi Shimon is among this group of five, and they wonder how to find him. They leave the she-mule to find the path on its own and it takes them straight to Rabbi Shimon and his disciples. Rabbi Shimon opens by saying that "A psalm. O sing to Hashem a new song, for He has done marvellous things" was chanted by the cows, who mooed the song to all who came out to welcome the ark.

293. רִבִּי פִּנְחָס הֲוָה אָזִיל לְמֶחֱמֵי בְּרָתֵּיהּ, אִנְתּוּ דְּר׳ שִׁמְעוֹן, דַּהֲוַת בְּמַרְעָא. וַהֲווּ אָזְלֵי עִמֵּיהּ חַבְרַיָּיא, וְהוּא הֲוָה רָכִיב בְּחַמְרֵיהּ. עַד דַּהֲוָה אָזִיל בְּאָרְחָא, פָּגַע בִּתְרֵין עַרְבָאֵי, אָמַר לוֹן, בַּחֲקָל דָּא אִתְּעַר קָלָא מִיּוֹמִין דְּעָלְמָא. אָמְרוּ לֵיהּ, מִיּוֹמִין דְּעָלְמָא לֵית אֲנָן יַדְעִין. מִיּוֹמִין דִּילָן, אֲנָן יַדְעִין. דְּהָא יוֹמָא חַד, הֲווּ אִינּוּן לִסְטִין מְקַפְּחֵי אָרְחִין דְּגוּבְרִין בְּהַהוּא חַקְלָא, וּפַגְעוּ בְּאִינּוּן יוּדָאֵי, וְאָתוּ לְקַפְּחָא לוֹן. וְאִשְׁתְּמַע מֵרָחִיק בְּהַאי חֲקַל, קַל דַּחֲמָרָא דָּא, דְּנָהַק תְּרֵי זִמְנֵי, וְאָתָא שַׁלְהוֹבָא דְּאֶשָּׁא בְּהַהוּא קָלָא וְאוֹקִיד לוֹן. וְאִשְׁתְּזִיבוּ אִינּוּן יוּדָאֵי. אָ״ל. עַרְבָאֵי, בְּמִלָּה דָּא דְּקָא אֲמַרְתּוּן לִי, תִּשְׁתֵּזְבוּן יוֹמָא דָּא מִלִּסְטִין אַחֲרָנִין, דְּקָא מְחַכָּן לְכוּ בְּאָרְחָא.

293. Rabbi Pinchas was going to see his daughter, the wife of Rabbi Shimon, who was ill. The friends joined along with him and he was riding on his donkey. While still walking along on their journey, they met up with two Arabs. He asked them if any sound stirred in this field from ancient days. They said, From times past, we do not know. From our times, we do know, because one day, robbers spread out over the roads in that field and assaulted Jews, and intended to destroy them. From the distance, the voice of this donkey ON WHICH YOU RIDE was heard in this field. It brayed twice. A flame of fire came along with that sound and burned them and these Jews were saved. He said to them, Arabs, Arabs, IN THE MERIT of this episode that you related to me, you will be saved today from the other robbers that are awaiting you along the road.

294. בָּכָה ר׳ פִּנְחָס, אָמַר, מָארֵיהּ דְּעָלְמָא רַחֲשָׁא דְּנִיסָא דָּא עַבְדַּת בְּגִינִי, וְאִשְׁתֵּזְבוּן אִינּוּן יוּדָאֵי, וְלָא יְדַעְנָא. פָּתַח וְאָמַר, לְעוֹשֵׂה נִפְלָאוֹת גְּדוֹלוֹת לְבַדּוֹ כִּי לְעוֹלָם חַסְדּוֹ. כַּמָּה טִיבוּ עָבֵיד קוּדְשָׁא בְּרִיךְ הוּא עִם בְּנֵי נָשָׁא, וְכַמָּה נִסִּין אַרְחִישׁ לוֹן בְּכָל יוֹמָא, וְלָא יָדַע אֶלָּא אִיהוּ בִּלְחוֹדוֹי. ב״נ קָם בְּצַפְרָא, וְחִוְיָא אָתֵי לְקַטְלָא לֵיהּ, וּב״נ שַׁוֵּי רַגְלֵיהּ עַל רֵישֵׁיהּ, וְקָטִיל לֵיהּ, וְלָא יָדַע בֵּיהּ בַּר קוּדְשָׁא בְּרִיךְ הוּא בִּלְחוֹדוֹי, הֲוֵי, לְעוֹשֵׂה נִפְלָאוֹת גְּדוֹלוֹת לְבַדּוֹ. ב״נ אָזִיל בְּאָרְחָא, וְלִסְטִין מְחַכָּאן לְמִקְטְלֵיהּ, אָתָא אַחֲרָא וְאִתְיְיהִב כּוּפְרָא תְּחוֹתֵיהּ, וְהוּא אִשְׁתְּזִיב. לָא יָדַע טִיבוּ דְּעָבֵד לֵיהּ קוּדְשָׁא בְּרִיךְ הוּא, וְנִסָּא דְּאַרְחִישׁ לֵיהּ, בַּר אִיהוּ בִּלְחוֹדוֹי, הֲוֵי, לְעוֹשֵׂה נִפְלָאוֹת גְּדוֹלוֹת לְבַדּוֹ. לְבַדּוֹ עָבֵיד וְיָדַע. וְאַחֲרָא לָא יָדַע.

294. Rabbi Pinchas wept and said, Master of the universe, this miracle You performed for my sake; these Jews were saved, and I did not even know. He opened the discussion with the verse: "To Him who alone does great wonders: for His steadfast love endures forever" (Tehilim 136:4). How much good does the Holy One, blessed be He, do for people, and how many miracles does He perform for them every day. No one knows except He alone. A person gets up in the morning and a snake comes to kill him. The person places his foot on his head, WITHOUT INTENTION, and kills him. No one is aware of that except the Holy One, blessed be He, alone. "To Him who alone does great wonders": A person walks along the road and robbers lie in wait to kill him. Another one comes along and pays ransom instead for him, and he is saved. None knows of the kindness that the Holy One, blessed be He, did with him and the miracle that just occurred to him, but the Holy One, blessed be He, Himself. "To Him who alone does great wonders": He by Himself made it andknows, and no one else is even knows it.

295. אָמַר לְחַבְרַיָּיא, חַבְרַיָּיא מַה דְּשָׁאִילְנָא לְהָנֵי עַרְבָאֵי, דְּמִשְׁתַּכְּחֵי

תָּדִיר בְּחַקְלֵי, אִי קָלָא דְּחַבְרַיָּיא, דְּאִינּוּן מִשְׁתַּדְּלֵי בְּאוֹרַיְיתָא שָׁמְעוּ. דְּהָא ר׳ שִׁמְעוֹן וְר׳ אֶלְעָזָר בְּרֵיהּ, וּשְׁאָר חַבְרַיָּיא, אַזְלִין לְקַמָּן, וְלָא יַדְעִין מִנָּן, וְשָׁאִילְנָא לְהָנֵי עַרְבָאֵי עָלַיְיהוּ. דְּיָדַעְנָא דְּקָלֵיהּ דְּר״ש יַרְגִּיז חַקְלִין וְטוּרִין, וְאִינּוּן גָּלוּ לִי מַה דְּלָא יָדַעְנָא.

295. He said to his friends, Friends, what I inquired of these Arabs who are always present in the field WAS if they heard the voices of the friends who study and deal with the Torah. Rabbi Shimon and Rabbi Elazar, his son, and the rest of the friends are traveling in front of us and are not aware of us, and I inquired of those Arabs about them, since I know that Rabbi Shimon's voice shakes up the fields and the mountains. They told me something I did not know of, MEANING THAT MIRACLE.

296. עַד דַּהֲווּ אָזְלִין, אִינּוּן עַרְבָאֵי אַהַדְרוּ לְגַבֵּיהּ. אָמְרוּ לֵיהּ, סָבָא סָבָא אַנְתְּ שָׁאִילְתָּא לָן מִן יוֹמִין דְּעָלְמָא, וְלָא שָׁאִילְתָּא עַל יוֹמָא דָּא, דַּחֲמֵינָא תְּוְהָא עַל תַּוְהָא, חֲמֵינָא חַמְשָׁא בְּנֵי נָשָׁא יַתְבִין, וְחַד סָבָא בַּהֲדַיְיהוּ, וַחֲמֵינָא עוֹפֵי מִתְכַּנְּפֵי וְקָא פַּרְשִׂין גַּדְפִּין עַל רֵישַׁיְיהוּ, אִלֵּין אַזְלִין, וְאִלֵּין תָּבִין, וְטוּלָא לָא אִתְעֲבַר מֵעַל רֵישַׁיְיהוּ. וְהַהוּא סָבָא אָרִים קָלֵיהּ עָלַיְיהוּ, וְאִינּוּן שַׁמְעִין.

296. While still traveling, these Arabs returned to them. They said to him, Old man, you asked us if A VOICE WAS STIRRED IN THE FIELD from days gone by. But you have not asked us about this day. We noticed, TODAY, a wonderful marvel. We saw five people sitting together and an old man was with them. We saw birds gathering and extending their wings over their heads, some going and some returning, so the shadow did not pass away from over their heads. This old man raised his voice to them, and they listened.

297. אָמַר עַל דָּא שָׁאִילְנָא. עַרְבָאֵי עַרְבָאֵי תֶּהֱווֹן, וְאָרְחָא דָּא תְּהֵא מִתְקְנָא קַמַּיְיכוּ, בְּכָל מַה דְּתִבְעוּן. תְּרֵין מִלִּין אֲמַרְתּוּן לִי, דַּחֲדֵינָא בְּהוּ. אַזְלוּ. אָמְרוּ לוֹ חַבְרַיָּיא, הַהוּא אֲתָר דְּר״ש שָׁארִי בֵּיהּ, הֵיךְ אֲנַן יַדְעִין. אָמַר לוֹן שְׁבוֹקוּ לְמָארֵי פְּסִיעָן דִּבְעִירֵי, דְּהוּא יַדְרִיךְ פְּסִיעוֹי

לְתַמָּן. לָא הֲוֵי טָעִין חֲמָרֵיהּ, וַחֲמָרֵיהּ סָאטֵי מֵאָרְחָא תְּרֵין מִלִּין, וְאָזַל לְתַמָּן.

297. He said, It is about this that I inquired. Arabs, Arabs, go and this road should be ready for you with whatever you wish. You have told me two things that make me glad. They left. The friends said, How are we going to find where Rabbi Shimon is? He said to them, Leave that to the one who has dominion over the footsteps of the beasts. He will direct their steps towards that place. He did not lead his donkey yet his donkey, on its own, took a detour from the road about two miles, and went there.

298. שָׁארִי נָהִיק תְּלַת זִמְנִין, נָחַת ר׳ פִּנְחָס, אָמַר לְחַבְרַיָּיא, נִתְתָּקַן לְקַבְּלָא סְבַר אַפֵּי יוֹמִין, דְּהַשְׁתָּא יִפְקוּן לְגַבָּן אַנְפֵּי רַבְרְבֵי וְאַנְפֵּי זוּטְרֵי. שָׁמַע ר״ש נָהִיקוּ דַּחֲמָרָא, אָמַר לְחַבְרַיָּיא, נֵיקוּם דְּהָא קָלָא דְּחַמְרָא דְּסָבָא חֲסִידָא אִתְּעַר לְגַבָּן. קָם ר׳ שִׁמְעוֹן וְקָמוּ חַבְרַיָּיא.

298. The donkey began to bray three times. Rabbi Pinchas dismounted and said to his friends, Let's prepare welcome the countenance OF ATIK YOMIN, MEANING THE SHECHINAH, because now a great face and a small face are coming towards us, MEANING RABBI SHIMON AND HIS DISCIPLES. Rabbi Shimon heard the braying of the donkey and said to his friends, Let us rise, because the voice of the donkey of the pious old sage has risen towards us. Rabbi Shimon rose and the friends rose.

299. פָּתַח ר׳ שִׁמְעוֹן וְאָמַר, מִזְמוֹר שִׁירוּ לַיְיָ׳ שִׁיר חָדָשׁ כִּי נִפְלָאוֹת עָשָׂה וְגוֹ׳. מִזְמוֹר זָקִיף טַעֲמָא לְעֵילָּא. אֲמַאי. אֶלָּא רָשִׁים טַעֲמָא רַבָּא, דְּהָא אָתֵי הַהוּא מִזְמוֹר, מִתְעַטְּרָא בְּעִטְרָא עִלָּאָה לְעֵילָּא עַל רֵישֵׁיהּ וְאָתֵי זָקִיף. מַאן הֲוָה אָמַר שִׁירָה דָּא. אִינּוּן פָּרוֹת, בְּאִינּוּן גּוֹעִין דַּהֲווֹ גָּעָאן. שִׁירוּ לַיְיָ׳ שִׁיר חָדָשׁ. לְמַאן הֲווֹ אַמְרִין שִׁירוּ. לְכַמָּה רְתִיכִין, לְכַמָּה מְמָנָן, לְכַמָּה דַּרְגִּין, דַּהֲווֹ אָתָאן תַּמָּן וְנַפְקוּ לְקַבְּלָא לֵיהּ לַאֲרוֹנָא, וּלְהוֹן הֲווֹ אַמְרֵי.

299. Rabbi Shimon opened the discussion with the verse: "A psalm. O sing to Hashem a new song; for He has done marvelous things" (Tehilim 98:1). OVER THE WORD "A psalm," there is a vertical musical note, WHICH IS THE CANTILATION MARK CALLED 'PAZER'. HE ASKS: Why? HE REPLIES: This note is indicative of a great reason, because this psalm comes and gets adorned with a supernal crown above its head. THEREFORE, it receives ABOVE IT a vertical NOTE THAT IS THE MUSICAL NOTE PAZER. Who chanted this song? The cows, who mooed: "O sing to Hashem a new song." HE ASKS: To whom did they say this "sing"? HE REPLIES: To the many Chariots, many appointees, for the many levels that came by there and went out to welcome the ark. To them, they used to say "SING."

25. Masculine song - Feminine song

A Synopsis

Rabbi Shimon explains that the word 'shir' (song) is in the masculine form in "O sing to Hashem a new song" because it refers to the ark, Malchut, along with what is stored in it, Zeir Anpin, and Zeir Anpin is masculine. We learn that God originally had His right hand on the chest of his son, Yisrael, to protect him, but when Yisrael sinned He put His hand on his back to throw him to his enemies.

300. שִׁירוּ לַיְיָ׳ שִׁיר חָדָשׁ, דְּכַר. מ״ט הָכָא שִׁיר, וּמֹשֶׁה אָמַר שִׁירָה, נוּקְבָא אֶלָּא הָתָם בְּמֹשֶׁה אֲרוֹנָא לְחוֹדָא, זֹאת, נַפְקַת מִן גָּלוּתָא, הִיא וְאוּכְלוּסָהָא, וְלָא יַתִּיר. ובג״כ אֶת הַשִּׁירָה הַזֹּאת, נוּקְבָא. אֲבָל הָכָא אֲרוֹנָא, וּמַה דַּהֲוָה גָּנִיז בְּגַוֵּיהּ נָפִיק. וּבְגִין הַהוּא דַּהֲוָה גָּנִיז בְּגַוֵּיהּ, אִתְּמַר שִׁיר חָדָשׁ, דְּכַר.

300. "O sing to Hashem a new song (Heb. *shir*)" (Tehilim 98:1). THAT SONG IS masculine. HE ASKS: What is the difference that here *shir* IS IN MASCULINE FORM, while Moses said, *shirah,* feminine, AS IT SAYS, "THEN SANG...THIS SONG (HEB. *SHIRAH*)" (SHEMOT 15:1)? HE REPLIES: It is because there, with Moses, the ark was by itself, since *zot* (Eng. 'this'), MALCHUT THAT IS CALLED *'ZOT'* AND ALSO 'ARK', left the exile, she and her multitudes, THE SHECHINAH AND YISRAEL, and nothing else. Therefore, it says: "This (Heb. *zot*) song (Heb. *shirah*)," which is feminine, BECAUSE IT REFERS TO THE SHECHINAH, WHICH IS FEMININE. However, here, the ark came out, THAT IS MALCHUT, with what is stored in it, THAT IS ZEIR ANPIN, THAT IS MASCULINE, so it says: "a new *shir*," which is masculine.

301. כִּי נִפְלָאוֹת עָשָׂה, מַה דְּעֲבַד בַּפְּלִשְׁתִּים, וּמַה דְּעֲבַד בְּטַעֲוָותְהוֹן. הוֹשִׁיעָה לּוֹ יְמִינוֹ, לְמַאן. לְעַצְמוֹ. מַאן עַצְמוֹ. הַהוּא מִזְמוֹר עַצְמוֹ, וְרוּחָא עִלָּאָה קַדִּישָׁא גָּנִיז בֵּיהּ. יְמִינוֹ, הַהוּא דְּיָרִית סָבָא. וְדָא יְמִינוֹ, אַתְקִיף בְּהַהוּא מִזְמוֹר, וְלָא שָׁבִיק לֵיהּ בִּידָא דְּאַחֲרָא.

301. "For He has done marvelous things": That is what He did with the

Philistines and what He did to their deities. "His right hand...gained Him the victory" (Tehilim 98:1). Who? Meaning itself. Who is Itself? It is that psalm itself, WHICH IS THE SHECHINAH THAT IS REFERRED TO AS A PSALM because a supernal holy spirit, ZEIR ANPIN, was stored in it. "His right," WHAT IS IT? It is that quality that the old man inherited, ABRAHAM, THAT IS CHESED. That right holds on to that psalm and does not abandon it to the hands of another.

302. הָכָא אִית לְגַלָּאָה מִלָּה חֲדָא, כָּל זִמְנָא דְּהַהוּא יְמִינָא, הֲוָה לְאַרְחָשָׁא נִיסָא, הֲוָה אַתְקִיף בְּהַאי מִזְמוֹר, וְשַׁוֵּי לֵיהּ לְקַמֵּיהּ, לְאַתְקְפָא בֵּיהּ, כְּאַבָּא דְּאַתְקִיף יְמִינֵיהּ בְּחַדּוֹי דִּבְרֵיהּ לְקַמֵּיהּ, וְאָמַר מַאן הוּא דְּיִקְרַב לְגַבֵּי בְּרִי. כֵּיוָן דְּסָרַח לְגַבֵּי אֲבוֹי, שַׁוֵּי אֲבוֹי יְדוֹי עַל כַּתְפוֹי לַאֲחוֹרָא, וְשַׁדְיֵיהּ בִּידָא דְּשַׂנְאוֹי.

302. Here we should reveal one thing. As long as that right, CHESED, had WISHED to accomplish a miracle, it held unto that psalm. And it placed YISRAEL, IN WHOM THE SHECHINAH IS ATTIRED, before it to hold on to him, as a father whose right is held to the chest of his son in front of him and says, Who dares approach my son? As soon as he sins against his father, his father places his hands on his shoulders from the back and throws him to his enemies.

303. כִּבְיָכוֹל, בְּקַדְמֵיתָא כְּתִיב, יְמִינְךָ יְיָ׳ נֶאְדָּרִי בַּכֹּחַ. בַּכֹּחַ מַאן. הַהוּא דְּאִשְׁתְּמוֹדְעָא. בְּעַרַבְיָא קוֹרִין לְחַדּוֹי דְּבַר נָשׁ כֹּחַ. הַהוּא יְמִינָא נֶאְדָּרִי וְאַתְקִיף בְּכֹחַ. מַאן הוּא דְּיִקְרַב לְגַבֵּי בְּרִי. לְבָתַר מַה כְּתִיב, הֵשִׁיב אָחוֹר יְמִינוֹ מִפְּנֵי אוֹיֵב, שַׁוֵּי יְמִינֵיהּ עַל כִּתְפֵיהּ, וְדָחֵי לֵיהּ בִּידָא דְּשַׂנְאוֹי. בְּקַדְמֵיתָא יְמִינֵיהּ לְקַמֵּיהּ בְּחַדּוֹי, לְאַתְקְפָא בֵּיהּ. וּלְבָתַר לַאֲחוֹרָא עַל כַּתְפוֹי, לְדַחְיָיא לֵיהּ. וְהָכָא הוֹשִׁיעָה לּוֹ יְמִינוֹ וּזְרוֹעַ קָדְשׁוֹ, תְּרֵין דְּרוֹעִין לְאַתְקְפָא בֵּיהּ.

303. HE EXPLAINS HIMSELF. At first it says, so to speak, "Your right, Hashem, is glorious in power" (Ibid. 6). Who is "in power"? That is with that known POWER THAT IS YISRAEL. In Arabia, they call the chest of man "power." AND THE SCRIPTURE SAYS that right, WHICH IS CHESED, "is glorious" and holds to power, MEANING IN THE CHEST OF YISRAEL THAT IS CALLED 'POWER'. He says, Who is there that dare get close to my son? Afterward, it is written: "He has drawn back His right hand from before the enemy" (Eichah 2:3), because He placed His right on the shoulders OF YISRAEL and pushed them into the hands of those who hate them. At the beginning, His right hand was in front OF YISRAEL at his chest AREA, to hold on to him. Afterwards, His right was on his back over his shoulders, to push him. Here, IT SAYS, "His right hand, and His holy arm have gained Him the victory" (Tehilim 98:1). THAT MEANS with two arms, to keep him.

26. The braying of the donkey, who sang

A Synopsis

Rabbi Shimon says that the cows sang with their mooing, and they were not even accustomed to miracles; therefore Rabbi Pinchas' donkey was much more likely to be able to sing. We learn that God created a grade over the mouth of the she-mule, and at the correct time God opened the abyss in which that grade was kept, and the grade emerged to rule over the she-mule; thus the she-mule was able to talk. Similar things are said about the mouth of the earth and the mouth of the well, and we are told that all of them were created on the eve of Shabbat at twilight. When the Shabbat is sanctified, the mouth of Hashem ascends to dominate all the powers. Next we hear how Rabbi Pinchas sends away all the birds who are circling over the rabbis to provide shade; Rabbi Shimon tells the birds that he will call for them again on a hot day. The rabbis sit under three shady trees near a spring.

304. דְּאִי אִינּוּן פָּרוֹת דְּלָא אִתְרְגִילוּ בְּנִסִּין, אֶלָּא הַהִיא שַׁעֲתָא בְּגוֹעָא דִּלְהוֹן אָמְרוּ שִׁירָתָא. דָּא נְהִיקוּ דַּחֲמָרָא דְּסָבָא חֲסִידָא דְּרָגִיל בְּנִסִּין, עאכ"ו דְּאָמַר שִׁירָה. חַבְרַיָּיא, אִי תֵּימְרוּן דַּחֲמָרָא לָא הֲוָה אָרְחֵיהּ בְּכַךְ מִיּוֹמָא דְּאִבְרֵי עָלְמָא, פּוּקוּ וְחָמוּ אָתוֹן דְּבִלְעָם חַיָּיבָא, דְּנַצְּחַת לְרִבּוֹנָהּ בְּכֹלָּא. חֲמָרֵיהּ דְּרִבִּי פִּנְחָס בֶּן יָאִיר עאכ"ו. וְתוּ אָתוֹן דְּבִלְעָם כַּד מְלִילַת, מַלְאָכָא עִלָּאָה הֲוָה עָלָהּ מִלְעֵילָּא.

304. If those cows which had not been accustomed to miracles were singing only then with their mooing, how much more likely it is that the donkey of the pious old man, RABBI PINCHAS BEN YAIR, who was accustomed to miracles, would sing. Friends, if you say that this is not a custom of a donkey, since it first appeared on the face of the earth, TO CHANT ANY SONG, go take a look at the she-mule of the wicked Bilaam that has defeated her master outright. The donkey of Rabbi Pinchas ben Yair can most certainly sing. Furthermore, when the she-mule of Bilaam spoke, there was a supernal angel above her THAT SCARED HER; HOWEVER, NOBODY COULD SCARE THE DONKEY OF RABBI PINCHAS BEN YAIR.

305. הַשְׁתָּא אִית לְגַלָּאָה, חַבְרַיָּיא שִׁמְעוּ. פִּי הָאָתוֹן דְּאִבְרֵי ע"ש בֵּין הַשְּׁמָשׁוֹת, סַלְקָא בְּדַעְתַּיְיכוּ דְּפוּמָא הֲוָה פְּתִיחָא מֵהַהוּא זִמְנָא. אוֹ

תְּנַאי דְּאַתְנֵי קוּדְשָׁא בְּרִיךְ הוּא מֵהַהוּא זִמְנָא. לָאו הָכִי. וְרָזָא הָכָא דְּאִתְמְסַר לְחַכִּימֵי, דְּלָא מַשְׁגְּחָן לְטִפְּשׁוּ דְּלִבָּא. פִּי הָאָתוֹן, דַּרְגָּא דְּאַתְנֵי, הַהוּא עִלָּאָה דִּסְטָר נוּקְבֵי. הַהוּא הֲוָה דְּשַׁרְיָא עַל הַהוּא אָתוֹן, וּמַלִּיל עָלָהּ. וְכַד בָּרָא קוּדְשָׁא בְּרִיךְ הוּא לְהַאי דַּרְגָּא, דְּאִקְרֵי פִּי הָאָתוֹן, סָתַם לֵיהּ בְּגוֹ נוּקְבָּא דִּתְהוֹמָא רַבָּא, וְאַסְתִּים עָלֵיהּ עַד הַהוּא זִמְנָא. כַּד מָטָא הַהוּא זִמְנָא, פָּתַח הַהוּא נוּקְבָּא, וְנָפַק וְשָׁרָא עָלָהּ, וּמַלִּילַת.

305. Now there is something that needs to be revealed, friends. Listen. The mouth of the she-mule that was created on the eve of Shabbat at twilight, could you ever think that it was open from that period on? Or rather, THE MEANING IS THAT the Holy One, blessed be He, made a condition from that time on? It is not so and there is a secret reason here that was passed on to the wise, who do not pay attention to the foolish at heart. The mouth of the she-mule is a level of asses, that higher POWER of the female aspect, the one that prevailed over that she-mule, BECAUSE THERE IS NOTHING BELOW THAT DOES NOT HAVE AN ANGEL OVER IT THAT IS APPOINTED FROM ABOVE. He talked over her AND IS CONSIDERED THE MOUTH OF THAT SHE-MULE. When the Holy One, blessed be He, created that level that is called the mouth of the she-mule, He plugged it up in the hole of the great abyss and kept it covered until that time. When that time arrived, He opened that hole OF THE GREAT ABYSS. It emerged and prevailed over that she-mule, OF BILAAM, and it talked.

306. כְּגַוְונָא דָּא, וַתִּפְתַּח הָאָרֶץ אֶת פִּיהָ. אֶת, לְאַסְגָּאָה דוּמָ״ה דְּאִיהוּ פִּי הָאָרֶץ. אֶת פִּי הָאָתוֹן, לְאַסְגָּאָה קַמְרִיאֵ״ל, דְּאִקְרֵי פִּי הָאָתוֹן. פִּי הַבְּאֵר כְּגַוְונָא דָּא. מַאן פִּי הַבְּאֵר. הַהוּא דַּרְגָּא דַּהֲוָה מְמָנָא עָלֵיהּ לְתַתָּא, וְאִיהוּ תְּחוֹת פִּי יְיָ׳, וּמַאן אִיהוּ. יָהַדְרִיאֵ״ל שְׁמֵיהּ. תְּלַת פּוּמִין אִלֵּין, אִתְבְּרִיאוּ ע״ש בֵּין הַשְּׁמָשׁוֹת. בְּשַׁעֲתָא דְּקָדֵשׁ יוֹמָא סַלְּקָא פֶּה דִּמְמָנָא עַל כָּל שְׁאַר פּוּמִין, וּמַאן אִיהוּ. הַהוּא יוֹמָא דְּאִסְתַּלָּק וְאִתְקַדָּשׁ בְּכֹלָּא, הַהוּא דְּאִקְרֵי פִּי יְיָ׳. ע״ש בֵּין הַשְּׁמָשׁוֹת, אִבְרוּן שְׁאַר פּוּמִין. אִתְקַדָּשׁ יוֹמָא סָלִיק פּוּמָא דְּשַׁלִּיט עַל כֹּלָּא פִּי יְיָ׳.

306. Similar to this is the meaning of: "And the earth opened (*et*) her mouth" (Bemidbar 16:32). The particle "*Et* (lit. 'the')" is meant to include THE ANGEL Dumah, which is CONSIDERED the mouth of the earth. "(*et*) The mouth of the she-mule" comes to add THE ANGEL Kamriel, who is considered the mouth of the she-mule. Similarly is the mouth of the well. Who is the mouth of the well? It is that level that is appointed over it from below, which is underneath the mouth of Hashem. Who does this refer to? THAT IS THE ANGEL whose name is Yehadriel. These three mouths, THE MOUTH OF THE EARTH, THE MOUTH OF THE SHE-MULE, THE MOUTH OF THE WELL, were created on the eve of Shabbat at twilight. At the time that the day was sanctified, the mouth that is appointed over all the other mouths ascended. Who is that? That is the day that ascended and was sanctified in everything, the same that is called 'the mouth of Hashem', WHICH IS MALCHUT. At twilight of Shabbat eve, the rest of the mouths were created, MEANING THE ANGELS THAT LEAD THEIR BRANCHES THAT ARE IN THIS WORLD, WHICH ARE THE WEEKDAY POWERS. When the day was sanctified, the mouth ascended that rules and dominates over all THE POWERS, which is the mouth of Hashem.

307. אַדְּהָכִי, חָמוּ לְר׳ פִּנְחָס דַּהֲוָה אָתֵי, מָטוּ לְגַבֵּיהּ, אָתָא ר׳ פִּנְחָס וּנְשָׁקֵיהּ לְר״ש. אָמַר, נְשַׁקְנָא פִּי יְיָ׳, אִתְבָּסַּם בְּבוּסְמִין דְּגִנְתָּא דִּילֵיהּ. חֲדוּ כַּחֲדָא, וְיָתְבוּ. כֵּיוָן דְּיָתְבוּ פָּרְחוּ כָּל אִינּוּן עוֹפִין דַּהֲווֹ עַבְדֵי טוּלָא, וְאִתְבָּדָרוּ. אַהְדָּר רֵישֵׁיהּ ר״ש, וְרָמָא לוֹן קָלִין וְאָמַר, עוֹפֵי שְׁמַיָּא לֵית אַתּוּן מַשְׁגִּיחִין בִּיקָרָא דְּמָרֵיכוֹן דְּקָאֵים הָכָא. קַיְימוּ, וְלָא נָטְלוּ מִדּוּכְתַּיְיהוּ, וְלָא קָרִיבוּ לְגַבַּיְיהוּ. א״ר פִּנְחָס אֵימָא לוֹן דְּיָהֲכוּן לְאָרְחַיְיהוּ, דְּהָא לָא יָהֲבִין לוֹן רְשׁוּ לְאַהְדְּרָא.

307. In the meanwhile, they saw Rabbi Pinchas arriving. They went to him. Rabbi Pinchas approached and kissed Rabbi Shimon. He declared, I have kissed the mouth of Hashem and I was perfumed with the fragrances of His garden. They rejoiced together and sat down. As soon as they sat down, all those birds that created the shadow flew away and scattered. Rabbi Shimon turned back his head, raised his voice to them and said, birds of the sky, you are not careful about to the honor of your Master who stays here. The birds stopped in their flight and traveled no further from their location, but did not get closer to him. Rabbi Pinchas declared, Tell them that they may continue on their way, because they are not given permission to return.

308. אר״ש, יְדַעְנָא דְקוּדְשָׁא בְּרִיךְ הוּא בָּעֵי לְמֶרְחָשׁ לָן נִיסָא. עוֹפִין עוֹפִין זִילוּ לְאָרְחַיְיכוּ, וְאָמְרוּ לְהַהוּא דִּמְמָנָא עֲלַיְיכוּ, דְּהָא בְּקַדְמֵיתָא הֲוָה בִּרְשׁוּתֵיהּ, וְהַשְׁתָּא לָאו בִּרְשׁוּתֵיהּ קַיְימָא. אֲבָל סְלִיקְנָא לֵיהּ לְיוֹמָא דְטִנָּרָא, כַּד סָלִיק עִיבָא בֵּין שִׁינֵי תַּקִּיפִין, וְלָא מִתְחַבְּרָאן. אִתְבַּדָּרוּ אִינּוּן עוֹפֵי וְאָזְלוּ.

308. Rabbi Shimon said, I know that the Holy One, blessed be He, wishes to do a miracle for us, TO GIVE US SHADE FROM ANOTHER PLACE. Birds' of firds, go on your way and say to the one who is appointed over you that at first you were under his authority, AND IT WAS UP TO HIM TO SEND YOU TO GIVE ME SHADE. You are no longer under his authority, BECAUSE RABBI PINCHAS BEN YAIR RULES NOW AND HE HAS NO DESIRE FOR YOU. However, I will bring you on the day that is as harsh as a rock when a cloud will rise between the mighty teeth OF THE HOT RAYS OF THE SUN and they won't BE ABLE TO join AND CREATE A SHADE. The birds dispersed and left.

309. אַדְּהָכִי, הָא תְּלַת אִילָנִין, מִתְפַּשְּׁטָן בְּעַנְפִין לִתְלַת סִטְרִין עֲלַיְיהוּ, וּמַעְיָינָא דְמַיָּא נַבְעִין קַמַּיְיהוּ. חֲדוּ כֻּלְּהוּ חַבְרַיָּיא, וְחַדוּ ר׳ פִּנְחָס וְר״ש. אָמַר ר׳ פִּנְחָס טוֹרַח סַגִּי הֲוָה לְאִינּוּן עוֹפֵי בְּקַדְמֵיתָא, וְטוֹרַח בַּעֲלֵי חַיִּים לָא בָּעֵינָן. דְּהָא וְרַחֲמָיו עַל כָּל מַעֲשָׂיו כְּתִיב. אָמַר ר״ש, אֲנָא לָא אַטְרַחְנָא לוֹן. אֲבָל אִי קוּדְשָׁא בְּרִיךְ הוּא חָס עֲלָן לֵית אֲנָן יַכְלִין לְדַחְיָיא מַתְּנָן דִּילֵיהּ. יָתְבוּ תְּחוֹת הַהוּא אִילָנָא, וְשָׁתוּ מִן מַיָּא, וְאִתְהֲנוּ תַּמָּן.

309. Meanwhile, behold three trees spreading out their branches to the three directions over their head, WHICH COVERED THEM WITH SHADE. A spring of water flowed before them. All the friends rejoiced and Rabbi Pinchas and Rabbi Shimon were glad. Rabbi Pinchas said, Those birds before had to work hard TO CREATE A SHADE, and the toil of living animals I do not desire, because it says, "And His mercies are over all His works" (Tehilim 145:9). Rabbi Shimon replied, I have not bothered them. However, if the Holy One, blessed be He, had mercy on us AND DISPATCHED THESE BIRDS TO CREATE A SHADE OVER US, we have no right to refuse His gifts. They reposed underneath the shade of that tree, drank from the water and took pleasure there.

27. "A fountain of gardens"

A Synopsis

Rabbi Shimon tells Rabbi Pinchas that a spring in a garden is better than a spring in the desert because the former benefits grasses and fruits, flowers and plants; it is a well of life-giving water. The Congregation of Yisrael when gathered together are referred to as a spring of gardens, and Rabbi Shimon says that the five gardens in which God takes pleasure are Chesed, Gvurah, Tiferet, Netzach and Hod of Zeir Anpin. They receive water from the spring above them, Binah; the garden below them, Malchut, benefits from the five gardens. We hear that there are other gardens – the three worlds – underneath this garden, and they produce a variety of fruits. Rabbi Shimon says that sometimes Malchut is a spring and sometimes a well.

310. פָּתַח ר׳ פִּנְחָס וְאָמַר, מַעְיַן גַּנִּים בְּאֵר מַיִם חַיִּים וְנוֹזְלִים מִן לְבָנוֹן. מַעְיַן גַּנִּים, וְכִי לֵית מַעְיָין אֶלָּא הַהוּא מִן גַּנִּים, וְהָא כַּמָּה מַעְיָינִין טָבִין וְיַקִּירִין אִית בְּעָלְמָא. אֶלָּא לֵית כָּל הֲנָאוֹת שָׁוִין. אִית מַעְיָין דְּנָפִיק בְּמַדְבְּרָא, בַּאֲתַר יְבֵישָׁא, הֲנָאָה אִית לְמַאן דְּיָתִיב וְשָׁתֵי. אֲבָל מַעְיַן גַּנִּים, כַּמָּה אִיהוּ טַב וְיַקִּירָא, הַהוּא מַעְיָין עָבֵיד טִיבוּ לַעֲשָׂבִין וְאִיבִין, מַאן דְּקָרִיב עָלֵיהּ אִתְהֲנֵי בְּכֹלָּא. אִתְהֲנֵי בְּמַיָּא, אִתְהֲנֵי בַּעֲשָׂבִין, אִתְהֲנֵי בְּאִיבִין. הַהוּא מַעְיָין מִתְעַטְּרָא בְּכֹלָּא. כַּמָּה וְורְדִין, כַּמָּה עֲשָׂבִין דְּרֵיחָא סַחֲרָנֵיהּ, כַּמָּה יָאוּת הַהוּא מַעְיָין, מִשְּׁאַר מַעְיָינִין, בְּאֵר מַיִם חַיִּים.

310. Rabbi Pinchas opened the discussion saying, "A fountain of gardens, a well of living waters, and streams from Lebanon" (Shir Hashirim 4:15). "A fountain of gardens": HE INQUIRES: Does he not have a spring except from gardens? There are so many good and valuable springs in the world. HE RESPONDS: All pleasures are not equal. There is a spring that emerges in the desert, in a dry place, and there is enjoyment in it for whoever sits down and drinks. However, how much better and more precious is that fountain of gardens. It benefits the grasses and the fruits. Whoever gets close to it enjoys everything; he has pleasure from the water, enjoys the grass and benefits from the fruits. That spring is adorned by everything - many roses, many fragrant plants and grasses surrounding it. How worthy is this spring above all other springs. It is a well living water.

311. וְהָכִי אוֹקִימְנָא כֹּלָּא בִּכְנֶסֶת יִשְׂרָאֵל קָאָמַר, אִיהִי מַעְיָין גַּנִּים. מַאן גַּנִּים. חָמֵשׁ גַּנִּים אִית לֵיהּ לְקוּדְשָׁא בְּרִיךְ הוּא, דְּקָא מִשְׁתַּעְשְׁעָא בְּהוּ. וּמַעְיָינָא חֲדָא עִלָּוַויְיהוּ, דְּקָא אַשְׁקֵי לוֹן, וְרַוֵּי לוֹן, טָמִיר וְגָנִיז, וְכֻלְּהוּ עַבְדִּין פֵּירִין וְאֵיבִין. גִּנְתָּא חֲדָא אִית לְתַתָּא מִנַּיְיהוּ, וְהַהוּא גִּנְתָּא נָטִיר סַחֲרָא מִכָּל סִטְרִין דְּעָלְמָא. תְּחוֹת הַאי גִּנְתָּא, אִית גַּנִּים אַחֲרָנִין, עַבְדִּין אֵיבִין לִזְנַיְיהוּ.

311. This is how we established it regarding the Congregation of Yisrael, WHICH IS MALCHUT, which is referred to as a fountain of gardens. Who are the gardens? HE RESPONDS: The Holy One, blessed be He, has five gardens, WHICH ARE CHESED, GVURAH, TIFERET, NETZACH AND HOD OF ZEIR ANPIN, in which He takes pleasure. One spring above them, THAT IS, BINAH, is hidden and stored away. It waters and saturates them, and all produce fruits and plants. There is a garden below them, WHICH IS MALCHUT, THAT RECEIVES FROM THE FIVE GARDENS. That garden is protected and surrounded from all directions. Underneath this garden, there are other gardens, IN BRIYAH, YETZIRAH AND ASIYAH, that produce a variety of fruits.

312. וְהַאי גִּנְתָּא, אִתְהַפָּךְ וַהֲוֵי מַעְיָין דְּאַשְׁקֵי לוֹן, בְּאֵר מַיִם חַיִּים, כַּד אִצְטְרִיךְ הֲוֵי מַעְיָין, וְכַד אִצְטְרִיךְ הֲוֵי בְּאֵר, מַה בֵּין הַאי לְהַאי. לָא דָּאמֵי, כַּד אִתְמַשְׁכוּן מַיָּא מֵאֵלַיְיהוּ, לְכַד שַׁאֲבִין מַיָּא לְאַשְׁקָאָה. וְנוֹזְלִים מִן לְבָנוֹן, מַאי נוֹזְלִים. אִלֵּין נוֹזְלִים אָהַדְרוּ לְמַעְיָין, כַּד נַבְעִין מַיִין וְנוֹזְלִים טִפִּין מִלְּעֵילָּא אִלֵּין בָּתַר אִלֵּין, מַיִין מְתִיקָן, דְּנַפְשָׁא אַזְלָא אֲבַתְרַיְיהוּ. כַּךְ אִינּוּן חָמֵשׁ מְקוֹרִין, דְּנָפְקוּ מִן לְבָנוֹן, אִתְעֲבֵידוּ נוֹזְלִים בְּהַאי מַעְיָין. כַּךְ קוּדְשָׁא בְּרִיךְ הוּא רָחִישׁ לָן נִיסָּא בַּאֲתָר דָּא, קָרֵינָא עַל מַעְיָינָא דָּא קְרָא דָּא.

312. That garden, WHICH IS MALCHUT, turns into and becomes a watering spring TO ALL THE GARDENS IN BRIYAH, YETZIRAH AMD ASIYAH, a well of living water. When it needs to, it is a spring and when it needs, it is a well.

What is the difference between the two? HE REPLIES: Water that flows by itself, LIKE IN A WELL, is not like water that is drawn up to give drink AS IN THE GARDEN. "And streams from Lebanon": What is the meaning of "streams"? HE RESPONDS: These waters again become a spring when water flows and drops fall down from above, fresh water for which the soul longs. So these are the five sources, WHICH ARE CHESED, GVURAH, TIFERET, NETZACH AND HOD OF ZEIR ANPIN, that emerge from Lebanon, WHICH IS BINAH. They become streams in this spring, WHICH IS MALCHUT, WHERETO THEY FLOW DROP BY DROP. So, too, the Holy One, blessed be He, has produced a miracle for us at this place. THAT IS WHY I read this verse about this spring.

28. "When you shall besiege a city many days"

A Synopsis

Rabbi Shimon opens by talking about the great value of the Torah. Like the spreading branches of a tree, the words of Torah include the literal meaning of the text, homiletic discourses, hints that allude to wisdom, numerical values, hidden and concealed secrets one on top of the other, forbidden and permissible. And the person who studies Torah is therefore like a great tree. God protects this tree from destruction even in a period of Judgment. Rabbi Shimon says that ever since the destruction of the temple God has only what is offered up for him in the way of Torah studies and the insights that are constantly renewed by the scholars. We are also informed that these scholars give advice to the people, who have their sins forgiven due to their acceptance of that advice. Rabbi Shimon changes the topic to the evil eye, and says that Joseph moved in front of his mother so the wicked one (Esau) could not look at her, and that Joseph inflated his own size to accomplish this. When Bilaam lifted up his eyes he could not give the evil eye to the tribe of Joseph because the evil eye has no effect on them. When Bilaam's eye sharpened, Rachel (who is Malchut) spread her wings over the children of Yisrael to protect them. Thus Joseph first protected his mother and then his mother protected him and his tribe.

313. תּוּ פָּתַח וְאָמַר, כִּי תָצוּר אֶל עִיר יָמִים רַבִּים לְהִלָּחֵם עָלֶיהָ לְתָפְשָׂהּ וְגוֹ', כַּמָּה טָבִין אִינּוּן אָרְחִין וּשְׁבִילִין דְּאוֹרַיְיתָא, דְּהָא בְּכָל מִלָּה וּמִלָּה, אִית כַּמָּה עֵיטִין, כַּמָּה טָבִין לִבְנֵי נָשָׁא, כַּמָּה מַרְגְּלָאן דְּקָא מְנַהֲרָן לְכָל סְטָר, וְלֵית לָךְ מִלָּה בְּאוֹרַיְיתָא, דְּלֵית בָּהּ כַּמָּה בּוּצִינִין מְנַהֲרָן לְכָל סְטָר. הַאי קְרָא אִיהוּ כְּפוּם פְּשָׁטֵיהּ. וְאִית בֵּיהּ כְּפוּם מִדְרָשֵׁיהּ. וְאִית בֵּיהּ חָכְמְתָא עִלָּאָה, לְאִזְדַּהֲרָא לְמַאן דְּאִצְטְרִיךְ. זַכָּאָה חוּלָקֵיהּ מַאן דְּאִשְׁתְּדַל בְּאוֹרַיְיתָא תָּדִיר.

313. Again, he opened the discussion saying, "When you shall besiege a city many days, in making war against it to take it..." (Devarim 20:19). How wonderful are the ways and paths of the Torah, since in every single word there is much advice and so many benefits to people, so many gems that sparkle in every direction. There is no detail in the Torah that does not contain many candles giving light to all directions. This scriptural verse is in accord with its literal meaning. It contains much in accordance with discourses and it has higher wisdom to admonish whoever requires it. Happy is the lot of he who regularly strives in the Torah.

314. מַאן דְּאִשְׁתְּדַל בָּהּ, מַה כְּתִיב בֵּיהּ, כִּי אִם בְּתוֹרַת יְיָ׳ חֶפְצוֹ וּבְתוֹרָתוֹ יֶהְגֶּה יוֹמָם וָלָיְלָה, וְהָיָה כְּעֵץ. אֲמַאי דָּא סָמִיךְ לְדָא. אֶלָּא מַאן דְּאִשְׁתְּדַל בְּאוֹרַיְיתָא יוֹמָם וָלָיְלָה, לָא לֶיהֱוֵי כְּאָעָא יְבֵישָׁא, אֶלָּא כְּעֵץ שָׁתוּל עַל פַּלְגֵי מָיִם. מַה אִילָן אִית בֵּיהּ שָׁרָשִׁין, וְאִית בֵּיהּ קְלִיפִּין, וְאִית בֵּיהּ מוֹחָא, וְאִית בֵּיהּ עַנְפִּין, וְאִית בֵּיהּ טַרְפִּין, וְאִית בֵּיהּ פַּרְחִין, וְאִית בֵּיהּ אִיבָּא. שִׁבְעַת זִינִין אִלֵּין, סַלְּקִין לְשִׁבְעָה עָשָׂר, לְשַׁבְעִין. אוּף מִלִּין דְּאוֹרַיְיתָא אִית בְּהוּ פְּשָׁטָא דִּקְרָא. דְּרָשָׁא. רֶמֶז, דְּקָא רָמִיז חָכְמְתָא. גִּימַטְרִיָּיאוֹת. רָזִין טְמִירִין. רָזִין סְתִימִין אִלֵּין עַל אִלֵּין. פָּסוּל וְכָשֵׁר. טָמֵא וְטָהוֹר. אִיסּוּר וְהֶיתֵּר. מִכָּאן וּלְהָלְאָה, מִתְפַּשְּׁטָאן עַנְפִּין לְכָל סְטָר. וְהָיָה כְּעֵץ וַדַּאי, וְאִי לָאו, לָאו אִיהוּ חָכָם בְּחָכְמְתָא.

314. It is written about whoever strives in the Torah: "But his delight is in the Torah of Hashem; and in His Torah he meditates day and night. And he shall be like a tree" (Tehilim 1:2). HE INQUIRES: Why is: "AND HE SHALL BE LIKE A TREE" adjoining this? It is because whoever toils in the Torah day and night will not be like dry wood, but rather "he shall be like a tree planted by streams of water" (Ibid.). Just like a tree has roots, has bark, has a marrow and branches and leaves, grows flowers and produces fruit, these seven types amount to seven TIMES ten, TOTALING seventy. THAT IS THE SECRET OF THE SEVEN SFIROT, CHESED, GVURAH, TIFERET, NETZACH, HOD, YESOD AND MALCHUT, OF WHICH EACH ONE IS COMPRISED OF TEN. Torah words include also the literal meaning of the text, homiletic discourses, hints that allude to wisdom, numerical values, hidden secrets and concealed secrets, one on top of the other, faulty and approved, unclean and clean and forbidden and permissible. From here on, the branches extend to every direction. "And he shall be like a tree" assuredly, but if not, IF HE DOES NOT POSSESS ALL THESE BRANCHES, he is not a man of wisdom.

315. ת״ח, כַּמָּה חֲבִיבִין אִינּוּן דְּמִשְׁתַּדְּלֵי בְּאוֹרַיְיתָא קַמֵּי קוּדְשָׁא בְּרִיךְ

הוּא, דַּאֲפִילּוּ בִּזְמְנָא דְּדִינָא תַּלְיָא בְּעָלְמָא, וְאִתְיְיהִיב רְשׁוּ לִמְחַבְּלָא לְחַבְּלָא, קוּדְשָׁא בְּרִיךְ הוּא פָּקִיד לֵיהּ עָלָוַויְיהוּ, עַל אִינּוּן דְּקָא מִשְׁתַּדְּלֵי בְּאוֹרַיְיתָא. וְהָכִי אָ״ל קוּדְשָׁא בְּרִיךְ הוּא, כִּי תָצוּר אֶל עִיר, בְּגִין חוֹבֵיהוֹן סַגִּיאִין דְּחָטָאן לְקַמָּאי, וְאִתְחַיְּיבוּ בְּדִינָא. יָמִים רַבִּים, מַאי רַבִּים. תְּלָתָא יוֹמִין, דָּא בָּתַר דָּא, דְּאִשְׁתְּמוֹדְעָא דֶּבֶר בְּמָתָא. מְנָלָן דְּיָמִים רַבִּים תְּלָתָא יוֹמִין אִינּוּן, דִּכְתִּיב וְאִשָּׁה כִּי יָזוּב זוֹב דָּמָהּ יָמִים רַבִּים. וְכִי יָמִים רַבִּים אִינּוּן. אֶלָּא תְּלָתָא יוֹמִין דָּא בָּתַר דָּא, אִקְרֵי יָמִים רַבִּים. אוּף הָכִי כִּי תָצוּר אֶל עִיר יָמִים רַבִּים, תְּלָתָא יוֹמִין דָּא בָּתַר דָּא, דְּאִשְׁתְּמוֹדְעָא דֶּבֶר בְּמָתָא. תָּא וְאַפְקִיד לָךְ עַל בְּנֵי בֵּיתִי. לֹא תַשְׁחִית אֶת עֵצָהּ, דָּא ת״ח דְּאִיהוּ בְּמָתָא, דְּאִיהוּ אִילָנָא דְּחַיֵּי, אִילָנָא דְּיָהִיב אִיבִּין.

315. Come and see how beloved are those who study the Torah before the Holy One, blessed be He. Even when Judgment impends upon the world and permission is given to the destroyer to destroy, the Holy One, blessed be He, commands THE DESTROYER concerning those occupied with Torah. Thus speaks the Holy One, blessed be He, TO THE DESTROYER, “‘When you shall besiege a city” (Devarim 20:19), because of their many sins and iniquities to Me, and because they were found guilty in judgment.’ “Many days”: What is many? It is three consecutive days when the plague is known throughout the city. How do we know that “many days” are three days? Because it is written: “And if a woman have an issue of her blood many days” (Vayikra 15:25). Are they, then, many? Only IF SHE SEES BLOOD three days in a row is it called “many days.” Here too, “when you shall besiege a city many days” means three consecutive days, by which the plague is established to exist in the city. THE HOLY ONE, BLESSED BE HE, SAYS TO THE DESTROYER, ‘Come and I will give instructions regarding the members of My household. “You shall not destroy its tree”’ (Devarim 20:19): that is the Torah student that resides in the city, who is the Tree of Life, a tree that gives fruit.

316. ד״א אֶת עֵצָהּ, הַהוּא דְּיָהִיב עֵיטָא לְמָתָא, לְאִשְׁתְּזָבָא מִן דִּינָא, וְאוֹלִיף לוֹן אָרְחָא דְּיְהָכוּן בָּהּ, וְעַל דָּא לֹא תַשְׁחִית אֶת עֵצָהּ לִנְדּוֹחַ עָלָיו גַּרְזֶן, לְנַדְחָא עָלֵיהּ דִּינָא, וְלָא לְאוֹשָׁטָא עָלֵיהּ חַרְבָּא מְלָהֲטָא,

חַרְבָּא מְשַׁנְּנָא, הַהִיא דְּקָטְלָא לְשְׁאַר אִינְשֵׁי דְּעָלְמָא. כִּי מִמֶּנּוּ תֹאכֵל. וְכִי הַהוּא מְחַבְּלָא אָכִיל מִנֵּיהּ. לָא. אֶלָּא כִּי מִמֶּנּוּ תֹאכֵל, הַהִיא טִנְרָא תַּקִּיפָא, הַהִיא דְּכָל רוּחִין תַּקִּיפִין וְקַדִּישִׁין נָפְקִין מִנָּהּ, דְּלֵית הֲנָאָה וְתִיאוּבְתָּא לְרוּחַ קוּדְשָׁא בְּהַאי עָלְמָא, אֶלָּא אוֹרַיְיתָא דְּהַהוּא זַכָּאָה, כִּבְיָכוֹל אִיהוּ מְפַרְנֵס לָהּ, וְיָהֵיב לָהּ מְזוֹנָא בְּהַאי עָלְמָא, יַתִּיר מִכָּל קָרְבְּנִין דְּעָלְמָא.

316. Another explanation: "Its tree" is the one who gives counsel (Heb. *etzah*) to the inhabitants of the city on how to avoid the judgment, and teaches them the way to follow. Hence, "you shall not destroy its tree (Heb. *etzah*) by forcing an ax against it" (Ibid.), meaning to force sentence upon him and not to draw upon him the fiery sword, a sharp sword, that kills the rest of the people "for you may eat of it" (Ibid.). HE ASKS: Does the destroyer then eat FROM THE TORAH SCHOLAR? HE RESPONDS: No, but rather "for you may eat of it" MEANS that hard rock, the one from where all the holy, strong and mighty spirits emerge. SHE, MALCHUT, WILL EAT OF HIM, because the Holy Spirit THAT IS MALCHUT has no other pleasure or desire in this world, except for the Torah words of the righteous who sustain her, so to speak, and provide her food in this world more than all the offerings in the world.

317. בְּקָרְבָּן מַה כְּתִיב. אָכַלְתִּי יַעְרִי עִם דִּבְשִׁי אִכְלוּ רֵעִים. וּמִיּוֹמָא דְּאִתְחָרַב בֵּי מַקְדְּשָׁא, וּבָטְלוּ קָרְבְּנִין, לֵית לֵיהּ לְקוּדְשָׁא בְּרִיךְ הוּא, אֶלָּא אִינּוּן מִלִּין דְּאוֹרַיְיתָא, וְאוֹרַיְיתָא דְּאִתְחַדְּשָׁא בְּפוּמֵיהּ, בְּג"כ כִּי מִמֶּנּוּ תֹאכֵל, וְלֵית לָהּ מְזוֹנָא בְּהַאי עָלְמָא, אֶלָּא מִמֶּנּוּ, וּמֵאִינּוּן דִּכְוָותֵיהּ. וְכֵיוָן דְּמִמֶּנּוּ תֹאכֵל, וְאִיהוּ זָן לָהּ, אוֹתוֹ לֹא תִכְרוֹת, הֱוֵי זָהִיר בֵּיהּ, דְּלָא תִּקְרַב בֵּיהּ.

317. It is written regarding the offering: "I have eaten my honey comb with my honey... Eat, O dear ones" (Shir Hashirim 5:1). From the day the Temple was destroyed and the sacrifices ceased, the Holy One, blessed be He, has only words of Torah and the Torah new insights from the mouth OF THE TORAH SCHOLAR. Due to this, IT IS WRITTEN: "For you may eat of it," since she has no other sustenance except from his and those like him.

Since she will eat from it and he sustains her, THEREFORE, "you shall not cut it down." Be careful that you do not come close to him.

318. כִּי הָאָדָם עֵץ הַשָּׂדֶה, דָּא אִקְרֵי אָדָם דְּאִשְׁתְּמוֹדַע עֵילָּא וְתַתָּא. עֵץ הַשָּׂדֶה, אִילָנָא רַבְרְבָא וְתַקִּיף דְּהַהוּא שָׂדֶה אֲשֶׁר בֵּרֲכוֹ יְיָ'. דָּא סָמִיךְ עָלֵיהּ, אִילָן דְּאִשְׁתְּמוֹדַע לְהַהוּא שָׂדֶה תָּדִיר. לָבֹא מִפָּנֶיךָ בַּמָּצוֹר, מִלָּה דָּא אַהְדָּר לְרֵישָׁא דִּקְרָא, דִּכְתִּיב לֹא תַשְׁחִית אֶת עֵצָהּ, הַהוּא דְיָהִיב לוֹן עֵיטָא, וְאַתְקִין לְמָתָא, לָבֹא מִפָּנֶיךָ בַּמָּצוֹר, אִיהוּ יָהִיב לוֹן עֵיטָא, לְאִתָּקְנָא וּלְאָהַדְרָא בְּתִיּוּבְתָּא, וְאַתְקִין לֵיהּ מָאנֵי זַיְינִין, בּוּקִינָס וְשׁוֹפָרִין. לָבֹא מִפָּנֶיךָ, מַאי לָבֹא מִפָּנֶיךָ. לָבֹא לְקַמָּאי, וּלְאַעֲלָא מִפָּנֶיךָ. מִקַּמֵּי דְּחִילוּ דִּילָךְ. בַּמָּצוֹר, בַּאֲתָר דְּעִלָּאִין וְתַתָּאִין לָא יַכְלִין לְאַעֲלָא תַּמָּן. וּמַאן אִיהוּ. דַּרְגָּא דְּבַעֲלֵי תְּשׁוּבָה עָאלִין תַּמָּן, וּמַאן אִיהוּ. תְּשׁוּבָה. דָּא אִיהוּ מָצוֹר, אֲתָר תַּקִּיף, וְטִנָּרָא תַּקִּיפָא.

318. "For is the tree of the field a man" (Devarim 20:19), meaning that the Torah scholar who is famous above and below is called 'man'. "The tree of the field" is a mighty great tree of "a field, which Hashem has blessed" (Beresheet 27:27), WHICH IS MALCHUT THAT IS CONSIDERED A FIELD. It depends on it for support, BECAUSE THE TORAH SCHOLAR SUSTAINS HER, since he is the tree that is constantly known to the field. "That it should be besieged by you" (Devarim 20:19) refers to what is written at the beginning of the verse: "You shall not destroy its tree (Heb. *etzah*)," meaning the person who gives them advice (Heb. *etzah*) and improves the city inhabitants, giving them counsel, "that it should be besieged by you," that is, to repair and do repentance, and to prepare for themselves weapons, trumpets and horns. What is the meaning of "that it should (lit. 'come') be beseiged by you"? That is to "come" before and enter; "by you": with the fear of you. "Besieged" refers to a place where the higher and lower beings are unable to enter. What is it? That is the level into which the ones who repent enter. What is that? That is repentance, WHICH IS BINAH, a besieged place, meaning a fortified area and a strong rock.

319. וְכֵיוָן דְּעֵיטָא דָּא נַטְלִין, אֲנָא מְכַפֵּר לְחוֹבַיְיהוּ וְאִתְקַבְּלָן בְּרַעֲוָא לְקַמָּאי. וְכָל דָּא פָּקִיד קוּדְשָׁא בְּרִיךְ הוּא, עַל אִינּוּן דְּמִשְׁתַּדְּלֵי

בְּאוֹרַיְיתָא. בְּג״כ זַכָּאִין אִינּוּן דְּקָא מִשְׁתַּדְּלֵי בְּאוֹרַיְיתָא, אִינּוּן דְּמִשְׁתַּדְּלֵי בְּאוֹרַיְיתָא אִינּוּן אִילָנִין רַבְרְבִין בְּהַאי עָלְמָא.

319. 'Because they accept that advice FROM THE SAGE, I forgive their iniquities and they will be received willingly into My presence.' All this the Holy One, blessed be He, instructs for those who strive in Torah and, because of this, happy and praiseworthy are those who study Torah. Those who are occupied in the Torah are great trees in this world.

320. חָמוּ, מַה עֲבַד קוּדְשָׁא בְּרִיךְ הוּא דְּנָטַע אִילֵין אִילָנִין, זַכָּאָה אָרְחָא דָּא, וְלָא דַּי אִילָנָא חֲדָא, אֶלָּא תְּלָתָא אִילָנִין רַבְרְבִין, פְּרִיסָן עַנְפִּין לְכָל סְטָר, עֲבַד לָן קוּדְשָׁא בְּרִיךְ הוּא. יְהֵא רַעֲוָא קַמֵּי שְׁמַיָּא, דְּלָא יִתְעֲדוּן לְעָלְמָא אִילָנִין אִלֵּין, וְדָא מַעְיָינָא, מֵאֲתָר דָּא וְעַד יוֹמָא קַיְימִין תַּמָּן, וְהַהוּא מַעְיָינָא דְּמַיָּא. וּקְרָאן לוֹן בְּנֵי נָשָׁא, נְצִיבוּ דְּר׳ פִּנְחָס בֶּן יָאִיר.

320. Look what the Holy One, blessed be He, accomplished by planting these trees. Praised is this path. One tree would not have been sufficient, but rather three huge trees spreading their branches to every direction is what the Holy One, blessed be He, produced for us. Let it be the will of heaven that these trees, and this fountain, shall never be missing in this area. Until this day, these trees and water fountain are still present there. And the people call them the pillar of Rabbi Pinchas ben Yair.

29. "And he lifted up his eyes, and saw the women and the children"

A Synopsis

Rabbi Shimon gives an explanation of the title verse, wherein he says that the accuser sees Yisrael anguished from fasting and believes that they are fasting because they are afraid of him. We read how and why God protects innocent children during Yom Kippur, so that they are not punished for the sins of Yisrael. The innocent children are the Torah scholars, to whom God has told His secrets. No evil eye can have any power over them. Next we hear that the three trees that are sheltering the rabbis bend down individually over their heads immediately after Rabbi Shimon says that the three trees are the secret of the Patriarchs.

321. פָּתַח ר״ש וְאָמַר, וַיִּשָּׂא אֶת עֵינָיו וַיַּרְא אֶת הַנָּשִׁים וְאֶת הַיְלָדִים וַיֹּאמֶר מִי אֵלֶּה לָּךְ וַיֹּאמַר הַיְלָדִים אֲשֶׁר חָנַן אֱלֹהִים אֶת עַבְדֶּךָ. ת״ח, הַהוּא רָשָׁע דְּעֵשָׂו, יָהִיב עֵינוֹי לְעַיְּינָא עַל נָשִׁין, וּבְגִינֵיהּ אַתְקִין תִּיקוּנוֹי. יַעֲקֹב, שַׁוֵּי שְׁפָחוֹת בְּקַדְמֵיתָא, וּבְנֵיהוֹן לְבָתַר, דְּחָשִׁיבוּ יַתִּיר. לֵאָה אֲבַתְרַיְיהוּ, וּבְנָהָא לְבָתַר. לְבָתַר יוֹסֵף, וּבַתְרָהּ רָחֵל, וְהוּא עָבַר לִפְנֵיהֶם.

321. Rabbi Shimon opened the discussion with the verse: "And he lifted up his eyes, and saw the women and the children; and said, 'Who are those with you?' And he said, 'The children which Elohim has graciously given Your servant'" (Beresheet 33:5). Come and see that the wicked one allowed his eyes to gaze at the women. Due to him, JACOB had to make some arrangements. Jacob placed the handmaidens in front, and their sons, who were a little more important, behind them. Leah followed behind them, and her sons were behind her. Behind them was Joseph and behind him Rachel. And he HIMSELF went in front of all of them.

322. כַּד סָגִידוּ כֻּלְּהוֹן, מַה כְּתִיב. וַתִּגַּשְׁנָה הַשְּׁפָחוֹת הֵנָּה וְיַלְדֵיהֶן וַתִּשְׁתַּחֲוֶיןָ. וּלְבָתַר כְּתִיב, וַתִּגַּשׁ גַּם לֵאָה וִילָדֶיהָ וְיִשְׁתַּחֲווּ וְאַחַר נִגַּשׁ יוֹסֵף וְרָחֵל וְגוֹ׳. וְהָא יוֹסֵף לְבַתְרַיְיתָא הֲוָה, וְרָחֵל לְקַמֵּיהּ. אֶלָּא בְּרָא טָבָא, בְּרָא רְחִימָא, צַדִּיקָא דְּעָלְמָא, יוֹסֵף, כֵּיוָן דְּחָמָא עֵינֵיהּ דְּהַהוּא רָשָׁע מִסְתָּכַּל בְּנָשִׁין, דָּחִיל עַל אִמֵּיהּ, נָפִיק מֵאֲבַתְרָהּ, וּפָרִישׂ דְּרוֹעוֹי

וְגוּפֵיהּ, וְכַסֵּי עֲלָהּ, בְּגִין דְּלָא יִתֵּן הַהוּא רָשָׁע עֵינוֹ בְּאִמֵּיהּ. כַּמָּה אִתְסְגֵי, שִׁית אַמִּין לְכָל סְטַר, וְחָפָא עֲלָהּ, וְלָא יָכִיל עֵינֵיהּ דְּהַהוּא רָשָׁע לְשַׁלְטָאָה עֲלָהּ.

322. (THIS IS ANOTHER VERSION, EXPLAINING DIFFERENTLY). After they all bowed down, it is written: "Then the handmaidens came near, they and their children, and they bowed themselves" (Ibid. 6). Afterward, it says, "And Leah also with her children came near, and bowed themselves: and after came Joseph near and Rachel, and they bowed themselves" (Ibid. 7). HE ASKS: But Joseph was last behind Rachel and Rachel was in front of him, AND NOT JOSEPH IN FRONT OF RACHEL. HE REPLIES: It is just that when this good son, beloved son, the righteous in the world, Joseph, noticed that the eyes of the wicked were staring at the women, he was fearful for his mother. THEN he came out from behind her and spread his arms and his body and covered her, so that wicked one would not place his eyes on his mother. How much did he inflate his size? Six cubits to each direction, so he covered her up so that the eyes of the wicked one shall have no effect over her. CONSEQUENTLY, AT THE START, JOSEPH WAS INDEED BEHIND HER, AS IS WRITTEN EARLIER. HOWEVER, HE LATER CAME OUT FROM BEHIND HER AND WENT IN FRONT OF HER.

323. כְּגַוְונָא דָּא, וַיִּשָּׂא בִּלְעָם אֶת עֵינָיו, עֵינוֹ כְּתִיב, הַהוּא עֵינָא בִּישָׁא דְּבָעָא לְאִסְתַּכְּלָא עֲלַיְיהוּ. וַיַּרְא אֶת יִשְׂרָאֵל שׁוֹכֵן לִשְׁבָטָיו. מַהוּ שׁוֹכֵן לִשְׁבָטָיו. אֶלָּא שִׁבְטָא דְּיוֹסֵף הֲוָה תַּמָּן, וְשִׁבְטָא דְּבִנְיָמִין. שִׁבְטָא דְּיוֹסֵף, דְּלָא שַׁלְטָא בְּהוּ עֵינָא בִּישָׁא, דִּכְתִּיב בֵּן פּוֹרָת יוֹסֵף. מַאן בֵּן פּוֹרָת. דְּאִתְסְגֵי לְכַסָּאָה עַל אִמֵּיהּ. בֵּן פּוֹרָת עֲלֵי עָיִן, דְּלָא שַׁלְטָא בֵּיהּ עֵינָא בִּישָׁא. שִׁבְטָא דְּבִנְיָמִין, דִּכְתִּיב בֵּיהּ וּבֵין כְּתֵפָיו שָׁכֵן. וּכְתִיב יִשְׁכּוֹן לָבֶטַח. מַאי לָבֶטַח. דְּלָא דָּחִיל מֵעֵינָא בִּישָׁא, וְלָא דָּחִיל מִפִּגְעִין בִּישִׁין.

323. Similar to this, "Bilaam lifted up his eyes" (Bemidbar 24:2). It is written "eye": that refers to the evil eye that wished to stare at them, MEANING THAT HE ROUSED AGAINST THEM THAT EVIL KLIPAH CALLED 'EVIL EYE'. "And he saw Yisrael abiding according to their tribes" (Ibid.): What is the meaning of "according to their tribes"? HE REPLIES: It only refers to the tribes of Joseph and Benjamin that were there. Upon the tribe of Joseph, no evil eye can have any effect, as is written: “Joseph is a fruitful bough” (Beresheet 49:22). What does “a fruitful bough” mean? It means that he increased and spread about to cover his mother FROM THE EVIL EYE OF ESAU, AS MENTIONED EARLIER. “A fruitful bough by a well” means that no evil eye can affect him. It is written about the tribe of Benjamin: “And he shall dwell between his shoulders” (Devarim 33:12) and: “He shall dwell in safety” (Ibid.). What does “in safety” indicate? It means that he has no fear of the evil eye and is not afraid of any evil plague.

324. אָמַר הַהוּא רָשָׁע, אֲנָא אַעֲבָר שׁוּרָה דָּא, דְּלָא אִתְקַיְּימוּן, וַאֲנָא אִסְתָּכַּל כַּדְקָא יָאוּת. רָחֵל הֲוַת תַּמָּן, חָמָאת דְּעֵינָא דְּהַהוּא רָשָׁע מְשַׁנְּנָא לְאַבְאָשָׁא, מַה עַבְדַּת. נַפְקַת וּפְרִישַׁת גַּדְפָּהָא עָלַיְיהוּ, וְחַפָּאת עַל בְּרָהָא. הה״ד וַיִּשָּׂא בִלְעָם אֶת עֵינָיו וַיַּרְא אֶת יִשְׂרָאֵל. כֵּיוָן דְּחָמָא רוּחַ דְּקוּדְשָׁא, עֵינָא מְשַׁנְּנָא, מִיַּד וַתְּהִי עָלָיו רוּחַ אֱלֹהִים. עַל מַאן. עַל יִשְׂרָאֵל. דְּפָרִישׁ גַּדְפּוֹי, וְחָפָא עֲלֵיהוֹן. וּמִיַּד תָּב הַהוּא רָשָׁע לַאֲחוֹרָא.

324. The wicked one said, I will remove AND MAKE VOID this line OF THE TRIBES OF JOSEPH AND BENJAMIN, so that they will not last IN THE WORLD, and I will gaze at them WITH MY EVIL EYE as is required. Rachel was present there and noticed that the eye of the wicked one was focussed to do harm. What did she do? She came out and spread her wings over them, which covered over her children. This is what it says: “And Bilaam lifted up his eyes, and he saw Yisrael.” Once the Holy Spirit, WHICH IS MALCHUT CALLED ‘RACHEL’, noticed the focussed eye OF BILAAM, instantly “the spirit of Elohim came upon him.” Upon whom WAS THE SPIRIT OF ELOHIM? THAT MEANS upon Yisrael, THAT THE SPIRIT OF ELOHIM spread its wings and covered over them. Immediately, the wicked one retreated.

325. בְּקַדְמֵיתָא בְּרָא חָפָא עַל אִמֵּיהּ. וְהַשְׁתָּא אִימָּא חָפָאת עַל בְּרָא. אָמַר קוּדְשָׁא בְּרִיךְ הוּא, בְּהַהִיא שַׁעֲתָא דְּחָפָא אִיהוּ עַל רָחֵל אִמֵּיהּ, דְּלָא יִשְׁלוֹט עֵינָא דְּהַהוּא רָשָׁע עָלָהּ, חַיֶּיךָ, בְּשַׁעֲתָא דְּיֵיתֵי עֵינָא בִּישָׁא אַחֲרָא לְאִסְתַּכְּלָא עַל בָּנֶךָ וְעַל בְּנֵי, אִמָּךְ תֵּחָפֵי עָלַיְיהוּ. אַתְּ חָפִית עַל אִמָּךְ, אִמָּךְ תֵּחָפֵי עָלַיְיהוּ. אַתְּ חָפִית עַל אִמָּךְ, אִמָּךְ תֵּחָפֵי עֲלָךְ.

325. At first, the son was covering his mother and now the mother covered her son. At that time when JOSEPH covered his mother, Rachel, so the evil eye of the wicked one would not harm her, the Holy One, blessed be He, said TO JOSEPH, 'Upon your life, when an evil eye approaches to gaze at your children and Mine, your mother will cover over them. You covered over your mother and your mother will cover you.'

326. וַיִּשָּׂא אֶת עֵינָיו וַיַּרְא אֶת הַנָּשִׁים. הַאי קְרָא, בְּרָזָא דְּחָכְמְתָא אִתְּמַר, בְּיוֹמָא דְּכִפּוּרֵי, דִּבְנֵי עָלְמָא קַיְימֵי בְּדִינָא, וְיִשְׂרָאֵל תַּיְיבִין בְּתִיּוּבְתָּא קַמֵּי קוּדְשָׁא בְּרִיךְ הוּא, לְכַפְּרָא עַל חוֹבַיְיהוּ. וְהַהוּא מְקַטְרְגָא קַיְּימָא עָלַיְיהוּ, דְּחָשִׁיב לְאוֹבָדָא לוֹן עַל חוֹבַיְיהוּ, שַׁלְחֵי לֵיהּ הַהוּא דּוֹרוֹנָא, וּכְדֵין כְּתִיב, כִּי אָמַר אֲכַפְּרָה פָנָיו בַּמִּנְחָה הַהוֹלֶכֶת לְפָנַי. לְבָתַר דִּמְקַבֵּל הַהוּא מְקַטְרְגָא לְהַהוּא דּוֹרוֹנָא, אִתְהַפָּךְ לְהוּ סַנֵּיגוֹרָא.

326. "And he lifted up his eyes, and saw the women and the children" (Beresheet 33:5). This verse was said in the secret of wisdom on Yom Kippur (Day of Atonement), when people stand for trial, and Yisrael repent before the Holy One, blessed be He, to be forgiven for their iniquities and the accuser standing over them, planning to destroy them due to their iniquities, they send him that gift, MEANING THE GOAT FOR AZAZEL. Then it is written: "For he said, 'I will appease him with the present that goes before me'" (Beresheet 32:21). After the accuser receives this gift, he reverses himself and becomes his advocate.

327. זָקִיף וְחָמֵי לוֹן לְיִשְׂרָאֵל, כֻּלְּהוּ מִתְעַנָּן בְּתַעֲנִיתָא, יְחֵפֵי רַגְלִין. חָמֵי נָשִׁין, חָמֵי יַנּוּקִין, כֻּלְּהוּ בְּתַעֲנִיתָא, כֻּלְּהוּ נְקִיִּים בְּנַקְיוּ. וַיֹּאמֶר מִי אֵלֶּה לָךְ. שְׁמָא קַדִּישָׁא לָךְ. מִי אֵלֶּה לָךְ. שָׁאִיל עַל יַנּוּקֵי, וְאָמַר הַיְלָדִים אֲשֶׁר חָנַן אֱלֹהִים אֶת עַבְדֶּךָ. וְכִי אֲמַאי אִצְטְרִיךְ לְאָתָבָא לֵיהּ כְּלוּם. אֶלָּא כֵּיוָן דִּמְקַבֵּל הַהוּא שׁוֹחַד, אִתְהַפָּךְ לְהוּ סַנֵּיגוֹר. זָקִיף עֵינוֹי, וְחָמֵי לוֹן לְיִשְׂרָאֵל כְּגַוְונָא דָּא, חָשִׁיב דִּבְגִין דְּחִילוּ דִּילֵיהּ אִינּוּן קַיְימִין כַּךְ.

327. THE ACCUSER raises HIS EYES and sees Yisrael are fasting and are bare footed. He sees women and he sees children; all are fasting, all are radiant with purity. "And he said, 'Who (Heb. *mi*) are those (Heb. *eleh*) with you?'" (Ibid. 5), MEANING the Holy Name ELOHIM THAT IS DERIVED FROM *MI ELEH*; THEY ARE with you, YISRAEL. He asked about the children, and he replied, "The children that Elohim has graciously given your servant" (Beresheet 33:5). HE ASKS: Did he need to answer him anything? HE REPLIES: Since he accepted that bribe, MEANING THE SCAPEGOAT, he turned to be a good advocate for them. He raised his eyes and saw Yisrael in this way and thought that, due to the fear of him, LEST HE MAKE ACCUSATIONS ABOUT THEM, they were in such a state OF FASTING AND REPENTANCE.

328. שָׁאִיל עַל יַנּוּקֵי, וְאָמַר מִי אֵלֶּה לָךְ. מַהוּ מִי אֵלֶּה לָךְ. אֶלָּא אָמַר, תִּינַח אַתּוּן דְּחַבְתּוּן קַמֵּי מַלְכָּא. אֲבָל אִלֵּין יַנּוּקֵי, אֲמַאי קַיְימִין הָכִי, מִי אֵלֶּה לָךְ. וַיֹּאמַר הַיְלָדִים, רוּחַ קֻדְשָׁא אָמַר, וְעַ״ד זָקִיף טַעֲמָא. וַיֹּאמַר הַיְלָדִים. בְּאֹרַח סָתִים אֲשֶׁר חָנַן אֱלֹהִים אֶת עַבְדֶּךָ, וְכִי רוּחַ הַקֹּדֶשׁ אָמַר אֶת עַבְדֶּךָ. אֶלָּא רוּחַ קֻדְשָׁא אָמַר, אִלֵּין אִינּוּן יַנּוּקֵי דְּלָא חָאבוּ, וְלָא טָעִימוּ טַעֲמָא דְּחֶטְאָה, וּמָסַר לוֹן קוּדְשָׁא בְּרִיךְ הוּא, בִּידָא דְּהַהוּא מְמָנָא דִּילָךְ, וְקָטִיל לוֹן בְּלָא חוֹבָא, כד״א וּמִיַּד עוֹשְׁקֵיהֶם כֹּחַ. וְדָא הוּא אֶת עַבְדֶּךָ.

328. ANOTHER EXPLANATION: He asked about the children and said, "Who are these with you?" What is the meaning of: "Who are these with you"? HE REPLIES THAT what he meant IS THE FAST AND REPENTANCE befits you, because you sinned against the King. Why are these children in a situation like this, FASTING, and "Who are these with you"? "And he said, 'The children'": The Holy Spirit said this; therefore, there is a vertical tonal pause, ZAKEF GADOL, ON TOP OF "And he said," AND ON TOP OF "the children" without specifying, TO INDICATE THAT THE HOLY SPIRIT SPOKE SO. "That Elohim has graciously given your servant": HE INQUIRES: Did then the Holy Spirit say TO ESAU, "your servant"? HE RESPONDS: The Holy Spirit said, These are the children who have not had a taste of sin IN THEIR FIRST INCARNATION. The Holy One, blessed be He, placed them in the hands of your minister and he killed them without them having sinned, as it says, "And on the side of their oppressors there was power" (Kohelet 4:1). That is the meaning of, "your servant."

329. כֵּיוָן דְּשָׁמַע מֵאִינּוּן יַנּוּקֵי, מִיַּד סָלִיק לְגַבֵּי קוּדְשָׁא בְּרִיךְ הוּא, וְאָמַר, מָארֵיהּ דְּעָלְמָא, כָּל אָרְחָךְ בְּדִינָא דִּקְשׁוֹט, וְאִי דִּינָא שַׁרְיָא עַל יִשְׂרָאֵל בְּגִין חוֹבֵיהוֹן אִיהוּ, יַנּוּקִין דִּלְהוֹן דְּלָא חָאבוּ לְקָמָךְ, אֲמַאי מַסְרַת לוֹן לְקַטְלָא לוֹן בְּלָא חוֹבָא. וְקוּדְשָׁא בְּרִיךְ הוּא נָטִיל מִלּוֹי בְּכַךְ, וְחָס עֲלַיְיהוּ. וְהַהִיא שַׁעֲתָא, לָא הֲוֵי אַסְכָּרָא בַּתִּינוֹקוֹת.

329. As soon as he heard about these children, he immediately ascended to the presence of the Holy One, blessed be He, and said, Master of the universe, all Your ways are just and true. If there is any judgment that prevails upon Yisrael, that would be for their own sins. Why did You hand their children who have not sinned over to be killed? The Holy One, blessed be He, accepts thus his words and has compassion on them. At that time, IN YOM KIPPUR, children do not suffer from diphtheria.

330. וְהַהוּא מְקַטְרְגָא נָטִיל קִנְאָה מֵהַהוּא מְמָנָא דִּתְחוֹת יְדֵיהּ. אָמַר, וְכִי לִי יָהִיב קוּדְשָׁא בְּרִיךְ הוּא אִינּוּן דְּמִתְלַבְּשָׁן בְּחֶטְאִין וְחוֹבִין, וּלְהַהוּא מְמָנָא דִּילִי מָסַר יַנּוּקִין בְּלָא חוֹבָא, דְּלָא טַעֲמוּן טַעֲמָא דְּחוֹבָה. מִיַּד אָזַל לְאַפָּקָא לוֹן מִתְּחוֹת יְדֵיהּ, וְלָא יִשְׁלוֹט בְּהוּ. וְעַ"ד אַקְדִּים לֵיהּ וְאָ"ל, הַיְלָדִים אֲשֶׁר חָנַן אֱלֹהִים אֶת עַבְדֶּךָ. לְהַהוּא עַבְדֶּךָ, בְּלָא חוֹבָא וּבְלָא חַטָּאָה. וּבְגִין דְּלָא יְהֵא שִׁבְחָא לַמְּמָנָא דִּילֵיהּ יַתִּיר מִנֵּיהּ, בָּעָא לְאַפָּקָא לוֹן מִן יְדוֹי.

330. The accuser becomes jealous about this chieftain appointed under him and says, Did the Holy One, blessed be He, give men children that carry upon themselves sins and iniquities? To the chieftain He handed children without sin, who don't even know the taste of sin. He immediately goes and removes them from his hand, so he should not have any control over them. Therefore, THE HOLY SPIRIT proceeded and said, "The children that Elohim has graciously given your servant," to that servant, MEANING HE GRACIOUSLY GAVE HIM CHILDREN THAT ARE without taste of any iniquity or sin. And so that the appointed one shall not have more praise than him, he wishes to remove them from his hand.

331. כַּד סַלְּקִין צְלוֹתִין דְּיִשְׂרָאֵל בְּיוֹמָא דָא קַמֵּי קוּדְשָׁא בְּרִיךְ הוּא,

מַה כְּתִיב וְהוּא עָבַר לִפְנֵיהֶם. הָא רוּחַ קוּדְשָׁא אַעְבַּר לְקָמַיְיהוּ, כד"א וַיַּעֲבוֹר מַלְכָּם לִפְנֵיהֶם וְהוּא וַדַּאי עָבַר לִפְנֵיהֶם. וַיִּשְׁתַּחוּ אַרְצָה שֶׁבַע פְּעָמִים, רוּחַ קוּדְשָׁא, אַזְעַר גַּרְמֵיהּ לְגַבֵּי עֵילָּא ז' זִמְנִין, לְגַבֵּי ז' דַּרְגִּין עִלָּאִין דְּעָלֵיהּ, וְאַקְטִין גַּרְמֵיהּ, לְאַכְלְלָא לוֹן עִמֵּיהּ כָּל חַד וְחָד. עַד גִּשְׁתּוֹ עַד אָחִיו, לְהַהוּא דַּרְגָּא דְּרַחֲמֵי, דְּהָא בֵּן וּבַת אִינּוּן. בֵּן, בְּנִי בְכוֹרִי יִשְׂרָאֵל. בַּת, כ"י. רוּחַ קוּדְשָׁא עָבֵיד אַזְעִירוּ דְּגַרְמֵיהּ, עַד גִּשְׁתּוֹ.

331. When the prayers of Yisrael ascend on that day to the Holy One, blessed be He, what is written? "And he passed over before them" (Beresheet 33:3). Here, the Holy Spirit, THAT IS MALCHUT, passed in front of them, as it says, "And their king passed on before them" (Michah 2:13) and he definitely crossed over in front of them. "And bowed himself to the ground seven times" (Beresheet 33:3): the Holy Spirit, THAT IS MALCHUT, diminished itself towards the one above, ZEIR ANPIN, seven times, corresponding to the seven higher grades, CHESED, GVURAH, TIFERET, NETZACH, HOD, YESOD AND MALCHUT OF ZEIR ANPIN, that are above it and diminished itself, to include them with it, each and every one. "Until he came near to his brother" (Ibid.), meaning to that level of Mercy THAT IS ZEIR ANPIN, WHICH IS CONSIDERED THE BROTHER OF THE HOLY SPIRIT, WHICH IS MALCHUT since they son and daughter TO BINAH, AND THEREFORE, THEY ARE BROTHERS. ZEIR ANPIN IS CALLED 'son', as it says, "Yisrael is My son, My firstborn" (Shemot 4:22); THAT IS ZEIR ANPIN CONSIDERED YISRAEL. Daughter is the Congregation of Yisrael, MEANING MALCHUT. The Holy Spirit caused a diminishing of itself until its approach TO ITS BROTHER, ZEIR ANPIN.

332. כֵּיוָן דְּמָטָא לְגַבֵּיהּ, תָּבַע מִינֵּיהּ, וְאוֹדַע לֵיהּ צַעֲרָא דִּבְנַיְיהוּ לְתַתָּא. וְתַרְוַויְיהוּ עָאלִין לְהֵיכָלָא טְמִירָא גְּנִיזָא דְּיוֹם הַכִּפּוּרִים, אִימָּא דִּלְהוֹן, וְתַבְעִין עַל יִשְׂרָאֵל לְכַפְּרָא לוֹן, כְּדֵין כְּתִיב כִּי בַיּוֹם הַזֶּה יְכַפֵּר עֲלֵיכֶם לְטַהֵר אֶתְכֶם וְגוֹ'. אֲכַפֵּר עֲלֵיכֶם לָא כְּתִיב, אֶלָּא יְכַפֵּר עֲלֵיכֶם.

332. As soon as MALCHUT reached him, ZEIR ANPIN, she beseeched him and informed him of the distress of their children below, IN THIS WORLD. Both ZEIR ANPIN AND MALCHUT entered the hidden and concealed chamber of Yom Kippur, THAT IS BINAH, their mother, SINCE ON YOM KIPPUR, MALE AND FEMALE ASCEND TO IMA and beg forgiveness for

Yisrael. Then it says, "For on that day will He forgive you, to cleanse you..." (Vayikra 16:30). It does not say, 'I will forgive', but rather "He," in the THIRD PERSON HINTING AT BINAH.

333. וְהַשְׁתָּא הַיְלָדִים, אִלֵּין חַכִּימִין דְּהָכָא, קוּדְשָׁא בְּרִיךְ הוּא יָהַב לוֹן רָזִין דְּאוֹרַיְיתָא, לְאִתְעַטְּרָא בְּהוּ, וּלְאִשְׁתַּדְּלָא בְּהוּ. עֵינָא בִּישָׁא לָא שַׁלְטָא עֲלַיְיהוּ, בְּגִין עֵינָא טָבָא, רוּחַ קוּדְשָׁא דְּר׳ פִּנְחָס, דְּשַׁרְיָא עֲלַיְיהוּ. אָתָא ר׳ פִּנְחָס וּנְשָׁקֵיהּ. אָמַר, אִלְמָלֵא לָא אֲתֵינָא אָרְחָא דָּא, אֶלָּא לְמִשְׁמַע מִלִּין אִלֵּין, דַּי לִי. זַכָּאָה אָרְחָא דָּא דְּאָתֵינָא לְגַבָּךְ.

333. Now, the Holy One, blessed be He, granted the children, that are the sages present here, secrets of the Torah, to be adorned with them and become engage in them. No evil eye has power over them, due to the benevolent eye and the Holy Spirit of Rabbi Pinchas that dwells upon them. Rabbi Pinchas approached and kissed RABBI SHIMON. He said, Had I come only to listen to these words, it would have been sufficient for me. Praised is this road upon which I came to you.

334. וְקוּדְשָׁא בְּרִיךְ הוּא הָכָא, דְּאִסְתָּכַּם עִמָּנָא. וְלָא דַּי אִילָנָא חַד, אֶלָּא תְּלַת. אֲבָל מַעְיָינָא דָּא, דִּיּוּקְנָא עִלָּאָה הוּא, לְגַבֵּי הַהוּא מַעְיָינָא דְּטָמִיר וְגָנִיז. תְּלַת אִילָנִין אִלֵּין, תְּלַת אֲרָזִין אִינּוּן, דְּאִקְרוּן אַרְזֵי לְבָנוֹן. וְאִינּוּן דִּיּוּקְנָא דִּתְלַת אִילָנִין רַבְרְבִין, רָזָא דַּאֲבָהָן. זַכָּאָה חוּלָקָנָא בְּהַהִיא שַׁעֲתָא.

334. The Holy One, blessed be He, is here agreeing with us. He not only granted us one tree, but HE EVEN GAVE US three TREES. However, this fountain is of a higher form, in accord with that hidden and concealed fountain THAT IS BINAH. These three trees are the cedars called 'the cedars of Lebanon', and are in the form of three great trees, which are the secret of the Patriarchs – MEANING CHESED, GVURAH AND TIFERET OF ZEIR ANPIN CALLED 'PATRIARCHS' AND CALLED THE CEDARS OF LEBANON, BECAUSE THEY EMANATE FROM BINAH CALLED 'LEBANON'. Praised is our lot at that time.

335. אַרְכִּינוּ אִילָנִין, חַד עַל רֵישֵׁיהּ דְּר׳ שִׁמְעוֹן, וְחַד עַל רֵישֵׁיהּ דְּרִבִּי

פִּנְחָס, וְחַד עַל רֵישֵׁיהּ דְּר׳ אֶלְעָזָר. אִתְפְּשָׁטוּ עַנְפִּין, לְכָל סְטַר, עַל רֵישֵׁיהוֹן דְּחַבְרַיָּיא, בָּכָה רִבִּי פִּנְחָס וְאָמַר, זַכָּאָה חוּלָקִי וְזַכָּאִין עֵינַי דְּחָמָאן כַּךְ. וְלָא עַל דִּידָךְ וְעַל דִּידִי חַדֵּינָא בִּלְחוֹדַיְיהוּ, אֶלָּא עַל רִבִּי אֶלְעָזָר בְּרָנָא קָא חַדֵּינָא, דְּחָשִׁיב אִיהוּ קַמֵּי מַלְכָּא קַדִּישָׁא כְּחַד מִינָן. קָם וּנְשָׁקֵיהּ. אָמַר רִבִּי שִׁמְעוֹן, אֶלְעָזָר קוּם בְּקִיּוּמָךְ, וְאֵימָא לְקַמֵּי מָארָךְ מִלִּין דִּילֵיהּ. קָם רִבִּי אֶלְעָזָר.

335. The trees bent over, one over the head of Rabbi Shimon, one over the head of Rabbi Pinchas and one over the head of Rabbi Elazar. The branches extended in every direction over the heads of the friends. Rabbi Pinchas wept and said, Praised is my lot and praised are my eyes that saw this. I am rejoicing not only about mine and yours but I am also rejoicing about Rabbi Elazar, our child, that he is as considered before the Holy King as one of us, BECAUSE ONE OF THE TREES BENT OVER HIS HEAD, THE SAME AS IT DID OVER THE HEADS OF RABBI SHIMON AND RABBI PINCHAS. He rose and kissed him. Rabbi Shimon declared, Elazar, stand up inyour place and cite in the presence of your Master some of His teachings, MEANING SOME WORDS OF TORAH. Rabbi Elazar rose.

30. "What have I done to you? and wherein have I wearied you?"

A Synopsis

Rabbi Elazar tells us how compassionate God is to His sons even when they have sinned. He says that God feels their pain if He punishes them, so that finally He begs them to act righteously.

336. פָּתַח וְאָמַר עַמִּי זְכָר נָא מַה יָּעַץ בָּלָק מֶלֶךְ מוֹאָב וְגוֹ'. עַמִּי, כַּמָּה קוּדְשָׁא בְּרִיךְ הוּא אַבָּא רַחֲמָן עַל בְּנוֹי, אע"ג דְּחָאבוּ גַּבֵּיהּ, כָּל מִלּוֹי בִּרְחִימוּ לְגַבַּיְיהוּ, כְּאַבָּא לְגַבֵּי בְּרֵיהּ. חָטֵי בְּרֵיהּ לְגַבֵּי אֲבוֹי, אַלְקֵי לֵיהּ, כ"כ דְּאַלְקֵי לֵיהּ לָא תָּב מֵאָרְחֵיהּ, נָזִיף בֵּיהּ בְּמִלִּין וְלָא קַבִּיל. אָמַר אֲבוֹי, לָא בָּעֵינָא לְמֶעְבַּד לִבְרִי כְּמָה דְּעָבֵדְנָא עַד יוֹמָא. אִלּוּ אַלְקֵיֵיהּ יְהֵא חָשִׁישׁ בְּרֵישֵׁיהּ, הָא כְּאִיבָא דִּילֵיהּ גַּבָּאי, אֱהֵא נָזִיף בֵּיהּ, הָא דִּיוּקְנֵיהּ מִשְׁתַּנְיָא, מַה אַעְבִּיד, אֶלָּא אֵיזִיל וְאֶתְחַנַּן לְגַבֵּיהּ, וְאֵימָא לֵיהּ מִלִּין רְכִיכִין, בְּגִין דְּלָא יִתְעֲצַב.

336. He opened the discussion with the verse: "O My people, remember now what Balak, king of Moab devised" (Michah 6:5). "My people;" how much is the Holy One, blessed be He, compassionate to His children, even though they sinned against Him. All His words to them are with love, like a father to his son. If a son sins against his father and he beats him yet as much as he beats him he doesn't repent his ways; if he scolds him with words but he does not accept from him, his father then says, I do not wish to continue to do to my son as I have done until now. If I beat him, his head will hurt and his pain will be upon me. If I scold him, his expression will be strange. What shall I do? I can only go and beg of him and speak to him softly, so he should not get saddened.

337. כֵּן בְּכָל זִינִין, אָזִיל קוּדְשָׁא בְּרִיךְ הוּא בְּיִשְׂרָאֵל. שָׁארִי עִמְּהוֹן אַלְקָאָה וְלָא קַבִּילוּ. נָזִיף בְּהוּ, וְלָא קַבִּילוּ. אָמַר קוּדְשָׁא בְּרִיךְ הוּא, חֲמֵינָא בִּבְרִי, דִּבְגִין מַלְקִיוּתָא דְּלָקֵינָא לוֹן, אִינּוּן חַשְׁשׁוּ בְּרֵישֵׁיהוֹן. וַוי, דְּהָא מִגּוֹ כְּאִיבָא דִּלְהוֹן, חֲשִׁישְׁנָא אֲנָא. דִּכְתִּיב, בְּכָל צָרָתָם לוֹ צָר. נָזִיפְנָא בְּהוּ, אֶשְׁתַּנָּא דִּיוּקְנָא דִּלְהוֹן, דִּכְתִּיב, חָשַׁךְ מִשְּׁחוֹר תָּאֳרָם לֹא נִכְּרוּ בַּחֻצוֹת. וַוי כַּד אִסְתְּכָלִית בְּהוּ, וְלָא אִשְׁתְּמוֹדָעוּ. הַשְׁתָּא,

30. "What have I done to you? and wherein have I wearied you?"

אֱהֵא מִתְחַנְּנָא לְגַבַּיְיהוּ גּוֹ תַּחֲנוּנִים. עַמִּי מֶה עָשִׂיתִי לְךָ וּמָה הֶלְאֵיתִיךָ. בְּרִי יְחִידָאָה דִּילִי, חֲבִיבָא דְּנַפְשָׁאִי, חָמֵי מַה עֲבָדִית לָךְ, שַׁלִּיטִית לָךְ עַל כָּל בְּנֵי הֵיכָלֵי, שָׁלִיטִית לָךְ עַל כָּל מַלְכִין דְּעָלְמָא, וְאִי עֲבָדִית לָךְ עוֹבָדִין אַחֲרָנִין, עֲנֵה בִּי, אַנְתְּ הֲוֵי סָהִיד בִּי.

337. In all these ways, the Holy One, blessed be He, conducted Himself towards Yisrael. He began by hitting them but they did not submit. He scolded them but they did not submit. The Holy One, blessed be He, then said, I see about My children that, due to the beatings they had from Me, their heads hurt. Woe is their pain which I also feel, as it says, "In all their afflictions He was afflicted" (Yeshayah 63:9). If I scold them, their expression will change, as it says, "Now their visage is blacker than coal; they are not known in the streets" (Eichah 4:8). Woe, when I gaze at them and I do not recognize them. Now, I will just beseech them, "O My people, what have I done to you? and wherein have I wearied you?" (Michah 6:3). My only son, My soul's beloved, look what I have caused you. I have set you up to rule over all the members of the palace. I have set you up to dominate over all the king of the world. And if I have done any other things, answer Me. You can testify against Me.

338. עַמִּי זְכָר נָא מַה יָּעַץ בָּלָק מֶלֶךְ מוֹאָב וּמֶה עָנָה אוֹתוֹ בִּלְעָם בֶּן בְּעוֹר. זְכָר נָא, הֲוֵי דָּכִיר בְּמָטוּ מִינָךְ. מַה יָּעַץ הַשְׁתָּא אִית לְאִסְתַּכְּלָא, מַה הֲוָה עֵיטָא דְּבָלָק עַל עַמָּא קַדִּישָׁא וְאוֹרַיְיתָא לָא חֲשִׁיבַת לֵיהּ לְבָלָק כְּלוּם, כְּמָה דַּהֲוָה לְלָבָן, דִּכְתִּיב אֲרַמִּי אוֹבֵד אָבִי.

338. "O My people, remember now what Balak, king of Moab devised, and what Bilaam, the son of Beor answered him." "Remember now": Remember, I pray you, "what...devised." Now we should observe what the advice of Balak was against the holy people. The Torah did not consider Balak as anything in comparison to Laban, as it says, "An Arammian wished to destroy my father" (Devarim 26:5). (THE REST IS MISSING)

31. "And from the hills I behold him" – And I extend a step outward

A Synopsis

We hear the esoteric meaning of the title verse, part of which has to do with the coming of Messiah son of David and also the emergence of Messiah son of Joseph who will die and be killed but will later rise to life again.

339. אֲשׁוּרֶנּוּ וְגוֹ׳, צִיּוּרָא וּדְיוּקְנָא דַּאֲבוֹי, אִתְרְשִׁים בֵּיהּ מַמָּשׁ. וּמֵהַהוּא זִמְנָא דַּהֲוָה בִּמְעָהָא דְּאִמֵּיהּ, מִסִּטְרָא דִּילָהּ, אִתְמְתַּח וְאוֹשִׁיט פְּסִיעָה לְבַר יַתִּיר. כִּי מֵרֹאשׁ צוּרִים אֶרְאֶנּוּ, דָּא דִּיוּקְנָא וְצִיּוּרָא דַּאֲבוֹי מַמָּשׁ. כֵּיוָן דַּהֲוָה בִּמְעָהָא דְּאִמֵּיהּ, אֲשׁוּרֶנּוּ, אוֹשִׁיט פְּסִיעָה לְבַר, ו׳ כְּגַוְונָא דָּא.

339. "I behold him..." (Bemidbar 23:9). HERE, the depiction and form of his father was really impressed upon him. And from the time he was in his mother's womb, from her side, he spread out and extended one more step outside. HE EXPLAINS: "For from the top of the rocks I see him" (Ibid.). That was the form and depiction of his actual father. When he was in his mother's womb, "I behold him." I will have extended a step outward, Vav, in this way.

340. וְדָא הוּא וּמִגְּבָעוֹת אֲשׁוּרֶנּוּ, בִּמְתִיבְתָּא עִלָּאָה, גִּבְעֹת חָסֵר ו׳. בִּמְתִיבְתָּא דִּרְקִיעָא, וּמִגְּבָעוֹת בְּאָת ו׳. וְאַשְׁלִים לִתְרֵין סִיטְרִין. חַד, דְּהָא הַאי גִּבְעַת לָא אִתְפָּרְשָׁא מִן בְּרָהּ לְעָלְמִין, וְלָא שַׁבְקָת לֵיהּ. וְעַ״ד אִתְכְּלִיל ו׳ בַּהֲדָהּ לְעָלַם. וְחַד, דְּהָא גִּבְעָה דִּלְתַּתָּא בְּרָהּ דְּאִתְכְּלִיל בָּהּ, אִצְטְרִיךְ לְזִמְנָא דְּאָתֵי כַּד יֵיתֵי מַלְכָּא מְשִׁיחָא, לְנַטְלָא לֵיהּ גִּבְעַת עִלָּאָה, וּלְאַעֲלָא לֵיהּ גּוֹ גַּדְפָּהָא, בְּגִין לְאַתְקְפָא לֵיהּ, וּלְאוֹקָמָא לֵיהּ בְּחַיִּין עִלָּאִין, וּמִנָּהּ יִפּוֹק בְּהַהוּא יוֹמָא מְשִׁיחָא דְּדָוִד.

340. That is the meaning of: "And from the hills I behold him." In the higher Yeshivah, the word "*geva'ot* (Eng. the hills)" is spelled without a Vav. In the heavenly Yeshivah, *geva'ot* has a Vav. The Vav is perfecting both sides, one, ZEIR ANPIN, because this hill never separates from its son,

THAT IS ZEIR ANPIN, and never abandons him. Therefore, the Vav is always part of it AND THAT IS WHY IT IS WRITTEN: "*GEVA'OT*" WITH A VAV. And one IS ABOUT MESSIAH, SON OF DAVID, because the lower hill, WHICH REFERS TO MALCHUT, has the son included in her, THAT IS MESSIAH, SON OF DAVID. In the future to come, when Messiah will come, that higher hill, THAT REFERS TO BINAH, needs to take and bring him inside her wings in order to strengthen him and place him in the higher life OF BINAH. From it will emerge on that day Messiah, son of David. THE VAV OF "*UMIGEVA'OT* (LIT. 'FROM THE HILLS')" IS ALLUDING TO HIM.

341. וְרָזָא דָּא, אֲסַפְּרָה אֶל חֹק יְיָ׳ אָמַר אֵלַי בְּנִי אַתָּה אֲנִי הַיּוֹם יְלִדְתִּיךָ. זַמִּין אֲנָא לוֹמַר לְהַהוּא אֲתָר דְּאִקְרֵי חֹק, וּלְבַשְּׂרָא לֵיהּ ה׳ אָמַר אֵלַי בְּנִי אַתָּה אֲנִי הַיּוֹם יְלִדְתִּיךָ. בְּהַהוּא יוֹמָא מַמָּשׁ, יָפִּיק לֵיהּ הַהוּא חֹק מִתְּחוֹת גַּדְפָהָא, בְּכַמָּה חַיִּין, בְּכַמָּה עִטְרִין, בְּכַמָּה בִּרְכָאן, כַּדְקָא יָאוּת.

341. That is the secret of, "I will tell of the decree: Hashem has said to me, 'You are My son; this day have I begotten you'" (Tehilim 2:7), WHICH IS EXPLAINED AS FOLLOWS: I will speak to this place that is called 'decree', THAT IS MALCHUT, and give the good tidings. "Hashem," THAT IS BINAH "has said to me, 'You are My son; this day have I begotten you'". THEREFORE, that very day, WHICH IS BINAH, produces that decree, THAT IS MALCHUT, from under her wings, OF BINAH, with much life, with many adornments and many blessings, as is proper.

342. וְהַהוּא חֹק לָא יִשְׁתְּאַר בִּלְחוֹדוֹי, יִתְכְּלִיל בֵּיהּ מְשִׁיחָא אַחֲרָא בְּרֵיהּ דְּיוֹסֵף, וְתַמָּן יִתְתָּקַף, וְלָא בַּאֲתָר אַחֲרָא. וּבְגִין דְּאִיהוּ גִּבְעָה תַּתָּאָה, דְּלֵית בָּהּ חַיִּין, יָמוּת מָשִׁיחַ דָּא, וְיִתְקְטִל, וִיהֵא מִית עַד דְּתִלְקוֹט חַיִּין גִּבְעָה דָּא, מֵהַהִיא גִּבְעָה עִלָּאָה, וִיקוּם.

342. That decree, WHICH IS MALCHUT, will not remain on its own, AFTER MESSIAH THE SON OF DAVID WILL EMERGE FROM IT. Because then, another Messiah, WHICH IS MESSIAH the son of Joseph, will be also be included in it, IN MALCHUT. There, IN MALCHUT, he will be fortified, and at no other place, THAT IS, NOT IN BINAH AS MESSIAH THE SON OF

DAVID, because this is a lower hill, MEANING MALCHUT, that has no life of its own, BECAUSE MALCHUT CONTAINS NOTHING ON HER OWN, EXCEPT WHAT ZEIR ANPIN GIVES HER, WHO DRAWS FROM BINAH AND GRANTS TO MALCHUT. MESSIAH THE SON OF JOSEPH WAS ATTACHED EXCLUSIVELY TO MALCHUT ALONE AND TO NO OTHER PLACE; THEREFORE, that Messiah will die and be killed, BECAUSE MALCHUT ON HIS OWN HAS NOTHING TO GRANT HIM. And he will remain dead until this hill, MALCHUT, will gather life from the higher hill, THAT IS BINAH, AND PROVIDE TO MESSIAH THE SON OF JOSEPH FROM THE LIGHTS OF BINAH. Then MESSIAH THE SON OF JOSEPH will rise TO LIFE.

343. ובג"כ, בִּמְתִיבְתָּא דִּרְקִיעָא וּמִגְּבָעוֹת שָׁלִים בְּאוֹת ו', עַל תְּרֵין סִטְרִין אִלֵּין. אֲבָל בְּמְתִיבְתָּא עִלָּאָה, חָסֵר, בְּלָא ו', לְאַחֲזָאָה מִלָּה דְּלֵית בָּהּ קוּשְׁיָא וְסָפֵק. הֶן עָם לְבָדָד יִשְׁכּוֹן, בְּיִחוּדָא, בְּלָא עִרְבּוּבְיָא אַחֲרָא.

343. Because of that, in the Yeshivah of the firmament, THE WORD, "*geva'ovt* (Eng. 'the hills')" is complete with the letter Vav THAT INDICATES both sides, ZEIR ANPIN AND MESSIAH. In the higher Yeshivah, the word *geva'ot* is missing the Vav, to indicate something about which there is no question or doubt. "It is a people that shall dwell alone" (Bemidbar 23:9), on their own, without any other admixture.

32. Top, trunk and path

A Synopsis

Because some of this section is missing it cannot all be summarized. It begins with a discussion about the name "Yud Hei Vav Hei our Elohim Yud Hei Vav Hei." We learn that the children of Yisrael have the Hebrew alphabet and language, and that higher secrets can be understood from the form of the letters; this understanding is not available to people of other nations, who have scripts that are merely inventions or agreements among them. The Zohar turns to the supernal creation of Zeir Anpin and Malchut, and lastly to the secret explanation of "And the number of the fourth part of Yisrael."

344. כָּל יִחוּדָא שְׁלִים, הָכָא אִיהוּ. יְיָ' אֱלֹהֵינוּ יְיָ'. דְּהָא רָזָא דִּילֵיהּ, מֵרֹאשׁ צוּרִים אִיהוּ, וְאִתְיַיחֵד בְּרֵישָׁא, בְּגִזְעָא וּשְׁבִילָא. יְיָ': דָּא רֵישָׁא עִלָּאָה, אֲוִירָא דְּסַלְּקָא. אֱלֹהֵינוּ: דָּא גִּזְעָא, דְּאִתְּמַר גֶּזַע יִשָׁי. יְיָ': דָּא שְׁבִילָא דִּלְתַּתָּא. וְעַל רָזָא דָּא אִתְיָיחַד בֵּיהּ כַּדְּקָא יָאוּת. וּבְגִין דְּאִתְמְתַּח בֵּיהּ שְׁבִילָא אִצְטְרִיךְ. רָזָא דְּאִתְגְּזַר בִּתְרֵי מְתִיבְתֵּי.

344. All the complete unity is here IN THE NAMES "Yud Hei Vav Hei our Elohim Yud Hei Vav Hei," because its secret is "from the top of the rocks" (Bemidbar 23:9) THAT IS SUPERNAL ABA. It was unified with the top, the trunk and path. Yud Hei Vav Hei is the highest peak of air that ascends, MEANING "TOP OF THE ROCKS" THAT IS ABA; our Elohim is the trunk, as is written: "The stem of Yishai" (Yeshayah 11:1), NAMELY BINAH. Yud Hei Vav Hei is the lower path, WHICH IS ZEIR ANPIN, VAV. By this secret, it was properly united with it and, because it spread out into it, INTO THE VAV, the path, IN THE SECRET MEANING OF THE STEP OUTWARD, there is a need...(MISSING THE CONTINUATION) the secret that was clarified in the two Yeshivot.

345. זַכָּאָה חוּלָקָךְ רִבִּי שִׁמְעוֹן, דְּזָכִית לְמִלִּין עִלָּאִין דְּמָארִיךְ, וּמָארָךְ אִתְרְעֵי בָּךְ, כַּמָּה שִׁיעוּרָא דִּמְתִיחָן דִּשְׁבִילָא דָּא בְּשִׁיעוּרָא עִלָּאָה, דְּרֵישָׁא וְגִזְעָא וּשְׁבִילָא, וְאִתְלַבְּשָׁן בִּמְתִיחוּ דָּא. וְעַ"ד מְתִיחוּ דְּא', שִׁיעוּרָא דְּשִׁית סִטְרִין. וְכֹלָּא אִתְיָחַד בְּהַאי אָת, ובג"כ, לְבָדָד יִשְׁכּוֹן כַּדְּקָא יָאוּת.

345. Happy is your lot, Rabbi Shimon, that you merited the higher matters of your Master. Your Master is pleased with you. How much the measure of the expansion of this path is by higher measurement, in the top, the trunk and the path, and they were attired in this extension. Therefore, the first extension is the measure of the six ends and everything was unified into this letter. Due to this, it properly "shall dwell alone..."(BECAUSE THE BEGINNING IS MISSING, IT IS IMPOSSIBLE TO EXPLAIN IT).

346. וּבַגּוֹיִם לֹא יִתְחַשָּׁב, יִשְׂרָאֵל אִית לוֹן כְּתָב וְלָשׁוֹן. וּבְכָל אָת, יַכְלִין לְאִסְתַּכְּלָא בְּדִיּוּקְנָא וְצִיּוּרָא כַּדְּקָא יָאוּת. אֲבָל בַּגּוֹיִם עכו״ם, לֹא יִתְחַשָּׁב. רָזָא דְּנָא, בְּגִין דְּלֵית לוֹן כְּתָב וְלָשׁוֹן, וְלֵית לוֹן לְאִסְתַּכְּלָא וּלְמִנְדַּע כְּלוּם, דְּהָא הֶבֶל הֵמָּה מַעֲשֵׂה תַּעְתּוּעִים. וְלָא יִתְחָשָׁב רָזָא דְּנָא בְּמַחֲשָׁבָה וּבְאַסְתַּכְּלוּתָא דִּלְהוֹן, הוֹאִיל וְלֵית לוֹן כְּתָב. זַכָּאִין אִינּוּן יִשְׂרָאֵל.

346. "And shall not be reckoned among the nations" (Ibid.): Yisrael have a script and a language. In each letter, it is possible to observe the form and proper depiction, IN ORDER TO UNDERSTAND THE HIGHER SECRETS IN THEM. However, it "shall not be reckoned among the nations," because they do not possess the script and language, ORIGINALLY DEPICTED IN ACCORDANCE WITH HIGHER FORMS. They have nothing by which to observe and know anything, THROUGH THE SHAPE OF THEIR SCRIPT, because "they are vanity, the work of delusion" (Yirmayah 10:15), SINCE THEIR SCRIPT AND LANGUAGES ARE MERELY AGREEMENTS, WHEREBY PEOPLE HAVE DECIDED UPON A SPECIFIC LANGUAGE AND SCRIPT. This secret "shall not be reckoned" in their way of thinking and observation, OF THEIR LETTER FORMS, because they do not have a script. Happy are Yisrael.

347. מִי מָנָה עֲפַר יַעֲקֹב וּמִסְפָּר אֶת רוֹבַע יִשְׂרָאֵל. הַהוּא נְקוּדָה עִלָּאָה, רֵישָׁא וְגִזְעָא וּשְׁבִילָא, בִּטְמִירוּ אִיהוּ, וְלָא קַיְּימָא לְשָׁאֲלָא לְבַר. אֲבָל מִשַּׁעֲתָא דְּשָׁארִי לְאִתְבְּנָאָה, וּלְמֶעְבַּד הֵיכָלָא בִּרְעוּתֵיהּ, וְאִקְרֵי מִ״י, שָׁארִי לְאִתְבְּנָאָה, דִּיּוּקְנָא, דִּילֵיהּ מַמָּשׁ. אַפִּיק נוּקְבָא דִּילֵיהּ, בְּדִיּוּקְנָא דְּאִמֵּיהּ.

347. "Who can count the dust of Jacob, and the number of the fourth part of Yisrael" (Bemidbar 23:10). That higher point, WHICH IS SUPERNAL ABA AND IMA, which top, trunk and path, ARE THE BEGINNING, MIDDLE AND END, MEANING CHOCHMAH, BINAH, DA'AT, CHESED, GVURAH, TIFERET, NETZACH, HOD AND YESOD, is hidden. It is not available for questioning. From the moment it began to be built and to become a chamber in accordance with His wish and be referred to as "Who," THAT IS YISRAEL-SABA AND TEVUNAH, its form OF ABA AND IMA began to be actually built, WHICH IS ZEIR ANPIN. FOLLOWING THAT, it produced his female, MEANING MALCHUT, in the form of His mother, THAT IS YISRAEL-SABA AND TEVUNAH, WHICH IS BINAH.

348. מַאי מִי. דָּא רֵישָׁא וְגִזְעָא וּשְׁבִילָא. וְאִתְפָּשַׁט לְאִתְבְּנָאָה בִּפְשִׁיטוּ דְּחַד הֵיכָלָא, לִתְרֵין סִטְרִין בָּאנֵי. ואע"ג דְּאַפִּיק לְיִשְׂרָאֵל. דְּאִיהוּ ו', אוּף הָכִי אַפִּיק לְנוּקְבָּא דִּילֵיהּ כַּחֲדָא, וְאַזְמְנָהּ לְגַבֵּיהּ. מָנָה, כד"א וַיְמַן לָהֶם הַמֶּלֶךְ וּמִשְׁלוֹחַ מָנוֹת. יָהַב לֵיהּ נְבַזְבְּזָא רַב וְיַקִּירָא, וְאַפִּיק לָהּ כַּחֲדָא מִנֵּיהּ. בְּהַהוּא פְּשִׁיטוּ דְּאִתְפְּשַׁט אַפִּיק תַּרְוַויְהוּ כַּחֲדָא, בְּשַׁעֲתָא חֲדָא.

348. What is this "Who"? It is the top, the trunk and the path, MEANING THE TOP, MIDDLE AND END, WHICH ARE CHOCHMAH, BINAH, DA'AT, CHESED, GVURAH, TIFERET, NETZACH, HOD AND YESOD OF YISRAEL-SABA AND TEVUNAH, that spreads out, so that a chamber may be built by extension. It built in two directions, TO ZEIR ANPIN AND MALCHUT, so that even though it took out Yisrael that is Vav, ZEIR ANPIN, it ALSO took out the female together and invited her to itself. "Who can count (Heb. *manah*)" MEANS, as it says, "And the king appointed them (Heb. *vayeman*)" (Daniel 1:5), AND ALSO "sending choice portions (Heb. *manot*)" (Ester 9:22), MEANING THAT "WHO," WHICH IS YISRAEL-SABA AND TEVUNAH, gave him, ZEIR ANPIN, a very valuable gift, WHICH IS MALCHUT, and let it out together with him. In the same extension that it expanded, it took both of them out together in the same moment.

349. וּמִסְפָּר אֶת רוֹבַע יִשְׂרָאֵל, רוֹבַע יִשְׂרָאֵל רָזָא דָּא בְּגִינָךְ ר' אִתְמְסַר, זַכָּאָה חוּלָקָךְ. רוֹבַע יִשְׂרָאֵל, רְבִיעִית, מִן מְדִידוּ דְּיִשְׂרָאֵל,

אִיהוּ בְּרִית. אֲמַאי אִקְרֵי רוֹבַע. אֶלָּא שִׁיעוּרָא דְּגוּפָא אַרְבַּע בְּרִיתוֹת הֲוֵי בְּשִׁיעוּרָא דִּילֵיהּ. וּבְרִית רוֹבַע אִיהוּ בְּשִׁיעוּרָא דִּמְדִידוּ דְּגוּפָא. כֹּלָּא אַפִּיק מִי.

349. The secret meaning of, "And the number of the fourth part of Yisrael" is passed on for your sake, Rabbi. Praised is your lot. "The fourth part of Yisrael" MEANS one quarter of the measure of Yisrael, WHICH IS ZEIR ANPIN CALLED 'YISRAEL' that is the covenant, MEANING YESOD OF ZEIR ANPIN. Why is it referred to by "fourth part"? Because in the measure of the body is four covenants. The member of the covenant is a quarter in measuring the body and all of it is produced by "who" THAT IS BINAH. THEREFORE, IT SAYS, "WHO CAN COUNT THE DUST OF JACOB, AND THE NUMBER OF THE FOURTH PART OF YISRAEL," BECAUSE "WHO" HAS BROUGHT FORTH EVERYTHING.

33. "My voice shall You hear in the morning, Hashem"

A Synopsis

Rabbi Elazar talks about the title verse, saying that 'morning' is the morning of Abraham that is Chesed, when people should pray because it is a time of goodwill for everyone. All those who have sinned should pray for forgiveness. We hear about Refael who carries all remedies and healing in his hand, and about how God looks for merit in people at the time of morning prayer. Rabbi Shimon tells his son that there are two mornings, one of Abraham and one of Joseph: both are of Chesed but the latter is revealed through the illumination of Chochmah. We hear that when God first made light it was too bright for the worlds to bear it, so He made successive levels of light to be clothed in it in order for it to be brought down to a level that the worlds could withstand. Joseph receives all the higher light, so his brightness radiates from one end of the world above to the other.

350. ר"א הֲוָה אָזִיל לְמֶחֱמֵי לְר' יוֹסֵי חָמוּי, ר' אַבָּא וְחַבְרוֹי אַזְלוּ עִמֵּיהּ. פָּתַח ר' אֶלְעָזָר וְאָמַר, יְיָ' בֹּקֶר תִּשְׁמַע קוֹלִי וְגוֹ'. יְיָ' בֹּקֶר מַאי בֹּקֶר. אֶלָּא דָּא בֹּקֶר דְּאַבְרָהָם, דְּאִתְּעַר בְּעָלְמָא. דִּכְתִּיב, וַיַּשְׁכֵּם אַבְרָהָם בַּבֹּקֶר. דְּהָא כַּד אָתֵי צַפְרָא, הַהוּא בֹּקֶר אִתְּעַר בְּעָלְמָא, וְהוּא עִידָּן רַעֲוָא לְכֹלָּא, וּלְמֶעְבַּד טִיבוּ לְכָל עָלְמָא, לְזַכָּאִין וּלְחַיָּיבִין. וּכְדֵין עִידָּן צְלוֹתָא הוּא, לְמִצְלֵי קַמֵּי מַלְכָּא קַדִּישָׁא.

350. Rabbi Elazar was journeying to see his father-in-law, Rabbi Yosi. Rabbi Aba and the friends went with him. Rabbi Elazar opened the discussion with the verse: "My voice shall You hear in the morning, Hashem" (Tehilim 5:4). What is the meaning of "morning"? HE RESPONDS: It refers to the morning of Abraham, WHO IS CHESED, that was roused in the world, as is written: "And up Abraham rose early in the morning" (Beresheet 22:3). When that morning arrived, that morning, THAT IS CHESED, awakens in the world, which is a time of goodwill for all, and a time to do kindness throughout the world, to the righteous and the wicked. Then it is a proper time period for prayer, to pray before the Holy King.

351. וְעַ"ד, בְּשַׁעֲתָא דְּאָתֵי צַפְרָא, כָּל אִינּוּן אֲסִירֵי מַלְכָּא, אַשְׁכָּחוּ נַיְיחָא, עִידָּן צְלוֹתָא אִיהוּ עֲלַיְיהוּ. וכ"ש אִינּוּן דְּתַיְיבִין בְּתִיוּבְתָּא,

וּבְעָאן בְּעוּתְהוֹן לְקַמֵּי מַלְכָּא קַדִּישָׁא. בְּגִין, דְּהַאי שַׁעֲתָא, חַד מְמָנָא נָפִיק לְסְטַר דָּרוֹם, וּרְפָאֵל שְׁמֵיהּ, וְכָל זִינֵי אַסְוָותָא בִּידוֹי. וּמִסְּטַר דָּרוֹם, נָפַק חַד רוּחָא, וּמַטֵי לְגַבֵּי הַהוּא מְמָנָא, דִּמְמָנָא עַל אַסְוָותָא. וְכַד מָטֵי צְלוֹתָא לְקַמֵּי קוּדְשָׁא בְּרִיךְ הוּא, פָּקִיד לְבֵי דִּינָא דִּילֵיהּ, דְּלָא יִפְתְּחוּן בְּדִינָא, בְּגִין דְּחַיִּים בִּידָא דְּקוּדְשָׁא בְּרִיךְ הוּא, וְלָא בִּידַיְיהוּ.

351. Therefore, during that time when that morning arrives, all the King's captives, MEANING THOSE WHO SIN AND ARE BOUND IN THE CHAINS OF SIN, find rest. It is a time for them to say prayers, and most certainly for those who repent and ask their request in the presence of the Holy King. In that time, a chieftain comes out to the south side, THAT IS CHESED, and his name is Raphael. there are all kinds of remedies in his hand. From the south side, THAT IS CHESED, a spirit leaves and reaches the chieftain appointed over healing, THAT IS RAPHAEL. When the prayer reaches the Holy One, blessed be He, He instructs the members of His court not to begin the trial, because life is in the hands of the Holy One, blessed be He, and not in their hands.

352. וּמִגּוֹ דְּאִיהוּ עִידָּן רַעֲוָא, בָּעָא קוּדְשָׁא בְּרִיךְ הוּא זְכוּתָא דְּהַהוּא ב"נ, אִי יִשְׁתְּכַּח בִּצְלוֹתָא, אוֹ דְּאִיהוּ מָארֵיהּ דִּתְיוּבְתָּא, חָס עָלֵיהּ. בְּהַהִיא שַׁעֲתָא קָל צִפֳּרִין דִּמְקַנְּנָן אִשְׁתְּמָעוּ, דִּכְתִּיב אֲשֶׁר שָׁם צִפֳּרִים יְקַנֵּנוּ. וְאִינּוּן צִפֳּרִין אוֹדָאן וּמְשַׁבְּחָן לְקוּדְשָׁא בְּרִיךְ הוּא. וְהַהוּא אַיֶּלֶת הַשַּׁחַר אִתְּעַר בְּעָלְמָא וְאָמַר, מָה רַב טוּבְךָ אֲשֶׁר צָפַנְתָּ לִּירֵאֶיךָ וְגוֹ'. כְּדֵין הַהוּא מְמָנָא נָפִיק, וְעָבֵיד כָּל מַה דְּאִתְפְּקַד.

352. Because it is a time of favor, the Holy One, blessed be He, looks to find merit for that person. If he is at prayer or he is repenting, He has compassion on him. At that time, the voice of nesting birds is heard, as is written: "Where the birds make their nests" (Tehilim 104:17), because these birds thank and praise the Holy One, blessed be He. The morning gazelle woke up in the world said, "O how great is Your goodness, which You have laid up for those who fear You..." (Tehilim 31:20). Then the appointee OVER HEALING goes forth and does all that he is instructed to do.

353. וְאִי תֵּימָא דְּזִינֵי אַסְוָותָא בִּידוֹי כְּמָה דְּאָמָרָן. לָאו הָכִי. דְּהָא

אַסְוָותָא לָא הֲוֵי, אֶלָּא בִּידוֹי דְּמַלְכָּא קַדִּישָׁא. אֲבָל בְּשַׁעֲתָא דְּפָקִיד קוּדְשָׁא בְּרִיךְ הוּא אַסְוָותָא לְהַהוּא בַּר נַשׁ, אִיהוּ נָפִיק, וְכָל אִינּוּן מְקַטְרְגִין דִּמְמָנָן עַל מַרְעִין בִּישִׁין, דַּחֲלִין מִנֵּיהּ. כְּדֵין הַהוּא רוּחָא דְּקָא נָסַע מִסִּטְרָא דְּדָרוֹם, אוֹשִׁיט לֵיהּ לְהַהוּא ב״נ, וְהָא אַסְוָותָא אִשְׁתְּכַח, וְכֹלָּא בִּידוֹי דְּקוּדְשָׁא בְּרִיךְ הוּא.

353. If you think that the types of healing are in the power OF THE APPOINTEE as we mentioned, it is not so, because remedy is only in the hands of the Holy King. However, at the moment when the Holy One, blessed be He, instructs a remedy for that person, the appointee goes out and all the prosecutors that are appointed for awful diseases fear him. Then the spirit that travels from the south side, THAT IS THE SPIRIT OF CHESED, extends THAT CHESED to that person and behold, there is healing. HOWEVER, all is in the hand of the Holy One, blessed be He.

354. וְעַ״ד כְּתִיב, יְיָ׳ בֹּקֶר תִּשְׁמַע קוֹלִי. וְלָא כְּתִיב יְיָ׳ תִּשְׁמַע קוֹלִי. אֶלָּא לְגַבֵּי בֹּקֶר דְּאַבְרָהָם קָאָמַר. בֹּקֶר אֶעֱרָךְ לְךָ וַאֲצַפֶּה. תְּרֵי בֹּקֶר אֲמַאי. אֶלָּא חַד בֹּקֶר דְּאַבְרָהָם. וְחַד בֹּקֶר דְּיוֹסֵף. דִּכְתִּיב הַבֹּקֶר אוֹר, וּמְתַרְגְּמִינָן צַפְרָא נְהִיר, נְהִיר וַדַּאי. אֶעֱרָךְ לְךָ וַאֲצַפֶּה, אֶעֱרָךְ לְךָ מַהוּ. אֶלָּא אֲסַדֵּר לְךָ בּוּצִינָא דִּילָךְ לְאַדְלָקָא. כד״א עָרַכְתִּי נֵר לִמְשִׁיחִי. וּלְגַבֵּי בֹּקֶר דְּיוֹסֵף קָאָמַר, דְּהַהוּא סִדּוּרָא דְּבוּצִינָא דִּילֵיהּ הוּא.

354. Therefore, it is written: "My voice shall You hear (in) the morning, Hashem" instead of simply saying, 'My voice shall You hear, Hashem,' because he spoke to that morning of Abraham. "(In) the morning I will direct my prayer to You; and will wait expectantly" (Tehilim 5:4). HE ASKS: Why is morning said twice? HE RESPONDS: It is because one morning is the one of Abraham, THAT IS CHESED, and one morning is of Joseph, as is written: "As soon as the morning was light" (Beresheet 44:3). The Targum translates it as: "the morning shines," for it definitely gives light. AND THE DIFFERENCE IS THAT THE MORNING OF ABRAHAM IS CHESED, WHICH IS CONCEALED FROM CHOCHMAH, AND THE MORNING OF JOSEPH IS OF CHESED THAT IS REVEALED THROUGH THE ILLUMINATION OF CHOCHMAH. "I will direct my prayer to You; and will wait expectantly": What is the meaning OF, "I WILL DIRECT MY PRAYER TO YOU"? It is, I will prepare Your candle to light up with, as it says, "I have set up a lamp for My anointed" (Tehilim 132:17). That refers to that morning of Joseph, because this preparation of the candle is his.

355. וַאֲצַפֶּה, מַהוּ וַאֲצַפֶּה. הָא כָּל בְּנֵי עָלְמָא מְצַפָּאן וּמְחַכָּאן לְטִיבוּ דְּקוּדְשָׁא בְּרִיךְ הוּא, וַאֲפִילוּ בְּעִירֵי דְּחַקְלָא, וּמָה שְׁבַחָא דְּדָוִד יַתִּיר מִכֹּל בְּנֵי עַלְמָא, אֶלָּא, מִלָּה דָּא שָׁאִילְנָא, וְהָכִי אָמְרוּ לִי, וְאִיהִי מִלָּה קְשׁוֹט דְּאָתֵי מֵרָחִיק. נְהוֹרָא קַדְמָאָה דְּבָרָא קוּדְשָׁא בְּרִיךְ הוּא, הֲוָה נָהִיר עַד דְּלָא הֲווֹ יַכְלִין עָלְמִין לְמִסְבְּלֵיהּ. מָה עֲבַד קוּדְשָׁא בְּרִיךְ הוּא, עָבֵד נְהוֹרָא לִנְהוֹרֵיהּ, לְאִתְלַבְּשָׁא דָּא בְּדָא. וְכֵן כָּל שְׁאַר נְהוֹרִין, עַד דְּעָלְמִין כֻּלְּהוּ אִתְקָיְימוּ בְּקִיּוּמַיְיהוּ, וְיַכְלִין לְמִסְבַּל.

355. IT SAYS, "and will wait expectantly." HE ASKS: What is the meaning of: "and will wait expectantly"? Aren't all the inhabitants of the world hoping and waiting for the kindness of the Holy One, blessed be He, even the beasts? In what is that praise of David better than everyone's in the world? HE REPLIES: I have inquired about this matter and this was the reply, which is a matter of truth that comes from a distance. THAT IS THE SECRET OF CHOCHMAH, AS IT SAYS, "I SAID LET ME BECOME WISE, BUT IT WAS FAR FROM ME" (KOHELET 7:23). The first light that the Holy One, blessed be He, created was so bright that the worlds could not stand it. What did the Holy One, blessed be He, do? He made light to His light, so that they could be attired with one another, and similarly with all the rest of the lights. THAT IS, EACH HIGHER LIGHT IS CLOTHED WITH A LEVEL THAT IS LOWER THAN IT, until all the worlds are maintained and can withstand it.

356. ובג"כ אִתְפְּשָׁטוּ דַּרְגִּין, וְאִתְלַבָּשׁוּ נְהוֹרִין, וְאִינּוּן אִקְרוּן כְּנָפַיִם עִלָּאִין, עַד דְּמָטוּ לְהַאי בֹּקֶר דְּיוֹסֵף, וְאִיהוּ נָטִיל כָּל נְהוֹרִין עִלָּאִין, וּמִגּוֹ דְּכָל נְהוֹרִין עִלָּאִין בֵּיהּ תַּלְיָין, זִיוֵיהּ סָלִיק מִסַּיְיפֵי עָלְמָא עַד סַיְיפֵי עָלְמָא דִּלְעֵילָּא, עַד דְּעָלְמִין דִּלְתַתָּא לָא יַכְלִין לְמִסְבַּל. אָתָא דָּוִד וְאַתְקַן הַאי בּוּצִינָא, חוּפָּאָה לְהַאי בֹּקֶר דְּיוֹסֵף, לְאִתְחַפָּאָה בֵּיהּ, וּלְקַיְּימָא עָלְמִין דִּלְתַתָּא, בְּסִדּוּרָא דְּבוּצִינָא דָּא וְעַל דָּא כְּתִיב, בֹּקֶר

אֶעֱרָךְ לְךָ וַאֲצַפֶּה. כד"א, וַיְצַפֵּהוּ זָהָב טָהוֹר. וּבְגִין דְּהַהוּא בּוּצִינָא דְּדָוִד אִיהִי, וּבָהּ תַּלְיָיא, אָמַר דְּאִיהוּ לִיהֱוֵי חוּפָּאָה לְהַאי בֹּקֶר. אָתָא רִבִּי אַבָּא וּנְשָׁקֵיהּ, אָמַר אִלְמָלֵא לָא נָפַקְנָא בְּאָרְחָא, אֶלָּא לְמִשְׁמַע מִלָּה דָּא דַּיִי.

356. That is why all the levels were spread out and all the lights were clothed. These GARMENTS, WHEREIN THE LOWER DRESSES UP THE HIGHER, are called 'supernal wings' until they reach that morning of Joseph. And he receives all the higher lights, BECAUSE YESOD IS COMPRISED AND COMPOSED OF ALL THE LIGHTS HIGHER THAN IT. Due to the fact that all the higher lights depend on it, its brightness radiates from one end of the world to the other end of the world above, until the worlds below IT can not withstand it. David came and prepared the candle, which is a cover for the morning of Joseph, to cover it to allow the maintenance of the worlds that are lower by the setting of that candle. That is why it is written, "In the morning I will direct my prayer to You; and will wait (Heb. *atzapeh*) expectantly," as it says, "And he overlaid it (Heb. *yetzapehu*) with pure gold" (Shemot 37:2). That candle is of David, THE CHARIOT OF MALCHUT, upon which he is dependent, and he said it should be the cover over this morning OF JOSEPH. Rabbi Aba approached and kissed him. He said, Had I gone out on my journey only to hear this one thing, it would have been sufficient reason for me.

34. The son of Rabbi Yosi of Peki'in

A Synopsis

A dove lands in front of Rabbi Elazar and he sends it with a message to his father-in-law Rabbi Yosi to say that he should be prepared for a miracle in three days time. Before leaving, the dove says that someone else has died in Rabbi Yosi's place. Rabbi Elazar and Rabbi Aba make a detour to visit the house of Rabbi Yosi of Pekiin who has died instead of Rabbi Yosi. They find the Rabbi's small son in terrible grief; he won't allow anyone else near the body, and he keeps telling God that He should have taken him and his sister instead of their father. A voice says to Rabbi Yosi of Pekiin that he has been given another 22 years of life and that thirteen other people have died in his place; this will give him time to bring up and teach his son. Rabbi Yosi is returned to life and there is much rejoicing. He tells the others what happened when he was in the world beyond and how much his son's action of offering to give up his life in exchange for him led to God's mercy.

357. עַד דַּהֲווּ אָזְלֵי, הָא יוֹנָה חַד מָטָא לְגַבֵּי רִבִּי אֶלְעָזָר. שָׁרִיאַת, וְקָא מְצַפְצְפָא קַמֵּיהּ. אָמַר רִבִּי אֶלְעָזָר, יוֹנָה כְּשֵׁרָה מְהֵימְנַת הֲוֵית תָּדִיר בִּשְׁלִיחוּתֵיךְ, זִילִי וְאֵימָא לֵיהּ, הָא חַבְרַיָּיא אָתָאן לְגַבָּךְ, וַאֲנָא עִמְּהוֹן. וְנִסָּא יִתְרְחִישׁ לֵיהּ לִתְלָתָא יוֹמִין, וְלָא יִנְפּוֹל עָלֵיהּ דְּחִילוּ, דְּהָא בְּחֶדְוָה אֲנָן אַזְלִין לְגַבֵּיהּ. אָתִיב זִמְנָא אַחֲרָא וְאָמַר, לָא חַדֵּינָא סַגְּיָא, וּבָאִישׁ בְּעֵינָי סַגִּי, עַל חַד רִמּוֹנָא מַלְיָא דְּאִתְיְהִיב תְּחוֹתֵיהּ, וְיוֹסֵי שְׁמֵיהּ. אַזְלַת הַהִיא יוֹנָא מִקַּמֵּיהּ, וְאִינּוּן חַבְרַיָּיא אַזְלוּ.

357. During their travel, a dove reached Rabbi Elazar. She landed and chirped before him. Rabbi Elazar declared, Worthy dove, you are always faithful in your mission. Go and inform him, RABBI YOSI, RABBI ELAZAR'S FATHER-IN-LAW, to be prepared for the friends that are coming to you, and tell him I am with them. A miracle will occur to him in three days and he shall have no fear, because we are coming to him with gladness. He replied again and said, I am not too happy, because I am very badly disturbed about one full pomegranate that was placed below him in his stead, MEANING THAT SOMEONE ELSE DIED IN HIS PLACE; his name is also Yosi. The dove left his presence and the friends left.

358. אָמַר רִבִּי אַבָּא לְר׳ אֶלְעָזָר, מַאי הַאי, תַּוְּוהְנָא סַגִּי, מִמָּה דַּחֲמֵינָא. אָ״ל, יוֹנָה דָּא אָתָאת לְגַבָּאי בִּשְׁלִיחוּתֵיהּ דְּרִבִּי יוֹסֵי חָמֵי, דְּאִיהוּ בְּבֵי מַרְעֵיהּ, וְיָדַעְנָא מֵהַאי יוֹנָה דְּאִשְׁתְּזִיב, וְחִלּוּפָא אִתְיְיהִיב עָלֵיהּ וְאִתְּסֵי.

358. Rabbi Aba said, Rabbi Elazar, what is this great wonder that I have observed? He said to him, This dove came to me on a mission from Rabbi Yosi, my father-in-law, who is in his sick chamber. I learned from this dove that he is already saved, and a substitute was given in his stead, MEANING TO SAY ANOTHER PERSON IS GOING TO DIE INSTEAD OF HIM, and he got well.

359. עַד דַּהֲווֹ אָזְלוּ, הָא עוּרְבָא חַד קָאֵים לְקַמַּיְיהוּ, קָרָא בְּחֵילָא, וּמְצַפְצְפָא צִפְצוּפָא סַגִּי. אָמַר רִבִּי אֶלְעָזָר, לְהָכִי אַתְּ קַיְּימָא, וּלְהָכִי אַנְתְּ מִתַּקַּן, זִיל לְאָרְחָךְ, דְּהָא יְדַעְנָא. אָמַר ר׳ אֶלְעָזָר, חַבְרַיָּיא נֵיזִיל וְנִגְמוֹל חֶסֶד לְרִמּוֹנָא, דַּהֲוָה מַלְיָא מִכֹּלָּא, וְרִבִּי יוֹסֵי דִּפְקִיעִין שְׁמֵיהּ אִיהוּ, דְּהָא אִסְתַּלָּק מֵעָלְמָא דֵּין, וְלֵית מַאן דְּחָזֵי לְאִשְׁתַּדְּלָא בֵּיהּ, וְאִיהוּ קָרִיב לְגַבָּן.

359. While still journeying, behold, a raven appeared to them. It cried out and crowed loudly. Rabbi Elazar said, This is your duty, and for that reason you were created, MEANING TO BRING BAD TIDINGS. Get going on your way, I already know. Rabbi Elazar said, Let us go and do an act of kindness for that pomegranate that was full of everything; Rabbi Yosi of Peki'in was his name, who departed from this world and no one is worthy to make an effort for his sake. And he is close by.

360. סָטוּ מֵאָרְחָא, וְאָזְלוּ לְתַמָּן. כֵּיוָן דְּחָמוּ לוֹן כָּל בְּנֵי מָאתָא, נַפְקוּ לְגַבַּיְיהוּ. וְעָאלוּ תַּמָּן בְּבֵי רִבִּי יוֹסֵי דִּפְקִיעִין, אִינּוּן חַבְרַיָּיא אִלֵּין. בְּרָא זְעֵירָא הֲוָה לֵיהּ לְרִבִּי יוֹסֵי, וְלָא שָׁבִיק לְבַר נָשׁ דְּיִמְטֵי לְעַרְסָא דַּאֲבוֹי, בָּתַר דְּמִית. אֶלָּא הֲוָא בִּלְחוּדוֹי הֲוָה סָמִיךְ לֵיהּ, וּבָכֵי עָלֵיהּ, פּוּמֵיהּ בְּפוּמֵיהּ מִתְדַּבְּקָא.

360. They detoured from the road and went there. When the townspeople saw them, they all went to welcome them, and these friends entered the house of Rabbi Yosi of Peki'in. Rabbi Yosi had a little boy who wouldn't allow anyone to get close to the bed of his father after he died. He alone was by it, crying over him with his mouth over his mouth.

361. פָּתַח הַהוּא יַנּוּקָא וְאָמַר, מָארֵיהּ דְּעָלְמָא, כְּתִיב בְּאוֹרַיְיתָא, כִּי יִקָּרֵא קַן צִפּוֹר לְפָנֶיךָ וְגוֹ׳, שַׁלֵּחַ תְּשַׁלַּח אֶת הָאֵם וְגוֹ׳. הֲוָה גָּעֵי הַהוּא יַנּוּקָא וּבָכֵי, אָמַר, מָארֵיהּ דְּעָלְמָא, קַיֵּים מִלָּה דָּא דְּאוֹרַיְיתָא, תְּרֵין בְּנִין הֲוֵינָא מֵאַבָּא וְאִמִּי, אֲנָא וַאֲחָתִי זְעֵירְתָּא מִנַּאי. הֲוָה לָךְ לְמֵיסַב לָן, וּלְקַיְּימָא מִלָּה דְּאוֹרַיְיתָא. וְאִי תֵּימָא מָארֵיהּ דְּעָלְמָא, אֵם כְּתִיב, וְלָא אָב, הָא הָכָא כּוֹלָּא הוּא, אַבָּא וְאִמָּא. אִימָּא מִיתַת, וּנְסִיבַת לָהּ מֵעַל בְּנִין. הַשְׁתָּא אַבָּא דַּהֲוֵי חָפֵי עֲלָן, אִנְסִיב מֵעַל בְּנִין, אָן דִּינָא דְּאוֹרַיְיתָא. בָּכוּ ר׳ אֶלְעָזָר וְחַבְרַיָּיא, לָקֳבֵל בְּכִיָּה וְגָעוּ דְּהַהוּא יַנּוּקָא.

361. The child opened with, Master of the universe, it says in the Torah: "If a bird's nest chance to be before you...but you shall surely let the mother go..." (Devarim 22:6). The child was crying and weeping. He said, Master of the universe, abide by that matter that is in the Torah. We were two children to my father and mother, myself and my younger sister. You should have taken us, and acted in accordance with the words of the Torah, AS IT SAYS, "BUT YOU SHALL SURELY LET THE MOTHER GO, AND TAKE THE YOUNG TO YOU" (IBID. 7). If you should say, Master of the universe, it says "mother" and not "father," this is the same, my father and mother, as mother died and You have taken her away from the children, and now, my father also, who was our protection, You took away from the children. Where is the just sentence in the Torah? Rabbi Elazar and his friends cried before the grief and tears of the child.

362. פָּתַח ר׳ אֶלְעָזָר וְאָמַר, שָׁמַיִם לָרוּם וָאָרֶץ לָעוֹמֶק וְגוֹ׳. עַד דַּהֲוָה אָמַר ר׳ אֶלְעָזָר קְרָא דָּא, הֲוָה עַמּוּדָא דְּאֶשָּׁא פָּסִיק בֵּינַיְיהוּ, וְהַהוּא יַנּוּקָא הֲוָה דָּבִיק בְּפוּמֵיהּ דַּאֲבוּי, וְלָא הֲווֹ מִתְפָּרְשָׁאן. א״ר אֶלְעָזָר, אוֹ בָּעֵי קוּדְשָׁא בְּרִיךְ הוּא לְמִרְחָשׁ נִיסָא, אוֹ בָּעֵי דְּלָא יִשְׁתְּדַל בַּר נָשׁ אַחֲרָא עָלֵיהּ, אֲבָל עַל מִלִּין דְּהַהוּא יַנּוּקָא וְדִמְעוֹי, לָא יָכִילְנָא לְמִסְבַּל.

362. Rabbi Elazar opened the discussion with the verse: "The heaven for height, and the earth for depth" (Mishlei 25:3). While Rabbi Elazar was saying this verse, a pillar of fire separated them FROM THE DEPARTED, but the child was still attached to the lips of his father and did not separate. Rabbi Elazar said, THIS IS WHY THE PILLAR OF FIRE SEPARATED; either the Holy One, blessed be He, wishes to perform a miracle AND REVIVE HIM, or He desires that no one else deal with him. However, I cannot bear to see the child's tears or to hear what he is saying.

363. עַד דַּהֲווֹ יַתְבִין, שָׁמְעוּ חַד קָלָא, דַּהֲוָה אָמַר, זַכָּאָה אַנְתְּ רַבִּי יוֹסֵי, דְּמִלִּין דְּהַאי גַּדְיָא זְעֵירָא, וְדִמְעוֹי, סָלִיקוּ לְגַבֵּי כֻּרְסְיָיא דְּמַלְכָּא קַדִּישָׁא, וְדָנוּ דִּינָא, וּתְלֵיסָר בְּנֵי נָשָׁא אַזְמִין קוּדְשָׁא בְּרִיךְ הוּא לְמַלְאַךְ הַמָּוֶת בְּגִינָךְ, וְהָא עֶשְׂרִין וּתְרֵין שְׁנִין אוֹסִיפוּ לָךְ, עַד דְּתוֹלִיף אוֹרַיְיתָא, לְהַאי גַּדְיָא שְׁלֵימָא, חֲבִיבָא קַמֵּי קוּדְשָׁא בְּרִיךְ הוּא.

363. While still sitting, they heard another voice that said, Blessed are you, Rabbi Yosi, that the speeches of the young goat kid and his tears rose to the throne of the Holy King and pronounced the sentence. And the Holy One, blessed be He, handed thirteen people for your sake to the Angel of Death, TO REDEEM YOU. Behold, they have added 22 years to your life, so you will have time to teach the young kid, perfect and beloved before the Holy One, blessed be He.

364. קָמוּ ר׳ אֶלְעָזָר וְחַבְרַיָּיא, וְלָא שָׁבְקוּ לְבַר נָשׁ לְמֵיקַם בְּבֵיתָא, מִיַּד חָמוּ הַהוּא עַמּוּדָא דְּאֶשָּׁא דְּסָלִיק, וְר׳ יוֹסֵי פָּתַח עֵינוֹי. וְהַהוּא יַנּוּקָא דָּבִיק פּוּמֵיהּ בְּפוּמֵיהּ. א״ר אֶלְעָזָר, זַכָּאָה חוּלָקָנָא דַּחֲמֵינָא תְּחִיַּית הַמֵּתִים, עֵינָא בְּעֵינָא. קְרִיבוּ לְגַבֵּיהּ, וַהֲוָה הַהוּא יַנּוּקָא נָאִים, כְּמָה דְּגָוַע מֵהַאי עָלְמָא, אָמְרוּ זַכָּאָה חוּלָקָךְ רַבִּי יוֹסֵי, וּבָרִיךְ רַחֲמָנָא דְּאַרְחִישׁ לָךְ נִיסָּא, עַל גַּעְיָא וּבִכְיָיא דִּבְנָךְ, וּבְמִלּוֹי, דְּהָכִי דָּחִיק בְּמִלִּין שַׁפִּירִין לִתְרַע שְׁמַיָּא, בְּמִלּוֹי וּבְדִמְעוֹי אוֹסִיפוּ לָךְ חַיִּין.

364. Rabbi Elazar and the friends rose, and did not allow anyone to stay in the house. They immediately saw the pillar of fire was gone. Rabbi Yosi opened his eyes and the child was still glued with his lips to his lips. Rabbi

Elazar said, Blessed is our lot that we witnessed the resurrection of the dead eye to eye. They approached him and the child fell asleep, as if he was expiring from this world. They said, Blessed is your lot, Rabbi Yosi, and blessed is the Merciful One, who performed a miracle for your sake due to the crying and weeping of your son, and his words. Life was added to you for his words, that he was pressing with beautiful speeches to the gates of heaven in his pleading and tears.

365. נְטָלוּהוּ לְהַהוּא יַנּוּקָא, וּנְשָׁקוּהוּ וּבָכוּ עִמֵּיהּ מֵחֶדְוָה סַגִּיא. וְאַפְקוּהוּ לְבֵיתָא אַחֲרָא, וְאַתְעֲרוּ עֲלֵיהּ, וְלָא אוֹדְעוּ לֵיהּ מִיַּד, אֶלָּא לְבָתַר הָכִי. חֲדוּ תַּמָּן תְּלָתָא יוֹמִין, וְחַדִּישׁוּ בַּהֲדֵי הַהוּא רִבִּי יוֹסֵי, כַּמָּה חִדּוּשִׁין בְּאוֹרַיְיתָא.

365. They took the child and kissed him and cried with him due to great joy. They removed him to another house and woke him up FROM HIS SLEEP. They did not inform him immediately OF HIS FATHER'S REVIVAL, but later on. They rejoiced there for three days and uncovered, with Rabbi Yosi, many new insights in the Torah.

366. אָמַר לוֹן ר' יוֹסֵי, חַבְרַיָּיא, לָא אִתְיְהִיבַת לִי רְשׁוּ לְגַלָּאָה מֵהַהוּא דַּחֲמֵינָא בְּהַהוּא עָלְמָא, אֶלָּא לְבָתַר תְּרֵיסַר שְׁנִין. אֲבָל תְּלַת מְאָה וְשִׁתִּין וַחֲמֵשׁ דִּמְעִין, דְּאוֹשִׁיד בְּרִי, עָאלוּ בְּחוּשְׁבְּנָא קָמֵי מַלְכָּא קַדִּישָׁא, וְאוֹמֵינָא לְכוּ חַבְרַיָּיא, דִּבְשַׁעֲתָא דְּפָתַח בְּהַהוּא פְּסוּקָא, וְגָעָא בְּאִינּוּן מִלִּין, אִזְדַּעְזְעוּ תְּלַת מְאָה אַלְפֵי סַפְסְלֵי דַּהֲווֹ בִּמְתִיבְתָּא דִּרְקִיעָא, וְכֻלְּהוּ קַיְימֵי קַמֵּיהּ דְּמַלְכָּא קַדִּישָׁא, וּבָעוּ רַחֲמֵי עָלַי, וְעָרְבוּ לִי. וְקוּדְשָׁא בְּרִיךְ הוּא אִתְמְלֵי רַחֲמִין עָלַי.

366. Rabbi Yosi said to them, Friends, I was not given authority to reveal what I observed in that world, until twelve years later. However, the 365 tears that my son spilled came into account before the Holy King. And I tell you friends, at the time MY SON opened up with that verse MENTIONED ABOVE and cried out with these words, 300,000 benches that were in the Yeshivah of heaven were shaken. All THE SOULS stood before the Holy King and asked for compassion towards me, and guaranteed for me THAT I

WOULD NOT SIN DURING THAT TIME. The Holy One, blessed be He, was filled with compassion for me.

367. וְשַׁפִּיר קַמֵּיהּ, אִינּוּן מִלִּין, וְהֵיךְ מָסַר נַפְשֵׁיהּ עָלַי. וְחַד אַפּטְרוֹפְּסָא הֲוָה קַמֵּיהּ, וְקָאָמַר, מָארֵי דְעָלְמָא, הָא כְּתִיב מִפִּי עוֹלְלִים וְיוֹנְקִים יִסַּדְתָּ עוֹז לְמַעַן צוֹרְרֶיךָ לְהַשְׁבִּית אוֹיֵב וּמִתְנַקֵּם. יְהֵא רַעֲוָא קַמָּךְ, זְכוּ דְאוֹרַיְיתָא, וּזְכוּ דְהַהוּא רַבְיָא, דְקָא מָסַר נַפְשֵׁיהּ עַל אֲבוּהָ דְתֵחוּס עָלֵיהּ, וְיִשְׁתֵּזִיב.

367. The words OF MY SON were pleasing to Him, and the way in which he surrendered his own life for me. A guardian was present there, A PROTECTOR AND DEFENSE COUNSELOR, who said, Master of the universe, does it not say, "Out of the mouth of babes and sucklings have You founded strength because of Your enemies, that You might still the enemy and the avenger" (Tehilim 8:3)? May it please You that through the merit of the Torah, and the merit of that child who was ready to give his soul for his father's sake, You would have mercy on him and he would be saved.

368. וּתְלֵיסַר בְּנֵי נָשָׁא אַזְמִין לֵיהּ תְּחוֹתַי, וְעִרְבוֹנָא יָהַב לֵיהּ, מִדִּינָא תַּקִּיפָא דָא. כְּדֵין קָרָא קוּדְשָׁא בְּרִיךְ הוּא לְמַלְאַךְ הַמָּוֶת, וּפָקִיד לֵיהּ עָלַי, דְלֵיתֵב לְבָתַר עֶשְׂרִין וּתְרֵין שְׁנִין, דְּהָא לָאו עִרְבוֹנָא קַמֵּיהּ, אֶלָּא לִיתוּב לִידוֹי, מַשְׁכּוֹנִין דַּהֲווֹ בִּידוֹי, הַשְׁתָּא חַבְרַיָּיא, בְּגִין דְחָמָא קוּדְשָׁא בְּרִיךְ הוּא דְאַתּוּן זַכָּאֵי קְשׁוֹט, אִתְרְחִישׁ נִיסָא לְעֵינַיְיכוּ.

368. And thirteen people were summoned in my stead, who were granted TO THAT ANGEL OF DEATH as pledge, MEANING AS RANSOM IN HIS STEAD, TO REMOVE ME from this harsh sentence. Then, the Holy One, blessed be He, called on the Angel of Death and instructed him concerning me to return after 22 years, because THE THIRTEEN PEOPLE PLACED IN MY STEAD were not considered REAL surety INSTEAD OF ME TO EXCUSE ME FROM DEATH FOREVER. They were merely placed in his hands as a pledge, MEANING TO SAY THAT EITHER WAY, THESE THIRTEEN WOULD HAVE DIED EVENTUALLY, AND THEY WERE IN THE HANDS OF THE ANGEL OF DEATH, EXCEPT THAT THEY DIED BEFORE. THEREFORE THEY COULD

NOT BE A DEPOSIT AND PLEDGE FOREVER, TO GIVE HIM LEAVE OF DEATH; THEY HAVE ONLY EXTENDED HIS TIME FOR A PERIOD OF 22 YEARS. Now, friends, because the Holy One, blessed be He, saw that you were truly righteous, the miracle occurred before your eyes.

35. "Hashem kills, and gives life"

A Synopsis

Rabbi Yosi asks how Hashem can kill when the name Yud Hei Vav Hei is an elixir of life in which death does not exist. Rabbi Shimon explains that He kills the body but gives life to the soul. He lowers the soul to Sheol to purify it and then raises it up to its place in the Garden of Eden. Rabbi Yosi concludes by saying that for the next 22 years he is no longer allowed to work at ordinary things of the world, but he has to study the matters that follow from what he learned in the supernal realm.

369. פָּתַח ר׳ יוֹסֵי וְאָמַר, יְיָ׳ מֵמִית וּמְחַיֶּה מוֹרִיד שְׁאוֹל וַיָּעַל. הַאי קְרָא אִית לְאִסְתַּכְּלָא בֵּיהּ, וְכִי יְיָ׳ מֵמִית, וְהָא שְׁמָא דָּא סַמָּא דְּחַיִּין אִיהוּ לְכֹלָּא. וּמִלָּה דָּא דְּמוֹתָא, לָא שַׁרְיָא בֵּיהּ, וּבְכָל אֲתָר שְׁמָא דָּא יָהִיב חַיִּין לְכָל עָלְמָא, מַהוּ יְיָ׳ מֵמִית, חַשְׁבִין בְּנֵי נָשָׁא דְּאִיהוּ קָטִיל לְכָל בְּנֵי נָשָׁא. אֶלָּא יְיָ׳ מֵמִית וַדַּאי דְּאִיהוּ עָלֵיהּ, לָא יַכְלִין כָּל מְקַטְרְגִין דְּעָלְמָא לְנַזְקָא לֵיהּ, בְּשַׁעֲתָא דְּאִסְתָּלִיק מִנֵּיהּ, מִיָּד כָּל מְקַטְרְגִין יַכְלִין לֵיהּ, וּמִית בַּר נָשׁ. לָאו הָכִי.

369. Rabbi Yosi opened the discussion with the verse: "Hashem kills, and gives life: He brings down to the grave and brings up" (I Shmuel 2:6). This verse requires more study. Does Hashem kill? Behold, this name, YUD HEI VAV HEI, is an elixir of life to everyone and this thing, death, does not prevail in it. Everywhere this name provides life to the whole world. What then is the meaning of "Hashem kills" that people could think that He kills all human beings? Certainly the name Yud Hei Vav Hei kills. How does it cause death? You might think to say that when it leaves a person HE DIES, because while it is still prevailing over him none of the accusers could do damage to him, but when it departs all the prosecutors immediately overcome him and the person dies. Yet this is not so.

370. אֶלָּא יְיָ׳ מֵמִית, לְמַאן מֵמִית. לְהַהוּא מְשִׁיכוּ דְּסִטְרָא אַחֲרָא בִּישָׁא. כֵּיוָן דִּמְשִׁיכוּ דְּסִטְרָא בִּישָׁא, חָמֵי לֵיהּ לְזִיו יְקָרֵיהּ דְּקוּדְשָׁא בְּרִיךְ הוּא, מִיַּד מִית. וְלֵית לֵיהּ קִיוּמָא אֲפִילוּ רִגְעָא חֲדָא. כֵּיוָן דְּהַהוּא

מְשִׁיכוּ דִּסְטָר אַחֲרָא מִית וְאִתְעֲבָר מִן עָלְמָא, מִיַּד מְחַיֶּה. לְמַאן מְחַיֶּה. לְהַהוּא מְשִׁיכוּ דְּרוּחַ קֻדְשָׁא, דְּאָתֵי מִסִּטְרָא דִּקְדוּשָּׁה, מְחַיֶּה לֵיהּ, וְאוֹקִים לֵיהּ בְּקִיּוּמָא שְׁלִים. כֹּלָּא עָבֵיד קוּדְשָׁא בְּרִיךְ הוּא בִּזְמְנָא חֲדָא. וּמַה דְּאָמַר מוֹרִיד שְׁאוֹל וַיָּעַל. מוֹרִיד לְהַהוּא רוּחַ קַדִּישָׁא לִשְׁאוֹל, וְעָבֵיד לֵיהּ תַּמָּן טְבִילָה, לְאִתְדַּכָּאָה, וּמִיַּד סָלִיק לֵיהּ, וְעָאל לַאֲתָר דְּאִצְטְרִיךְ בְּגַן עֵדֶן.

370. HE REPLIES: Yet "Hashem kills." Whom does He kill? The extension of that Other Side, MEANING THE BODY, because, when that extension of the Other Side sees the glorious glow of the Holy One, blessed be He, it instantly dies, and can not exist even an instant. As soon as the extension of the Other Side is dead and removed from the world, He immediately "gives life." To whom does He give life? To that extension of the Holy Spirit that is derived from the side of holiness, MEANING THE SOUL. He revives it and sustains it in a perfect existence and all is accomplished by the Holy One, blessed be He, at the same time. THAT IS, HE KILLS THE BODY AND REVIVES THE SOUL AND THAT IS WHY IT IS WRITTEN: "HASHEM KILLS, AND GIVES LIFE." And it is written: "He brings down to the grave (Heb. *Sheol*) and brings up," which means that He lowers that Holy Spirit, MEANING THE SOUL, to Sheol and bathes it there IN THE FIRE THAT IS IN SHEOL to purify it. He instantly raises it and brings it to its appropriate place in the Garden of Eden.

371. וַאֲנָא, חַבְרַיָּיא, בְּהַהוּא שַׁעֲתָא דְּאִסְתַּלַּקְנָא מֵעָלְמָא, רוּחָא דִּילִי אִסְתַּלַּק וְדָמַךְ מִיַּד, עַד שַׁעֲתָא זְעֵירָא דְּאַחְיָיא לִי קוּדְשָׁא בְּרִיךְ הוּא, וְגוּפָא הֲוָה מִית. בְּשַׁעֲתָא דְּפָתַח בְּרִי בְּאִינּוּן מִלִּין, כְּדֵין פַּרְחָה נִשְׁמָתֵיהּ, וְאִעֲרָעַת בְּנִשְׁמְתָא דִּילִי, דַּהֲוָה סַלְּקָא מִגּוֹ דַּכְיוּ וּמִגּוֹ טְבִילָה, וְעָאלַת בַּאֲתָר דְּעָאלָת, וְתַמָּן אִתְדָּן דִּינָהָא, וְאִתְיְיהִיבוּ לִי עֶשְׂרִין וּתְרֵין שְׁנִין דְּחַיִּין, בְּגִין דְּמְעִין וּמִלִּין דִּבְרִי, מִכָּאן וּלְהָלְאָה, אִית לִי לְאִשְׁתַּדְּלָא בְּמַה דַּחֲמֵינָא, דְּהָא לֵית לִי לְאִשְׁתַּדְּלָא בְּמִלִּין דְּהַאי עָלְמָא. כֵּיוָן דַּחֲמֵינָא מַה דַּחֲמֵינָא, וּבָעֵי קוּדְשָׁא בְּרִיךְ הוּא דְּלָא יִתְאֲבִיד וְיִתְנְשֵׁי מִנַּאי כְּלוּם.

371. And myself, my friends, during that period when I left the world my spirit was gone and departed immediately until a little later when the Holy One, blessed be He, brought me back to life. During that time, my body was dead. When my son began with these utterances, his soul escaped and flew to meet my soul that was rising from its immersion, AS MENTIONED ABOVE, and re-entered wherever it did. There, they sentenced and judged it and I was given 22 years of life for the sake of my son's words and tears. From here on, I need to strive in what I observed there, because I am no longer allowed to strive after worldly matters. After seeing what I saw, the Holy One, blessed be He, wishes me not to forget anything.

36. “Yah has chastised me severely”

A Synopsis

Rabbi Yosi says that David went through all kinds of trials but God always saved him because of his confidence in the world above. David reasoned that he had already received all his punishments in this world so he was purified and would not be punished in the world above.

372. פָּתַח וְאָמַר, יַסּוֹר יִסְּרַנִּי יָהּ וְגוֹ׳, דָּוִד מַלְכָּא אָמַר דָּא, עַל כָּל מַה דַּעֲבַד בְּהַאי עָלְמָא, וְאָמַר עַל אַבְטָחוּתָא דַּהֲוָה לֵיהּ בְּהַהוּא עָלְמָא. עַל כָּל מַה דְּאַעְבָּר בְּהַאי עָלְמָא, דִּרְדִיפוּ לֵיהּ, וַהֲוָה עָרִיק בְּאַרְעָא נוּכְרָאָה, בְּאַרְעָא דְּמוֹאָב, וּבְאַרְעָא דִּפְלִשְׁתָּאֵי, וּמִכֻּלְּהוּ שֵׁזִיב לֵיהּ קוּדְשָׁא בְּרִיךְ הוּא, וְלָא שָׁבִיק לֵיהּ לְמוֹתָא, וְאָמַר עַל אַבְטָחוּתָא דְּהַהוּא עָלְמָא.

372. He opened with the verse: “Yah has chastised me severely: but He has not given me up to death” (Tehilim 118:18). King David said, “YAH HAS CHASTISED ME SEVERELY” about all that he had done in this world and he said about the confidence he had in that world, “BUT HE HAS NOT GIVEN ME UP TO DEATH.” For from everything that happened to him in this world – that he was pursued and he escaped from all his pursuers to a strange land, in the land of Moab, and in the land of the Philistines – the Holy One, blessed be He, has saved him and did not leave him to die. He said, “BUT HE HAS NOT GIVEN ME UP TO DEATH” about his confidence in that world, THE ETERNAL.

373. אָמַר דָּוִד, אִי הָכָא חַבְנָא לְגַבֵּי קוּדְשָׁא בְּרִיךְ הוּא, הָכָא אַלְקֵינָא, וְקַבִּילְנָא עוֹנְשָׁא דִּילִי, וְאַדְכֵּי לִי מִכָּל מַה דְּחַבְנָא, וְלָא שָׁבִיק עוֹנְשָׁא דִּילִי לְהַהוּא עָלְמָא, בָּתַר מִיתָה. וַדַּאי יַסּוֹר יִסְּרַנִּי יָהּ, בְּהַאי עָלְמָא, בְּגִין לְנַקָּאָה לִי. וְלַמָּוֶת לֹא נְתָנָנִי, בְּהַהוּא עָלְמָא, לְנַטְלָא נִקְמָתָא מִנַּאי, וַאֲנָא, הָא קוּדְשָׁא בְּרִיךְ הוּא, אַנְקֵי לִי זִמְנָא חֲדָא בְּהַאי עָלְמָא, מִכָּאן וְהָלְאָה אִצְטְרִיכְנָא דְּלָא אֱהֵא בְּכִסּוּפָא בְּעָלְמָא דְּאָתֵי.

373. David said, If I sinned here against the Holy One, blessed be He, I have already been smitten here and have received my punishment. He purified me from all my sins and did not leave my punishments to that world that is after my death. Definitely, "Yah has chastised me severely" in this world to cleanse me. "But He has not given me up to death" in that world to take revenge from me there. RABBI YOSI RETURNED TO TALK ABOUT HIMSELF AND SAID, As for myself, the Holy One, blessed be He, has already cleansed me once in this world. From here on, I need to be careful AND WATCH OUT that I should not be shamed in the World to Come.

37. "Our father died in the wilderness"

A Synopsis

Rabbi Yosi's son talks about why Zelofehad's daughters mentioned that their father died in the wilderness when in fact many many of the children of Yisrael had died in the wilderness. He says that they died after the sin of the golden calf and before the Torah was given to them. Zelofehad was not acquainted with the Torah, and he led those who spoke out against Moses, so his daughters thought that Moses hated him. The women did not speak solely in front of Moses but only before the other chieftains as well so that they would be sure of having impartial judgment. In his humility Moses then disqualified himself from judging their case, but brought it before God instead. The Rabbi's son says that Zelofehad died through the words of his mouth but that his father Rabbi Yosi was raised back to life through the words of his son's mouth. The other rabbis talk about staying in Rabbi Yosi's house for seven days until his soul has settled back into place, but they decide to go see Rabbi Elazar's father-in-law first and then return. Rabbi Aba and Rabbi Elazar realize that the wisdom of the children of this generation will never be seen again until the coming of Messiah.

374. פָּתַח הַהוּא יַנּוּקָא בְּרֵיהּ וְאָמַר, אָבִינוּ מֵת בַּמִּדְבָּר וְהוּא לֹא הָיָה בְּתוֹךְ הָעֵדָה וְגוֹ׳. אָבִינוּ, הָא טַעֲמָא לְעֵילָּא, אָרִיךְ מִלָּה וּמָשִׁיךְ לָהּ, אִי חֲסִידִין קַדִּישִׁין, כַּמָּה מְשִׁיכוּ דְּצַעֲרָא בְּמִקְרֵי אָבִינוּ. לֵית צַעֲרָא, וְלֵית כְּאֵבָא דְּרוּחָא וְנַפְשָׁא, אֶלָּא כַּד קָרָאן הָכִי, אָבִינוּ, בִּכְאֵבָא מִלִּבָּא. מֵת בַּמִּדְבָּר, וְכִי אַחֲרָנִין לָא מִיתוּ בְּמַדְבְּרָא, דְּהָכָא רָשִׁים לֵיהּ, וְאָמַר דְּאִיהוּ מֵת בַּמִּדְבָּר, וְהָא אֲלַף וְרִבְבָן מִיתוּ בְּמַדְבְּרָא.

374. The child, his son, opened the discussion with the verse: "Our father died in the wilderness, and he was not in the company of them..." (Bemidbar 27:3). There is a cantilation mark above "Our father," MEANING 'ZARKA', WHOSE MUSICAL NOTATION lengthens the pronunciation of the word. Aha, devout holy ones, how much the pain is drawn out when reading "Our father." There is no pain or hurt of the spirit and soul, except when it is read like that, "Our father," when it is hurting from the heart. "Died in the wilderness": HE ASKS, Did not others die in the wilderness? Why is he marked by saying that he died in the wilderness? There were thousands and tens of thousands that died in the wilderness.

375. אֶלָּא כַּמָּה בְּנֵי נָשָׁא עַרְטִילָאִין עַל דָּא, מִנְּהוֹן אַמְרֵי דְּהוּא מְקוֹשֵׁשׁ עֵצִים הֲוָה, דִּכְתִּיב כִּי בְחֶטְאוֹ מֵת. וּמִנְּהוֹן אַמְרֵי הָכִי, וּמִנְּהוֹן אַמְרֵי הָכִי, וַאֲנָא הָכִי אוֹלִיפְנָא, יוֹמָא דְּאַבָּא נָפַל בְּבֵי מַרְעֵיהּ, אוֹלְפֵי לִי דָּא. וַאֲנָא חֲמֵינָא מַה דַּחֲמֵינָא, דְּפָקִיד לִי אַבָּא דְּלָא לְגַלָּאָה. אֶלָּא כַּמָּה וְכַמָּה הֲווּ דְּמִיתוּ בְּמַדְבְּרָא, וְלָא עַל חוֹבָא דְּקֹרַח, וְלָא עַל חוֹבָא דִּמְרַגְּלִים, כַּד אִתְגְּזַר גְּזֵרָה, אֶלָּא קוֹדֶם מַתַּן תּוֹרָה, וּבָתַר עֶגְלָא דְּעָבְדוּ, אִינּוּן מַטְעֵי עָלְמָא, וְאִינּוּן דְּאִתְמְשָׁכוּ אֲבַתְרַיְיהוּ.

375. HE RESPONDS: It is just that so many people are naked without it. Some of them say that he was a gatherer of wood, ZELOPHEHAD, because it says, "But he died in his own sin" (Ibid.). Some say this way and some say that way. I learned on the day my father fell on his sickbed; they taught me this, and I saw that which I saw, which my father forbade me from revealing. AND I WAS TAUGHT that there were many, many who died in the desert, and not on account of the sins of Korah or on account of the sin of the spies, when the decree was pronounced THAT ALL WILL DIE OUT IN THE WILDERNESS. But THEY DIED prior to the giving of the Torah and after those who misled the world, MEANING THE MIXED MULTITUDES, and those who followed them, made the golden calf. ZELOPHEHAD COULD HAVE BEEN AMONG THOSE, BUT THERE IS NO PROOF FROM THE VERSE: "BUT HE DIED IN HIS OWN SIN," THAT HE WAS THE GATHERER OF WOOD.

376. אֲבָל טַעֲנָה דְּטָעִינוּ אִינּוּן בְּנָתִין, דְּמִית בַּמִּדְבָּר, אִיהוּ, וַהֲוָה צְלָפְחָד רַב לְבֵי יוֹסֵף, וּמִגּוֹ דְּלָא יָדַע אָרְחוֹי דְּאוֹרַיְיתָא כַּדְּקָא יָאוּת, לָא הֲוָה נָשִׂיא. וְהוּא הֲוָה דְּלָא נָטַר פּוּמֵיהּ וּמִלּוֹי לְקָבְלֵיהּ דְּמֹשֶׁה, וְעָלֵיהּ כְּתִיב, וַיָּמָת עָם רָב מִיִּשְׂרָאֵל. גְּבַר דְּלָא יָדַע אוֹרַיְיתָא, וְאִיהוּ רַב מִשְׁפָּחָה. רַב דְּזַרְעָא דְּיוֹסֵף, מִבְּנוֹי דִּמְנַשֶּׁה. וּבְגִין דְּחָב בְּמַדְבָּר בְּמִלּוּלָא לְגַבֵּי מֹשֶׁה, חָשִׁיבוּ דְּמֹשֶׁה אַנְטִיר דְּבָבוּ. ובג״כ קְרִיבוּ לְקַמֵּיהּ דְּמֹשֶׁה, וְאֶלְעָזָר, וְכָל הַנְּשִׂיאִין, וְכָל רֵישֵׁי אֲבָהָן, וְלָא מַלִּילוּ עִם מֹשֶׁה אֶלָּא לְקַמַּיְיהוּ, בְּגִין דְּקַנִּיאוּ קִנְאָה מִנֵּיהּ.

376. However, the plea that these daughters pleaded was that he died in the wilderness. He, who was Zelophehad, a chief in the house of Joseph, and who was not properly versed in the manners of the Torah, was not THEREFORE a prince. And he was the one who did not watch his lips and speech against Moses, AS IT SAYS, "AND THE PEOPLE SPOKE AGAINST ELOHIM, AND MOSES..." (BEMIDBAR 21:5). ZELOPHEHAD WAS THE SPOKESMAN and about him, it is written: "And many (Heb. *rav*) people of Yisrael died" (Ibid. 6) BECAUSE HE WAS a man that was not versed in Torah. He was a chief (Heb. *rav*) of a family, a chieftain from the descendants of Joseph and an offspring of Menashe. Because he sinned in the wilderness by speaking against Moses, HIS DAUGHTERS thought that Moses harbored hatred AGAINST HIM. Therefore, they brought forward their complaints before Moses and Elazar and all the tribal heads and family chieftains. They did not speak with Moses alone but in their presence, because they were jealous of him.

377. מִכָּאן, מַאן דְּחָיִישׁ מִן דַּיָּנָא, יְקָרֵב אַחֲרָנִין, וְיִסְגֵּי בְּגוּבְרִין בַּהֲדֵי הַהוּא דַּיְּינָא, בְּגִין דְּיִשְׁמְעוּן דִּינָא מִנֵּיהּ, וְיִדְחַל מִנַּיְיהוּ, וְלָא יְהֵא בֶּן אֶלָּא כַּדְּקָא יָאוּת, וְאִי לָא, יִדְחֵי לֵיהּ מִן דִּינָא. וְאִינּוּן לָא יָדְעוּ דְּהָא מֹשֶׁה עָנָו מְאֹד מִכָּל הָאָדָם אֲשֶׁר עַל פְּנֵי הָאֲדָמָה. וְלָא יָדְעוּ דְּמֹשֶׁה לָאו הָכִי.

377. From here, it is understood that whoever has doubts about the judge shall bring forward other JUDGES and increase the number of people to be with that judge, who will listen to the trial proceedings. And he will have fear of them and he will not have a choice but to judge properly. If he does not, they will reject him from judging. But they did not know that "Moses was very meek, more so than all the men that were upon the face of the earth" (Bemidbar 12:3). They did not know that Moses was not like that.

378. כֵּיוָן דְּחָמָא מֹשֶׁה כַּךְ, אָמַר חֲמֵינָא דְּכֹל כְּנוּפְיָא דְּגוּבְרִין רַבְרְבִין מִיִּשְׂרָאֵל, וְכָל רֵישֵׁי אֲבָהָן וְכָל נְשִׂיאֵי כְּנִשְׁתָּא, עָלַי קְרִיבוּ. מִיַּד אִתְפְּרַשׁ מֹשֶׁה מִן דִּינָא, הה"ד וַיַּקְרֵב מֹשֶׁה אֶת מִשְׁפָּטָן לִפְנֵי יְיָ'. עַנְוְותָנוּתָא דְּמֹשֶׁה, אַקְרִיב אֶת מִשְׁפָּטָן לִפְנֵי יְיָ'. דַּיָּינִין אַחֲרָנִין, אָרְחָא דָּא לָא נַטְלֵי, דאע"ג דִּכְנוּפְיָא סַגֵּי עֲלֵיהוֹן. אִינּוּן דַּיְינֵי אִקְרוּן עַזֵּי פָּנִים, לֵית בְּהוּ מֵעַנְוְותָנוּתָא דְּמֹשֶׁה כְּלָל. זַכָּאָה חוּלָקֵיהּ דְּמֹשֶׁה. חֲדוּ ר"א וְחַבְרַיָּיא.

378. When Moses saw this, he said, I see that all this gathering of great men, from Yisrael, and all the heads of the families and the heads of the congregation approach me. Then Moses immediately disqualified himself from judging, as it is written: "And Moses brought their cause before Hashem" (Bemidbar 27:5). Other judges do not behave this way, even if there is a great gathering upon them. Those judges are considered insolent, not having any of the humility that Moses had. Praised is the lot of Moses. Rabbi Elazar and the friends were glad.

379. אָמַר הַהוּא יַנּוּקָא, אַהֲדַרְנָא לְמִלִּין קַדְמָאִין. אָבִינוּ מֵת בַּמִּדְבָּר אָבִינוּ הַאי טַעֲמָא דָּאמֵי, לְנָחָשׁ תַּלְיָיא עַל קְדָלֵיהּ, וּמָשִׁיךְ זַנְבֵּיהּ בְּפוּמֵיהּ, בְּטַעְמָא, דְּהַהוּא דְּאִתְמְשַׁךְ עָלֵיהּ לְעֵילָּא. מֵת בַּמִּדְבָּר, בְּמִלּוּלָא דְּפוּמֵיהּ. אִתְבְּהִיל הַהוּא יַנּוּקָא בִּבְהִילוּ, וְאַתְקִיף בְּקוּדְלָא דַּאֲבוֹי, וּבָכָה וְאָמַר, צְלָפְחָד דָּא בְּמִלּוּלָא מִית, וְאַנְתְּ אַבָּא בְּמִלּוּלָא אַהֲדַרַת לְעָלְמָא דָּא. אַהְדָּר אֲבוֹי וְנָשִׁיק לֵיהּ, וְגָפִיף לֵיהּ. בָּכוּ ר׳ אֶלְעָזָר, וְחַבְרַיָּיא כֻּלְּהוּ, וַאֲבוֹי בָּכָה בַּהֲדַיְיהוּ, נְטָלוּהוּ כֻּלְּהוּ וּנְשָׁקוּהוּ בְּפוּמוֹי, עַל רֵישֵׁיהּ, וְעַל עֵינוֹי, וַאֲבוּהּ הֲוָה בָּכֵי בַּהֲדֵיהּ.

379. The child said, I am returning to the earlier topic, to talk about this pausal note, MEANING THE 'ZARKA' ֮, THAT IS ON THE WORD OF "OUR FATHER" IN, "Our father died in the wilderness." ITS SHAPE is comparable to a snake that hangs on his back and pulls his tail into his mouth. AND THIS DRAWING THAT IS on the musical note OF ZARKA that is drawn over THE WORD "OUR FATHER," CAUSED ZELOPHEHAD TO die "in the wilderness" through the words of his own mouth. The child hurried up quickly and held on to the back of the neck of his father, cried and said, This Zelophehad died through talking and you, my father, returned to this world through talking, MEANING THROUGH THE WORDS AND TEARS OF THE CHILD. His father hugged and kissed him again. Rabbi Elazar and the friends all cried, and the father cried along with them. They all took him and kissed him all over his lips, over his head and over his eyes, and his father was crying with him.

380. אָ״ל רִבִּי אֶלְעָזָר, בְּרִי, הוֹאִיל וְאַמְרַת מִלָּה דָּא, מַהוּ כִּי בְחֶטְאוֹ מֵת. אָמַר הַהוּא יַנּוּקָא, אַבָּא, אַבָּא, בְּחַד מִלָּה סַגִּי לוֹן, כֵּיוָן דְּהַהוּא נָחָשׁ דְּכָרִיךְ בִּזְנָבֵיהּ לְעֵילָּא, מָשִׁיךְ טַעֲמָא בְּחֶטְאוֹ, מַאי בְּחֶטְאוֹ.

בְּחֶטְאוֹ דְּהַהוּא נָחָשׁ. וּמַאי אִיהוּ. מִלּוּלָא דְּפוּמֵיהּ, כִּי בְחֶטְאוֹ מֵת, טַעֲמָא דְּהַהוּא מְשִׁיכוּ דְּהַהוּא נָחָשׁ דְּכָּרוּךְ בִּזְנָבֵיהּ, בְּחֶטְאוֹ וַדַּאי.

380. Rabbi Elazar said to him, My son, since you spoke about this matter, SAY, What is the meaning of: "But he died in his own sin"? The child said, Father, THEY ASK WHY one word, "HE DIED," was not enough for them. WHAT WAS THE NEED FOR THEM TO SAY THAT HE DIED IN THE DESERT AND ALSO THAT HE DIED BECAUSE OF HIS SIN? IT IS ONLY that IN THE DEPICTION OF THE ZARKA THAT IS OVER THE WORD "OUR FATHER," the snake that was wrapped around his tail above, lengthens the pronunciation. THEREFORE, IT IS WRITTEN: "In his own sin." What is "in his own sin"? It is in the sin of that snake. What is it? It is the speech in his mouth THAT HE SPOKE AGAINST MOSES. The reason "But he died in his own sin" extends from the snake that is wrapped around its tail, SINCE HE DREW THE POWER OF DEFILEMENT FROM THAT PRIMORDIAL SNAKE BY SPEAKING AGAINST MOSES. That is certainly "his own sin."

381. נַטְלֵיהּ ר׳ אֶלְעָזָר בְּתוּקְפֵּיהּ, בֵּין דְּרוֹעוֹי, וּבָכוּ כֻּלְּהוּ חַבְרַיָּיא. אָמַר לוֹן, רַבָּנָן, שְׁבוֹקוּ לִי בַּהֲדֵי אַבָּא, דְּעַד כְּעַן לָא אִתְיַישְׁבָא רוּחִי. א״ר אֶלְעָזָר לְר׳ יוֹסֵי, אִימָּא כַּמָּה יוֹמִין וְשָׁנִין לְהַאי יַנּוּקָא. אָמַר לוֹן, חַבְרַיָּיא, בְּמָטוּ מִנַּיְיכוּ לָא תִּבְעוּן דָּא, דְּהָא עַד לָא מָטוּ עֲלוֹי חָמֵשׁ שְׁנִין.

381. Rabbi Elazar took him on his lap and in his arms, and all the friends cried. The CHILD said to them, Sages, leave me with my father, because my mind has not settled down yet. Rabbi Elazar said to Rabbi Yosi, What is the age of the child in days and years? He replied to them, Friends, do not ask me this, because he still has not reached his fifth birthday.

382. א״ל ר׳ אֶלְעָזָר, ח״ו, דְּהָא בְּעֵינָא טָבָא אַשְׁגַּחְנָא בֵּיהּ. וּמַה דְּאַמְרַת חָמֵשׁ שְׁנִין, אִינּוּן חָמֵשׁ שְׁנִין אֲשֶׁר אֵין חָרִישׁ וְקָצִיר. דְּלָא תִּקְצוֹר לֵיהּ לְעָלְמִין. א״ר אֶלְעָזָר לְר׳ אַבָּא, נֵיתִיב הָכָא עַד ז׳ יוֹמִין, בְּגִין דְּאִתְיַישְׁבָא בֵּיתָא. דְּהָא כָּל שִׁבְעָה יוֹמִין דְּנִשְׁמְתָא נַפְקַת מִן גּוּפָא, אַזְלַת עַרְטִילָאָה. וְהַשְׁתָּא דְּאָהַדְרַת, עַד כְּעַן לָא אִתְיַישְׁבַת

בְּדוּכְתָּהָא, עַד שִׁבְעָה יוֹמִין.

382. Rabbi Elazar said, Heaven forbid, I am considering it only with a benevolent eye. And you mentioned five years: these are "five more years, in which there shall neither be ploughing nor harvest" (Beresheet 45:6), AND YOU TOO will never reap him. Rabbi Elazar said to Rabbi Aba, Let us stay here up to seven days, in order that THE SOUL should settle down in the house, because during the seven days after the soul left the body, it walks about naked. Now THAT THE SOUL OF RABBI YOSI LEFT AND returned it may not get settled back into its place until seven days have passed .

383. אָמַר ר׳ אַבָּא, כְּתִיב פָּתוֹחַ תִּפְתַּח אֶת יָדְךָ לְאָחִיךָ לַעֲנִיֶּךָ וּלְאֶבְיוֹנְךָ, קְרָא דָּא, הָא תָּנֵינָן לֵיהּ, דְּלָא יִשְׁבּוֹק ב״נ עַנְיָא דִּילֵיהּ, וְיָהִיב לְאַחֲרָא. הָא ר׳ יוֹסֵי חָמוּךְ בְּבֵי מַרְעֵיהּ, נֵיזִיל וְנִגְמוֹל חֶסֶד עִמֵּיהּ. וּבָתַר דְּנֶהְדַּר, נֵיעוּל בְּהַאי. וְהָא כָּל זִמְנָא דְּנֵהַךְ וְנֶהְדָּר בְּאָרְחָא דָּא, נֶחֱמֵי תְּחִיַּית הַמֵּתִים. א״ר אֶלְעָזָר וַדַּאי הָכִי הוּא, נְשָׁקוּהוּ לְהַהוּא יַנּוּקָא, בֵּרְכוּהוּ וְאַזְלוּ.

383. Rabbi Aba said that it is written: "You shall open your hand wide to your brother, to your poor, and to your needy" (Devarim 15:11). We have already taught this verse, that it is imperative for a person not to abandon his poor and give to other poor. Here, Rabbi Yosi, your father-in-law is also in his sick bed. Let's go and do a kindness for him. When we return, we will enter here FOR A SECOND TIME. As long as we come and go this way, we will witness the resurrection of the dead. Rabbi Elazar said, That is certainly so. They kissed the child, blessed him and left.

384. אָמַר ר׳ אַבָּא, תַּוַּוהְנָא עַל דַּרְדְּקֵי דְּדָרָא דָּא, כַּמָּה תַּקִּיפָא חֵילַיְיהוּ, וְאִינּוּן טְנָרִין רַבְרְבִין רָאמִין. אָמַר ר׳ אֶלְעָזָר, זַכָּאָה חוּלָקֵיהּ דְּאַבָּא, מָארֵיהּ דְּדָרָא דָּא. דְּהָא בְּיוֹמוֹי, בָּעֵי קוּדְשָׁא בְּרִיךְ הוּא לְאַתְקְנָא, תְּרֵין מְתִיבְתִּין דִּילֵיהּ, וּלְמֶעְבַּד לוֹן יְשׁוּבָא רַבְרְבָא וְעִלָּאָה כַּדְקָא יָאוּת. דְּהָא לָא יְהֵא כְּדָרָא דָּא, עַד דְּיֵיתֵי מַלְכָּא מְשִׁיחָא. אַזְלוּ.

384. Rabbi Aba said, I wonder about the children of this generation. How strong they are, like high and mighty mountains. Rabbi Elazar said, Praised is my father's lot, that he is the leader of this generation. During his lifetime, the Holy One, blessed be He, wishes to establish His two Yeshivot and wants to make them into a great and lofty settlement, because there will not be another generation like this until the coming of King Messiah. They left.

38. Due to eleven causes, plagues come

A Synopsis

Rabbi Aba lists the eleven causes of plagues that he was taught about in the Mishnah. The first of these causes is idol worship, and he equates being "in disorder" with leprosy. He also talks about the second cause, that is cursing the Holy Name.

385. עַד דַּהֲווּ אָזְלֵי, אָמַר רִבִּי אַבָּא, הָא תָּנֵינָן, עַל חַד סְרֵי מִלִּין נִגְעִין אַתְיָין עַל בְּנֵי נָשָׁא. וְאִלֵּין אִינּוּן: עַל עֲ״ז. וְעַל קִלְלַת הַשֵּׁם. וְעַל גִּלּוּי עֲרָיוֹת. וְעַל גְּנֵיבָה. וְעַל לָשׁוֹן הָרָע. וְעַל עֵדוּת שָׁקֶר. וְעַל דַּיָּינָא דִּמְקַלְקֵל יַת דִּינָא. וְעַל שְׁבוּעַת שָׁוְא. וְעַל דְּעָאל בִּתְחוּמָא דְּחַבְרֵיהּ. וְעַל דִּמְחַשֵּׁב מַחֲשָׁבִין בִּישִׁין. וְעַל דִּמְשַׁלֵּחַ מְדָנִים בֵּין אַחִים. וְאִית דְּאַמְרֵי, אַף עַל עֵינָא בִּישָׁא. וְכֻלְּהוּ תָּנֵינָן בְּמַתְנִיתָא.

385. While traveling, Rabbi Aba said, We have already learned that, due to eleven causes, plagues come about to people. They are due to idol worship, cursing the Holy Name, incest, theft, the evil tongue, bearing false testimony, a judge who is crooked in a trial, swearing falsely, one who encroaches on his friend's boundary rights, one who contemplates evil thoughts and ideas, and one who instigates quarrels between brothers. Some say also due to the evil eye, and we were taught all this in the Mishnah.

386. עֲ״ז מִנָּיִן. דִּכְתִּיב וַיַּרְא מֹשֶׁה אֶת הָעָם כִּי פָרוּעַ הוּא כִּי פְרָעֹה אַהֲרֹן. מַאי כִּי פָרוּעַ הוּא. דְּאַלְקוּ בְּצָרַעַת. כְּתִיב הָכִי כִּי פָרוּעַ הוּא, וּכְתִיב הָתָם, וְהַצָּרוּעַ אֲשֶׁר בּוֹ הַנֶּגַע בְּגָדָיו יִהְיוּ פְרוּמִים וְרֹאשׁוֹ יִהְיֶה פָרוּעַ. וְעַל קִלְלַת הַשֵּׁם, דִּכְתִּיב הַיּוֹם הַזֶּה יְסַגֶּרְךָ יְיָ׳ בְּיָדִי, וּכְתִיב, וְהִסְגִּירוֹ הַכֹּהֵן.

386. Idol worship: How do we know THAT DUE TO THAT CAUSE PLAGUES COME? Because it is written: "And when Moses saw that the people were in disorder; for Aaron had made them disorderly" (Shemot 32:25). What is the meaning of, "were in disorder"? It means that they were inflicted with leprosy. It is written here, "were in disorder (Heb. *paru'a*)" and it is written there, "And the diseased man in whom the plague is, his clothes shall be rent, and the hair of his head shall grow long (Heb. *paru'a*)..." (Vayikra 13:45). JUST LIKE IT MEANS LEPROSY THERE, HERE TOO IT IS LEPROSY. About cursing the name of Hashem, HOW DO WE KNOW? It is because it is written: "This day will Hashem deliver you (Heb. *yesagercha*) into my hand" (I Shmuel 17:46), MEANING THE PHILISTINE WHO WAS REVILING AND CURSING THE NAME. It is written ABOUT THE LEPER: "And the priest shall shut him up (Heb. *hisgiro*)" (Vayikra 13:5). WE UNDERSTAND FROM THIS COMPARISON BY ANALOGY. JUST LIKE IT WAS REGARDING LEPROSY THERE, HERE TOO IT HAS TO DO WITH LEPROSY.

39. The eye of David and the eye of Bilaam

A Synopsis

Rabbi Elazar says that David killed the Philistine by looking at him with an evil eye, and this caused leprosy on his forehead; thus the stone was sunk into his forehead. We hear that David's eye was beautiful and gazed with love on those who feared sin, but that the wicked were afraid of him. The eye of Bilaam, on the other hand, was entirely wicked. Next Rabbi Elazar says that the punishment for all the other causes of plagues listed earlier is always leprosy. He tells Rabbi Aba how Bilaam perpetrated all these sins, and that Bilaam tried to draw the abundance of Yisrael to his own evil side.

387. אָמַר ר׳ אַבָּא, מִלָּה דָּא לָא אִתְיַישְׁבָא, וְאִצְטְרִיךְ לְעַיְּינָא בֵּיהּ. א״ר אֶלְעָזָר, הָכִי הוּא וַדַּאי, פְּלִשְׁתִּי דָּא קָרִיב לְיִיחוּסָא דְּדָוִד הֲוָה, וּבְרָהּ דְּעָרְפָּה הֲוָה, וְהַיְינוּ דִּכְתִּיב, מִמַּעַרְכוֹת פְּלִשְׁתִּים, אַל תִּקְרֵי מִמַּעַרְכוֹת, אֶלָּא מִמְּעָרוֹת פְּלִשְׁתִּים, דְּשַׁוְיוּהָ לְאִמֵּיהּ כִּמְעַרְתָּא דָּא. וְכֵיוָן דִּכְתִּיב וַיְקַלֵּל הַפְּלִשְׁתִּי אֶת דָּוִד בֵּאלֹהָיו, אִסְתָּכַּל בֵּיהּ דָּוִד בְּעֵינָא בִּישָׁא. וּבְכָל אֲתָר דַּהֲוָה מִסְתַּכֵּל בְּעֵינָא בִּישָׁא, כָּל זִינֵי צָרַעַת אִתְמַשְׁכָן מְעֵינֵיהּ דְּדָוִד. וְהָכִי הֲוָה בְּיוֹאָב, כֵּיוָן דְּאִסְתָּכַּל בֵּיהּ דָּוִד בְּעֵינָא בִּישָׁא, מַה כְּתִיב, וְלֹא יִכָּרֵת מִבֵּית יוֹאָב זָב וּמְצוֹרָע וְגוֹ׳.

387. Rabbi Aba said, This matter REGARDING THE PHILISTINE has not suited me, and I need to study it further. Rabbi Elazar said, It is definitely so. This Philistine was close to the lineage of David and was the son of Orpah. That is the meaning of what is written: "Out of the ranks (Heb. *ma'arachot*) of the Philistines" (I Shmuel 17:23). Do not pronounce "*ma'arachot,*" but read 'from the caves (Heb. *me'arot*) of the Philistines', because he caused shame to his mother, making her as a cave, because it is written: "And the Philistine cursed David by his Elohim" (Ibid. 43). David gazed at him with an evil eye and anywhere THAT DAVID was gazing with an evil eye, all kinds of leprosy flowed from the eyes of David. This is the way it was regarding Joab. As soon as David gazed at him with an evil eye, it is written: "And let the house of Joab never lack such as are afflicted with an issue, or with leprosy..." (II Shmuel 3:29).

388. וְהָכָא בְּפְלִשְׁתִּי דָא, כֵּיוָן שֶׁקִּלֵּל אֶת הַשֵּׁם, אִסְתַּכַּל בֵּיהּ בְּעֵינָא בִּישָׁא, וְחָמָא בְּמִצְחֵיהּ דְּאִצְטְרַע. מִיַּד וַתִּטְבַּע הָאֶבֶן בְּמִצְחוֹ, וְאִתְדַּבְּקַת הַצָּרַעַת בְּמִצְחוֹ. וְכֹלָּא הֲוָה אִשְׁתְּקַעַת עֵינָא בִּישָׁא דְּצָרַעַת בְּמִצְחוֹ, וְאִשְׁתְּקַעַת אַבְנָא מַמָּשׁ בְּמִצְחוֹ, וַדַּאי מְצוֹרָע הֲוָה.

388. Here with this Philistine, as soon as he cursed the Name, David looked at him with an evil eye and saw on his forehead that he became leprous. Immediately, "the stone buried itself in his forehead" (I Shmuel 17:49), because the leprosy was stuck to his forehead. All this was DUE TO the impression of the evil eye of the leprosy in his forehead, that this stone was actually sunk into his brow. IT IS definite that he was a leper.

389. רָשָׁע חַיָּיבָא דְּבִלְעָם, עֵינָא דִּילֵיהּ, הֲוָה בְּהִפּוּכָא מֵעֵינָא דְּדָוִד עֵינָא דְּדָוִד הֲוָה מְרֻקָּמָא מִכָּל זִינֵי גַּוְונִין, לָא הֲוָה עֵינָא בְּעָלְמָא שַׁפִּירָא לְמֶחֱזֵי, כְּעֵינָא דְּדָוִד. כָּל גַּוְונִין דְּעָלְמָא מְנַצְצָן בֵּיהּ, וְכֹלָּא בִּרְחִימוּ לְמַאן דְּדָחִיל חַטָּאָה, דִּכְתִּיב יְרֵאֶיךָ יִרְאוּנִי וְיִשְׂמָחוּ. חַדָּאן כַּד חָמָאן לִי. וְכָל אִינּוּן חַיָּיבִין דַּחֲלִין מִקַּמֵּיהּ.

389. The wicked man Bilaam's eye was the opposite of David's eye. David's eye was embroidered in all kinds of colors, and there was no eye in the world as beautiful as David's. All the colors in the world sparkled in it and it was filled with love towards anyone who feared sin, as is written: "They who fear You will see me and be glad" (Tehilim 119:74). That is, they became happy when they looked at him and all those wicked USED TO BE fearful of him.

390. אֲבָל עֵינוֹי דְּבִלְעָם חַיָּיבָא, עֵינָא בִּישָׁא בְּכֹלָּא, בְּכָל אֲתָר דַּהֲוָה מִסְתַּכַּל, כְּשַׁלְהוֹבָא שָׁצֵי לֵיהּ. דְּהָא לֵית עֵינָא בִּישָׁא בְּעָלְמָא, כְּעֵינָא דְּהַהוּא רָשָׁע, דְּאִיהוּ בְּהִפּוּכָא מֵעֵינוֹי דְּדָוִד.

390. However, the eye of the wicked Bilaam was evil in every way. Anywhere he gazed was destroyed as with a flame, since there does not exist such an evil eye in the world as the eye of that wicked one, which was the opposite of David's eye.

391. עַל גִּלּוּי עֲרָיוֹת, דִּכְתִּיב וְשִׂפַּח יְיָ׳ קָדְקוֹד בְּנוֹת צִיּוֹן. וּכְתִיב וְלַשְׂאֵת וְלַסַּפַּחַת. עַל הַגְּנֵבָה, דִּכְתִּיב הוֹצֵאתִיהָ נְאֻם יְיָ׳ צְבָאוֹת וּבָאָה אֶל בֵּית הַגַּנָּב וְגו׳ וְכִלַּתּוּ וְאֶת עֵצָיו וְאֶת אֲבָנָיו. מַאן הוּא מִלָּה דִּמְכַלֶּה עֵצִים וַאֲבָנִים. דָּא צָרַעַת. דִּכְתִּיב, וְנָתַץ אֶת הַבַּיִת אֶת אֲבָנָיו וְאֶת עֵצָיו.

391. HOW DO WE KNOW THAT THE PUNISHMENT for incest IS LEPROSY? It is written REGARDING INCEST: "Therefore Hashem will smite with a scab the crown of the head of the daughters of Zion" (Yeshayah 3:17). It is written REGARDING LEPROSY: "And for a swelling, and for a scab..." (Vayikra 14:56). AS IT REFERS TO LEPROSY, HERE TOO IT REFERS TO LEPROSY. HOW DO WE KNOW THAT ONE CONTRACTS LEPROSY for thievery? Because it is written: "'I have now produced it,' says Hashem Tzva'ot, and it shall enter into the house of the thief...and shall consume it with the timber of it and the stones of it..." (Zecharyah 5:4). What is it that destroys timbers and stones – leprosy, as is written: "And he shall break down the house, the stones of it, and its timber" (Vayikra 14:45).

392. עַל לָשׁוֹן הָרָע, דִּכְתִּיב וּתְדַבֵּר מִרְיָם וְאַהֲרֹן בְּמֹשֶׁה וְגו׳, וּכְתִיב וַיִּפֶן אַהֲרֹן אֶל מִרְיָם וְהִנֵּה מְצוֹרַעַת. עַל עֵדוּת שֶׁקֶר, בְּגִין דְּסָהִידוּ יִשְׂרָאֵל שֶׁקֶר, וְאָמְרוּ אֵלֶּה אֱלֹהֶיךָ יִשְׂרָאֵל, בְּקָל תַּקִּיף, דִּכְתִּיב קוֹל מִלְחָמָה בַּמַּחֲנֶה. בג״ד, וִישַׁלְּחוּ מִן הַמַּחֲנֶה כָּל צָרוּעַ וְכָל זָב וְגו׳.

392. HOW DO WE KNOW THAT ONE COONTRACTS LEPROSY for the evil tongue? Because it is written: "And Miriam and Aaron spoke against Moses..." (Bemidbar 12:1) and it is written further: "And Aaron looked upon Miriam, and behold, she was leprous" (Ibid. 10). For false testimony, HOW DO WE KNOW THAT ONE CONTRACTS LEPROSY? We find that Yisrael testified falsely and said, "These are your Elohim, Yisrael" (Shemot 32:4) in a loud voice, as is written: "There is a noise of war in the camp" (Ibid. 17). Thus, "they put out of the camp everyone with leprosy and everyone that has an issue..." (Bemidbar 5:2). BOTH CASES THE TERM OF "CAMP" IS USED TO INDICATE AN ANALOGY BETWEEN THEM.

393. עַל דַּיָּין דִּמְקַלְקֵל דִּינָא, דִּכְתִיב כֶּאֱכוֹל קַשׁ לְשׁוֹן אֵשׁ וַחֲשַׁשׁ וְגוֹ' וּפִרְחָם כָּאָבָק יַעֲלֶה וְגוֹ', מַאי טַעֲמָא. כִּי מָאֲסוּ אֵת תּוֹרַת יְיָ' צְבָאוֹת. וְאֵין פִּרְחָם, אֶלָּא צָרַעַת. דִּכְתִיב, וְאִם פָּרוֹחַ תִּפְרַח הַצָּרַעַת. עַל דְּעָאל בִּתְחוּמָא דְּחַבְרֵיהּ מְנַיִן. מֵעוּזִיָּהוּ. דְּעָאל בִּתְחוּמָא דִּכְהוּנָה. דִּכְתִיב, וְהַצָּרַעַת זָרְחָה בְמִצְחוֹ. וְעַל דִּמְשַׁלֵּחַ מְדָנִים בֵּין אַחִים. דִּכְתִיב וַיְנַגַּע יְיָ' אֶת פַּרְעֹה, דְּאִיהוּ שָׁלַח מְדָנִים בֵּין אַבְרָהָם וְשָׂרָה. וְעַל עֵינָא בִּישָׁא, כְּמָה דְּאִתְּמָר. וְכֻלְּהוּ הֲווֹ בֵּיהּ בְּהַהוּא רָשָׁע דְּבִלְעָם.

393. About a judge who distorts justice, HOW DO WE KNOW THAT ONE CONTRACTS LEPROSY? Because it is written "As the fire devours the stubble, and as the chaff...and their blossom shall go up as dust ..." (Yeshayah 5:24). What is the reason? "Because they have cast away the Torah of Hashem Tzva'ot" (Ibid.). And 'blossom' means none other than leprosy, as is written: "And if the leprosy breaks (lit. 'blossoms') out abroad" (Vayikra 13:12). If one infringes on boundary rights of his neighbor, HOW DO WE KNOW THAT ONE CONTRACTS LEPROSY? From Uzziah, who infringed on the rights of the priesthood, as it is written: "The leprosy broke out on his forehead" (II Divrei Hayamim 26:19). HOW DO WE KNOW THAT someone who incites strife among brothers CONTRACTS LEPROSY? Because it is written: "And Hashem plagued Pharaoh" (Beresheet 12:17), BECAUSE he caused quarrel between Abraham and Sarah. About an evil eye, HOW DO WE KNOW? This is as we already studied THAT DAVID'S EVIL EYE WAS INFLICTING WITH LEPROSY THOSE WHO DID NOT FEAR HASHEM, SO WE HAVE PROOF THAT THE EVIL EYE CAUSES LEPROSY. All this was applicable to the wicked Bilaam.

394. ת"ח, מַה כְּתִיב, פְּתוֹרָה אֲשֶׁר עַל הַנָּהָר. מַאי עַל הַנָּהָר. דְּיָהַב עֵינָא בִּישָׁא, עַל הַהוּא נָהָר, דְּקַיְּימָא בְּהוּ בְּיִשְׂרָאֵל. דִּכְתִיב הִנְנִי נוֹטֶה אֵלֶיהָ כְּנָהָר שָׁלוֹם. וְהוּא אָתָא בְּהַהוּא פְּתוֹרָא, וְאִגְרֵי בְּהוּ.

394. Come and see that it is written: "To Petor, which is by the river" (Bemidbar 22:5). What is the meaning of "by the river"? HE RESPONDS: He set his evil eye on the river that is in Yisrael, WHICH IS YESOD IN ZEIR ANPIN, as is written: "Behold, I will extend peace to her like a river" (Yeshayah 66:12). Bilaam came upon Petor, WHICH IS MALCHUT OF THE

OTHER SIDE, and was provoking them.

395. א״ר אַבָּא, כָּל הָנֵי מִלִּין הֲווֹ וַדַּאי בְּבִלְעָם. אֲבָל גִּלּוּי עֲרָיוֹת מִנַּיִן, דִּכְתִּיב, הֵן הֵנָּה הָיוּ לִבְנֵי יִשְׂרָאֵל בִּדְבַר בִּלְעָם לִמְסָר מַעַל בַּיְיָ׳ וְגוֹ׳. הָא הָכָא עֲ״ז וּגְלוּי עֲרָיוֹת. סַהֲדוּתָא דְּשִׁקְרָא, דִּכְתִּיב וְיוֹדֵעַ דַּעַת עֶלְיוֹן, וְדַעַת בְּהֶמְתּוֹ לָא הֲוָה יָדַע. קִלְקֵל יַת דִּינָא, דִּכְתִּיב לְךָ אִיעָצְךָ. דְּהָא בְּדִינָא קַיְּימָא, וְיָהַב עֵיטָא בִּישָׁא לְאַבְאָשָׁא, וְסָטֵי מִן דִּינָא, וְאַמְלִיךְ בִּישִׁין עָלַיְיהוּ.

395. Rabbi Aba said, Certainly all these things applied to Bilaam, but how do we know that he, BILAAM, was also involved in sexually indecent behavior? HE REPLIES: Because it says, "Behold, these caused the children of Yisrael, through the counsel of Bilaam, to revolt against Hashem..." (Bemidbar 31:16). We have here idol worship OF PEOR and sexual immorality OF KOZBI, DAUGHTER OF TZUR. HOW DO WE KNOW THAT false testimony APPLIED TO BILAAM? Because it is written: "And knows the knowledge of the most High" (Bemidbar 24:16) and yet he did not know even the thoughts of his beast, BECAUSE HE COULD NOT FIGURE OUT WHY HIS SHE-MULE DETOURED FROM THE ROAD. HOW DO WE KNOW THAT the distortion of justice ALSO APPLIED TO BILAAM? Because it is written: "Come therefore, and I will advise you" (Ibid. 14), for it was still debated AND IMPENDS ON judgment IF YISRAEL IS GUILTLESS OR NOT. Yet he gave bad advice to harm YISRAEL and that is a perversion of justice AND DIDN'T CARE IF HE DID IT and counseled harmful things about them.

396. עָאל בִּתְחוּמָא דְּלָאו דִּילֵיהּ, דִּכְתִּיב וָאַעַל פָּר וָאַיִל בַּמִּזְבֵּחַ, וּכְתִיב אֶת שִׁבְעַת הַמִּזְבְּחוֹת עָרַכְתִּי. מְשַׁלֵּחַ מְדָנִים בֵּין אַחִים, בֵּין יִשְׂרָאֵל לַאֲבִיהֶם שֶׁבַּשָּׁמַיִם. לָשׁוֹן הָרָע, לָא הֲוָה בְּעָלְמָא כְּגִינֵיהּ. קִלְלַת הַשֵּׁם, דִּכְתִּיב וְאָנֹכִי אִקָּרֶה כֹּה. וְכֻלְּהוּ הֲווֹ בֵּיהּ. עֵינָא בִּישָׁא כְּמָה דְּאִתְּמַר. וְכֹלָּא עַל הַהוּא נָהָר דְּיִשְׂרָאֵל, יָהַב עֵינוֹי לְאִתְגָּרָא בֵּיהּ. אֶרֶץ בְּנֵי עַמּוֹ, וְכִי לָא יְדַעְנָא דְּאֶרֶץ בְּנֵי עַמּוֹ הִיא. אֶלָּא רָזָא דָּא, דְּכָל בְּנֵי עַמּוֹ מִתְדַּבְּקָן בֵּיהּ וְהָא אִתְּמַר.

396. He infringed on what was beyond his boundary rights. HOW DO WE

KNOW THAT ABOUT BILAAM? Because it is written: "And I have offered upon every altar a bullock and a ram" (Bemidbar 23:4) and it is written: "I have prepared the seven altars" (Ibid.). YET THE OFFERING OF SACRIFICES BELONGED TO THE PRIESTS AND NOT TO HIM. And inciting strife between brothers APPLIED TO HIM AS WELL, BECAUSE HE CAUSED STRIFE between Yisrael and their Father in heaven. Evil tongue APPLIED TO HIM, since no one in the world was A MASTER OF THE EVIL TONGUE as he was, SINCE ALL HIS POWER WAS IN HIS MOUTH. The curse of the Holy Name APPLIED TO HIM, as is written: "While I go to the meeting yonder (Heb. *coh*)" (Ibid.), WHICH MEANS THAT HE WISHED TO UPROOT MALCHUT CALLED *COH* FROM YISRAEL. All these things were in him, and the evil eye as we learned, and everything was directed against the river of Yisrael THAT IS YESOD OF ZEIR ANPIN. He set his eyes on it to provoke it, TO BEND ITS ABUNDANCE TO HIS OWN EVIL SIDE. "To the land of the children of his people" (Bemidbar 22:5): HE ASKS: Don't we know that this was the land of the children of his people? HE RESPONDS: That is only the secret meaning, that which all the members of his people were attached to it, as we have studied already.

40. “Of him who has an evil eye”

A Synopsis

Rabbi Yosi says that Balak realized that he and his people would fall into the hands of Yisrael because he ‘saw’ this. Bilaam’s knowledge was of the kind that was only understood at night when the lower Sfirot and the asses of the Klipot have dominion.

397. וַיַּרְא בָּלָק בֶּן צִפּוֹר וְגוֹ׳. רִבִּי יוֹסֵי פָּתַח, אַל תִּלְחַם אֶת לֶחֶם רַע עָיִן וְגוֹ׳. דָּא בִּלְעָם, דְּבָרִיךְ לְהוּ לְיִשְׂרָאֵל. וְאַל תִּתְאָו לְמַטְעַמּוֹתָיו, דָּא בָּלָק, דְּקוּדְשָׁא בְּרִיךְ הוּא לָא אִתְרְעֵי לְאִינּוּן עִלָּוָון דְּאַתְקִין קַמֵּיהּ.

397. “And Balak the son of Tzipor saw...” Rabbi Yosi opened the discussion with the verse: “Do not eat the bread of him who has an evil eye” (Mishlei 23:6). That applies to Bilaam, WHO WAS EVIL-EYED, and he blessed Yisrael. “Nor desire his dainties” (Ibid.) applies to Balak, for whose burnt offerings that he offered before Him, the Holy One, blessed be He, had no desire.

398. ת״ח, בְּשַׁעֲתָא דְּחָמָא בָּלָק דְּהָא סִיחוֹן וְעוֹג אִתְקְטָלוּ, וְאִתְנְסִיבַת אַרְעֲהוֹן, חָמָא מַה חָמָא, דְּאִיהוּ אָמַר וַיַּרְא. אֶלָּא חָמָא בְּחָכְמְתָא דִּילֵיהּ, דְּאִיהוּ, וַחֲמִשָּׁה עִלָּאֵי דְּמִדְיָן, וְעַמֵּיהּ, נַפְלִין בִּידָא דְּיִשְׂרָאֵל. חָמָא, וְלָא יָדַע, וְעַל דָּא אַקְדִּים לְבִלְעָם, דְּחֵילֵיהּ בְּפוּמֵיהּ, כְּגַוְונָא דְּיִשְׂרָאֵל דְּחֵילֵיהוֹן בְּפוּמֵיהוֹן.

398. Come and see, when Balak saw that Sihon and Og were killed and their country was taken, he saw ONE MORE THING. HE ASKS: What did he see THAT THE SCRIPTURE says, “saw”? It is only that he saw in his wisdom he and the five top chiefs of Midian and his people were falling into the hands of Yisrael. He saw, yet did not know CLEARLY. Therefore, he first approached Bilaam, whose power was in his mouth TO BLESS AND CURSE, like Yisrael, whose power is in their mouth.

399. וַאֲפִילוּ בִּלְעָם תָּאִיב הֲוָה יַתִּיר מִבָּלָק. וְהַהִיא יְדִיעָא דְּאִיהוּ הֲוָה יָדַע, בְּלֵילְיָא הֲוָה יָדַע, בְּגִין דְּאִינּוּן כִּתְרִין תַּתָּאִין וַחֲמָרֵי, לָא שְׁכִיחוּ

אֶלָּא בְּמִשְׁמָרָה רִאשׁוֹנָה דְּלֵילְיָא, וְעַ"ד הֲוָה לֵיהּ אֲתָנָא, דְּהַאי גִּיסָא, לְאִתְחַבְּרָא חֲמָרֵי בַּהֲדָהּ בְּרֵישָׁא דְּלֵילְיָא.

399. Bilaam was even more loathsome than Balak. Whatever he knew, he knew only at night. These lower Sfirot and the asses OF THE KLIPOT prevail only at the first watch of the night. AND ON THE FIRST WATCH, A SHE-MULE BRAYS. Therefore, he had an she-mule of that side, so the donkeys could join with her in the beginning of the night.

41. "And Elohim came to Bilaam," refers to the appointed minister

A Synopsis

We are told that the Elohim that came to Bilaam and to Laban was their appointed minister. Bilaam used the power of his she-mule to remove himself from the power of God and operate under his own authority. Rabbi Yitzchak relates what Rabbi Yehuda told him about the ten lower Sfirot of the right and the ten of the left. We learn from Rabbi Yosi that Joseph studied the wisdom of the lower Sfirot of the Other Side while he was in Egypt. Rabbi Shimon tells the others that in the future God will tie up the she-mule that is Yisrael's accuser so that he can no longer harm them. We hear about the Sfirot that pertain to divination and the Sfirot that pertain to enchantment; the ox comes from the aspect of enchantment and the she-mule comes from the angle of divination. This is why Bilaam used the she-mule in his witchcraft to remove himself from God's power. We hear about the angel of compassion that stood in Bilaam's way when he tried to leave God's jurisdiction, and how the angel confounded Bilaam's wisdom and deflected him from his path of witchcraft.

400. וְאִי תֵּימָא, הָא כְּתִיב וַיָּבֹא אֱלֹהִים אֶל בִּלְעָם לַיְלָה. הָכִי הוּא וַדַּאי, וְאוּקִימְנָא הַהוּא מְמָנָא דִּמְמָנָא עֲלַיְיהוּ, וְהוּא הֲוָה אָתֵי לְקַבְלֵיהּ. כְּגַוְונָא דָּא וַיָּבֹא אֱלֹהִים אֶל לָבָן הָאֲרַמִּי וְגוֹ'. וְכֹלָּא חַד מִלָּה. בְּגִין דָּא אִיהוּ אָמַר לְרַבְרְבֵי בָּלָק לִינוּ פֹּה הַלַּיְלָה.

400. You may wonder why we find written: "And Elohim came to Bilaam at night" (Bemidbar 22:9). That is certainly how it is and we already explained that this is the minister that was appointed over them. And he approached him. Similarly, "Elohim came to Laban the Aramnian..." (Beresheet 31:24) and it all was the same meaning. IT REFERS TO THEIR APPOINTED MINISTER, BECAUSE ELOHIM IS A COMMON NAMESAKE USED EVEN FOR PEOPLE. Therefore, he said to the princes of Balak, "Lodge here this night" (Bemidbar 22:8).

401. כֵּיוָן דַּהֲוָה אָתֵי הַהוּא מְמָנָא, בִּלְעָם הֲוָה אָתֵי לְגַבֵּי אֲתָנֵיהּ, וַעֲבַד עוֹבַדְיָה, וְאָמַר מִלֵּי, וּכְדֵין אַתְנָא אוֹדְעָא לֵיהּ. וְאִיהוּ אַחְזֵי עוֹבָדָא לְמִשְׁרֵי עֲלוֹי הַהוּא רוּחָא. וּמַאי אַחְזֵי. הוּא הֲוָה יָדַע דַּחֲמָרֵי שָׁטָאן

וְשָׁרָאן בְּקַדְמֵיתָא דְּלֵילְיָא, כְּדֵין אַחְזֵי עוֹבָדָא, וְקָאֵים לַאֲתָנֵיהּ בַּאֲתָר מְתַתְקָן, וְעָבֵד עוֹבָדוֹי וְסִדֵּר מִלּוֹי. וּכְדֵין הֲוָה אָתֵי מַאן דְּאָתֵי, וְאוֹדַע לֵיהּ עַל יְדָא דְּהַהִיא אָתוֹן.

401. When that appointed minister used to arrive, Bilaam came in to his she-mule and performed his deeds, and spoke his spells. Then the she-mule would inform him. He also demonstrated acts, so that this spirit should dwell on him. What did he demonstrated? He knew that she-mules wander around and prevail at the beginning of the night. He then showed that accomplishment and placed his she-mule at a prepared spot LINED UP AGAINST THE SHE-MULES, and accomplished his work. He set the order of his speeches, and he used the she-mule to tell whoever came in WHATEVER WAS NEEDED.

402. כֵּיוָן דְּלֵילְיָא חַד אָ״ל לֹא תֵלֵךְ עִמָּהֶם, מ״ט תָּב תִּנְיָינוּת לְהַאי. אֶלָּא אִינּוּן בִּרְשׁוּתָא דִּלְעֵילָּא קַיְימֵי, וְהָא תָּנֵינָן, בַּדֶּרֶךְ שֶׁאָדָם רוֹצֶה לָלֶכֶת בָּהּ מוֹלִיכִין וְכוּ׳. בְּקַדְמֵיתָא כְּתִיב, לֹא תֵלֵךְ עִמָּהֶם. כֵּיוָן דְּחָמָא קוּדְשָׁא בְּרִיךְ הוּא, דִּרְעוּתָא הוּא לְמֵיהַךְ. אָ״ל קוּם לֵךְ אִתָּם וְאַךְ אֶת הַדָּבָר וְגוֹ׳. מָה עֲבַד בִּלְעָם כָּל הַהוּא לֵילְיָא הֲוָה מְהַרְהֵר וְאָמַר וּמָה אָן הוּא יְקָרָא דִּילִי, אִי בְּקִטוּרָא אַחֲרָא אִתְקַטַּרְנָא. אַשְׁגַּח כָּל הַהוּא לֵילְיָא בְּחַרְשׁוֹי, וְלָא אַשְׁכַּח סִטְרָא, דִּיְהֵא הוּא בִּרְשׁוּתֵיהּ, אֶלָּא מִסִּטְרָא דַּאֲתָנֵיהּ.

402. HE INQUIRES: Since one night he already told him, "You shall not go with them" (Ibid. 12), what is the reason that he returned the second time? HE RESPONDS: It is only that they were under jurisdiction of the high authority and we were taught, 'in the path man wishes to follow he is led.' At first, it is written: "You shall not go with them." However, when the Holy One, blessed be He, saw that he wanted to SO, He told him "Rise up, and go with them; but only that word..." (Bemidbar 22:20). What did Bilaam do? All that night he was contemplating and thinking, saying, Where then is my honor if I am bound, THAT IS, TO A HIGHER AUTHORITY? He studied his witchcraft all night but could not find an angle that would place him under his own authority, except from the aspect of his she-mule, MEANING THAT WITH THE POWER OF HIS SHE-MULE, HE WOULD BE

DISCONNECTED FROM HIGHER AUTHORITY AND COME INTO HIS OWN AUTHORITY.

403. וְהַיְינוּ דא״ר יִצְחָק אָמַר ר׳ יְהוּדָה, בְּאִלֵּין כִּתְרִין תַּתָּאִין אִית יְמִינָא וְאִית שְׂמָאלָא. מִסִּטְרָא דִּימִינָא חֲמָרֵי, כְּמָה דְּאוֹקִימְנָא. וּמִסִּטְרָא דִּשְׂמָאלֵי אֲתָנֵי וְתָאנָא, עֲשָׂרָה אִינּוּן לִימִינָא, וַעֲשָׂרָה לִשְׂמָאלָא. וְדָא הוּא דא״ר יוֹסֵי, יוֹסֵף כַּד אִתְפְּרַשׁ מֵאֲבוֹי, יָדַע בְּחָכְמְתָא דִּלְעֵילָּא, בְּרָזָא דְּכִתְרִין קַדִּישִׁין עִלָּאִין. כֵּיוָן דַּהֲוָה בְּמִצְרַיִם, אוֹלִיף בְּהַהִיא חָכְמְתָא דִּלְהוֹן, בְּאִינּוּן כִּתְרִין תַּתָּאִין, הֵיךְ אֲחִידָן אִינּוּן דִּימִינָא, וְאִינּוּן דִּשְׂמָאלָא. עֲשָׂרָה דִּימִינָא וַעֲשָׂרָה דִּשְׂמָאלָא חֲמָרֵי וַאֲתָנֵי. וּבְגִין כַּךְ רָמַז לַאֲבוֹי מִמָּה דְּאוֹלִיף תַּמָּן, דִּכְתִּיב וּלְאָבִיו שָׁלַח כְּזֹאת עֲשָׂרָה חֲמוֹרִים וְגוֹ׳.

403. That is what Rabbi Yitzchak said in the name of Rabbi Yehuda regarding these lower Sfirot: there is right and there is left. From the right side are the donkeys, WHICH ARE MALES, as we explained, and from the left side are the she-mules THAT ARE THE FEMALES. We have learned that there are ten to the right and ten to the left. THAT IS, CORRESPONDING TO THE TEN SFIROT OF HOLINESS, since "THE ELOHIM HAS MADE THE ONE AS WELL AS THE OTHER" (KOHELET 7:14). That is what Rabbi Yosi said: When Joseph left his father, he was knowledgeable in the higher wisdom in the secret meaning of the holy supernal Sfirot. When he was in Egypt, he studied also their wisdom of the lower Sfirot OF THE OTHER SIDE, how these of the right and these of the left are linked. That is the ten of the right and the ten of the left, the male and female asses. That is why he told his father what he had learned there, as is written: "And to his father he sent after this manner; ten asses..." (Beresheet 45:23).

404. א״ר יוֹסֵי, אִינּוּן דִּימִינָא כְּלִילָן כֻּלְּהוּ בְּחַד, דְּאִקְרֵי חֲמוֹ״ר. וְהַאי הוּא הַהוּא חֲמוֹר, דִּכְתִּיב לֹא תַחֲרוֹשׁ בְּשׁוֹר וּבַחֲמוֹ״ר יַחְדָּיו. וְהַאי הוּא חֲמוֹר, דְּזַמִּין מַלְכָּא מְשִׁיחָא לְמִשְׁלַט עָלֵיהּ, כְּמָה דְּאוֹקִימְנָא. וְאִינּוּן דִּשְׂמָאלָא, כְּלִילָן כֻּלְּהוּ בְּחַד דְּאִקְרֵי אָתוֹן, דְּהָא מִסִּטְרָהָא נָפִיק עִירֹה, קְטְרוּגָא דְּדַרְדְּקֵי, כְּמָה דְּאוֹקִימְנָא. וְהַיְינוּ דִּכְתִּיב, עָנִי וְרוֹכֵב עַל חֲמוֹר

וְעַל עַיִר בֶּן אֲתוֹנוֹת, אֲתָנֹת חָסֵר, עַשְׂרָה דִּכְלִילָן כְּחַד.

404. Rabbi Yosi said, These TEN of the right are all comprised in that one that is called 'donkey'. That is the same donkey of which is written: "You shall not plow with an ox and an donkey together" (Devarim 22:10). That is the same donkey which King Messiah will handle, as was explained, BASED ON THE MEANING OF THE VERSE: "HUMBLE, AND RIDING UPON AN DONKEY" (ZECHARYAH 9:9). These TEN of the left are all comprised in the one that is called 'the she-mule', because from her side emanates Iroh that harms children, THAT IS, a COLT (HEB. *IR*), THE FOAL OF AN DONKEY, as we studied. This is what is written: "Humble, and riding upon an donkey, and upon a colt, the foal of an she-mule (Heb. *atonot*)." It spells *atonot*, with out Vav OF PLURAL INDICATION, because the ten are all included in one SHE-MULE, AS MENTIONED ABOVE.

405. וְדָא הוּא דאר"ש, מַאי דִּכְתִּיב אֹסְרִי לַגֶּפֶן עִירֹה. אֹסְרִי לַגֶּפֶן, זַמִּין קוּדְשָׁא בְּרִיךְ הוּא לְקַשְׁרָא בְּגִינֵיהוֹן דְּיִשְׂרָאֵל דְּאִקְרוּן גֶּפֶן. עִירֹה. דְּאִיהוּ קַטֵּיגוֹרָא דִּילְהוֹן, וּבְגִין דְּאִקְרוּן שׂוֹרֵק, דִּכְתִּיב וְאָנֹכִי נְטַעְתִּיךְ שׂוֹרֵק. בְּנִי אֲתֹנוֹ, הַהוּא דְּנָפִיק מִסִּטְרָא דְּהַאי אָתוֹן.

405. Rabbi Shimon said that it is written: "Binding his foal to the vine" (Beresheet 49:11). "Binding...to the vine," MEANS THAT for the sake of Yisrael, who are called 'grapevine', AS IT IS WRITTEN: "YOU HAVE BROUGHT A VINE OUT OF EGYPT" (TEHILIM 80:9), the Holy One, blessed be He, will tie up this *Iroh*, who is the accuser that harms them, since YISRAEL are called "noble vine," as it is written: "And I had planted you a noble vine" (Yirmeyah 2:21). IT IS WRITTEN: "His ass's colt TO THE CHOICE VINE" (Beresheet 49:11), meaning the one who comes from that ass's side. HE WILL BIND HER AND SUBDUE HER.

406. וְהָנֵי י' מִימִינָא, וְי' מִשְּׂמָאלָא, וְאִתְכְּלִילָן בְּהָנֵי תְּרֵי, כֻּלָּא אִינּוּן מִשְׁתַּכְחֵי בְּקֶסֶ"ם. וְאִית עַשְׂרָה אַחֲרָנִין דִּימִינָא וַעֲשָׂרָה דִּשְׂמָאלָא, דְּמִשְׁתַּכְחֵי בְּנַחַ"שׁ. וע"ד כְּתִיב, כִּי לֹא נַחַשׁ בְּיַעֲקֹב וְלֹא קֶסֶם בְּיִשְׂרָאֵל. מ"ט, בְּגִין כִּי יְיָ' אֱלֹהָיו עִמּוֹ. מסטר דְּנָחָ"שׁ, נָפַק שׁוֹ"ר, מִסִּטְרָא דְּקֶסֶ"ם, נָפַק חֲמוֹ"ר. וְדָא הוּא שׁוֹר וַחֲמוֹר, וְעַ"ד בִּלְעָם, כֵּיוָן

דְּיָדַע דְּאִתְקְשַׁר בִּרְשׁוּתָא אַחֲרָא, וְאָ"ל אַךְ אֶת הַדָּבָר וְגוֹ', אַבְאִישׁ לֵיהּ, וְאָמַר, וּמַה אָן הִיא יְקָרָא דִּילִי. מִיָּד אִסְתָּכַּל בְּחַרְשׁוֹי, וְלָא אַשְׁכַּח דִּיהֵא בִּרְשׁוּתֵיהּ, אֶלָּא הַאי אָתוֹן.

406. The ten from the right and ten from the left that are included in these two, WHICH ARE THE MALE AND FEMALE DONKEY, AS MENTIONED BEFORE, all pertain to divination. There are ten others of the right and ten of the left that pertain to enchantment. Therefore, it is written: "Surely there is no enchantment in Jacob, nor is there any divination in Yisrael" (Bemidbar 23:23). What is the reason? Because "Hashem Elohim is with him" (Ibid. 21), from the aspect of enchantment comes the ox. From the aspect of divination comes the donkey. That is the meaning of "ox and an donkey." Therefore, because Bilaam knew that he was bound to the other authority THAT IS HIGHER, it said to him: "But only that word..." He found this bad, saying to himself, Where is my honor? Immediately, he examined his witchcraft but could not come up with ANYTHING that would REINTRODUCE HIM to his authority, except this she-mule.

407. מִיָּד וַיָּקָם בִּלְעָם בַּבֹּקֶר וַיַּחֲבוֹשׁ אֶת אֲתוֹנוֹ לְמֶעְבַּד רְעוּתֵיהּ בָּהּ, וּרְעוּתָא דְּבָלָק. וְעַל דָּא וַיִּחַר אַף אֱלֹהִים כִּי הוֹלֵךְ הוּא. הוּא דַּיְיקָא, דְּאַפִּיק גַּרְמֵיהּ מֵרְשׁוּתֵיהּ, מִמַּה דְּאָמַר לֵיהּ וְאַךְ אֶת הַדָּבָר וְגוֹ'. ת"ח דְּהָכִי הוּא, דְּהָא בְּקַדְמֵיתָא יָהַב לֵיהּ רְשׁוּתָא, וְאָמַר קוּם לֵךְ אִתָּם, הַשְׁתָּא דְּהֲוָה אָזִיל, אַמַּאי וַיִּחַר אַף אֱלֹהִים. אֶלָּא בְּגִין דְּהוֹלֵךְ הוּא, הוּא בִּרְשׁוּתֵיהּ דִּילֵיהּ, לְנָפְקָא מֵהַהוּא דְּאָמַר לֵיהּ וְאַךְ אֶת הַדָּבָר.

407. Instantly, "Bilaam rose up in the morning, and saddled his she-mule" (Bemidbar 22:21) to do his desire with her and the desire of Balak. Therefore, "Elohim's anger burned because he went" (Ibid. 22), "he" precisely, because he has removed himself from His authority, WITH THE HELP OF HIS SHE-MULE, AS MENTIONED EARLIER from what he was told: "but only that word WHICH I SHALL SAY TO YOU, SHALL YOU DO" (Ibid. 20). Come and see that this is how it was: because he was granted permission at first and was told to "stand up and go with them," now that he was going, why did "Elohim's anger burned"? It is because "he" in his own authority was going to exclude himself from the One who said to him, "But only that word..."

408. אָמַר לֵיהּ קוּדְשָׁא בְּרִיךְ הוּא, רָשָׁע, אַתְּ מְתַקֵּן וּמְזָרֵז זַיְינָךְ לְנָפְקָא מִן רְשׁוּתִי, חַיֶּיךָ אַנְתְּ וַאֲתָנָךְ בִּרְשׁוּתִי תֶּהֱווֹן. מִיַּד וַיִּתְיַצֵּב מַלְאַךְ יְיָ׳. מַאי וַיִּתְיַצֵּב. א״ר אַבָּא, נָפַק וְקָאֵים בְּאוּמְנוּתָא אַחֲרָא, מֵאוּמָנוּתָא דִּילֵיהּ, דְּהַאי מַלְאָכָא דְּרַחֲמֵי הֲוָה. וְהַיְינוּ דְּאָמַר ר׳ שִׁמְעוֹן, חַיָּיבַיָּא מְהַפְּכֵי רַחֲמֵי לְדִינָא. לְשָׂטָן לוֹ, דְּהָא לָא אוּמָנוּתָא דִּילֵיהּ הֲוָה.

408. The Holy One, blessed be He, said to him, 'Wicked one, you are hurrying and preparing your gear and hastening to leave My authority. I promise on your life, that you and your she-mule will remain in My control.' Soon, "the angel of Hashem stood" (Bemidbar 22:22). What is the meaning of: "stood"? Rabbi Aba said, He deviated from his usual skill and adopted another skill, because he was an angel of Mercy AND NOT OF JUDGMENT, AS BILAAM. That is what Rabbi Shimon meant when he said, 'The wicked transform Mercy into Judgment.' Therefore, it is written: "as an adversary" (Ibid.), BUT NOT FOR ANOTHER, because that was not his wont, SINCE HE WAS OF THE ATTRIBUTE OF MERCY.

409. אָמַר רִבִּי אֶלְעָזָר, לָא שָׁנֵי מַלְאָכָא, וְלָא נָפַק מֵאוּמָנוּתָא דִּילֵיהּ, אֶלָּא בְּגִין דַּהֲוָה הַאי מַלְאָכָא מִסִּטְרָא דְּרַחֲמֵי, וְקָאֵים לַקֳבְלֵיהּ, סָתִיר חָכְמְתָא דִּילֵיהּ, וְקִלְקֵל רְעוּתֵיהּ. הה״ד לְשָׂטָן לוֹ. לוֹ הֲוָה שָׂטָן, וְאִשְׁתְּכַח שָׂטָן, אֲבָל לְאַחֲרָא לָא הֲוָה שָׂטָן.

409. Rabbi Elazar says, The angel did not act differently and did not leave his usual practice. It is only that the angel was from the merciful side and stood against him. He was confounding his wisdom and disturbing his wishes. That is the meaning of, "as an adversary." To him, he was an adversary and presented himself as an adversary, but to someone else he was not considered an adversary.

410. תָּאנָא, אר״ש, כַּמָּה חַכִּים הֲוָה בִּלְעָם בְּחַרְשׁוֹי, עַל כָּל בְּנֵי עָלְמָא, דְּהָא בְּשַׁעֲתָא דְּאַשְׁגַּח, לְאַשְׁכְּחָא עֵיטָא לְנָפְקָא מֵרְשׁוּתֵיהּ דְּקוּדְשָׁא בְּרִיךְ הוּא, מֵהַהִיא מִלָּה דִּכְתִּיב, וְאַךְ אֶת הַדָּבָר וְגוֹ׳. אִסְתָּכַּל בְּחַרְשׁוֹי, וְלָא אַשְׁכַּח בַּר הַהִיא אָתוֹן, מַה כְּתִיב, וַיַּחֲבוֹשׁ אֶת אֲתוֹנוֹ, אַטְעִין לָהּ בְּכָל חַרְשִׁין, וּבְכָל קְסָמִין דַּהֲוָה יָדַע, וְאָעִיל בָּהּ, וְאַכְלִיל

לָהּ מִכֻּלְּהוּ, בְּגִין לְמֵילָט לְהוּ לְיִשְׂרָאֵל. מִיָּד וַיִּחַר אַף אֱלֹהִים כִּי הוֹלֵךְ הוּא. הוּא דַּיְיקָא כְּמָה דְּאִתְּמַר. מָה עֲבַד קוּדְשָׁא בְּרִיךְ הוּא, אַקְדִּים לְמַלְאָכָא דְּרַחֲמֵי. לְקַיְּימָא לָקֳבְלֵיהּ, וְיַסְתִּיר חֲרָשׁוֹי וְקִסְמוֹי.

410. We studied that Rabbi Shimon said, How much wiser Bilaam was with his witchcraft than other people in the world. When he was looking for an idea new to escape the jurisdiction of the Holy One, blessed be He, the words: "But only the word," he then took stock of his witchcraft but could not find anything besides this she-mule THROUGH WHICH HE COULD BE HELPED TO ESCAPE THE AUTHORITY OF THE HOLY ONE, BLESSED BE HE. It is written: "And saddled his she-mule." He loaded his she-mule with all types of magic and sorcery with which he was familiar, put it on her and made her part of all of them in order to curse Yisrael. Instantly, "Elohim's anger burned because he went." "He" is specific, as we were taught THAT "HE" INDICATES THAT HE LEFT HIS JURISDICTION, AS MENTIONED EARLIER. What did the Holy One, blessed be He, do? He put before him an angel of Mercy that would stall and oppose him, and confound his witchcraft and sorcery.

411. ות"ח, דְּעַד הַשְׁתָּא לָא כְּתִיב יְיָ' וְלָא אִתְחֲזֵי בְּקִסְמוֹי וְחַרְשׁוֹי. וְהָא אוּקְמוּהָ. וְהַשְׁתָּא כֵּיוָן דְּאַתְקִין אֲתָנֵיהּ, וְזֵרְזָה בְּתִקּוּנֵי חֲרָשׁוֹי, בְּסִטְרָא דְּדִינָא לְמֵילָט לְיִשְׂרָאֵל, אַקְדִּים קוּדְשָׁא בְּרִיךְ הוּא לְמַלְאָכָא דְּרַחֲמֵי לָקֳבְלֵיהּ, וּבִשְׁמָא דְּרַחֲמֵי, בְּגִין לִסְתּוֹר חָכְמְתָא דִּילֵיהּ, וּלְאַסְטָאָה לַאֲתָנֵיהּ מֵהַהוּא אָרְחָא, כְּמָה דִּכְתִּיב, וַתֵּט הָאָתוֹן מִן הַדֶּרֶךְ. מִן הַדֶּרֶךְ דַּיְיקָא. וְעַל דָּא לָא כְּתִיב וַיִּתְיַצֵּב מַלְאַךְ הָאֱלֹהִים, וַיַּעֲמוֹד מַלְאַךְ הָאֱלֹהִים, אֶלָּא מַלְאַךְ יְיָ' דְּרַחֲמֵי.

411. Come and see: Until now, it is not written Hashem, because it is not seen in his witchcraft and sorcery, as we have already explained. When he had prepared his she-mule and readied her with appropriate witchcraft, with the aspect of Judgment to curse Yisrael, the Holy One, blessed be He, prepared the angel of Mercy against him prior to that, and with the name of Mercy to confound his wisdom and to divert his she-mule from that direction, as is written: "And the she-mule turned aside out of the way" (Bemidbar 22:23). "Out of the way" is precise, MEANING FROM HIS PATH

OF WITCHCRAFT. That is why it does not say, 'The angel of Elohim', but rather "the angel of Hashem," Which is Mercy.

412. אָמַר קוּדְשָׁא בְּרִיךְ הוּא, רָשָׁע, אַתְּ אַטְעֲנַת לַאֲתָנָךְ בְּחַרְשָׁךְ, בְּכַמָּה סִטְרֵי דְּדִינֵי לְקָבֵל בָּנַי. אֲנָא אַעְבָּר טְעוּנָךְ, וְיֵהָפֵךְ מֵאָרְחָא דָּא, מִיָּד אַקְדִּים מַלְאָכָא דְּרַחֲמֵי לְשָׂטָן לוֹ. לוֹ דַּיְיקָא. כְּמָה דְּאִתְּמַר.

412. The Holy One, blessed be He, said, 'Wicked man, you have loaded your she-mule with your witchcrafts, with several aspects of judgments against My children. I will remove your load and remove you from this path.' Immediately, He advanced the angel of Mercy "as an adversary against him," "against him" is precise as we studied AND NOT AGAINST ANYONE ELSE, AS MENTIONED EARLIER.

42. "And the she-mule saw the angel of Hashem"

A Synopsis

When Rabbi Yitzchak wonders why the she-mule was able to see the angel and yet the supposedly wise Bilaam was not, Rabbi Yosi says the wicked should not gaze at a holy sight. They talk about Bilaam falling down before he saw his visions, and having his eyes open at the time, but as they do not know the correct interpretation of this they go to see Rabbi Shimon.

413. וַתֵּרֶא הָאָתוֹן אֶת מַלְאַךְ יְיָ׳ וְגוֹ׳. אָמַר רִבִּי יִצְחָק, וְכִי אֲמַאי חָמָאת הִיא, וּבִלְעָם דַּהֲוָה חַכִּים כָּל כַּךְ לָא חָמָא. אָמַר רִבִּי יוֹסֵי, ח״ו דְּהַהוּא רָשָׁע יִסְתַּכֵּל בְּחֵיזוּ קַדִּישָׁא. אָמַר לֵיהּ, אִי הָכִי, הָא כְּתִיב נוֹפֵל וּגְלוּי עֵינָיִם. אָמַר לֵיהּ לָא שְׁמַעְנָא בְּהָא מִידִי וְלָא אֵימָא. א״ל אֲנָא שְׁמַעְנָא, דְּכַד הֲוָה אִצְטְרִיךְ לְאִסְתַּכְּלָא, הֲוָה נָפִיל וְחָמֵי. וְהַשְׁתָּא לָא אִצְטְרִיךְ לְאִסְתַּכְּלָא.

413. "And the she-mule saw the angel of Hashem..." (Bemidbar 22:25). Rabbi Yitzchak said, How come THE SHE-MULE saw and Bilaam, who was so wise, did not see? Rabbi Yosi said, Heaven forbid that the wicked should gaze at a holy sight, THAT HE SHOULD BE ABLE TO PERCEIVE AN ANGEL OF HASHEM. He said to him, If so, why is it written: "Falling down, but having his eyes open" (Bemidbar 24:4)? He said to him, I have not heard anything about this, so I say nothing. He said, I heard that when he needed to see, he fell, and then saw. BY THE ANGEL, he was not ment to look AND THAT IS WHY HE DIDN'T SEE.

414. אָמַר לֵיהּ, אִי הָכִי, בְּדַרְגָּא עִלָּאָה יַתִּיר הֲוָה עַל כָּל נְבִיאֵי מְהֵימְנוּתָא, דְּאִיהוּ גְּלוּי עֵינַיִם, חָמֵי וְאִסְתַּכַּל בִּיקָרָא דְקוּדְשָׁא בְּרִיךְ הוּא. וְהָא ר׳ שִׁמְעוֹן אָמַר, בִּלְעָם בְּחַרְשׁוֹי, הֲוָה יָדַע בְּאִינּוּן כִּתְרִין תַּתָּאִין דִּלְתַתָּא, כְּמָה דִּכְתִּיב וְאֶת בִּלְעָם בֶּן בְּעוֹר הַקּוֹסֵם, קוֹסֵם קַרְיֵיהּ קְרָא, דְּטִנּוּפָא דְּטִנּוּפֵי, הֵיךְ יִסְתַּכַּל בִּיקָרָא דְּמָארֵיהּ. וְעוֹד, הָא אָמַר רִבִּי שִׁמְעוֹן, בְּחֵיזוּ חַד דְּחָזָא לְפוּם שַׁעֲתָא, דִּכְתִּיב וַיְגַל יְיָ׳ אֶת עֵינֵי בִלְעָם, אִתְעֲקִימוּ עֵינוֹי, וְאַתְּ אַמְרַת דַּהֲוָה חָמֵי בִּגְלוּי דְּעַיְינִין,

וְאִסְתְּכַּל בִּיקָרָא דקוּדְשָׁא בְּרִיךְ הוּא.

414. He said to him, If so, then BILAAM was in a higher level than all the other faithful prophets, because he was "having his eyes open," seeing and observing the glory of the Holy One, blessed be He. Didn't Rabbi Shimon say that Bilaam with his witchcraft understood the lower Sfirot below, as it is written: "Bilaam also, of the son of Beor, the soothsayer" (Yehoshua 13:22). The scripture calls him "soothsayer"; that is, soiled filth, and how could he gaze at the glory of his Master? Furthermore, didn't Rabbi Shimon say that when he beheld for a short while, as is written: "Then Hashem opened the eyes of Bilaam," his eyes squinted and you say that he had to see with his eyes open, observing the glory of the Holy One, blessed be He.

415. א"ל, אֲנָא אַהֲדַרְנָא לָקֳבְלָךְ. דִּידִי וְדִידָךְ בָּעֵי צָחוּתָא. וַדַּאי רָזֵי אוֹרַיְיתָא עִלָּאִין, וְלָא יַכְלִין בְּנֵי עָלְמָא לְמֵיקַם עֲלַיְיהוּ. בְּגִין כַּךְ אָסִיר לְאַקְדְּמָא בְּמִלָּה דְּאוֹרַיְיתָא, עַד דְּיִשְׁמַע מִלָּה וְיֵדַע לָהּ עַל בּוּרְיֵיהּ. אָתוּ לְקַמֵּיהּ דר"ש אָמְרוּ מִלָּה קַמֵּיהּ.

415. He said to him, I take back what I said against you. My words and yours need to be polished AND CLARIFIED. The secrets of the Torah are definitely lofty and ordinary people cannot understand them. It is therefore not permissible to proceed to expound on a topic in Torah before hearing and understanding the matter properly and clearly. They came to Rabbi Shimon and discussed the matter with him.

43. Aza and Azael, “falling down, but having his eyes open”

A Synopsis

Rabbi Shimon explains to the rabbis that when God wished to create man many of the angels told Him that man would sin, and others asked him, ‘What is man, that you are mindful of him?’ God said that He wished to create man, and that man would be in their own image and would have wisdom higher than the angels. When Adam sinned, Aza and Azel complained to God about it, so He dropped them from heaven and reduced their holiness. Angels are capable of enduring only through the higher light that sustains them, and when their level was dropped the glow of their light was reduced. Rabbi Shimon talks about the manna that fell to feed the children of Yisrael in the wilderness, and says that it was from the dew that filtered down; when it encountered the air of this world its glow was reduced and it solidified. He goes on to say that when God saw how Aza and Azael were misleading the world He buried them in the dark mountains, from where they still teach people witchcraft and divinations; Laban and Bilaam learned from them. When Torah says that Bilaam heard “the words of El” this meant the words that Aza and Azael related of God’s words that they had learned when still in heaven. Rabbi Shimon tells us that “falling down” refers to Aza and “having his eyes open” refers to Azael. He concludes by saying that the Shechinah dwells only in a holy place that is deserving of it.

416. פָּתַח וְאָמַר, מָה אֱנוֹשׁ כִּי תִזְכְּרֶנּוּ וְגוֹ׳, הַאי קְרָא אוּקְמוּהָ, דִּמְמָנָן דְּעָלְמָא אֲמָרוּהָ, בְּשַׁעֲתָא דְּסָלִיק בִּרְעוּתֵיהּ דְּקוּדְשָׁא בְּרִיךְ הוּא לְמִבְרֵי אֱנָשָׁא. קְרָא לְכִתּוֹת כִּתּוֹת דְּמַלְאֲכֵי עִלָּאֵה, וְאוֹתִיב לוֹן קַמֵּיהּ. אָמַר לוֹן, בָּעֵינָא לְמִבְרֵי אָדָם. אָמְרוּ קַמֵּיהּ, וְאָדָם בִּיקָר בַּל יָלִין וְגוֹ׳. אוֹשִׁיט קוּדְשָׁא בְּרִיךְ הוּא אֶצְבְּעָא דִּילֵיהּ, וְאוֹקִיד לוֹן. אוֹתִיב כִּתּוֹת אַחֲרָנִין קַמֵּיהּ, אָמַר לוֹן בָּעֵינָא לְמִבְרֵי אָדָם. אָמְרוּ קַמֵּיהּ, מָה אֱנוֹשׁ כִּי תִזְכְּרֶנּוּ. מַה טִיבוּ דב״נ דָּא. אָמַר לוֹן, ב״נ דִּיְהֵא בְּצַלְמָא דִּידָן, דִּיְהֵא חָכְמְתָא דִּילֵיהּ, עִלָּאָה מֵחָכְמָתְכוֹן.

416. He opened the discussion with the verse: “What is man, that You are mindful of him...” (Tehilim 8:5). It was explained that the ministers said this at the time when it was the Holy One, blessed be He, wish to create man.

THEN He called many groups of the ministering angels and sat them in His presence. He told them, 'I wish to create man', and they said, "Nevertheless man abides not in honor..." (Tehilim 49:13). The Holy One, blessed be He, extended His finger and put them in fire. He had other classes sit in His presence. He said to them, 'I wish to create man'. They replied, "What is man, that You are mindful of him"? What are the functions of this man? He replied to them' I WISH TO CREATE MAN, who will be in Our image, and whose wisdom will be above your wisdom'.

417. כֵּיוָן דְּבָרָא אָדָם, וְחָטָא, וְנָפִק בְּדִימוּס קַמֵּיהּ, אָתוּ עֲזָ"א וַעֲזָ"אֵל, אָמְרוּ קַמֵּיהּ, פִּתְחוֹן פֶּה אִית לָן גַּבָּךְ, הָא ב"נ דְּעַבְדַּת חָטֵי קַמָּךְ. אָמַר לְהוּ, אִלְמָלֵי תֶּהֱווֹן שְׁכִיחֵי גַּבַּיְיהוּ וְכוּ'. מַה עֲבַד קוּדְשָׁא בְּרִיךְ הוּא. אַפִּיל לוֹן מִדַּרְגָּא קַדִּישָׁא דִּלְהוֹן מִן שְׁמַיָּא.

417. As soon as Adam was created and sinned, and left His presence with his verdict, Aza and Azael approached. They said to Him, We have a redress to complain about to You. Here is the man that You created and he sinned against You. He replied to them, 'If you would have been with them, you would have been worse than him.' What did the Holy One, blessed be He, do? He threw them down from heaven from their level of holiness.

418. אָמַר ר"ש, הַשְׁתָּא אַהֲדַרְנָא לְתִיּוּבְתַּיְיכוּ. דְּבִלְעָם אָמַר נוֹפֵל וּגְלוּי עֵינָיִם, אִי נֵימָא דְּלָא הֲוָה הָכִי, וְשַׁבּוּחֵי קָא מְשַׁבַּח גַּרְמֵיהּ, הֵיךְ יִכְתּוֹב קוּדְשָׁא בְּרִיךְ הוּא מִלָּה כְּדִיבָא בְּאוֹרַיְיתָא. וְאִי מִלָּה דִּקְשׁוֹט הִיא, הֵיךְ יִשְׁתַּבַּח הַהוּא רָשָׁע בְּדַרְגָּא עִלָּאָה עַל כָּל נְבִיאֵי מְהֵימְנוּתָא. וְעוֹד, דְּהָא לָא שַׁרְיָא קְדוּשָׁה דִּלְעֵילָּא, אֶלָּא בְּאַתְרֵיהּ דְּאִתְחֲזֵי לֵיהּ.

418. Rabbi Shimon said, Now I will return to your question, what Bilaam was saying, "falling down, but having his eyes open." If we say that this was not so, BUT RATHER he praised himself, how would the Holy One, blessed be He, write a lie in the Torah? If it was true, how could the wicked one boast of the highest level, above all the prophets of the Faith? In addition, doesn't higher holiness dwell only on a place that is appropriate for it, AND NOT ON THIS DEFILED MAN?

419. הַשְׁתָּא אַהֲדַרְנָא לְמִלָּה קַדְמָאָה. בָּתַר דְּאַפִּיל לוֹן קוּדְשָׁא בְּרִיךְ

הוּא, מֵאֲתָר קַדִּישָׁא דִּלְהוֹן. טָעוּ בָּתַר נְשֵׁי עָלְמָא, וְאַטְעוּ עָלְמָא. הָכָא אִית לְאִסְתַּכְּלָא, וְהָא כְּתִיב עוֹשֶׂה מַלְאָכָיו רוּחוֹת וְגוֹ'. וְהָא אִלֵּין מַלְאֲכִין הֲווֹ, אֵיךְ יָכִילוּ לְאִתְקַיְּימָא בְּאַרְעָא. אֶלָּא ת"ח, כָּל אִינּוּן דִּלְעֵילָּא, לָא קַיְימִין, וְלָא יַכְלִין לְמֵיקָם, בַּר בִּנְהוֹרָא עִלָּאָה דְּנָהִיר לוֹן, וְקַיִּים לוֹן. וְאִי פָּסִיק מִנַּיְיהוּ הַהוּא נְהוֹרָא דִּלְעֵילָּא, לָא יַכְלִין לְמֵיקָם. כָּל שֶׁכֵּן אִלֵּין דְּאַפִּיל לוֹן קוּדְשָׁא בְּרִיךְ הוּא. וּפָסַק מִנַּיְיהוּ הַהוּא נְהוֹרָא דִּלְעֵילָּא, דְּאִשְׁתָּנֵי זִיוַויְיהוּ. וְכַךְ נַחְתּוּ וְשָׁלִיט בְּהוּ אֲוִירָא דְּעָלְמָא, אִשְׁתָּנוּ בְּדַרְגָּא אַחֲרָא.

419. Now, Let me return to the former subject. After the throwing down OF AZA AND AZAEL from their holy level by the Holy One, blessed be He, they whored after the women of the world and misled the world. Here we need to observe, as we find written: "Who makes the winds His messengers..." (Tehilim 104:4). Here, these angels were messengers. How could they exist on the earth? HE REPLIES: Just come and see. All the angels above exist, and can only exist by the higher light that illuminates for them and sustains them. If that light of the above is cut off from them, they cannot exist. Most certainly, these ANGELS, which the Holy One, blessed be He, threw down, and from whom He removed that high light, their glow changed. CONSEQUENTLY, when they fell and were under the dominance of the atmosphere, they transformed to another level.

420. ת"ח, מַנָּא דַּהֲוָה נָחִית לְהוּ לְיִשְׂרָאֵל בְּמַדְבְּרָא, הַהוּא מַנָּא הֲוָה, מִטַּלָּא דִּלְעֵילָּא, דַּהֲוָה נָחִית מֵעַתִּיקָא סְתִימָא דְּכָל סְתִימִין. וְכַד הֲוָה נָחִית, הֲוָה נְהוֹרֵיהּ נָהִיר בְּכֻלְּהוּ עָלְמִין, וּמִנֵּיהּ אִתְּזָן חֲקַל דְּתַפּוּחִין, וּמַלְאֲכֵי עִלָּאֵי. וְכַד הֲוָה נָחִית לְתַתָּא, וְשָׁלִיט בֵּיהּ אֲוִירָא דְּעָלְמָא, אִגְלִיד, וְאִשְׁתָּנֵי זִיוֵיהּ, וְלָא הֲוָה זִיוֵיהּ אֶלָּא כְּמָה דִּכְתִּיב וְהַמָּן כִּזְרַע גַּד הוּא וגו', וְלָא יַתִּיר. וְכָל שֶׁכֵּן מַלְאֲכִין, כֵּיוָן דְּנַחְתּוּ וְשָׁלִיט בְּהוּ אֲוִירָא, אִשְׁתָּנוּ מֵהַהוּא דַּרְגָּא קַדְמָאָה דַּהֲווֹ.

420. Come and see the manna that came down for Yisrael in the wilderness. That manna was from the celestial dew that filtered down from the most concealed Atik, THAT IS, KETER. When it came down, its light was illuminating throughout the worlds and from it was sustained and fed the field of apple trees, THAT IS MALCHUT, and the higher angels. When the manna came down and the air of the world affected it, it gelled and its glow changed. It was not glowing any more, only as it says, "And the manna was like coriander seed ..." (Bemidbar 11:7). The atmosphere had even more of an effect on the angels THAT WERE THROWN DOWN BY THE HOLY ONE, BLESSED BE HE. As soon as they descended, they were transformed from that earlier level in which they were.

421. מָה עֲבַד קוּדְשָׁא בְּרִיךְ הוּא. חָמָא דְּאַטְעֲיָין עָלְמָא, קָשַׁר לוֹן בְּשַׁלְשְׁלָאֵי דְּפַרְזְלָא בְּטוּרָא דַּחֲשׁוֹכָא, בְּאָן אֲתָר יַתְבֵי. בְּעֲמִיקָא דְּטוּרֵי. אוֹתִיב לֵיהּ לַעֲזָ״א, וּרְמֵי חֲשׁוֹכָא דְּאַנְפִּין. בְּגִין דְּהַהִיא שַׁעֲתָא דְּקָשַׁר לוֹן קוּדְשָׁא בְּרִיךְ הוּא, אִתְתָּקַף וְאַרְגִּיז כְּלַפֵּי מַעֲלָה, וְקוּדְשָׁא בְּרִיךְ הוּא אָפִּיל לֵיהּ בְּעוּמְקָא עַד קְדָלֵיהּ, וְזָרִיק חֲשׁוֹכָא בְּאַנְפּוֹי. עֲזָאֵ״ל דְּלָא אִתְתָּקַף, אוֹתְבֵיהּ גַּבֵּיהּ, וְנָהִיר לֵיהּ חֲשׁוֹכָא.

421. What did the Holy One, blessed be He, do? He saw that they, AZA AND AZAEL, were misleading the world. He bound them with chains of iron in the dark mountains. Where are they situated? In the valley of the mountains. He placed Aza there and threw darkness in his face, because when the Holy One, blessed be He, bound them, he strengthened himself to provoke anger to the higher. AS A RESULT, the Holy One, blessed be He, dropped him down to his neck and threw darkness in his face. He placed Azael, who did not strengthen himself, next to Aza and illuminated the darkness for him.

422. וּבְנֵי עָלְמָא דְּיַדְעִין אַתְרַיְיהוּ, אַתְיָין לְגַבַּיְיהוּ, וְאוּלְפִין לוֹן לִבְנֵי נָשָׁא חַרְשִׁין וּנְחָשִׁין וּקְסָמִין. וְאִינּוּן טוּרֵי חֲשׁוֹכָא, אִקְרוּן הַרֲרֵי קֶדֶם. מ״ט. בְּגִין דַּחֲשׁוֹכָא אַקְדִּים לִנְהוֹרָא. ובג״כ, טוּרֵי חֲשׁוֹכָא, הַרֲרֵי קֶדֶם אִקְרוּן. לָבָן וּבִלְעָם מִנַּיְיהוּ אוּלְפֵי חַרְשִׁין. וְהַיְינוּ דְּאָמַר בִּלְעָם, מִן אֲרָם יַנְחֵנִי בָּלָק מֶלֶךְ מוֹאָב מֵהַרְרֵי קֶדֶם וְגוֹ'.

422. People that know the location OF AZA AND AZAEL visit them. They teach people witchcraft, enchantments and divinations. These dark mountains are referred to as the mountains of old. What is the reason? Because the darkness preceded the light. That is why the dark mountains are called “Mountains of old.” Laban and Bilaam learned witchcraft from them and that is what Bilaam said, “Balak the king of Moab has brought me from Aram, out of the mountains of old” (Bemidbar 23:7).

423. ת"ח, בִּלְעָם הֲוָה קָא מְשַׁבַּח גַּרְמֵיהּ מֵהַאי אֲתָר, וְאָמַר נְאֻם שׁוֹמֵעַ אִמְרֵי אֵל וְגוֹ'. בְּגִין דַּעֲזָ"א וַעֲזָאֵ"ל, אַמְרֵי לְאִינּוּן בְּנֵי עָלְמָא, מֵאִילֵּין מִלִּין עִלָּאִין, דַּהֲווֹ יַדְעֵי בְּקַדְמֵיתָא לְעֵילָּא. וּמִשְׁתָּעֵי מֵעָלְמָא קַדִּישָׁא דַּהֲווֹ בֵּיהּ, הה"ד שׁוֹמֵעַ אִמְרֵי אֵל. שׁוֹמֵעַ קוֹל אֵל, לָא כְּתִיב, אֶלָּא אִמְרֵי אֵל, אִינּוּן אֲמִירָן דְּאַמְרֵי מִנֵּיהּ. מַאן דְּאָתֵי מִפִּרְקָא, וְשָׁאֲלִין לֵיהּ מֵאָן אַתְּ אָתֵי. אָמַר, מִלְּמִשְׁמַע מִלִּין דְּמַלְכָּא קַדִּישָׁא. כַּךְ נְאֻם שֹׁמֵעַ אִמְרֵי אֵל. וְיוֹדֵעַ דַּעַת עֶלְיוֹן, דַּהֲוָה יָדַע שַׁעֲתָא דְּתַלְיָא דִּינָא בְּעָלְמָא, וּמְכַוֵּין שַׁעֲתָא בְּחַרְשׁוֹי.

423. Come and see that Bilaam used to praise himself from this location, and said, “The saying of him who hears the words of El...” (Bemidbar 24:16). Aza and Azael used to tell people about these higher matters which they knew earlier WHEN THEY WERE above IN HEAVEN. They used to relate information from the holy world where they were. That is what it says, “Who hears the words of El.” It is not written: ‘who hears the voice of El’, but rather, “the words of El.” These are the speeches and stories that AZA AND AZAEL used to relate of Him, OF EL, SIMILAR TO someone who comes from listening to a discourse IN A SEMINAR. They ask him, Where did you come from? He says, From listening to the speeches of the Holy King. The same is the meaning of: “who hears the words of El” and “knows the knowledge of the most High” (Ibid.) that he knew the times when Judgment impends on the world and focuses on that time with his witchcraft.

424. אֲשֶׁר מַחֲזֵה שַׁדַּי יֶחֱזֶה, מַאן מַחֲזֵה שַׁדַּי. אִלֵּין אִינּוּן נֹפֵל וּגְלוּי עֵינָיִם. וְאִלֵּין אִינּוּן עֲזָ"א וַעֲזָאֵ"ל. נֹפֵל: דָּא עֲזָ"א, דְּאָעְמִיק לֵיהּ קוּדְשָׁא בְּרִיךְ הוּא בְּעוּמְקָא חֲשׁוֹכָא, וְיָתִיב בְּעוּמְקָא עַד קְדָלֵיהּ כִּדְקָאַמְרָן, וַחֲשׁוֹכָא אִזְדְּרַק בְּאַנְפּוֹי. וְעַל דָּא אִקְרֵי נוֹפֵל. נָפַל זִמְנָא חֲדָא מִן שְׁמַיָּא, וְנָפַל זִמְנָא אַחֲרָא, לְבָתַר, בְּעוּמְקָא דַּחֲשׁוֹכָא. עֲזָאֵ"ל: הוּא גְּלוּי עֵינַיִם, דְּהָא לָא אִזְדְּרַק חֲשׁוֹכָא עָלֵיהּ, דְּלָא אִתְתָּקַף, וְלָא אַרְגִּיז כְּהַהוּא דִּלְעֵילָּא. וּבִלְעָם קָרֵי לוֹן מַחֲזֵה שַׁדַּי, דְּאִינּוּן נֹפֵל וּגְלוּי עֵינָיִם.

424. "Who sees the vision of Shadai" (Ibid.). What is "the vision of Shadai"? These are "falling down" and "having his eyes open," which refer to Aza and Azael. "Falling down" is Aza. WHY WAS HE CALLED "FALLING"? That is because the Holy One, blessed be He, stuck him into the depths of darkness where he stays with it up to his neck, as we mentioned, and darkness gets hurled into his face. That is why he is referred to by "falling down," because he fell from heaven and next he fell once more into the depths of darkness. Azael is "having his eyes open," because he was not covered with darkness, because he neither provoked nor angered like the one before, MEANING AZA. Bilaam referred to them by the words, "the vision of Shadai," which are "falling down" and "having his eyes open."

425. וּבְהַהוּא זִמְנָא, לָא אִשְׁתְּאַר בְּעָלְמָא, דְּיִשְׁתְּכַח גַּבַּיְיהוּ, בַּר אִיהוּ. וּבְכָל יוֹמָא, הֲוָה אַסְתִּים בְּאִינּוּן טוּרֵי עִמְּהוֹן. הה"ד, יַנְחֵנִי בָלָק מֶלֶךְ מוֹאָב מֵהַרְרֵי קֶדֶם. מֵהַרְרֵי קֶדֶם וַדַּאי, וְלָא מֵאֶרֶץ בְּנֵי קֶדֶם.

425. During that time, there was nobody in the world who was with them, AZA AND AZAEL, except for him, BILAAM, who would daily shut himself with them in those mountains. That is why it says, "Balak the king of Moab has brought me from Aram, out of the mountains of old," surely from "the mountains of old," WHICH ARE THE MOUNTAINS OF THE DARKNESS, AS MENTIONED, and not from the land of the people of the east (also: 'of old').

426. אר"ש, כַּמָּה זִמְנִין אֲמֵינָא מִלָּה דָּא, וְלָא מִסְתַּכְּלֵי חַבְרַיָּיא, דְּהָא קוּדְשָׁא בְּרִיךְ הוּא לָא שַׁרְיָא שְׁכִינְתָּא, אֶלָּא בַּאֲתָר קַדִּישָׁא, בַּאֲתָר דְּאִתְחֲזֵי לְשַׁרְיָא עֲלוֹי. וְכֵן קוּדְשָׁא בְּרִיךְ הוּא מַכְרִיז וְאָמַר, לֹא יִמָּצֵא בְךָ מַעֲבִיר בְּנוֹ וְגוֹ'. וְהוּא אָתֵי לְאִתְעָרְבָא בַּהֲדַיְיהוּ. אֶלָּא זַכָּאָה חוּלָקֵיהוֹן דְּיִשְׂרָאֵל, דְּקוּדְשָׁא בְּרִיךְ הוּא קַדִּישׁ לוֹן לְשַׁרְיָא בֵּינַיְיהוּ. וְהַיְינוּ דִּכְתִּיב, כִּי יְיָ' אֱלֹהֶיךָ מִתְהַלֵּךְ בְּקֶרֶב מַחֲנֶיךָ וְגוֹ'. וּבְגִין דְּהוּא מִתְהַלֵּךְ בְּקֶרֶב מַחֲנֶיךָ, כְּתִיב וְהָיָה מַחֲנֶיךָ קָדוֹשׁ וְגוֹ'. וּכְתִיב וִהְיִיתֶם קְדוֹשִׁים וְגוֹ'. וּכְתִיב אַל תִּטַּמְּאוּ בְּכָל אֵלֶּה וְגוֹ'. וּכְתִיב וָאָקֻץ בָּם וְגוֹ'. דְּלָא יָכִילְנָא לְקָרְבָא גַּבַּיְיהוּ, וְשָׁרוּ לִי לְבַר. זַכָּאָה חוּלָקֵהוֹן דְּיִשְׂרָאֵל, וְזַכָּאָה חוּלָקֵהוֹן דִּנְבִיאֵי מְהֵימְנֵי קַדִּישֵׁי, דְּאִינּוּן קַדִּישִׁין, וְאִית לוֹן

חוּלָקָא לְאִשְׁתַּמְשָׁא בִּקְדוּשָּׁה עִלָּאָה.

426. Rabbi Shimon said, How many times I have said this and the friends do not observe that the Holy One, blessed be He, allows His Shechinah to dwell only in a holy place, a place that is fit to rest on. That is how the Holy One, blessed be He, proclaims and says, "There must not be found among you anyone that makes his son or his daughter to pass..." (Devarim 18:10). And he, BILAAM, comes to mix among them. Praised is the lot of Yisrael that the Holy One, blessed be He, sanctified them to dwell among them. That is the meaning of: "For Hashem, your Elohim walks in the midst of your camp..." (Devarim 23:15). Because He walks in the midst of your camp, it is written: "Therefore shall your camp be holy" (Ibid.), and: "And be holy ..." (Vayikra 20:7). It is also written: "Defile not yourselves in any of these things..." (Vayikra 18:24), and: "and therefore I abhorred them..." (Vayikra 20:23), because I can not come near to them and they cause Me to dwell without. Praised is Yisrael's lot and praised is the holy faithful prophets' lot. They are sanctified and they have a part to benefit in the higher holiness.

44. "And the she-mule saw the angel of Hashem," part two

A Synopsis

Rabbi Shimon says that the mission of the angel was intended both to help the she-mule and to punish Bilaam. From the rabbis we learn several meanings of this event and of the ass's deviation from the path of witchcraft. Rabbi Aba talks about the four colors that adorn Malchut when she wants to unite with Zeir Anpin, and about the twelve boundaries. We hear the esoteric description of the rows of towers and the movement of the wheels and the ascension and descent of the crowns. When the mating draws blessings from above those blessings all flow to the children of Yisrael, who send part of them to sustain the other nations. That residue is the meaning of "a path of the vineyards," toward which Bilaam had turned his she-mule. The angel blocked that path to prevent him from drawing energy from there. Rabbi Chiya tells us that the speech of the she-mule made Bilaam realize that his power had been broken, since it was God who made the she-mule speak. Because Bilaam responded to the silly she-mule he showed himself to be a fool.

427. וַתֵּרֶא הָאָתוֹן אֶת מַלְאַךְ יְיָ׳ נִצָּב בַּדֶּרֶךְ וְחַרְבּוֹ שְׁלוּפָה בְּיָדוֹ, בַּדֶּרֶךְ, בְּהַהוּא אָרְחָא דַּהֲוָה אִשְׁתְּקַע בְּגַוָּוה. וְחַרְבּוֹ שְׁלוּפָה בְּיָדוֹ, וְכִי אִי אִיהוּ נָפִיק לְקָבֵיל הַאי אָתוֹן, מַאי בָּעֵי חַרְבָּא. וְאִי אִיהוּ נָפִיק לְקָבְלֵיהּ דְּבִלְעָם, אֲמַאי חָמָאת אֲתָנֵיהּ, וְאִיהוּ לָא חָמָא. אֶלָּא כֹּלָּא אִזְדְּמַן. הַהוּא מַלְאָכָא מִזְדְּמַן לְקָבְלֵיהּ דְּאָתוֹן, לְאַפָּקָא לָהּ מִן הַהוּא אָרְחָא דְּאִתְטְעַן בָּהּ. וּבְמָה. בְּרַחֲמֵי. וְאִזְדְּמַן לְקָבְלֵיהּ דְּבִלְעָם, לְאַעְנְשָׁא לֵיהּ, עַל דְּאִיהוּ הֲוָה בָּעֵי לְמֵיהַךְ בִּרְשׁוּתֵיהּ, וְלָא בִּרְשׁוּתָא דִּלְעֵילָּא.

427. "And the she-mule saw the angel of Hashem standing in the way, and his sword drawn in his hand" (Bemidbar 22:23). "In the way" means in that path into which he was sinking, THE WAY OF WITCHCRAFT AND SORCERY. "And his sword drawn in his hand": HE ASKS, If his mission was against the she-mule, what need was there for the sword? If his intentions were against Bilaam, why did the see him but Bilaam was unable to perceive him? HE RESPONDS: It must be that his mission was intended against all, BOTH TO THE SHE-MULE AND BILAAM. The angel came before the she-mule to help her out from the way loaded on her, MEANING THE WITCHCRAFT AND SORCERY THAT WERE PLACED ON THE SHE-MULE. How DID HE RELIEVE HER? With compassion. And he stood against Bilaam to punish him for his intention to follow his own authority rather than a higher authority.

428. א״ר יוֹסֵי, הַשְׁתָּא אִית לְשָׁאֲלָא, אִי מִלּוֹי הֲווֹ אַתְיָין מִסִּטְרָא דְּכִתְרִין תַּתָּאִין, וְלָא מֵאֲתָר אַחֲרָא, אֲמַאי כְּתִיב וַיָּבֹא אֱלֹהִים אֶל בִּלְעָם וְגוֹ׳, וְאַךְ אֶת הַדָּבָר וְגוֹ׳. א״ר יִצְחָק הָכִי אוֹלִיפְנָא. דְּהַאי אֱלֹהִים דְּהָכָא כֻּלְּהוּ מַלְאָכָא הֲוָה. וְהַהוּא אִיהוּ אֲתָר דְּאָתֵי מִסִּטְרָא דְּדִינָא קַשְׁיָא, דְּבֵיהּ אֲחִידָן חֵילָא וְתוּקְפָּא דְּאִינּוּן כִּתְרִין תַּתָּאִין, דְּהֲוָה מִשְׁתַּמֵּשׁ בְּהוּ בִּלְעָם. ובג״כ, וַיָּבֹא אֱלֹהִים אֶל בִּלְעָם. וַיֹּאמֶר אֱלֹהִים אֶל בִּלְעָם. דִּלְזִמְנִין אִתְקְרֵי מַלְאָכָא בִּשְׁמָא עִלָּאָה.

428. Rabbi Yosi said, Now there is room to question if BILAAM'S utterances were from the aspects of the lower Sfirot and not from an other place, as it is written: "And Elohim came to Bilaam...but only that word...." (Bemidbar 22:20) Rabbi Yitzchak said, This is how I learned that all these references to Elohim here were referring to an angel, who came from the aspect of harsh Judgment, to which are linked the power and strength of the lower crowns of which Bilaam made use. Hence, IT IS WRITTEN: "And Elohim came to Bilaam," and, "And Elohim said to Bilaam" (Ibid. 12), because an angel is sometimes referred to by a supernal name.

429. וַתֵּט הָאָתוֹן מִן הַדֶּרֶךְ, סָטָאת מִן הַהוּא אָרְחָא, דַּהֲוַת טְעִינָא מִסִּטְרָא דְּדִינָא קַשְׁיָא, לְקַבְלֵיהוֹן דְּיִשְׂרָאֵל. וּבְמָה חָמָא בִּלְעָם, דְּהִיא סָטָאת מֵהַהוּא אָרְחָא. אֶלָּא הָכִי אר״ש, דַּאֲפִילּוּ בְּאָרְחָא, בָּעָא לְאַבְאָשָׁא לְהוּ לְיִשְׂרָאֵל, בְּחֵילָא דַּאֲתָנֵיהּ. וְכֵיוָן דְּלָא סָלִיק בִּידוֹי, מַה כְּתִיב, וַיַּךְ אֶת הָאָתוֹן בַּמַּקֵּל. אַטְעָן לָהּ, וְאַלְבָּשׁ לָהּ, בִּזְרוּזֵי דִּינָא קַשְׁיָא תַּקִּיפָא. הה״ד בַּמַּקֵּל. בַּמַּקֵּל דַּיְיקָא. דְּאִיהוּ דִּינָא קַשְׁיָא תַּקִּיפָא. בְּמַקְלוֹ לָא כְּתִיב, אֶלָּא בַּמַּקֵּל.

429. "And the she-mule turned aside out of the way" (Ibid. 23), meaning that she deviated from the aspect that she was encumbered with, the aspect of harsh Judgment against Yisrael. HE ASKS: How did Bilaam perceive that she deviated from that path? Rabbi Shimon only meant to say that, even along the road, he wished to harm Yisrael with the strength of his she-mule. Since he was unable to, it is written, "And he struck the she-mule with a staff" (Ibid. 27), MEANING THAT he burdened her and loaded her with the powers of harsh and forceful judgment. That is why it is written, "with a staff" and "staff" is precise, which alludes to powerful and harsh Judgment. It is not written: 'his staff', but rather "a staff," WHICH INDICATES THAT WELL-KNOWN STAFF THAT IS HARSH JUDGMENT.

430. פּוּק חָמֵי, כַּמָּה תַּקִּיפָא חָכְמְתָא דְּהַהוּא רָשָׁע, וְתִיאוּבְתָּא דִּילֵיהּ לְאַבְאָשָׁא לְהוֹן לְיִשְׂרָאֵל, דְּאִיהוּ אַשְׁגַּח לְנָפְקָא מֵרְשׁוּתָא דִּלְעֵילָּא, בְּגִין דְּתִיאוּבְתֵּיהּ לְאִתְיַיקְּרָא, וּלְאַבְאָשָׁא לְהוּ לְיִשְׂרָאֵל.

430. Come out and see how powerful and effective was the wisdom of the wicked one and his passion to harm Yisrael, because he was careful to leave the authority above, THAT PREVENTS HIM FROM THAT due to his passion to have honor and to harm Yisrael.

431. וַיַּעֲמוֹד מַלְאַךְ יְיָ' בְּמִשְׁעוֹל הַכְּרָמִים וְגוֹ'. מַה כְּתִיב לְעֵילָּא, בְּקַדְמֵיתָא כְּתִיב, וַתֵּט הָאָתוֹן מִן הַדֶּרֶךְ וַתֵּלֶךְ בַּשָּׂדֶה, וַתֵּלֶךְ בְּאֹרַח מֵישָׁר, מִסִּטְרָא דְּשָׂדֶה, וְאִרְכִּינַת מִמַּה דַּהֲוָה בָּהּ. וַיַּךְ בִּלְעָם אֶת הָאָתוֹן לְהַטּוֹתָהּ הַדָּרֶךְ לְאַסְטָאָה לָהּ מֵהַהוּא אָרְחָא דְּשָׂדֶה. אָמַר רִבִּי יוֹסֵי, בֵּין מַלְאָכָא וּבֵין בִּלְעָם הֲוַת אֲתָנָא בְּעָאקוּ. לְבָתַר כַּד חָמָא בִּלְעָם, דְּלָא הֲוָה יָכִיל, כְּדֵין וַיַּךְ אֶת הָאָתוֹן בַּמַּקֵּל. כְּמָה דְּאִתְּמַר.

431. "But the angel of Hashem stood in a path of the vineyards..." (Bemidbar 22:24). What is written above? At first, it is written: "And the she-mule turned aside out of the way, and went into the field," meaning it followed a straight course in the side of field, WHICH IS MALCHUT, and deviated from what was instilled in her, FROM THE COURSE OF WITCHCRAFT WITH WHICH BILAAM HAD BURDENED HER. "And Bilaam smote the she-mule, to turn her into the way" (Ibid. 23), meaning to diverge from that course of the field, WHICH IS MALCHUT OF HOLINESS, TO THE COURSE OF HIS WITCHCRAFT. Rabbi Yosi said, Between the angel and

Bilaam, the she-mule found herself in great distress. Afterward, when Bilaam realized that he was unable TO DEVIATE HER FROM THE COURSE OF THAT FIELD, then "he struck the she-mule with a staff," as we explained, THAT STAFF REFERS TO HARSH JUDGMENT.

432. וַיַּעֲמוֹד מַלְאַךְ יְיָ׳ וְגוֹ׳. א״ר אַבָּא, כַּמָּה אִית לָן לְאִסְתַּכְּלָא בְּמִלֵּי דְּאוֹרַיְיתָא, הָנֵי קְרָאֵי רְמִיזֵי בְּחָכְמְתָא עִלָּאָה. וְכִי לְמַגָּנָא נָפַק הַאי מַלְאָכָא, לְאִתְחֲזָאָה לְחַד אֲתָנָא. אוֹ לְמֵיקָם בֵּין כַּרְמַיָּיא לָקֳבְלָהּ, זִמְנָא הָכָא וְזִמְנָא הָכָא. אֶלָּא כֹּלָּא רָזָא עִלָּאָה הוּא, וְכֹלָּא בָּעֵי קוּדְשָׁא בְּרִיךְ הוּא בְּגִין לְאַגָּנָא עֲלַיְיהוּ דְּיִשְׂרָאֵל, וְלָא יִשְׁלְטוּ בְּהוּ זִינִין בִּישִׁין, בְּגִין דְּאִינּוּן חוּלָקֵיהּ דקוּדְשָׁא בְּרִיךְ הוּא.

432. "But the angel of Hashem stood..." Rabbi Aba said, How important it is for us to pay attention to the words of the Torah. These verses are imbued with higher wisdom. Is it in vain that this angel comes out, to be seen to one she-mule, or to stand against her between the vineyards, now here and now there? It is only that it is a higher secret and with everything, the Holy One, blessed be He, wished to protect Yisrael, so they would not be controlled by evil beings because they are the lot of the Holy One, blessed be He.

433. וַיַּעֲמוֹד מַלְאַךְ יְיָ׳ וְגוֹ׳. תָּאנָא, מִסִּטְרָא דְּאִמָּא, כַּד אִיהִי מִתְעַטְּרָא, נָפְקִין בְּעִטְרָהָא אֲלַף וַחֲמֵשׁ מְאָה סִטְרֵי גְּלִיפִין בְּתַכְשִׁיטָהָא. וְכַד בָּעָאת לְאִזְדַּוְּוגָא בְּמַלְכָּא, מִתְעַטְּרָא בְּחַד עַטְרָא דְּאַרְבַּע גְּוָונִין. אִינּוּן גְּוָונִין מִתְלַהֲטָן בְּאַרְבַּע סִטְרֵי עָלְמָא, כָּל גְּוָונָא וּגְוָונָא מִתְלַהֲטָא תְּלַת זִמְנִין בְּהַהוּא סִטְרָא. דְּאִינּוּן תְּרֵיסָר תְּחוּמֵי גְּלִיפִין. וְעָאלִין וְאִתְכְּלִילוּ בִּתְרֵיסַר אַחֲרָנִין.

433. "But the angel of Hashem stood in a path of the vineyards." We were taught that when she, MALCHUT, is adorned from the aspect of Ima, in her decorations appear 1,500 aspects engraved on her ornaments. When she, MALCHUT, wants to unite with the king, THAT IS ZEIR ANPIN, she gets adorned with a crown of four colors. Those colors glow in the four directions of the world, and each and every color glows three times in its direction, which are the twelve marked boundaries. They come to be included in twelve others.

434. בְּרֵישָׁא דְּעַטְרָא, אִית ד׳ שׁוּרִין לְד׳ סִטְרִין, וְאִינּוּן מִגְדָּלוֹת, כד״א מִגְדְּלוֹת מֶרְקָחִים. מַהוּ מֶרְקָחִים. כְּמָה דְּאַתְּ אָמֵר, מִכָּל אַבְקַת רוֹכֵל. וְעַל כָּל מַגְדְּלָא וּמַגְדְּלָא ג׳ פִּתְחִין, קְבִיעִין בְּאַבְנִין טָבָן, מִכָּל סִטְרָא וְסִטְרָא. הַאי עַטְרָא, נְהִירָא בְּדִלּוּגִין דְּאוֹפִיר, בְּגִין יְקָרָא דְּמַלְכָּא, כְּמָה דִּכְתִּיב אוֹקִיר אֱנוֹשׁ מִפָּז וְגוֹ׳.

434. At the top of that crown, there are four rows to four directions – NORTH, SOUTH, EAST, WEST – which are ROWS OF towers, as it says, "Banks (also: 'towers') of fragrant flowers" (Shir Hashirim 5:13). What is "fragrant"? It is as it says, "With all powders of the merchant" (Ibid. 3:6). On each tower are three portals, set with fine stones around each side. This crown shines with engravings of precious gold of Ophir for the glory of the King, as is written: "I will make men more rare than fine gold; and mankind, than the pure gold of Ophir" (Yeshayah 13:12).

435. תְּחוֹת עַטְרָא, תַּלְיָין זָגֵי דְּדַהֲבָא בְּסַחֲרָנָהָא, זָגָא דְּדַהֲבָא מִסִּטְרָא דָּא, וְזָגָא דְּדַהֲבָא מִסִּטְרָא דָּא, וְחַד רִמּוֹנָא. בְּגוֹ הַהוּא רִמּוֹנָא, אִית בָּהּ אֲלַף זָגִין, וְכָל זָגָא מִנַּיְיהוּ, מִתְלַהֲטָא בְּסוּמָקָא בְּחִוָּורָא. הַהוּא רִמּוֹנָא אִתְפְּלַג בִּפְלוּגִין אַרְבַּע, וְקַיְּימָא פְּתִיחָא, לְאִתְחֲזָאָה זָגָהָא. תְּלַת מְאָה וְעֶשְׂרִין וַחֲמֵשׁ זָגִין לְסִטְרָא דָּא, וְכֵן לְכָל סִטְרָא וְסִטְרָא, עַד דְּמִתְלַהֲטָן אַרְבַּע סִטְרֵי עָלְמָא, מֵחֵיזוּ דְּכָל פִּלְכָּא וּפִלְכָּא, וְאִינּוּן אִקְרוּן פֶּלַח הָרִמּוֹן. כְּמָה דִּכְתִּיב, כְּפֶלַח הָרִמּוֹן רַקָּתֵךְ מִבַּעַד לְצַמָּתֵךְ.

435. Under the crown, gold bells are suspended all around, a gold bell from this side, a gold bell from that side, and one pomegranate. Within that pomegranate, there are a thousand bells and each one of those bells glows in red and in white. That pomegranate is divided into four segments and stays open to display its bells. There are 325 bells to this side and similarly to each and every side until all the four directions in the world glow from the display of each individual segment. They are referred to as "a piece of a pomegranate," as is written: "Your cheek is like a piece of a pomegranate within your locks" (Shir Hashirim 4:3).

436. אַרְבַּע גַּלְגַּלִּין בְּפִלְכֵי אַרְבַּע, נַטְלִין בְּגַלְגּוּלָא לְהַהוּא עַטְרָא, וְכַד

נַטְלֵי לָהּ, אִזְדַּקְּפָן לְעֵילָא. עַד דְּמָטוּ לְגַלְגּוּלָא דְּפִלְכָּא עִלָּאָה, דְּנָהִים יְמָמָא וְלֵילְיָא, מִתְחַבְּרָן כָּל אִינּוּן פִּלְכִין, וְנַטְלִין לְעַטְרָא, וְזַקְפָן לָהּ. וְקָלָא דְּאִינּוּן גַּלְגַּלִּין, אִשְׁתְּמַע בְּכֻלְּהוּ רְקִיעִין. לְקַל נְעִימוּתָא מִתְרַעֲשִׁין כָּל חֵילֵי שְׁמַיָא, וְכֻלְּהוּ שָׁאֲלִין דָּא לְדָא, עַד דְּכֻלְּהוּ אַמְרֵי בָּרוּךְ כְּבוֹד יְיָ' מִמְּקוֹמוֹ.

436. The four wheels in the four segments OF THE POMEGRANATE take, through rolling, that crown. When they have taken it, they elevate themselves upwards, until they reach wheels in the upper segment, that moans day and night. THEN all these segments join and take that crown and lift it upright and the sound of these wheels reverberates throughout the firmaments. Hearing this melodious sound, all the legions of heaven are excited and all ask one another about it, until all recite and proclaim: "Blessed be the glory of Hashem from His place" (Yechezkel 3:12).

437. כַּד מִזְדַּוֵּוג מַלְכָּא בְּמַטְרוֹנִיתָא, סַלְּקָא עַטְרָא דָּא, וְאִתְיַשָּׁבַת בְּרֵישָׁא דְּמַטְרוֹנִיתָא. כְּדֵין נָחִית חַד עַטְרָא עִלָּאָה, קְבִיעָא דְּכָל אֶבֶן טָבָא, וְחֵיזוּר וְשׁוֹשָׁן, בְּסַחֲרָנָהָא. בְּשִׁית גַּלְגַּלִּין אַתְיָא, לְשִׁית סִטְרִין דְּעָלְמָא, שִׁית גַּדְפִּין דְּנֶשֶׁר נַטְלִין לָהּ. חַמְשִׁין עֲנָבִין סַחֲרָנָהָא, דְּגָלִיף בָּהּ אִימָּא עִלָּאָה. קְבִיעָאן בְּאֶבֶן טָבָא, חִוָּור וְסוּמָק יָרוֹק וְאוּכָם תְּכֵלָא וְאַרְגְּוָונָא. שִׁית מְאָה וּתְלַת עֲשַׂר זִוּוִין, לְכָל סִטְרָא וְסִטְרָא.

437. When the King, THAT IS ZEIR ANPIN, units with the Matron, THAT IS MALCHUT, this crown is elevated and set on the head of the Matron, ONLY WHEN ZEIR ANPIN IS JOINED WITH MALCHUT. Then one higher crown descends, ALSO TO ZEIR ANPIN, that is set around with every fine gem, and bulbs and flowers. It is equipped with six circles to the six directions of the world, carried by the six wings of the eagle; fifty grapes are surrounding THAT CROWN, engraved on it by supernal Ima, BINAH. They are set with precious gems, WHOSE COLORS ARE white, red, green, black and purple, with 613 lights to each and every direction.

438. אֶלֶף וְשִׁית מְאָה מִגְדָּלִין, לְכָל סִטְרָא וְסִטְרָא. וְכָל מַגְדְּלָא וּמַגְדְּלָא, טוּרִין קְבִיעִין. פַּרְחִין לְעֵילָּא, אִשְׁתְּאֲבָן בְּפִתּוֹרָא דְּאִימָּא

עִלָּאָה, בְּמִשְׁחָא רְבוּת דִּילָהּ. כְּדֵין אִימָּא, בִּלְחִישׁוּ, נָגִיד מַתְּנָן עִלָּאִין, וְשָׁדַר וְקָבַע לוֹן בְּהַהוּא עֲטָרָא. לְבָתַר אַנְגִּיד נַחֲלֵי דִּמְשַׁח רְבוּת קַדִּישָׁא, עַל רֵישָׁא דְּמַלְכָּא. וּמֵרֵישֵׁיהּ, נָחִית הַהוּא מִשְׁחָא טָבָא עִלָּאָה, עַל דִּיקְנֵיהּ יַקִּירָא. וּמִתַּמָּן נָגִיד עַל אִינּוּן לְבוּשֵׁי מַלְכָּא. הה״ד, כַּשֶּׁמֶן הַטּוֹב עַל הָרֹאשׁ יוֹרֵד עַל הַזָּקָן וְגו׳.

438. There are 1,600 towers to each and every direction and each individual tower is MADE OF permanently set rows (Heb. *turim*), MEANING THAT EACH TOWER IS SURROUNDED WITH A FEW HOUSES, DERIVED FROM *TURIM*. They blossom above and get their sustenance from the table of supernal Ima, WHO IS BINAH, from her anointing oil. Then the supernal Ima quietly bestows supernal gifts, sends them and sets them into that crown. Afterward, she endows abundant rivers of holy anointing oil on the King's head, ZEIR ANPIN. From His head, that supernal, precious oil flows down on His glorious beard and from there it flows over the King's garments. That is what is written: "It is like the precious ointment upon the head, running down upon the beard..." (Tehilim 133:2).

439. לְבָתַר אִתְהַדָּר עֲטָרָא, וּמְעַטְּרָא לֵיהּ אִימָּא עִילָּאָה בְּהַהוּא עֲטָרָא, וּפְרִישָׂא עָלֵיהּ, וְעַל מַטְרוֹנִיתָא, לְבוּשֵׁי יְקָר בְּהַהוּא עֲטָרָא. כְּדֵין קָלָא אִשְׁתְּמַע בְּכֻלְּהוּ עָלְמִין, צְאֶינָה וּרְאֶינָה וְגו׳. כְּדֵין חֶדְוָותָא הוּא בְּכָל אִינּוּן בְּנֵי מַלְכָּא. וּמַאן אִינּוּן. כָּל אִינּוּן דְּאָתוּ מִסִּטְרַיְיהוּ דְּיִשְׂרָאֵל. דְּהָא לָא מִזְדַּוְּוגֵי בְּהוּ, וְלָא קַיְימִין עִמְּהוֹן, בַּר אִינּוּן יִשְׂרָאֵל, דְּאִינּוּן בְּנֵי בֵּיתָא, וּמְשַׁמְּשֵׁי לְהוּ. כְּדֵין בִּרְכָאן דְּנָפְקֵי מִנַּיְיהוּ, דְּיִשְׂרָאֵל הוּא.

439. Afterwards, the crown returns. Supernal Ima decorates ZEIR ANPIN with this crown and spreads over ZEIR ANPIN and over Malchut glorious garments with that crown. Then the sound reverberates throughout the worlds: "Go forth, O daughters of Zion, and behold King Solomon with the crown, with which his mother crowned him" (Shir Hashirim 3:11). KING SOLOMON IS ZEIR ANPIN AND HIS MOTHER IS BINAH. She then rejoices with all the King's children. Who are they? They are all those who come from the side of Yisrael, because they do not join with them WITH THE UNION OF ZEIR ANPIN AND MALCHUT. None stay with them except

Yisrael, who are of her household and serve them, WHICH MEANS THEY RAISE MAYIN NUKVIN (FEMALE WATERS) THROUGH THEIR TORAH STUDY AND PRAYER THAT AWAKEN THE UNION. As a consequence, the blessings that emerge from them, FROM THE UNION OF ZEIR ANPIN AND MALCHUT, belong to Yisrael.

440. וְיִשְׂרָאֵל נַטְלִין כֹּלָּא, וּמְשַׁדְּרֵי חוּלָקָא מִנֵּיהּ לִשְׁאַר עַמִּין, וּמֵהַהוּא חוּלָקָא אִתְזָנוּ כָּל אִינּוּן שְׁאַר עַמִּין. וְתָאנָא, מִבֵּין סִטְרֵי חוּלָקֵהוֹן דִּמְמָנָן עַל שְׁאַר עַמִּין, נָפִיק חַד שְׁבִיל דָּקִיק, דְּמִתַּמָּן, אִתְנְגִיד חוּלָקָא לְאִינּוּן תַּתָּאֵי, וּמִתַּמָּן מִתְפְּרַשׁ לְכַמָּה סִטְרִין. וְדָא קָרֵינָן לֵיהּ תַּמְצִית, דְּנָפִיק מִסִּטְרָא דְּאַרְעָא קַדִּישָׁא.

440. And Yisrael take everything, MEANING ALL THE BLESSINGS THAT RESULT FROM THE ILLUMINATION OF THE UNION OF ZEIR ANPIN AND MALCHUT. They send part of them to the rest of the nations and from that part are sustained all the rest of the nations. We have learned that the parts of the lower beings, MEANING THE OUTER FORCES, AND THE OTHER NATIONS OF THE WORLD, are drawn from a very fine path which emerges from between the aspects of the portions of the ministers of the heathen nations. From there, it separates to several directions. That is what we called 'the residue' that emanates from the side of the Holy Land, THAT IS MALCHUT.

441. וְעַל דָּא עָלְמָא כּוּלֵּיהּ מִתַּמְצִית דְּאֶרֶץ יִשְׂרָאֵל קָא שָׁתֵי. מַאן א"י. הָא אוֹקִימְנָא. וּבֵין לְעֵילָּא, וּבֵין לְתַתָּא, כָּל אִינּוּן שְׁאַר עַמִּין עכו"ם, לָא אִתְזָנוּ אֶלָּא מֵהַהוּא תַּמְצִית. וְלָא תֵּימָא דְּאִינּוּן בִּלְחוֹדוֹי, אֶלָּא אֲפִילּוּ אִינּוּן כִּתְרִין תַּתָּאִין, מֵהַהוּא תַּמְצִית שַׁתְיָין. וְדָא הוּא בְּמִשְׁעוֹל הַכְּרָמִים, שְׁבִיל מֵרַבְרְבֵי שְׁאַר עַמִּין דְּמִתְבָּרְכָן מִנֵּיהּ.

441. Therefore, the whole world drinks from the residue of the land of Yisrael. What is that land of Yisrael? We have already explained THAT THE LAND OF YISRAEL IS MALCHUT. Both above and below, all the rest of the heathen nations are sustained only from that residue. Do not think it is just they themselves, for even the lowest Sfirot drink from that residue. This is the meaning of "a path of the vineyards." That is the path from the chief ministers of the rest of the nations, who are blessed from it.

442. כַּד חָמָא הַהוּא מַלְאָכָא, דְּהָא בִּלְעָם אַסְטֵי לְאָתוֹן לְהַהוּא שְׁבִילָא, דִּכְתִּיב לְהַטּוֹתָהּ הַדָּרֶךְ, מִיַּד וַיַּעֲמוֹד מַלְאַךְ יְיָ׳ בְּמִשְׁעוֹל הַכְּרָמִים, לְאַסְתְּמָא שְׁבִילָא, דְּלָא יִסְתַּיְּיעוּן בֵּיהּ אִינּוּן שְׁאַר עַמִּין עכו״ם, וְאִינּוּן כִּתְרִין תַּתָּאִין. וְאָזְלָא הָא, כְּהָא דְּאָמַר רַבִּי יִצְחָק, כְּתִיב שָׂמוּנִי נוֹטֵרָה וְגוֹ׳, לְנַטְרָא וּלְבָרְכָא לִשְׁאַר עַמִּין בְּגָלוּתָא. וְיִשְׂרָאֵל דְּאִינּוּן כַּרְמִי שֶׁלִּי, לֹא נָטַרְתִּי, בְּגִין דְּאִינּוּן בְּגָלוּתָא, וְלָא מִתְבָּרְכִין כַּדְּקָא חָזֵי.

442. When the angel saw that Bilaam had turned his she-mule towards that path, THAT IS REFERRED TO AS "A PATH OF THE VINEYARD" IN ORDER TO CONVEY FROM THERE THE POWER TO CURSE YISRAEL, It says, "To turn her into the way." THIS INDICATES THE PATH PRACTICED BY THE OUTER FORCES, WHICH IS A PATH OF THE VINEYARD, THROUGH WHICH THEY RECEIVE ALL THEIR SUSTENANCE. Instantly, "the Angel of Hashem stood in a path of the vineyards" to block that path, so the rest of the heathen nations would not be able to be helped by it nor would the lower Sfirot OF THE OUTER FORCES. "A PATH OF THE VINEYARDS" accords with the words of Rabbi Yitzchak that it is written, "They made me the keeper of the vineyards" (Shir Hashirim 1:6), meaning to preserve and bless, during the exile, the rest of the nations THAT ARE CALLED "VINEYARDS." "I have not kept" (Ibid.) Yisrael who are "my own vineyard" (Ibid.), because they are in exile, and are not properly blessed as they deserve.

443. גָּדֵר מִזֶּה וְגָדֵר מִזֶּה. אָמַר ר׳ אַבָּא, הֵיךְ יָכִיל הַהוּא מַלְאָכָא לְאַסְתְּמָא הַהוּא שְׁבִילָא. אֶלָּא בְּגִין דְּסִיוּעָא אַחֲרָא הֲוָה לֵיהּ, קוּדְשָׁא בְּרִיךְ הוּא וּכְנֶסֶת יִשְׂרָאֵל. ר׳ יְהוּדָה אָמַר, אוֹרַיְיתָא מְסַיְּיעָא לֵיהּ, דִּכְתִּיב מִזֶּה וּמִזֶּה הֵם כְּתוּבִים.

443. "A wall being on that side, and a wall on that side" (Bemidbar 22:24). Rabbi Aba said, How was it possible for the angel to block that path? HE REPLIES: It is only because he had another help, which was the Holy One, blessed be He, and the Congregation of Yisrael, WHICH IS MALCHUT. Rabbi Yehudah said, The Torah helped him out, because it is written: "On the one side and on the other were they written" (Shemot 32:15).

444. בְּהַהִיא שַׁעֲתָא מַה כְּתִיב. וַתֵּרֶא הָאָתוֹן וְגוֹ', וַתִּלָּחֵץ אֶל הַקִּיר, מַאי וַתִּלָּחֵץ אֶל הַקִּיר. כד"א מְקַרְקַר קִיר וְגוֹ'. קִיר: פַּטְרוֹנָא, הַהוּא דְּשַׁלְטָא עֲלַיְיהוּ. וַתִּלְחַץ אֶת רֶגֶל בִּלְעָם אֶל הַקִּיר, הִיא לָא יָהֲבָא לֵיהּ סִיּוּעָא כְּלַל. וּבְעָקוּתָא, אַשְׁדְּרַת לֵיהּ לְהַהוּא קִיר. וְרַמְזָא לֵיהּ הַאי, כְּדֵין וַיּוֹסֶף לְהַכּוֹתָהּ בְּהַאי סִטְרָא.

444. At that time, it is written: "And when the she-mule saw...she thrust herself to the wall" (Bemidbar 22:25). What is the meaning of, "she thrust herself to the wall"? HE RESPONDS: IT IS as is written: "A breaking down of walls" (Yeshayah 22:5). THAT WALL MEANS A PROTECTIVE WALL. HERE TOO, a wall MEANS a guardian, which is that FORCE which protects them. "And crushed Bilaam's foot against the wall" (Ibid.) MEANS that she, THE SHE-MULE, gave him no help at all, but in her distress she sent him to the wall, WHO IS THE CHIEF MINISTER THAT PROTECTS THEM. That is what she intimated to him, BY PRESSING HERSELF TO THE WALL. Then "he struck her again" (Ibid.) at that LEFT side.

445. וַיּוֹסֶף מַלְאַךְ יְיָ' עֲבוֹר וַיַּעֲמוֹד בְּמָקוֹם צַר וְגוֹ'. בְּהַהִיא שַׁעֲתָא, אַסְתִּים לָהּ כָּל אָרְחִין, וְכָל סִיּוּעִין, דְּלָא אִשְׁתְּכַח בָּהּ מִכָּל סִטְרָא דְּעָלְמָא סִיּוּעָא. כְּדֵין וַתִּרְבַּץ תַּחַת בִּלְעָם. כַּד חָמָא בִּלְעָם דְּלָא הֲוָה יָכִיל, מַה כְּתִיב. וַיִּחַר אַף בִּלְעָם וַיַּךְ אֶת הָאָתוֹן בַּמַּקֵּל, כְּמָה דְּאִתְּמַר, דְּאַטְעַן לָהּ, וְאַלְבַּשׁ לָהּ, בְּזִירוּזֵי דִּינָא קַשְׁיָא תַּקִּיפָא.

445. "And the angel of Hashem went further, and stood in a narrow place" (Ibid. 26). At that time, THE ANGEL closed up all the routes and supporting courses, so she would not have any help whatsoever from any side in the world. Then "she lay down under Bilaam" (Ibid. 27), MEANING SHE COUND NOT EVEN HINT TO FIND HELP, AS SHE DID BEFORE, SO HE WOULD ASK HELP FROM THE WALL, AS MENTIONED ABOVE. When Bilaam saw that he was powerless, it is written: "And Bilaam's anger burned, and he struck the she-mule with a staff" (Ibid.). We were taught that he loaded her and coursed her with weapons of forceful harsh Judgment, AS WE MENTIONED THERE.

446. וַיִּפְתַּח יְיָ' אֶת פִּי הָאָתוֹן וְגוֹ'. הַיְינוּ חַד מֵאִינּוּן מִלִּין, דְּאִתְבְּרִיאוּ

עֶרֶב שַׁבָּת בֵּין הַשְּׁמָשׁוֹת. א״ר יִצְחָק, מַאי סַגֵּי הַאי לְבִלְעָם, אוֹ לָאָתוֹן, אוֹ לְיִשְׂרָאֵל. בְּהָנֵי מִלִּין. א״ר יוֹסֵי, דְּחַיְיכִין בֵּיהּ אִינּוּן רַבְרְבִין דַּהֲווֹ עִמֵּיהּ, וְכַד מָטוּ לְבָלָק, אָמְרוּ לֵיהּ, וְכִי לְהַאי שַׁטְיָא שַׁדְרַת לְיָקְרָא, לָא תִּשְׁכַּח בֵּיהּ מַמָּשׁוּת, וְלָא בְּמִלּוֹי. וּבְאִינּוּן מִלָּה דַּאֲתָנָא, אִתְבְּזָא מִן יְקָרֵיהּ. ר׳ חִיָּיא אָמַר אִלְמָלֵי לָא אַמְרַת אֲתָנָא הַאי, לָא שָׁבִיק בִּלְעָם הַהוּא דִּילֵיהּ, וּבְמִלֵּי דַּאֲתָנָא יָדַע דְּאִתְּבַר חֵילֵיהּ.

446. “And Hashem opened the mouth of the she-mule...” (Ibid. 28): That is one of those things that were created on the eve of Shabbat at twilight. Rabbi Yitzchak said, What benefit is there from this, to Bilaam or to the she-mule or to Yisrael, in these speeches OF THE SHE-MULE? Rabbi Yosi said, The princes that were with him had a good laugh at him. When they reached Balak, they said to him, You will not find any substance in the speeches of this fool you sent us to call on; CONSEQUENTLY, with the utterances of his she-mule, he was disgraced. Rabbi Chiya said, If the she-mule was not spoken up with this, Bilaam would not have abandoned what was his. It is only through the utterances of his she-mule that he realized his power had been broken.

447. ר׳ אַבָּא רָמֵי, כְּתִיב וַתִּפְתַּח הָאָרֶץ וְגוֹ׳. וּכְתִיב וַיִּפְתַּח יְיָ׳ אֶת פִּי וְגוֹ׳. מַאי שְׁנָא אֶרֶץ מֵאָתוֹן, דְּלָא כְּתִיב בָּהּ וַיִּפְתַּח יְיָ׳ אֶת פִּי הָאָרֶץ. אֶלָּא, הָתָם מֹשֶׁה גָּזַר עַל פּוּמָא, וּפַתְחַת, וְעַבְדַת אַרְעָא פִּקוּדָא דְּמֹשֶׁה, וְלָא יַאוּת דְּקוּדְשָׁא בְּרִיךְ הוּא יַעֲבֹר פִּקוּדֵיהּ, דְּהָא מֹשֶׁה גָּזַר וּפָקִיד, וּפָצְתָה הָאֲדָמָה אֶת פִּיהָ. וְעַ״ד הִיא עַבְדַת פִּקוּדוֹי. דִּכְתִּיב וַתִּפְתַּח הָאָרֶץ אֶת פִּיהָ. אֲבָל הָכָא, לָא אִשְׁתְּכַח מַאן דְּגָזַר, אֶלָּא רְעוּתָא דְּקוּדְשָׁא בְּרִיךְ הוּא הֲוָה, וְהוֹאִיל וּרְעוּתֵיהּ הֲוָה בְּכַךְ, כְּתִיב וַיִּפְתַּח יְיָ׳ אֶת פִּי הָאָתוֹן. מִנֵּיהּ אָתָא מִלָּה, וּמִנֵּיהּ אִשְׁתְּכַח.

447. Rabbi Aba asked a difficult question. It is written: “and the earth opened her mouth” (Bemidbar 16:32) and it is written: “And Hashem opened the mouth of the she-mule.” Why the difference between the earth and the she-mule? It is not written REGARDING THE EARTH that ‘Hashem opened the mouth of the earth’. HE RESPONDS: It is only that there, it was Moses’ decree that the earth should open her mouth. And the earth performed the command of Moses by opening. It is not proper that Hashem should carry out an instruction commanded by Moses, seeing that Moses has decreed and instructed: "and the earth opens her mouth" (Ibid. 30). Hence, THE EARTH performed the command OF MOSES, as written: "And the earth opened her mouth." However, here, there was no one who had decreed, but it was only the wish of the Holy One, blessed be He. Since that was His desire, it is written: "And Hashem opened the mouth of the she-mule." It originated with Him and through Him, it occurred.

448. ר׳ יְהוּדָה אָמַר, אִסְתַּכַּלְנָא בְּפָרָשְׁתָא דָּא, וּבְאִלֵּין מִלִּין, וְאִתְחֲזְיָין דְּלָאו מִלִּין דִּצְרִיכִין אִינּוּן. וְכִי מֵאַחַר דִּכְתִּיב וְיִּפְתַּח יְיָ׳ אֶת פִּי הָאָתוֹן, בַּעְיָין לְמֶהֱוֵי אִינּוּן מִלִּין מִלֵּי מְעַלְיָיתָא, מִלֵּי דְּחָכְמְתָא, וְאִי כְּמָה דְּאַתְעֲרוּ חַבְרָנָא, דְּאִיהוּ מְשַׁבַּח דְּסוּסְיָא דִּילֵיהּ רָעֵי בִּרְטִיבָא, וְהִיא תָּבַת וְאַמְרַת, הֲלֹא אָנֹכִי אֲתוֹנְךָ. מֵהָכָא הֲוָה לָהּ לְמִפְתַּח, וְהִיא לָא פָּתְחָה אֶלָּא מֶה עָשִׂיתִי לְךָ. וְאִי הָכִי, אֲמַאי קָא טָרַח קוּדְשָׁא בְּרִיךְ הוּא, לְמִפְתַּח פּוּמָהּ לְהָנֵי מִלִּין.

448. Rabbi Yehuda said, I have studied this passage ABOUT THE "MOUTH OF THE SHE-MULE" and these words. These words seem not to be the needed ones, as it says, "And Hashem opened the mouth of that she-mule." It would have been more appropriate to have these utterances in matters of greater importance, words of wisdom. And if it is as the friends said, that Bilaam was taking pride in that his horse was in the pasture, AND THEREFORE HE HAD TO TAKE THE SHE-MULE, AND THE SHE-MULE has spoken up and said: "Am I not your she-mule, upon which you have ridden all your life to this day?" (Ibid. 30) THEN this is where she should have made her opening statement, but she merely started with: "What have I done to you" (Ibid. 28). If so, why did the Holy One, blessed be He, bother Himself to open her mouth with these words?

449. אָמַר רִבִּי אַבָּא, וַדַּאי בְּאִלֵּין מִלִּין אוֹלִיפְנָא דַּעְתָּא דְּבִלְעָם, דְּלָאו כְּדַאי הוּא לְמִשְׁרֵי עָלֵיהּ רוּחַ קוּדְשָׁא, וְאוֹלִיפְנָא, דְּהָא לֵית יָכִילוּ בְּאַתְנֵיהּ, לְאַבְאָשָׁא אוֹ לְאוֹטָבָא. וְאוֹלִיפְנָא מֵהַאי אָתוֹן, דְּהָא לֵית חֵילָא בִּבְעִירֵי לְאַשְׁרָאָה עֲלַיְיהוּ דַּעְתָּא שְׁלִים. ת״ח, בִּלְעָם, בְּהַהִיא

מִלָּה דַּאֲתָנֵיהּ, וּבְהַהוּא דַּעְתָּא טִפְּשָׁא לָא יָכִיל לְמֵיקָם. בְּדַעְתָּא עִלָּאָה עַל אַחַת כַּמָּה וְכַמָּה.

449. Rabbi Aba said, It is definite that through these words OF THE SHE-MULE, I would have learned the thoughts of Bilaam, that he was not worthy to have the Holy Spirit rest on him. I also learned that his she-mule had no power to do good or evil. I further learned from this she-mule that beasts do not have the strength, to instill them with full understanding AND CONSEQUENTLY SHE SPOKE NO WORDS OF WISDOM. Come and see that Bilaam could not comprehend the speech of his she-mule nor the silly thoughts OF HIS SHE-MULE. How much more would he be uncomprehending of the knowledge of the most High, YET HE CLAIMED THAT HE "KNOWS THE KNOWLEDGE OF THE MOST HIGH" (BEMIDBAR 24:16).

450. וַתֹּאמֶר לְבִלְעָם מֶה עָשִׂיתִי לְךָ. וְכִי בִּרְשׁוּתִי הֲוָה לְמֶעְבַּד טַב וּבִישׁ. לָאו. דְּהָא בְּעִירֵי לָא מִתְנַהֲגָן, אֶלָּא בְּמָה דְּנַהֲגוּ לוֹן. ואע"ג דְּהַהִיא אֲתָנָא בְּעַקְתָּא יַתִּיר, לָאו בִּרְשׁוּתָהּ הִיא, דְּהָא הוּא אַטְעִין לָהּ בְּחַרְשׁוֹי, וּבִרְשׁוּתֵיהּ קַיְּימָא.

450. "And she said to Bilaam, 'What have I done to you?'" MEANING THAT SHE SAID TO HIM, IS it within my power to do any good or harm - no, because beasts behave only the way they are led to behave. Although that she-mule was in great distress, she had no control on her own because Bilaam had loaded her with his magic and she remained under his authority.

451. וַיֹּאמֶר בִּלְעָם לָאָתוֹן כִּי הִתְעַלַּלְתְּ בִּי. הֲוָה לֵיהּ לְחַיְּיכָא מִנָּהּ, וְהוּא אָתִיב לְקַבְּלָא טִפְּשׁוּתָא דְּמִלָּהָא, כְּדֵין חַיְּיכוּ מִנֵּיהּ, וְאִתְקְלִיל בְּעֵינַיְיהוּ, וְיָדְעוּ דְּאִיהוּ שַׁטְיָא. וּמָה אָמַר. כִּי הִתְעַלַּלְתְּ בִּי לוּ יֶשׁ חֶרֶב בְּיָדִי. אָמְרוּ, שַׁטְיָא דָּא אִיהוּ יָכִיל לְשֵׁיצָאָה עַמִּין בְּפוּמֵיהּ, הֵיךְ לָא יָכִיל לְשֵׁיצָאָה לְאַתְנֵיהּ, וְהוּא בָּעֵי חַרְבָּא. וְאוֹלִיפְנָא, דְּלֵית חֵילָא בִּבְעִירֵי לְאַשְׁרָאָה עָלַיְיהוּ רוּחָא אַחֲרָא, דְּאִי יֵימְרוּן בְּנֵי נָשָׁא, אִי יְמַלְּלוּן בְּעִירֵי, כַּמָּה דַּעְתָּא שְׁלִים יִפְּקוּן לְעָלְמָא, פּוּק וְאוֹלִיף מֵהַאי

אֲתָנָא, דְּהָא קוּדְשָׁא בְּרִיךְ הוּא אַפְתַּח פּוּמָהּ, חָמֵי מִלּוֹי.

451. "And Bilaam said to the she-mule, 'Because you have mocked me'" (Bemidbar 22:29). He should have laughed her off, but instead, he responded with illogic. Then they laughed at him and he was degraded in their eyes, IN THE EYES OF THE PRINCES THAT ACCOMPANIED HIM, and they realized that he was a fool. What did he say, "Because you have mocked me, I would there were a sword in my hand..." (Ibid.). THE PRINCES said, This fool BOASTS that he could destroy nations with his mouth, but he can not even destroy his she-mule, and he needs a sword. We have further learned that beasts do not have that power required to have them be endowed with another spirit OF WISDOM. If people say, If the beasts could talk, how much perfected knowledge would come to the world, they should go learn from that she-mule, whose mouth the Holy One, blessed be He, opened to see how she spoke.

45. "When Balak took Bilaam"

A Synopsis

We are told that Bilaam went up to the altars of Ba'al because he foresaw that Yisrael would come to worship Ba'al in the future. Bilaam wanted to provoke a quarrel with Yisrael yet he saw he could not because of their friendship with God, so he made a sacrifice to God that was rejected. Bilaam told Balak to restrain Malchut with his witchcraft, and, if he could do that, he himself would nullify the blessings he had given Yisrael. Yet Rabbi Yitzchak says that Yisrael could be cursed neither from the aspect of the patriarchs nor the matriarchs. The rabbis talk about various sections of this scripture – the top of the rocks, the dust of Jacob, and the fourth part of Yisrael. In the end we hear that Bilaam saw that even with all his witchcraft and his offerings he would be unable to sever Yisrael from God, so he was powerless. He had tried to breach Yisrael's defences at the level of Jacob and at the level of Israel, but was unable to because neither level is ever involved in evil actions. We hear that there are two Klipot of iniquity and perverseness that correspond to enchantment and divination; Bilaam thought these would be the right weapons against Jacob and Israel, but he was wrong. The rabbis say that Yisrael is as strong as a lion and will conquer the heathen nations in the future. Rabbi Aba also refers to the form of a lion that appears on top of acceptable burnt offerings. If the form of a dog appeared on the fire it meant that Yisrael must repent. Rabbi Elazar returns to the story of Bilaam and tells Rabbi Yosi that at the moment Bilaam turned his evil eye to Yisrael, God protected them by covering them with His spirit. Bilaam praised Yisrael so that his evil eye would be more effective and they would be more vulnerable to it, but God did not allow him to harm Yisrael. Yisrael is never afraid, even in exile, because they have the strength of a lion due to their study of the Torah and their obedience to its laws.

452. וַיְהִי בַבֹּקֶר וַיִּקַּח בָּלָק אֶת בִּלְעָם וְגוֹ'. ר' יִצְחָק אָמַר, בָּלָק חַכִּים הֲוָה בְּחַרְשִׁין, יַתִּיר מִבִּלְעָם, בַּר דְּלָא הֲוָה מְכַוּוֹן שַׁעֲתָא לְלַטְיָיא. מָשָׁל וְכוּ'. בג"כ וַיִּקַּח בָּלָק אֶת בִּלְעָם וְגוֹ'. הוּא הֲוָה אַתְקִין לֵיהּ וְאָחִיד לֵיהּ לְכֹלָּא.

452. "And it came to pass on the morrow, when Balak took Bilaam..."

(Bemidbar 22:41). Rabbi Yitzchak said, Balak was wiser in magic than Bilaam, except that he was unable to figure out the most opportune time to curse, LIKE BILAAM. Therefore, "Balak took Bilaam." He was preparing him and holding to him in everyway.

453. וַיַּעֲלֵהוּ בָּמוֹת בָּעַל. מַאי וַיַּעֲלֵהוּ בָּמוֹת בָּעַל. אֶלָּא אַשְׁגַּח בְּחַרְשׁוֹי, בְּמַאי סִטְרָא יִתְאֲחִיד בְּהוּ, וְאַשְׁכַּח דִּזְמִינִין יִשְׂרָאֵל לְמֶעְבַּד בָּמוֹת, וּלְמִפְלַח לַבַּעַל. כְּמָה דִּכְתִּיב, וַיֵּלְכוּ אַחֲרֵי הַבַּעַל. וַיַּרְא מִשָּׁם קְצֵה הָעָם, חָמָא רַבְרְבֵי דְּעַמָּא, וּמַלְכָּא דִּלְהוֹן, דְּפָלְחִין לֵיהּ, כְּמָה דִּכְתִּיב וְיִקְרְאוּ בְּשֵׁם הַבַּעַל, וּכְתִיב אִם יְיָ׳ הָאֱלֹהִים וְגו׳. כֵּיוָן דְּחָמָא בִּלְעָם, דִּזְמִינִין יִשְׂרָאֵל לְהַאי, מִיַּד וַיֹּאמֶר בִּלְעָם אֶל בָּלָק בְּנֵה לִי בָזֶה שִׁבְעָה מִזְבְּחֹת.

453. "And brought him up into the high altars of Ba'al" (Ibid.). What is the meaning of: "And brought him up into the high altars of Ba'al"? HE RESPONDS: It is that he observed which aspect OF YISRAEL he should grasp on to with his witchcraft. And he discovered that Yisrael were going to build altars and serve the Ba'al, as it says, "And served the Ba'al" (II Melachim 17:16). "That thence he might see the utmost part of the people" (Bemidbar 22:41): he noticed the chiefs of the people and their king worshipping him, as it is written: "And they called on the name of the Ba'al" (I Melachim 18:26) and: "If Hashem be Elohim..." (Ibid. 21). As soon as Bilaam saw that Yisrael were going for it in the future, immediately "Bilaam said to Balak, 'Build me here seven altars'" (Bemidbar 23:1).

454. ר׳ יוֹסֵי וְר׳ יְהוּדָה, חַד אָמַר לָקֳבְלֵי מַדְבְּחָן דְּקַדְמָאֵי, אַקְרִיב אִינּוּן שִׁבְעָה מַדְבְּחָן. וְחַד אָמַר, בְּחָכְמְתָא עָבֵד כֹּלָּא, וְאַשְׁכַּח דְּחוּלָקְהוֹן דְּיִשְׂרָאֵל בְּשִׁבְעָה דַּרְגִּין אִתְקְשָׁרוּ. בְּגִין כַּךְ אַסְדַּר שִׁבְעָה מַדְבְּחָן.

454. Rabbi Yosi and Rabbi Yehuda were talking. One said that in accordance with the earlier altars, THAT WERE PREPARED by the ancestors, he offered sacrifices ON seven altars. And one said that he did everything with wisdom, because he found that Yisrael's lot was tied to the seven levels, CHESED, GVURAH, TIFERET, NETZACH, HOD, YESOD AND MALCHUT. Therefore, he said, Let me set up seven altars.

455. לב״נ דַּהֲוָה לֵיהּ רְחִימָא חַד, דְּשָׁבַק לֵיהּ אֲבוֹי. וּבְנֵי נָשָׁא מִסְתְּפוּ לְקַטְטָה בַּהֲדֵיהּ, בְּגִין הַהוּא רְחִימָא. לְיוֹמִין, אָתָא ב״נ חַד, וּבָעָא לְאִתְעָרָא קְטָטוּ בַּהֲדֵיהּ. אָמַר, מַה אַעְבֵּיד, אִי אִתְעַר בֵּיהּ קְטָטָא, הָא הַהוּא רְחִימָא דְּאִתְקְשַׁר בַּהֲדֵיהּ, וְלָא יָכִילְנָא, אָמַר מָה עֲבַד, שָׁדַר לֵיהּ דּוֹרוֹן לְהַהוּא רְחִימָא. אָמַר הַהוּא רְחִימָא, וְכִי מָה אִית לֵיהּ לְהַאי ב״נ גַּבָּאי, יְדַעְנָא דִּבְגִין הַהוּא בַּר רְחִימָאי הוּא. אָמַר, הַאי דּוֹרוֹן לָא יֵיעוּל קַמָּאי, זְמִינוּ לֵיהּ לְכַלְבֵּי וְיֵכְלוּנֵיהּ.

455. THIS IS COMPARABLE to a person who had a friend, whose father left him. People were afraid to quarrel with him on account of that friendship. Sometime later, a person came and wanted to quarrel with him. He thought to himself, What should I do? If I provoke him into a quarrel, here he has a friend, and I shall not prevail. What did he do? He sent a gift to the friend. The friend thought to himself, What does this fellow have to do with me? I understand that it is on account of my friend's son, WHOM HE WISHES TO HARM. He said, This gift is not acceptable to me. Call the dogs, and let them eat it.

456. כַּךְ בִּלְעָם, אָתָא לְאִתְעָרָא קְטָטוּ בְּהוּ בְּיִשְׂרָאֵל, וְחָמָא דְּלָא יָכִיל בְּגִין הַהוּא רְחִימָא עִלָּאָה דִּלְהוֹן, שָׁארֵי לְתַקְּנָא קַמֵּיהּ דּוֹרוֹן. אָמַר קוּדְשָׁא בְּרִיךְ הוּא, רָשָׁע וּמַה אִית לָךְ גַּבָּאי, אַתְּ בָּעֵי לְאִזְדַּוְּוגָא בְּבָנַי, הֲרֵי דּוֹרוֹנָךְ זַמִּין לְכַלְבֵּי. ת״ח, מַה כְּתִיב, וַיִּקָּר אֱלֹהִים אֶל בִּלְעָם. וְאר״ש, לָשׁוֹן קֶרִי וְטוּמְאָה. דּוֹרוֹנָךְ לְאִלֵּין אִתְמְסַר וְלָא יֵיעוּל קַמָּאי.

456. So, Bilaam too came along to provoke a quarrel with Yisrael and saw that he could not, because of that supernal friend of theirs. He began preparing a gift for Him, WHICH IS THE SACRIFICIAL OFFERINGS. The Holy One, blessed be He, said, 'Wicked one, what do you have to do with Me? You wish to be associate with My children. Behold, your gift is being given to the dogs.' Come and observe that it is written: "And Elohim met (Heb. *vayikar*) Bilaam" (Bemidbar 23:16). Rabbi Shimon said *VAYIKAR* is

derived from the same root as nightly pollution (Heb. *keri*) and defilement. Behold, your gift is presented to those, and does not enter before Me.

457. ר׳ אַבָּא אָמַר, וַיִּקָּר: כד״א, לִפְנֵי קָרָתוֹ מִי יַעֲמוֹד. הוּא הֲוָה זַמִּין, דִּבְהַהוּא דוֹרוֹן, יָכִיל בְּהוּ בְּיִשְׂרָאֵל. מַה כְּתִיב. וַיִּקָּר אֱלֹהִים. קָרִיר גַּרְמֵיהּ מִן דָּא דְּהֲוָה חָשִׁיב. וַיִּקָּר אֱלֹהִים, כְּמָה דְּאִתְּמַר, דְּאִתְּעַר עָלֵיהּ מִסִּטְרָא דִּמְסָאֲבוּתָא.

457. Rabbi Aba said, *vayikar* is like it says: "Who can stand before His cold (Heb. *karato*)?" (Tehilim 147:17). He was confident that he would be able to overcome Yisrael with that gift. It is written: "And Elohim met (Heb. *vayikar*)"; He cooled Himself from what he, BILAAM, was thinking. IN ADDITION, "And Elohim met" is as we were taught, that the aspect of defilement was roused against him.

458. רִבִּי אֶלְעָזָר אָמַר, וַיִּקָּר, בִּלְעָם חָשִׁיב דִּבְהַהוּא דוֹרוֹן יֵיעוּל לְאַבְאָשָׁא לְהוּ לְיִשְׂרָאֵל, וְקוּדְשָׁא בְּרִיךְ הוּא אַעְקָר לֵיהּ מִקַּמֵּיהּ לְהַהוּא דוֹרוֹן. וְאַעְקַר לֵיהּ לְבִלְעָם, מִמַּה דְּהֲוָה חָשִׁיב. וְאַעְקַר לֵיהּ מֵהַהוּא דַּרְגָּא, הה״ד וַיִּקָּר. כד״א יִקְּרוּהָ עוֹרְבֵי נַחַל. אָמַר לֵיהּ, רָשָׁע, לֵית אַנְתְּ כְּדַאי לְאִתְקַשְּׁרָא בַּהֲדָאי וּלְמֵיעַל קַמָּאי. דוֹרוֹנָךְ לְכַלְבֵּי אִתְמְסַר.

458. Rabbi Elazar said that va*yikar* MEANS THAT Bilaam believed he would be able to harm Yisrael with that gift. The Holy One, blessed be He, eradicated that gift from His presence, expunged Bilaam from such thoughts and uprooted him from that level. That is what is meant by *vayiker*, as it says, "The ravens of the valley shall pick it up (Heb. *yikruha*)" (Mishlei 30:17). He said to him, 'Wicked one, you are not worthy to be associated with Me or to enter into My presence. Your gift will be given to the dog.'

459. אָמַר ר׳ שִׁמְעוֹן, ת״ח, הַאי רָשָׁע, גַּעֲלָא דְּכַלְּבָא הֲוָה. דְּלָא תִּשְׁכַּח בְּכָל פָּרַשְׁתָּא דָּא, וַיֹּאמֶר יְיָ׳ אֶל בִּלְעָם, אוֹ וַיְדַבֵּר יְיָ׳, ח״ו. מַה כְּתִיב. וַיָּשֶׂם יְיָ׳ דָּבָר בְּפִי בִלְעָם וְגוֹ׳, כְּמַאן דְּשַׁוֵּי חִסְמָא בְּפוּם חֲמָרָא, דְּלָא יִסְטֵי הָכָא אוֹ הָכָא, כַּךְ וַיָּשֶׂם יְיָ׳ דָּבָר בְּפִי וְגוֹ׳.

459. Rabbi Shimon said, Come and see that this wicked one was the abomination of everyone, because you will not find in the entire passage of the episode such expressions as: "And Hashem spoke to Bilaam" or "And Hashem said." Heaven forbid. It is written: "And Hashem put a word in the mouth of Bilaam...," which is like someone who puts the bridle bit into the mouth of the she-mule to restrain it from diverting this way or that. So too is the meaning of: "And Hashem put a word in the mouth..."

460. אָ"ל קוּדְשָׁא בְּרִיךְ הוּא, רָשָׁע, אַתְּ חָשִׁיב דְּעַל יְדָךְ יְהֵא וְיִתְקַיֵּים בִּרְכָה בְּבָנַי, אוֹ אִתְּכָא. לָא צְרִיכִין אִינּוּן לָךְ, כְּמָה דְּאַמְרִין לַצִּרְעָה וְכוּ'. אֶלָּא אַתְּ שׁוּב אֶל בָּלָק, וְכַד תִּפְתַּח פּוּמָךְ, לָא יְהֵא בִּרְשׁוּתָךְ. וְלָא בְּפוּמָךְ תַּלְיָיא מִלּוּלָא, אֶלָּא וְכֹה תְדַבֵּר. הֲרֵי כֹּ"ה, דִּזְמִינָא לְבָרְכָא לוֹן. כֹּה, תְּמַלֵּל בִּרְכָה דִּבְנַי, דְּכַד תִּפְתַּח פּוּמָךְ, הִיא תְּמַלֵּל מִלִּין, לְאִתְקַיְּימָא עַל בְּנַי, דְּלָא אֶשְׁבּוֹק מִלִּין לָךְ.

460. The Holy One, blessed be He, said to him, 'Wicked one, do you really think that it depends on you if the blessings will be fulfilled in My children or not? They do not need you. They say to a bee: NOT FROM YOUR STING AND NOT FROM YOUR HONEY, but rather "go back to Balak" (Bemidbar 23:16). When you open your mouth, it will not be in your control and it will not depend on your mouth, but only "say thus (Heb. *coh*)." For *coh*, WHICH IS THE SHECHINAH, is prepared to bless them and *coh* will express the blessing of My children. When you open your mouth, She will speak the words that will come true in My children, and I will not leave these matters in your hand.'

461. ת"ח, דְּכַךְ הוּא, כֵּיוָן דְּאָתָא לְבָלָק, וּבָלָק שָׁמַע כָּל אִינּוּן מִלִּין, הֲוָה חָשִׁיב דְּהָא מִפּוּמֵיהּ דְּבִלְעָם נָפְקִין, אָמַר, לָקוֹב אוֹיְבַי לְקַחְתִּיךָ. אָמַר בִּלְעָם. סַב אִלֵּין חַרְשִׁין בִּידָךְ, בְּגִין לְאַעְכָּבָא הָכָא לְהַאי כֹּה, וְאִי אַתְּ תֵּיכוּל לְאַעְכְּבָא לָהּ בְּהַאי חַרְשִׁין, אֲנָא אַעֲקַר לָהּ מֵאִינּוּן מִלִּין דְּהִיא אָמְרָה.

461. Come and see that this is how it was. As soon as BILAAM came to Balak and Balak heard all these things, WITH WHICH HE BLESSED YISRAEL,

Balak first thought that they emerged from Bilaam's mouth. He said, "I called you to curse my enemies..." and Bilaam replied, Take this witchcraft into your hand to restrain here this *coh*, WHICH IS MALCHUT. If you will be capable of holding her back with this sorcery, I will expunge all these words that She said from her, MEANING HE WILL NULLIFY THE BLESSINGS THAT SHE SAID, AS MENTIONED ABOVE.

462. מַה כְּתִיב, הִתְיַצֵּב כֹּה עַל עוֹלָתֶךָ, בְּהַאי, וּבְאִלֵּין חַרְשִׁין, תְּעַכֵּב לָהּ, וְאָנֹכִי אִקָּרֶה כֹּ״ה, כְּלוֹמַר, אַעְקָר לָהּ מֵאִלֵּין מִלִּין. אָ״ל קוּדְשָׁא בְּרִיךְ הוּא, רָשָׁע, אֲנָא אַעְקָר לָךְ. מַה כְּתִיב בַּתְרֵיהּ. וַיִּקָּר אֱלֹהִים אֶל בִּלְעָם. וְהַהוּא דָּבָר אָרִים קָלָא, בְּמִלּוּלֵי דְּכֹ״ה. וַיֹּאמֶר שׁוּב אֶל בָּלָק וְכֹה תְּדַבֵּר, כֹּ״ה תְּדַבֵּר וַדַּאי.

462. It is written: "Stand thus (Heb. *coh*) by your burnt offering" (Bemidbar 23:15). Through this and through these magical practices, you will restrain Her *COH*, WHICH IS MALCHUT, "while I go to the meeting yonder (lit. 'meet *coh*')," meaning to say I will uproot Her from these words THAT WERE SAID BY HER. The Holy One, blessed be He, said to him, 'Wicked one, I will uproot you.' It is said afterwards: "And Elohim met Bilaam" (Bemidbar 23:16). That matter will raise its voice with the speeches of *coh* and that is what is written: "And said, 'Go back to Balak, and say thus (Heb. *coh*)'". "And say thus (*coh*)" is exact.

463. ת״ח, בְּקַדְמֵיתָא לָא כְּתִיב הִתְיַצֵּב כֹּה עַל עוֹלָתֶךָ, אֶלָּא הִתְיַצֵּב עַל עוֹלָתֶךָ וְאֵלְכָה אוּלַי יִקָּרֶה יְיָ׳ לִקְרָאתִי. כֵּיוָן דְּחָמָא דְּכֹ״ה אָמַר אִינּוּן בִּרְכָאן, כְּדֵין אָמַר הִתְיַצֵּב כֹּ״ה עַל עוֹלָתֶךָ, וְאָנֹכִי אִקָּרֶה כֹּ״ה.

463. Come and see: The first time it is not written: 'Stand thus (Heb. *coh*) by your burnt offering', but rather "Stand by your burnt offering, and I will go: perhaps Hashem will come to meet me" (Ibid. 3). However, when he realized that *coh* spoke those blessings, he then said, "Stand thus (*coh*) by your burnt offering, while I go to the meeting yonder," MEANING AS EXPLAINED IN THE PREVIOUS DISCUSSION.

464. לְכָה אָרָה לִּי יַעֲקֹב, כְּלוֹמַר, לְקוּט. רִבִּי יוֹסֵי אָמַר, אַשְׁדֵּי לוֹן

מֵהַהוּא דַּרְגָּא דְּאִינּוּן קַיְימֵי, כד"א צִדָּה אוֹרֶה. אָמַר, אִי תֵּיכוּל לְמִשְׁדֵּי לוֹן מֵהַהוּא דַּרְגָּא דִּלְהוֹן, הָא כֻּלְּהוּ אִתְעֲקָרוּ מֵעָלְמָא. וּלְכָה זוֹעֲמָה יִשְׂרָאֵל, יִשְׂרָאֵל דִּלְעֵילָּא, דְּיִשְׁתְּכַח רוּגְזָא קַמֵּיהּ, כד"א וְאֵל זוֹעֵם בְּכָל יוֹם.

464. "Come, curse (Heb. *ara*) me Jacob" (Ibid. 7). *ARA* means 'pick', DERIVED FROM: "I HAVE GATHERED (HEB. *ARITI*) MY MYRRH WITH MY SPICE" (SHIR HASHIRIM 5:1). Rabbi Yosi said, He threw them off from that level where they stood before, as it is written: "And I will shoot (Heb. *ore*) on the side of it" (I Shmuel 20:20), MEANING SHOOT AND HURL THEM AWAY. He said, If you will be able to hurl them off that level, THAT IS MALCHUT, all of them will be uprooted from the world. "And come, denounce Yisrael" (Bemidbar 23:7) REFERS TO Yisrael above, WHICH IS ZEIR ANPIN, WHO SHOULD CAUSE HIM TO BE ANGRY, meaning anger AND INDIGNATION shall be before Him, as it says, "And an El who has indignation every day" (Tehilim 7:12).

465. כִּי מֵרֹאשׁ צוּרִים וְגוֹ'. א"ר יִצְחָק, מֵרֹאשׁ צוּרִים, אִלֵּין אִינּוּן אֲבָהָתָא. דִּכְתִּיב הַבִּיטוּ אֶל צוּר חוּצַּבְתֶּם. וּמִגְּבָעוֹת אֲשׁוּרֶנּוּ, אִלֵּין אִמָּהָן, בֵּין מֵהַאי סִטְרָא וּבֵין מֵהַאי סִטְרָא, לָא יַכְלִין לְאִתְלַטְיָיא.

465. "For from the top of the rocks I see him..." (Bemidbar 23:9). Rabbi Yitzchak said, This refers to the patriarchs, as it is written: "Look to the rock whence you are hewn" (Yeshayah 51:1). "And from the hills I behold him" (Bemidbar 23:9): this refers to the matriarchs. They could be cursed neither from this aspect OF THE PATRIARCHS nor from that OF THE MATRIARCHS.

466. ר' אַבָּא אָמַר, כִּי מֵרֹאשׁ צוּרִים, מַאן יָכִיל לְהוּ לְיִשְׂרָאֵל, דְּהָא הוּא אָחִיד מֵרֵישָׁא דְּכָל צוּרִים נָפְקִין, וּמַאן אִינּוּן צוּרִים. גְּבוּרָן. דְּהָא כָּל דִּינִין דְּעָלְמָא מֵאִינּוּן גְּבוּרָן נָפְקֵי, וְאִינּוּן אִתְאַחֲדָן בְּהוּ. וּמִגְּבָעוֹת אֲשׁוּרֶנּוּ, אִלֵּין שְׁאַר מַשִׁרְיָין דְּאִתְאַחֲדָן בְּהוּ. הֶן עָם לְבָדָד וְגוֹ'. כד"א ה' בָּדָד יַנְחֶנּוּ.

466. Rabbi Aba said that "top of the rocks" means who has power against Yisrael, since they are attached and emanate from the top of the rocks. Who are the rocks? They are Gvurot, because all the judgments in the world emerge from the Gvurot and they are attached onto them. "And from the hills I behold him": These are the rest of the camps that are linked to them, TO THE GVUROT, "it is a people that shall dwell alone" (Ibid.). It is the same as it is written: "So Hashem alone did lead him" (Devarim 32:12).

467. מִי מָנָה עֲפַר יַעֲקֹב וְגוֹ׳, הָא אוּקְמוּהָ. אֶלָּא א״ר יוֹסֵי, תְּרֵין דַּרְגִּין אִינּוּן, יַעֲקֹב וְיִשְׂרָאֵל. בְּקַדְמֵיתָא יַעֲקֹב, וּלְבָתַר יִשְׂרָאֵל. ואע״ג דְּכֹלָּא חַד, תְּרֵין דַּרְגִּין אִינּוּן, דְּהָא דַּרְגָּא עִלָּאָה יִשְׂרָאֵל הוּא.

467. "Who could count the dust of Jacob" (Bemidbar 23:10). This was already explained. However, Rabbi Yosi said, There are two levels, Jacob and Israel. At first, WHEN HE IS AT THE SIX ENDS, HE IS CONSIDERED Jacob and later on, WHEN HE ATTAINS THE FIRST THREE SFIROT, HE IS Iisrael. Although it is all the same, they are two grades. The higher grade is Israel AND THE GRADE OF JACOB IS LOWER.

468. מִי מָנָה עֲפַר יַעֲקֹב וְגוֹ׳. לְתַתָּא, מַאן הוּא עָפָר. ר׳ שִׁמְעוֹן אָמַר, הַאי דִּכְתִּיב בֵּיהּ יִתֵּן כֶּעָפָר חַרְבּוֹ וְגוֹ׳. מַאן חַרְבּוֹ. הָא יְדִיעָא, דִּכְתִיב חֶרֶב לַיְיָ׳ מָלְאָה דָם. עָפָר, הַהוּא אֲתָר דְּאִתְבְּרֵי מִנֵּיהּ אָדָם הָרִאשׁוֹן, דִּכְתִיב וַיִּיצֶר יְיָ׳ אֱלֹהִים אֶת הָאָדָם עָפָר וְגוֹ׳. וּמֵהַהוּא עָפָר, כַּמָּה חַיָּילִין, וְכַמָּה מַשִׁרְיָין נָפְקוּ, כַּמָּה טַפְסִין, כַּמָּה גַּרְדִּינֵי נְמוּסִין, כַּמָּה גִּירִין, כַּמָּה בַּלִיסְטְרָאוֹת, כַּמָּה רוּמְחִין, וְסַיְיפִין, וְזַיְינִין, אִשְׁתְּכָחוּ מֵהַהוּא עָפָר. מִי מָנָה כד״א, הֲיֵשׁ מִסְפָּר לִגְדוּדָיו.

468. "Who can count the dust of Jacob." HE ASKS: What is the dust below IN THE LEVEL OF JACOB? Rabbi Shimon says, It is written about it: "His sword makes them as dust" (Yeshayah 41:2). Who is His sword? It is known THAT IT IS MALCHUT, as is written: "The sword of Hashem is filled with blood" (Yeshayah 34:6), BECAUSE MALCHUT IS CONSIDERED "THE SWORD OF HASHEM." Dust refers to the place from which Adam was created, as it is written: "And Hashem Elohim formed man of the dust of the ground" (Beresheet 2:7). From that dust emerge many legions and many camps, many levels, many law investigators, many arrows, many projectile stones and many spears, swords and weapons. "Who can count" is as it says, "Is there any number to His armies?" (Iyov 25:3).

469. וּמִסְפָּר אֶת רוֹבַע יִשְׂרָאֵל. רֹבַע יִשְׂרָאֵל הִיא הֵ״א, וְחַד מִלָּה הִיא. רוֹבַע יִשְׂרָאֵל, כד״א רוֹבֵץ תַּחַת מַשָּׂאוֹ, רְבִיעַ הֲדָא הוּא דִּכְתִּיב, מִטָּתוֹ שֶׁלִּשְׁלֹמֹה. ד״א רֹבַע, כְּמוֹ רְבִיעִית מִיִּשְׂרָאֵל לְתַתָּא, רֹבַע אִתְקְרֵי לְפוּם כִּתְרִין מַשְׁמַע דָּוִד, דְּאִיהוּ רַגְלָא רְבִיעָאָה דְּכוּרְסְיָיא.

469. "And the number of the fourth part of Yisrael" (Bemidbar 23:10). The quarter of Yisrael is the Hei OF YUD HEI VAV HEI, BECAUSE YISRAEL, WHICH IS ZEIR ANPIN, CONTAINS THE FOUR LETTERS OF THE NAME YUD HEI VAV HEI, OF WHICH MALCHUT IS THE FOURTH LETTER. THEREFORE, IT IS CALLED "THE FOURTH PART (HEB. *ROVA*) OF YISRAEL." It is one WITH THE DUST OF JACOB, WHICH IS ALSO MALCHUT, EXCEPT THAT DUST IS MALCHUT OF JACOB, AND A FOURTH PART IS MALCHUT OF YISRAEL. A fourth of Yisrael is as it says, "Lying under its burden" (Shemot 23:5), WHOSE ARAMAIC TRANSLATION IS *RAVI'A*. THUS "THE FOURTH PART OF YISRAEL," MEANS THE LYING DOWN OF YISRAEL, THAT IS, THE BED OF YISRAEL, WHICH IS MALCHUT, WHICH IS CALLED 'BED'. This refers to that which is written: "his litter, that of Solomon" (Shir Hashirim 3:7), WHICH IS MALCHUT. Another explanation of "fourth part": Like the fourth from Yisrael down, NAMELY MALCHUT, WHICH IS BELOW ZEIR ANPIN THAT IS CALLED YISRAEL, BEING THE FOURTH UNDERNEATH IT. For it is called 'a fourth part' in the sequence of the Sfirot. From this, we under that David, WHICH IS MALCHUT, is the fourth leg of the throne, SINCE CHESED, GVURAH AND TIFERET OF ZEIR ANPIN ARE THE THREE LEGS OF THE THRONE, WHICH IS BINAH, AND MALCHUT IS A FOURTH TO THEM.

470. ד״א מִי מָנָה עֲפַר יַעֲקֹב וְגוֹ׳, כָּל אִינּוּן דַּחֲשִׁיבִין עַפְרָא, כְּמָה דְּאוֹקִימְנָא. וּמִסְפָּר אֶת רֹבַע יִשְׂרָאֵל, דִּכְתִּיב הֲיֵשׁ מִסְפָּר לִגְדוּדָיו. רֹבַע יִשְׂרָאֵל כְּמָה דְּאוֹקִימְנָא. ד״א מִי מָנָה עֲפַר, אִינּוּן פִּקּוּדִין דְּאִינּוּן בְּעַפְרָא, בִּזְרִיעָה, בִּנְטִיעָה, בְּחַצְדָּא, וְהָא אוּקְמוּהָ חַבְרַיָּיא. וּמִסְפָּר אֶת רֹבַע, כד״א בְּהֶמְתְּךָ לֹא תַרְבִּיעַ.

470. Another explanation of: "Who can count the dust of Jacob." "Dust" are all those who are considered as dust, MEANING THAT EMANATE FROM MALCHUT THAT IS CALLED "DUST," as we explained. "And the number of the fourth part of Yisrael" is meant in the same sense, as is written: "Is there any number to His armies?" "The fourth part of Yisrael" MEANS as we explained. THE ONLY DIFFERENCE IS THAT THE WORDS "IS THERE ANY NUMBER TO HIS ARMIES" NOW REFERS TO THE QUARTER OF YISRAEL AND NOT TO THE DUST OF JACOB. Another explanation: "Who can count the dust of Jacob" refers to the precepts applying to the dust, like sowing, planting, harvesting, as was already explained by the friends. "And the number of the fourth part of Yisrael" REFERS TO THE PRECEPTS APPLYING TO THE LIVESTOCK, as it says, "You shall not let your cattle gender with a diverse kind (Heb. *tarbia*)" (Vayikra 19:19).

471. וְיִשָּׂא מְשָׁלוֹ וַיֹּאמַר. וַיְדַבֵּר לָא כְּתִיב, מַאי וְיִשָּׂא מְשָׁלוֹ. רִבִּי חִיָּיא אָמַר, הוּא הֲוָה זָקִיף קָלָא לְגַבֵּי הַהוּא מְמַלֵּל, וְיִשָּׂא מְשָׁלוֹ בִּלְעָם. וַיֹּאמַר הַאי כֹּה כְּמָה דִּכְתִּיב וְכֹה תְּדַבֵּר, וַאֲמִירָה מִנָּהּ הֲוָה.

471. "And he took up his discourse, and said..." (Bemidbar 23:7). HE INQUIRES: It is not written, 'he spoke', THAT WOULD MEAN THAT HE SPOKE. THEN what is the meaning of: "And he took up his discourse," INDICATING THAT HE MADE THE SPEECH AND NOBODY ELSE? Rabbi Chiya said, He was just raising his voice towards the speaker THAT IS MALCHUT CALLED *COH*. THAT IS THE MEANING OF: "And he took up his discourse." This was Bilaam WHO TOOK UP HIS DISCOURSE; "and said," which refers to *Coh*. SHE SPOKE, as is written: "And say thus (Heb. *coh*)." MALCHUT, THAT IS CALLED *COH* WILL DO THE SPEAKING. And the speech was from her.

472. ת"ח, כֵּיוָן דְּחָמָא בִּלְעָם דִּבְכָל חֲרָשׁוֹי וּבְכָל הַהוּא דּוֹרוֹן, לָא יָכִיל לְאַעְקְרָא הַהוּא כֹּה, כד"א וְאָנֹכִי אִקָּרֶה כֹּה, אַעְקָר לְהַאי כֹּה. אָ"ל קוּדְשָׁא בְּרִיךְ הוּא, רָשָׁע, אַנְתְּ סָבוּר לְאַעְקְרָא לָהּ, אֲנָא אַעְקָר לָךְ מִשַּׁלְשׁוּלָךְ, מַה כְּתִיב. וַיִּקָּר אֱלֹהִים אֶל בִּלְעָם, כְּמָה דְּאִתְּמַר. לְבָתַר, כֵּיוָן דְּחָמָא דְּלָא יָכִיל, הָדַר וְאָמַר, וּבֵרֵךְ וְלֹא אֲשִׁיבֶנָּה, וְלֹא אֲשִׁיבֶנּוּ מִבָּעֵי לֵיהּ. אֶלָּא וְלֹא אֲשִׁיבֶנָּה וַדַּאי, לְהַהִיא דִּכְתִּיב כֹּה, וְכֹה תְּדַבֵּר.

לֵית אֲנָא יָכִיל לְאַהֲדְרָא לָהּ.

472. Come and see, when Bilaam saw that even with all his witchcraft and all that offering, MEANING THE SACRIFICES THAT HE OFFERED, he was unable to uproot that *coh*, as it says, "While I go to the meeting yonder (Heb. *coh*)," to uproot *coh*. The Holy One, blessed be He, then said to him, 'Wicked one, you are planning to annihilate her. I will extricate you from your chain, MEANING HE WILL UPROOT HIM FROM THE SOURCE. It is written: "And Elohim met (Heb. *vayikar*) Bilaam," as we explained THAT IT IS DERIVED FROM "THE RAVENS OF THE VALLEY SHALL PICK IT OUT (HEB. YIKRUHA)" (MISHLEI 30:17), PICK HIM OUT OF HIS LEVEL. Following this, when he realized that he could not, he again said, "And he has blessed; and I cannot reverse it (her)." It should have read: 'I cannot reverse him', but "reverse her" is more precise, because it refers to her about whom the word *coh* is used, as "And say thus (Heb. *coh*)," REFERS TO MALCHUT, ABOUT WHOM HE SAID, I cannot reverse her FROM YISRAEL.

473. אָמַר בִּלְעָם, בִּתְרֵין דַּרְגִּין בָּעֵינָא לְאַעֲלָא בְּהוּ. בָּעֵינָא לְאַעֲלָא בְּהוּ מִדַּרְגָּא דְּיַעֲקֹב, וְלָא יְכִילְנָא. בָּעֵינָא לְאַעֲלָא בְּהוּ מִסִּטְרָא אַחֲרָא דְּיִשְׂרָאֵל, וְלָא יְכִילְנָא. מַאי טַעֲמָא. בְּגִין דִּשְׁמָא דָּא אוֹ דָּא, לָא אִתְקְשַׁר בְּזִינִין בִּישִׁין, הה"ד לֹא הִבִּיט אָוֶן בְּיַעֲקֹב וְגוֹ'.

473. Bilaam said, Into two levels I tried to enter. I tried to enter into them from the level of Jacob but I could not. I tried to enter them from another side, FROM THE LEVEL of Yisrael, but I did not succeed. What is the reason? It is because neither level is involved in evil species. This is what is written: "He has not beheld iniquity in Jacob nor has he seen perverseness in Yisrael" (Bemidbar 23:21).

474. תָּאנָא, תְּרֵין דַּרְגִּין אִינּוּן: נַחַשׁ, וְקֶסֶם. לָקֳבְלֵיהוֹן: עָמָל, וְאָוֶן. אָמַר בִּלְעָם, הָא וַדַּאי אַשְׁכַּחְנָא לָקֳבְלֵי דְּהָנֵי יַעֲקֹב וְיִשְׂרָאֵל. אָוֶן, לָקֳבְלֵיהּ דְּיַעֲקֹב, דְּאִיהוּ קָטִיר בְּנַחַשׁ. עָמָל, לָקֳבְלֵיהּ דְּיִשְׂרָאֵל, דְּאִיהוּ קָטִיר בְּקֶסֶם. כֵּיוָן דְּחָמָא דְּלָא יָכִיל, אָמַר, וַדַּאי לֹא הִבִּיט אָוֶן בְּיַעֲקֹב וְגוֹ'. מ"ט. בְּגִין דַּיְיָ' אֱלֹהָיו עִמּוֹ וְגוֹ'.

474. We studied earlier that there are two levels, enchantment and divination. Corresponding to them are TWO KLIPOT OF iniquity and perverseness. Bilaam thought to himself, I definitely discovered the adversaries of Jacob and Yisrael, since iniquity is THE KLIPAH against Jacob that is connected WITH THE SORCERY CALLED 'enchantment'. Perverseness is THE KLIPAH against Yisrael that is connected to 'divination'. When he realized that he could not succeed, he said, Most certainly, "he has not beheld iniquity in Jacob nor has he seen perverseness in Yisrael." What is the reason? Because "Hashem his Elohim is with him..."

475. וְאִי תֵּימָא, בְּהָנֵי לָא יָכִילְנָא. בְּקֶסֶם וְנַחַשׁ יָכִילְנָא. כְּתִיב כִּי לֹא נַחַשׁ בְּיַעֲקֹב וְגוֹ׳. וְלֹא עוֹד, אֶלָּא דְּכָל חֵילִין דִּלְעֵילָּא, וְכָל מַשִּׁרְיָין כֻּלְּהוּ, לָא יַדְעֵי וְלָא מִסְתַּכְּלֵי בְּנִמּוּסָא דְּמַלְכָּא עִלָּאָה, עַד דְּשָׁאֲלֵי לְהָנֵי תְּרֵי יַעֲקֹב וְיִשְׂרָאֵל. וּמַאי אַמְרֵי. מַה פָּעַל אֵל. אָמַר רִבִּי אֶלְעָזָר, כָּל הָנֵי מִלִּין, כֹּה אָמַר, וְהוּא אָרִים קָלָא לָקֳבְלָהּ, וְלָא יָדַע מַאי הוּא, וְלָא אִשְׁתְּמַע בַּר קָלֵיהּ.

475. If you will say that with these, INIQUITY AND PERVERSENESS, I cannot succeed, but with enchantment and divination I will succeed, it is written: "Surely there is no enchantment in Jacob, nor is there any divination in Yisrael" (Ibid. 23). Not only this, but all the legions above and all the camps are unaware, nor do they look at the customs of the King up high until only after they ask for these two LEVELS of Jacob and Yisrael. What are they saying? "What El has performed" (Ibid.). Rabbi Elazar said, All these matters were spoken by *Coh*, THAT IS MALCHUT, AND BILAAM JUST raised his voice towards her, having no idea what it was all about, and nothing was heard of him save his voice.

476. הֶן עָם כְּלָבִיא יָקוּם וְגוֹ׳, מַאן עַמָּא תַּקִּיפָא כְּיִשְׂרָאֵל. בְּשַׁעֲתָא דְּאִתְנְהִיר צַפְרָא, קָם וּמִתְגַּבָּר כְּאַרְיָא, לְפוּלְחָנָא דְּמָארֵיהוֹן, בְּכַמָּה שִׁירִין, בְּכַמָּה תּוּשְׁבְּחָן. מִשְׁתַּדְּלֵי בְּאוֹרַיְיתָא כָּל יוֹמָא, וּבְלֵילְיָא לֹא יִשְׁכַּב וְגוֹ׳. כַּד בָּעֵי ב״נ לְמִשְׁכַּב עַל עַרְסֵיהּ, מְקַדֵּשׁ שְׁמָא עִלָּאָה, אַמְלִיךְ לֵיהּ לְעֵילָּא וְתַתָּא. כַּמָּה גַּרְדִּינֵי נִמּוּסִין מִתְקַשְּׁרָן קַמַּיְיהוּ,

בְּשַׁעֲתָא דְּפַתְחִין פּוּמְהוֹן עַל עַרְסַיְיהוּ, בִּשְׁמַע יִשְׂרָאֵל. וּבָעָאן רַחֲמֵי קָמֵי מַלְכָּא קַדִּישָׁא, בְּכַמָּה קְרָאֵי דְּרַחֲמֵי.

476. "Behold, the people shall rise up as a great lion..." (Ibid. 24). Which nation is as strong as Yisrael? When the morning light breaks to shine, he rises and gains strength like a lion for the devotional service of his Master with many songs and praises, studying Torah all day. At night, he "shall not lie down until he eat of the prey" (Ibid.). When a person wishes to lie down on his bed, he sanctifies the Holy Name and proclaims Him King above and below. How many instigators of laws come together before them at the time they open their mouths on their bed with Sh'ma Yisrael, and beg for compassion before the Holy King with several verses of mercy.

477. ר' אַבָּא אָמַר, הֶן עָם כְּלָבִיא יָקוּם. זְמִינִין הַאי עַמָּא, לְמֵיקָם עַל כָּל עַמִּין עכו"ם, כְּאַרְיֵה גִּיבָּר וְתַקִּיף, וְיִתְרְמֵי עֲלַיְיהוּ. אָרְחַיְיהוּ דְּכָל אַרְיָיוָותָא לְמִשְׁכַּב עַל טַרְפַּיְיהוּ, אֲבָל עַמָּא דָּא לָא יִשְׁכַּב, עַד יֹאכַל טֶרֶף.

477. Rabbi Aba said, "Behold, the people shall rise up as a great lion" MEANS this nation is will rise in the future over all heathen nations like a powerful mighty lion, and will hurtle HIMSELF over them. It is the manner of all lions to lie down over their prey; however, this nation "shall not lie down until he eat of the prey."

478. ד"א הֶן עָם כְּלָבִיא יָקוּם, לְקָרְבָא קָרְבְּנִין וְעִלָּוָון קָמֵי מַלְכְּהוֹן, עַל גַּבֵּי מַדְבְּחָא. וְתָאנָא, בְּשַׁעֲתָא דְּקוּרְבְּנָא אִתּוֹקַד עַל גַּבֵּי מַדְבְּחָא, הֲוֹו חָמָן דְּיוּקְנָא דְּחַד אַרְיֵה רְבִיעַ עַל הַהוּא קָרְבְּנָא, וְאָכִיל לֵיהּ.

478. Another explanation of: "Behold, the people shall rise up as a great lion" to bring offerings and burnt offerings before the King on the altar. We have learned that, at the time the offering is being burnt on the altar, they perceived a form of a lion reclining over the sacrifice and eating it.

479. וְאָמַר רִבִּי אַבָּא, אוּרִיאֵ"ל מַלְאָכָא עִלָּאָה הֲוָה, וְחָמָאן לֵיהּ

בְּדִיוּקְנָא דְּאַרְיָא תַּקִּיפָא, רְבִיעַ עַל מַדְבְּחָא, וְאָכִיל לוֹן לְקָרְבְּנִין. וְכַד יִשְׂרָאֵל לָא הֲווֹ זַכָּאִין כָּל כַּךְ, הֲווֹ חָמָאן דִּיוּקְנָא דְחָד כַּלְבָּא חֲצִיפָא רְבִיעַ עָלֵיהּ, כְּדֵין הֲווֹ יַדְעֵי יִשְׂרָאֵל דְּבַעְיָין תְּשׁוּבָה, וּכְדֵין תַּיְיבַן. לֹא יִשְׁכַּב וְגוֹ', אִלֵּין קָרְבְּנִין דְּלֵילְיָא כְּגוֹן עַלָּוָון. וְדַם חֲלָלִים יִשְׁתֶּה, דְקוּדְשָׁא בְּרִיךְ הוּא אֲגַח קְרָבָא דִּלְהוֹן עַל שַׂנְאֵיהוֹן.

479. Rabbi Aba said, Uriel was a high angel and he was perceived in the form of a strong lion, reclining on the altar and consuming the sacrifices. When Yisrael were not so worthy, they used to perceive the form of some impudent dog reclining over it. Yisrael then realized that they had to repent, and they repented. "He shall not lie down until he eat of the prey" refers to the sacrifices that must be completely consumed by fire during the night, such as burnt offerings. "And drink the blood of the slain" (Bemidbar 23:4) means that the Holy One, blessed be He, will carry on battles with their enemies for them.

480. רִבִּי אֶלְעָזָר אָמַר, לֹא יִשְׁכַּב, מַהוּ לֹא יִשְׁכַּב. אֶלָּא בְּכָל לֵילְיָא וְלֵילְיָא, כַּד בַּר נָשׁ אִיהוּ אָזִיל בְּפִקּוּדֵי דְמָארֵיהּ, לָא שָׁכִיב עַל עַרְסֵיהּ, עַד דְּקָטִיל אֲלַף וּמְאָה וְעֶשְׂרִים וַחֲמֵשׁ, מֵאִינּוּן זַיְינִין בִּישִׁין, דְּשַׁרְיָין עִמֵּיהּ. רִבִּי אַבָּא אָמַר, אֲלַף אִינּוּן דִּסְטָר שְׂמָאלָא, דִּכְתִּיב יִפּוֹל מִצִּדְּךָ אֶלֶף. כְּמָה דִּכְתִּיב, יַעְלְזוּ חֲסִידִים בְּכָבוֹד וְגוֹ', רוֹמְמוֹת אֵל בִּגְרוֹנָם וְגוֹ', לַעֲשׂוֹת נְקָמָה וְגוֹ', הה"ד לֹא יִשְׁכַּב וְגוֹ' וְדָא הוּא לַעֲשׂוֹת בָּהֶם מִשְׁפָּט וְגוֹ'.

480. Rabbi Elazar said that it is written: "He shall not lie down." What is the meaning of, "He shall not lie down"? HE RESPONDS: It is only because every single night, when a person follows his Master commands, he does not lie down on his bed until he kills 1,125 of those evil species that dwell with him. Rabbi Aba said, A thousand are from the left side, as it is written: "A thousand shall fall at your side" (Tehilim 91:7) and it is also written: "Let the pious be joyful in glory, let them sing aloud upon their beds. The high praises of El are in their mouth, to execute vengeance upon the nations..." (Tehilim 149:5-7). Hence, it says, "He shall not lie down..." which is the meaning of, "To execute upon them the judgment..." (Ibid. 9).

481. אָמַר רִבִּי חִזְקִיָּה, לָקֳבְלֵי תְּלַת זִמְנִין דְּהוּא מָחָא לְאַתְנֵיהּ, וְאַטְעִין לָהּ בְּחַרְשׁוֹי, אִתְבָּרְכוּן יִשְׂרָאֵל תְּלַת זִמְנִין. רִבִּי חִיָּיא אָמַר, לָקֳבְלֵיה אִתְבָּרְכוּן יִשְׂרָאֵל תְּלַת זִמְנִין, דְּסַלְּקִין יִשְׂרָאֵל לְאִתְחֲזָאָה קַמֵּי מַלְכָּא קַדִּישָׁא.

481. Rabbi Chizkiyah said, In accordance with the three times that Bilaam beat his she-mule and loaded her with his witchcraft, Yisrael were blessed three times. Rabbi Chiya said, Corresponding to this, Yisrael got the blessing to go up three times a year and be seen in the presence of the Holy King.

482. וַיַּרְא בִּלְעָם כִּי טוֹב בְּעֵינֵי יְיָ׳ וְגוֹ׳, וְלֹא הָלַךְ כְּפַעַם בְּפַעַם לִקְרַאת נְחָשִׁים וְגוֹ׳. מַאי לִקְרַאת נְחָשִׁים. א״ר יוֹסֵי, דְּהָנֵי תְּרֵין זִמְנִין קַדְמָאֵי, הֲוָה אָזִיל בְּכָל חֲרָשׁוֹי, וּבָעָא לְמֵילָט לְיִשְׂרָאֵל. כֵּיוָן דְּחָמָא רְעוּתֵיהּ דקוּדְשָׁא בְּרִיךְ הוּא, דְּאָמַר שׁוּב אֶל בָּלָק, דְּהָא מִלּוּלָךְ לָא בַּעְיָין בָּנַי. מִלּוּלָא אוּחֲרָא זַמִּין מֵהַאי כֹּה, כְּמָה דִּכְתִּיב וְכֹה תְּדַבֵּר. כֹּה תְּדַבֵּר, וְלָא אַנְתְּ. כֹּה תְּדַבֵּר, דְּשַׁלְטָא עַל כָּל שַׁלִּיטִין חַרְשִׁין וְקִסְמִין וְזִינִין בִּישִׁין, דְּלָא יַכְלִין לְאַבְאָשָׁא לִבְנַי. כְּדֵין בָּעָא לְאִסְתַּכְּלָא בְּהוּ, בְּעֵינָא בִּישָׁא.

482. "And when Bilaam saw that it pleased Hashem to bless Yisrael, he went not, as at other times, to seek for enchantments..." (Bemidbar 24:1). HE INQUIRES: What is the meaning of: "to seek for enchantments"? Rabbi Yosi said, The first two times, he approached with all the implements of his witchcraft and desired to curse Yisrael. Then he realized the wish of the Holy One, blessed be He, who said, ""Go back to Balak," because My children have no need of your utterances. Another speech is forthcoming from this *Coh*, as it says, "And say thus (Heb. *coh*)." That means *Coh* will be speaking and not you. "And say thus (*coh*)," (or: '*coh* will speak'), because she governs all the rulers of witchcraft and sorcery and the variety of evils, so they are not able to harm My children.' He then wished to gaze at them with the evil eye.

483. ת״ח, הַאי רָשָׁע כַּד אִסְתַּכַּל בְּהוּ בְּיִשְׂרָאֵל, הֲוָה מִסְתַּכַּל בְּאִלֵּין

תְּרֵין דַּרְגִּין יַעֲקֹב וְיִשְׂרָאֵל, לְאַבְאָשָׁא לוֹן, אוֹ בְּהַאי אוֹ בְּהַאי בְּחַרָשׁוֹי, בְּגִין כַּךְ כָּל בִּרְכָּן וּבִרְכָּן יַעֲקֹב וְיִשְׂרָאֵל אִתְבְּרִיכוּ. וַיַּרְא בִּלְעָם כִּי טוֹב וְגוֹ'. בַּמֶּה חָמָא חָמָא דִּי בְּשַׁעֲתָא דְּאַנְפֵּי מַלְכָּא נְהִירִין, זִינִין בִּישִׁין לָא קַיְימֵי בְּקִיּוּמַיְיהוּ, וְכָל חַרְשִׁין וְכָל קִסְמִין לָא סַלְקָאן בְּחַרְשַׁיְיהוּ.

483. Come and see this wicked one. When he gazed at Yisrael, he looked into both of these levels – Jacob and Yisrael – to harm them with his witchcraft, either this one or that one. Therefore, at each and every blessing, both Jacob and Yisrael were blessed. "And when Bilaam saw that it pleased..." How did he see? HE RESPONDS: He noticed that when the King's face was shining, the variety of evils did not endure, and none of the magic and sorcery were successful in their witchcraft.

484. ת"ח, בְּהָנֵי תְּרֵי זִמְנֵי כְּתִיב וַיִּקָּר. וַיִּקָּר אֱלֹהִים. וַיִּקָּר יְיָ' אֶל בִּלְעָם וְגוֹ'. וּכְתִיב וְכֹה תְדַבֵּר. וְהַשְׁתָּא כֵּיוָן דְּחָמָא דְּהָא לָא אִשְׁתְּכַח רוּגְזָא, וְחַרְשׁוֹי לָא סַלְקִין, כְּדֵין וְלֹא הָלַךְ כְּפַעַם בְּפַעַם וְגוֹ'. כֵּיוָן דְּאַפְרִישׁ וְאִסְתַּלָּק גַּרְמֵיהּ מֵחַרְשׁוֹי, שָׁארִי בְּאִתְעָרוּתָא אַחֲרָא לְשַׁבְחָא לְיִשְׂרָאֵל. א"ר יְהוּדָה, מַאי אִתְעָרוּתָא הָכָא. אָ"ל, אִתְעָרוּתָא דְּרוּחָא חֲדָא מִסִּטְרָא דִּשְׂמָאלָא, הַהוּא דְּאִתְקְשָׁרוּ תְּחוֹתוֹי אִינּוּן זִינִין וְחָרְשִׁין דִּילֵיהּ.

484. Come and see: At those two times, it is written "met" once in, "And Elohim met" and once in, "And Hashem met Bilaam." Then it says, "And say thus (Heb. *coh*)." When he realized that no anger exists, and his witchcraft was not helping him, "he went not, as at other times..." As soon as he separated and removed himself from his magic, he began with another kind of rousing to praise Yisrael. Rabbi Yehuda said, What was this rousing here? He said to him, This was the rousing of a spirit of the left side, the one under whom all the varieties of his witchcraft are connected.

485. א"ר אֶלְעָזָר, הָכִי אוֹלִיפְנָא, דַּאֲפִילּוּ הַאי זִמְנָא לָא שַׁרְיָא בֵּיהּ רוּחָא דְּקוּדְשָׁא. אָ"ל ר' יוֹסֵי, אִי הָכִי, הָא כְּתִיב וַתְּהִי עָלָיו רוּחַ אֱלֹהִים, וּבְכָל אִינּוּן זִמְנִין אָחֲרָנִין לָא כְּתִיב בְּהוּ הָכִי. אָ"ל הָכִי הוּא. ת"ח, כְּתִיב טוֹב עַיִן הוּא יְבוֹרָךְ, וְהָא אוּקְמוּהָ אַל תִּקְרֵי יְבוֹרָךְ. אֶלָּא

יְבָרֵךְ. וּבִלְעָם הֲוָה רַע עַיִן, דְּלָא אִשְׁתְּכַח רַע עַיִן בְּעָלְמָא כְּוָותֵיהּ, דִּבְכָל אֲתָר דַּהֲוָה מִסְתָּכַּל בְּעֵינוֹי, הֲוָה מִתְלַטְיָיא.

485. Rabbi Elazar said, This is what I was taught, even the THIRD time the Holy Spirit did not dwell upon him. Rabbi Yosi inquired of him, If so, why is it written: "And the spirit of Elohim came upon him" (Ibid. 2) and all the other times, it is not written that way. He replied to him, That is the way it must be. Come and see that it is written: "He that has a generous eye shall be blessed" (Mishlei 22:9). It was already explained not to read, 'Shall be blessed', but rather "shall bless." Since Bilaam was so evil-eyed, that no one in the world was as evil-eyed as he. Everything at which he gazed with his eyes became cursed.

486. וְעַ"ד אָמְרוּ, הַאי מַאן דְּאַעְבַּר בְּרֵיהּ בְּשׁוּקָא, וּמִסְתַּפֵּי מֵעֵינָא בִּישָׁא, יְחֲפֵּי סוּדְרָא עַל רֵישֵׁיהּ, בְּגִין דְּלָא יָכִיל עֵינָא בִּישָׁא לְשַׁלְטָאָה עֲלֵיהּ. אוּף הָכָא, כֵּיוָן דְּחָמָא בִּלְעָם, דְּלָא יָכִיל בְּחַרְשׁוֹי וְקִסְמוֹי לְאַבְאָשָׁא לְיִשְׂרָאֵל, בָּעָא לְאִסְתַּכָּל בְּהוּ בְּעֵינָא בִּישָׁא, בְּגִין דִּבְכָל אֲתָר דַּהֲוָה מִסְתָּכַּל בְּעֵינוֹי בִּישִׁין, הֲוָה מִתְלַטְיָיא. ת"ח מַה רְעוּתֵיהּ דִּילֵיהּ לַקֳבְלֵהוֹן דְּיִשְׂרָאֵל, כְּתִיב וַיָּשֶׁת אֶל הַמִּדְבָּר פָּנָיו, כְּתַרְגּוּמוֹ, וְשַׁוֵּי לְעֶגְלָא דִּי עָבַדוּ יִשְׂרָאֵל בְּמַדְבְּרָא אַפּוֹהִי, בְּגִין דִּיהֵא לֵיהּ סְטַר סִיּוּעָא, לְאַבְאָשָׁא לְהוּ.

486. Therefore, they said, Whoever makes his son pass in the marketplace and has fear of the evil eye should cover the top of his head with a head scarf, so the evil eye will not affect him. As well, when Bilaam saw that he could not succeed with his magic and sorcery in harming Yisrael, he wanted to gaze on them with the evil eye, because everything he looked at with his evil eyes became cursed. Come and see what he planned against Yisrael. It is written: "But he set his face toward the wilderness" (Bemidbar 24:1), as the Targum translates THAT HE PUT HIS GAZE IN THE DIRECTION OF THE CALF THAT YISRAEL CREATED AND SINNED WITH IN THE DESERT, so that he may get allies to harm them.

487. הַשְׁתָּא חָמֵי מַה כְּתִיב, וַיִּשָּׂא בִלְעָם אֶת עֵינָיו וַיַּרְא אֶת יִשְׂרָאֵל.

בָּעָא לְאִסְתַּכְּלָא בְּהוּ בְּעֵינָא בִּישָׁא. בֵּיהּ שַׁעֲתָא, אִלְמָלֵא דְּאַקְדִּים לוֹן קוּדְשָׁא בְּרִיךְ הוּא אַסְוָותָא, הֲוָה מְאַבֵּד לוֹן בְּאִסְתַּכְּלוּתָא דְּעֵינוֹי. וּמַאי אַסְוָותָא יָהַב קוּדְשָׁא בְּרִיךְ הוּא לְיִשְׂרָאֵל בְּהַהִיא שַׁעֲתָא. דָּא הוּא דִּכְתִּיב וַתְּהִי עָלָיו רוּחַ אֱלֹהִים. וַתְּהִי עָלָיו, עַל יִשְׂרָאֵל קָאָמַר. כְּמַאן דְּפָרִישׁ סוּדְרָא עַל רֵישֵׁיהּ דְּיַנּוּקָא, בְּגִין דְּלָא יִשְׁלוֹט בְּהוּ עֵינוֹי.

487. See what is written: "And Bilaam lifted up his eyes, and he saw Yisrael" (Bemidbar 24:2), because he wished to gaze at them with the evil eye. At that very moment, if the Holy One, blessed be He, had not preceded him with the remedy, he could have destroyed them with the gaze of his eyes. Which remedy did the Holy One, blessed be He, grant to Yisrael at that very moment? It is written: "And the spirit of Elohim came upon him" and "came upon him" refers to Yisrael. The Holy One, blessed be He, extended and covered Yisrael over with the spirit of Elohim. It is in the same sense as a person spreads the scarf over the head of a child, so that no evil eye shall affect him.

488. כְּדֵין שָׁארִי וְאָמַר, מַה טוֹבוּ אֹהָלֶיךָ יַעֲקֹב. ת״ח, כָּל מַאן דְּבָעֵי לְאִסְתַּכְּלָא בְּעֵינָא בִּישָׁא, לָא יָכִיל, אֶלָּא כַּד מְשַׁבַּח וְאוֹקִיר לְהַהוּא מִלָּה, דְּבָעֵי לְאַלְטְיָיא בְּעֵינָא בִּישָׁא. וּמַה אָרְחֵיהּ. אָמַר, חָמוּ כַּמָּה טָבָא דָּא. כַּמָּה יָאָה דָּא. בְּגִין דְּיִשְׁלוֹט בֵּיהּ עֵינָא בִּישָׁא. אוּף הָכָא אָמַר, מַה טֹּבוּ אֹהָלֶיךָ יַעֲקֹב, כַּמָּה אִינּוּן יָאָן, כַּמָּה אִינּוּן שַׁפִּירָן, כַּמָּה נְטִיעָן שַׁפִּירָן דְּאִתְנְטָעָן מִנַּיְיהוּ, דַּמְיָין לְאִינּוּן נְטִיעִין דְּנָטַע קוּדְשָׁא בְּרִיךְ הוּא בְּגִנְתָּא דְּעֵדֶן יָאָיָין. מַאן יָהֵן, וְאִלֵּין נְטִיעָן אִשְׁתְּכָחוּ מֵאִינּוּן מִשְׁכְּנֵי, דִּבְהוּ.

488. He opened the discussion with the verse: "How goodly are your tents, O Jacob" (Ibid. 5). Come and see: Whoever wishes to gaze with an evil eye is not able to do so unless he praises and honors the one whom he wishes to curse with the evil eye. What is his usual method of operation? He says, How nice he is, how beautiful he is, in order that the evil eye would affect him. Here too, he said, "How goodly are your tents, O Jacob." How nice, how beautiful they are, how beautiful are the plants that have been planted from them. They are comparable to the pretty plantings that the Holy One, blessed be He, has planted in the Garden of Eden! Would that plantings shall come forth from these dwellings!

489. יִזַּל מַיִם מִדָּלְיָו וְגוֹ׳. לְב״נ דַּהֲוֵו לֵיהּ יְדָן שַׁפִּירָן, יָאָן לְמֶחֱזֵי. אַעְבָּר חַד ב״נ דְּעֵינָא בִּישָׁא, אִסְתָּכַּל בְּאִינּוּן יְדִין, נָקִיט בְּהוּ, שָׁארִי לְשַׁבְּחָא, אָמַר, כַּמָּה אִינּוּן שַׁפִּירָן, כַּמָּה אִינּוּן יָאָן, חָמוּ אֶצְבְּעָן מִגְּזֵרָה דְּשַׁפִּירוּ עִלָּאָה. לְבָתַר אָמַר, מַאן יִתֵּן יְדִין אִלֵּין דְּשַׁרְיָין בֵּין אַבְנִין יַקִּירִין, וּבִלְבוּשֵׁי יְקָר דְּאַרְגְּוָונָא בְּבֵיתֵיהּ לְאִשְׁתַּמְּשָׁא בְּהוּ, וְיֵהוֹן גְּנִיזִין בְּתֵיבוּתָא דִּילֵיהּ.

489. "He shall pour the water out of his bucket" (Ibid. 7). THIS IS like a man who had fine hands, beautiful in appearance. One person passed by, a man of the evil eye, gazed at these hands, grasped them and began to praise them, saying, How beautiful they are, how pretty. Look at the fingers cut out in the highest form of beauty. Then he is, Who shall give these hands to dwell among precious stones and expensive purple garments, AND BE in his house to use them and they shall be stored in his vault.

490. כַּךְ בִּלְעָם, שָׁרֵי לְשַׁבְּחָא, מַה טּוֹבוּ אֹהָלֶיךָ, חָמוּ כַּמָּה שְׁפִּירָן, כַּמָּה יָאָן וְכוּ׳, לְבָתַר אָמַר יִזַּל מַיִם מִדָּלְיָו, לָא יִשְׁתְּכַּח נְטִיעָא שַׁפִּירָא דָּא, נְטִיעָא דְּאוֹרַיְיתָא, לְבַר מֵאִינּוּן מַשְׁכְּנִין, וְזַרְעוֹ בְּמַיִם רַבִּים, דְּלָא יִסְגֵּי וְלָא יַרְבֵּי רוּחָא דְּקוּדְשָׁא.

490. Here, the same Bilaam began to praise: "How goodly are your tents, O Jacob, and your tabernacles, O Yisrael." How handsome they are and how fine. Afterward, "He shall pour the water out of his bucket," WHICH MEANS that you cannot find a nicer planting than this, the planting of Torah, outside of these dwellings. And "moistening his seed plentifully" (Ibid. 7), WHICH HE MEANT TO BE AMONG THE KLIPOT THAT ARE CALLED 'PLENTIFUL MIGHTY WATERS', MEANING TO SAY that the Holy Spirit should not grow and increase.

491. אָ״ל קוּדְשָׁא בְּרִיךְ הוּא, רָשָׁע, לָא יַכְלִין עֵינַיךְ לְאַבְאָשָׁא, הָא פְּרִיסוּ דְּקוּדְשָׁא עָלַיְיהוּ, כְּדֵין אָמַר, אֵל מוֹצִיאוֹ מִמִּצְרַיִם וְגוֹ׳, הָא לָא

יַכְלִין כָּל בְּנֵי עָלְמָא לְאַבְאָשָׁא לוֹן, דְּהָא חֵילָא תַּקִּיפָא עִלָּאָה אָחִיד בְּהוּ, וּמַאי אִיהוּ. אֵל מוֹצִיאוֹ מִמִּצְרַיִם. וְלֹא עוֹד, אֶלָּא כְּתוֹעֲפוֹת רְאֵם לוֹ, דְּלָא יָכִיל ב״נ לְאוֹשִׁיט יְדֵיהּ עָלֵיהּ, מִגּוֹ רוּמֵיהּ. וּמִדְּאִשְׁתְּכַח בִּזְקִיפוּ עִלָּאָה הָכִי, יֹאכַל גּוֹיִם צָרָיו וְגו׳. וְלֵית מַאן דְּיָכִיל לְאַבְאָשָׁא לוֹן.

491. The Holy One, blessed be He said to him, 'Wicked one, your eyes can do no harm, because there is a veil of the Holy Spirit over them'. He then said, "El brought him out of Egypt..." (Ibid. 8), WHICH MEANS none of the world's inhabitants will be able to harm them because a strong and powerful higher strength holds on to them. What is it? It is: "El brought him out of Egypt." Not only that, but "he has as it were the strength of a wild ox" (Ibid.) No person could extend his hands over him due to his height. Because he exists at such a height, "he shall eat up the nations his enemies" (Ibid.) and no one is able to harm them.

492. וַאֲפִילוּ בִּזְמְנָא דְּלָא זָקִיף, לָא יַכְלִין, הה״ד כָּרַע שָׁכַב. לָא דָּחִיל, בְּגִין דְּאִשְׁתְּכַח גִּיבָּר כַּאֲרִי וּכְלָבִיא, אֲפִילוּ כַּד אִינּוּן בֵּינֵי עֲמְמַיָּא, וְכָרַע וְשָׁכַב בֵּינַיְיהוּ, כַּאֲרִי הוּא יִשְׁתְּכַח בִּנְמוּסֵי אוֹרַיְיתָא, בְּאוֹרְחֵי אוֹרַיְיתָא. שׁוּלְטָנוּתָא אִית לְהוּ בְּמָארֵיהוֹן, דַּאֲפִילוּ כָּל מַלְכַיָּא דְּעָלְמָא, לָא יַעְקְרוּן לְהוּ. כְּאַרְיָא דָּא כַּד שָׁכִיב עַל טַרְפֵּיהּ, לָא יַכְלִין לְאַקָּמָא לֵיהּ מִנֵּיהּ, הה״ד כָּרַע שָׁכַב כַּאֲרִי וְגו׳.

492. Even at a time when he is not standing, they will not succeed AGAINST HIM. This is what is written: "He couched, he lay down" (Ibid. 9). EVEN THEN he is not afraid, because he is mighty "like a lion, and like a great lion" (Ibid.). This means that, even when he is IN EXILE among the nations and he crouches and lies among them like a lion, he will be familiar in the laws of the Torah and in the ways of the Torah. They have a government from their Master that all the kings of the world cannot uproot; it is comparable to the strength of the lion which can not be raised up from the prey that he is crouched over. It is written: "He couched, he lay down like a lion, and like a great lion: who shall stir him up?"

493. א״ר אֶלְעָזָר, לָא אִשְׁתְּכַח בְּעָלְמָא חַכִּים לְאַבְאָשָׁא, כְּבִלְעָם רְשִׁיעָא, דְּהָא בְּקַדְמֵיתָא הֲוָה אִשְׁתְּכַח בְּמִצְרַיִם, וְעַל יְדוֹי, קְשִׁירוּ

מִצְרָאֵי עֲלַיְיהוּ דְּיִשְׂרָאֵל קְשׁוּרָא, דְּלָא יִפְּקוּן מֵעַבְדוּתְהוֹן לְעָלְמִין. וְדָא הוּא דְּאָמַר, מָה אֵיכוּל לְאַבְאָשָׁא לְהוּ, דְּהָא אֲנָא עֲבִידְנָא דְּלָא יִפְּקוּן מֵעֲבִידְתָּא דְּמִצְרָאֵי לְעָלְמִין, אֲבָל אֵל מוֹצִיאוֹ, מִמִּצְרַיִם וְלָקֳבְלֵיהּ לָא יַכְלִין חַכִּמִין וַחֲרָשִׁין דְּעָלְמָא.

493. Rabbi Elazar said, You could not find in the world a wiser person to do harm than that wicked Bilaam. At first, he was in Egypt and, through him, the Egyptians plotted against Yisrael, so that they should never escape their slavery. And he said, how can I harm them? I was the one who caused them never to escape the slavery of Egypt, yet, "El brought him out of Egypt" and against Him, none of the wise men and sorcerers of the world could prevail.

46. Aza and Azael

A Synopsis

Rabbi Yehuda tells how Bilaam went to the mountains of darkness to consult with Aza and Azael. We hear what happens in those mountains and how Aza and Azael teach magic and sorcery to those who enter there. When Bilaam went there God confused all the magic in the world so it would be ineffective against His children, so Bilaam eventually gave Balak advice regarding the Midianite women in an attempt to hurt Yisrael. When God saw that he had given this advice He told Bilaam that he would be ensnared in his own plot, and indeed he was later killed in the vengeance against Midian.

494. וְעַתָּה הִנְנִי הוֹלֵךְ לְעַמִּי וְגוֹ׳ ר׳ יְהוּדָה פָּתַח, לֹא תַסְגִּיר עֶבֶד אֶל אֲדוֹנָיו וְגוֹ׳ עִמְּךָ יֵשֵׁב בְּקִרְבְּךָ. כַּמָּה חֲבִיבִין מִלֵּי דְּאוֹרַיְיתָא. כַּמָּה חֲבִיבָה אוֹרַיְיתָא קַמֵּי קוּדְשָׁא בְּרִיךְ הוּא. כַּמָּה חֲבִיבָה אוֹרַיְיתָא, דְּאוֹרִית לָהּ קוּדְשָׁא בְּרִיךְ הוּא לְכ״י. ת״ח, בְּשַׁעֲתָא דִּי נַפְקוּ מִמִּצְרָיִם. שְׁמַע בִּלְעָם דְּהָא חֲרָשׁוֹי וְקִסְמוֹי, וְכָל אִינּוּן קִשְׁרִין, לָא סְלִיקוּ בְּהוּ בְּיִשְׂרָאֵל, שָׁארִי לְגַרְדָּא גַּרְמֵיהּ, וּלְמֵירַט רֵישֵׁיהּ. אָזַל לְאִינּוּן טוּרֵי חֲשׁוֹכָא, וּמָטָא לְגַבֵּי אִינּוּן שַׁלְשְׁלָאֵי דְּפַרְזְלָא.

494. "And now, behold, I go to my people..." (Bemidbar 24:14). Rabbi Yehuda opened the discussion with the verse: "You shall not deliver to his master the servant...he shall dwell with you" (Devarim 23:16). How lovely are the words of the Torah before the Holy One, blessed be He, and how beloved is the Torah that he gave her as a legacy to the Congregation of Yisrael. Come and see: At the time they left Egypt, Bilaam heard that his witches and sorcerers, and all those ties THAT THEY PERFORMED, were not effective against Yisrael. He began to scratch himself and tear his hair out of his head. Then, he went to the mountains of darkness and reached the iron chains, WITH WHICH AZA AND AZAEL ARE BOUND.

495. וְכַךְ הוּא אָרְחָא דְּמַאן דְּמָטֵי גַּבַּיְיהוּ, כֵּיוָן דְּעָאל ב״נ בְּרֵישֵׁי טוּרַיָּא, חָמֵי לֵיהּ עֲזָאֵ״ל, הַהוּא דְּאִקְרֵי גְּלוּי עֵינַיִם. מִיַּד אָמַר לַעֲזָ״א, כְּדֵין יָהֲבִין קָלָא, וּמִתְכַּנְּשִׁין גַּבַּיְיהוּ חִוְיָין רַבְרְבֵי דִּמְתוֹקְדָן, וְסַחֲרִין

לוֹן. מְשַׁדְּרֵי אוּנִימְתָא זְעֵירְתָּא לְקַבְלֵיהּ דב״נ, וְתָנָא, כְּמִין שׁוּנְרָא, הִיא, וְרֵישֵׁהּ כְּרֵישָׁא דְּחִוְיָא, וּתְרֵין זַנְבִין בָּהּ, וִידָהָא וְרַגְלָהָא זְעִירִין. ב״נ דְּחָמֵי לָהּ, חָפֵי אַנְפּוֹי, וְהוּא מַיְיתֵי חַד קַטוּרְתָּא, מֵאוּקִידוּ דְּתַרְנְגוֹלָא חִוָּרָא, שָׁדֵי בְּאַנְפָּהָא וְהִיא אָתְיָת עִמֵּיהּ.

495. This is the manner of the one who reaches them. As soon as a person enters there, between the mountaintops, Azael, THAT ONE that is called "having his eyes open" (Bemidbar 24:4), notices him. He immediately informs Aza. They then give the sound signal and the great burning snakes gather to them and surround them. They send a TYPE OF small CREATURE CALLED 'Onimta' towards that person. We were taught that it is a cat-like animal with a narrow snake-like head. It has two tails and its hands and feet are tiny. A person who sees it covers his face and brings A VESSEL WITH ASHES THAT IS CALLED 'smoked shreds' from the burning of a white rooster and throws them in front of the Onimta, which then comes with him.

496. עַד דְּמָטֵי לְגַבֵּי רֵישָׁא דְּשַׁלְשְׁלָאֵי, וְהַהִיא רֵישָׁא דְּשַׁלְשְׁלָאֵי, נָעִיץ בְּאַרְעָא, וּמָטֵי עַד תְּהוֹמָא. וְתַמָּן בִּתְהוֹמָא. חַד סָמִיךְ, וְהוּא נָעִיץ בִּתְהוֹמָא תַּתָּאָה, וּבְהַהוּא סָמִיךְ אִתְקְשַׁר רֵישָׁא דְּשַׁלְשְׁלָאֵי. כַּד מָטֵי ב״נ לְרֵישָׁא דְּשַׁלְשְׁלָאָה, בָּטַשׁ בָּהּ ג׳ זִמְנִין, וְאִינּוּן קָרָאן לֵיהּ, כְּדֵין כָּרַע וְסָגִיד עַל בִּרְכּוֹי, וְאָזִיל וְאָטִים עֵינוֹי, עַד דְּמָטֵי גַּבַּיְיהוּ. כְּדֵין יָתִיב קַמַּיְיהוּ, וְכָל אִינּוּן חִוְיָין סָחֲרִין לֵיהּ מֵהַאי סִטְרָא וּמֵהַאי סִטְרָא. פָּתַח עֵינוֹי, וְחָמֵי לוֹן, אִזְדַּעְזָע, וְנָפַל עַל אַנְפּוֹי, וְסָגִיד לְקַבְלַיְיהוּ.

496. He goes until he reaches the top of the chains, because the top of those chains is stuck into the ground and reaches to the great depths. In the great depths, there exists a socket that is stuck into the lower depth, and into that socket the top of the chains is connected. When a person reaches the top of the chain, he knocks at it three times. They, AZA AND AZAEL, call for him. He then kneels on his knees, bows down and continues to close his eyes until he reaches them. He then sits up in front of them and all these snakes surround him from either side. Then he opens his eyes and sees them. He is shaken, and he falls on his face and bows towards them.

497. לְבָתַר אוֹלְפִין לֵיהּ חֲרָשִׁין וְקִסְמִין, וְיָתִיב גַּבַּיְיהוּ נ׳ יוֹמִין. כַּד

מָטָא זִמְנָא לְמֵיהַךְ לְאָרְחֵיהּ, הַהִיא אוֹנִימְתָא, וְכָל אִינּוּן חִוְיָין, אַזְלִין קַמֵּיהּ, עַד דְּנָפִיק מִן טוּרַיָּיא, בֵּין הַהוּא חֲשׁוֹכָא תַּקִּיפָא.

497. Afterwards, AZA AND AZAEL teach him magic and sorcery, and he stays with them for fifty days. When the time arrives to leave on his way, that LITTLE CREATURE CALLED 'Onimta' and all these snakes walk in front of him, until he leaves the mountain ranges from in between that heavy darkness.

498. וּבִלְעָם כַּד מָטָא גַּבַּיְיהוּ, אוֹדַע לוֹן מִלָּה, וְאַסְגַּר גַּרְמֵיהּ בְּטוּרַיָּיא עִמְּהוֹן. וּבָעָא לְקַטְרְגָא לוֹן, לְאָתָבָא לוֹן לְמִצְרַיִם. וְקוּדְשָׁא בְּרִיךְ הוּא בִּלְבֵּל וְקִלְקֵל כָּל חָכְמְתָא דְּעָלְמָא, וְכָל חֲרָשִׁין דְּעָלְמָא, דְּלָא יָכִילוּ לְקָרְבָא בַּהֲדַיְיהוּ.

498. When Bilaam reached AZA AND AZAEL, he told them WHAT HE NEEDED FROM THEM, locked himself with them in the mountains and asked to denounce YISRAEL and return them to Egypt. The Holy One, blessed be He, confused and impaired all the wisdoms in the world, and all the magic in the world, so they could not get close TO YISRAEL.

499. ת"ח, הַשְׁתָּא כֵּיוָן דְּחָמָא בִּלְעָם דְּלָא יָכִיל לְאַבְאָשָׁא לְיִשְׂרָאֵל, אַהְדָּר גַּרְמֵיהּ, וְאַמְלִיךְ לֵיהּ לְבָלָק, מַה דְּלָא בָּעָא מִנֵּיהּ, בְּגִין לְאַבְאָשָׁא לוֹן. וְעֵיטָא דִּילֵיהּ הֲוָה בְּאִינּוּן נוּקְבֵי דְּמִדְיָן דְּאִינּוּן שָׁפִּירָן, וְאִלְמָלֵא דְּאָ"ל מֹשֶׁה, לָא הֲוֵינָא יָדַע, דִּכְתִּיב הֵן הֵנָּה הָיוּ לִבְנֵי יִשְׂרָאֵל בִּדְבַר בִּלְעָם.

499. Come and see: When Bilaam realized that he was incapable of harming Yisrael, he returned to Balak and gave him advice in order to harm Yisrael, something he did not ask him to do. And his advice was regarding the Midianite women, who were beautiful. If not for the fact that Moses TOLD THIS TO US, we would not have known of it, because it is written: "Behold, these caused the children of Yisrael, through that counsel of Bilaam" (Bemidbar 31:16).

500. כֵּיוָן דְּחָמָא קוּדְשָׁא בְּרִיךְ הוּא עֵיטָא דִּילֵיהּ, אָמַר, הָא וַדַּאי גַּרְמָךְ

בְּעֵיטָךְ יִפּוֹל. מַה עָבֵד, הַהוּא חֵילָא דְּשָׁלַט עַל כָּל חֲרָשִׁין, אַחְמֵי לֵיהּ סוֹפָא דְּכֹלָּא. וְכִי אִית לְהוּ רְשׁוּתָא לְזִמַּן רָחִיק. א״ר יִצְחָק, עֵינָא חָמָא, וּמִלִּין אִתְמָרוּ מֵהַהוּא דְּקָאֵים עָלֵיהּ, וְהָא אוּקְמוּהָ. וַיִּשָּׂא מְשָׁלוֹ וַיֹּאמַר. מַאן דְּאִית לֵיהּ לְמֵימַר. מ״ט. בְּגִין דְּלָא יִתְקַיְּימוּן מִלִּין דְּגָעֲלָא, בִּרְעוּתָא עִלָּאָה, בְּדַעְתָּא עִלָּאָה בְּאוֹרַיְיתָא.

500. When the Holy One, blessed be He, saw his advice, He said, 'You will certainly get snared by your own plot' – BECAUSE HE WAS KILLED IN THE VENGEANCE AGAINST MIDIAN. What did the power controlling magic do, THAT IS MALCHUT, AS MENTIONED ABOVE? It showed him the final end. HE INQUIRES: Does he have permission to see into the distant future? Rabbi Yitzchak said, The eye saw and perceived; however, the actual statements were spoken by the one who is over him, MEANING IT CAME FROM MALCHUT. This was already explained in relation to the verse: "And he took up his discourse, and said..." WHO SPOKE? Whoever should have spoken, MEANING MALCHUT, AS WE MENTIONED THERE. Why is that so? So that disgusting statements BY BILAAM should not come true through the will of the most High, through the high knowledge of the Torah.

47. In the time of Messiah

A Synopsis

We are told what will happen at the time of Messiah when God is going to rebuild Jerusalem. The account presages the destruction of Rome and its ruler, and talks about many wars. The spirit of Messiah will destroy the enemies of Yisrael, and the righteous will be brought back to life. When the children of Yisrael leave their exile the Shechinah will go with them, and there will be great joy. At the time of redemption all blessings will freely flow to the righteous from the great deep springs of Chochmah and Binah.

501. אֶרְאֶנּוּ וְלֹא עַתָּה, דְּהָא מִלִּין אִלֵּין מִנַּיְיהוּ אִתְקָיָּימוּ בְּהַהוּא זִמְנָא, וּמִנַּיְיהוּ לְבָתַר, וּמִנַּיְיהוּ בְּזִמְנָא דְּמַלְכָּא מְשִׁיחָא. תְּנָן, זַמִּין קוּדְשָׁא בְּרִיךְ הוּא לְמִבְנֵי יְרוּשָׁלַםִ, וּלְאַחְזָאָה חַד כֹּכָבָא קְבִיעָא, מְנַצְּצָא בְּע׳ רָהֲטִין, וּבְע׳ זִיקִין נַהֲרִין מִנֵּיהּ בְּאֶמְצָעוּת רְקִיעַ, וְיִשְׁתָּאֲלוּן בֵּיהּ ע׳ כֹּכָבִין אַחֲרָנִין, וִיהֵא נָהִיר וְלָהִיט ע׳ יוֹמִין.

501. "I behold it, but it is not near" (Bemidbar 24:17), because some of these matters came true at that time and some of them are for future times, in the period of King Messiah. We learned that the Holy One, blessed be He, will build Jerusalem and display a fixed star that sparkles with seventy moving PLANETS and with seventy winds that display light from it in the center of the firmament. Another seventy stars will be instructed and guided by it, and it will be glowing and blazing seventy days.

502. וּבְיוֹמָא שְׁתִיתָאָה, יִתְחֲזֵי בְּכ״ה יוֹמִין לְיַרְחָא שְׁתִיתָאָה, וְיִתְכְּנִישׁ בְּיוֹמָא שְׁבִיעָאָה, לְסוֹף ע׳ יוֹמִין, יוֹמָא קַדְמָאָה יִתְחֲזֵי בְּקַרְתָּא דְּרוֹמָא. וְהַהוּא יוֹמָא יִנְפְּלוּן ג׳ שׁוּרִין עִלָּאִין מֵהַהִיא קַרְתָּא דְּרוֹמִי, וְהֵיכְלָא רַבְרְבָא יִנְפּוֹל, וְשַׁלִּיטָא דְּהַהִיא קַרְתָּא יְמוּת. כְּדֵין יִתְפָּשַׁט הַהוּא כֹּכָבָא לְאִתְחֲזָאָה בְּעָלְמָא. וּבְהַהוּא זִמְנָא יִתְעֲרוּן קְרָבִין תַּקִּיפִין בְּעָלְמָא, לְכָל ד׳ סִטְרִין, וּמְהֵימְנוּתָא לָא יִשְׁתְּכַח בֵּינַיְיהוּ.

502. On Friday, on the twenty-fifth day to the sixth month, the star will be seen. It will be gathered on the seventh day at the ending of the seventy days. IT WILL BE COVERED AND NOT SEEN. On the first day, it will be seen in the city of Rome and, on that day, three higher walls will fall from the city of Rome, and the great palace WHICH IS THERE will fall. The governor of that city will die. Then that star will spread and extend to be seen in the world. During that time, great and mighty wars will be stirring in the world to all four directions, and there will be no faith among them.

503. וּבְאֶמְצָעוּת עָלְמָא, כַּד יִתְנְהִיר הַהוּא כֹּכָבָא, בְּאֶמְצָעוּת רְקִיעָא. יְקוּם מַלְכָּא חַד רַב וְשָׁלִיט בְּעַלְמָא, וְיִתְגָּאֶה רוּחֵיהּ עַל כָּל מַלְכִין, וְיִתְעַר קְרָבִין בִּתְרֵין סִטְרִין, וְיִתְגַּבָּר עֲלַיְיהוּ.

503. In the center of the world, when that star will shine in the centre of heaven, a great king and ruler will rise in the world. He will have haughty disposition over all the kings and provoke war on the two sides, and will overpower them.

504. וּבְיוֹמָא דְּיִתְכַּסֵּי כֹּכָבָא, יִזְדַּעְזַע אַרְעָא קַדִּישָׁא מ"ה מִילִין, סַחֲרָנֵיהּ אֲתָר דַּהֲוָה בֵּי מַקְדְּשָׁא. וּמְעַרְתָּא חֲדָא מִן תְּחוֹת אַרְעָא יִתְגְּלֵי. וּמֵהַהִיא מְעַרְתָּא יִפּוּק אֶשָּׁא תַּקִּיפָא לְאוֹקְדָא עָלְמָא. וּמֵהַהִיא מְעַרְתָּא יִסְגֵּי חַד עַנְפָּא, רַבְרְבָא עִלָּאָה, דְּיִשְׁלוֹט בְּכָל עָלְמָא, וְלֵיהּ אִתְיְהִיב מַלְכוּתָא. וְקַדִּישֵׁי עֶלְיוֹנִין יִתְכַּנְּשׁוּן גַּבֵּיהּ. וּכְדֵין יִתְגְּלֵי מַלְכָּא מְשִׁיחָא בְּכָל עָלְמָא, וְלֵיהּ אִתְיְהִיב מַלְכוּתָא.

504. During the day when that star will be covered, the Holy Land will shudder and shake 45 miles around the area of the Temple, and a cave underneath the ground will be discovered. From that cave will emanate a fire to burn the world. And from that cave will grow one great lofty branch that will dominate over the entire world, and the kingdom will be granted to him. The most high saints will be gathering to him. Then, Messiah will be revealed in the entire world and the kingdom will be granted to him.

505. וּבְנֵי עָלְמָא בְּשַׁעֲתָא דְּיִתְגְּלֵי, יֶהוֹן מִשְׁתַּכְּחִין בְּעַקְתָּא בָּתַר עַקְתָּא. וְשַׂנְאֵיהוֹן דְּיִשְׂרָאֵל יִתְגַּבְּרוּן, כְּדֵין יִתְעַר רוּחָא דִּמְשִׁיחָא עֲלַיְיהוּ, וִישֵׁיצֵי לֶאֱדוֹם חַיָּיבָא, וְכָל אַרְעָא דְּשָׂעִיר יוֹקִיד בְּנוּרָא. כְּדֵין

כְּתִיב, וְיִשְׂרָאֵל עוֹשֶׂה חָיִל. הה״ד, וְהָיָה אֱדוֹם יְרֵשָׁה וְהָיָה יְרֵשָׁה שֵׂעִיר אוֹיְבָיו. אוֹיְבָיו דְּיִשְׂרָאֵל. וּכְדֵין וְיִשְׂרָאֵל עוֹשֶׂה חָיִל. וּבְהַהוּא זִמְנָא, יָקִים קוּדְשָׁא בְּרִיךְ הוּא לְמֵתַיָּיא דְּעַמֵּיהּ, וְיִתְנָשֵׁי מִנְּהוֹן מִיתָה, הה״ד יְמִין יְיָ׳ עֹשָׂה חָיִל. לֹא אָמוּת כִּי אֶחְיֶה. וּכְתִיב וְעָלוּ מוֹשִׁיעִים וְגוֹ׳. וּכְדֵין וְהָיָה יְיָ׳ לְמֶלֶךְ.

505. At the time of the revealing OF MESSIAH, the inhabitants of the world will find themselves in one distress after another and those who hate Yisrael will get stronger. Then the spirit of Messiah will stir against them, and will destroy the wicked Edom, and the entire land of Seir will go up in flames. Concerning that time, it is written: “And Yisrael shall do valiantly” (Bemidbar 24:18). That is the meaning of: “And Edom shall be his possession, Seir also, his enemies” (Ibid.), meaning the enemies of Yisrael. That is the meaning of: “And Yisrael shall do valiantly.” At that time, the Holy One, blessed be He, will raise TO LIFE the dead of His people and remove death from them. This is what it says, “The right hand of Hashem does valiantly. I shall not die, but live” (Tehilim 118:16-17). It is further written: “And liberators shall ascend...” (Ovadyah 1:21) and then: “And Hashem shall be king” (Zecharyah 14:9).

506. א״ר אַבָּא, מַאי דִּכְתִּיב כִּי בְשִׂמְחָה תֵצֵאוּ וְגוֹ׳. אֶלָּא כַּד יִפְקוּן יִשְׂרָאֵל מִן גָּלוּתָא, שְׁכִינְתָּא נָפְקָא עִמְּהוֹן, וְעִמָּהּ יִפְקוּן. הֲדָא הוּא דִּכְתִּיב, כִּי בְשִׂמְחָה תֵצֵאוּ. שָׂשׂוֹן דָּא קוּדְשָׁא בְּרִיךְ הוּא. ר׳ יִצְחָק אָמַר דָּא צַדִּיק. הֲדָא הוּא דִּכְתִּיב שָׂשׂוֹן וְשִׂמְחָה יִמָּצֵא בָהּ.

506. Rabbi Aba said, What is the meaning of, “For you shall go out with joy” (Yeshayah 55:12)? It only means that, when Yisrael leave the exile, the Shechinah will leave with them. They will leave together with Her. This is the meaning of: “For you shall go out with joy” WITH THE SHECHINAH THAT IS CALLED ‘GLADNESS’. “Joy” is referring to the Holy One, blessed be He. Rabbi Yitzchak said, That is referring to the Righteous, MEANING YESOD OF ZEIR ANPIN. This is the meaning of: “Joy and gladness shall be found in it” (Yeshayah 51:3), WHICH ARE YESOD AND MALCHUT.

507. אר״ש, צַדִּיק שָׂשׂוֹן אִקְרֵי. וּמִן יוֹמָא דְּכ״י נַפְלַת בְּגָלוּתָא.

אִתְמְנָעוּ בִּרְכָּן מִלְּנַחְתָּא לְעָלְמָא מֵהַאי צַדִּיק. בְּהַהוּא זִמְנָא מַה כְּתִיב, וּשְׁאַבְתֶּם מַיִם בְּשָׂשׂוֹן, דָּא צַדִּיק. מִמַּעַיְינֵי הַיְשׁוּעָה, אִלֵּין אַבָּא וְאִמָּא. ד״א, אִלֵּין נֶצַ״ח וְהוֹ״ד. וְכֹלָּא מִמַּבּוּעֵי נְבִיעִין עֲמִיקִן. כְּדֵין וְאָמַרְתָּ בַּיּוֹם הַהוּא אוֹדְךָ יְיָ׳ וְגוֹ׳, צַהֲלִי וָרֹנִּי יֹשֶׁבֶת צִיּוֹן וְגוֹ׳.

507. Rabbi Shimon said, The Righteous, THAT IS, YESOD OF ZEIR ANPIN, is called 'joy'. From that day onward, when the Congregation of Yisrael fell into the exile, the blessings were withheld from flowing down to the world from this Righteous. At that time OF REDEMPTION, it is written: "Therefore with joy shall you draw water" (Yeshayah 12:3). This refers to the Righteous CALLED 'JOY'. "Out of the wells of salvation" (Ibid.) refers to Aba and Ima, WHICH ARE CHOCHMAH AND BINAH, FROM WHERE THE YESOD DRAWS. Another explanation: "Out of the wells of salvation" IS REFERRING to Netzach and Hod, FROM WHOM YESOD RECEIVES. All RECEIVE from deep springs that flow, WHICH ARE CHOCHMAH AND BINAH. Then, it is written: "And in that day you shall say, Hashem, I will praise You..." (Ibid. 1), and: "Cry out and shout, you inhabitant of Zion..." (Ibid. 6).

בָּרוּךְ יְיָ׳ לְעוֹלָם אָמֵן וְאָמֵן. יִמְלוֹךְ יְיָ׳ לְעוֹלָם אָמֵן וְאָמֵן.

Blessed be Hashem for evermore. Amen, and Amen. Hashem reign for evermore. Amen, and Amen.

NOTES

NOTES

NOTES

NOTES

NOTES

NOTES

NOTES

NOTES

NOTES

NOTES

NOTES

NOTES

NOTES

NOTES

NOTES